JUDAISM AND CHRISTIAN ART

JUDAISM AND CHRISTIAN ART

Aesthetic Anxieties from the Catacombs to Colonialism

Edited by

Herbert L. Kessler

and

David Nirenberg

PENN

University of Pennsylvania Press

Philadelphia · Oxford

Published by
University of Pennsylvania Press
Philadelphia, Pennsylvania 19104-4112
www.upenn.edu/pennpress

Printed in the United States of America on acid-free paper

10 9 8 7 6 5 4 3 2 1

Library of Congress Cataloging-in-Publication Data
Judaism and Christian art : aesthetic anxieties from the catacombs to colonialism / edited by Herbert L. Kessler and David Nirenberg.
    p. cm.
    Includes bibliographical references and index.
    ISBN 978-0-8122-4285-0 (hardcover : alk. paper)
    1. Christian art and symbolism—Europe.   2. Judaism in art.   3. Art, European—Themes, motives.   I. Kessler, Herbert L., 1941–   II. Nirenberg, David, 1964–
N8180.J83   2011
704.9′482—dc22
                                                                                                2010023068

CONTENTS

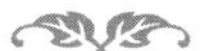

List of Illustrations — vii

Introduction
DAVID NIRENBERG — 1

Chapter 1. "Pharaoh's Army Got Drownded": Some Reflections on
Jewish and Roman Genealogies in Early Christian Art
JAŚ ELSNER — 10

Chapter 2. Unfeigned Witness: Jews, Matter, and Vision in
Twelfth-Century Christian Art
SARA LIPTON — 45

Chapter 3. Shaded with Dust: Jewish Eyes on Christian Art
HERBERT L. KESSLER — 74

Chapter 4. *Iudeus sacer*: Life, Law, and Identity in the "State
of Exception" Called "Marian Miracle"
FRANCISCO PRADO-VILAR — 115

Chapter 5. Abraham Circumcises Himself: A Scene at the Endgame
of Jewish Utility to Christian Art
MARCIA KUPFER — 143

Chapter 6. Frau Venus, the Eucharist, and the Jews of Landshut
ACHIM TIMMERMANN — 183

Chapter 7. Jewish Carnality, Christian Guilt, and Eucharistic Peril
in the Rotterdam-Berlin Altarpiece of the Holy Sacrament
MITCHELL B. MERBACK — 203

Chapter 8. The Ghetto and the Gaze in Early Modern Venice
DANA E. KATZ   233

Chapter 9. Through a Glass Darkly: Paths to Salvation in Spanish
Painting at the Outset of the Inquisition
FELIPE PEREDA   263

Chapter 10. Renaissance Naturalism and the Jewish Bible: Ferrara,
Brescia, Bergamo, 1520–1540
STEPHEN J. CAMPBELL   291

Chapter 11. Poussin's Useless Treasures
RICHARD NEER   328

Chapter 12. Eugène Delacroix's Jewish Wedding and the Medium
of Painting
RALPH UBL   359

Chapter 13. The Judaism of Christian Art
DAVID NIRENBERG   387

List of Contributors   429

Index   431

Acknowledgments   443

ILLUSTRATIONS

Figure 1.1. Sarcophagus of the Red Sea crossing, front, currently in
Archaeological Museum, Split   13

Figure 1.2. Sarcophagus of the Red Sea crossing, front, currently
serving as altar front in Arles   13

Figure 1.3. Sarcophagus of the Red Sea crossing, front, currently in
Museo Pio Cristiano in Rome   16

Figure 1.4. Sarcophagus of the Red Sea crossing, front, currently in
Musée Granet in Aix-en-Province   16

Figure 1.5. Sarcophagus of the Red Sea crossing, left side, showing
Moses before Pharaoh and the Israelites beginning their journey out
of Egypt   17

Figure 1.6. Sarcophagus of the Red Sea crossing, right side, showing
miracle of manna and quails and Moses making the bitter waters sweet   18

Figure 1.7. Sarcophagus of the Red Sea crossing, front, detail of the
Hebrews fleeing, Musée de l'Arles antique   20

Figure 1.8. Arch of Trajan at Beneventum   22

Figure 1.9. Relief panel showing Marcus Aurelius distributing largesse
to parents and children, Arch of Constantine, Rome.   23

Figure 1.10. Trajan's Column in Rome, relief showing Dacian families
with children in flight from Roman soldiers   24

Figure 1.11. Column of Marcus Aurelius in Rome, relief showing
mother and child in flight from Roman legionary   25

Figure 1.12. Tombstone of Petronia Grata in Turin, relief showing
Aeneas carrying his father, Anchises, and leading his son Iulus by the
hand   27

Figure 2.1. Old Testament prophets identical to New Testament apostles, First Bible of Charles the Bald 47

Figure 2.2. Romanesque archaizing depiction of a Hebrew prophet, Lobbes Bible 48

Figure 2.3. Eilbertus portable altar in Berlin 54

Figure 2.4. Christ in Majesty, the twelve apostles, and Gospel scenes, Eilbertus portable altar 55

Figure 3.1. David composing psalms, in St. Alban's Psalter 76

Figure 3.2. Christ in Majesty with prophets 81

Figure 3.3. Saint Etienne at Sens, altarpiece 84

Figure 3.4. Leviticus frontispiece 88

Figure 3.5. Titus returning with Jerusalem trophies 91

Figure 3.6. Reims, St. Remi, Moses and Aaron with brazen serpent 94

Figure 3.7. Moses and the brazen serpent 96

Figure 3.8. Felanitx, *Passio imaginis* altarpiece 98

Figure 3.9. Mandylion and Keramion 101

Figure 3.10. Ezekiel's vision of the Temple 103

Figure 4.1. *Lapidary*, Escorial, MS. H.I.15, folio 1r 117

Figure 4.2. *Lapidary*, Escorial, MS. H.I.15, folio 19r 118

Figure 4.3. *Cantigas de Santa Maria*, Florence, MS. B.R. 20, folio 119v 119

Figure 4.4. *Cantigas de Santa Maria*, MS. B.R. 20, folio 92r 120

Figure 4.5. *Cantigas de Santa Maria*, Escorial, MS. T.I.1, folio 39r 122

Figure 4.6. *Cantigas de Santa Maria*, MS. B.R. 20, folio 119v 123

Figure 4.7. *Cantigas de Santa Maria*, MS. T.I.1, folio 131r 125

Figure 4.8. *Cantigas de Santa Maria*, MS. T.I.1, folio 155v 127

Figure 4.9. *Cantigas de Santa Maria*, MS. T.I.1, folio 9v 130

Figure 4.10. *Bible moralisée*, Toledo, MS. 1, folio 53v 132

Figure 5.1. Luis de Guzmán sending his letter of commission to Moses Arragel; the rabbi at work between his censors; Alba Bible 147

Figure 5.2. Rabbi Moses Arragel's presentation of the commissioned
manuscript to Luis de Guzmán, Alba Bible   148

Figure 5.3. Arragel touching the feet of King Juan II of Castile,
Alba Bible   149

Figure 5.4. Jerusalem attacked by the nations, Alba Bible   155

Figure 5.5. Abraham circumcises himself, Alba Bible   159

Figure 5.6. Joshua leads the assault on Ai, Alba Bible   165

Figure 5.7. Abraham circumcises himself, Bible of Jean de Sy   169

Figure 5.8. Conclusion of the story of Hagar; God in the person
of Christ speaks with Abraham; Abraham circumcises himself;
Padua Bible   171

Figure 6.1. Poniky, St. Francis, Living Cross   184

Figure 6.2. Landshut, St. Martin, Living Cross   185

Figure 6.3. Detail of Synagoga from Landshut, St. Martin, Living Cross   185

Figure 6.4. Joseph Huber, longitudinal section of Landshut's
synagogue   187

Figure 6.5. Landshut, view of the Dreifaltigkeitsplatz   193

Figure 6.6. Wasserburg am Inn, St. James, Living Cross   195

Figure 6.7. Landshut, St. Martin, tabernacle altar   197

Figure 7.1. Dirc Bouts, *Altarpiece of the Holy Sacrament*   206

Figure 7.2. *Last Supper*, center panel of the *Rotterdam-Berlin Corpus
Christi Altarpiece*   208

Figure 7.3. *Israelite Passover*, left wing of the *Rotterdam-Berlin Corpus
Christi Altarpiece*   210

Figure 7.4. Detail of Judas from the *Rotterdam-Berlin Corpus Christi
Altarpiece*   212

Figure 7.5. Master Bertram of Minden, *Last Supper*, from Passion Altar   213

Figure 7.6. Detail of youthful apostle from the *Rotterdam-Berlin Corpus
Christi Altarpiece*   218

Figure 7.7. Master I. A. M. van Zwolle, *Last Supper*   219

Figure 7.8. Detail of brazen serpent sheet from the *Rotterdam-Berlin Corpus Christi Altarpiece*   221

Figure 8.1. The Ghetto Nuovo, Venice   234

Figure 8.2. Former gated entrance to the Ghetto Nuovo   235

Figure 8.3. Aerial view of the Venetian ghetto complex   236

Figure 8.4. Jacopo de' Barbari, *Venetie*   238

Figure 8.5. The Banco Rosso pawnshop, Ghetto Nuovo   239

Figure 8.6. Stairwell in the Venetian ghetto complex   240

Figure 8.7. Detail of Jacopo de' Barbari, *Venetie*   241

Figure 8.8. The Procuratie Vecchie, Piazza San Marco, Venice   243

Figure 8.9. Terrace at the Ghetto Nuovo   244

Figure 8.10. The Ghetto Vecchio, Venice   249

Figure 8.11. Bricked-up quays along the waterway, Ghetto Nuovo   250

Figure 9.1. Juan Sánchez de San Román, *Cristo Varón de Dolores*   266

Figure 9.2. School of Jan Van Eyck, *Portrait of Christ*   267

Figure 9.3. *Santo Rostro*   269

Figure 9.4. Virgin "de la Antigua"   271

Figure 9.5. Fray Alonso de Espina, "Fortalitium Fidei"   277

Figure 9.6. "Miracle of the Host" in Fray Alonso de Espina, "Fortalitium Fidei"   280

Figure 9.7. "Cristo de Burgos"   281

Figure 10.1. Garofalo, *Allegory of the Law and the Gospels*   292

Figure 10.2. Titian, *Resurrection*   298

Figure 10.3. Romanino, *Resurrection*   299

Figure 10.4. Romanino, *Mass of St. Apollonius*   301

Figure 10.5. Perugino, *Marriage of the Virgin*   302

Figure 10.6. Girolamo Savoldo, *Adoration of the Shepherds*   303

Figure 10.7. *Adoration of the Child*   304

Figure 10.8. Romanino, *Adoration of the Eucharist*   307

Figure 10.9. Moretto, *Last Supper*   310

Figure 10.10. Moretto, *Elijah and the Angel*   312

Figure 10.11. Moretto, *The Gathering of the Manna*   313

Figure 10.12. Marcantonio Raimondi after Raphael, *The Judgment of Paris*   314

Figure 10.13. Romanino, *Raising of Lazarus*   315

Figure 10.14. Moretto, *Elijah and the Angel*   317

Figure 10.15. After Lorenzo Lotto, *Judith Leaving the Philistine Camp*   318

Figure 10.16. Moretto, *Feast of the Paschal Lamb*   319

Figure 11.1. Nicolas Poussin, *Penance*   329

Figure 11.2. After Nicolas Poussin, *Penance*   330

Figure 11.3. Nicolas Poussin, frontispiece to *Biblia Sacra*   337

Figure 11.4. Simon Vouet, *Adoration of the Holy Name*   340

Figure 11.5. Philippe de Champaigne, *Christ at the House of Simon the Pharisee*   342

Figure 11.6. Nicolas Poussin, *Christ and the Woman Taken in Adultery*   344

Figure 11.7. Detail of Nicolas Poussin, *Christ and the Woman Taken in Adultery*   347

Figure 11.8. Torah pointer (*yad*)   349

Figure 11.9. Nicolas Poussin, *The Death of Saphira*   350

Figure 12.1. Eugène Delacroix, *A Jewish Wedding in Morocco*   360

Figure 12.2. Eugène Delacroix, *Women of Algiers in Their Apartment*   361

Figure 12.3. Eugène Delacroix, *Moroccan Sketchbook*   369

Figure 12.4. Eugène Delacroix, *The Jewish Bride*   370

Figure 12.5. Eugène Delacroix, *Front-Boeuf and Isaac of York*   375

Figure 12.6. Paolo Veronese, *Wedding at Cana*   379

Figure 13.1. School of Jan van Eyck, *The Fountain of Grace and the Triumph of the Church over the Synagogue*   404

Figure 13.2. Detail of school of Jan van Eyck, *The Fountain of Grace and the Triumph of the Church over the Synagogue*   405

INTRODUCTION

David Nirenberg

What does Judaism have to do with Christian art? Until recently, "nothing" seemed an unproblematic answer. Indeed, through much of the nineteenth and twentieth centuries there were many who would have added that Judaism had nothing to do with art *tout court*, whether Christian or any other sort. This was, of course, the position of many committed antisemites such as the composer Richard Wagner (1813–1883), who famously insisted—in his essay "Jewry in Music" (1850)—that Jews had never, could never, contribute to true art.[1] But plenty of Jews, from the most religious to the most assimilated, would themselves have agreed (although for different reasons) that Judaism and art, especially visual art, were originally and essentially at odds. The German convert Heinrich Heine (1797–1856) put it well, summarizing and subscribing to his teacher Hegel's views of the ancient Israelites: "In what a dreadful opposition they must have stood to colorful Egypt, the Temples of Joy of Astarte in Phoenicia, lovely, fragrant, Babylon, and finally to Greece, the flourishing home of art."[2]

Today such an answer is untenable. Unlike Kant, Hegel, and other founding fathers of art history and criticism, we no longer assume that the history of Judaism's relationship to art began or ended with its negation ("Thou shalt make no graven image"). We now treat aniconism—the supposed Jewish hostility to images—not as the essential Jewish attitude toward art, but as one potential among many, and understand that potential as itself an ever-changing product of a long history of interactions with other cultures and religions. In the third century, for example, those interactions produced the synagogue at Dura Europos, whose floor-to-ceiling wall paintings of scriptural narrative have entered most text books in the history of art. The present generation seems far more interested in the other potentials—that is, in the many histories of Jewish engagements with images—than in aniconism. The result is a plethora of books, journals, exhibits, and even museums dedicated to "Jewish art," a harvest whose bounty suggests that the topic is becoming a field, even if no one quite knows where its boundaries are.

But this book is about "Christian," not "Jewish" art, as its title makes clear. What does Judaism have to do with specifically Christian art? Here, too, recent generations have posed questions previously left unasked. We now know a great deal, for example, about the formal devices, iconographies, stereotypes, and caricatures developed by Christian artists of different times and places in order to depict Jews and Judaism. And with this knowledge has come a new awareness of how the representation of Jews and Judaism in Christian media—whether in the decorative programs of churches, manuscript illumination, liturgical theater, poetry, popular song, or sermon—helped to shape Christian perceptions of Judaism, and thereby transformed the possibilities of existence for Jews in Christendom.

The contributors to this volume all share the conviction that these questions of "Judaism *in* Christian art" need to be pursued in a more radical direction. They are not merely "minority" questions, relevant only to issues of Jewish-Christian relations, but are also critical questions about the nature of Christianity and of art. Given God's prohibitions on the worship of created things, can art ever be "Christian"? If so, what should that art look like, and how should it be looked at by Christians? These are some of the most basic questions about art that Christians learned to pose through figures of Judaism. To put our central claim bluntly: in all the Christian cultures explored in this book, from those of early Christianity to those of modern Europe, art defined and legitimated itself by rearticulating and representing its relationship to "Judaism," and thereby discovered the conditions of possibility for its own existence.

The articles that follow, albeit dedicated to different places, times, and genres of art, each demonstrate this point within its appropriate context. But it is also worth remembering that key aspects of these basic questions already existed in the earliest Christian communities. Those communities produced no art (or at least none that survives), but the importance of the texts they produced—those of the New Testament—for the future of art cannot be overestimated. For those texts are marked by the conviction—common to many strands of Hellenistic philosophy as well as of Judaism—that humanity's appetites for the beauty of things in this world are a powerful force drawing it away from divine truth, and orienting its attention to the works of man rather than the love of God.

The Gospel of Matthew's explanation of the visual danger is quite typical of these early Christian worries about aesthetics: "The eye is the lamp of the body.

DAVID NIRENBERG

So if your eye is sound, your whole body will be full of light; but if your eye is not sound, your whole body will be full of darkness. If then the light in you is darkness, how great the darkness!" (Matt. 6:22–23). One of that gospel's goals is to teach its readers how to make their eye sound: to teach it how to see through the outer, "fleshy" appearance of things, persons, texts, and into their "spiritual" interior. To that end, it often represents the error of preferring apparent to inner beauty, flesh to spirit, the life of this world to the life of the next, through figures of Judaism: "Alas for you, scribes, and Pharisees, you hypocrites! You are like whitewashed tombs that look handsome on the outside, but inside are full of the bones of the dead and every kind of corruption" (23:25–32).

The earliest Christian authors treated these aesthetic, epistemological, and ontological problems as "Jewish questions" because of the context in which they were writing. Living before what scholars today call the "parting of the ways" between Judaism and Christianity, many of them stood within both the "old Israel" and the "new," even as they sought to delineate dependences and differences between the two. If all Israel was instructed by the same prophetic tradition, why had only a fraction recognized and embraced Jesus as its messiah? What were the ongoing obligations of that reborn fraction to the traditions from which it sprang? And what of the gentile followers of Jesus? What was their proper relationship to the "old Israel" into which their savior had chosen to be born? It was in order to answer these and similar questions that the earliest followers of Jesus began to map the history of Israel, God's chosen people, onto the history of aesthetics.

St. Paul, himself both Pharisee and apostle to the gentiles, felt the pressure of these questions most acutely, and the influence of his writings transmitted his answers to the many future communities we call Christian. Given our subject, it is worth remembering that his most extended treatment of the relationship between the followers of the old covenant with Israel and the new—the Epistle to the Romans—begins as a comparative history of aesthetics. The gentiles, Paul explains in chapter 1, chose to worship created things rather than deduce from those things the existence of the true God ("Ever since the creation of the world his invisible nature, namely his eternal power and deity, has been clearly perceived in the things that have been made," Rom 1:18–20). To the Israelites, however, God gave the law, which was designed to teach them humanity's powerlessness to save itself by its own works from the "law of sin which dwells in [its] members"; and to announce the coming gift of God's love, the messiah who would redeem humanity from this impasse.

But when that redeemer came, most of Israel rejected him. It did so, according to Paul, because of its own errors of perception and cognition. It saw only

the outside of God's gifts—their literal, carnal, and ceremonial significance—
rather than their inner or spiritual meaning. It understood only the letter of
God's scripture, only the humanity of God's son. "To set the mind on the flesh
is death, but to set the mind on the spirit is life and peace" (8:6). Because of
this slavery to the flesh and to its senses, the bulk of Israel was cut off from
God's vine, making room for the in-grafting of the gentiles. Outcast Israel did
retain the honor of having received the promise ("As regards the gospel they
are enemies of God for your sake; but as regards election they are beloved for
the sake of their forefathers," 11:28). She was not condemned forever. At the
end of time "all Israel will be saved," and her reconciliation will bring "life for
the dead" (Rom. 11). But in the meantime, the Israelites who reject Jesus have
yet another aesthetic role to play. They are "vessels of wrath made for destruction, in order to make known the riches of his glory for the vessels of mercy"
(9:22–23). Their "blind eyes" and bent backs serve as a lesson to gentile Christians (like those among the Romans and the Galatians), a warning not to repeat
their ocular error of seeing only the letter of the law, the outer flesh rather than
the inner spirit. Already here, in this text from the first generation after the
death of Jesus, the Jews are becoming media, exemplary artifacts through which
God's teachings about vision becomes visible and the Christian eye learns how
to see.[3]

Unlike these New Testament texts, all surviving Christian art postdates the
"parting of the ways." Its producers live in a world—beginning in the third and
fourth centuries of the Common Era—in which the differences between "old
Israel" and "new" are more sharply defined, with the "new" politically and
demographically in the ascendant. Questions of Judaism no longer exert the
same pressure upon Christians that they had upon the apostolic communities.[4]
But as early Christianity, with its critical discourse of "flesh" and "spirit,"
expanded into the material culture of the Greco-Roman world and adopted
some of the representational practices of that world, the pressure from questions of art grows all the greater. What is the proper use of artifacts in Christian
worship? Did attention to the beautiful works of human hands constitute a
misplaced emphasis on the things of this world, or worse, a form of idolatry?
Does the decoration of churches and devotional objects orient the eye toward
darkness or toward light? And if decoration is allowed, what styles, motifs, and
symbols should it draw upon? Are those of ancient Israel permitted? And what
of those, vastly more numerous and prestigious, from the gentile cultures of the
ancient world?

In part because early Christians had addressed aesthetic questions in terms
of Judaism, later Christians did so as well. And from the beginning, we see
answers to these questions proffered in the works of art themselves. When—to

turn once more to Dura Europos—the painters of the Christian chapel avoid
picturing Christ on the focal wall, even while introducing him in the narratives
on the sides, they betray a sensitivity to issues posed by the Second Commandment similar to (and presumably in dialogue with) that of the Jews in their
nearby synagogue. And when Roman Christians adorned the walls of catacombs
with exempla from Hebrew Scripture, they were appropriating examples of Jewish salvation not only in order to supplant them with more esteemed pictures
of Christian eschatological belief, but also to assert a new lineage, and a new
place in salvation history, for Roman culture.

Since works of art have an a priori commitment to the legitimacy of their
own existence, texts may provide more extreme formulations of the problem.
The late fourth-century debate between St. Jerome and Nepotian over the decoration of churches provides a famous example. Nepotian invokes God's
approval of the precious objects in Jerusalem's Temple to justify Christian decoration. Jerome attacks precisely that point in his counterargument: "And let no
one allege against me the wealth of the temple of Judea, its tables, its lamps . . .
and the rest of its golden vessels." Those things of the Temple were, according
to Jerome, "figures typifying things still in the future." But for Christians, who
live in that future, "the Law is spiritual." If Christians "keep to the letter" in
this, they must keep it in everything and adopt the Jewish rituals: "Rejecting the
superstition of the Jews, we must also reject the gold; or approving the gold, we
must approve the Jews as well. For we must either accept them with the gold or
condemn them with it." St. Paul had condemned gentile Christians who
adopted Israelite practices of circumcision as "Judaizers" (Gal. 2:14). St. Jerome
tries to extend the condemnation to include decorators of churches.[5]

We can see from this one example that invocations of Judaism could justify
diametrically opposed positions toward Christian art. Where Nepotian stressed
the ongoing value of the Hebrew prophets' literal example in order to approve
of art and decoration, Jerome rejected it by insisting on the complete supersces-
sion of the letter by the spirit, casting any residual literalism as "Judaizing." But
of course the example is not exhaustive: there were countless other positions
available, as many as there were ways of thinking about the relationship between
the "Old Testament" and the "New." It is precisely because early Christian
questions about that relationship were so multiple, and so important to Christian understanding of the relationship between God and the material world,
that Jews and Judaism came to stand at the center of Christian thinking about
the dangers of aesthetics and the possibilities for art.

With a topic as vast as this, it would be vain to aim for comprehensive
coverage, but the essays collected here span a millennium and a half of Christian
culture. We begin (Chapter 1) with Jaś Elsner's study of fourth-century reliefs

of the Israelites crossing the Red Sea on fourth-century Christian sarcophagi—
"Pharaoh's Army Got Drownded"—in order to discover how Christian art created a distinctive space for itself within Roman culture by representing its
descent from Israel. And we finish (Chapter 12) deep in nineteenth-century
French colonial territory, with Ralph Ubl's reading of Eugène Delacroix's paintings of "A Jewish Wedding in Morocco" as a defense of the materiality of paint
and the medium of painting.

The sheer chronological range of the essays' subjects should make clear that
the importance of our topic is not limited to any particular period, or even to
what we would consider religious art. On the contrary, we hope that the cumulative impact of the chapters in this volume demonstrates that centuries of
thinking about art in terms of Judaism have made Judaism a critical figure for
modern as well as premodern aesthetics in the West, and for secular as well as
sacred. It is for this reason that the volume concludes with an essay—David
Nirenberg's "The Judaism of Christian Art"—that uses the figure of the Jew
to retrace the history of Western aesthetics, from the ancient world until the
present.

That said, a number of the essays in this volume focus on the timespan from
1000 to 1650, the periods called by art historians the "Middle Ages" and the
"Renaissance." Collectively, these essays seek to explain how Christian theology
and Christian art fashioned the Jews into—to quote Herbert Kessler's "Shaded
with Dust" (Chapter 3)—"the cohort of the 'eye of the body' on the battlefield
of Christian art, continuously engaged in combat with the Christian troops of
the 'eye of the heart.'" And they seek to demonstrate some of the ways in which
Christian art deployed these "Jewish" cohorts, in order to conquer, defend, and
explore its own territory.

Kessler's "Shaded with Dust" is a lapidary history of this deployment in the
early and high Middle Ages. It provides, together with Sara Lipton's "Unfeigned
Witness" (Chapter 2), the foundations for this temporal cluster, setting the
artifacts of emerging eleventh- and twelfth-century visual culture within the
context of theological debates about the "Jewish" dangers of vision and of
media. Lipton's essay elaborates one of the deepest piers in this foundation,
demonstrating how the Augustinian doctrine of the Jews as blind witnesses to
Christian truth was, in the twelfth century, put to the work of authenticating
textual and material representations of Christian sanctity. The Jewish witness in
the life of Saint Heribertus and the Hebrew prophets standing on the twelfth-
century Eilbertus Altar both emerge as defenders of the artifact, protecting the
work from the charge of "fiction" with which Christian critics of art could
reproach it.

                       DAVID NIRENBERG

The subsequent essays each explore a different aspect of the constantly evolving work that figures of Judaism did for Christian art. In Chapter 4, Francisco Prado-Vilar discovers, in the inclusion and exclusion of Jews from the illuminations of a sumptuous thirteenth-century Castilian manuscript of poetry devoted to the Virgin Mary, a strategy of biopolitical resistance to the reduction of the Christian body to "bare life." And we might add—although he does not claim it—that in the process he has also discovered a strategy by which the illuminations themselves resist the reduction of the image to bare matter and bare mimesis. Felipe Pereda's "Through a Glass Darkly: Paths to Salvation in Spanish Painting at the Outset of the Inquisition" (Chapter 9) presents us with a case from the same kingdom—Castile—some two centuries later, at a time when the conversion of tens of thousands of Jews to Christianity had fractured consensus about the "Christianity" of art. Pereda provides an illuminating case study of how a Christian culture refashioned its converts into the "Jewish" cohorts it needed to defend Christian art. Stephen Campbell (Chapter 10) addresses a fear of "Judaism" provoked not by old Jews or new converts, but by new "realist" styles of painting. Focusing on a group of mid-sixteenth-century Brescian painters that included Moretto—who explored Old Testament themes like the sacrifice of Isaac in order to differentiate his "sacred naturalism" from rival forms of realism that he associated with carnality, mimesis, and excessive mediation—he offers us a powerful example of how readily pictorial realism was assimilable in Christian thought to "Jewish" emphasis on material form rather than spiritual truth. Finally, at the very end of our Medieval and Renaissance cluster, the illegible Hebrew script that Poussin's Jesus writes in the dust of "The Woman Caught in Adultery" becomes for Richard Neer (Chapter 11) the founding charter of Christian history painting. It is in these letters, writes Neer, that Poussin "think[s] history painting's grounding laws of space, time, and legibility, laws that Poussin states precisely in order to transcend them in his figural juxtapositions."

The diversity of this volume is not only chronological: it also encompasses a great variety of objects and artifacts—from coffins to canvasses—some of which we moderns are not used to thinking of as art. In societies accustomed to imagining the earthly city in terms of the heavenly one, even the built environment can be considered a form of Christian art and thus engaged in terms of Judaism. In Achim Timmermann's "Frau Venus, the Eucharist, and the Jews of Landshut" (Chapter 6), we see a sculptural assault on Synagoga transform the orientation of the roads leading to a town square into a memorial of the expulsion of the Jews and a representation of the Church's victories over Judaism; while in Dana Katz's essay on the Venice ghetto (Chapter 8), Jewish skyscrapers become a painful provocation of the Christian gaze.

The one form of diversity we have not striven for is religious. A number of the authors represented here are experts in the history of Judaism and of Jewish art, but few real Jews people the pages of this volume: Jews who breathed air and lived history, as opposed to Jews as imagined by Christians and represented in Christian art. Occasionally we do find living Jews intervening in this work, as in the fifteenth-century case of Rabbi Moses Arragel, whose attempts to shape the program of the Alba Bible's Christian illuminators Marcia Kupfer discusses in Chapter 5. But the cultures, artists, and objects we are studying are primarily Christian because our focus is on the work that figures of Judaism do in Christian art, and on the ways in which that art deployed the perils and possibilities of Judaism in order to explore the perils and possibilities of its own practice.

It is worth stressing that this work did not depend on the presence of real, living Jews of flesh and blood. In fact, it was often carried out in places (such as medieval England and France, or early modern Spain and Germany) from which the Jews themselves had all been converted or expelled.[6] This is not to say that Christian representations of Judaism were unaffected by the existence and actions of real Jews; that (conversely) these representations had no real consequences for the possibilities of existence available to Jews; or that Jews did not engage with or contest Christian representations of Judaism. It is, however, to say that these topics are not the primary focus of this book. The essays below often point to these interdependences as they contextualize the Christian phenomenology they uncover. But their goal, and the common purpose of this volume, is the discovery of that Christian phenomenology itself. For only once that phenomenology is discovered does it become possible to see the vital role that anti-Jewish projection played in providing a protected ontological space for the creation of Christian art.

A Note on Terms

Although words such as "Jew," "Israelite," and "Hebrew" have acquired specific meanings in the historical disciplines of our day, the distinctions are not those of other times and places. For example, although by "Israelite" an English-speaking historian today might mean only a member of the ancient kingdom and not a rabbinic Jew, until the mid-twentieth century the word was used (and in some languages continues to be used) to designate contemporary Jews. We are confident that the terms are clear in context and have not been dogmatic about imposing uniformity. Similarly, where many Jews (or at least, Jewish scholars) prefer the term "Hebrew Bible" to "Old Testament" because of the latter's supersessionist implications, "Old Testament" remains in wide use among Christian scholars and in Christian culture, and therefore sometimes

DAVID NIRENBERG

appears in these pages. Finally, it is worth repeating that this is a book about Christian figures of Judaism. Those figures are historical realities of power and consequence, but they need not, and very often do not, correspond to real Jews or to what we know about historical Judaism. In this sense, we should imagine scare quotes around most uses of "Jew" and "Judaism" in this book, for we are writing about figures of Judaism created by Christians in order to think about art, not Jews or Judaism as they imagined or represented themselves.

NOTES

1. See Richard Wagner, "Das Judenthum in der Musik," published in 1850 under the pseudonym of K. Freigedank, in the *Neue Zeitschrift fuer Musik* 33, no. 19 (September 3), and no. 20 (September 6). A new edition appeared in 1869 (*Richard Wagner's Prose Works*, ed. and trans. W. A. Ellis [London, 1897]).

2. *Heine's Werke* (Berlin and Weimar, 1968), 5:197–98.

3. Paul invokes the blinding of the Jews' eyes in Romans 11:10, citing Psalm 68:23–24. Augustine will take up Paul's point, for example in *De civitate dei* 18.46: "But the rest are blinded, of whom it was predicted, 'Let their eyes be darkened lest they see.'" It should be stressed that in describing Paul's Jewish "vessels of wrath" as "exemplary artifacts," I do not mean to imply that Paul intended the exemplarity that later Christian thinkers—most famously St. Augustine—developed from them.

4. To say that these questions no longer exert the "same pressure" is not to say that they exert no pressure: in every period covered by this book, from the first century to the mid-twentieth, there is always a great deal of concern among both Christians and Jews about questions of difference and zones of indistinction. But the causes, contexts, and consequences of these anxieties are very different in the late fourth century of St. John Chrysostom, for example, from those in the mid-first century of St. Paul.

5. St. Jerome, Letter 52 (dated 394), chapter 10.

6. In the case of fifteenth-century Spain (studied in Chapter 9), the Judaism that was thought to threaten Christian art was believed to come from "New Christians," converts from Judaism and their descendents. This does not mean, of course, that the converts considered themselves Jews or thought of themselves as Judaizing.

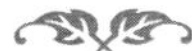

CHAPTER 1

"Pharaoh's Army Got Drownded": Some Reflections on Jewish and Roman Genealogies in Early Christian Art

Jaś Elsner

If I could, I surely would
Stand on the rock where Moses stood.
Pharoah's army got drownded—
Oh Mary, don't you weep.
Oh Mary don't you weep, don't you mourn,
Oh Mary don't you weep, don't you mourn,
Pharoah's army got drownded—
Oh Mary, don't you weep.
Mary wore three links of chain,
Every link was Jesus' name.
Pharoah's army got drownded—
Oh Mary, don't you weep.
Oh Mary don't you weep, don't you mourn,
Oh Mary don't you weep, don't you mourn,
Pharoah's army got drownded—
Oh Mary, don't you weep.
Mary wore three links of chain,
Every link was freedom's name.
Pharoah's army got drownded—
Oh Mary, don't you weep
Oh Mary don't you weep, don't you mourn,

Oh Mary don't you weep, don't you mourn,
Pharoah's army got drownded—
Oh Mary, don't you weep.
One of these nights about twelve o'clock,
This ol' world is gonna reel and rock.
Pharoah's army got drownded—
Oh Mary, don't you weep.
Oh Mary don't you weep, don't you mourn,
Oh Mary don't you weep, don't you mourn,
Pharoah's army got drownded—
Oh Mary, don't you weep.
Moses stood on the Red Sea shore,
Smotin' the water with a two by four.
Pharoah's army got drownded—
Oh Mary, don't you weep.
Oh Mary don't you weep, don't you mourn,
Oh Mary don't you weep, don't you mourn,
Pharoah's army got drownded—
Oh Mary, don't you weep.
—Negro spiritual, attested before the U.S. Civil War[1]

I open with a song that demonstrates the remarkable longevity of certain uses of imagery and allusion to scripture that are characteristic of Christianity from the early church until the present day.[2] This song appears, as it opens, to be about the Hebrews' liberation from Egyptian tyranny in the miraculous actions of Moses at the Red Sea shore. As soon as it reaches the chorus, this spiritual slides from a Jewish to a Christian thematics and instantly revises the Jewish narrative as a type or figure for a triumphant Christian story. That Christianity is explicitly affirmed in the second verse with "Jesus' name"; and the implicit model of one story being a cipher or symbol for another leads to the evocation of "freedom's name" in the third verse—signaling not only personal and collective spiritual freedom but also freedom from slavery (in the context of America in the 1860s, where the song is first attested) and freedom in relation to institutional prejudice and civil rights in later contexts of its singing and reception. But even before it gets to the chorus, in its very first verse, this spiritual performs that model of retrospective reading whereby what has just been articulated comes to have a different meaning, one that implicitly includes but expands upon the first apparent level of significance. "The rock where Moses stood" seems initially to refer to Sinai and the cleft of rock where Moses stood for his vision of God (Exod. 33:18–23) and to receive the tablets of the Law; it is only in the light of the chorus that it must (also) mean the Red Sea shore.

The most interesting and sophisticated biblical play in this song is the injunction to Mary in the chorus. For Mary (in Greek, *Mariam*) is the name both of Jesus' mother and of Mary the Prophetess, sister of Moses and Aaron (translated in most English versions as Miriam to differentiate her from the Virgin, but in fact the name is identical both in Greek and in Jerome's Latin Vulgate, where it is rendered as Maria). The instruction to Mary not to weep and not to mourn not only refers to the Passion of Christ and the image of the mourning Mother of God but also to Mary the Prophetess, who "took a timbrel in her hand; and all the women went out after her with timbrels and with dances. And Mary answered them, Sing ye to the Lord, for he hath triumphed gloriously; the horse and his rider hath he thrown into the sea" (Exod. 15:20–21). Mary must not weep and mourn *because* Pharaoh's army got drownded, because, that is, not only were the Jews saved by Moses but all men were saved by Jesus and all the imprisoned by the coming of "freedom's name." The negative form of the injunction—"Oh Mary don't you weep, don't you mourn"— deftly allows it to refer both to Miriam's celebratory singing and dancing *and* to Mary's sadness at the Crucifixion and death of Our Lord.[3]

The Red Sea Sarcophagi

Among historiated Christian sarcophagi, only one narrative theme has the distinction of developing an iconography that occupies the full visual field of the main front of the coffin exclusively and without being juxtaposed against varieties of other Old or New Testament (or apocryphal) scenes.[4] This is the late fourth-century rendition of the crossing of the Red Sea (Exod. 14:15–15:22), of which examples survive from Rome, southern France, and Split—some made in Rome and then exported, and others probably made in Gaul.[5] The Theodosian rendering of the theme is a developed version of earlier fourth-century experiments with the subject on a smaller scale and as one narrative among several on a sarcophagus' main face.[6] Interestingly, the theme is also popular in early Christian poetry.[7]

While the examples from the 380s and 390s show some iconographic variation, they fit into broadly a standard scheme (Figure 1.1). On the left hand side (from the viewer's perspective), the Egyptian army—mounted and in late Roman military dress—ride out of the city gates in pursuit of the Israelites. Beneath them are a series of small-scale reclining personifications that appear to represent the land of Egypt and the Red Sea.[8] At the head of the Egyptian cavalry, about a third of the way along the frieze of the sarcophagus front,

JAŚ ELSNER

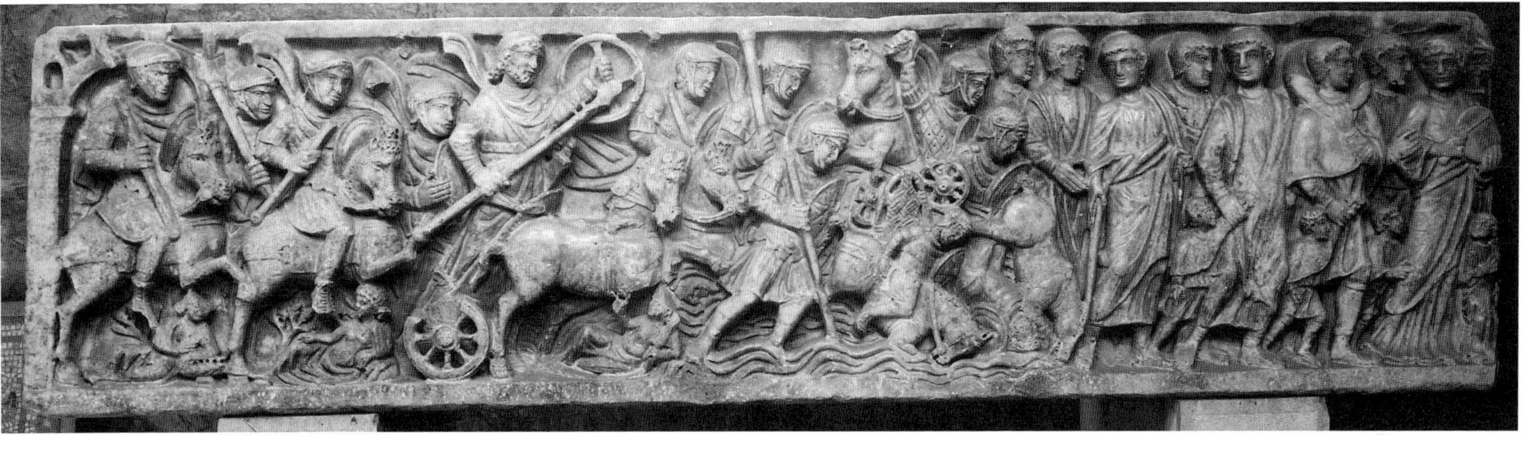

1.1. Sarcophagus of the Red Sea crossing, front, c. 380–90 A.D. Marble (from Carrara). Probably from a Roman workshop. Archaeological Museum, Split (where it was in the Franciscan Church as early as the fourteenth century). Photo courtesy DAI Rome, Inst. Neg. 1982.2071 (Schwanke).

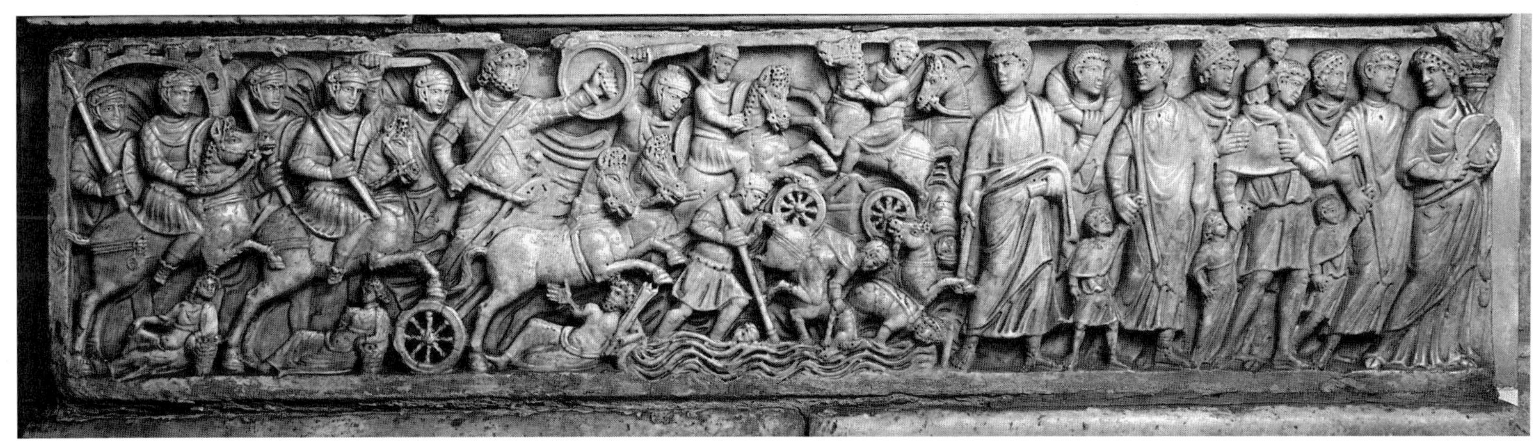

1.2. Sarcophagus of the Red Sea crossing, front, c. 380–90 A.D. Marble. Probably from a Roman workshop. Currently serving as the altar front in the Grignan chapel in the church of St. Trophime in Arles. Photo courtesy DAI Rome, Inst. Neg. 1960.1813 (Böhringer).

comes Pharaoh dressed as a Roman emperor and riding in a chariot bearing a round shield in his outstretched left hand and spear in his right.[9] The center of the visual plane shows the Egyptian army plunging to its death in a chaos of overturned figures, all on a smaller scale than the riding Egyptians to the left or the escaping Hebrews to the right. In only one example, the great sarcophagus now in the church of St. Trophime in Arles (Figure 1.2), is Pharaoh himself certainly shown again, tumbling beneath the waves, his head immediately beneath Moses' staff but still at the front of his now shattered troops.[10] On the right-hand side of the visual field Moses strikes the sea with his staff, causing disaster to fall upon the Egyptians while the Israelites flee to safety. It is the imagery of the saved Jews on which I primarily focus in this chapter. This is characterized by several features—a mix of men, women, and children escaping, also the figure of Miriam singing and dancing with her "timbrel" in celebration (Exod. 15:20–21).

The full visual field in these sarcophagi offers a frame of repeated mounted figures on the left and repeated walking figures on the right with a chaos of falling and overturning figures in the center. In the most splendid surviving example, the sarcophagus from St. Trophime in Arles, the three small-scale personifications beneath the horses on the left might be said to balance the three smaller-scale figures of children walking beside their Hebrew parents on the right, but in fact the number of Hebrew children varies from one to four in the different sarcophagi within the corpus (as the number of personifications varies from one to three). A contrast nonetheless is drawn between reclining symbols of the old order and the youth, the future, of the saved Israelites. There is a polarity between armed men and horses to the left and unarmed men, women, and children to the right in which victory goes to those without weapons (a sufficient structural differentiation to enable interpretation of the sort unleashed on the Bible by the anthropologist Edmund Leach, if one were so inclined).[11] Indeed, kinship is a specific issue underlined among the saved Hebrews—not just by the imagery of family couples and generations but also by the image of Miriam and its allusion to a text that specifically affirms the fact that she is sister of Aaron. Certainly the figures of Moses and Pharaoh, one with his staff and the other with sword or spear, are in counterpoint.[12] So, too, are the images of Pharaoh and Miriam, each of whom bears a round object (shield or timbrel) aloft.[13] The water symbolism has allowed the option of inferring a baptismal meaning to this imagery, alongside more liturgically based interpretations as well as the rather fanciful comparison of the Red Sea crossing with Constantine's victory over Maxentius at the Milvian Bridge.[14] In some sarcophagi, the move is from culture to nature—Pharaoh's army leaving its city gates to perish in the waters as the Hebrews advance into the wilderness.[15] But

JAŚ ELSNER

in others, culture makes an odd entry into the natural, right-hand side of the field. In the great, now fragmented version in Metz, a pillar with a capital that sprouts flames is carved into the background at the point where Pharaoh's army perishes and Moses' staff touches the waters (a literal rendition of the pillar of cloud by day and fire by night—in Greek, *stylos*—which goes before the Israelites in their flight through the wilderness [Exod. 13:21–22] and moves from before the Hebrews to behind them when they cross the Red Sea, giving light to the Jews but darkness to Pharaoh's army [Exod. 14:19, 24]).[16] In a fragmentary example from the Villa Doria Pamphili in Rome, a triumphal arch has been carved over the figure of Moses—signaling a kind of divine doorway into the wilderness of Sinai, perhaps, or emphasizing Moses' most spectacular miracle.[17] Strangest are two cases in Nimes and Rome (Figure 1.3) where the entire narrative takes place before a background of arches, columns, and colonnades, and indeed the wilderness in which the Jews would wander for forty years seems more urban than the Egypt they are escaping.[18]

The subject is certainly not confined only to sarcophagi in early Christian art. Its key appearance in Rome was in the lost frescoes of narrative themes from Genesis and Exodus on the right wall of the nave of Old St. Peter's, where the Red Sea crossing uniquely occupied two pictorial panels in an expansion of a given subject that may have inspired the exceptional size of the rendition on our sarcophagi.[19] The date of the St. Peter's frescoes is not certain—but they are probably later than the traditional Constantinian foundation of the church,[20] and if the date of the Vatican basilica is in fact mid- to late fourth century rather than Constantinian,[21] then they may be very close to the sarcophagi. Among surviving images, the Red Sea crossing appears in catacomb painting—most notably in two fourth-century images from cubiculum C and cubiculum O, respectively, in the Via Latina Catacomb in Rome,[22] on the early fifth-century wooden doors of the church of Santa Sabina in Rome,[23] and in the program of fifth-century mosaics in the nave of the basilica of Santa Maria Maggiore in Rome.[24] In a fragmentary and abbreviated form, it survives also in a remarkable fourth-century textile, probably from Egypt, now in Bern, depicting various Old Testament scenes.[25] There is an illumination of the Red Sea crossing in the late sixth- or seventh-century Latin manuscript known as the Ashburnham Pentateuch, which may or may not reflect an earlier tradition of illustration.[26]

If we turn to the full visual context in which this large-scale scene of the Red Sea crossing—occupying the whole face of a sarcophagus front—is set, it is unfortunate that only a few examples survive where the sides of the sarcophagus are also preserved. Some have nonfigural carving on the ends.[27] The great example at Split (Figure 1.1), which is unusual in having all four faces carved, offers no narrative scheme on its other sides, nor any obvious connection of their

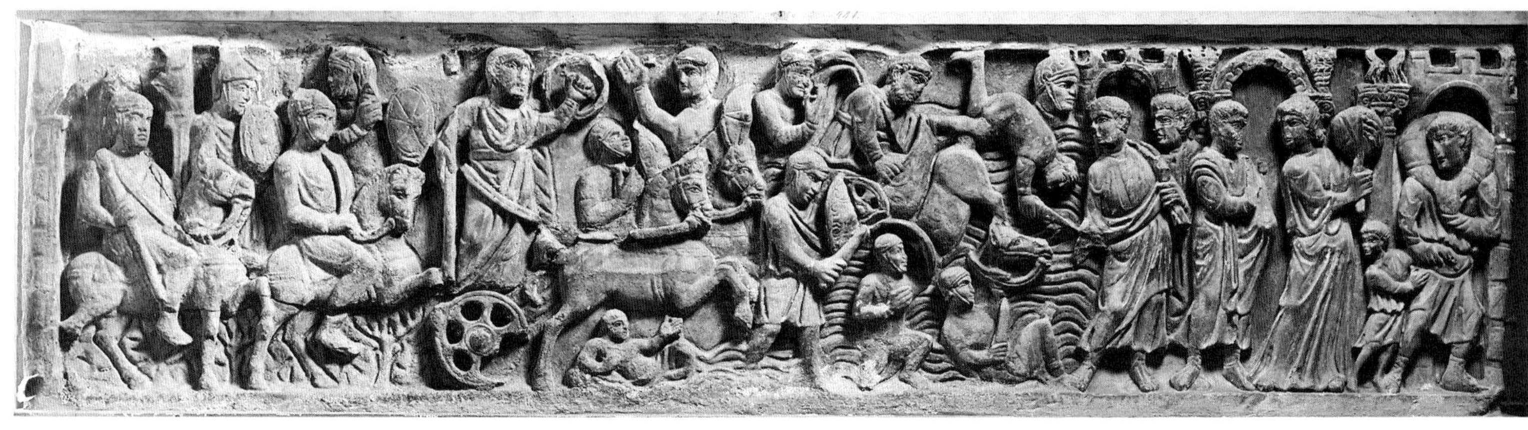

1.3. Sarcophagus of the Red Sea crossing, front, c. 380–90 A.D. Marble. Probably made in Rome. Museo Pio Cristiano, Vatican City, Rome. Photo courtesy DAI Rome, Inst. Neg. 03223.

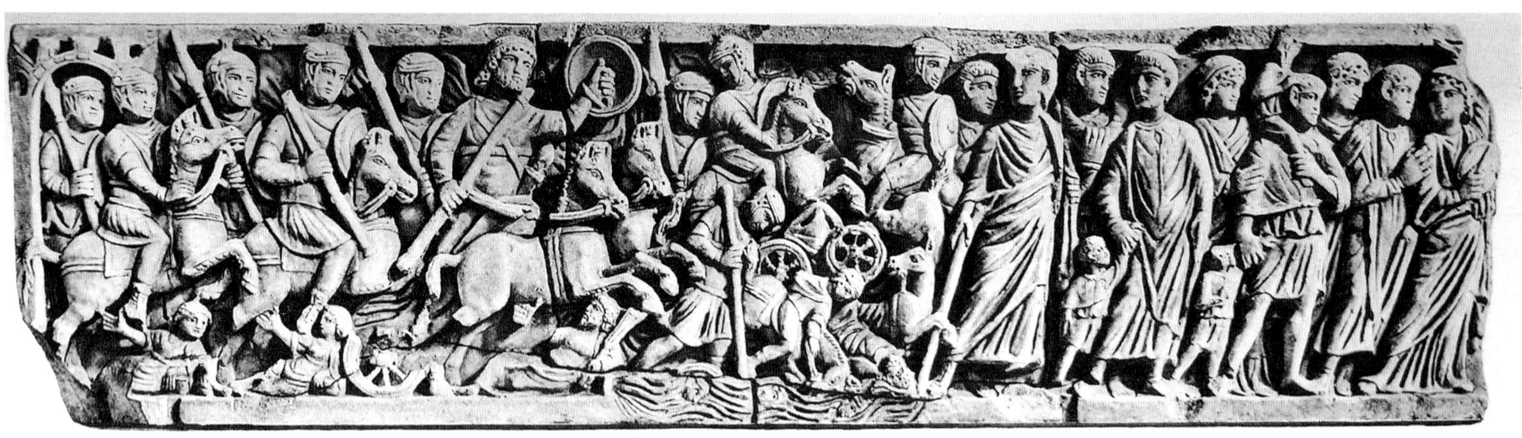

1.4. Sarcophagus of the Red Sea crossing, front, c. 380–90 A.D. Marble. Probably from a Roman workshop. Musée Granet, Aix-en-Provence (brought to Aix in the sixteenth century from Alyscamps in Arles). Photo after G. Wilpert, *I Sarcophagi Cristiani Antichi* (Rome, 1929), cxxxxvii, 1.

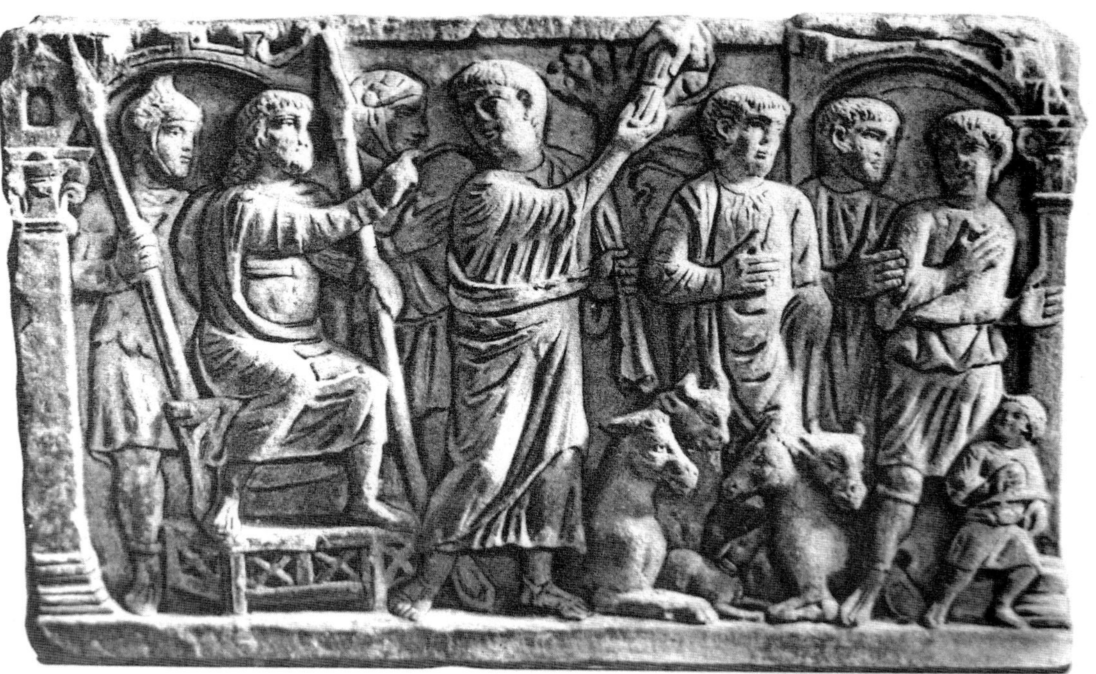

1.5. Sarcophagus of the Red Sea crossing, as in Figure 1.4. Left side, showing Moses before Pharaoh and the Israelites beginning their journey out of Egypt. Photo after G. Wilpert, *I Sarcophagi Cristiani Antichi* (Rome, 1929), cxxxxvii, 2.

imagery with that of the Red Sea crossing.[28] On the right end, two male figures bearing scrolls stand between a large cross topped with the christogram in a wreath, while the left end has a repeated conch-shaped decorative pattern typical of sarcophagi of this period. The back shows a female orant in the center and two standing male figures (that on the right with a scroll) at the ends with panels of strigillation in between. While this is a typical scheme in many carved sarcophagi of the late fourth century,[29] a reading that played on the Red Sea theme of the front might see the orant as a figure for Miriam/Mary, the saints to the right and left as figures for the saved (as in the Israelites) and the undulating strigillation as imaging the waters of the Red Sea. Needless to say, such interpretative possibilities—while opened by the very juxtaposition of the imagery before the gazes of beholders—are unprovable. By contrast, the sarcophagus at Aix-en-Provence is extremely interesting in keeping firmly to the Mosaic narrative (Figure 1.4).[30] The left end (Figure 1.5) shows Pharaoh enthroned, presumably at the point where he orders Moses to take the Israelites out of Egypt (Exod. 12:31–2). Moses turns toward Pharaoh but reaches up to receive a scroll from Heaven—in one sense a reference to his repeated instructions from God

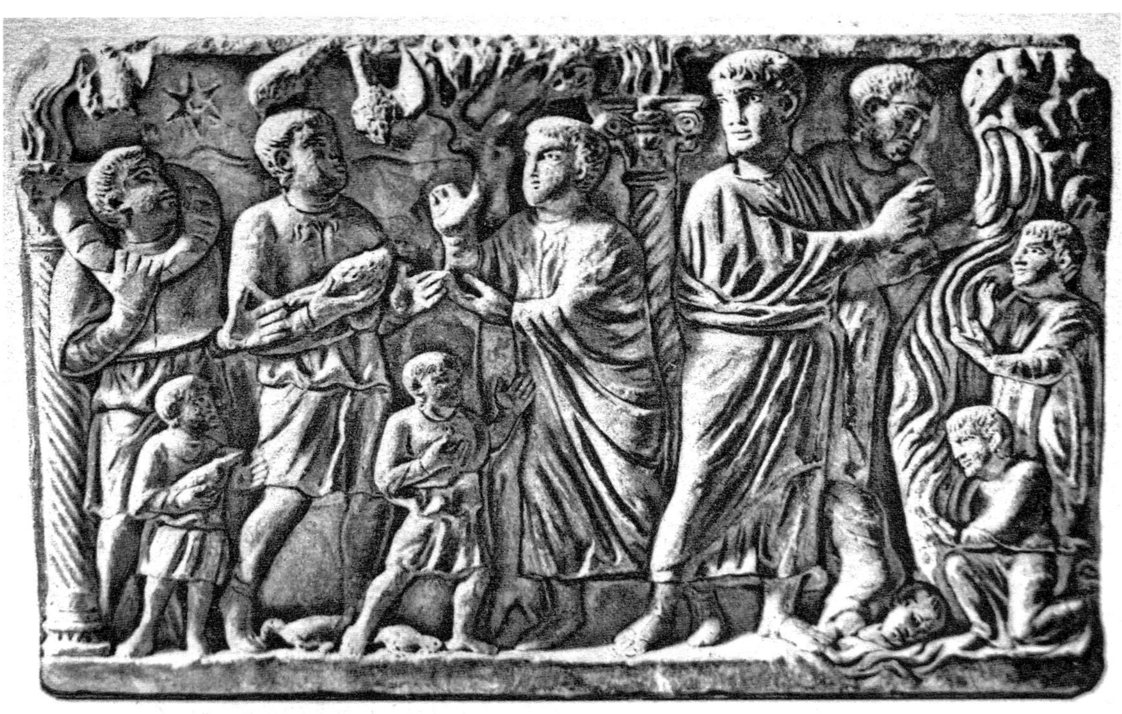

1.6. Sarcophagus of the Red Sea crossing, as in Figure 1.4. Right side, showing the miracle of manna and quails and Moses making the bitter waters sweet. Photo after G. Wilpert, *I Sarcophagi Cristiani Antichi* (Rome, 1929), cxxxxvii, 3.

but also a proleptic signal beyond this stage in the story toward his receiving the tablets of the Law on Sinai (Exod. 34:1–27). To the right, the Hebrews begin their journey out of Egypt. On the right end (Figure 1.6) are two of Moses' miracles in the wilderness—each inaugurated by the column of fire. On the left is the miracle of quails and manna (Exod. 16:4–36); on the right Moses making the bitter waters sweet (Exod. 15:23–27). Here, the ends are made to bleed into the Red Sea narrative of the front, with the Israelites leaving Egypt (on the left) already presaging the crossing of the Red Sea and the walking men and children in the scene of the miracle of quails and manna on the right end effectively carrying on the imagery of the escaping Israelites from the right side of the front.[31] There is a certain amount of play with scriptural chronology (the water miracle precedes that of manna and quails in the text, but comes afterward in the image; the allusion to the tablets of the Law points well ahead in the Exodus narrative). The key point, however, is that the Red Sea theme was highly adaptable to appearing as an isolated subject, a point within a longer, scripturally based narrative that firmly kept to an Old Testament model,[32] or as an image that could be juxtaposed against and beside more directly Christian imagery.

Some Iconographic Appropriations

To return to the Red Sea image, I want to press more carefully the representation of the liberated Israelites on the right-hand side of the visual field (Figure 1.7). What is immediately noticeable is the familial emphasis with men, women, and children all prominent in the crowd of refugees. Familial imagery does to some extent also mark the iconography of the Red Sea crossing in other media—such as mosaics and paintings.[33] What has been less remarked on is the iconographic origins of these figures in the sarcophagi in relation to earlier mainstream Roman art. In particular, where children are carried or held by an adult, it is always by a male. The children on these sarcophagi come in four types—which never appear all together in any of our surviving examples. A child may walk alone, may be held by a parental hand, may be carried on a father's shoulders, and—in the most striking image, since it has a very deep past in Roman visual culture—a father may both carry a child on his shoulders and hold a second child by the hand. The surviving examples are best illustrated by means of Table 1.1.

This imagery is carefully chosen and has deep resonances in Roman art. It might be said to come in two categories—the celebratory and the traumatic. In the case of the celebratory, there are two potential visual genealogies for the representation of the fleeing Hebrews: the processional relief in which children move alongside their parents (most notably in the great friezes of the Ara Pacis Augustae)[34] and the presence of children in scenes of imperial benefaction. In such canonical state reliefs as the so-called *alimenta* panel from the Arch of Trajan at Beneventum (Figure 1.8),[35] or the *liberalitas* relief from what was once an arch of Marcus and Commodus (Figure 1.9),[36] which is now on the attic story of the Arch of Constantine in the Roman Forum, parents and children constitute the recipients of imperial largesse.[37] By contrast with the Ara Pacis, where no children are carried, in the two benefaction reliefs we already have most of the adult/child combinations found on the sarcophagi. The Beneventum panel has a child standing alone before the emperor (who has lost his head), a child on his father's shoulders, and a father striding away with one child on his shoulders and another held by the hand. The Marcus relief has one child on his or her father's shoulders (the image is so damaged we cannot tell the gender) and one male child held by his ear. The parents and children in these panels become symbols of that euergetic culture that defines the proper

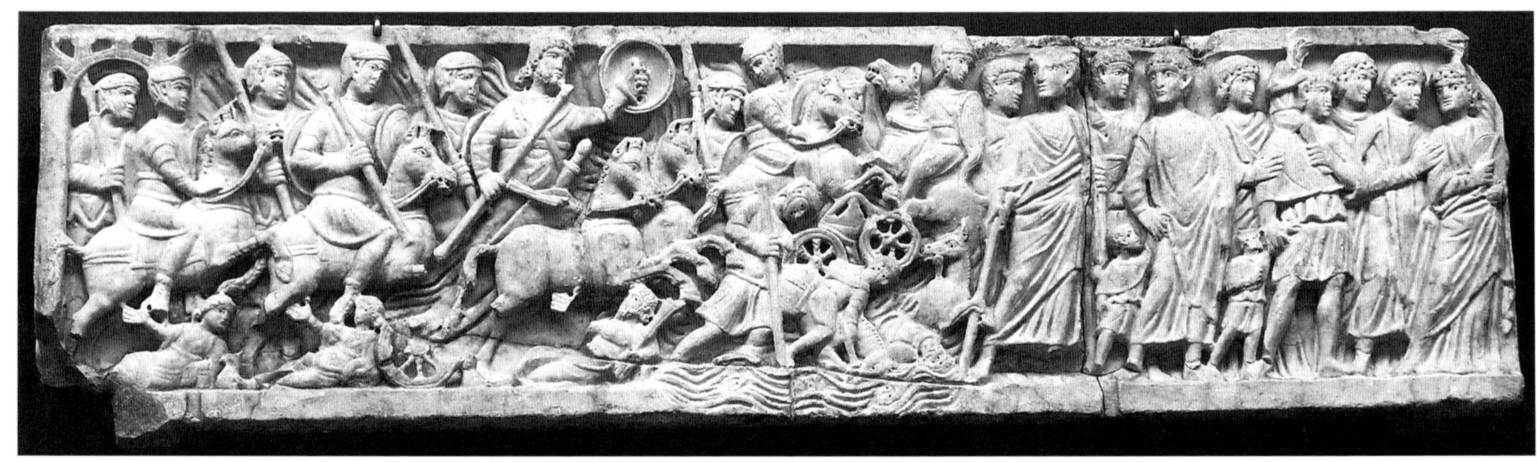

1.7. Sarcophagus front showing the Red Sea crossing, detail of the Hebrews fleeing, c. 380–90 A.D. Marble. Probably made in Rome. Musée de l'Arles antique, Arles (originally from St-Honorat-des-Alyscamps). Photo: Jaś Elsner.

Table 1.1.   Children and Adults in the Red Sea Crossing Sarccophagi

	Child walking alone	Hand-held child	Child on shoulders	Child on shoulders and child hand-held
Aix Rep III, 21/ Rizzardi 1		1	1	
Aix Rep III, 27/ Rizzardi 2		1	1	
Arles Rep III, 43/ Rizzardi 5		1		1
Arles Rep III, 44/ Rizzardi 11		1		1
Arles (St Trophime) Rep III, 119/ Rizzardi 3		2		1
Metz Rep III, 340/ Rizzardi 14	1	1		1
Moustiers Ste Marie Rep III, 356/ Rizzardi 15		1	1	
Nimes Rep III, 16/ Rizzardi 414		2		
Rome Rep I, 64/ Rizzardi 26		1		
Rome Rep I, 953/ Rizzardi 28		2	1	
Split Rep II, 146/ Rizzardi 29	2	2		

workings of empire, with the emperor himself providing for his people and ensuring their continuance through future generations. The mood music here is fundamentally positive and inclusive, though no one has satisfactorily explained why the man with the child on his shoulders and another held with his right hand should stride so purposefully *away* from the imperial presence in the benefaction scene on the Beneventum Arch. It is highly relevant that imperial largesse is at play here—and especially the distribution of piles of grain in the Beneventum scene. Many of the sarcophagi feature a male figure carrying a rolled cloak on his shoulders (and sometimes leading a child by the hand), which appears to play an iconographic variation on the image of the father with a child on his shoulders.[38] But it also, brilliantly, gives visual form to the text of Exodus 12:34: "And the people took their dough before it was leavened, their kneading troughs being bound up in their clothes upon their shoulders."

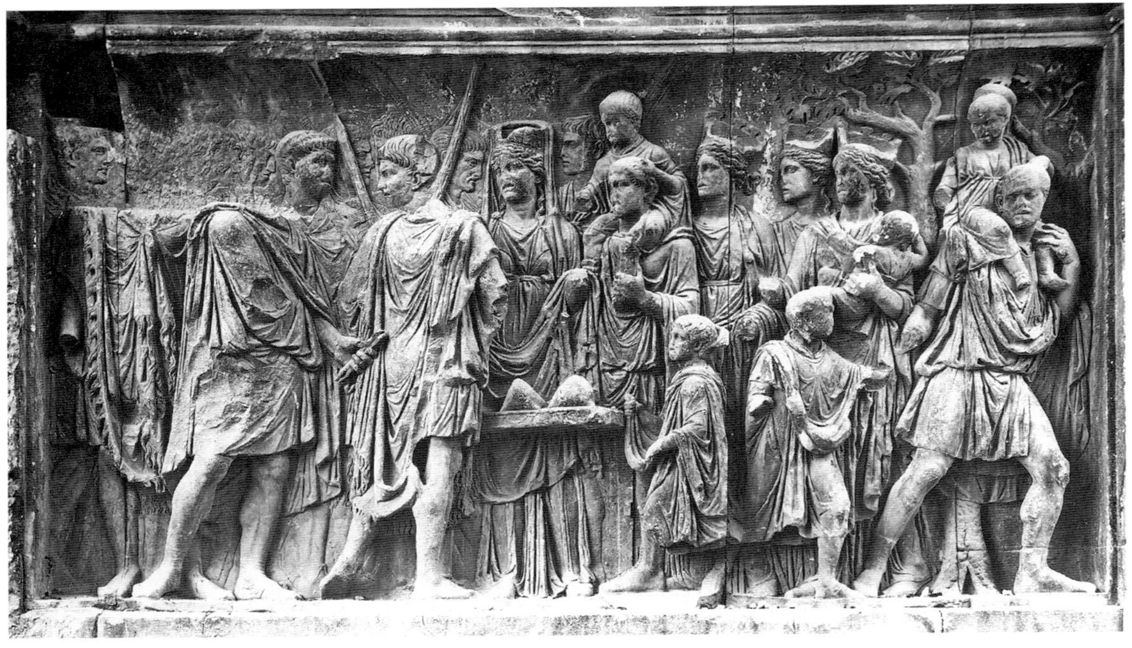

1.8. Arch of Trajan at Beneventum, c. 114–18 A.D. Marble relief panel showing Trajan (to the left, his head now missing) distributing the *alimenta* to fathers and children. From the central passageway. Photo: Alinari/Art Resource, New York.

The right end of the Aix sarcophagus plays further on this theme by having God provide His own divine *alimenta* to the Hebrews by means of the miracle of manna and quails. Effectively, the imperial benevolence theme implicit in the Roman iconography of parents and children is adapted to a Christian dispensation in which one greater than the emperor bestows miraculous gifts that surpass the mundane lotteries of pagan times.

If we turn to the traumatic, we find parents and children—and especially parents carrying children—in scenes of war and the results of war. Specifically, the Columns of Trajan and Marcus both have numerous scenes of fleeing and defeated non-Romans dragging or carrying their children away from the carnage.[39] For example, the Dacians in scene LXXVI of Trajan's Column—either fleeing the battleground or evacuating their lands at the behest of the conquering Romans—include the figure of a bearded man urgently dragging his child by the arm as well as walking children, babes in their mothers' arms and a toddler carried on its father's shoulders (Figure 1.10).[40] Scene XXXIX shows two Dacian men carrying children on their shoulders, a woman with a babe in arms and an older man shepherding a child as they retreat to a Roman encampment in the wake of three of their leaders who surrender to the emperor.[41] Scene XXX shows the

    JAŚ ELSNER

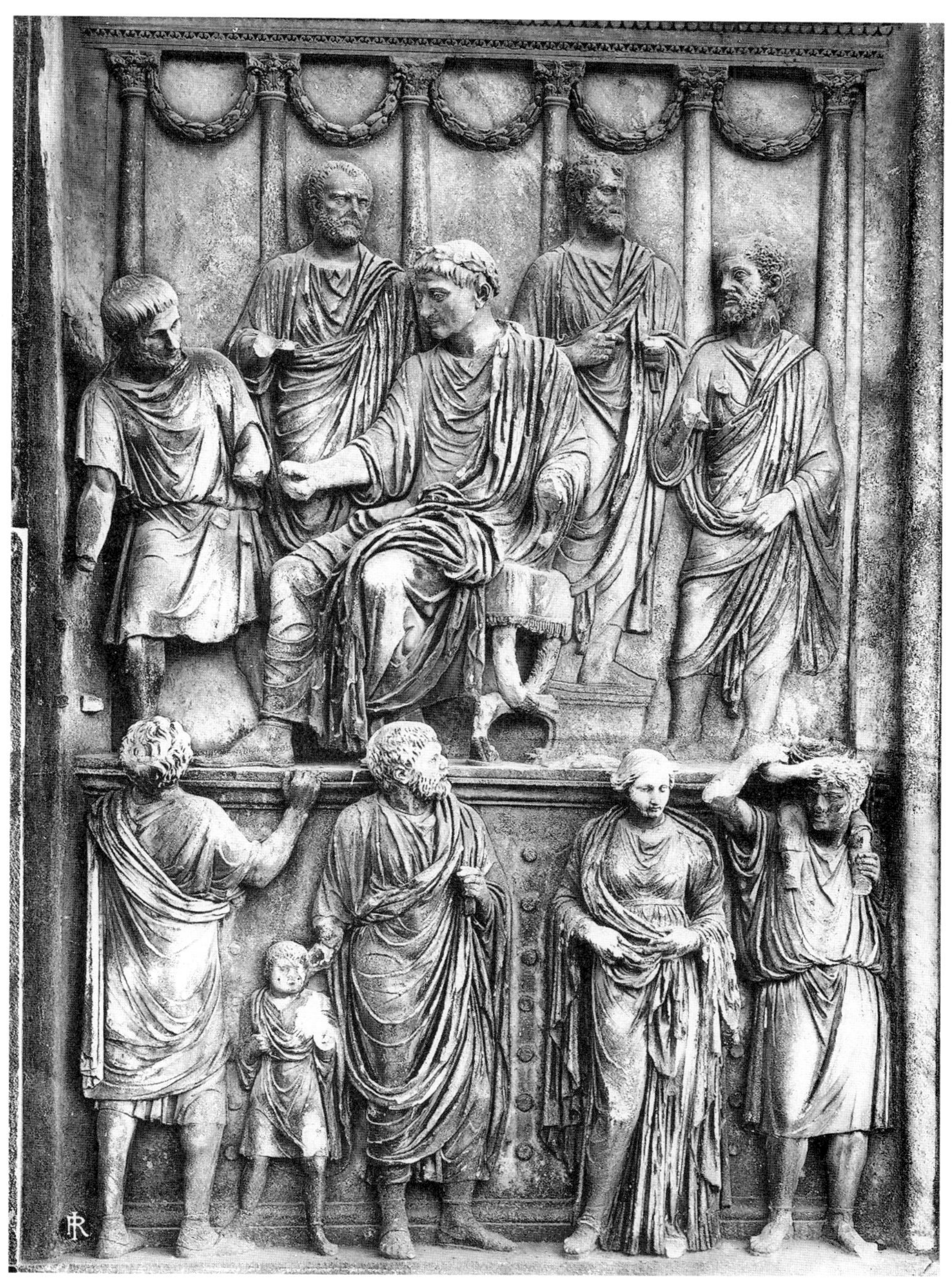

1.9. Marble relief panel showing Marcus Aurelius (his head replaced in the eighteenth century by a head of Constantine) distributing largesse to parents and children. Originally from the Arch of Marcus and Commodus (whose image was placed alongside that of Marcus but was carefully removed after his *damnatio* in 192 A.D), c. 176–80 A.D. Now in the upper storey of the Arch of Constantine in Rome, north side. Photo: Alinari/Art Resource, New York.

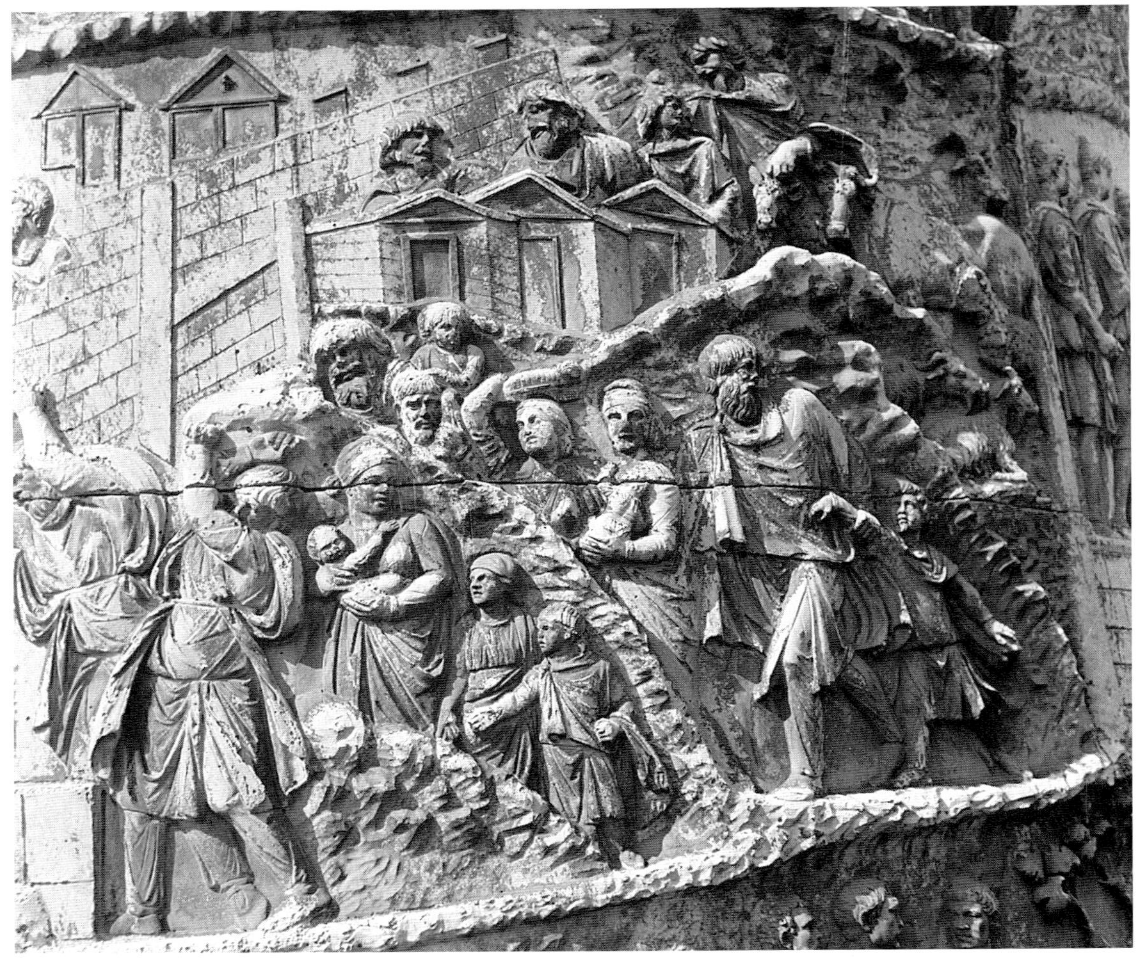

1.10. Trajan's Column, Rome, c. 110–15 A.D. Relief in marble (scene LXXVI) showing Dacian families with children in flight from Roman soldiers. Photo courtesy DAI Rome, Inst. Neg. 1941.1474 (Deichmann).

Roman cavalry burning a village, with the men fleeing—one of whom leads a child by the shoulders—while Trajan receives a group of captured women and children, one with a child on its mother's shoulders.[42] The last scene with human figures of the frieze on Trajan's column, CLIV, now in very bad condition, seems to depict a final snapshot of defeated Dacians fleeing their conquered homeland with an adult dragging a child by the arm.[43] The violence is still greater on the Aurelian Column, with women and children especially in a central role; indeed, it is perhaps a deliberate part of the upping of the violence and pathos in this monument that children under attack are invariably depicted with women rather than with men, as is usual on Trajan's column or the Red Sea sarcophagi.[44] Scene

JAŚ ELSNER

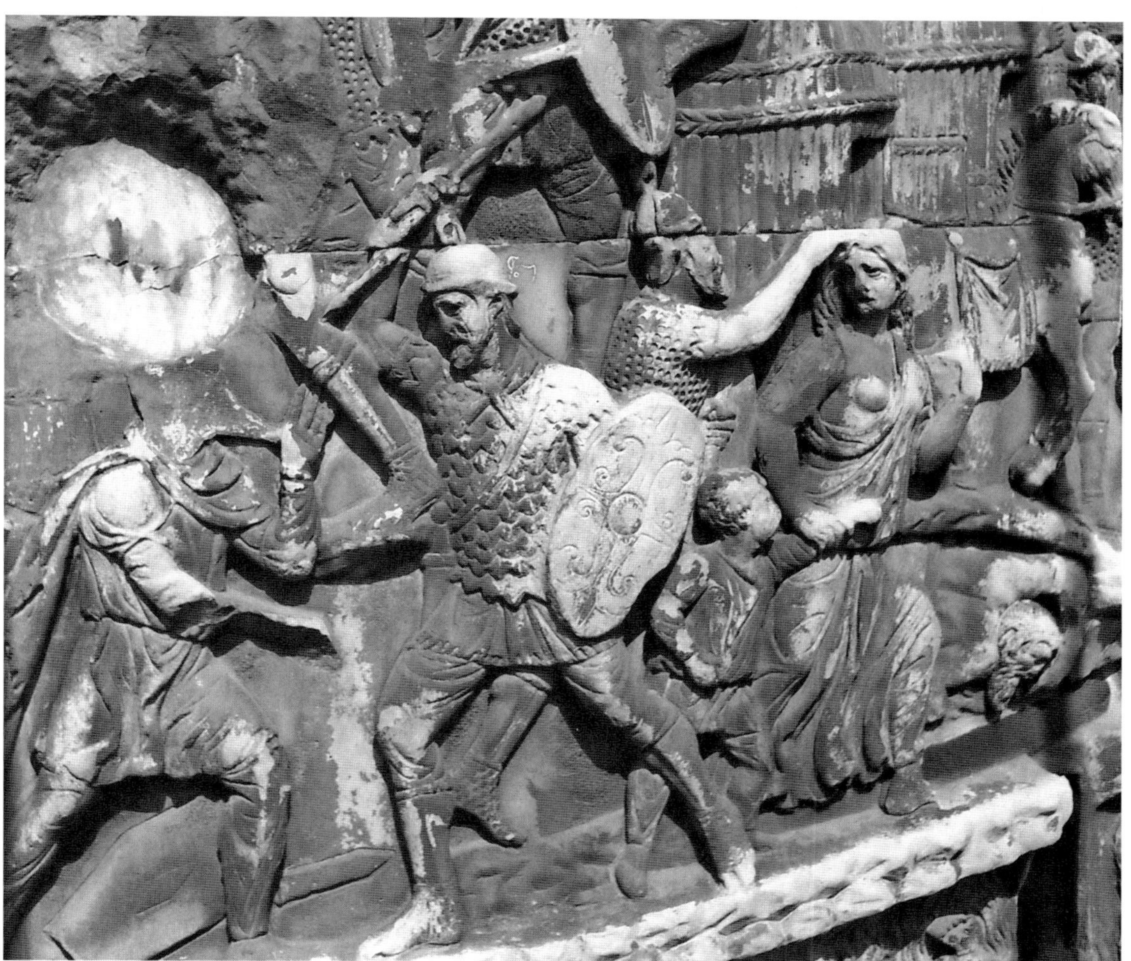

1.11. Column of Marcus Aurelius in Rome, c. 180–92 A.D. Relief in marble (scene XX) showing a mother and child in flight from a Roman legionary. Photo courtesy DAI Rome, Inst. Neg. 1943.0083 (Felbmeier).

XX (Figure 1.11), for example, has a woman with disheveled hair and bared breast grasping her child by the arm and attempting to flee a village as a Roman soldier drags her by the hair and a corpse lies fallen behind.[45] Again, the borrowing of these motifs in the Red Sea sarcophagi is strikingly well motivated. What are the Hebrews, after all, but a throng of defenseless, victimized, non-Roman refugees in flight from a powerful and tyrannical imperium? But the difference is that, unlike all these defeated barbarians, their flight is a miraculous triumph, and the pagan world they are fleeing is one they will supplant.

The deep past of this imagery reaches back to one of the most canonical and, we may even say, iconic visual formulations of Roman identity at the dawn of the imperial era. In the Forum of Augustus in Rome, built by the first Roman emperor at the end of the first century B.C. around the temple of Mars Ultor, which had been built to celebrate the vengeance wreaked on Julius Caesar's assassins, there were two principal exedrae with bronze statues of the *summi viri*, or great men, of the Republic (on the southeast side) and the major figures of the Julio-Claudian clan, now the new imperial dynasty (on the northwest side).[46] These two series of statues culminated in major bronze images of Romulus (in the southeast) and Aeneas, the legendary founder of the Julio-Claudians (in the northwest).[47] The image of Aeneas showed the founder of Rome fleeing the sack of Troy with his father Anchises on his shoulders and holding his son Ascanius (or Iulus) by the hand.[48] This visual formula (itself adapting an iconic motif used by Augustus' adoptive father, Julius Caesar)[49] was frequently replicated in all kinds of media,[50] from the acroteria of the temple of the deified Augustus in Rome,[51] to large-scale public statuary in the provinces,[52] via paintings and caricatures in Pompeii,[53] to private altars and grave reliefs (Figure 1.12),[54] to lamps, coins and gems.[55] Of course, the Aeneas theme is fundamentally different from the images of parents with children that we have been looking at, since Aeneas carries his father on his shoulders and not his son. But it seems to me hard to deny that this iconic visual formula was adapted for the creation of the group on the right of the benefaction relief at Beneventum and hence for the group of a father with a child on his shoulders and leading a child by the right hand on the Red Sea sarcophagi.[56] Again, if the Aeneas group lies behind the fleeing Hebrews in the Red Sea scheme, it is strikingly well chosen. Aeneas and his family are refugee Trojans fleeing carnage to set up a new city in a new land and develop a new triumphant identity that will become Rome; the Jews, more complexly, flee carnage in a land to which they are visitors in order to make the long trek back to their homeland where they too will create a new identity around a holy city and temple. But in so far as all this is really about the Christians, it has the new faith's triumphalism dressed in the refugee iconography of the pagan Roman world out of which and over which Christianity is stepping.

It might be added that these two models of representing parents and children—that is, the act of imperial benefaction and the movement of barbarian peoples—were combined in an intriguing lead proof for the reverse of a large gold medallion of the very late third century, the so called "plomb de Lyon."[57] Although now in very poor condition, its complex imagery is not entirely clear but appears to show two tetrarchic emperors in the upper tier receiving a group of figures with an adult carrying a child on his (or her?) shoulders and a second child who may be held by the hand walking away to the right (as on the Beneventum relief). In the lower tier, a group of what have been interpreted as barbarians including a child (the same group as in the upper tier?) cross a bridge

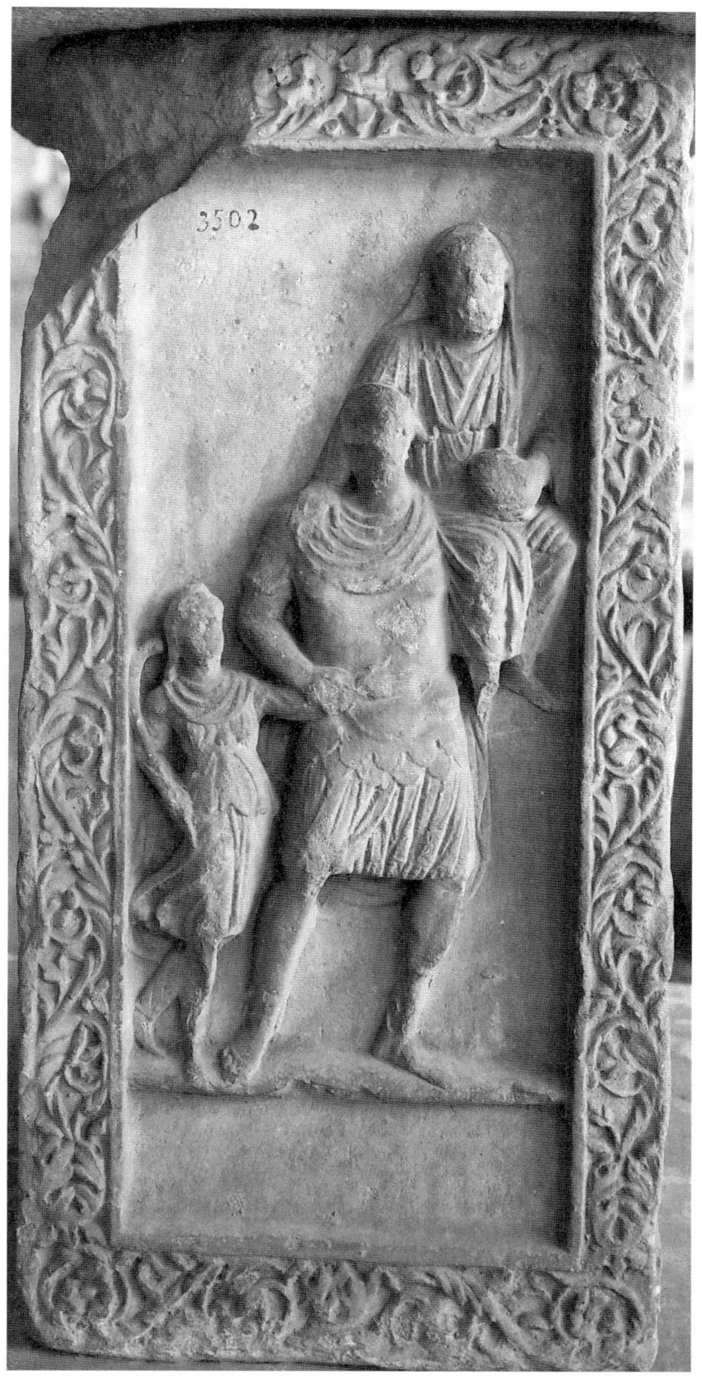

1.12. Marble tombstone of Petronia Grata, first century A.D. Relief showing Aeneas carrying his father, Anchises, and leading his son Iulus by the hand, based on the statue group in the Forum of Augustus. Archaeological Museum, Turin. Photo courtesy DAI Rome, Inst. Neg. 1930.0232 (Franck).

over the Rhine (labeled) in order to enter Mainz, which is labeled MONGOTIA-
CUM. While specific interpretations differ, there is broad consensus that the
imagery refers to the resettling of peoples in Gaul, probably barbarians, by the
emperors as an act of largess—a policy conducted by the tetrarchs. For our
purposes, what is significant here is that the two tropes of the "traumatic" and
the "celebratory" are combined in late antiquity, in this case with none of the
edge of the Red Sea sarcophagi; nonetheless, they presage their creativity with
traditional and familiar motifs that were certainly known to whomever made
the die whose lead proof was later lost in the Soane.

The imagery of the Egyptian army riding out to attack the Israelites and that
of the carnage in the waters seem to me to be less complex in their allusions
but no less deeply embedded in earlier visual models. The most obvious of these
are the early fourth-century friezes of the Arch of Constantine, whose east and
west sides give plenty of models of soldiers riding out to war (with rounded
helmets such as those that characterize the sarcophagi in the siege of Verona
panel on the south side) and whose image of the battle of the Milvian Bridge
on the south gives a parallel for armies drowning in water.[58] This has, of course,
been long recognized by that strand of scholarship (misguided, in my view)
that has seen the sarcophagi as deliberately alluding to or even representing
Constantinian triumph.[59]

Competitive Genealogies: The Genesis of Christian Art

Let us take a step back from a deliberately close-focused analysis of specific
details in a group of related objects. What does this evidence tell us? So far, this
paper has commented on two things: first, an iconography or subject matter
that is strikingly Jewish, and second, a series of formal appropriations and commentaries on the arts of the past that are strikingly Roman. In effect, the Red
Sea sarcophagi address directly one of the most interesting and problematic
aspects in all Christian art—and indeed in late antique culture more generally—
namely, the ways Christianity dealt with a fundamental genealogical oddity,
which might be described as having not one father but two. The emblem of
this—and the way a newly Christian culture signaled its shift from the norms
of pre-Christian Greco-Roman origins—might be the genealogical transformation in the official arts of Constantine during the span of his reign. From the
emperor's affirmation of a genealogy of Roman imperialism looking back to his
great predecessors Trajan, Hadrian, and Marcus in his arch in Rome, Constantine moved to affirming a new lineage in the midst of Christian sainthood, a
genealogy rooted in Jewish and Christian scripture and hagiography, in the
monuments and relics among which he chose to be buried in his (otherwise

JAŚ ELSNER

probably rather traditional)[60] mausoleum in Constantinople.[61] The genealogical problem is itself a double one, since it concerns both actual origins (the real roots and causes of what became Christian art—oddly a somewhat mythical topic since we are never going to have the evidence that could conclusively and objectively prove an origin) and the Christians' conception of their origins (a matter of changing rhetoric, polemic, and identity for many centuries and still in the present day).

The Red Sea sarcophagi come to the question of genealogy at a later moment than Constantine—in roughly the 380s. They give evidence of an identification with the triumphantly fleeing Hebrews that treats the Christians' ancestral Judaism with an idealization that is surprising (given the antisemitism already traceable in numerous early Christian texts).[62] They combine this with a persistent classicism in relation to their referencing of the arts of the Roman past that is at the very least highly aggressive. If Jewish subject matter signals Christian triumph, then the clothing of it in the forms of Roman art signifies that this triumph is over Rome.

In respect of their relations to Roman art, the Red Sea Sarcophagi show a much greater bite, thoughtfulness of appropriation, and polemicism of intent than has been granted to "Theodosian Classicism." Usually, the classicism of the later fourth century, an established theme in academic interpretation for over a hundred years, is treated as the rather loose reference in fourth-century art to stylistic treatments, artistic forms, or traditional subject matter (the latter frequently mythological and hence non-Christian), all of which are redolent of earlier periods in Roman artistic production, and specifically of the pre-Christian past.[63] What we see in the Red Sea imagery is something much more trenchant. These sarcophagi show a clear and conscious use of carefully selected earlier motifs, founded on a wide-ranging and rigorous visual antiquarianism centered on objects available in Rome and Beneventum, which chose relevant imagery from the imperial pagan past and replicated it with some aplomb to make constitutively and even aggressively differentiated statements about the triumphalist identity of the new dispensation. The Red Sea sarcophagi appear to play on a series of key characteristics of Roman visual imagery in the imperial period. Their engagement with the past draws on the discursive quality of Roman art, perhaps excessively defined as a "language" in Tonio Hölscher's classic treatment of the 1980s,[64] taking particular motifs from earlier art and reconfiguring them for specific effects. The use of the children motifs applies to the arts of the past some of the more polemical features of Roman imagery, in which—both in the political and the religious spheres—iconographies were specifically targeted to make propagandist points against the positions they were supposed to embody or support.[65] A good example, specifically associated with the iconic image of Aeneas carrying Anchises, is the coinage issued by Augustus' rival Sextus Pompeius (ca. 67–36 B.C.) in Sicily, which represented the myth of two Catanean brothers showing their *pietas* by rescuing their aged parents from an eruption of Etna. In Pompeius' version, where the head of his father Pompey the Great appears on the obverse, the coins engage in an act of iconographic one-upmanship (two brothers and two parents instead of the single figure of Aeneas carrying Anchises) in the propaganda competitions around claims of *pietas* against Caesar and his heir Octavian.[66] In pitting such iconographic polemicism against the arts of the pagan past rather than contemporary visual statements, the Red Sea sarcophagi participate in, and might even be said to extend, a kind of appropriative and targeted classicism that in my view is well attested in Roman art before the fourth century,[67] though many of its studies (as in the arena of Roman copying and what is now called "emulation") are much too soft-focused about its potential polemical and self-assertive proper-ties, as evidenced for instance by the images we have been studying here.[68]

It might be objected, following Paul Veyne's famous intervention in the literature on Trajan's Column, that many of the objects I am implying here were carefully studied and responded to in the fourth century, were not in fact very visible, indeed hardly visible at all.[69] But if there was a moment in antiquity when we might have expected the columns of Trajan and Marcus to have been extensively studied, perhaps even with the use of scaffolding, it is at the point when they were themselves replicated by order of Theodosius and his son Arcadius, who commissioned historiated columns with helical friezes in imita-tion of the Trajanic and Aurelian monuments to be set up in Constantinople (in 386 and 402, respectively).[70] Indeed, the kind of antiquarian classicism that resulted on the level of entire monuments in the replication of the Roman cochliate columns in Constantinople is a side of the same phenomenon as the targeted assertion of triumphant Christian identity in the Red Sea crossing, in the form of the liberated Israelites dressed up iconographically in some of the most normative of traditional motifs of pagan Roman victory.[71] However, it appears from the drawings that survive of the Arcadian column (which was at least sketched in some detail before its destruction in modern times) that the iconography of children in flight, which we have seen was so marked in the two Roman columns, was avoided in Constantinople.

But if the choice of visual motifs is a systematic reversal of how such types were made to play in normative Roman art, then the choice of subject matter (and its exclusively Old Testament emphasis) appears to affirm a Jewish geneal-ogy to the same extent that the way this subject is represented appears to reject a Roman one. These sarcophagi show, as we have seen, a distinct interest in emphasizing the pictorial narrative of Exodus so that it takes over the entire main face of the sarcophagus and, in the case of the example from Aix, over the whole carved visual field comprising the front and both sides. Unlike much early Christian art in this period, these sarcophagi appear to play up Judaic subjects and to play down Christian typological comparison or juxtaposition. Yet is there anything Jewish about them? We have seen that the iconography systematically borrows from earlier imperial Roman types to make quite specific points of difference—especially in the imagery of the victorious Hebrews by contrast with the scenes of defeated barbarians or Roman populace receiving imperial handouts on which they are based. Likewise, the Egyptian foe of the Israelites appears to resemble not so much prehistoric or biblical Egyptians as near-contemporary Romans (or Roman pagans). The message is resoundingly clear—a Christian people has walked through a miracle, from oppression by pagan persecutors to freedom. Yet all this is clothed, as it were, in the context of an Old Testament narrative about the Jews. We return to the interesting problematic of the Negro spiritual with which we began—a song in which the one great story of Jewish triumph in scripture is appropriated to a theme of Christian salvation.

It is necessary to note that, earlier than our sarcophagi and indeed before any other surviving imagery of the Red Sea crossing, the subject appears in an unequivocally Jewish liturgical setting as the most extensive of all the painted themes in the Dura Europos synagogue of roughly 240 A.D.[72] There are many differences between this image and all the later examples—most notably its right-to-left orientation (following the direction in which Hebrew is read), its unusually large scale for the three-times repeated figure of Moses, its representation of the Israelites as armed (following Exodus 13.18, mistranslated in the Septuagint, leading to the Jews' being pictured as defenseless refugees in the Roman tradition).[73] As in the sarcophagi, the Jews include one prominently placed child led by the hand as well as men carrying bags of flour over their shoulders.[74] All this is to say that the Red Sea theme—along with a good many other Old Testament subjects—had a vibrant and independent existence in art executed for the decoration (which may be to imply the visual sanctification) of Jewish liturgical space. Whatever the range of its possible meanings in this context and for the Jewish viewers of Dura (for instance, historical, allegorical, liturgical),[75] the meanings generated for Christian viewers in the Theodosian period by the representation of the same textual source on the Red Sea sarcophagi were substantively different.

What the sarcophagi offer is not the usual art-historical model of antisemitism in the choice to represent Jews negatively in art.[76] Nor is it the expected late antique positing of a Jewish type to be fulfilled and surpassed by the new Christian dispensation.[77] Rather, the pointedly rendered Jewish theme of the

Red Sea crossing comes to constitute a cipher—empty of its own intrinsic or independent meaning (such as the meanings that might have been imputed to the Dura Synagogue frescoes before their destruction in about 256 or 257 A.D.). Despite their existence as the careful illustration of a scriptural text—careful, because quite specific and deliberate choices have been made as to what not to depict and which elements to synthesize into a continuous visual field—the Red Sea crossing sarcophagi represent not the text of Exodus as a manifestly or meaningfully *Jewish* scripture, but rather Exodus as a site of Christian exegetic and interpretative investment. Judaism—as in the song with which we started, in which the rock where Moses stood and the drowning of Pharaoh's army could bleed so swiftly into the injunction to Mary not to weep—is a kind of empty figure into which and around which a series of entirely Christian meanings must inevitably resonate.

In the period of the making of this group of sarcophagi, Moses' actions by the Red Sea shore (and indeed everything else in the Old Testament) might be said to have been in the grip of a crisis of competitive Christian interpretation. To judge by the range of allusion and the radically different directions in which interpretative meaning was developed in the Patristic writings of the later fourth and early fifth centuries, there was no single authoritative version but rather the willingness to take such Old Testament narratives and subject them to creative exegesis in relation to a variety of potential agendas.[78] Let us take three examples. Here is Ambrose of Milan (bishop from 374 to 397) writing in Latin probably in the 380s,[79] at the time when the Red Sea sarcophagi were made:

> Happiness can be known even in the midst of sufferings. . . . Think of the happiness Moses had—there was nothing meager about that was there? There he was, surrounded by the Egyptian hordes, with no way of escape, cut off by the sea—but he earned such favour by the godly spirit he showed that he found a path for himself and our Father's people to pass through the waters on foot. Did he ever show greater courage than he did at that moment, when he was completely hemmed in, and the dangers could not have been greater? He refused to give up hope of salvation, and in the end he brought off great triumph.(*De Officiis* 2.10)

By contrast, take Gregory of Nyssa (bishop ca. 371–95) writing in Greek around 390:[80]

> No one who hears this should be ignorant of the mystery of the water. He who has gone down into it with the army of the enemy emerges alone, leaving the enemy's army drowning in the water. For who does

JAŚ ELSNER

not know that the Egyptian army—those horses, chariots and their drivers, archers, slingers, heavily armed soldiers, and the rest of the crowd in the enemies' line of battle—are the various passions of the soul by which man is enslaved? . . . So all such things rush into the water with the Israelite who leads the way in the baleful passage. Then as the staff of faith leads on and the cloud provides light, the water gives life to those who find refuge in it but destroys their pursuers . . . after we have drowned the whole Egyptian person (that is every form of evil) in the saving baptism we emerge alone, dragging along nothing foreign in our subsequent life.(*De Vita Moysis* 2. 121–26)

These are remarkably different takes on a single biblical narrative. Of course, they have different rhetorical functions in the two texts, where the example of the Red Sea crossing is for specific exemplary purposes. Ambrose takes Moses as a model of human action—a paradigm of the ways happiness may triumph in suffering, through faith and an exhortation to courage and the hope of salvation in adversity. Gregory, building on a familiar typology whereby the Red Sea crossing was read as a type of baptism following Paul's comment "and were all baptized unto Moses in the cloud and in the sea" (I Cor. 10.2),[81] takes the story as a figure not only for baptism as such but for the spiritual sense of salvation and purification of the individual for which baptism is itself a symbol and also a significant ritual. Just as the sarcophagi make choices about which features of the story to include, so Gregory chooses specific elements—the list of the various components of the Egyptian army that serve as "passions of the soul," Moses' "staff of faith," the cloud—in order to build his interpretation.

The key point is that the Red Sea narrative—whether as exemplary scriptural story or as work of art—is consistently and creatively appropriated for a range of Christian exegetic meanings. A striking commentary on the potential excess of such meanings and the need for interpretative restraint is offered by Augustine in his *City of God*, composed between Alaric's sack of Rome in 410 and 426:[82]

For they [i.e., others with whom Augustine does not agree] think that the plagues in Egypt, of which there were ten before the people of God began their exodus, should be interpreted as meaning that the last persecution by Antichrist should be taken as figured in the eleventh plague, in which the Egyptians, while pursuing the Hebrews with enmity, perished in the Red Sea, while the people of God passed through on dry land. But I do not think that those events in Egypt were prophetic symbols of these persecutions, although those who think so evidently have matched them one by one with far-fetched ingenuity, yet not so much by prophetic inspiration as by speculation of the human mind, which sometimes attains to truth but sometimes goes astray. (*De Civitate Dei* 18.52)

This is a fascinating passage about the ground rules for exegesis and about the need for "prophetic inspiration" in understanding scripture (as much as in its production). But for our purposes here, it demonstrates the range, types, and vibrancy of Christian interpretative engagements, as well as their speculative flavor and the failure of some to carry conviction.

The Red Sea theme, in these patristic accounts, and the Red Sea sarcophagi which make that theme visual are a good example of that characteristic Christian treatment of Jewish models as a series of "paradigms to think with." In the case of the Hebrews' flight from Egypt, they are part of the preparation for the ground in which grew subsequently a series of distinctive and distinctively Christian identifications with the fleeing Israelites—from the Orange Calvinists of seventeenth-century Netherlands to the enslaved blacks of the southern United States in the nineteenth century and the song with which I began.[83] The role of Judaism—whose subject matter exclusively occupies these objects' main visual field—is ironically as an empty vessel to be filled with a complex nexus of Christian projections and transferences. Their Judaism—and that of the story they tell—is a cipher absent of any intrinsic or original meaning but correspondingly rich and open to a multitude of competitive Christian understandings.

I maintain that we are dealing with a fundamental problem in the genesis of Christian culture in the West. The issue is how to build upon two not wholly compatible pasts—that Jewish and scriptural world out of which Christianity as a religious sect emerged and that Roman imperial system (not just a government but a universalizing literary, educational, and artistic establishment) whose every reflex Christianity borrowed and transformed. The clash of paternities, in the case of these sarcophagi, takes a very interesting bifurcation into idealization (of the Israelites) and denigration (of Roman models). These are hardly separable forms of anxiety about genealogical origins.[84] It is of no surprise that the later development of the assimilation of these themes in Christian culture moved from a positive identification with the Jews as an ideal model to a targeted and denigrating antisemitism not so different from the response to Roman origins in the objects we have been studying. The fact that Christian culture—both in art and its writing—constitutively placed both Judaism and the classical past in the position of its parents or at least of its privileged ancestors was hardly a discouragement to the oedipal ramifications of its relationships with both. No wonder it was to be in equal measures extraordinarily creative and spectacularly conflicted about dealing with this lineage.

More to the point, in relation to our own assessments (dare I say, projections?) of this genesis, modern scholarship is no less entangled in the meshes of its own Christian paternity—its own heritage and relations with ancestral Christian positions from "Catholic" to "Protestant"—than were the early Christians enmeshed in the web of parental Judaism and Romanitas.[85] Jewish scholars—so significant among the art historians of the twentieth century concerned with study of Roman, Jewish, and early Christian art—offer no less complicated a set of investments.[86] That is to say, our own accounts of themes so fraught—so idealized by some and excoriated by others—as the origins of Christianity (in the case of this paper, the genealogies of Christian art) and the relation of those origins to Judaism (Jewish art) and to Rome (which is to say to pagan Roman art) are no less invested, identified, and convoluted than the complexities I have been attempting to examine in the Red Sea sarcophagi. That, I suppose, is what makes the topic so compelling.

It is notable that a version of genealogical anxiety is already tacitly present in the Roman material borrowed and adapted by the Red Sea sarcophagi. The coins of Julius Caesar and Sextus Pompeius show a backward-looking notion of genealogical *pietas* with children carrying their parents. The Augustan adaptation added a forward generational thrust by adding Aeneas's son and heir to the pair of Aeneas and Anchises. The Augustan figuration—looking forward and back—is replaced in the high empire by the Trajanic and Aurelian models of fathers carrying and holding children, an iconography that looks forward to the replication of *pietas* in the succeeding generations rather than specifically claiming it for the present. It is this version that the Christians adopted. But it is interesting that they should have seized upon a complex theme that developed and changed markedly as republic became empire and as empire settled into the natural pattern of government. Inscribed into the shifts here, in their Christian appropriation, is the difference between a Christianity looking back to its Classical and Jewish parentage and one looking away from it into the future of its children. The triumphant Hebrews of the sarcophagi certainly take the second of these options.

It is striking that the genealogical problem I have been stressing—a problem so deep and so familiar that every Old Testament reference in a Christian context is effectively complicit in it—should be explicitly raised in the song with which I started. The spiritual embodies and transfers the relations of lineage implicit in placing Moses on the Red Sea shore beside Mary and her three links of chain in the image of Mary's mourning (or not mourning) for Jesus, her son. Even as the song repeatedly enjoins Mary not to weep, not to mourn, it conjures the image of the weeping mother over her dead child and the tears that lie in genealogy on both sides of the parent/child divide.

NOTES

This chapter was written for the Third Lavy Colloquium on Judaism and Christian Art, organized with great panache by Herb Kessler and David Nirenberg. I am grateful to them not only for the invitation but also for their acute questioning and suggestions, as well as to other participants at the event at Johns Hopkins University and the anonymous readers for the University of Pennsylvania Press. My thanks go to John Ma and Jonathan Prag for advice on specific points, as well as to Allen Brent, Milette Gaifmann, Rolf Schneider, Charles Barber, Ed Watts, and Christine Kondoleon for allowing me to try out versions at, respectively, Cambridge, Yale, Munich, Notre Dame, The Shifting Frontiers Conference at Indiana, and the Museum of Fine Arts in Boston.

ABBREVIATIONS

Rep. I: G. Bovini and H. Brandenburg, *Repertorium der Christlich-Antiken Sarkophage I: Rom und Ostia*, Mainz, 1967

Rep. II: J. Dresken-Weiland, *Repertorium der Christlich-Antiken Sarkophage II: Italien mit einem Nachtrag Rom und Ostia, Dalmatia, Museen der Welt*, Mainz, 1998

Rep. III: B. Christern-Briesenick, *Repertorium der Christlich-Antiken Sarkophage III Frankreich, Algerien, Tunisien*, Mainz, 2003

1. I give the version sung by Pete Seeger in *American Favorite Ballads,* vol. 1 (Smithsonian Folkways Recordings, SFW CD 40150, 2002), recorded in 1957. There are many variants and combinations. See, e.g., N. White, *American Negro Folk Songs* (Cambridge, Mass., 1928), 58–59, 60–63; H. Odun and G. Johnson, *Negro Workaday Songs* (Chapel Hill, N.C., 1926), 190.

2. For a study of the typological uses of Exodus in the early church, see J. Daniélou, *Sacramentum Futuri: Études sur les origines de la typologie biblique* (Paris, 1950), 131–200. On Exodus in relation to modern revolutionary movements, see M. Walzer, *Exodus and Revolution* (New York, 1985).

3. For Miriam as a type of Mary, see, e.g., Gregory of Nyssa, *De Virginitate* 19, with the parallels cited in Grégoire de Nysse, *Traité de la virginité*, ed. M. Aubineau (Paris, 1966), 486–87. For a survey of Miriam in Patristic writing and archaeology, see J. Doignon, "Miryam et son tambourin," *Studia Patristica* 4 (1961), 70–77. For Miriam the singer as muse of Christian poetry, see Sidonius Apolinaris, *Euchariston ad Faustum Episcopum* (poem 16), vv. 1–10. For some anthropological reflections on the complexities of the multiple Marys in the Bible, see E. Leach, "Why did Moses have a sister?," in E. Leach and D. Aycock, *Structuralist Interpretations of Biblical Myth* (Cambridge, 1983), 33–66.

4. So T. Mathews, *The Clash of Gods: A Reinterpretation of Early Christian Art* (Princeton, 1993), 75; also G. Noga-Banai, *Prolegomena to the Study of Sarcophagus Production in Rome under Pope Damasus* (Jerusalem, 2007), 10n29.

5. C. Rizzardi, *I sarcophagi paleocristiani con rappresentazione del passagio del Mar Rosso* (Faenza, 1970), collects and catalogues twenty-nine examples (cf. G. Koch, *Fruhchristlich Sarkophage* [Munich, 2000], 42–43, 313–14). Of these, a number are fragmentary. On the iconography and its textual referents, see P. van Moorsel, "Rotswonder of doortocht door de Rode

Zee," *Mededelingen van het Nederland Historisch Instituut, Rome* (s'Gravenhage, 1966), 55–89. My position on provenance represents a modern consensus—see, e.g., Koch (2000), 299 and 490–92, with a recent general review of the issue being F. Baratte, "Les sarcophages romains: Problèmes et certitude," *Perspective* 1 (2006), 38–54, esp. 46–49. Rizzardi (1970), 137, argued for Rome as the origin in contrast to earlier literature, e.g., the position of M. Lawrence, "Columnar Sarcophagi in the Latin West," *Art Bulletin* 14 (1932), 101–85, who argues for a number of ateliers in Gaul producing sarcophagi (including the Red Sea examples) and exporting them to Rome and Dalmatia.

6. E.g., Rizzardi (1970), nos. 4 [Rep. III, no. 41], 10 [Rep. III, no. 162], 12 [Rep. II, no. 249], 13 [Rep. III, no. 203], 17 [Rep. II, no. 12], 18 [Rep. I, no. 899], 24 [Rep. I, no. 41], 27 [Rep. I, no. 712]. For discussion of the chronology, see Rizzardi (1970), 110–12. On the novelty of the Theodosian treatment, see F. Gerke, "Der Verhältnis von Malerei und Plastik in der Theodosianisch-Honorianischen Zeit," *Rivisita di archeologia Cristiana* 12 (1935), 119–63, esp. 123–28. Noga-Banai (2007) plausibly emphasizes a local Roman connection with the papacy of Damasus rather than the principate of Theodosius.

7. E.g., Prudentius, *Cathemerinon* 5.45–80; *Hamartigena* 460–77; *Dittochaeon* 9; *Peristephanon* 5.481–84.

8. Some of the nonfragmentary examples show three personifications: Rizzardi (1970), nos. 3 [Rep. III, no. 119], 5 [Rep. III, no. 43], 11 [Rep. III, no. 44], 14 [Rep. III, no. 340—now fragmentary, but see the drawing at taf. 84.1], probably 21 [Rep. I, no. 809, but this is fragmentary], and 29 [Rep. II, no. 146]. Some show only one personification, of the Red Sea: Rizzardi (1970), nos. 16 [Rep. III, no. 414] and 26 [Rep. 1, no. 64]. The example in Aix-en-Provence has two personifications—Rizzardi (1970), no. 1 [Rep. III, no. 21]. In the case of multiple personifications, the land of Egypt is female and the Red Sea male. On the meaning of the personifications, see Rizzardi (1970), 34, 41–42, and Noga-Banai (2007), 10, who suggests fertility for the female ones.

9. On Pharaoh as Roman emperor, see Mathews (1993), 76.

10. See Rizzardi (1970), 42; Mathews (1993), 76; and Rep. III, p. 74.

11. See Leach and Aycock (1983), and E. Leach, "Fishing for Men on the Edge of the Desert," in Robert Alter and Frank Kermode, eds., *The Literary Guide to the Bible* (Cambridge, Mass., 1987), 579–99.

12. On the "faceoff" of Moses and Pharaoh, see Mathews (1993), 76. For Moses' staff and its magical meanings, see Mathews (1993), 72–77.

13. The now fragmentary Metz sarcophagus (Rizzardi [1970], no. 14 = Rep. III, no. 340)—if we are to believe a drawing of the eighteenth century—appears to have had a christogram inscribed onto Miriam's timbrel. Even if we believe the drawing, the date of this inscription is impossible to ascertain. But it would not only make the contrast of Miriam and Pharaoh that much more pointed; it would also brilliantly anticipate the conflation of not-mourning Mary and Miriam in the Negro spiritual with which I began. See J. Doignon, "Le monogramme cruciforme du sarcofage paléochrétien de Metz représentant le passage de la Mer Rouge," *Cahiers Archéologiques* 12 (1962), 65–87.

14. For a summary of these interpretations and a bibliography, see Rizzardi (1970), 19–31.

15. E.g., the examples from Split (Rizzardi [1970], no. 29, and Rep. II, no. 146), from Aix (Rizzardi [1970], no. 1 and Rep. III, no. 21), and three from Arles (Rizzardi [1970], nos. 3, 5, and 11 (Rep. III, nos. 119, 43, and 44).

16. The Metz sarcophagus is Rizzardi (1970), no. 14 and Rep. III, no. 340. A pillar with flames above it (cf. Exod. 13:21) appears in a number of the Red Sea sarcophagi—in the Nimes and Rome examples discussed below (Rizzardi [1970], no. 16 [Rep. III no. 414] and Rizzardi (1970), no. 26 [Rep. I, no. 64]) as well as at the right side of sarcophagi at Split

(Rizzardi [1970], no. 29 [Rep. II, no. 146]), Arles Museum (Rizzardi [1970], 11 [Rep. III, no. 44]), St. Trophime (Rizzardi [1970], no. 3 [Rep. III, no. 119]) and Aix (Rizzardi [1970], no. 1 [Rep. III, no. 21]), where it also figures twice in the image on the right-hand side. Parallels appear in the Bern tapestry (below. n. 25), the Dura Europos Synagogue (below, n. 72) and the Ashburnham Pentateuch, where the pillar of cloud is provided with a titulus saying "columna nubis" (below, n. 26)

17. The Doria-Pamphili fragment is Rizzardi (1970), no. 28 and Rep. I, no. 953—wrongly labeled 954 in the plates volume.

18. Nimes: Rizzardi (1970), no. 16 and Rep. III, no. 414; the Rome example: Rizzardi (1970), no. 26 and Rep. I, no. 64.

19. Our principal source is G. Grimaldi, *Descrizione della basilica antica di S. Pietro in Vaticano*, ed. R. Niggl (Vatican, 1972), 140, with discussion by H. Kessler, *Old St. Peter's and Church Decoration in Medieval Italy* (Spoleto, 2002), 9, 53, 76–77, 98–99. Note that the Red Sea theme did not appear in the very close replica (also probably fourth century and now lost) of the St. Peter's frescoes in the basilica of St. Paul Outside the Walls in Rome (ibid., 82, 99) but is reproduced in the fifteenth-century cycle of mural copies of the St Peter's cycle in the Oratory of the Annunicata in Cori (ibid., 54, 101, and plate 3.9).

20. On the date, see Kessler (2002), 77: "not long after the basilica's completion during the third quarter of the fourth century."

21. See G. W. Bowersock, "Peter and Constantine," in W. Tronzo, ed., *St. Peter's in the Vatican* (Cambridge, 2005), 5–15.

22. See A. Ferrua, *Le pitture della nuova catacomba di Via Latina* (Vatican City, 1960), 54–55, 81–82; L. Kötzsche-Breitenbruch, *Die Neue Katakombe an der Via Latina in Rom* (Munster, 1976), 79–83; A Ferrua, *The Unknown Catacomb* (Florence, 1990), 88–89 (cubiculum C), 144–45 (cubiculum O).

23. See G. Jeremias, *Die Holztür der Basilika S. Sabina in Rom*, Tubingen, 1980, 26–32.

24. See B. Brenk, *Die frühchristlichen Mosaiken in S Maria Maggiore zu Rom*, Wiesbaden, 1975, 84–87, 120.

25. See L. Kötzsche, "Die neuerworbene Wandbehang mit gemalten alttestamentlichen Szenen in der Abegg-Stiftung (Bern)," in C. Moss and K. Kiefer, eds., *Byzantine East, Latin West: Art Historical Studies in Honor of Kurt Weitzmann* (Princeton, 1995), 65–74; S. Schrenk, *Textilen des Mittelmeerraumes aus Spätanike bis frühislamischer Zeit* (Riggisberg, 2004), 65–70; L. Kötzsche, *Der Bemalte Behang in der Abegg-Stiftung in Riggisberg: Eine alttestamentliche Bildfolge des 4 Jahrhunderts (Riggisberger Berichte 11)* (Riggisberg, 2004), 172–79.

26. Paris, Bibliothèque nationale lat. Nouv. Acq. 2334, fol. 68r, with O. von Gebhardt, *The Miniatures of the Ashburnham Pentateuch* (London, 1883), 22, and D. Verkerk, *Early Medieval Bible Illumination and the Ashburnham Pentateuch* (Cambridge, 2004), 85–89, with substantive worries about the long history of scholarship that assumes the influence of Jewish manuscripts at 4–32.

27. Notably the example from Arles Museum (Rizzardi [1970], 11 [Rep. III, no. 44]) and the half sarcophagus now at Moustiers Ste. Marie (Rizzardi [1970], 15 [Rep. III, no. 356]).

28. See Rep. II, no. 146, pp. 51–52. Rizzardi (1970), 107–8.

29. E.g., Rep. II, nos. 111, 112, 113, 148, and Rep. III, nos. 31, 76, 77, 80, 81, 126, 160, for the general scheme; Rep, III, nos. 76 and 355 for the type with a female orant at the center.

30. See Rep. III, 9–10, Rizzardi (1970), 36. The photographs of the sides in Rep. III (taf. 6) are poorly angled. Better are those in J. Wilpert, *I sarcophagi cristiani antichi* (Rome, 1929), vol. 1, taf. 97.2 (right side) and 97.3 (left side).

31. For some play with manna, see J. Z. Smith, *Relating Religion* (Chicago, 2004), 118–25.

32. To use a Christian terminology for the Jewish Bible, as I do throughout, given that the Jews of this paper exist entirely within a Christian *imaginaire*.

     J A Ś   E L S N E R

33. The man next to Moses in the Sta Maria Maggiore mosaic panel holds a child by the hand, see Brenk (1975), 85; an Israelite man to the right in the Red Sea image carries a child on his shoulders in Cubiculum C (but not Cubiculum O) of the Via Latina Catacomb, though I have found no discussion or description of this vignette. A child appears in the earlier Jewish painting from the Dura Europos Synagogue (see n. 72 below). The fourth-century representation at St Peter's certainly had children, if we are to judge by the fifteenth-century image at Cori—but how far its numerous children and women carrying children reflect the original is impossible to determine. See Kessler (2002), plate 3.9, for a plate of the Cori fresco.

34. On children in the Ara Pacis processional friezes, see D. Kleiner and B. Buxton, "Pledges of empire: The Ara Pacis and the Donations of Rome," *American Journal of Archaeology* 112 (2008), 57–89, with extensive and up-to-date bibliography. The availability and visibility of the Ara Pacis in the later fourth century A.D. (and indeed before the unearthing of its friezes in 1568) is not known or knowable, but a strong case has been made on the basis of drill and chisel marks for the restoration of the monument in the late antique period. See N. Hannestad, *Tradition in Late Antique Sculpture* (Aarhus, 1994), 20–54, and D. Conlin, *The Artists of the Ara Pacis* (Chapel Hill, N.C., 1997), 47–52.

35. The literature on the alimenta panel is vast. Standard are P. Veyne, "Une hypothèse sur l'arc de Bénévent," *MEFRA* 72 (1960), 191–220, esp. 197–200; F. Hassel, *Der Trajansbogen in Benevent* (Mainz, 1966), 9–10; M. Rotili, *L'arco di Traiano a Benevento* (Rome, 1972), 87–89; K. Fittschen, "Das Bildprogramm des Trajansbogens zu Benevent," *Archäologische Anzeiger* (1972), 742–88, esp. 748–50; T. Lorenz, *Leben und Regierung Trajans auf den Bogen von Benevent* (Amsterdam, 1973), 24–29; W. Gauer, "Zur Bildprogramm des Trajansbogens von Benevent," *Jahrbuch des deutschen Archäologischen Instituts* 89 (1974), 308–35, e.g., 328; M. Torelli, "'Ex his castra, ex his tribus replebuntur': The Marble Panegyric on the Arch of Trajan at Beneventum," in D. Buitron-Oliver, ed., *The Interpretation of Architectural Sculpture in Greece and Rome* (Washington, D.C., 1997) (*Studies in the History of Art* 49), 145–78, esp. 145–47; C. Heitz, "Der Kaisers neue Kinder: Romanitas und Barbarentum am Trajansbogen von Benevent," *Römische Mitteilungen* 112 (2005–6), 207–24.

36. On the Liberalitas panel see I. Scott Ryberg, *Panel Reliefs of Marcus Aurelius* (New York, 1967), 73–76; H. von Heintze, "Zum Relief mit der *Liberalitas* das Marc Aurel," in J. Bibauw, ed., *Hommages à Marcel Renard* (Brussels, 1969), 662–74; E. Angelicoussis, "The Panel Reliefs of Marcus Aurelius," *Römische Mitteilungen* 91 (1984), 141–205, esp. 154–59; G. Koeppel, "Die historischen Reliefs der römischen Kaiserzeit IV," *Bonner Jahrbuch* 186 (1986), 1–90, esp. 72–75. If von Heintze is right about the excision of Commodus from this panel after his *damnatio memoriae* in 192 (as I accept), then the father/child imagery in this relief in its original form is further extended into the imperial family as well as the recipients of their largesse.

37. Specifically on the images of children in these two panels, see S. Currie, "The Empire of Adults: The Representation of Children on Trajan's Arch at Beneventum," in J. Elsner, ed., *Art and Text in Roman Culture* (Cambridge, 1996), 152–81, esp. 168–72; J. Uzzi, *Children in the Visual Arts of Imperial Rome* (Cambridge, 2005), 41–52; N. Kampen, *Family Fictions in Roman Art* (Cambridge, 2009), 55–58 (esp. 57–58 on Beneventum).

38. For this iconography, see J. Lassus, "Quelques representations du 'Passage de la Mer rouge' dans l'art Chrétien et d'occident," *Mélanges d'archéologie et d'histoire* 46 (1929), 159–81, esp. 164. See the fifth-century scene in the wooden doors of Sta Sabina for a parallel.

39. I use the standard numbering of scenes in the fundamental publications: C. Cichorius, *Der reliefs der Traiansäule* (Berlin, 1896–1900), and E. Petersen, *Die Markus-säule auf der Piazza Colonna in Rom* (Munich, 1896). Essential for Trajan's column now are S. Settis,

ed., *La colonna Traiana* (Turin, 1988), and F. Coarelli, *The Column of Trajan* (Rome, 2000), for outstanding post-restoration photographs. Essential for Marcus's column are C. Caprino et al., *La colonna di Marco Aurelio* (Rome, 1955), and J. Scheid and V. Huet, eds., *Autour de la colonne aurélienne* (Turnhout, 2000).

40. See Currie (1996), 160–61; Uzzi (2005), 124–26; Kampen (2009), 46–47, 51–53.

41. Uzzi (2005), 91–92; Kampen (2009), 49–50. The presence of a father carrying a child on his shoulders in a submission scene goes back at least to the late Augustan or Julio-Claudian Boscoreale cups of the first century A.D. See A. Kuttner, *Dynasty and Empire in the Age of Augustus* (Berkeley, 1995), 95; Uzzi (2005), 89; Kampen (2009), 58–60. This relief on a silver cup may reflect a lost state relief of the Augustan period (see Kuttner [1995], 1, 193–98) and I agree with Kuttner (1995), 111–17, that this image belongs broadly to a propaganda of inclusivity and benevolence rather than trauma.

42. Settis (1988), 221; Currie (1996), 159–60; Uzzi (2005), 90–91; Kampen (2009), 47–48.

43. Uzzi (2005), 126–27; Kampen (2009), 55.

44. See, e.g., P. Zanker, "Die Frauen und Kinder der Barbaren aud Markussäule," in Scheid and Huet (2000), 163–74; M. Beard, "The Spectator and the Column: Reading and Writing the Language of Gesture," in Scheid and Huet (2000), 265–82; S. Dillon, "Women on the Columns of Trajan and Marcus Aurelius and the Visual language of Roman Victory," in S. Dillon and K. Welch, eds., *Representations of War in Ancient Rome* (Cambridge, 2006), 244–71; Kampen (2009), 62.

45. See F. Pirson, "Style and Message in the Column of Marcus Aurelius," *Papers of the British School at Rome* 64 (1996), 139–79, esp. 142–48, for detailed visual analysis, and Uzzi (2005), 130. For further examples on the Aurelian column, see Uzzi (2005), 96–98, 129–35 with bibliography.

46. On the Forum of Augustus, see P. Zanker, *Forum Augustum* (Tubingen, 1968); J. Ganzert and V. Kockel, "Augustus Forum und Mars-Ultor-Tempel," in *Kaiser Augustus und die verlorene Republik* (Berlin, 1988), 149–200; V. Kockel, *Lexicon Topographicum Urbis Romae* 2 (1995), 285–95; K. Galinsky, *Augustan Culture* (Princeton, 1996), 197–213; M. Spannagel, *Exemplaria Principis: Untersuchungen zu Entstehung und Ausstatung des Augustusforums* (Heidelberg, 1999); J. Geiger, *The First Hall of Fame: A Study of the Statues in the Forum Augustum* (Leiden, 2008).

47. On these statues, see A. Degrassi, *Inscriptiones Italicae,* 13.3 (Rome, 1937), 1–36; S. Rinaldi Tufi, "Frammenti delle statue dei *summi viri* nel foro di Augusto," *Dialoghi di archeologia* n.s. 3 (1981), 69–84; D. Favro, *The Urban Image of Augustan Rome* (Cambridge, 1996), 126–27, 230–31; Spannagel (1999), 256–358; Geiger (2008), 117–62.

48. See, e.g., M. Cammagio, "Le statue di Enea e Romolo nel foro di Augusto," *Atti dell' Accademia Pontoniana* 58 (1928), esp. 131 and 144; J. Gagé, "Romulus-Augustus," *Mélanges d' archéologie et d'histoire* 47 (1930), 138–81, esp. 141–42; Zanker (1968), 17–18; J. de Rose Evans, *The Art of Persuasion: Propaganda from Aeneas to Brutus* (Ann Arbor, Mich., 1992), 114–18; Spannagel (1999), 162–77, 206–23 (esp. on the question of *pietas*). For the inscription, see A. Degrassi, *Inscriptiones Italicae* 13.3 (Rome, 1937), 9–11. For some iconographic roots of this motif, see K. Schauenburg, "Äneas und Rom," *Gymnasium* 67 (1960), 176–91.

49. See H. Grueber, *Coins of the Roman Republic in the British Museum* (London, 1920), vol. 2, 469.

50. See esp. F. Canciani, "Aineias," *Lexicon Iconographicum Mythologiae Classicae* 1 (1981), 381–96, esp. 386–90, and Spannagel (1999), 365–96, whose catalogue stretches to 141 examples in all media; also K. Galinsky, *Aeneas, Sicily and Rome* (Princeton, 1969), 3–10.

51. See P. Hill, *The Monuments of Ancient Rome as Coin Types* (London, 1989), 19–21. Galinsky (1996), 204, wrongly assumes that the coins that provide evidence for these acroteria depict the temple of Mars Ultor rather than that of Divus Augustus.

52. See Canciani (1981), 390, and additionally the marble group discovered in the forum of Roman Merida, with J. de la Barrera Antón and W. Trillmich, "Eine Widerholhung der Aeneas-Gruppe vom Forum Augustum samt ihrer inschrift in Mérida (Spanien)," *Römische Mitteilungen* 103 (1996), 119–38; Spannagel (1999), 365–69.

53. See Canciani (1981), 388; Spannagel (1999), 381–83. On the famous image from Pompeii over the shopfront of IX.13.5, see V. Sampaolo, "Fullonica di Ululitremulus," *Pompei: Pitture e Mosaici* 10 (Rome, 1003), 357–60; P. Zanker, "Bilderzwang: Augustan Political Symbolism in the Private Sphere," in J. Huskinson, M. Beard, and J. Reynolds, eds., *Image and Mystery in the Roman World* (Gloucester, 1988), 1–22, esp. 1–2; B. Kellum, "Concealing/ Revealing: Gender and the Play of Meaning in the Monuments of Augustan Rome," in T. Habinek and A. Schiesaro, eds., *The Roman Cultural Revolution* (Cambridge, 1997), 158–81, esp. 173–77.

54. E.g., the Carthage altar found in 1916 now in Tunis, with W. Herrmann, *Römische Götterältare* (Regensburg, 1961), 126–32, esp. 129, with bibliography at 126, or the cippus of Petronia Grata in Turin with H. Dütschke, *Antike Bildwerke in Oberitalien* 4 (Leipzig, 1880), 35–36, no. 48.

55. Canciani (1981), 388–90, gives a good conspectus. See Hill (1980), 90–91, for the coins struck in the reign of Antoninus Pius to celebrate the 900th anniversary of the foundation of Rome.

56. We do not know to which direction the original Aeneas group turned. The fresco from the house of Fabulus Ululitremulus (Pompeii IX.13.5) has the group walking to the left, but most versions—the Campanian parody, the Bonn and Merida groups, the Turin cippus, the Antonine coin type, as well as the terracotta lamps—have them striding to the right like the Beneventum group and the sarcophagi groups.

57. See P. Bastien, "Le medallion de plomb de Lyon," *Numismatique romain: Éssais, recherches et documents* 18 (Wetteren, 1989), 1–45, with bibliography. My thanks to Ralph Mathesen for pointing this out to me.

58. See H. P. L'Orange and A. von Gerkan, *Die spätantike Bildschmuck des Konstantinsbogens* (Berlin, 1939), 51–59 and 72–78 for the east and west sides, 65–71 for the battle in the water.

59. See Rizzardi (1970), 22–24, for a summary, and most recently Noga-Banai (2007), 11–12, 17–22.

60. Here I agree with C. Mango, "Constantine's Mausoleum and the Translation of Relics," *Byzantinische Zeitschrift* 83 (1990), 51–62, 434.

61. See the discussion of J. Elsner, "From the Culture of *Spolia* to the Cult of Relics: The Arch of Constantine and the Genesis of Late Antique Forms," *Papers of the British School at Rome* 68 (2000), 149–84, esp. 177.

62. See, e.g., J. Wilken, *John Chrysostom and the Jews* (Berkeley, 1983), 116–27, and for a nuanced view of Chrysostom's homilies against the Judaisers, see C. Shepardson, "Continually Contested Places: John Chrysostom's *Adversus Iudaeos* Homilies and the Spatial Politics of Religious Controversy," *Journal of Early Christian Studies* 15 (2007), 483–517, with extensive bibliography at n. 11, pp. 485–86.

63. See esp. B. Kiilerich, *Late Fourth Century Classicism in the Plastic Arts: Studies in the So-called Theodosian Renaissance* (Odense, 1993), esp. 9–18, for an earlier bibliography and an attempt at a definition, generally 244–51 and 220–34, of "Classicistic currents of the fourth century."

64. T. Hölscher, *Römische Bildsprache als semantisches System* (Heidelberg, 1987), trans. as *The Language of Images in Roman Art* (Cambridge, 2004). See my comments in J. Elsner, "Classicism in Roman Art," in J. Porter, ed., *Classical Pasts* (Princeton, 2006), 271–97, esp. 274–75.

65. For political imagery, see, e.g., P. Zanker, *The Power of Images in the Age of Augustus* (Ann Arbor, Mich. 1988), 33–79; for religions see, e.g., J. Elsner, "Cultural Resistance and the Visual Image: The Case of Dura Europos," *Classical Philology* 96 (2001), 269–304, esp. 281–301.

66. See, e.g., G. Marrone, "Pietas di Ottaviano e pietas di Sesto Pompeio," in G. Marrone, ed., *Temi Augustei* (Amsterdam, 1998), 7–20; A. Powell, "'An Island Amid the Flame': The Strategy and Imagery of Sextus Pompeius, 43–37 BC," in A. Powell and K. Welch, eds., *Sextus Pompeius* (London, 2002), 103–34, esp. 121, 123–27; E. M. Zarrow, "Sicily and the Coinage of Octavian and Sextus Pompey: Aeneas or the Catanean Brothers?" *Numismatic Chronicle* 163 (2003), 123–35. This story was still remembered in statuary and verse at the end of the fourth century A.D.: see Claudian's minor poem 17 (e.g., in vol. 2 of the Loeb edition).

67. See esp. Elsner (2006), 271–76, for a sketch of a definition.

68. The new scholarly consensus on Roman copying as "emulation" is in my view much too bland. Emulation is one of the aspects of the appropriation of the past, but a nuanced rejection of the past is equally possible—as in the case of the Red Sea sarcophagi. On emulation, see E. Gazda, "Roman Sculpture and the Ethos of Emulation: Reconsidering Repetition," *Harvard Studies in Classical Philology* 97 (1995), 121–56; the various studies in E. Gazda, ed., *The Ancient Art of Emulation* (Ann Arbor, Mich., 2002); and E. Perry, *The Aesthetics of Emulation in the Visual Arts of Ancient Rome* (Cambridge, 2005); with the thoughtful review of C. Hallett, "Emulation versus Replication: Redefining Roman Copying," *JRA* 18 (2005), 419–35, esp. 428–35. For some attempts to look beyond emulation in Greek and Roman replication to such issues as religion, subjectivity, quotation, excess in referencing the past, and reception, see the essays assembled in *Art History* 29.2 (April 2006).

69. See P. Veyne, *La société romaine* (Paris, 1991), 320–42, some of which was published in English as "Conduct without Belief and Works of Art without Viewers," *Diogenes* 143 (1988), 1–22. On the Column of Marcus (largely accepting Veyne's position) see J. Elsner, "Frontality in the Column of Marcus Aurelius," in J. Scheid and V. Huet, eds., *Autour de la colonne Aurélienne* (Tournhout, 2000), 251–64, esp. 257 and n. 33.

70. See J. Kollwitz, *Oströmische Plastik der theodosianischen Zeit* (Berlin, 1941), 3–69; G. Giglioli, *La colonna di Arcadio a Constantinopoli* (Naples, 1953); G. Becatti, *La colonna coclide istoriata* (Rome, 1960), esp. 83–150 (on Theodosius), 151–264 (on Arcadius), and 265–88 (on both); S. Sande, "Some New Fragments from the Column of Theodosius," *Acta ad atrium historiam pertinentia* 1 (1981), 1–78; Kiilerich (1993), 50–64.

71. In general the literature on copying has too much been concerned with statuary and sculpture, only very little with painting and hardly at all with the replication of three dimensional and large scale monuments and the ideological implications of such activity.

72. See C. Kraeling, *The Excavations at Dura-Europos: Final Report VIII.I: The Synagogue* (New Haven, 1956), 74–86; E. R. Goodenough, *Jewish Symbols of the Greco-Roman Period* (New York, 1964), vol. 10, 105–39; K. Weitzmann and H. Kessler, *The Frescoes of the Dura Synagogue and Christian Art* (Washington, D.C., 1990), 38–52.

73. Kraeling (1956), 80–1 and n. 237; Goodenough (1964), 118–19.

74. Kraeling (1956), 79–80; Goodenough (1964), 117–18.

75. For a survey and discussion, see, e.g., A. J. Wharton, *Refiguring the Post-Classical City* (Cambridge, 1995), 38–51.

76. For the western Middle Ages, see, e.g., M. Rubin, *Gentile Tales: The Narrative Assault on Late Medieval Jews* (Philadelphia, 2004), 144–89; R. Mellinhoff, *Antisemitic Hate Signs in Hebrew Illuminated Manuscripts from Medieval Germany* (Jerusalem, 1999); S. Lipton, *Images of Intolerance: The Representation of Jews and Judaism in the Bible moralisée* (Berkeley, 1999); and a number of the essays in this volume. For modernity, see, e.g., the essays in L. Nochlin and T. Garb, eds., *The Jew in the Text* (London, 1995).

77. See for instance, M. Miles, "Sta Maria Maggiore's Fifth Century Mosaics: Triumphal Christianity and the Jews," *Harvard Theological Review* 86 (1993), 155–75. Generally on visual typology, see S. Schrenk, *Typos und Antitypos in der frühchristlichen Kunst* (Munster, 1995), and C. Tkacz, *The Key to the Brescia Casket: Typology and the Early Christian Imagination* (Paris, 1992), 51–62.

78. *Pace* the persistent strand in scholarship to interpret the Red Sea crossing as a baptismal type—on which see Rizzardi (1970), 24–29, and Noga-Banai (2007), 13–15.

79. For date, see Ambrose, *De Officiis*, ed. I. Davidson (Oxford, 2001), 3–5.

80. For date, see W. Jaeger, *Two Rediscovered Works of Ancient Christian Literature: Gregory of Nyssa and Macarius* (Leiden, 1954), 118–19.

81. This trope has a long history in the Patristic interpretation of the Red Sea crossing— see, e.g., F. Dölger, "Der Durchzug durch das Rote Meer als Sinnbild der christlichen Taufe," *Antike und Christentum* 2 (1930), 63–69; P. Lundberg, *La typologie baptismale dans l'ancienne église* (Uppsala, 1942), 116–45; J. Daniélou, *Bible et liturgie* (Paris, 1951), 119–35. Note that in his *De Virginitate* Gregory makes no use of baptismal interpretation when discussing the Red Sea crossing (at 4.6 and 18.5). See the discussion of Aubineau (1966), 113–15.

82. See, e.g., C. Harrison, *Augustine: Christian Truth and Fractured Humanity* (Oxford, 2000), 194–97.

83. See on Holland, e.g., S. Schama, *The Embarrassment of Riches* (New York, 1987), 104–21. Note that these examples of idealization are distinctively Protestant.

84. See especially Melanie Klein, *Envy and Gratitude: A Study of Unconscious Sources* (London, 1957), 24–27, also 62–64; with, e.g., J. Kristeva, *Melanie Klein* (New York, 2001), 102–3, and L. Alford, *Melanie Klein and the Critical Social Theory* (New Haven, Conn., 1989), 88–89, in relation to groups. My invocation of psychoanalysis here is not as a psychological *deus ex machina* designed to solve the problems of history with some trans-historical psychic truth, but because psychoanalytic writing provides perhaps the deepest engagement (both empirical and conceptual) of twentieth-century thinking with the problems of how identity is formed through genealogical relationships and projections. Note this is a rather different position from the account of genealogy as "light-hearted positivism" used to highlight the fabrication of identities "in piecemeal fashion from alien forms" in the work of Michel Foucault. See the discussion of H. Dreyfus and P. Rabinow, *Michel Foucault: Beyond Structuralism and Hermeneutics* (London, 1982), 104–17, quotes (themselves from Foucault) on 105 and 107. I might add also that Klein's thinking—as a Jewish Austrian exile writing in the postwar London of the 1950s—may not explicitly refer to the Holocaust but is clearly driven by it in relation to the problems of envy as directed to groups as well as individuals. It thus signals the fact that all thinking on the topics governing this essay, and the others in this volume, is both from a place "after the Holocaust," and inevitably partial insofar as it foregrounds the Jews over all the other ancestors and alterities that Christianity depends upon but has chosen to elide.

85. In general see the outstanding discussion of J. Z. Smith, *Drudgery Divine: On the Comparison of Early Christianities and the Religions of Late Antiquity* (Chicago, 1990); on matters of art, see J. Elsner, "Archaeologies and Agendas: Reflections on Late Ancient Jewish and Early Christian Art," *Journal of Roman Studies* 93 (103), 114–28.

86. I have no space here to explore this theme at length or with the depth it deserves. I would argue that before the Nazi takeover in Germany and before the state of Israel, Jewish scholars—often so assimilated into their host cultures within the European Diaspora as to have converted to Christianity—effectively ventriloquized the ideologies that framed the scholarly fields in which they worked. That model of "Jewish" scholarship was transformed with the Holocaust, the fundamental and too often unvoiced subtext of any post-1945 study

of Jews or Christian relations with Jews, and the creation of a Jewish state. Note that Israeli art historians' ethnic claims to an indigenous ancient "Jewish art," archaeologically attested in Palestine, borrowed (in my opinion quite shockingly) all their terms from Nazi art history, inverting the negative scholarship of race into a positive scholarship of ascendant and ideological Zionism (see briefly Elsner [2003], 120–25, esp. at the bottom of 122). Post-1945 scholarship by Jewish art historians is thus profoundly implicated in the extent to which individuals consciously or unconsciously uphold a prewar Diaspora identity of strong assimilation or a pro-Israeli (Zionist) one, or any point in between. What we define as "Jewish" in relation to art historians is also complicated—ranging from people of Jewish extraction or origin (sometimes who only discover themselves so late in life) to converts (both to and from Judaism) to Israelis (both secular and religious) to "out-Jews," in Daniel Boyarin's cute phrase.

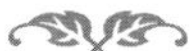

CHAPTER 2

Unfeigned Witness: Jews, Matter, and Vision in Twelfth-Century Christian Art

Sara Lipton

When around the year 1120 the Benedictine monk Rupert of Deutz rewrote the *Vita* of his abbey's sainted founder, Archbishop Heribert of Cologne (d. 1021), he added a novel and curious detail.[1] The miraculous heavenly light that accompanied the birth of the future saint was no longer seen solely by the Christian mother and midwives, as in the original text, but was now also witnessed by a Jew.[2] Moreover, according to Rupert, this Jew enjoyed the privilege of being the first to voice the meaning of the blessed vision, telling the boy's father: "Surely [by this light] you may know that [*he who*] *is born to you will fill you with joy, and he will make his family shine with the great splendor of his name.*"[3] At roughly the same time that Rupert inserted this Jewish witness into Heribert's life story, images of Jews began to proliferate in Christian art. In this essay I argue that this coincidental creation of the visionary and the visible Jew was not fortuitous. Rather, a constellation of specific intellectual, ecclesiastical, and devotional trends combined to provoke a fundamental reorientation of the age-old theological concept of "Jewish witness," and to lay new stress on Jewish vision. Although in Christian polemic the Jews were traditionally characterized as "blind," Christian art and texts in the twelfth century began to highlight Jewish sight, and "seeing" Jews became central objects of the Christian gaze.

Becoming Visible: Identifiable Jews in Christian Art

As is well known, Christian theology adopted a bifurcated approach to Jews and Judaism. Although polemicists from the Gospels through John Chrysostom and well beyond routinely castigated "the Jews" for their blindness, Jews were also regarded as crucial witnesses to and signs of Christian truth.[4] As expounded by Saint Augustine, Jews filled this role by virtue of their possession of Scripture, their descent from those present at the Crucifixion, and their subsequent state of subjugation, which testified to Christian triumph.[5] In spite of this conceptual centrality, however, for the first half of the Middle Ages Jews played little role in Christian art. Israelites indistinguishable from their gentile foes and prophets identical to apostles (Figure 2.1) occasionally inhabited illuminated pages of Scripture, but before the eleventh century Old Testament illustration was rare, and there was no such thing as a visually distinct Jew.[6] Only with the creation of great Romanesque Bibles in the 1080s did a specific "Jewish" iconography finally appear, as illuminators adopted peaked Persian hats, scrolls, pseudo-classical drapery, and beards to signal the antiquity of Hebrew prophecy (Figure 2.2).[7] Within a few decades, archaizing depictions of Hebrew prophets and patriarchs were widespread, and the scroll, beard, and pointed hat had become familiar and consistent enough to constitute identifying marks of Jewishness.[8]

An obvious starting point for any investigation into the new prominence of imagery from Hebrew Scripture is contemporary biblical scholarship. The first half of the twelfth century was a time of intense activity in the area of exegesis: typological interpretation (which read the Old Testament as foreshadowing Christian history) was elaborated, new layers of signification were articulated, and new approaches to the "letter" were developed.[9] Major works of biblical commentary, in particular the heavily typological *Glossa ordinaria* (created at Laon c. 1100–1140), the even more typological and wildly idiosyncratic readings of Rupert of Deutz himself, and the literal-historical approach pioneered by Hugh of St.-Victor (d. 1141) and his Victorine School, all devised sophisticated new methods for teasing out the relationship between Old Law and New, matter and spirit, sign and meaning.[10] These works affirmed the ongoing value of the Old Testament, but also highlighted the extent to which Jews, misled by their "carnal" attachment to the "letter" of Scripture, were "blind" to its true spiritual import.[11] Castigation of the Jews' "superficial" and "material" understanding, linked to their stereotypical greed and carnality, thus came to form a conventional component of high medieval Christian interpretation.[12]

These developments are frequently cited to explain the growing prominence in the twelfth century of Old Testament visual imagery. Just as the Jews' language, texts, and heritage were rendered ever more central to Christian study, scholars have assumed, so naturally their Scriptures and persons figured more centrally in Christian art.[13] It is certainly clear that contemporary exegesis—and the anti-Jewish polemic that so often accompanied it—must be considered an

SARA LIPTON

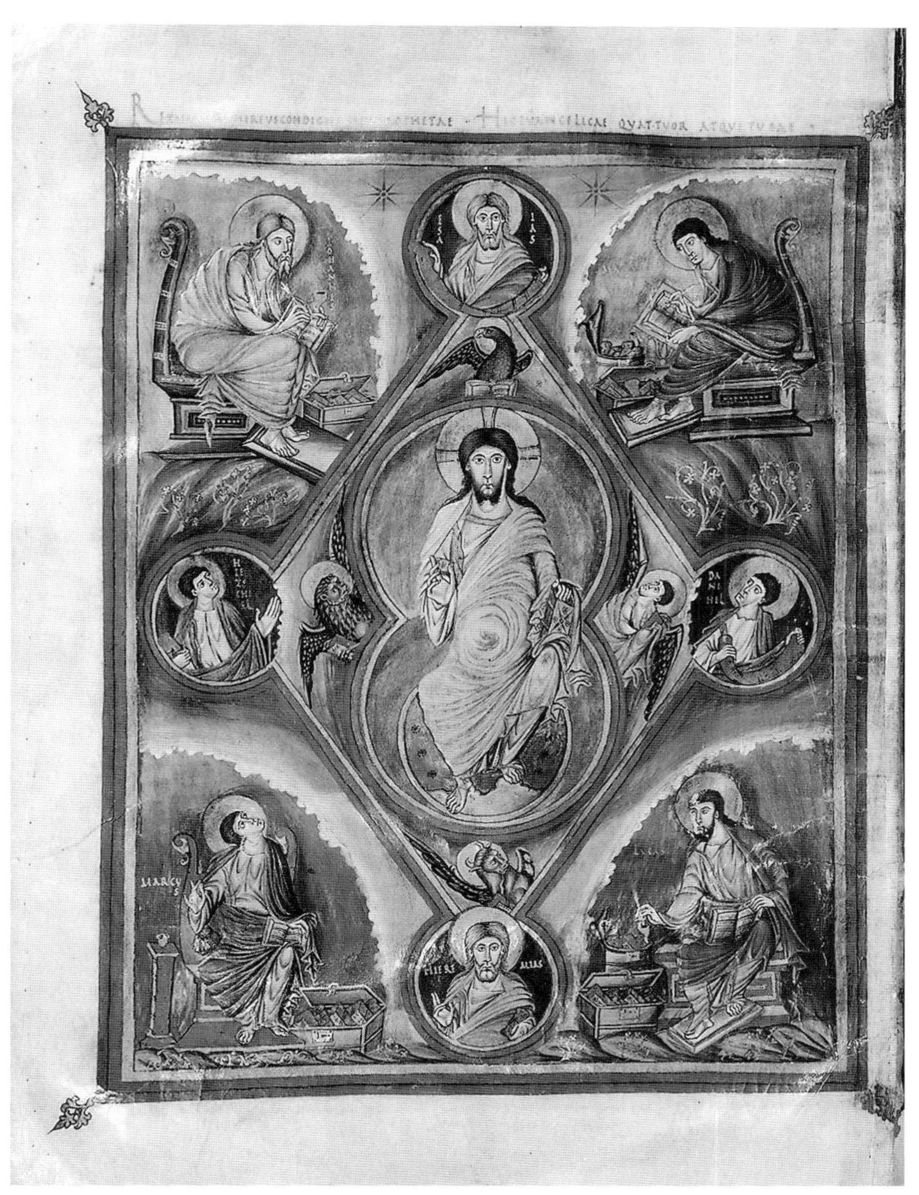

2.1. Old Testament prophets identical to New Testament apostles (compare Ezekiel and Mark, Daniel and Matthew). First Bible of Charles the Bald, frontispiece to the Gospels. Tours, 845. Paris, Bibliothèque nationale de France, ms. Lat. 1, fol. 329v. Photo courtesy Bibliothèque nationale de France.

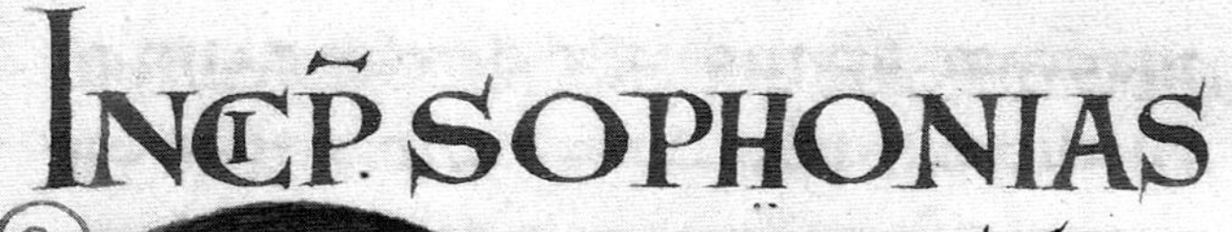

2.2. A Romanesque archaizing depiction of a Hebrew prophet. Lobbes Bible, initial to Sophonias (Zephaniah). Lobbes, Belgium, 1084. Tournai, Bibliothèque du Séminaire, cod. 1, fol. 270. Photo © KIK-IRPA, Brussels.

essential context for our images. Typological imagery undoubtedly draws on typological biblical commentary,[14] and the exegesis of Rupert of Deutz has been shown to have influenced several works of art.[15] Nonetheless, simply citing contemporary exegesis cannot satisfactorily explain *why* the new intellectual trends were so rapidly and widely transposed into visual imagery, much less account for the spread of a specific "Jewish" iconography or illuminate how it was understood. To begin to answer these questions we need to pay careful attention to the full range of issues addressed in text, image, and object, and ask what *work* representations of Jews were designed to do. Rupert of Deutz's story of the witnessing Jew provides significant guidance concerning these questions; it is to this story that I now turn.

The Vita Heriberti: The Jew as Outside Witness

The first striking feature of the revised *Vita* is the fact that Rupert's account of the miraculous birth inverts the standard Christian characterization of Jewish perception as mired in carnal error.[16] Rupert writes: "On the night when [Heribert] was poured out from the maternal womb, an immense heavenly light shone there, which some sleeping people saw with the *eyes of the heart,* and some waking people saw with the *eyes of the body.*" One might expect that the Jew, stereotypically associated with the flesh, was one of the waking witnesses who saw with "the eyes of the body," but this is not the case. Rupert's narrative continues: "The father of the infant was sleeping, and with him a certain one of his friends (yet a Jew), who had come to him for customary conversation or friendly business. Sleeping together at that hour in which in the light of the happy birth came forth, each [of these two men] saw the same dream. Awaking, they spoke immediately to one another, each . . . relating his own dream. . . . [The Jew] narrated first. [He dreamt that] the bed, in which the beloved wife lay in childbirth, [seemed] to open at the front, and a radiance bright as the midday sun was admitted and shone." The Jew then interprets the vision as an omen of Heribert's future "splendor."[17]

Rupert was well aware that his monastic audience would be startled by his casting of a Jew in such a pivotal role, and he hastens to explain. Without the Jew, he asserts, the miracle would not have been credible: "Indeed, it would, perhaps rightly, have seemed unbelievable to anyone, if *only* the light of spiritual grace, which Judaic blindness knows not, had been fit to be conferred on [Heribert]. A Jew may well seem to be an unworthy sharer of the same luminous dream that the Christian father deserved to see. But the elect and glorious *son of light* [Heribert] was able to shine both with the interior gift of eternal light . . . and [also] with the external prosperity of temporal glory."[18] That is to say,

in Rupert's view, the miracle might have been disputed had Heribert's greatness
been signaled *only* through *invisible* grace, via a purely private and internal
vision. Perceptible physical phenomena were far more persuasive. Apparently
many Christians, even Christian monks, were like spiritually blind Jews: in need
of concrete signs.

Rupert's concern that Christians would question a spiritual sign of sanctity
may seem somewhat surprising, but it was very much in accord with contemporary trends. In the later eleventh century, as part of the papal reform program,
the newly rediscovered Roman law and the revived discipline of dialectic began
to be applied to canonization procedures.[19] Standards of proof changed and
tightened; both the type of testimony that could be adduced and the type of
person who was allowed to testify were subject to more rigorous regulation.[20]
In a significant epistemological shift, mere rumor, second-hand testimony, and
even written depositions were no longer deemed adequate forms of evidence.[21]
Witnesses had to be personally present at a hearing; there had to be at least two
witnesses to any event; they had to have direct, sensory experience of the facts
to which they were testifying; and they had to be of respectable social rank,
unimpeachable character, and demonstrated impartiality.[22] Women were dis-
paraged as unreliable, open to persuasion, and prone to fancy.[23] Personal visions
were considered a particularly suspect source of knowledge. A report of the 1131
canonization of St. Godehard of Hildesheim explains the reasons for such cau-
tion: "It was decreed at that time that on account of the illusions of demons
which frequently happened . . . in these matters, no one should be canonized
except by apostolic authority and after his life had been examined by duly quali-
fied persons."[24]

This, then, suggests one motivation for Rupert's revision: the account of
Heribert's birth provided by his mid-eleventh-century source no longer satisfied
twelfth-century legal requirements. As servants, members of the subject's household or family, and as women, the midwives and even Heribert's mother failed
to meet the standards for suitable witnesses. (The fact that canonists' disapproval of female testimony seems often to have been ignored in practice does
not negate the basic point. Rupert would have wanted his account to reflect the
ideal.) Only male witnesses could provide convincing testimony. Since men
were generally excluded from birthing chambers, the miraculous physical light
accompanying the birth could not be directly perceived by a male witness; hence
its reception in dream form. Heribert's aristocratic father could not be the sole
male witness to his son's miraculous splendor, however, and in any case as a
close relative, he was an overly partisan and therefore less than ideal witness.[25]
The best possible confirmation of the heavenly grace conferred upon Heribert
was the simultaneous revelation of the dream to a figure with no such intimate

ties. And who could be more disinterested on the subject of Christian sainthood than a Jew? The visitor may have been a friendly familiar of the household, but as a Jew he was still inevitably an outsider (as Rupert put it: "a friend, yet a Jew" [*amicus, Iudeus tamen*]). Hence his usefulness. As a canon law compiled in the 1070s stated, quoting 1 Timothy 3:7: "[for a bishop's probity to be assured] it is necessary that he have good testimony from those who are outside."[26]

The Vita Heriberti: The Jew as Material Witness

The significance of the Jew in Rupert's narrative can hardly be reduced to mere forensic convenience, however. Rupert explicitly indicates that as a formulaic embodiment of materiality, the Jew was *uniquely* suited to testify not only to Heribert's miraculous birth, but also to his future glory. Rupert comments, "Who, indeed, does not know the splendor of the great church of Cologne, how . . . it glittered also in temporal resources and honors? Since therefore [Heribert] was destined to be so preeminent in rank, and since *this light* of the Lord *was destined to have been exalted upon* so great *a candelabrum* . . . it ought not seem unworthy that a Jew, too, should have received the portent of his future brightness."[27] Heribert's temporal greatness, then, vindicated the Jew's mundane reading of the miraculous sign ("he will make his family shine with the great splendor of his name").

Rupert thus uses Heribert's birth miracle to mount a defense of ecclesiastical splendor—a quality that was under attack by ascetic reformers.[28] Wealth and worldliness are—as they had long been in Christian polemic—associated with the Jew, but here they are nevertheless accorded positive valence, qualifying as the fitting attributes of an ecclesiastical saint. Nor was this the first time that Rupert wielded a Jew, or at least Judaic references, in this way. Faced with the reformers' denigration of custom (Pope Gregory VII famously noted that "Christ did not say, 'I am custom . . .'"), defenders of monastic and ecclesiastical splendor needed to cite a more powerful precedent than simply longstanding practice. Rupert found it in the Hebrew Scriptures: in his commentary *On the Divine Offices* (written c. 1112), he compared ornately decorated altars and churches to the Jerusalem Temple itself.[29] It is surely not by chance that in the *Vita* Rupert describes Heribert as a great *candelabrum*—the kind of church furnishing under increasing attack by critics of ecclesiastical excess, and often associated with Hebrew ritual.[30] In his *Apologia* of 1125, for example, Bernard of Clairvaux, greatest of the Cistercian reformers, lamented: "Churches are decorated, not simply with jeweled crowns, but with jeweled wheels illuminated as much by their precious stones as by their lamps. We see *candelabra* like big bronze trees, marvelously wrought, their gems glowing no less than their flames. . . . [These things] seem to me in some sense a revival of ancient Jewish rites."[31]

Rupert turns this "judaizing" strategy on its head. Most scholars agree that Rupert's rewriting of the *Vita,* which far more than the earlier version emphasizes Heribert's humility and likeness to the apostles, was intended to condemn the ambition, pride, and venality of over-worldly prelates.[32] But he also seeks to demonstrate that one can and must distinguish unrestrained worldliness from appropriate grandeur. The Jew's participation in Heribert's miraculous birth heralds the temporal majesty rightly claimed by a great ecclesiastical lord, and rightly displayed in a great ecclesiastical foundation. Rupert, then, introduced the Jew for more than his juridical utility. He was using this exemplar of antique materiality to uphold the value of material splendor.

But we are still not quite done with Rupert and his Jew. Eager as he was to demonstrate and defend Heribert's earthly grandeur, and thereby to justify the artistic grandeur of the monastery founded by Heribert (his own Abbey of Deutz), Rupert was of course even more committed to affirming the saint's spiritual perfection. He did this by interrupting his chronological narrative to relate a second, wondrous event that took place when Heribert was twenty-four. Rupert concludes his discussion of the Jew's prophesy of Heribert's future temporal splendor by noting: "This he could say by gazing at the light or glory only of the secular world. But *Christ, the true light* and glory *of the heavens* miraculously fulfilled the miraculous prediction [of Heribert's spiritual splendor]. For [twenty-four years later] on [Christmas night], during the sacred celebration of the Mass, when we sing 'The light will shine today over us,' Heribert, carrier of the true light, was consecrated a priest. Who will doubt that this happened through providence or the same arrangement of God, with which care or grace he first sent out the afore-mentioned sign, when he was being born?"[33] This second miracle—the fact that the service sung during Heribert's consecration mentions a shining light—contrasts starkly with the first. It involves no bodily sight, only proper (spiritual) understanding of breath and sound. As opposed to the first, well-attested event, we have here no mention of witnesses, proof, discussion, or interpretation. And yet no suspicion whatever is attached to this miracle; this time Rupert explicitly rules out the possibility of doubt. And, finally, of course, this is a miracle in which the Jew plays no part. He is physically absent, and his prediction of Heribert's future familial glory made no mention of spiritual exaltation.

In sum, Rupert's tale uses the witnessing Jew to present a complex epistemology of faith, one, I should add, by no means unique to Rupert.[34] Two sources of knowledge are recognized: sensory experience and inward spiritual enlightenment. Both are valid. Indeed, the former provides an instructive, even necessary model and metaphor for, and offers a pathway to, the latter. Although spiritual understanding is manifestly a higher form of knowledge, it is inaccessible to most Christians, and the human need for concrete signs is accepted, and even enshrined in canon law.[35] Thus, the Jew, whose "vision" and understanding are traditionally—and notoriously—material and corporeal, can still provide valuable and valued witness, even of Christian truths. During those rare moments when a few select Christians are able to achieve purely spiritual *intellectus* (exemplified by the saint's consecration), the Jew again provides testimony—in the form of his absence and/or oblivion. In this imperfect world, in which the seeking Christian stands ever poised at the juncture of flesh and spirit, one figure stands at the crossroads and indicates the road not to be taken: the figure of the Jew.[36]

The Eilbertus Altar: Unfeigned Prophecy
and Fashioned Words

In Rupert's *Vita* the testifying Jew remains a purely textual sign. But he would soon be given visible form. As we have seen, in the first decades of the twelfth century a host of Hebrew characters made their way into Christian art. A stunning work of art from Rupert's hometown helps explain the introduction and clarify the function of such representations. Within twenty or so years of the rewriting of the *Vita Heriberti,* the makers of this object mobilized Old Testament prophets in support of corporeal perception, creating visual parallels to Rupert's Jewish witness.

The object in question is a portable altar from Cologne dating to c. 1130–50 (Figure 2.3).[37] On the altar table are depicted Christ in Majesty surrounded by the evangelists' symbols, the twelve apostles holding scrolls and seated on thrones, and scenes from the life, Passion, and Resurrection of Christ (Figure 2.4). These are all quite standard images for an altarpiece. Around the sides are sixteen standing Hebrew prophets and kings holding inscribed scrolls.[38] This is, according to Robert Favreau, an entirely new kind of iconography for portable altars, which had not previously featured figures from Hebrew Scripture.[39] The Hebrews' inscriptions are in many cases also unprecedented and have never been fully explained.[40] The kings and prophets are framed above and below by a larger inscription. It reads: "Filled with the doctrine of faith, the twelve fathers bear witness that the prophetical words are not fictions [*ficta non esse prophetica dicta*]. Inspired by heaven, they prophesied about Christ; they foretold those things which were to come after."[41] The "twelve fathers" presumably refers to Daniel, Isaiah, Jeremiah, Ezekiel, Hosea, Malachi, Jonah, Nahum, Joel, Obadiah,

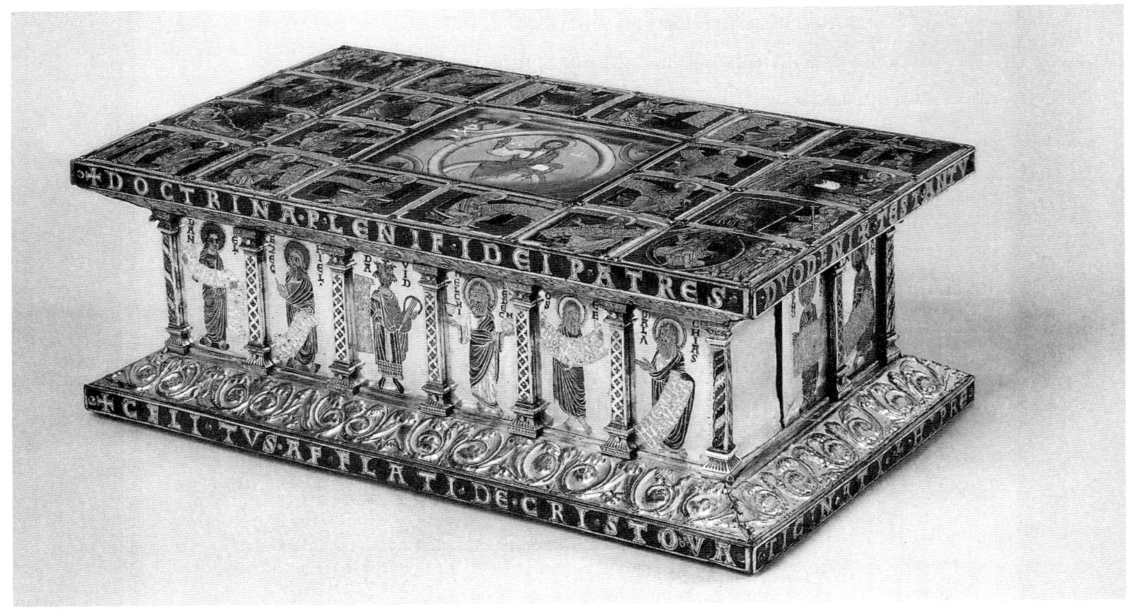

2.3. The Eilbertus portable altar. Oak, copper gilt, enamel. Cologne, c. 1130–50. Berlin, Kunstgewerbemuseum, Staatliche Museen, Inv. W 11. Photo: Bildarchiv Preussischer Kulturbesitz/Art Resource, New York.

Zechariah, and Zephaniah. Balaam was considered a false prophet, although he predicted the rising "star," and the remaining three are kings.

This inscription seems on the surface to be a straightforward articulation of Christian exegesis: as far back as the recorded words of Jesus, and most powerfully in the epistles of Paul, the Old Testament was read as foretelling the coming of Christ. As presented here on the altar and embodied by the Hebrew prophets, this is powerful and positive witness indeed: the fathers' testimony is said to be "inspired by heaven," and their portrayal is respectful and dignified. David is crowned and wears a chlamys and robe, Solomon is crowned and cloaked, while the remaining Hebrews are identical in physiognomy and dress to the apostles themselves: bareheaded, bearded, and dressed in togas, but also (unusually) barefoot—a mark of asceticism that, together with the signs of wisdom, displays the purity and truth of their words, their *dicta non ficta*.

Yet for all the visual serenity and conceptual concordance between old and new apparent here, there is a discordant note, a defensive tone embedded in that phrase: *dicta non ficta*. Why should our altar feel the need to proclaim so forcefully that prophecy is not fictive? In fact, the phrase did not originate in medieval Cologne; it is a paraphrase of words penned by Saint Augustine as Christian Rome was beset on all sides, and also, in his view, from within. They

SARA LIPTON

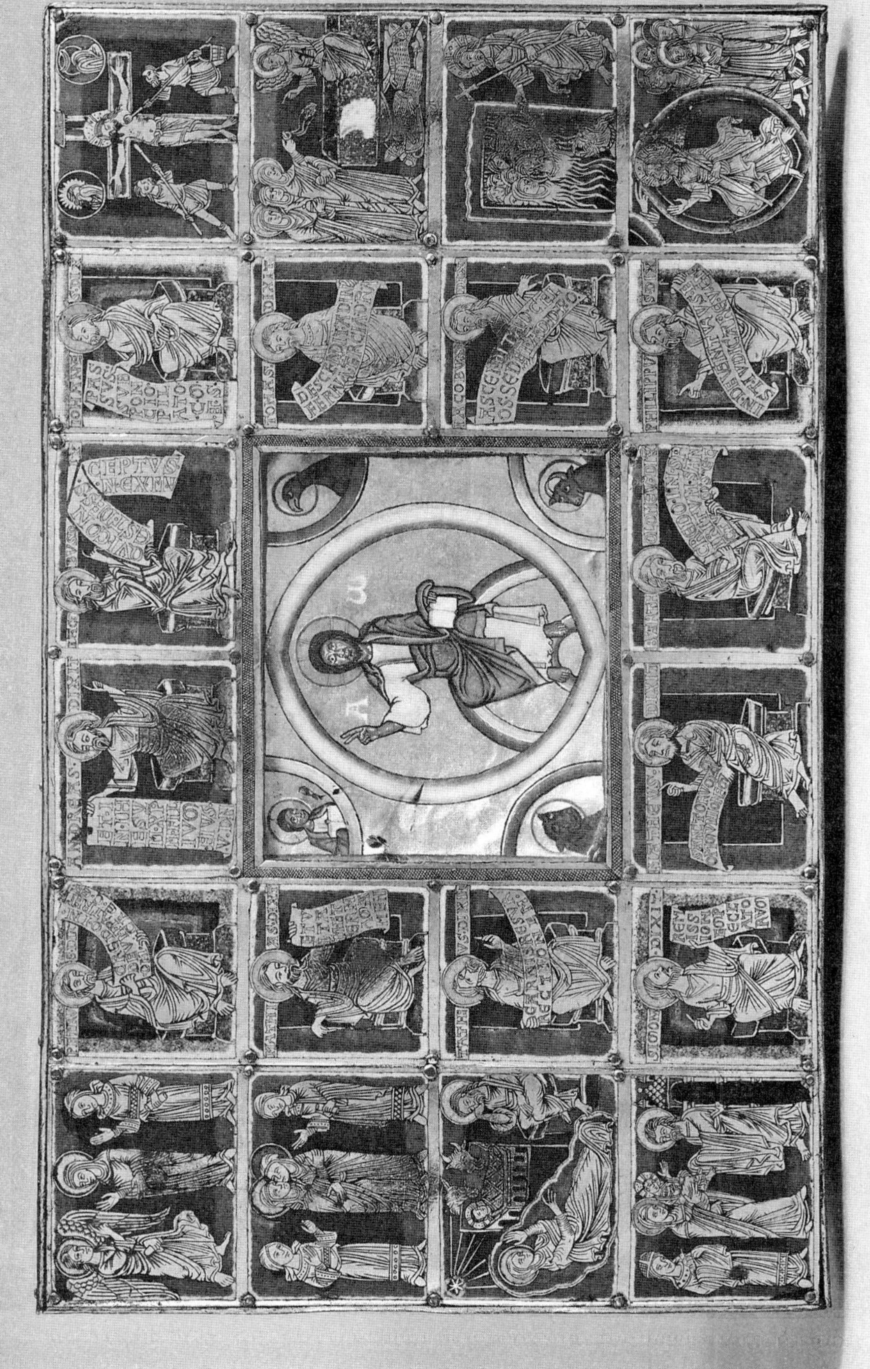

2.4. Christ in Majesty, the twelve apostles, and Gospel scenes. Eilbertus portable altar, tabletop. Cologne, c. 1130–50. Berlin, Kustgewerbemuseum, Staatliche Museen, Inv. W 11. Photo: Bildarchiv Preussischer Kulturbesitz/Art Resource, New York.

appear in *Contra Faustum* 16.21, a work written c. 387 to refute dualist Manichaean charges that the Hebrew Scriptures were blasphemous nonsense, and that Catholics had forged both the Old Testament Christological prophecies and the Gospel passages that echo them. According to Augustine, the Jews' Scriptures disprove such accusations: "It is a great confirmation of our faith that such important testimony is borne by enemies. The . . . Gentiles cannot suppose these testimonies to Christ to be [our] recent forgeries [*non possunt putare confictum*]; for they find them in books held sacred for so many ages by those who crucified Christ."[42] The passage is repeated in slightly modified form in *City of God* 18.46: "[The Jews] were dispersed through the lands, so that indeed there is no place where they are not, and [they] are thus by their own Scriptures a testimony that we have not forged the prophecies about Christ [*prophetias nos non finxisse*]."[43] This is part of the famous "Augustinian justification" or "doctrine of tolerance," which explained why Jews continued to reside in Christian lands. Augustine's valuation of Jewish testimony, however, had not been much invoked in Christian texts in the intervening centuries, which actually cited Gregory the Great and Roman law far more than Augustine when justifying toleration of Jews within Christendom.[44] It seems strange for our altar to echo this defense of the antiquity and verity of Scripture, in the heart of the Holy Roman Empire, at the height of the age of faith. Why, and to whom, does our inscription insist that the words of prophecy were not forged?

It is unlikely that this defense of prophecy was aimed in the first instance at Jews. Typological exegesis is, indeed, in function and often in intention a rebuttal of Jewish literalistic interpretation, and Jews certainly disputed Christological readings of Hebrew prophecy. But they did not as a rule allege that the Hebrew prophetical books were forged by Christians. Augustine (and others) wielded typology against gnostics, and there were some dualistic heresies plaguing Cologne at this time.[45] But they were small voice, and unlikely to be a central concern of the clerics who made this altar. I think, rather, that the defense of the antiquity and authenticity of prophecy is directed toward a more powerful chorus in the mid-twelfth-century Rhineland: the very same critics of ecclesiastical ostentation who provoked Rupert's revisions. (In fact, Rupert of Deutz may have been the first high medieval exegete to revive the exact wording of Augustine's justification. In his commentary on the story of Cain, he echoes Augustine's reading in *Contra Faustum* 12, and then quotes the justification from *Contra Faustum* 16.)[46]

When Augustine repeated his discussion of Jewish testimony in *City of God*, he added a further comment: "And very many [Israelites], considering [their own dispersal], even before His passion, but chiefly after His resurrection, believed in Him. . . . But the *rest are blinded,* of whom it was predicted, 'Let

     SARA LIPTON

their table be made before them a trap, and a retribution, and a stumbling-block. Let their eyes be darkened lest they see.'"[47] Testimony, then, is here conflated with visual perception. This is, of course, an extremely common, even ubiquitous conflation: throughout western history knowing has been construed as seeing and vice versa.[48] But what was to Augustine primarily a metaphor for religious insight takes on rather more pointed resonance when inscribed on a three-dimensional, image-soaked, enameled and gilt altar table.[49] Let us look again that word *ficta*. It is usually translated as "false," "feigned," or "fictive," but, as the past participle of *fingere,* it literally means "formed," "fashioned," "molded," "sculpted." How is one to take it here? Certainly the words of prophecy are neither "false" nor "fictions," but on this particular object, the prophecies—the words of the prophets, the words of the Apostles, and the Gospel deeds that fulfilled them—are nevertheless indisputably "formed" and "fashioned." It is *these* "fashioned" words and works, I believe, that need to be defended. The altar is intervening in a debate, not about Scripture, but about art. The contested text whose antiquity and authenticity must be upheld is the object itself.

In placing the antique authority of the Hebrew prophets and the spiritual usefulness of material artifice at the center of a debate about luxurious art, the Eilbertus Altar was joining a broad discussion. Rupert of Deutz's linkage of ecclesiastical ornamentation with Old Testament grandeur was by no means an isolated example. As Conrad Rudolph, Jean-Claude Schmitt, and Herbert Kessler have all demonstrated, ancient Hebrew precedent was rhetorically central to the Benedictine-Cistercian debate over art and excess; it featured equally prominently in contemporary quarrels between regular canons and cloistered monks over their respective callings.[50] Hebrew Scripture figured in these debates in two distinct ways. On the one hand, as Rupert's invocation of the Temple indicated, Hebrew antiquity conveyed authority (one superior to the previously privileged custom), which both sides were eager to claim. The writings of Abbot Suger of Saint-Denis (d. 1151), the most famous art patron of the twelfth century, are crammed with parallels for and justifications of his projects drawn from Hebrew Scripture.[51] But traditionalists did not monopolize scriptural citation. The pro-reform (although himself Benedictine) Abbot William of St. Thierry (d. 1148) also invoked the authority of Hebrew precedent, defending the Carthusian way of life against accusations of novelty by saying that the new monks were merely emulating Elijah and Elisha.[52]

On the other hand, Christian exegetical practice, and especially the temporal tension inherent in typological thinking, which simultaneously insisted on the ongoing relevance of the past and the linear march of time, considerably complicated the question of Hebrew precedent.[53] Christianity insisted that in spite of the ongoing validity of the Old Testament, most aspects of antique Hebrew observance had been either "spiritualized" or utterly superseded. Monastic reformers thus frequently cast their project as a contest between the pure spirituality of the New Dispensation and the corrupt, overly ritualistic materiality of the Old.[54] As we have seen, Bernard of Clairvaux criticized church ornamentation as disturbingly suggestive of "ancient Jewish rites." When secular clerics and Cluniacs excused their wealth by noting that Abraham, Isaac, Jacob, and other holy Hebrews possessed earthly riches, the Cistercian Idung of Prüfening (fl. c. 1155) criticized their biblical understanding and their hermeneutical method: "Just as Christ told the Jews: 'you err, not knowing scripture,' so the Cistercian says to the Cluniac: 'you err, not knowing scripture.'" And he added, quoting Saint Jerome: "Those things in Old Testament times were just the shadow of future things. All things happened to [the patriarchs] in figures. . . . Let us repudiate therefore gold with the rest of the Jewish superstitions; or if one loves gold, then one loves also the Jews."[55] The traditionalists, not to be cowed, threw accusations of "Judaizing" interpretation back upon their critics, charging them with excessive literalism and legalism. Cardinal Matthew of Albano (d. 1134), a Benedictine and proponent of monastic tradition and moderation, chastised reformist abbots for making cloister life more onerous by warning: "Dear brothers, when you multiply the mandates, you multiply the transgressions. As Paul said: 'The Law indeed brings wrath.'"[56] And lest the point be lost, he turned Christ's own imprecations against his adversaries: "Let not that Lord's reproach apply to you: 'Woe to you, scribes and pharisees—who took the key of knowledge, so that neither you enter, nor do you permit others to enter!'"[57] (The reformist abbots in turn echoed the implicit anti-Judaism of the Gospels in their reply to Cardinal Matthew, complaining to him, "You spit in our face!" [i.e., as the Jews did to Christ].)[58]

If the status of letter was under continual debate, the status of the "thing" proved equally problematic. Reformers insisted that signs—whether the words of Scripture or an image in a church—were to be valued for what they signified, not in their own right.[59] Paintings were an acceptable form of representation because they made no claim to innate, material worth.[60] Gold and silver objects, by contrast, were as liable to be valued for their matter and their craftsmanship as for what they represented. For this reason Bernard of Clairvaux and William of St.-Thierry both warned about the dangers of craftsmanship and "artifice"—a hypocritical attempt on the part of humans to usurp the beauty of nature and borrow the shine of the sun. In doing so, they consciously echoed Hebrew Scripture: Bernard's "miro artificis opere" and William's "per manus artificium" both recall terms used in Jeremiah to condemn Israelite materialism.[61] And three-dimensional images, whether precious metalwork objects or rough wood or stone sculptures, struck many Christians as uncomfortably, even dangerously akin to idols.[62] The initial shock of the cleric Bernard of Angers (c. 1020) at his first encounter with the cult of the statue of Ste. Foi at Conques is well known.[63] By the year 1100, concern about possible idolatrous misuse of images led to the incorporation of disclaimers of divinity into images themselves: an inscription on the north portal of the early twelfth-century Church of San Miguel, Estella warns: "The image that you see, is neither God nor man. But he whom the sacred image figures, is both God and man."[64] Christians felt particularly vulnerable to Jewish mockery of the new devotional and representational practices: many contemporary texts incorporate defenses of images directed against real or imagined Jews. A central concern of Rupert's *Dialogue Between Jews and Christians,* for example, was to refute the charge that Christian veneration of images—especially the image of Christ—amounted to idolatry. In the text, the Christian discussant repeats longstanding Christian explanations of the efficacy of image: "While we externally image forth [Christ's] death through the likeness of the cross, we [are kindled] inwardly to love of him." He then criticizes the Jews for their "blindness," by which he means their inability to recognize the spiritual in the material.[65]

The debate over church ornament and monastic and ecclesiastical image-based practices thus quickly mutated into a debate over who was most "Jewish"—in their manner of worship, in their interpretation of the letter, and in their approach to matter.[66] We have moved from ritual to representation: what began as a disagreement over wealth and gold, clothing and prayer, eventually inspired competing verbal and visual semiotic approaches. One man's "shine" is another man's "shadow," and the ongoing validity of the "figure" (biblical or artistic) poses a problem of pressing import. In Idung's *Dialogue,* the Cluniac defender of art was silenced, offering no response to his interlocutor's critique. In real life, however, as we have seen, the traditionalists responded vigorously, accusing their critics—whether Cistercian or Jewish—of not knowing the difference between *spurs to* devotion and *objects of* devotion, in the process articulating a legitimizing theory of luxurious matter and a theology of "spiritual seeing."[67] But the proponents of sumptuous decoration and visual devotion did more than argue the efficacy of art. In perhaps the most eloquent of all their responses, they created art.[68]

The Eilbertus Altar: Visible Witness and Invisible Truth

And so the visible Jewish witness is born. Just as Rupert invented a Jew whose vision and presence attested to the truth of tangible signs, and whose blindness and absence then attested to the higher truth of invisible ones, so our altarpiece forges prophets to point the way by look, word, and deed . . . and then to fall behind.

The prophets witness by look: their very visual similarity to the apostles, their haloed and hatless heads, affirm that they have received divine revelation. They do differ from the Apostles in one way, however: in their posture. The Apostles are all seated, whereas the prophets all stand, a contrast that perforce draws attention to their stances.[69] This composition cannot have been dictated solely by the form of the altar—there are plenty of twelfth-century portable altars with seated figures on their sides.[70] Rather, the positioning of the figures, presided over by an image of Christ enthroned, echoes Matthew 19:27–29: "When the Son of Man sits on the Throne of His Glory, you who have followed me will also sit on twelve thrones, judging the twelve tribes of Israel." This text was quoted by Bernard of Clairvaux in 1147, when he scolded the secular clergy in Cologne for leading a "disordered" or "pattern-less" (*informem*) life. According to Bernard, Christ's prophecy signifies that monks would one day be exalted over and allowed to sit in judgment upon secular clerics.[71] An earlier interpretation, found in Jerome and echoed by the ninth-century exegete Christian of Stavelot, had read the text as predicting that believers would judge unbelievers, especially the Jews.[72] Bernard was thus implicitly comparing secular clerics to unbelieving Jews. The Eilbertus Altar, then, may be seen as offering a retort on the part of Cologne churchmen—secular canons or traditionalist monks—to Bernard's charge, replacing the analogy "apostles are to Hebrews as reformers are to traditionalists/Jews" with the equation "apostles are to Hebrews as those who draw spiritual insight from corporeal vision, are to those who see only literally." It thus serves to indict all those who cannot spiritually appreciate the object, as themselves matter-bound.

The prophets witness with words: the inscriptions almost all in some way relate light, sight, and shine to knowledge of God, and equate corporeal vision with religious faith. Thus Jeremiah's scroll asserts: "He *was seen* on earth and conversed with men."[73] Jacob's verse proclaims, "*I saw* the Lord face to face."[74] Zechariah announces: "He who will have touched you, touches the *pupil of my eye*."[75] Isaiah exclaims to his viewer, "*Behold!* A virgin will conceive and bear a son" as he curves his body to the right and gestures toward the Annunciation, visible just above him and to his right, on the top of the altar.[76] The phrase flourished by Ezekiel, "I will sanctify my name, which was polluted among the nations," while apparently unrelated to vision, continues in the next verse: "The nations will know that I am the Lord when I will be sanctified in you *before their eyes*."[77] Malachi assures his viewers, "For you who fear God, the *sun of justice* will rise."[78] Nahum predicts: "The Lord has restored the pride [or: *splendor*] of Jacob like the pride [or: *splendor*] of Israel."[79] Joel's inscription invokes an image associated with darkness and blindness: "The beasts have rotted in their dung."[80] The scroll of Zephaniah reads, "Morning after morning, the lord will bring his judgment *into the light,* and it [or he] will not be hidden."[81] The verse of Obadiah proclaims, "Those exiles from Jerusalem who are in the Bosphorus will possess the cities of the South."[82] Although this inscription is labeled by Favreau "particularly obscure," the South was inevitably associated with light, and Favreau himself records that Rupert of Deutz comments in relation to this passage, "The Bosphorus signifies the pagans nations, who are without knowledge of God, in the obscurity of cold, but who *will find the light.*"[83] Balaam, as is customary, holds his sole true prophecy: "There shall arise a *star* from Jacob, and a man shall rise out of Israel," lines that are in Scripture preceded by a verse that (in Christian exegesis) simultaneously affirms the truth of Hebrew prophecy, the insufficiency of the Judaic era, and the visible reality of the Incarnation: "*I shall see him, but not now; I shall behold him, but not near.*'"[84] It is difficult to find a reference to shine or vision in the verse flourished by Hosea: "The number of the sons of Israel will be like the sands of the sea,"[85] but the ever sight-sensitive Rupert of Deutz managed to do so: "And in the end the aquatic sand of the sea will be separated by the *shining stars* of heaven." Rupert explained that in this verse Hosea was predicting that great things would arise out of the seed of Abraham.[86] And Daniel's phrase, "When the holy of holies comes, unction will cease," while recalling Christian polemical assertions of the Hebrews' supersession, also paraphrases a verse that explicitly equates justice and knowledge with vision and prophecy: "Seventy weeks are shortened upon thy people . . . that iniquity may be abolished; and everlasting justice may be brought; and *vision and prophecy may be fulfilled;* and the saint of saints may be anointed."[87]

The prophets witness with deeds: each points upward toward the truth, makes an expressive gesture, or holds objects that prefigure the Christian liturgy (especially as observed in traditional, ornament-laden churches). Thus Isaiah gestures toward the Annunciation image enameled on the top of the golden altar as he foretells the Incarnation. Melchizedek displays bread and wine, or rather a golden paten and chalice, symbols of the body and blood of Christ consumed in the Mass, but also the type of luxury items so frequently criticized by reformers. David grasps his harp, indicative alike of the Hebrew Psalms and of the music that played so central a role in Benedictine worship, and which was frequently criticized by reformers. (The Cistercian Aelred of Rielvaux, for example, railed against the use of musical instruments in church as overly Hebraic, exclaiming: "Where does it come from, since types and figures have already ceased, where does it come from, that there are in church so many instruments, so many cymbals?!"[88])

The prophets fall behind, or rather remain below: they function as supports for the altar table, but their view of the top is blocked, and they cannot see either the painted image of Christ or the Body that is daily sacrificed upon it.

This last, visible act of negative witness—the prophets' physical inability to see the Body of Christ, which they nonetheless spiritually foresaw through heavenly inspiration—rounds out their usefulness to the Christian viewer. For he, too, cannot "see" the Body of Christ, in the sense of perceiving flesh, limbs, and so on; he needs to look with "the eyes of faith" if he is to discern Christ in the consecrated bread. Although Christian imagery had linked the Eucharist to Old Testament figures as early as the sixth century,[89] the growing theological consensus in favor of complete transubstantiation (which insisted that the bread and wine of the Mass actually turned into the physical, if disguised, body and blood of Christ) rendered issues of matter, vision, and representation more significant—and vexing—than ever before.[90] The central sacrament of medieval Christianity now required the same ability to transcend mundane perception and "see spiritually," as did religious art.[91] And it was subject to the same criticisms, by internal Christian sectarian critics as well as by external ones.[92] It is for this reason that a defense of the sacrament written by the Cistercian Baldwin of Canterbury (d. 1190) reads very much like defenses of religious art in general, and the inscription on the Eilbertus Altar in particular: "nothing [in the sacrament] is false, feigned, counterfeit, or faked by magical manipulations. There is truth in that which is evident, and in that which is hidden." And to provide a model for how Christians might "see" what cannot be seen, he cites the prophets: "The law and prophets bear witness to future promise (in the shadows)." But he also indicts those who could not learn to see properly: "The Pharisees, who did not believe, were made more blind."[93]

The imagery of the Eilbertus Altar, then, embodies Christian theology regarding Jewish prophecy—its truth, its centrality, its incompleteness without Christ. But it also embodies, and links Hebrew prophecy to, one specific—and embattled—stream of Christian thought promoting the spiritual efficacy of luxurious matter and bodily perception. The ancient Hebrew prophets, who forecast the coming of Christ in words and imagery drawn from their own pre-Christian world, demonstrate that splendor *can* lead to salvation, if viewed with properly spiritual vision. But the altar is also preserving, and enshrining in its very form, the difference between "types" and "figures" on the one hand (represented by the Hebrew prophets and kings) and the transcendent truth they herald (represented by the invisible godhead above them). Each time the celebrant leans over the shining surface of this altar, its words, images, composition, and very shape instruct him in the correct path to knowledge of God. He is to move progressively upward from corporeal sight (the beauty of the object and the appearance of the prophets), through visual imagination (the inspired words of the prophets), to the climax of the Christian Mass: ingestion of the unseeable Body of Christ.[94] This last act foreshadows the ultimate goal of the Christian believer: to come as close as is possible in this flawed, flesh-bound world to purely image-less *intellectus* or understanding.

Conclusion

It is natural and tempting to link the new prominence of Hebrew figures in twelfth-century art with contemporary anti-Jewish polemic, and to see these images as early harbingers of the growing intolerance that came to mark high medieval Christendom. But although it is clear that these works of art are strongly influenced by debates over scriptural interpretation and reflect deep disapproval of Jewish literal understanding, exegesis on its own cannot explain material and visual innovation. Differences in medium and audience must be taken into account; the function of images must be considered. I have suggested that the most immediate and compelling context for the new imagery is the challenge posed by ecclesiastical reform to traditional ritual and splendor, and the corresponding need felt by many twelfth-century monks, priests, and prelates to articulate a space within Christian spirituality for sensory perception and embodied existence. That is, the primary realm in which religious images must be understood is the realm in which religious imagery was used: Christian devotion. I have no wish to fall into Marc Bloch's "fetish of single cause."[95] But it is necessary to look at *when* and *where* images were made, *how* images work, and *why* they do what they do. The Eilbertus Altar was made in the Rhineland by and for secular clerics or Benedictine monks: men who, like Rupert of Deutz, continued to be moved by ritual and grandeur, and who, while committed to reform and purification, spurned the more ascetic and potentially dualistic practices and ideals of the Cistercians. Adopting and adapting the very judaizing label assigned them by their critics, they used Judaic imagery to demonstrate the difference between purely materialistic appreciation of matter and spiritually motivated use of matter.

Jewish prophets appear as venerable and authoritative witnesses to the antiquity, sanctity, and efficacy of luxurious matter and corporeal vision. Their function is not to rehabilitate the Jew as a spiritual witness, but to rehabilitate the realm long associated with Jews (the external, glorious, temporal, image-saturated world so inimical to early Cistercians) as a valid part of Christianity. By peopling innovative objects with visibly antique Hebrew figures, art makers and patrons could simultaneously claim prophetic authority for their artistic innovations, and point to contemporary Jews' carefully preserved though (from the Christian perspective) woefully misunderstood ancient Scriptures for affirmation. That is, the witnessing Jew appears *in* art in order to provide historical, scriptural, and epistemological justification *for* art, and to justify the very artworks in which he appears.

Although we cannot see the artistic representation of the Jew as a straightforward reflection of contemporary attitudes toward Jews, the *Vita Heriberti* and the Eilbertus Altar can help illuminate developments in contemporary Christian thought about the Jews. As Rupert of Deutz and his brethren asserted the testimonial value of matter, the power of Old Testament imagery, and the spiritual status of vision, Augustine's long-dormant articulation of Jewish witness acquired new relevance and force. Ideas that had previously been exclusively textual and largely metaphorical were given visual expression and tangible form. And, in turn, these images subtly affected the realm of ideas: an inevitable (and perhaps unintended) side effect of their representational strategy is to demonstrate graphically the Jews' own stagnancy, sterility, materiality, subordination, and supersession. These themes had always been present in Christian thought, of course, but they received new emphasis in twelfth-century texts, for reasons that are perhaps now somewhat clearer. The final lesson of this examination of twelfth-century text and image, then, is a historiographical one: just as Rupert of Deutz wrote a Jew into his source in order to illuminate Christian history, so by investigating the changing iconography of the Jew we can illuminate the history of Jews *and* of Christians in medieval Europe.

NOTES

1. John van Engen, *Rupert of Deutz* (Berkeley: University of California Press, 1983), 225–26. Heribert had founded the abbey in c. 1003. The original *Vita* had been written c. 1045–56 by a Deutz monk named Lambert: Lantbert vom Deutz, *Vita Heriberti, Miracula Heriberti, Gedichte, Liturgische Texte*, ed. Bernhard Vogel, MGH Scriptores 73 (Hanover: Hahnsche Buchhandlung, 2001), 135–201.

2. Rupert of Deutz, *Vita Heriberti: Kritische Edition mit Kommentar und Untersuchungen*, ed. Peter Dinter (Bonn: Röhrscheid, 1976), 1.4–8, p. 34. The original version of the miracle is in Lantbert vom Deutz, *Vita Heriberti*, 141–42.

3. The italicized citations are from Luke 1:35 and Acts 2:28.

4. See, for example, Matt. 15:14. On Jewish witness see the elegant—if schematic—overview by Anna Abulafia, "Christians and Jews in the High Middle Ages: Christian Views of Jews," in *The Jews of Europe in the Middle Ages,* ed. Christoph Cluse (Turnholt: Brepols, 2004), 19–28.

5. Most notably in *De civitate dei* 18.46 (ed. B. Dombart and A. Kalb [Stuttgart: Teubner, 1981], 2.328); discussed further in note 43 below. On Augustine and the Jews, see Paula Fredrikson, "Augustine and Israel: *Interpretatio ad litteram,* Jews, and Judaism in Augustine's Theology of History," *Studia patristica* 38 (2001): 119–35, and Jeremy Cohen, *Living Letters of the Law: Ideas of the Jew in Medieval Christianity* (Berkeley: University of California Press, 1999), 23–71.

SARA LIPTON

6. The Old Law was symbolized by the personification of Synagoga. On the absence of Jews in early medieval art, see Bernhard Blumenkranz, *Le juif médiéval au miroir de l'art chrétien* (Paris: Études augustiniennes, 1966).

7. On these developments, see Sara Lipton, *Dark Mirror: Jews, Vision, and Witness in Medieval Christian Art, 1000–1500* (New York: Metropolitan Books, forthcoming), chap. 1. Bearded and scroll-bearing prophets had occasionally appeared in Carolingian and Ottonian manuscripts, but before 1100 their appearance was not standardized; it was equally common for Hebrew prophets to be depicted as clean-shaven.

8. See, for example, the prophets on the western portal of the cathedral of Modena (consecrated 1106), the famous sculpted prophets at the monastery of Moissac (c. 1100), the jamb sculptures at Cremona (c. 1107–17), the nine prophets at Verona (1139), and many more. For a discussion of the spread of images of prophets, see Jean-Pierre Caillet, "La réappropriation du prophétisme par les imagiers chrétiens du XIIe siècle," *Le Monde de la Bible* 131 (2000): 47–53. Hats were less ubiquitous signs but were also common. Wide-brimmed pointed hats appear on the heads of Hosea, Jonah, and Daniel in the earliest stained glass windows that survive intact, on the south side of the nave of Augsburg Cathedral (c. 1100 or 1130); Ezekiel and Micah wear rounded, peaked caps in the Bury Bible (c. 1130–35); and Saint Joseph, Simon the Pharisee, Joseph of Arimathea, and Nicodemus all wear knobbed or peaked caps in the St. Albans Psalter (c. 1120–30).

9. See Beryl Smalley, *The Study of the Bible in the Middle Ages*, 3rd ed. (Oxford: Blackwell, 1983), and Nikolaus M. Häring, "Commentary and Hermeneutics," in *Renaissance and Renewal in the Twelfth Century*, ed. Robert L. Benson and Giles Constable (Cambridge, Mass.: Harvard University Press, 1982), 173–200.

10. On typology, see J. Daniélou, *Sacramentum futuri. Études sure les origines de la typologie biblique (Études de théologie historique)* (Paris: Beauchesne, 1950); G. W. H. Lampe and K. J. Woollcombe, *Essays on Typology* (London: SCM Press, 1957); and G. von Rad, "Typological Interpretation of the Old Testament," *Interpretation* 15 (1961): 174–92. On the *Glossa Ordinaria*, see Smalley, *Study of the Bible*, 46–66; Ermenegildo Bertola, "La 'Glossa Ordinaria' ed i suoi problemi," *RTAM* 45 (1978): 34–78; and Robert Wielockx, "Autour de la *Glossa Ordinaria*," *RTAM* 49 (1982): 222–28. On Rupert's exegesis, see van Engen, *Rupert of Deutz*, and David E. Timmer, "Biblical Exegesis and the Jewish-Christian Controversy in the Early Twelfth Century," *Church History* 58 (1989): 309–21. On St.-Victor, see Smalley, *Study of the Bible*, 83–195, and Jean Chatillon, "La culture de l'école de Saint-Victor au 12e siècle," in *Entretiens sur la Renaissance du 12e siècle*, ed. M. de Gandillac and E. Jeauneau (The Hague: Mouton, 1968), 156–58.

11. On the connections between Bible study and anti-Judaism, see Jeremy Cohen, "Scholarship and Intolerance in the Medieval Academy: The Study and Evaluation of Judaism in European Christendom," *American Historical Review* 91 (1986): 592–613. On Rupert's anti-Jewish exegesis, see van Engen, *Rupert of Deutz*, 241–48; Timmer, "Biblical Exegesis;" and Maria Lodovica Arduini, *Ruperto di Deutz e la controversia tra cristiani ed ebrei nel secolo XII* (Rome: Istituto storico italiano per il Medio Evo, 1979). On Victorine exegesis and the Jews, see Rebecca Moore, *Jews and Christians in the Life and Thought of Hugh of St.-Victor* (Atlanta: Scholar's Press, 1998).

12. See Anna Sapir Abulafia, *Christians and Jews in the Twelfth-century Renaissance* (London: Routledge, 1995).

13. Nigel Morgan, "The Iconography of Twelfth-century Mosan Enamels," in *Rhein und Maas: Kunst und Kultur 800–1400* (Cologne: Schnütgen-Museum, 1973), 2.263–75: "Typological was art presumably stimulated by Bible scholarship such as at Laon (*Glossa Ordinaria*)" (263). Caillet, "La réappropriation," likewise links prophetic imagery to biblical study. Robert

Favreau, "Controverses judéo-chrétiennes et iconographie. L'apport des inscriptions," *Comptes rendus des séances de l'année. Académie des inscriptions et belles-lettres* (2001): 1267–1303, attributes the prominence of prophets to the spread of textual Jewish-Christian polemic, but does not discuss the intellectual context for or uses of such polemic.

14. See P. Bloch, "Typologische Kunst," in *Lex et Sacramentum im Mittelalter,* ed. P. Wilpert (Berlin: de Gruyter, 1969), 127–42.

15. See H. Silvestre, "Trois témoignages mosans du début du XIIe siècle sur le crucifix de l'arc triomphal," *Revue des archaeologues et historiens d'art de Louvain* 9 (1976): 225–31; Rhabanus Haacke, "Rupert von Deutz: Kräfte der Bilde und neue Rationalität," in *Grosse Gestalten Christlicher Spirtualität,* ed. Josef Sudbrack and James Walsh (Würzburg: Echter, 1969), 113–21; and Michael Curschmann, "Imagined Exegesis: Text and Picture in the Exegetical Works on Rupert of Deutz, Honorius Augustodunensis, and Gerhoh of Reichersberg," *Traditio* 44 (1988): 145–69. Sermons, too, influenced art: verses from the so-called Quodvultdeus "Sermon Against the Jews" were inscribed nearly verbatim on several twelfth-century monuments. According to Dorothy Glass, "Pseudo-Augustine, Prophets, and Pulpits in Campania," *Dumbarton Oaks Papers* 41 (1987): 215–226, the sermon was first translated into sculpture by Nicolaus at Piacenza, Verona, and Ferrara c. 1110–30; it also influenced the sculpture of Notre-Dame-la-Grande in Poitiers (226).

16. Like almost all Christian commentators, Rupert in his exegesis had often associated the Jews' literal interpretation with moral carnality, assigning them the major "worldly" sins: greed, lust, and pride. This last quality is presented by Rupert as the efficient cause of the Jews' exegetical blindness: "They are blinded by the pride of those who are wise with their own wisdom and prudent in their own eyes." *Anulus sive Dialogus inter Christianum et Iudaeum,* ed. Rhabanus Haacke, in Arduini, *Ruperto di Deutz,* 183–242 (quotation at 203). See Timmer, "Biblical Exegesis," 315. In Rupert, the Jews' pride is primarily intellectual: they are the "sapientes et prudentes" of Matt. 11:25; see also Rupert of Deutz, *De Sancta Trinitate et operibus eius,* ed. R. Haacke, CCCM 21 (Turnholt: Brepols, 1971), 125.

17. *Vita Heriberti,* ed. Dinter, 33–35.

18. Ibid. *Iudaica cecitas* is from Rom. 11:25.

19. See W. Ullman, "Medieval Principles of Evidence," *Law Quarterly Review* 62 (1946): 77–87; H. L. Ho, "The Legitimacy of Medieval Proof," *Journal of Law and Religion* 19 (2003): 259–98; K. W. Nörr, "Institutional foundations of the new jurisprudence," in *Renaissance and Renewal,* 324–37; James A. Brundage, *Medieval Canon Law* (London: Longman, 1995), 120–53; Linda Fowler-Magerl, *Ordines iudiciarii and libelli de ordine iudiciorum (from the Middle of the Twelfth to the end of the Fifteenth Century),* Typologie des sources du moyen âge occidental, 63 (Turnholt: Brepols, 1994); and Elisabeth van Houts, "Gender and Authority of Oral Witnesses in Europe (800–1300)," *Transactions of the Royal Historical Society,* 6th ser. 9 (1999): 201–20.

20. Ho, "Legitimacy," 294: "The power of medieval witness-proof lay in the witness's standing as a direct source of knowledge, on his character and social rank, and on his having 'invoked the deity to the truth of' his assertions." See also James A. Brundage, "Juridical Space: Female Witnesses in Canon Law," *Dumbarton Oaks Papers* 52 (1998): 147–56.

21. For an interesting study of legal culture around 1000, see Jeffrey A. Bowman, *Shifting Landmarks: Property, Proof, and Dispute in Catalonia around the Year 1000* (Ithaca, N.Y.: Cornell University Press, 2004).

22. In the 1090s Pope Urban II refused to canonize a Breton saint on the grounds that proper witnesses had not been produced. In 1139, Innocent II refused to canonize Edward the Confessor on the same grounds. This may have been a political decision, but the grounds he cited must have been widely accepted: E. W. Kemp, "Pope Alexander III and the Canonization of Saints: The Alexander Prize Essay," *Transactions of the Royal Historical Society,*

   SARA LIPTON

4th series, 27 (1945): 13–28. In 1050, Pope Leo articulated idea that a saint needed "human corroboration" before his sanctity could be assured: Jay Rubenstein, "Liturgy against History: The Competing Visions of Lanfranc and Eadmer of Canterbury," *Speculum* 74 (1999): 279–309.

23. Brundage, "Juridical Space," and van Houts, "Gender and Authority."

24. Quoted in Kemp, "Pope Alexander III," 15.

25. John T. Gilchrist, *The Collection in Seventy-four Titles: A Canon Law Manual of the Gregorian Reform* (Toronto: Pontifical Institute of Mediaeval Studies, 1980), 99: "The influence of relationship, friendship and lordship often impedes the truth" (Titulus 5, Capitula 48).

26. "Oportet autem illum et testimonium habere bonum ab iis qui foris sunt." For its incorporation into canon law, see Gilchrist, *The Collection,* 163 (Titulus 20, Capitula 169).

27. *Vita Heriberti,* ed. Dinter, 34–35.

28. The benefits reaped by so many monasteries from the economic flourishing of the later eleventh and early twelfth centuries generated a strong reaction, known as the "monastic crisis of prosperity." New monastic orders (particularly the Carthusians, founded 1084, and the Cistercians, founded 1098) critiqued the excesses even of secular clerics, and promoted greater simplicity in lifestyle, liturgy, art, and architecture. So, for example, the earliest account of the first Carthusians, written in 1104, notes that they allowed no gold or silver ornaments in their church, except for a silver chalice (Guibert de Nogent, PL 156:853ff.). The phrase "monastic crisis of prosperity" was coined by Jean Leclerq; see Conrad Rudolph, *The 'Things of Greater Importance': Bernard of Clairvaux's Apologia and the Medieval Attitude toward Art* (Philadelphia: University of Pennsylvania Press, 1990), 3–4. On reformers' criticisms, see Jean Leclerq, "La crise du monachisme aux XIe et XIIe siècles," *Bulletino dell'Instituto storico italiano per il medio evo 70* (1958): 19–41, and John van Engen, "The 'Crisis of Cenobitism' Reconsidered," *Speculum* 61 (1986): 269–304.

29. *Liber de divinis officiis* 2.23, ed. Rhabanus Haacke, CCCM 7 (Turnholt: Brepols, 1967), 10–12. See also John van Engen, "Theophilus Presbyter and Rupert of Deutz: Arts and Benedictine Theology," *Viator* 11 (1980): 147–64.

30. See for example Exod. 25:31. On the monastic debate over art, see especially Conrad Rudolph, *Artistic Change at St-Denis: Abbot Suger's Program and the Early Twelfth-Century Controversy over Art* (Princeton, N.J.: Princeton University Press, 1990), and Rudolph, *Things of Greater Importance.*

31. *Apologia* XII.28, in Rudolph, *Things of Greater Importance,* 10. Bernard also contrasts Hebrew chandeliers and candelabra with Christian asceticism in *Liber ad milites Templi de laude novae militiae* 9, in *S. Bernardi Opera,* ed. J. Leclercq and H. M. Rochais (Rome: Editiones Cistercienses, 1963), 3.206–239 (quotation at 222).

32. Van Engen, *Rupert of Deutz,* 226, and *Vita Heriberti,* ed. Dinter, 126.

33. *Vita Heriberti,* ed. Dinter, 35.

34. On visual devotion, see Jeffrey Hamburger, *Visual and the Visionary: Art and Female Spirituality in Late Medieval Germany* (New York: Zone Books, 1998); Barbara Newman, *God and the Goddesses: Vision, Poetry, and Belief in the Middle Ages* (Philadelphia: University of Pennsylvania Press, 2003); Peter Dinzelbacher, *Vision und Visionsliteratur im Mittelalter* (Stuttgart: Hiersemann, 1981). For further discussion of Rupert's approach to visual devotional aids and religious epistemology, see my "Sweet Lean of His Head: Writing about Looking at the Crucifix in the High Middle Ages," *Speculum* 80 (2005): 1172–1208.

35. Neither route to knowledge is completely autonomous: waking witnesses see spiritual light with their physical bodies, and sleeping witnesses see secular light in their dreaming minds. This almost inextricable intertwining of the external and the ineffable is reflected in

the living world: Heribert is simultaneously majestic lord and humble saint; the Christian reader is simultaneously skeptical and devout.

36. The same argument, expressed in almost identical words, appears in David Nirenberg, "Christian Sovereignty and Jewish Flesh," in *Rethinking the Medieval Senses*, ed. S. Nichols, A. Kablitz, and A. Calhoun (Baltimore: Johns Hopkins University Press, 2008), 154–85: "At the crossroads of [the relationship between the material world and the divine Word], representing the possibility of confusion in its purest form, they placed the Jews." I thank David Nirenberg for this reference.

37. Welfenschatz, Berlin, Kunstgewerbemuseum, W11. See Anton Legner, *Romanische Kunst im Deutschland* (Munich: Hirmer, 1982), 185; Otto von Falke, R. Schmidt, and G. Swarzenski, *Der Welfenschatz* (Frankfurt-am-Main: Frankfurter Verlagsanstalt, 1930), no. 17; Dietrich Kötzsche, "Zur Stand der Forschung der Goldschmiedekunst des 12. Jahrhunderts im Rhein-Maas-Gebiet," in *Rhein und Maas*, 2.191–236; Dietrich Kötzsche, "Goldschmiedekunst," in *Die Zeit der Staufer. Geschichte-Kunst-Kultur* (Stuttgart: Württembergisches Landesmuseum, 1977), 1.391–93; Stefan Soltek, "Kölner romanische Tragaltäre," in *Ornamenta ecclesiae. Kunst und Künstler der Romanik* (Cologne: Stadt Köln, 1985).

38. Daniel, Isaiah, Jeremiah, Ezekiel, David, Melchisedek, Osee (Hosea), Malachi, Jonah, Nahum, Solomon, Joel, Abdias (Obadiah), Zechariah, Zephaniah, and Balaam.

39. Robert Favreau, "Les autels portatifs et leurs inscriptions," *Cahiers de civilisation médiévale* 46 (2003): 327–52 (quotations at 327, 337). For a comprehensive catalogue of portable altars, see Michael Budde, *Altare portatile: Kompendium der Tragaltäre des Mittelalters 600–1600* (Münster: published by author, 1998). For a thoughtful study of portable altars in their liturgical contexts, see Eric Palazzo, *L'Espace rituel et le sacré dans le christianisme: La liturgie de l'autel portative dans l'antiquité et au moyen âge* (Turnholt: Brepols, 2008). I thank Herb Kessler for this reference.

40. Favreau, "Les autels portatifs," 340, notes that all these texts "strongly assert the superiority of the Christian faith over Israelite law," but confesses himself otherwise baffled by the selection of unprecedented and often obscure verses. In "Controverses judéo-chrétiennes," 1282, Favreau points out that the verses on the scrolls of Isaiah, Jeremiah, and Daniel are identical to the verses cited in the pseudo-Augustinian anti-Jewish sermon now attributed to Quodvultdeus, which was incorporated into the Nativity liturgy and, eventually, the *Drama of the Prophets*. The other thirteen inscriptions, however, do not appear in the sermon or the drama.

41. "Doctrina pleni fidei patres duodeni testantur, ficta non esse prophetica dicta/Celitus afflati de christo vaticinati/ hi predixerunt que post ventura fuerunt."

42. *Contra Faustum* 16.21: "nihil de illo ad tempus possunt putare confictum," ed. J. Zycha, CSEL 25 (Vienna: F. Tempsky, 1891–92). See also 13.10: "One might rather fear that the inquirer . . . would say that the Christians composed those writings when the events described had already begun to take place . . . were it not for the widely spread and widely known people of the Jews. . . . From the Jewish manuscripts we prove that these things were not written by us to suit the event, but were long ago published and preserved as prophecies in the Jewish nation." Augustine was primarily interested in defending Christianity against pagan critics who mocked its novelty, by invoking texts known to be ancient. But he was doing more than relying on the Jews' antiquity. Like Rupert after him, he was relying on their status as outsiders: he knew his Bible, and may well have been thinking of 1 Tim. 3:7 ("It is necessary to have witness from outsiders"). But Augustine was a professor of rhetoric, and he also knew his rhetoric and law. The Roman rhetorician Quintilian wrote (*Institutio Oratorio* V.i.1–2) that witness testimony, one of the most persuasive forms of evidence, was classified as "inartificial proofs" (*inartificiales*), that is, proofs external to the speaker's art,

and drawn into the service of a case from without. Augustine, then, may have been invoking Quintilian when defending the prophetical books as "non confictum." See also Aristotle's *Poetics*, 1451b: "Non ficta fabula, sed vera historia."

43. *De civitate dei* 18.46, ed. Dombart and Kalb, 2.328. The passage explains the role of Jews in salvific history: "[The Jews] were dispersed through the lands (so that indeed there is no place where they are not), and [they] are thus by their own Scriptures a testimony [*testimonio*] that we have not forged the prophecies about Christ."

44. I owe this observation to Kenneth Stow, whom I thank for the insight and for encouraging me to think further about the Augustinian legacy. See his "Conversion, Apostasy, and Apprehensiveness: Emicho of Flonheim and the Fear of Jews in the Twelfth Century," *Speculum* 76 (2001): 911–33; also his review of Amnon Linder, *Jews in Legal Sources of the Early Middle Ages* in *Jewish Quarterly Review* n.s. 89 (1999): 460–65. For a different view of the influence of Augustine's doctrine of tolerance in the Middle Ages, see Cohen, *Living Letters of the Law,* and Abulafia, *Christians and Jews,* 65–66.

45. For example, by Irenaeus of Lyon, in his *Adversus Haereticos,* Book 4. On dualist heretics in Cologne in the 1140s and 1150s, see R. I. Moore, *The Birth of Popular Heresy* (London: Edward Arnold, 1975), 72–75, and Malcolm Lambert, *Medieval Heresy: Popular Movements from the Gregorian Reform to the Reformation,* 3rd ed. (Oxford: Blackwell, 2002), 62–64. Everwin of Steinfeld, the Cologne cleric who reported on dualist heretics in Cologne in 1143–44, dwelled less on their unorthodox ideas than on their critique of monastic wealth—a charge that stung precisely because it echoed perfectly orthodox critics (see Lambert, *Medieval Heresy,* 63). The dualistic tendencies inherent in Catholic thought—and brought to the fore in Catholic reformist debates and in Catholic critiques of Jewish materialism—made it all the more necessary to stress the heterodoxy of dualism, and all the more crucial to identify a "proper" Christian approach to matter, distinct from the mistaken Jewish approach.

46. *In Genesim* 4.6 in *De Sancta Trinitate,* ed. Haacke, CCCM 21, 288. See Gilbert Dahan, "L'exégèse de l'histoire de Cain et Abel du XIIe au XIVe siècle en Occident," in *RTAM* 49 (1982): 21–89 and 50 (1983): 5–68. The only other contemporary citation of which I am aware was written by Hervé de Déols (d. c. 1150), a Cluniac monk who had studied in the schools, translated the highly visual pseudo-Dionysian treatise on *Celestial Hierarchy,* commented on Scripture, and influenced art: "The crime of [the Jews] is the salvation of the Gentiles, since because of the killing of the Savior they are dispersed, they bear the Holy Scriptures for all nations, they are testimony for us, that we have not forged the prophecies about Christ, and they corroborate the faith of the gentiles" (PL 181:751). On Hervé's influence on art, see Marcia Kupfer, "Spiritual Passage and Pictorial Strategy in the Romanesque Frescoes at Vicq," *Art Bulletin* 68 (1986): 35–53. On Hervé's literary work, see Germain Morin, "Un critique en liturgie au douzième siècle. Le traité inédit de Hervé de Bourgdieu," *Revue bénédictine* 24 (1907): 36–61.

47. *De civitate dei* 18.46, ed. Dombart and Kalb, 2.328–29. Augustine was citing Rom. 11:7–10, which was, in turn, quoting Ps. 68:23–24.

48. See Roland Recht, *Le croire et le voir: L'art des cathédrales (XIIe–XVe siècles)* (Paris: Gallimard, 1999); Jeffrey Hamburger, "Body vs. Book: The Trope of Visibility in Images of Christian-Jewish Polemic," in *Ästhetik des Unsichtbaren: Bildtheorie und Bildgebrauch in der Vormoderne,* ed. David Ganz and Thomas Lentes (Berlin: Reimer, 2004), 1.113–45; Gudrun Schleusner-Eicholz, *Das Auge im Mittelalter* (Munich: W. Fink, 1985).

49. The medieval Latin word for portable altar is "tabula."

50. Rudolph, *Things of Greater Importance* and *Artistic Change at St-Denis;* Jean-Claude Schmitt, *Le corps des images: essais sur la culture visuelle au moyen âge* (Paris: Gallimard,

2002); Herbert L. Kessler, *Spiritual Seeing: Picturing God's Invisibility in Medieval Art* (Philadelphia: University of Pennsylvania Press, 2000). On canons' invocation of Aaron and the Levites as their forerunners, see Caroline Walker Bynum, *Jesus as Mother: Studies in the Spirituality of the High Middle Ages* (Berkeley: University of California Press, 1982), 29. The treatise *On the Various Orders and Professions of the Church,* dating to c. 1125–30, sets up an elaborate series of correspondences between different Christian Orders and Old Testament groups; see PL 213:810–34; discussed by M. D. Chenu, *Nature, Man, and Society in the Twelfth Century: Essays on New Theological Perspectives in the Latin West* (Chicago: University of Chicago Press, 1968), 150.

51. See Suger of Saint-Denis, *De Administratione,* ed. and trans. Erwin Panofsky, *Abbot Suger on the Abbey Church of St. Denis and Its Art Treasures,* 2nd ed. by Gerda Panofsky-Soergel (Princeton, N.J.: Princeton University Press, 1979), and Rudolph, *Artistic Change at Saint-Denis.*

52. William of St. Thierry, *The Golden Epistle: A Letter to the Brethren at Mont Dieu,* vol. 4 of *The Works of William of St. Thierry,* trans. Theodore Berkeley (Spencer, Mass.: Cistercian Publications, 1971), 12. On William's attitude toward religious images, see Jeffrey F. Hamburger, "A *Liber Precum* in Sélestat and the Development of the Illustrated Prayer Book in Germany," *Art Bulletin* 73 (1991): 209–36 (quotation at 233).

53. Chenu, *Nature, Man, and Society,* 149–50 and 156, notes the temporal complexity inherent in the Christian notion of typology: the "ages of the fathers" was superseded, but also actively present.

54. See van Engen, "The 'Crisis of Cenobitism,'" and Adriaan H. Bredero, *Cluny et Cîteaux au douzième siècle: L'histoire d'une controverse monastique* (Amsterdam: APA-Holland University Press, 1987).

55. Idung, *Dialogus* 1.6 and 1.36, in R.B.C. Huygens, ed., "Le moine Idung et ses deux ouvrages," in *Studi medievali* 13 (1972): 291–470. Idung was quoting St. Jerome, who in his *Letter to Nepotian* says, "Either we reject gold together with other superstitions of the Jews, or if the gold is pleasing, the Jews must also be pleasing" (Ep. 52:10, in CSEL 54, 433).

56. Stanislaus Ceglar, "Guillaume de Saint-Thierry et son rôle directeur aux premiers chapitres des abbés bénédictins, Reims 1131 et Soissons 1132," in *Saint Thierry: Une abbaye du VIe au XXe siècle. Actes du Colloque international d'Histoire monastique, Reims-Saint-Thierry, 11 au 14 octobre 1976* (Saint-Thierry: Association des Amis de l'Abbaye de Saint-Thierry, 1979), 299–350 (quotation at 324).

57. Ibid. See also André Wilmart, "Une riposte de l'ancien monachisme au manifeste de Saint Bernard," *Revue Bénédictine* 46 (1934): 296–344: "There are some improvident people [Cistercian reformers] who impose hard laws, like those of the Pharisees, on the weak, when even perfect people can scarcely fulfill them" (313).

58. Wilmart, "Une riposte," 300. See also Nicholas of Clairvaux (d. 1180), *Epistola* 8: "And finally with common accord we leave all things, and fly from the Old Testament and the shadow of the Cluniacs up into Cistercian purity [of the New]." PL 196: 1603.

59. See Stephen G. Nichols, *Romanesque Signs: Early Medieval Narrative and Iconography* (New Haven, Conn.: Yale University Press, 1983). For a sensitive discussion of the "matter of matter," see Herbert L. Kessler, *Seeing Medieval Art* (Peterborough, Ont: Broadview Press, 2004), 19–43.

60. Rudolph, *Things of Greater Importance,* 59, notes that Cistercian Statutes 10 and 20 forbade the use of gold and silver in most liturgical objects, but allowed a painted image of Christ on the crucifix.

61. Rudolph, *Things of Greater Importance,* 60. See Jer. 10:3–11.

62. See Sara Lipton, "Images and Their Uses," in *The Cambridge History of Christianity: Christianity in Western Europe c. 1000–c.1500,* ed. Miri Rubin and Walter Simons (Cambridge:

Cambridge University Press, 2009), 254–83, for further discussion of concern over potentially idolatrous image veneration.

63. *The Book of Sainte Foy*, trans. Pamela Sheingorn (Philadelphia: University of Pennsylvania Press, 1995).

64. Calvin B. Kendall, *The Allegory of the Church: Romanesque Portals and Their Verse Inscriptions* (Toronto: University of Toronto Press, 1998), no. 47. On the origins, intellectual context, and conceptual implications of this distich, see the fine study by Herbert L. Kessler, *Neither God nor Man: Words, Images, and the Medieval Anxiety about Art* (Freiburg: Rombach, 2007). See also Ragne Bugge, "*Effigiem Christi, qui transis, semper honoria.* Verses condemning the cult of sacred images in art and literature," *Acta archaeologiam et artium historiam pertinentia* 6 (1975): 127–39, and Hamburger, *The Visual and the Visionary*, 186.

65. *Anulus*, in Arduini, *Ruperto di Deutz*, 183–242. Elsewhere Rupert recounted a powerful spiritual vision inspired by an image of Christ. On these texts, and Rupert's attitude to art in general, see Lipton, "The Sweet Lean of His Head." Jewish criticisms of Christian images also figure in the *Dialogue* of Gilbert Crispin and Anselm, *Cur Deus Homo*.

66. This helps explain a fact noted by van Engen, *Rupert of Deutz*, 241, that Benedictine monks were in the forefront of the Christian-Jewish debate in the first half of the twelfth century. Being accused of "Jewishness" made it all the more important that they distinguish themselves from Jews.

67. See especially Kessler, *Spiritual Seeing*; Bruno Reudenbach, "'Ornatus materialis domus dei': Die Theologische Legitimation handwerklicher Künste bei Theophilus," in *Studien zur Geschichte der europäischen Skulptur im 12./13. Jahrhundert*, ed. Herbert Beck and Kerstin Hengevoss-Dürkopp (Frankfurt: Henrich, 1994), 1.1–16; and Peter Diemer, "Suger von Saint-Denis und die Künstschätze seines Klosters," in *Beschreibungskunst-Kunstbeschreibung. Ekphrasis von der Antike bis zur Gegenwart*, ed. Gottfried Boehm and Helmut Pfotenhauer (Munich: Wilhelm Fink, 1995), 177–216.

68. Indeed, Bernard of Clairvaux seems to have worried about the eloquence of the sculpted figure: see his retort to Abelard, quoted in Caroline Walker Bynum, *Wonderful Blood: Theology and Practice in Late Medieval Northern Germany and Beyond* (Philadelphia: University of Pennsylvania Press, 2007), 230 and 344n6: "Does the fashioned thing/figure/image/sculpture ever say to the one who fashioned it, why did you shape me thus?" ("Numquid dicit figmentum ei qui se finxit: quid me finxisti sic?"). S. Bernardi, *Epist.* 190, chap. 8. (*Opera* 8:34).

69. This contrast appears in other locations, as well, of course. The Apostles are seated and the prophets are standing on the Heribert Shrine, which also dates to mid-century Cologne. On the facade of Chartres Cathedral (c. 1145), Old Testament kings and prophets on the door jambs are standing while the Apostles on the lintel above are seated.

70. See, for example, the portable altar made in Cologne, c. 1160, now in the Treasury of the abbey of St. Vitus, Mönchengladbach (*Rhein und Maas* 1.271).

71. The accusation is mentioned in the preface to the *Liber miraculorum* (Book VI of Geoffrey of Auxerre's *Vita prima Bernardi*): John van Engen, "'God is no Respecter of Persons': Sacred Texts and Social Realities," in *Intellectual Life in the Middle Ages: Essays Presented to Margaret Gibson*, ed. Lesley Smith and Benedicta Ward (London: Hambledon Press, 1992), 243–64 (quotation at 243). Bernard's Cologne discourse also quotes Isaiah 26:10: "Let us pity the impious—he will not discern justice, and in the land of the holy ones he acted iniquitously, and *he will not see the glory of God.*"

72. PL 106:1253.

73. "Visus est in terris et cum hominibus conversatus est." This is not from Jeremiah, in fact, but from Baruch 3:38. The verse features prominently in the section of Rupert's *Anulus* devoted to defending veneration of the crucifix: Arduini, *Ruperto di Deutz*, 232–36.

74. "Vidi dominum facie ad faciem." Gen. 32:30.

75. "Qui tetigerit vos tanget pupillam oculi mei." Zech. 2:8.

76. "Ecce virgo concipiet [et] pariet filium." Is. 7:14.

77. "Sanctificabo nomen meum quod pollutum est inter gentes . . . [ut sciant gentes quia ego Dominus, ait Dominus exercituum, cum sanctificatus fuero in vobis coram eis]." Ezek. 36:23.

78. "Vobis timentibus deum orietur sol justitiae." Mal. 4:2.

79. "Reddidit deus superbiam Jacob sicut superbiam Isarel [*sic*]." Nahum 2:2. Since the next verse describes the flaming shields and scarlet armor of the Israelites, a translation that underscores the visual manifestations of pride seems warranted. Favreau, "Les autels portatifs," 339, relates this verse to Rupert of Deutz's *Commentary on the Twelve Minor Prophets* (PL 168: 549).

80. "Computruerunt jumenta in stercore suo." Joel 1:17. In Tob. 2:11, dung falls on the eyes of Tobias and blinds him. The thrust of Joel 1 is to lament the loss of beauty: "Yea and the beasts of the field have looked up to thee, as a garden bed that thirsts after rain, for the springs of waters are dried up, and fire has devoured the beautiful places of the wilderness" (Joel 1:20).

81. "Mane, mane judicium suum dabit dominus in lucem et non abscondetur." Zeph. 3:5.

82. "Transmigratio Jerusalem que est in Bosphori possidebit civitates austri." Obad. 1:20.

83. Favreau, "Les autels portatifs."

84. "[Videbo eum, sed non modo: intuebor illum, sed non prope.] Ex Jacob stella prodiet et de Israhel homo surget." Num. 24:17. As Favreau, "Les autels portatifs" notes, the scriptural "a scepter will rise" (*consurget virga*) is here, as in the liturgy, replaced with the phrase "a man will rise" (*exsurget homo*).

85. "Erit numerus filiorum is[r]ahel quasi arena maris." Hos. 1:10.

86. *Commentary on Osee* (PL 168:29). Also noteworthy is Augustine's discussion of the verse in *Contra Faustum* (chap. 89). There Augustine proves that the Old Testament was fulfilled in the New, by pointing to the citation of Hosea in Romans 9:23–26: "What if God, willing to show his wrath, and to make his power known, endured with much patience vessels of wrath, fitted for destruction, That he might show the riches of his glory in vessels of mercy, which he hath prepared unto glory?" Sand is, of course, the fundamental ingredient of enamel, which is made of glass.

87. Favreau, "Les autels portatifs," 338, plausibly suggests that "Cum venerit sanctus sanctorum cessabit un[c]tio" was inspired by Dan. 9:24, and identifies several anti-Jewish texts that cite the verse. The three remaining inscriptions are somewhat more difficult to relate to vision or shine. The scroll of Solomon reads: "Per sapientiam sanati sunt qui placuerint domino a principio" (Sap. 9:19). It may be included because of a verse that comes three lines earlier: "Et quae in prospectu sunt invenimus cum labore" ("And we find with labor those things that are in sight") (Sap. 9:16). Alternatively, it may refer to a comment of Augustine related to this verse: "Quod autem Christus est veritas, quod idem ostenditur cum splendor Patris nuncupatur; non est enim quidquam in circuitu solis, nisi splendor ipse quem gignit: quid ergo potuit apertius et clarius ex Vetere Testamento huic sententiae consonare, quam illud quod dictum est . . . et paulo post, 'per sapientiam sanati sunt'" (PL 32:1323). See, too, a treatise ascribed to Cyprian, which remarks, "Per sapientiam sanati sunt: ambulantes in tenebris sibimetipsis lumen non possunt ostendere, nisi ultroneum seipsum non videntibus offerat lumen. Ita humanum caecitas ad Deum non dirigit viam, nisi ipse lucernam legis ostendat" (PL 4:848). Jonah's scroll reads, "Tolle animam meam quoniam melior est mi[hi] mors quam vita" (Jon. 4:3). Again, a neighboring verse (Jon. 4:5) refers to

darkness and sight: "Et egressus est Jonas de civitate, et sedit contra orientem civitatis: et fecit sibimet umbraculum ibi, et sedebat subter illud in umbra, donec videret quid accideret civitati" ("Then Jonas went out of the city, and sat toward the east side of the city: and he made himself a booth there, and he sat under it in the shadow, till he might see what would befall the city"). And Rupert commented regarding this verse: "Verba eius prae oculis habere debemus" (PL 168:434). David's verse (Ps. 93:12, "Beatus est quam tu erudieris domine," "Blessed is he whom you will instruct, Lord") is likewise perplexing, though it is located close to others that emphasize that physical vision is a gift of God and related to knowledge: "He that planted the ear, shall he not hear? or he that formed the eye, does he not consider? He that chastises nations, shall he not rebuke: he that teaches man knowledge?" (Ps. 93:9–10). And Rupert comments of this verse: "Suaviter namque et magna cum deliciarum multitudine summam sapientiam cito discit ille ad quem fit Verbum Domini, quia videlicet hoc Verbum *lux vera* est, *quae illuminat omnem hominem venientem in hunc mundum* (John 1), et dum infulget humanae menti, repente illuminat, repente docet" (PL 168:15).

88. *Speculum Caritatis* 2.23, in *The Mirror of Charity,* trans. Elizabeth Connor (Kalamazoo, Mich.: Cistercian Publications, 1990).

89. See Sabine Schrenk, *Typos und Anti-typos in der frühchristlichen Kunst* (Münster: Aschendorffsche Verlagsbuchhandlung, 1995), 9–51.

90. Jean Wirth, *L'image à l'époque romane* (Paris: Les Éditions du Cerf, 1999), 91. Chenu, *Nature, Man, and Society,* 152–53, notes that explication of the Mass with reference to Old Testament sacrifices intensified in the twelfth century.

91. An inscription on a nearly contemporary portable altar also from Cologne, the Gregory Portable altar by Fridericus of St. Pantaleon (c. 1160), is explicit in this regard: "Quicquid in altari tractatur materiali / Cordis in altari conpletur spirituali. / Hostia visibilis mactatur operta figura, / Immolat hanc pura devotio mentis in ara" ("Whatever is handled on the material altar / Is fulfilled in the spiritual altar of the heart / With the figure veiled, the visible host is immolated / Pure devotion sacrifices this [host] on the altar of the mind").

92. Miri Rubin, *Corpus Christi: The Eucharist in Late Medieval Culture* (Cambridge: Cambridge University Press, 1992), 24–25.

93. Baldwin of Canterbury, *Spiritual Tractates,* trans. David N. Bell (Kalamazoo, Mich.: Cistercian Publications, 1986), 1.43–54.

94. Palazzo, *L'Espace rituel,* 36–37, notes that the images on liturgical artworks are constitutive elements of ritual and serve as models for the man who participates in the liturgy.

95. Marc Bloch, *The Historian's Craft* (New York: Vintage, 1964), 193.

CHAPTER 3

Shaded with Dust: Jewish Eyes on Christian Art

Herbert L. Kessler

The wide range of people, subjects, and monuments considered in this volume reflect myriad ways in which diverse Christian cultures used Jews and Judaism to construct their own claims about the material and sensual world. Many of the themes treated by the various authors were already fully realized in the art and discussions about art during the Middle Ages; therefore, it seems useful to consider the subject under several broad rubrics: the perceived tension during the Middle Ages between material instruments and Jewish and Christian spirituality, the claim that Christianity had replaced Jewish law and the related assertion that material images resulted from a natural evolution away from "blind" Judaism, and the odd but telling contradiction that figured Jews as iconoclasts and at the same time as idolaters.

Pugna spiritualis

A miniature in a twelfth-century copy of Prudentius's *Psychomachia* in London (British Library, Cotton MS Titus D XVI, fol. 6) reminds us that, throughout the Middle Ages, the role of material images remained contentious within Christianity.[1] Drawn by the so-called "Alexis Master," who was also responsible for some of the miniatures in the famous St. Alban's Psalter in Hildesheim (Dombibliothek, St. Godehard, MS. 1),[2] the illustration departs from both the fifth-century text accompanying it and the pictorial tradition initially engendered by Prudentius's allegory of Christian virtue overcoming vice.[3] Labeled "faith advances and mutilates the eyes,"[4] it represents a personification of Christian belief trampling the fallen "Worship-of-the-Old-Gods" and plunging a lance into the organ used to worship idols rather than into the mouth "that was sated with the blood of beasts." At a time when the Eucharist had long since replaced the ancient blood offerings, looking at material images still provoked a struggle with faith during the twelfth century.

That "pugna spiritualis," or spiritual battle, is depicted literally in the St. Alban's Psalter itself (p. 72; Figure 3.1). On the opening page of Psalms, a picture of two knights in combat illustrates an accompanying written gloss that, among other topics, asserts faith's power to protect believers in the "divine battle foretold in the scriptures to come about between the holy church and the antichrist":

> Whoever wishes to be a son of God and a worthy heir of the heavens, and whoever wishes to gain the glory and inheritance which the devils lost when they fell from the kingdom of God, by night and day let him watch in eye and heart that war and (fight for) justice which he here observes drawn out. Just as these visible arms have been prepared with iron and wood, so that they may bring about evil and human slaughter, likewise on the other hand it is necessary for each one of us who is established in war and penitence, to be armed with faith and love, so that we may approach the heavenly blessings and obtain the angelic crown of life. . . . Just as they do not cease from reaching out mutually with the eye of the body to all their limbs, we likewise, on the other hand, with the eyes of the heart must always keep watch with all virtue (with the eyes of the heart) against our adversary who is constantly lying in wait to ambush us.[5]

The struggle between the "eye of the body" using "visible arms" and the "eye of the heart" drawing strength from "faith and love" underlay not only the illuminations in the St. Alban's Psalter but also other Christian art, as Caesarius of Arles already recognized in the fifth century when he banished art from the cloister: "Waxed curtains ought never to be hung, nor painted pictures affixed, nor ought any paintings be made on the walls and in the rooms, because that ought not to be in the monastery which does not please the spiritual but only the human eye."[6] Had that not been so, Jews would have played a very different role in Christian art, if any at all.

Jews constituted the cohort of the "eye of the body" on the battlefield of Christian art, continuously engaged in combat with the Christian troops of the "eye of the heart." Writing at the close of the *Dialogus contra Iudaeos* a few years before the St. Alban's Psalter was illuminated, Peter Alfonsi provided an explicit instance of how the struggle was understood.[7] His own Jewish combatant

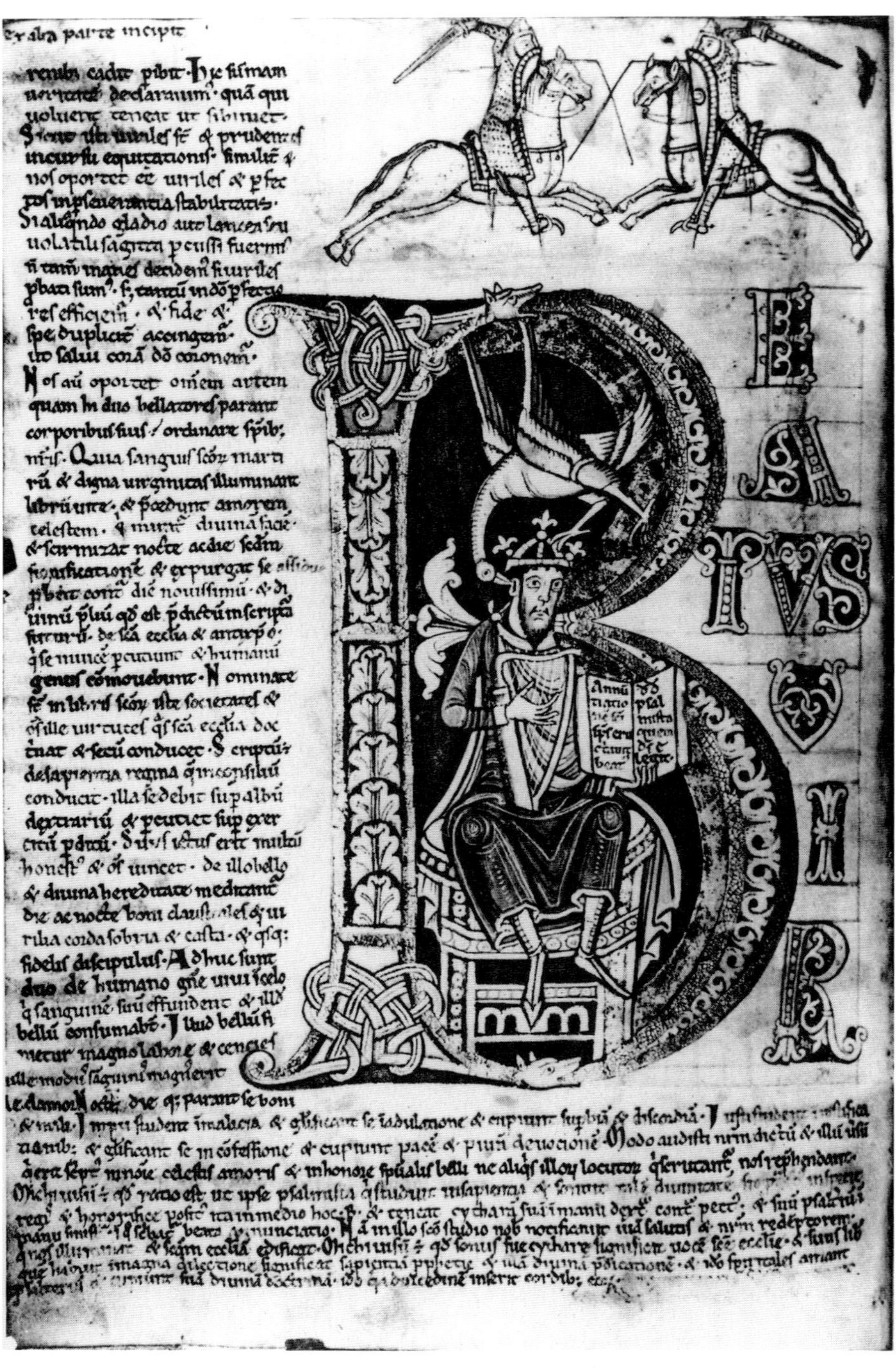

3.1. St. Alban's Psalter. Dombibliothek Hildesheim, HS St. Godehard 1, p. 72. David composing psalms. Photo courtesy Dombibliothek Hildesheim.

named Moses begins the discussion of art by emphasizing a Crucifix's physical aspect: "You act against God and all the prophets, namely, you cut down a tree in a grove, and then afterwards you seek out a carpenter, who chisels it, sculpts it, and forms it into the appearance of a man, smoothes it and paints it, and you place the image in a very high place in your churches and adore it."[8] To this Peter responds: "We, when genuflecting before the Cross, never adore the Cross or the image placed on it, but instead we adore God the Father and his Son Jesus Christ. . . . In the same way, the sons of Gad and the sons of Reuben constructed an altar across the Jordan in the image of that altar in Jerusalem, so that their children and wives, who could not go up to Jerusalem, might look upon it for a testimony only and as a reminder of the other one."[9] In the next century, during a disputation on Mallorca in 1286, Ingetus Contardus used the same argument to repel his Jewish challenger with a terse claim that the church allows images, "so that seeing them with the eyes of the body, they might see with the eyes of the heart, and be reminded of the passion of Christ, which he suffered for our salvation and for the redemption of humankind, as the prophets attest."[10]

A principal source of these claims is the assertion promulgated by Gregory the Great in support of art that even while corporeal sight engages the attention of the faithful, it has the potential to channel the mind upward.[11] Gregory's influential argument was included in a letter written in 599–600 after the pope had learned that Serenus, the Bishop of Marseilles, "burning with uncontrolled zeal, [had begun] breaking the statues of the saints with the rather weak excuse that they ought not to be worshipped"; responding to Serenus, the father of the church famously explained:

> For the worship of a picture is one thing but learning what should be worshipped through the story of the picture is something else. For what writing provides for readers, this a picture provides for uneducated people looking at it, for in it the ignorant see what they should follow and the illiterate read the same from it. Thus a picture serves as a text, especially for pagans (gentes). And you should have paid great attention to this, as you live among pagans, to avoid creating an impediment for ferocious minds, while you are rashly inflamed by righteous zeal. And so you should not break what has been placed in churches not for adoration but simply to instruct the minds of the ignorant.[12]

Peter Brown has argued that Gregory's "gentes" were, in fact, Jews and that the Pope's response should be understood in the context of the slightly later arguments recorded within the *adversos Iudaios* corpus in the eastern Mediterranean.[13] If Brown is right, then Gregory's arguments are central to an understanding of the problem considered in this volume; what became the most consequential of all justifications of Christian art in the Latin West would have to be understood within debates about Judaism.

Whether or not Gregory had Jews in mind when he wrote to Bishop Serenus, his letter promoted the possibility that Christians might reject art altogether if they chose to; indeed, its implication that the literate do not need pictures actually promotes aniconism in certain circles. The "artlessness" so often attributed to Judaism was not an essential issue for Gregory or other Christians who, during the course of centuries, opposed art or at least remained indifferent to material images. Caesarius of Arles was one;[14] as Sara Lipton's contribution to this volume documents, so were later theologians, especially monks; and so too, Stephen Campbell shows in his essay, in the early sixteenth century, Judaism enabled Catholics to arm themselves against the Protestant onslaught against art.

A clear preference for physical representations of Christ and his saints came to be asserted officially only at the end of the seventh century in Canon 82 of the Quinisext Council (692), specifically in the context of a Judaism characterized as a cult of "ancient symbols and shadows."[15] By the time of Byzantine iconoclasm (730–87, 815–43), therefore, those who opposed images could be labeled "Judaizers," a scriptural neologism that David Nirenberg discusses in Chapter 13 of this volume. After the conflict was finally resolved, sacred Christian art became an essential element of devotion.[16]

Although in the Latin West, Gregory's edict generally prevailed, many voices still spoke out against art, among them Theodulf of Orleans, Agobard of Lyons, and Claudius of Turin during the Carolingian period, and, most famously, Bernard of Clairvaux later. Writing less than a decade before the St. Alban's Psalter was being illuminated in the 1130s, Bernard conceded the utility of pictures in secular churches but he opposed it in monasteries. Indeed, turning Gregory's dictum on its head, Bernard lamented that "a variety of contradictory forms is seen that one would rather read in the marble [sculptures] than in books, and spend the whole day wondering at every single one of them than in meditating on the law of God."[17] The concern, it should be noted, was not with religious imagery alone and the attendant risk of idolatry, but with art more generally with its capacity to disrupt a viewer's spiritual concentration.

It may, in fact, have been in reaction to just such pressures by Bernard of Clairvaux (and others) that the designer of the St. Alban's Psalter inserted an excerpt of Gregory's defense of art into his manuscript, not only in the original Latin but also in an Old French translation.[18] Clearly the "gentes/genz" referred to in these texts were not understood in the twelfth-century abbey to be Jews or pagans; rather, the statement in favor of art was directed to the cloistered religious who would use the Psalter, that is, the group that Bernard was to claim could only be distracted by its rich ornamentation. This point is reinforced by the erroneous ascription of the quotation to a different letter Gregory had written, addressed not to a bishop but rather to the hermit Secundinus.[19] Like the gloss, mounted warriors, and sequence of pictures at the start of the Psalter, Gregory's authoritative text was thus most likely part of a Benedictine strategy to win the battle about art and other material instruments that various monastic groups were waging at the time. Perhaps, as in its original context, an idea of Judaism still played a role in this secondary citation; for Bernard had, himself, inserted the debate about art into a Jewish context: "To me [church ornament] somehow represent the ancient rite of the Jews. . . . They stimulate the devotion of a carnal people with material ornaments because they cannot do so with spiritual ones."[20]

The Law Foolishly Given to the Jews: Art as Supersession

The St. Alban's Psalter is, of course, essentially a book of Hebrew Scripture; and the supplementary texts and pictures are centered on a Jewish person, David, who was believed to be both the human ancestor of Jesus and the author of the sacred hymns that were regarded as prophecy of Christ. The gloss leaves no doubt about David's roles: "The blessed psalmist David, whom God has chosen, has gushed forth the annunciation of the Holy Spirit'. For in that holy zeal he has made known to us the way of salvation and our redeemer, who enlightens us and builds up the holy church. It has seemed to me that the sound of his harp signifies the voice of the holy church, and his book, which he held in great affection, signifies the wisdom of prophecy, and that divine prediction, and for that reason spiritual people love the psalter and desire its own divine teaching, because it sows sweetness in their hearts."[21] To convey David's dual role, the king is portrayed being inspired by the dove of the Holy Spirit, in a manner, it should be noted, that recalls traditional depictions of Pope Gregory.

In the St. Alban's Psalter, the psalms themselves are presented as prophecies of Christ also through a series of full-page miniatures that precedes the David initial and the one hundred historiated initials that follow it.[22] After two pictures of the Fall of Adam and Eve and Expulsion from Paradise—humankind's sin brought about through the carnal eye that had made the Incarnation necessary—it presents a sequence of pictures representing Christ meeting the disciples on the way to Emmaus with its subtext about physical blindness and spiritual recognition within the quire containing Gregory's letter, the mounted warriors, and David composing the poems framed by the gloss about spiritual seeing.[23] These pictures serve to elevate a literal reading of Hebrew Scripture and to make evident the fundamental spiritual claims of Christian art.

Like other pictures, they do this by engaging Christian supersession as set out in the Prologue to John's Gospel, linking art directly to the Incarnation: "So the Word became flesh; he came to dwell among us, and we saw his glory, such glory as befits the Father's only Son, full of grace and truth. . . . For while the Law was given through Moses, grace and truth came through Jesus Christ" (John 1:14–16). The concept is illustrated literally in the opening of a twelfth-century Byzantine Gospel book in Florence (Biblioteca Laurenziana, Cod. Plut. VI 32, fols. 7v and 8r), which opposes a depiction of Moses receiving the covenant inscribed on stone tablets to Christ Emmanuel in heaven, the Word incarnate made visible in a picture.[24]

Supersession was the most common method for engaging Judaism in works of Christian art.[25] Ingetus still enlisted it at Mallorca when he averred to the attestation of the prophets; his contemporary, William Durandus of Mende, explained the purpose of such prophets in Christian art in his influential *Rationale divinorum officiorum*: "Before the coming of Christ, the faith was shown figuratively, and many things remained unclear; to represent this, the Patriarchs and Prophets are painted with scrolls, as if to denote this imperfect knowledge."[26] Supersession established dominance over the Augustinian "witnesses" still among the living; as Mitchell Merback elucidates in his analysis of the Rotterdam-Berlin altarpiece; like the Passover Seder in relation to the Eucharist, Jewish types figured in Christian art are, in essence, anti-Jewish because they best Hebrew Scripture even while they appropriate it.

More usually, "prophetism" is rendered indirectly. In its most elemental form, it sets portraits of Hebrew prophets offering excerpts from their own writings in opposition to depictions of Christ, understood to be fulfillments of those writings. In the San Paolo Bible of c. 870 (Rome, Monastery of St. Paul's Outside the Walls, fol. 117v), for instance, the miniature that serves doubly as the frontispiece to Isaiah and the introduction to all the other prophetic books that follow pictures Achaz and his soldiers ushering forth the virgin (who will conceive a son) before Isaiah and, above, the sixteen prophets gesturing toward the celestial Deity.[27] The lower half thus pictures the Christian hermeneutical interpretation of the Jewish text while the upper portion envisions its full realization in the living God. A similar example comes out of Bernard's own Cistercian world, an early twelfth-century manuscript of Jerome's commentaries on Daniel, the minor prophets, and Ecclesiastes in Dijon (Bibl. municipale, MS. 132, fol. 12r; Figure 3.2).[28] Bearing books inscribed with their names and a few words from their prophecies, the twelve prophets are portrayed looking toward a great red, blue, and white mandorla in which Christ is pictured enthroned

HERBERT L. KESSLER

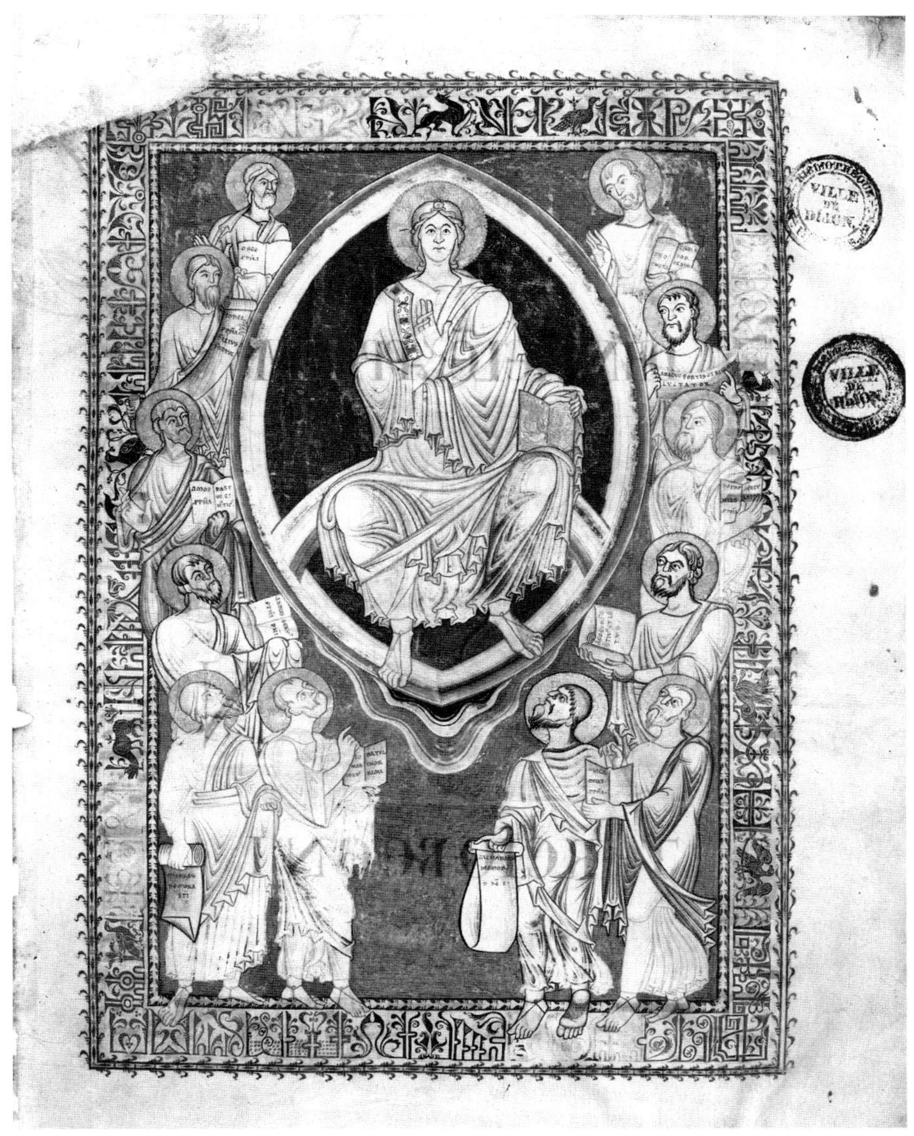

3.2. Bibliothèque municipale de Dijon, MS. 132, fol. 12r. Christ in majesty with prophets. Photo courtesy E. Juvin.

on a rainbow, blessing and proffering on his knee a golden codex. The nearly transparent figures may reflect Cistercian reluctance to render sacred images in full materiality; and other features betray a common Christian concern with art's materiality. Other than the haloes, the book that Christ displays is the only surface covered with gold, a pure, analphabetic visualization of the words often displayed in such pictures: *Ego sum lux mundi*, a distinct contrast to the texts

evoked by the abbreviated inscriptions proffered by the prophets. The mandorla
is solid green; and Christ is pictured resting his left foot on a blue form that
must refer to the sapphire footstool that was commonly used in depictions of
the Maiestas Domini to represent the firmament separating heaven from earth.
Painted so that it bleeds into the miniature's lower realm, in which the prophets
are portrayed against purple-stained parchment (itself an old metaphor of
Christ's flesh)[29] and growing into an amorphous cloud that also absorbs the
mandorla's white and red colors, this blue shape thus figures art's own transforming potential. The very processes of painting are in this way mustered
simultaneously to realize both the prophets' essentially limited perception and
the way in which earthly matter can represent their visions. Even as it enables
the presentation of supersession, art's materiality is used here to demonstrate
its limited capacity to realize the supernatural.

Supersession underlay Christian art not only because it demonstrated that
Christianity has fully replaced Judaism (which itself generally opposed typological reading)—that is, Christianity has made it a dead witness—but also because
it embodied the very process by which a literal reading was transmuted into
something spiritual, how David's Psalms, for instance, were understood as
embodiments of divine inspiration, or how prophetic texts are realized in Jesus
Christ. Thus, Prudentius began his *Psychomachia* not with Christ, but with "the
faithful" patriarch Abraham who "showed the way of believing" through his
willingness to sacrifice Isaac, his war against insolent kings, his tithing Melchisedek, and his feeding of the three messengers, all figures of Christ that "we
must watch in the armor of our faithful hearts." Embracing supersession, the
Psychomachia figures events from Hebrew Scripture as a prelude to spiritual
faith.

Not surprising, Bernard of Clairvaux's famous opponent, Abbot Suger of
Saint-Denis, relied on supersession to advance his own arguments in favor of
art, which he advocated with uncommon vigor.[30] Suger began the discussion of
the stained glass windows in his abbey church with a claim about the inspiriting
capacity of supersession: "One of these [roundels], urging us onward from the
material to the immaterial, represents the Apostle Paul turning a mill, and the
Prophets carrying sacks to the mill." And he designed windows that themselves
manifested just how St. Paul's typological methods affected the spiritual ascent.
Thus, one of the roundels represents the episode reported in the Book of Numbers (Num. 21:6–9) and bears the caption prepared for its typological reading
in the Gospel of John: "Just as the brazen serpent slays all serpents, / So Christ,
raised on the Cross, slays His enemies" (Num. 21:6–9). The roundel also asserts
the power of material images to defeat evil by picturing four creatures at the

HERBERT L. KESSLER

bottom of the cross to evoke the beasts of Psalm 90(91); and it portrays Moses with Christ's facial features, including long hair parted in the middle and a neatly trimmed beard, with the result that looking at the picture actually demonstrates supersession: gazing at Moses one sees Christ.[31] The depiction of Moses receiving the law on an Egyptian textile (London, Victoria and Albert Museum) used the device already in the sixth century, playing on the name Jehoshua (Joshua-Jesus) to identify Moses' attendant on Mt. Sinai as Christ by means of a cross halo;[32] as Marcia Kupfer shows, the same mechanism was deployed in the fifteenth-century Alba Bible. The law given to the prophet (which included the prohibition of images) is here subjected to a spiritual reading by means of a picture. The verso of the Maiestas Domini in the Dijon Commentaries manuscript (fol. 12v) operates in the same way, portraying Daniel with Christ's features and signaling his victory over evil by showing him with his feet on one of the lions. As important, although Daniel's garments are tinted, the prophet-Christ is set against a richly colored letter *A* adorned with plants and birds to emphasize its earthly character and hence to effect the transition through an inspired author from holy text to celestial archetype. Moreover, Habbakuk arrives with ewer and bread, a reference to the Eucharist that is reinforced by the gesture of Daniel/Christ's raised hands—shown with palms turned outward and thumbs touching in a gesture that evokes the priest's when the Sacraments are transformed into Christ's body and blood.[33] A reading of the Daniel text, the picture thus presents the Jewish prophet's rescue from the beasts as an exemplum of Christian salvation provided by the priest through the Sacraments.

Lipton rightly points out that supersessionist seeing and reading had their own histories; for instance, on the Eilbertus portable altar that she studies in detail, the entire process was carefully staged to begin with corporeal sight (in which Judaism was integrated), continue with visual imagination, and lead ultimately to communion with God. And Kupfer shows that even when Jews actually participated in the production of a Christian work, as they did in the Duke of Alba's Bible, the trumping of Jewish literalism by Christian imagery serves the same purpose.

The main altar of the church of Saint Étienne at Sens exemplified many of the ways in which the incorporating of references to Judaism enabled Christian art to manifest the tenet of faith that the Incarnate Christ had fulfilled and abrogated the prophecies and cult of the Jews. Probably made in the middle of the twelfth century and melted down in 1760 to help fund the Seven Year War, it is now known through an engraving published in André du Sommerard's *Les arts au Moyen Age* and through a few related descriptions (Figure 3.3).[34] At the center, a relief presented God enthroned in Heaven, identified by such

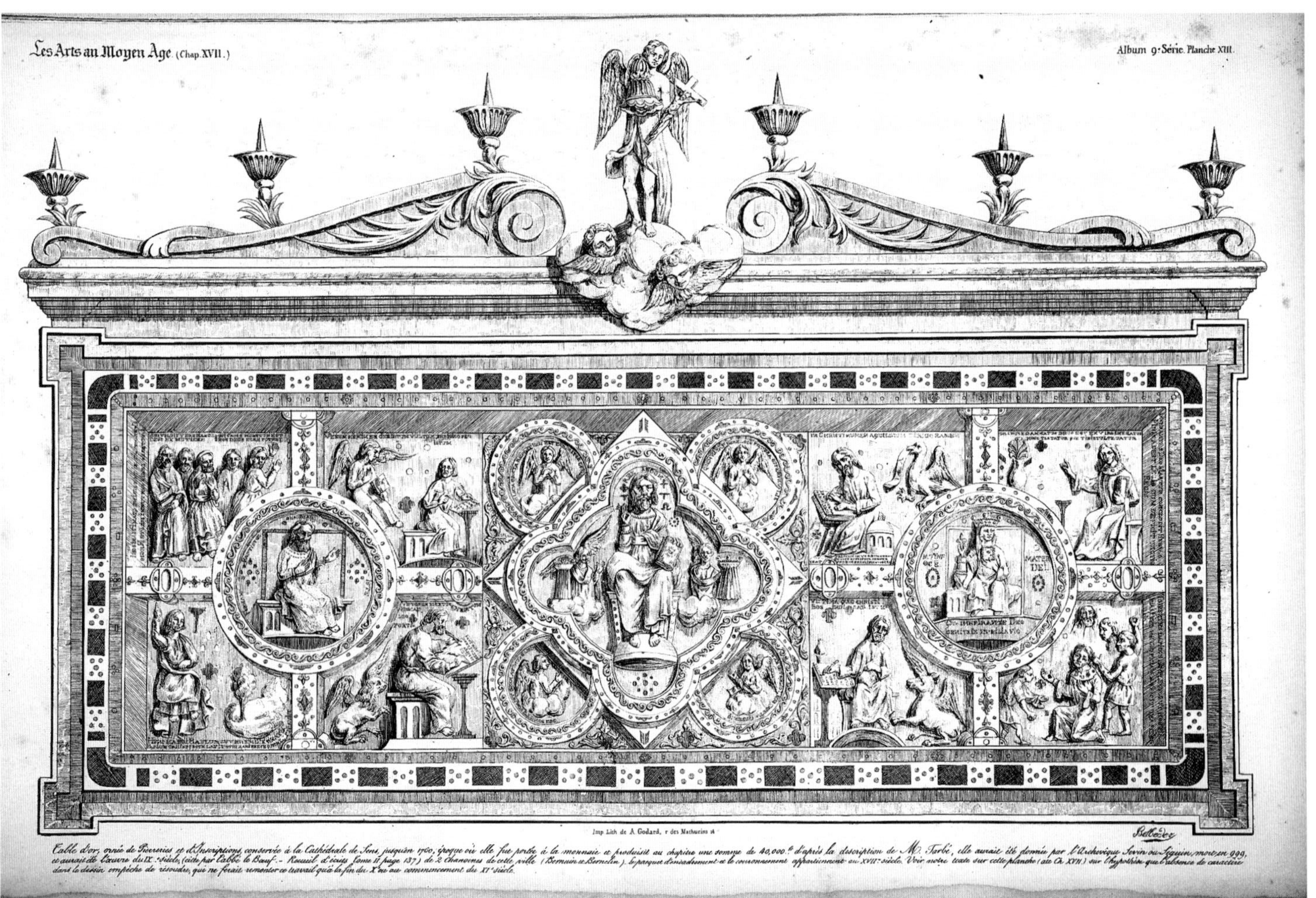

3.3. Saint Etienne at Sens, altarpiece (after Sommerard's *Les Arts au Moyen Age*).

inscriptions as the A and O, "Rex regum," and "Principium sine principio"; as in the Dijon Commentaries, God is pictured blessing and holding a book on his left knee, but here he is surrounded by angels, two beside him within the cosmic lozenge and four occupying the roundels attached to it. Anchoring the central image at the top were depictions of the protomartyr Stephen arguing the Christian interpretation of Hebrew Scripture before the Pharisees and scribes (identified as such) who respond heatedly. Stephen was shown a second time in the lower right being stoned by the Jews; and Paul, the most famous Jewish convert to Christianity, was portrayed as his counterpart, guarding the cloaks removed by the Jewish murderers.[35] In the Book of Acts, Stephen concludes his sermon: "How stubborn you are, heathen still at heart and deaf to the truth! . . . Was there ever a prophet whom your fathers did not persecute? They killed those who foretold the coming of the Righteous One; and now you have betrayed him and murdered him, you who received the Law as God's angels gave it to you, and yet have not kept it" (7:51–53). And on the Sens Altarpiece, captions accompanying the depictions based on this passage interpret the pictorial realizations of the Saint's preaching. In the upper left frame: "The Jews, not so much the scribes as the Pharisees, the doctors of the law, struggle with the soldier of the supreme king."[36] And above the Pharisees' heads, the tituli specify particular issues of contention: "Truly, God did not want to be born to a woman."[37] Who died on the cross cannot be God."[38] Stephen is presented responding to these claims by making the point again that the Jews do not understand their own scripture because they do not see Christ in it: "Born of a virgin, God was condemned to the cross. / This law attests to it, which foolishly was given to you [the Jews]."[39] And in the frame, the titulus draws a final judgment on Judaism: "Inspired by God, the martyr concludes that Jewish law / Is finished, since the royal unction had ended."[40]

Though planned for the specific context of the church of Saint Étienne where the Saint's relics were preserved and where the Virgin Mary and John the Baptist (also prominently pictured) were venerated, the altar thus emphasized Jews and the abrogation of Judaism. Moreover, as Robert Favreau has demonstrated, it does so in a way that corresponds to arguments found in the vast corpus of *adversos Iudaios* literature;[41] some of the inscriptions can be traced specifically to such texts as Quodvultdeus's *Sermon against the Jews*, and others betray more general connections to Jewish assertions about the virgin birth and the Crucifixion to which Guibert de Nogent, Gilbert Crispin, Peter Damian, Peter Alfonsi, and others had responded.[42] In other words, with its depictions and captions, the vast program of inscribed reliefs engages contemporary debates between Jews and Christians which, among other things, had focused on claims about Christ in relation to the Hebrew prophecies, and to which Rashi, Joseph Quimchi, and Jacob ben Reuben had responded.[43]

Most notable for our context, the Sens Altarpiece inserted art itself into this Christian-Jewish discourse. Thus, the inscription around the central figure of Christ invested the depiction with one of the standard Christian defenses of art promulgated during the Middle Ages, namely that, while limited to the material world, material images can also suggest the ineffable Deity: "Him that the superficial picture indicates is in this place, / Fills the entire place but is not localizable here."[44] As Favreau has shown convincingly, this claim, too, can be traced to the debates between Christians and Jews that almost always included arguments about art. Peter Alfonsi, for instance, had maintained that the material image is presented as merely the outward sign of God: "We . . . never adore the Cross or the image placed on it, but instead we adore God the Father and his Son Jesus Christ."

Moses' Icons

As they pertained to art, the dialogues between Christian and Jew relied not only on general claims of the replacement of Hebrew Scripture by the "New Testament" but also on specific assertions that Judaism's own material instruments prove that the prohibition in Mosaic Law of "carved images and likenesses of anything in the heavens above, or on earth below, or in the waters under the earth" was not to be taken literally, nor the injunction not to "bow down and worship them." Jews had themselves acknowledged the apparent contradiction between the so-called Second Commandment and examples within their scriptures that clearly undercut it; and such leading interpreters as Rashi, Maimonides, and Profiat Duran had mustered the Bible's apparent inconsistency to reject comprehensive aniconism.[45]

To justify their own art, particularly their representations of the Incarnate Deity, Christians seized on these sacred Jewish objects, the tablets of the Law, the brazen serpent that Moses set up in the desert, the Tabernacle and Temple and their appurtenances, and other objects mentioned in Hebrew Scripture that seemed to justify the use of material instruments, such as the altar set up by the tribes of Gad and Reuben that Peter Alfonsi cited. In the sixth century, Hypatius of Ephesus had already claimed in his letter to Julian, bishop of Atramytium, that "even the holy priest Moses, who issued these laws on God's prompting, set up, in the Holiest of Holies, golden images of the cherubim in beaten work."[46] A short time later, Leontius of Naples asserted: "You, Jew, also have other objects to remember God and glorify him: Moses' rod, tablets fashioned by God, the burning bush, the stone that was the source of water, the manna jar, ark, the

HERBERT L. KESSLER

altar, the veil that signifies God, etc."[47] The list of Jewish proof-things was expanded in a late seventh-century Armenian tract once attributed to Vrt'anes K'ert'ogh, which cited these Jewish objects and others to conclude that no literal adherence to "words of the Old Testament" is possible.[48] An illustration the text of Psalm 115.4—"Their idols are silver and gold made by the hands of men"—in the ninth-century Psalter on Mt. Athos (Pantocrator, MS 61, fol. 165r) pictures the argument literally;[49] in the wake of Iconoclasm, the Byzantine illuminator showed King David confronting John the Grammarian, the Iconoclastic patriarch pictured pointing to a statue of a naked man (his face recalling Christ's) atop a column, while David, with Besalel standing behind him, points upward toward the Tabernacle, its curtain colored blood red (an allusion to Hebrews 9–10 that likened it to Christ's flesh) and with the sacred vessels inside, hovered over by the cherubim (or rather seraphim), each with the four faces that became the Evangelist symbols.

It became standard to cite the Jewish *vasa sacra*, sometimes even referred to as "Moses' icons," to justify art in image-defenses during Iconoclasm and afterward.[50] Toward the end of the eleventh century, John Italos still argued that the law inscribed on stone tablets and other instruments ordained by God in Hebrew Scripture justify Christian images: "Images are of two kinds: either they are written words, as when God himself engraved the law on tablets of stone, and old holy books he commanded to be written, or they are material contemplations, as when God arranged everything together, the manna jar and rod kept in the ark as a memorial. According to the custom of excellent men, we make and set up holy and venerable icons."[51] Representations of the Incarnation, Christ's human death, and the Son returned to the heavenly throne not only demonstrated Christian supersession, therefore, but also raised de facto the relationship of images to the aniconic material objects of Jewish worship. The frontispiece before the Book of Leviticus in the mid-tenth-century Bible of Leo Patricius (Vatican, Biblioteca Apostolica, MS Reg. gr. 1b; fol. 85v; Figure 3.4) offers a literal example of how this worked.[52] Carrying a pyx and swinging a censer, Aaron is shown before the Levites bearing the Ark of the Covenant into the Holy Land, followed by Moses, explained by a two-part caption: "In this way, the priests and the Levites mystically prefigure the treasure of the Old [Law] as a progression towards Christ, the [treasure] of the New [Law]. As the plaques of the Law were [kept] inside, so too Christ issues forth from the Virgin as a diptych-nature, adding human to the divine." The Great Entrance of the Byzantine liturgy, as pictured for instance in the Menologion of Basil II (Vatican, MS gr. 1613, fol. 142r), is here mapped onto the Jewish procession, made explicit by the apsidal building in the background, which is thus simultaneously the Promised Land of Hebrew Scripture toward which the Jews are going and

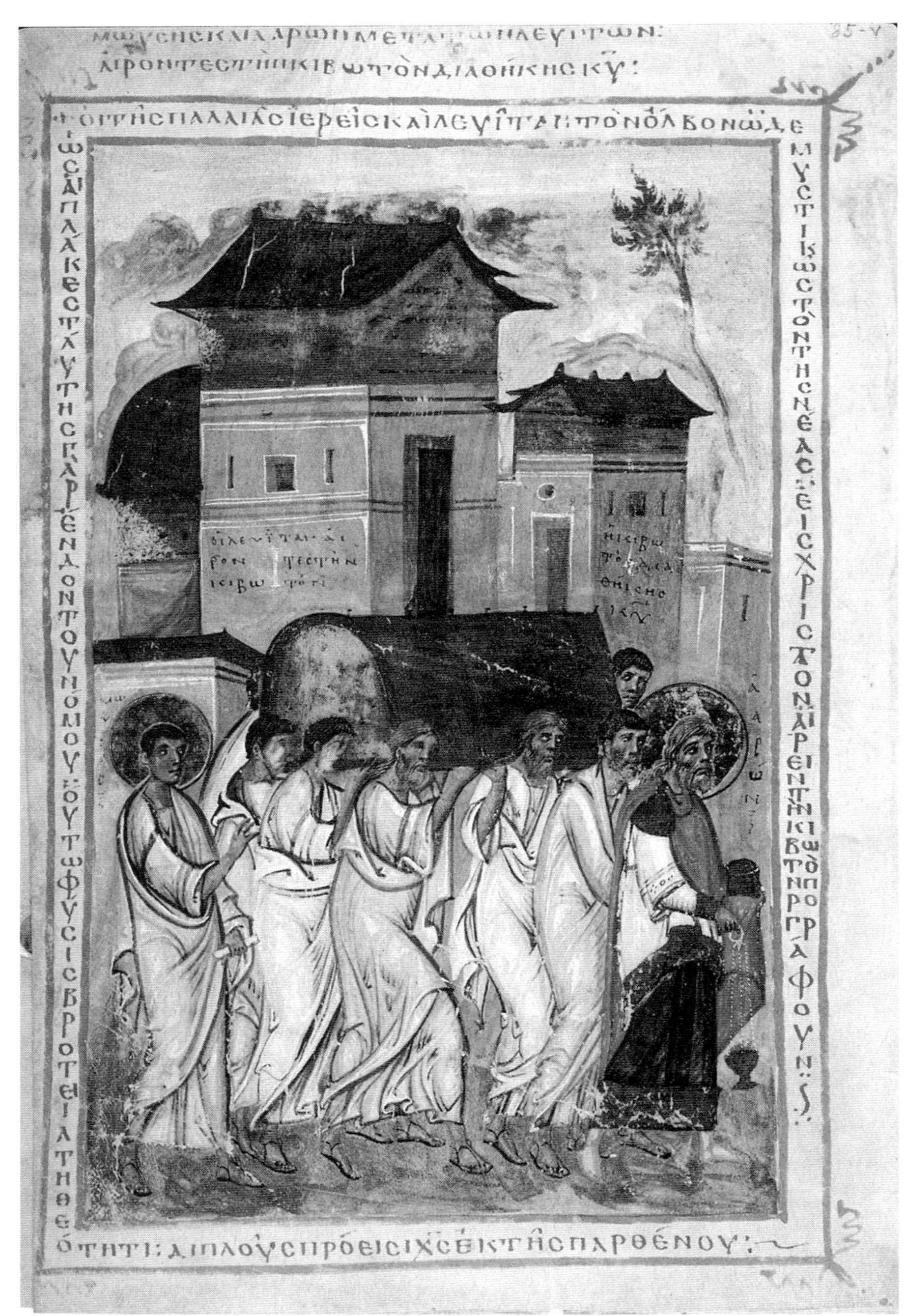

3.4. Vatican, Biblioteca Apostolica, MS Reg. gr. 1b, fol. 85v. Leviticus frontispiece. Photo courtesy Biblioteca Vaticana.

the church that, in Christianity, had replaced it. Looking at a historical episode from the "Old Testament" in a picture, one is thus led to see its Christian fulfillment. The similar illustration in the slightly later Vatican Octateuch (BAV, Cod. gr. 746, fol. 443r) actually represents the Deesis on the front of the Ark of the Covenant,[53] drawing the specific parallel between the Ark of the Covenant, secreted within the Holy of Holies in the Tabernacle and sprinkled with the blood of sacrificed animals once a year, and Christ's eternal sacrifice that offers Christians expiation for sin.

The pictorial argument hinged on the conviction set out in the New Testament that God had abrogated the covenant with the Jews and hence its cult objects when he assumed flesh, suffered death, and returned to the right hand of his Father. The Epistle to Hebrews likens Christ's flesh to the curtain that once divided the outer courtyard from the Holy of Holies housing the mercy throne where God had communicated with the Chosen People; and the Gospel of Mark links Christ's body with the Temple implements when it describes the "curtain of the temple torn in two from top to bottom" at the very moment Christ died on the cross. A series of miniatures devoted to individual Jewish *vasa sacra* in a composite Palaeologan manuscript destroyed during the tragic fire in the Smyrna (formerly Evangelical School, MS B.8) makes the point explicit that Judaism authorized Christian icons.[54] Among the pictures is one of Moses and Aaron flanking the jar of manna beneath a painting of the Hodegetria; the vessel of the food sent by God to his chosen people in the desert and safeguarded in the Temple's sancta sanctorum is likened to a painting of Mary, who was the container of the incarnate food for the new people of God. Anticipating Parmigianino's Madonna of the Long Neck (Florence, Galleria degli Uffizi),[55] the jar with its long handles and full, oval body creates a visual parallel to Mary's encompassing arms and full, curving torso. Jewish artifact generates Christian art.

As in Byzantium, the defense of Christian art through reference to the material objects authorized by Hebrew Scripture was consistently deployed also in the Latin West.[56] Apparently already aware in far-off Northumbria by 731 of eastern Iconoclasm, Bede cited the decorations of Solomon's temple and went on: "Moses himself who at the Lord's command first of all made cherubim on the propitiatory and later a brazen serpent in the desert so that by gazing at it the people might be healed of the poison of the wild serpents. For if it is permissible to raise up the brazen serpent on a tree that the Israelites might live by looking at it, why is it not permissible that the exaltation of the Lord our savior on the cross whereby he conquered death be recalled to the minds of the faithful pictorially, or even his other miracles and cures whereby he wonderfully triumphed over the same author of death."[57] Nearly four centuries later, Gilbert

Crispin began his defense of art against his Jewish interlocutor by citing the cherubim and other adornments mentioned in Exodus and 1 Kings, as well as the visions of Isaiah (6:1–2) and Ezekiel (1:10); and about the same time, Rupert of Deutz, trying to explain Christian art to the Jew, Herman of Scheda, cited the example Peter Alfonsi also used, the altar set up by Joshua (Josh. 22:22–27), concluding: "We also, for a like reason, hold the cross of Christ in great reverence because of the one hanging on it, but in no way do we render it the worship owed divinity."[58] And writing c. 1235 in a tract entitled *The Book of God's Wars*, William, archbishop of Bourges, concluded his debate:

> The Jews shout to me and curse: How dare you comment on the Law, given that you adore images of wood and stone, transgressing what is written: "Let all who worship images, who vaunt their idols" (Ps. 97:7) and more: "Their makers grow to be like them, and so do all who trust them" (Ps. 115:8). Therefore, you alone are cursed.
>
> I responded to them: Is Moses cursed, the legislator who made two cherubim, that is, two angels of gold? No! Obviously, the two cherubim and the Ark of the Covenant symbolize the two angels that were at the Lord's tomb, "one at the head and one at the feet" (John 20:12). The Law was in the Ark of the Covenant, which was conceived as a defense and figure of the Lord's tomb, in which our good Legislator was thrown.[59]

Following such arguments, a miniature before the Book of Leviticus in the Bible of San Paolo fuori le mura (fol. 32r) challenges the viewer to discover meaning through a process of visual scrutiny. The caption on the facing page asserts that "the whole ordinance of Leviticus [is] figurative in all ways"; and the painting transforms a literal depiction of the Jewish blood sacrifices made before the desert Tabernacle and the sanctuary itself into a prophecy of Christ's sacrifice that had replaced them by setting up the menorah, the altar with the Ark of the Covenant, a chandelier, and the tent (topped by a cross) along a central axis in the form of a green-colored cross. Toward the end of the twelfth century, Adam Scot of Dryburgh also connected the desert Tabernacle to the church and the human soul and, in turn, to the three modes of reading scripture.[60] Judaism provides the material for the spiritual understanding of art.

On the Sens altarpiece, too, reference is made to the relationship of Jewish implements to Christian art in the two angelic beings flanking Christ that allude to the cherubim that hovered above the Ark of the Covenant as in the San

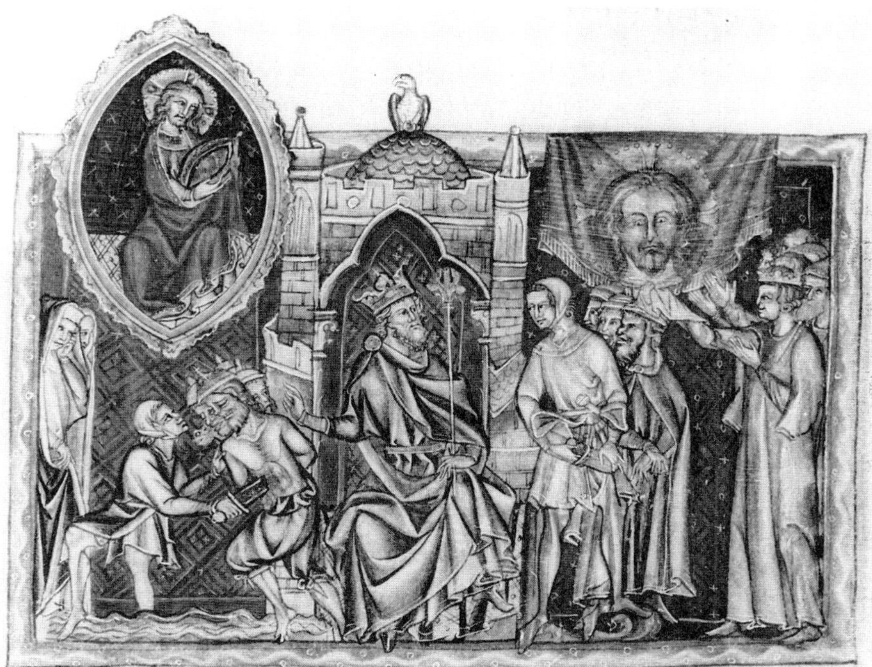

3.5. Lisbon, Gulbenkian Collection, MS L.A. 139, fol. 13r. Titus returning with Jerusalem trophies. Photo courtesy Gulbenkian Collection.

Paolo Bible; and in a miniature accompanying Revelation 6:12–17 in an English Apocalypse (Lisbon, Gulbenkian Collection, MS L.A. 139, fol. 13r; Figure 3.5) painted a century later, the trope is developed further to demonstrate the triumph of Christian imagery over Judaism. Illustrating Berengaudus's commentary on the breaking of the sixth seal,[61] one miniature portrays the Emperor Vespasian enthroned in the center before the city of Rome welcoming his troops back from the conquest of Jerusalem and ordering them to execute the captured Jews who are pictured, at the left, being dumped into the Tiber. The crowned Titus bears the Temple curtain, the red-colored cloth here emblazoned by the face of Christ, shown specifically as a Roman bust supported from beneath but identified with the Veronica, the face of Christ transferred directly to a cloth and, according to legend, "transported to Rome from Jerusalem [where] it cured Tiberius from leprosy, and revenge was accomplished against the Jews for the death of Christ." The miniature sets up a complex play between Christ in heaven and his image introduced on earth at the moment the Temple was destroyed, and between the Jews captured and executed by the Romans at the precise moment the physical icon is accepted by Christianity. Perhaps nowhere more clearly, Christian art is rendered as a trophy of the Roman victory over the Jews, and hence provides another instance of the dual genealogy of Christian art that Jaś Elsner shows was engaged in the complex process of exegesis from an early date, evident in the scenes of the Israelites pictured fleeing Egypt on fourth-century Red Sea sarcophagi.

Of all the material instruments of the Jews, the brazen serpent was particularly important for art, not only because it was cited as a typology of the Crucifixion already in John's Gospel, but also because it invested the opposition of true faith and false belief in the very act of looking at an object sanctioned by God. Bede listed it among the justifications for art; and Suger developed it to make the point clear that while the people who believed (i.e., Christians) are able to see beyond the material object itself to find its spiritual message, those who lacked faith (Jews and others) cannot because they remain locked in literal reading and seeing. Thus, his roundel pictures of Moses pointing out the brazen serpent to a group of faithful at the left who clap their hands in prayer, while the unbelievers at the right react in astonishment; and, formed as a finely wrought metalwork basilisk and displayed atop a column (the customary perch for idols), the "serpent" evokes the dangers of looking at material images as an end in itself, a concern that Nirenberg traces back to Augustine and that Merback discusses in the context of Moses' serpent. Indeed, the serpentine form (often mimicked in Christ's own body) introduces the notion of oscillation discussed in totally different contexts by Dana Katz and Ralph Ubl.[62] The Book of Chronicles reports that Hezekiah had to destroy the brazen serpent because the Israelites were worshipping it as an idol (2 Chron. 18:4). A Crucifix nested in the basilisk's wings provides the proper alternative; an image of Christ's death gives life to those who believe.

Christ had himself introduced the brazen serpent typology in response to the questioning of a "Pharisee and member of the Jewish Council," Nicodemus: "If you disbelieve me when I talk to you about things on earth, how are you to believe if I should talk about the things of heaven? No one ever went up into heaven except the one who came down from heaven, the Son of Man whose home is in heaven. This Son of Man must be lifted up as the serpent was lifted up by Moses in the wilderness, so that everyone who has faith in him possess eternal life" (John 3:15).

     HERBERT L. KESSLER

As a result of this encounter with Jesus, Nicodemus converted to Christianity and came ultimately to assist, after the Crucifixion, in the deposition and burial. In turn, Nicodemus became the prototypical Christian artist. Thus, in the mid-ninth-century Drogo Sacramentary (Paris, BnF MS lat. 9428, fol. 43v), he is portrayed as *Ecclesia*'s counterpart (and surrogate for the personification of *Sinagoga*) in the Crucifixion scene that adorns the O of the Palm Sunday prayer.[63] According to a legend first introduced at the Second Ecumenical Council held at Nicaea in 787 to defend images,[64] Nicodemus carved a wood Crucifix based on the accurate memory of his body that he retained when he lowered Christ from the cross.[65] The brazen serpent also forms a kind of halo for the crucified Christ on the magnificent ivory cross in the Cloisters in New York, entangled with inscriptions that reiterate the arguments about Christian art.[66] From its reappearance in the 1960s, the Cloisters Cross has been associated with Christian-Jewish disputes, including especially central issues about the Incarnation, namely God's generation from a woman and his suffering on the cross, themes presented as well on the Sens Altarpiece. Recently, Charles Little and Elizabeth C. Parker have introduced St. Anselm's *Cur Deus Homo* into the discussion of the discussion of the Cloisters Cross, a dialogue in which a monk named Boso takes on the role usually assigned a Jewish interlocutor, another instance in which monastic opposition to art is presented in the guise of Jewish skepticism.[67]

In the chevet of St. Remi at Reims, moreover, the brazen serpent serves as a fulcrum to transform an entire church into a spiritual reading (as the Leo Bible does figuratively). Building on Anne Prache's work, Madeline Caviness has shown that the decorative complex engaged Peter of Celle's exegesis of the Tabernacle of Moses, featuring David and Moses among other Old Testament figures in the pavement, a seven-branched candlestick to the left of the altar, and sculpted consoles carved with Old Testament personages.[68] One pair of sculptures (Figure 3.6) depicts Aaron at the left holding his rod and wearing a pointed hat and large breastplate and Moses at the right bearing the tablets of the Law (adorned with the abstract ornament), flanking the brazen serpent.[69] A titulus above Aaron "in cruce regnum" alludes to Christ's promise on the cross to the Good Thief that "today you shall be with me in Paradise"[70] and implies movement from carnal to spiritual seeing; and the placement of the (now extensively restored) serpent atop an actual colonette depicts the church building itself as a part of the anagogical ascent from the carnal Temple with its appurtenances to the spiritual Christian church. The theme was continued in the chandelier recalling the Heavenly Jerusalem and ultimately in the stained glass windows that, picking up on the brazen serpent rendered in stone, feature the crucified Christ. The brazen serpent was a type of the most important Christian image;

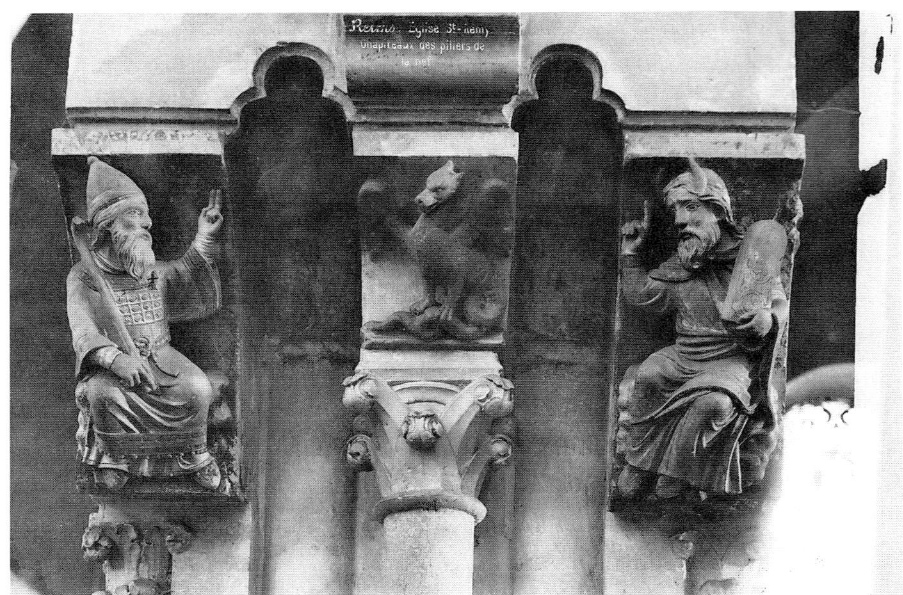

3.6. Reims, St. Remi, chevet sculpture. Moses and Aaron with brazen serpent. © Ministère de la Culture/Médiathèque du Patrimoine, Dist. RMN/Art Resource, New York.

and Christ's dialogue with Nicodemus was a prototype for the discussion about art incorporated in the *adversus Iudaios* literature and, even more important, for art's potential utility as an instrument for conversion, as discussed by Francisco Prado-Vilar and Felipe Pereda in this volume.

The arguments that, especially through its various *vasa sacra*, Judaism had actually prepared the way for Christian art did not go unanswered. Throughout the *Opus caroli*, Theodulf of Orleans, for example, vociferously denied the claims that Judaism provided arguments to support Christian pictures; and, reacting against mosaics he had seen in Rome during a journey in 800 featuring Christ flanked by his saints, he set up a mosaic in the apse of his chapel at Germigny des Prés that featured the Ark of the Covenant hovered over by the cherubim and two angels, in order to make the point that the Jewish implements evoked the Divine, not by their material form or artistic transformation, but through mental contemplation.[71] And more than three centuries later, indeed possibly with the monastery of St. Remi specifically in mind, Bernard of Clairvaux still thought of such justifications based on the Tabernacle/Temple with their ordained objects, when he denounced as "Jewish" the lavishly adorned churches that the bishops build.[72] Both Theodulf and Bernard maintained that art could appeal only to the human eye but could not, as the titulus

     HERBERT L. KESSLER

on the Sens altarpiece proclaims, indicate the ineffable. Theodulf had argued that "whoever affirms that man was made in the likeness and image of God in the way that an artisan makes an image of man, reveals that he imagines something corporeal in the Deity, which is sinful to believe" (*Opus caroli*, Book 1, chap. 7); and not only did he cite Hezekiah's need to destroy the brazen serpent, but he also taunted Christians who think they might be saved by pictures, urging them to venerate the images when they become ill and see if they are cured as the Israelites were when they looked upon the monument Moses set up in the desert.[73] Bernard denounced "carnal people [who need] material ornaments because they cannot do so with spiritual ones."

Jews were considered to be these carnal viewers par excellence.[74] Just as they had refused to find God in the person of Christ, they could not discover the spirit that imbued material images. In the ninth century, Claudius of Turin inserted the idea into the debate about art: "For the Word came into the world by Mary, clad in flesh, but seeing was not understanding. All saw the flesh, but knowledge of the divinity was given to a chosen few. Just so when the Word was shown to men through the lawgiver and the prophets, it was not shown them without suitable vesture. There it is covered by the veil of flesh, here by the letter."[75] In a picture epigram he composed around 1100 that recalls the sixth-century textile in the Victoria and Albert Museum, Hildebert of Le Mans made the same point about Jewish incapacity to look at God (also through images): "While Moses stood on the rock, he saw not God's face passing by but only the back part. Christ is the rock: Moses stands on it, with the Jewish people he believes in it. He does not see God's countenance: this people at present refuse to recognize Christ. He sees his back parts; after death, believing in Him, the most esteemed parts."[76] And Peter Alfonsi has his "Moses" exemplify Jewish materiality by describing Crucifixes as mere wood and paint worked by artisans. Writing in 1160, Jacob ben Reuben actually confirmed such a claim by having his own Jewish interlocutor react to the Christian charge that Moses' brazen serpent justified images of the Crucifixion with a sarcastic but altogether literal rebuttal: "Based on the implications of these verses, you claimed that your messiah looks like a serpent. Now, see the many ways in which you raised the question incorrectly. Our blessed Creator never forbade the making of statues and images. He only forbade the bowing down and worship."[77] A miniature in the bestiary of Guillaume le Clerc illuminated in London or Oxford between 1265 and 1270 (Paris, BnF, MS fr. 14969, fol. 9r; Figure 3.7) offers the Christian response to such Jewish claims.[78] At the left, it pictures the Christian faithful kneeling in prayer before a crucifix, the serpent in the form of a caladrius perched on top and Moses pointing up to it. At the right, it represents a devil pushing the Jews (wearing pointed caps) into a fiery Hell mouth because of

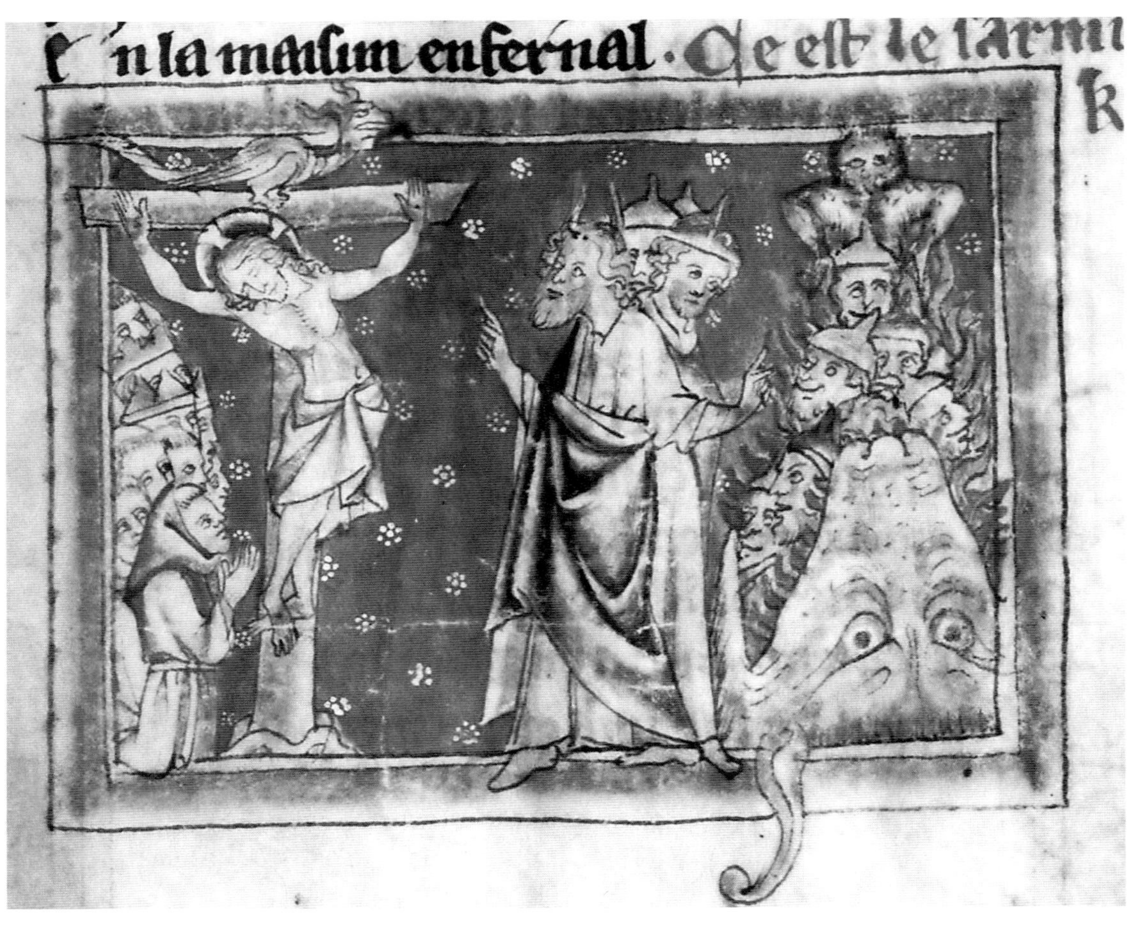

3.7. Paris, Bibliothèque nationale de France, MS fr. 14959, fol. 94. Moses and the brazen serpent. Photo courtesy BnF, Paris.

their lack of faith. Guillaume le Clerc explained the concept in his metrical paraphrase of the Physiologus text:

> This caladrius in truth is our savior Jesus,
> Who came of his great majesty to look upon the sickness
> Of the Jews, whom he had greatly loved and cared for and exhorted,
> So often fed and healed, so greatly honored and favored.
> And when he saw that they would die in unbelief in which they were,
> Saw their malice and their stubbornness, for their evil heart and sloth,
> From their gaze he turned his face.
> He visited our infirmities and bore our sins in his body
> On the sacred wood of the true cross, of which the devil is sore afraid.
> Thus it behooved him to do.

HERBERT L. KESSLER

Rejecting Christ and also images of Christ, the miniature shows, Jews are condemned to perdition.

Deeply embedded in writing and in art, the idea that Jews were blind literalists who failed to see God's spirit in images never vanished and, as Richard Neer documents, was reinvigorated in writings about art and painting itself following the Counter-Reformation.

Imagocides

The belief that Jews could see only the physical form of sacred images and not the archetype beyond them generated legends about Jews' destroying as idols Christian paintings and statues—part and parcel of similar claims about Host desecration and the blood libel itself that both Timmermann and Merback explore in this volume.[79] Of these legends, the most important was the story involving the crucifix fashioned by Nicodemus, also discussed here by Pereda. In the story, the crucifix was then passed onto Rabbi Gamaliel and, in turn, Zachaeus; eventually, it was discovered by Jews in a house in Beirut previously owned by a Christian who, believing it to be a mere statue, attempted to destroy it.[80] In so doing, the Jews reenacted on a material image what their forebears had allegedly done to Christ himself; indeed, the sculpture bled. Effecting cures (as the Veronica did for Vespasian), the crucifix converted the Jews to Christianity, thereby recapitulating what had happened in life to Nicodemus, even while proving the truth of Christian art.

In the 1440s, Guillem Sagrera carved a version of the legend on a stone altarpiece now in the sanctuary of San Salvador of Felanitx on Mallorca (Figure 3.8), which Carlos Espí Forcen has recently shown had originally been installed in the funerary chapel of Jordi Sabet in the nearby church of St. Michael.[81] The central axis of the great reredos starts at the altar itself, where the real body and blood of Christ were displayed, continues to the institution of the Eucharist at the Last Supper pictured in the predella and then through the Crucifixion, and ultimately reaches to the Resurrection where Christ's divine nature is affirmed. And this is flanked by six panels depicting the legend of the Beirut Crucifix, beginning at the upper left with the scene of the Christian praying beneath the crucifix before he sells his house to the Jews. It begins, in other words, with an example of proper interaction with a material image as the channel of contemplation of the Divine, continues with the very opposite image (set in a Jewish context) of Jews interrupting their carnal feasting when one of them notices the crucifix (the foremost tellingly shown pointing his knife toward the statue), and ends with a representation of the Jews stabbing the image. Set horizontally and actually replacing the banqueting table, the culminating depiction epitomizes

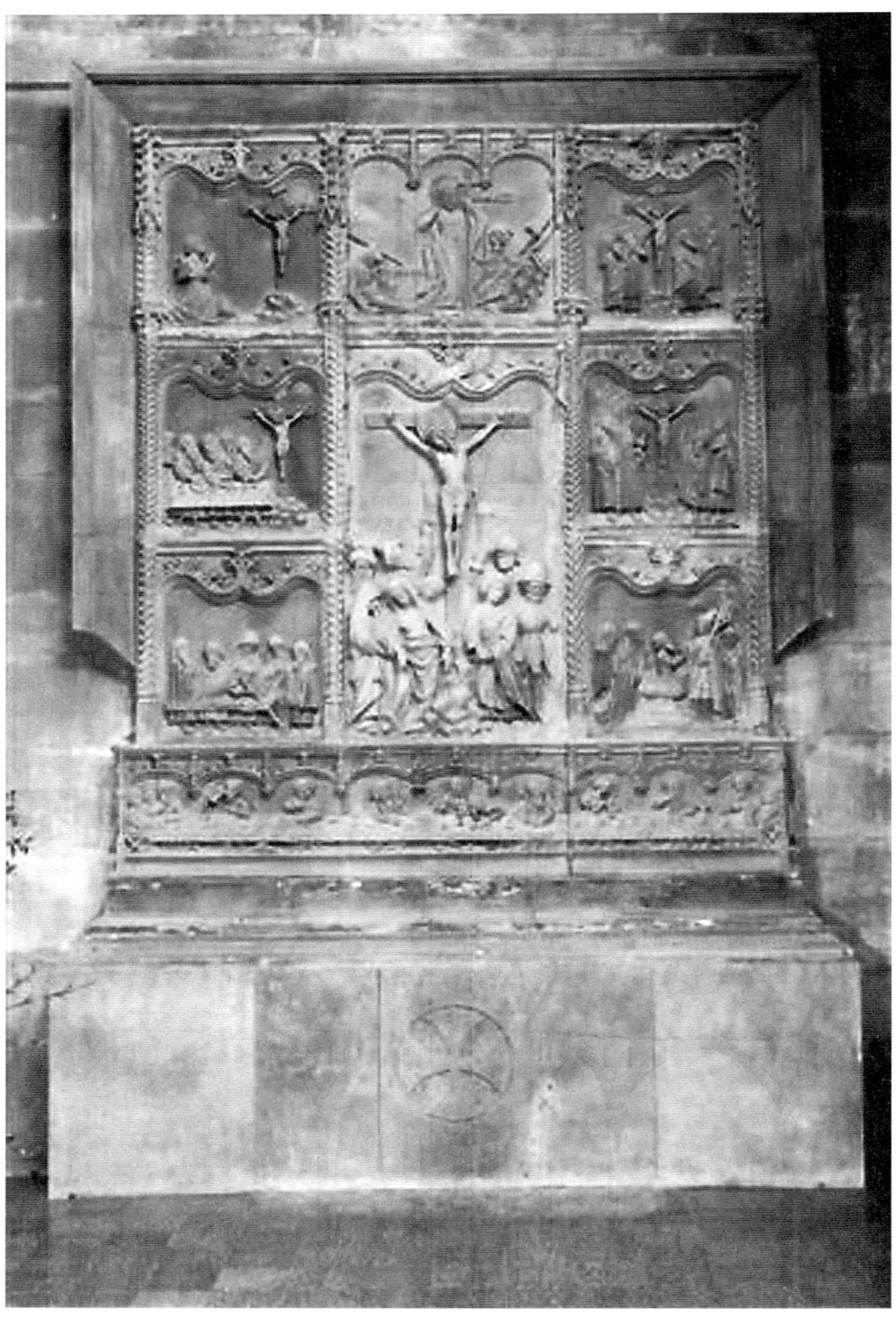

3.8. Guillem Sagera, altarpiece, Felanitx (Mallorca), San Salvador. *Passio imaginis.* Photo courtesy Iberimage, Madrid.

the perceived Jewish understanding of images as mere physical objects. Jewish desecration of the crucifix continues on the right with the Jews puncturing the Crucifixion just, as it was believed, their forebears had Christ himself. Next, the same Jews, converted by the blood that miraculously flowed from the image, save a sample in an ampoule and proclaim the image's power. The series concludes with the Jews being baptized by the town's bishop. Shortly before the campaign waged by Pedro González de Mendoza and Hernando de Talavera and discussed by Felipe Pereda in this volume, the issues of domestic images, Jewish desecration of crucifixes, miracles, and conversion are vividly depicted.

Visual parallels established between the Crucifixion at the center of the sculpture and the four uppermost depictions of the legend framing it leave no ambiguity about the intended identity of the work of art with the historical event or about Jewish attempts to destroy crucifixes and their original alleged act of deicide. Indeed, the rendering of the Jewish attack on the Beirut image at the lower left so resembles the carving of a statue that it sets up an association between the iconoclastic Jews and the image-making activities of the Jewish convert who first fashioned a crucifix. Nicodemus is, in fact, portrayed in the adjacent scene looking back and down at the base of the cross, the "prince of the Jews" who was shown the true meaning of the brazen serpent by Christ himself and who came to be identified as the archetypal sculptor.[82]

In this context, the emphasis on the Jews banqueting in the presence of the crucifix in the second episode serves to present the trope of Jewish carnality in contrast to Christ's sacred supper,[83] which provided the spiritual food continuously offered the faithful in the Sacraments. As both Achim Timmerman and Stephen Campbell show in their chapters, not long after the Felanitx altarpiece was made, Christian Sacraments were an issue in pre-Tridentine art in which, again, Judaism was implicated. Moreover, the chapel for which the altarpiece was made included capitals representing Christ's capture and flagellation, and—in the keystone of the vault—the Ascension; and it was opened by two prophets bearing passages from scripture, for instance, Zechariah with his "The Lord my God will appear with all the holy ones" (Zechariah 14:5). Thus, the story of the Beirut Crucifix was originally situated within an architectural and sculptural complex that began with references to supersession, continued with a historical narrative on the altarpiece, and was framed by depictions of Jewish conversion to Christianity by means of an image.

As pictured in the Catalan altarpiece, the legend of the Beirut Crucifix reinforced the general claim that Jews fell into idolatry because they could not see beyond art's physical presence; lacking faith, they could not move beyond it to the spiritual archetype. It realized Bernard's terse assertion that Jews regarded "material ornaments" in a manner that only "deflect[ed] the attention of those who pray and thus hinder their devotion." Just as they read their own scripture literally, that is, with no sense of its true meaning as a prophecy of Christ, Jews also could not affect the transfer from object to archetype, what Merback terms the foundational premise of Christian art the "phenomenological identity of earthly seeing and eschatological vision." Jews also were able to see physical images, to be sure; they simply were unable to comprehend them correctly, believing that material images appealed only to the eye of the body and could not engage the eye of the heart.

Occasionally, even Christians failed to make a sharp distinction between matter and image and that always caused problems. In Byzantium, Leo, Bishop of Chalcedon, precipitated a crisis at the end of the eleventh century, for instance, when he objected to the ecclesiastical *vasa sacra*'s being melted down to fund the emperor's war against Robert Guiscard because, he maintained, images imparted some degree of holiness to the matter in which they were impressed.[84] A church council was called in 1095 to reaffirm the orthodox position that icons were merely "likenesses appearing in the material" and were totally independent of their physical matter. (When the Archbishop of Sens ordered the melting down of the cathedral's altarpiece for its gold for a similar military purpose, he surely would not have believed that he was violating the saints pictured on it, for, like other Christians, he was able to distinguish the matter from its archetype.) An unusual double representation in a twelfth-century manuscript of John Climacus's *Heavenly Ladder* in the Vatican (Biblioteca Apostolica, Cod. Ross. 251, fol. 12v; Figure 3.9)[85] was painted in the wake of this controversy; the two originary icons in Byzantium (known as the Mandylion and Keramion) are labeled "Spiritual Tablets" to distinguish them from the material tablets given to Moses on Mt. Sinai (where Climacus had composed his own spiritual exercises in the sixth century). Believed to have been miraculously impressed in cloth and clay and pictured as being not in but on their material supports, they are understood to replace God's covenant with the Jews, which was inscribed on stone in written words. At the same time, an outline of the same face, barely visible beneath the blue ground between the two icons, declares that the painted faces are a prelude to what the devout will encounter in the aldilà.

In armis pectorum fidelium

Even while they were being attacked for alleged iconoclasm, Jews were also being accused of idolatry, a paradox Nirenberg explains in the final chapter of this volume. Already in the fourth century, John Chrysostom had scorned Jews as idol worshippers;[86] and the story of the Golden Calf, Hezekiah's destruction of the brazen serpent, and Ezekiel's vision of Jews worshipping the adornments

   HERBERT L. KESSLER

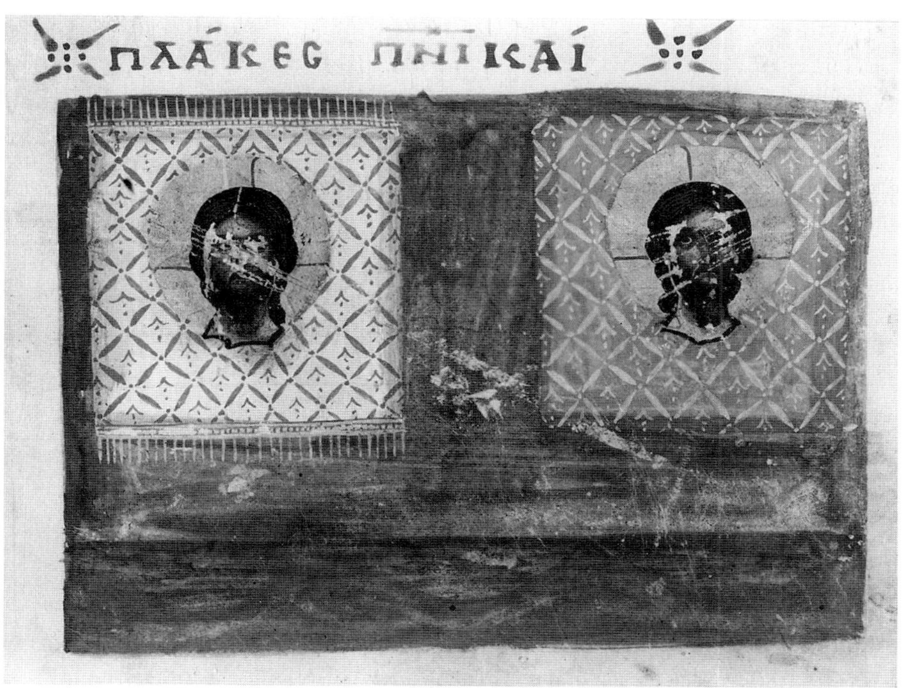

3.9. Vatican, BAV, Cod. Ross. 251, fol. 12v. Mandylion and Keramion. Photo courtesy Biblioteca Vaticana.

in Solomon's Temple continued to fuel Christian claims that they were prone to adore images. Citing the cherubim, for instance, Leontius of Naples noted that God had "showed Ezekiel the temple full of images and likenesses, of graven figures, of lions, palm trees, and men," which the prophet realized the Israelites were worshipping (Ezekiel 8:8–13), the same passage that may already have underlain the first Christian pronouncement on art, Canon 36 of the Synod of Elvira in 306.[87] Drawing on a conceit Nirenberg discusses, Isidore of Seville explained such seeing in terms of idolatry and the appeal of physical things as spiritual fornication: "They are not able to contemplate God who favor the desires of this world. Nor can he, whose eyes are shaded with dust, be able to perceive high things."[88] And at the end of the thirteenth century in the *Rationale* (the title of which itself derived from Aaron's ephod), Durandus argued that because of a Jewish propensity to worship those things "which the Lord your God created. . . . King Hezekiah broke to pieces the golden serpent that Moses had set up, because the people, contrary to the precept of the law, burnt incense before it."[89]

Jewish idolatry is the subject of a miniature painted c. 1000 in a manuscript of Haimo of Auxerre's *Commentaries on Ezekiel* in Paris (BnF, MS lat. 12302, fol. 1v; Figure 3.10), which makes the point vivid by showing the Jews in the Temple turning their backs on the (aniconic) Holy of Holies and engaging in such idolatrous acts as censing figures of reptiles, beasts, and vermin carved on the walls and women wailing for Tammuz figures as Adonis with his genitals exposed. What better illustration could there be of Bernard of Clairvaux's (later) claim that the monstrous and distracting decorations in Romanesque churches were examples of the Jewish rite!

The purported Jewish propensity to worship material images is the subject of a miniature in a fifteenth-century prayer book in Copenhagen (Kongelige Bibliotek, MS Gl. Kgl. S. 1605, fol. 20r). Illustrating the text of the commandment prohibiting image-worship, the miniature remarks on Jewish apostasy and Christian orthodoxy by picturing the Israelites dancing in joy around the Golden Calf, raised like a pagan idol on a pole, and ignoring Moses, who is shown in the background holding up the tablets of the Law,[90] and by framing it (and the text) with an elaborate late Gothic shrine that itself thematizes skillful manufacture and encloses a statue of Christ.[91]

Christians were never entirely immune to taking pictures as the actual embodiment of the figures they represented, that is, of confusing the material image with its archetype. The purposeful scrapings across the faces of Christ in the Vatican manuscript of the *Heavenly Ladder*, a monastic treatise that presumably had never passed into non-Christian hands, are traces of someone's rejection of images of Christ; and whoever effaced the miniature in the Pantocrator Psalter (presumably a monk) turned onto the painting of idols and, ironically, the portrait of the iconoclastic patriarch a vengeance similar to that of the iconoclasts. Giorgio Vasari records a parallel event when images of Jews were obliterated in a (lost) painting by Andrea del Castagno of the *Flagellation of Christ* because they were themselves considered evil: "The scribbling of children and other simple persons who have defaced the heads, the arms, and nearly all the faces of Jews, as a way of avenging the injuring done to our Lord."[92] This erasing of the pictured Jews served only to recall the spiritual nature of Christian art that Jews themselves mocked because they could not see beyond the physical object. Peter Alfonsi's Jew saw a crucifix only as a worked piece of wood; and Herman of Scheda, before his conversion, apprehended the depiction of the Crucifixion as simply the depiction of a man and the Majestas Domini as the result of an "artist's trick."[93]

Herman of Scheda, like other Jews, was denying the central tenet that enabled Christian art, namely, the faith that God had assumed flesh and was seen on earth. As the Pharisees on the Sens altarpiece declare, Jews rejected the Incarnation: "Truly, God did not want to be born to a woman" and "Who died on the cross cannot be God." Thus, Gilbert Crispin has his Jewish interlocutor

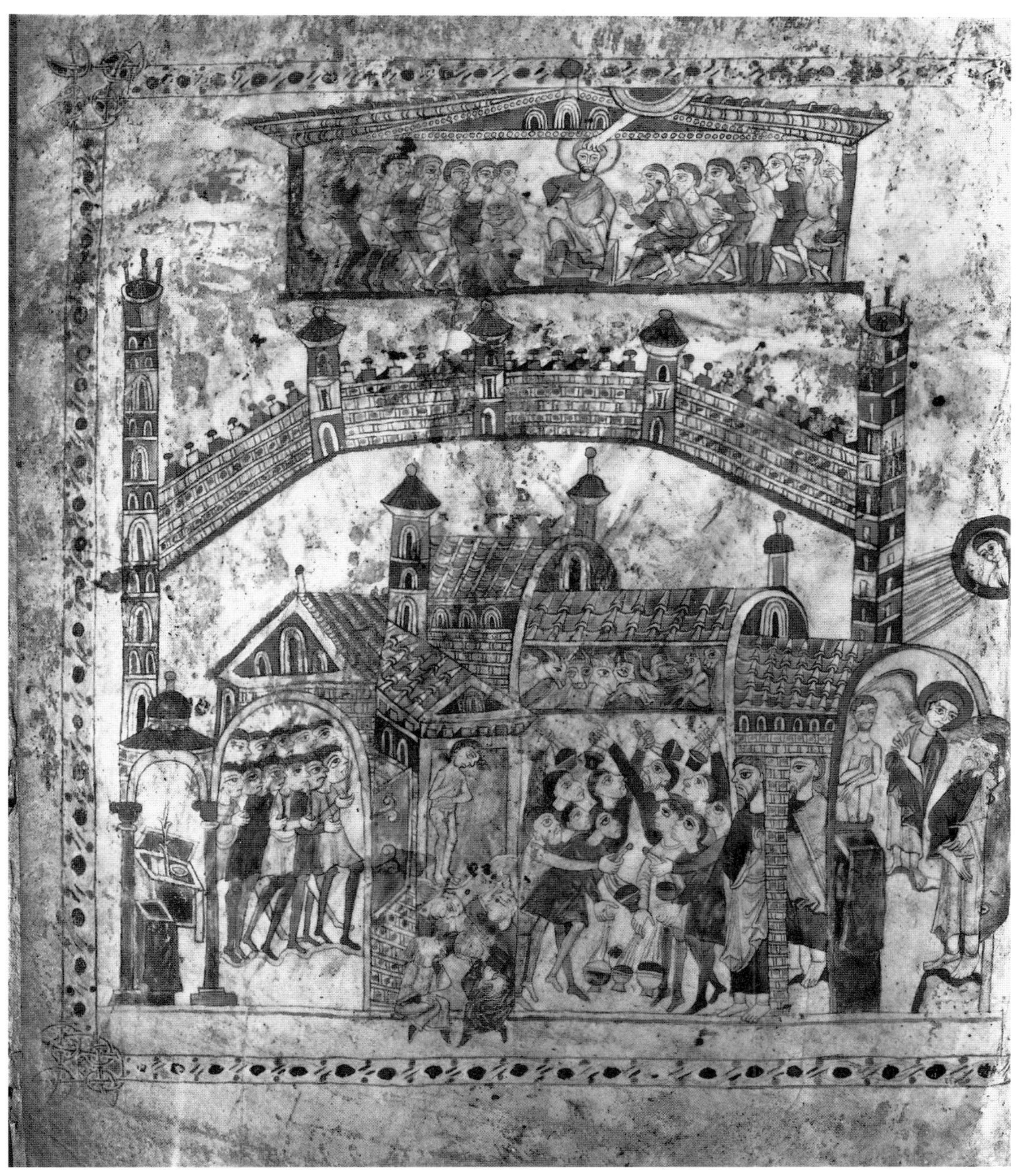

3.10. Paris, Bibliothèque nationale de France, MS lat. 12302, fol. 1v. Ezekiel's vision of the Temple. Photo courtesy BnF, Paris.

object especially to the depiction of God affixed with nails to a cross and suffering, and object equally to sculptures and paintings of the enthroned Deity majestically surrounded by the four beasts, to which he has the Christian respond with the usual citations of the decoration of the Tabernacle/Temple and defenses based on practice. Given the fact that much of Gilbert's *Disputatio* concerns the question of "cur Deus homo" based on Anslem, it is not surprising that the Christian's final response to his Jewish adversary invokes Christ's dual nature.[94] Peter of Celle explained this essential characteristic of Christian art: "Art first renders theology visible to the imagination and then raises the mind to spiritual qualities: If you believe you have only a likeness and not the truth itself, let the likeness lead you to the truth."[95] William of Bourges put it this way: "We do not believe in statues, but we adore and put our faith in the Keystone who entered the tomb of stone for us in order to open up our heart of stone." And in 1338, the sculptor Lando di Piero actually embedded the claim within a crucifix he had himself carved (Siena, Basilica della Osservanza): "This figure was completed in the likeness of Jesus Christ Crucified, true and living Son of God. And one should venerate Him and not this wood."[96]

The fact that even in the fourteenth century, an artist felt the need to assert the argument so often proffered by Christians in debates about art with Jews betrays the continuing anxiety about material images.[97] The claim that pictures, especially those of Christ's most humble aspect on the cross and his most glorified aspect in heaven, implicated the dual nature and hence create an anagogical pathway was frequently asserted in captions, for instance on the Sens Altarpiece, where Matthew at the upper left displayed a quotation from his Gospel: "So let your light shine before men, that they may see your good works, and glorify your Father who is heaven" (5:16) and John at the upper right declared: "But he that does truth, comes to the light, that his work may be made because they are done in God" (3:21). What is more, the book Christ held was inscribed with a free version of Isaiah 32:11, "Put a cloth round your waists and beat your breasts." Likewise, a widely circulated titulus composed around 1100 for a picture asserts: "Qui procul est oculis, procul est a limine cordis";[98] and another reduced the argument about Christ's two natures to "Materiam matri carnis dat, celica patri."[99] The best-known titulus was widely disseminated because it reduced the basic argument to a succinct distich: "It is neither God nor man, which you discern in the present figure, / But God and man, which the sacred image represents."[100] The transference necessary for religious imagery, the ascent from the corporeal eye and to the mind, was thus tied to art's "diptych" quality referred to in the titulus on the Leviticus page of the Leo Bible.

Not surprising, this premise of Christian art was a staple in the *adversos Iudaios* literature. Rupert of Deutz embedded the "neither God nor man" caption in his response to Herman of Scheda's admission that he was unable to move between the images of the dead Christ and the eternal Father in what may have been an early version of the Throne of Mercy (itself a typological image): "I discerned one and the same man abased and exalted, despised and lifted up, ignominious and glorious."[101] And in one manuscript, a gloss on the caption makes the point explicit: "against Jews, Saracens, and heretics who say that we adore idols."[102]

Like the witness at Heribert's birth that Lipton discusses, Jews (and other non-believers) thus verified art's fundamental sensual attractiveness and, at the same time, demonstrated the tenet that faith in the Incarnation alone saved Christians from the sin of idolatry. For instance, Guibert de Nogent argued in his *Tractatus de incarnatione contra Judeos* (III.9): "You attack us because we adore images of the Lord Jesus crucified, or even the wood of the cross itself, so as to accuse us of idolatry, like that which is prohibited by your law. But we adore nothing except the substance of God itself. Yet if we seem to venerate something extrinsic, we do not worship what is seen, rather we cling to the things that come from things unseen."[103] Just as they failed to recognize Jesus as God's truly begotten son, Christians argued, Jews could not comprehend images of him. Herman of Scheda admitted that he had been unable to grasp Rupert's argument in support of images because, when still a Jew, he "was not able to detect the light of truth with my mental eyes, darkened as they were by a cloud of Jewish blindness";[104] until he converted to Christianity, he was as blind as Worship-of-the-Old-Gods is in the London Prudentius. Throughout the Middle Ages and early modern period, looking at material images was itself a *psychomachia*, a struggle for the Christian soul on what Merback terms the "embattled terrain" of the sensual world, the afterlife, and the very history of faith. Herman embodies the struggle; when still a Jew he could not move from the physical depiction to the divine Archetype; once he came to believe in God-Made-Man, he could. It is no surprise, then, that c. 1300, the London Prudentius manuscript, with its remarkable image of Faith plunging a lance into Idolatry's eye, was bound together with a copy of the anonymous tenth-century *Altercatio Aecclesiae contra Sinagogam* and Gilbert Crispin's *Dialogus*, two tracts that pit Christian belief against the claims of Judaism, including those about art.

Like the *adversus Iudaios* tracts themselves, the battle between Christian faith and Jewish carnal vision was directed not to Jews but to those in the Christian community who would relegate material images to an inferior domain, monks such as Bernard of Clairvaux and literalists such as Alfonso de Madrigal el

Tostado, who insisted that art should avoid mystery and stay with history.[105] By figuring Jews simultaneously as both idolaters and iconoclasts, image makers throughout the centuries confirmed their own work's place as the perfect mediator between carnal seeing and spiritual elevation. Dust, the lowest possible material substance that formed Adam's body before God gave it a soul, still shaded Jewish eyes from the brilliant spirit of Christian art in which persons of faith alone could "detect the light of truth with mental eyes."

NOTES

1. Rudolph Stettiner, *Die illustrierten Handschriften des Prudentius* (Berlin, 1895–1915); Otto Homburger, *Die illustrierten Handschriften der Burgerbibliothek Bern* (Bern, 1962), Robert W. Baldwin, "'I slaughter barbarians': Triumph as a Mode in Medieval Christian," *Konsthistorisk tidskrift* 59 (1990): 225–42; Beate Fricke, "Fallen Idols and Risen Saints: Western Attitudes towards the Worship of Images and the 'cultura veterum deorum,'" in *Negating the Image: Case Studies in Iconoclasm,* ed. Anne McClanan and Jeffrey Johnson (London, 2006), 67–95, and Fricke, *Ecce Fides. Die Statue von Conques, Götzendienst, und Bildkultur im Westen* (Munich, 2007); Herbert L. Kessler, "Evil Eye(ing): Romanesque Art as a Shield of Faith," in *Romanesque Art,* ed. Colum Hourihane (University Park, Pa., 2008), 107–35.

2. See Otto Pächt, C. R. Dodwell, and Francis Wormald, *The St. Albans Psalter (Albani Psalter)* (London, 1960); Karen Haney, *The St. Alban's Psalter: An Anglo-Norman Song of Faith* (New York, 2002), Jane Geddes, *The St. Alban's Psalter: A Book for Christina of Markyate* (London, 2005); http://www.abdn.ac.uk/stalbanspsalter/; Kathryn Gerry, "The Alexis Quire and the Cult of Saints at St. Albans," *Institute of Historical Research* (London, 2008), 1–25.

3. Fricke, "Fallen Idols"; Kessler, "Evil Eye(ing)."

4. Fides pr[a]emit et fo[e]dit occulos.

5. Hic versus loquitur / de proceribus qui ex / alia parte positi s[un]t / De s[an]c[t]o terreno bello / in eccl[es]ia est co[m]parati[o, *trimmed off*] / & magna jocundita[s, *trimmed off*] / cu[m] ang[e]lis in celo. / Ideoq[ue] s[an]c[t]e figure in / sp[irit]u virili armate. / facte s[un]t Xpi [Christi] amice / et celestes allete [atlete] Q[ui] / cumq[ue] vult e[ss]e fili[us] / d[e]i & dignus heres ce / lo[rum] & qu[i]cu[m]q[ue] vult ad / imere gl[oria]m & here / ditate[m], q[ua]s diaboli a / regno d[e]i elapsi amise / r[un]t, nocte ac die oc / culo & corde speculet[ur] / illud bellu[m] & equitation[em, *trimmed off*] / q[uae] hic viderit p[ro]tract[a, *trimmed off*] / Sicut hec visibilia ar /ma ferrro & ligno s[un]t pa / rata ut malu[m] & hu / mana[m] occisione[m] facian[t, *trimmed off*] / similite[r] au[tem] que[m]qu[e] n[ost]r[u]m / in bello & penitentia / constitutu[m], fide & cari /tate oportet armari / ut celestib[us] bonis ap / p[ro]pinq[ue]m[us] & corona[m] vite / ang[e]lica[m] p[er]cipiam[us]. & / sic[ut] ipsi corporal[i]te[r] s[un]t tu / mentes sup[er]bia & male / dictione. similite[r] nos / sp[irit]ual-it[er] oportet e[ss]e / mansuetos in humili / tate & deica b[e]n[e]dictio[ne, *trimmed off*] / Sicut ipsi dati s[un]t in ira[m, *trimmed off*] / & visibile[m] rabie[m] corp[or]ali[ter, *trimmed off*] / similite[r] nos oportet / e[ss]e in pace & sapien / tia sp[irit]ualite[r]. Sicut ipsi / ad o[mni]a membra sua occ[u]lo / coporis n[on] sinunt in /vice[m] extende[re]. nos au[tem] / similit[er] occ[u]lis cordis c[um, *trimmed off*] / o[mn]i v[ir]tute se[m]p[er] oportet / [oculis cordis] circ[um]spice[re] / cont[ra] adv[er]sarium n[ost]rum / nob[is] i[n]sidiante[m] conti / nuo tempore. Adversari[us] n[oste]r optat & adestimat irruere sup[er] vertice[m] n[ost]r[u]m o[mn]e malu[m] q[uo]d orit[ur] in duello isto[rum]. Ipsi / occ[u]lis suis nu[m-]q[ua]m dant sopore[m] nec calcarib[us] oblivib[us] oblivione[m]. & cuspis n[ost]re meditationis se[m]p[er] habeat p[ro]vident[em, *trimmed off*] / ratione[m] & affec[tus] studii

HERBERT L. KESSLER

coortatione[m]. Uterq[ue] sit cert[us] in corde. q[uo]d n[isi] adversariu[m] suu[m] visibile[m] occid[erit, *trimmed off*] / ipse occidet[ur], nos au[tem] n[isi] adv[er]sariu[m] invisibile[m] int[er]fecerim[us], nos ipsi interficiem[ur] Qui vincit vere vivet. q[ui] frac[tis, *trimmed off*]; http://www.abdn.ac.uk/stalbanspsalter.

6. Nam nec vela cerata adpendi, nec tabulae pictae adfigi, nec in parietibus vel camaris ulla picture fieri debet: quia in monasterio, quod non spiritalibus, sed humanis tantum oculis placet, esse non debet; *Regulae monasticae*, ed. Germain Morin (Mareteoli, 1942), 2:114.

7. Petrus Alfonsi, *Dialogi contra Iudaios*, PL 157, cols. 670–71, trans. Irven M. Resnick (Washington, D.C., 2006), 271–72; see also Felipe Pereda, *Las imágenes de la Discordia. Politica y poética de la imagen sagrada en la España de 400* (Madrid, 2007).

8. MOYSES. Tale quid profecto est quod vos contra Deum et omnes prophetas facitis, videlicet quod in nemore arborem quamdam conciditis, et postea artificem lignarium, qui illam secet, sculpat, et in hominis speciem formet, poliat et depingat exquiritis, et imaginem illam in vestris Ecclesiis in celsiori videlicet loco construitis, et adoratis.

9. PETRUS. Ita et nos ante crucem genua flectentes, nequaquam crucem illam aut imaginem superpositam, imo Deum Patrem et Filium suum Jesum Christum adoramus. . . . Sed et filii Ruben altare construxerant trans Jordanem ad similitudinem altaris illius Hiericho, ut filii sui et uxores, qui ascendere non potuerunt illud aspicerent, in testimonium tantum alterius et cognitionem.

10. Et has ymagines, quas videtis in ecclesiis, non adoramus, sed sancta mater ecclesia in modum specula ipsas point, u teas videntes oculi corporals videant oculi cordis, et recordentur de passione Christi qui passus fuit pro salute nostra et pro redemptione humani generis, sicut prophete testantur. MGH. *Quellen zur Geistesgeschichte des Mittelalters*, vol. 15, ed. Ora Limor (Munich, 1994), 291–95. See Gilbert Dahan, *The Christian Polemic against the Jews in the Middle Ages*, trans. J. Gladding (Notre Dame, 1998), 26–27.

11. See Celia Chazelle, "Pictures, Books, and the Illiterate: Pope Gregory I's Letters to Serenus of Marseille," *Word and Image* 6 (1990): 138–53; Pascal Weitmann, *Sukzession und Gegenwart. Zu theoretischen Äusserungen über bildende Künste und Musik von Basileios bis Hrabanus Maurus* (Wiesbaden, 1997), 8–61; Herbert L. Kessler, "Gregory the Great and Image Theory in Northern Europe in the Twelfth and Thirteenth Centuries," in *A Companion to Medieval Art: Romanesque and Gothic in Northern Europe*, ed. C. Rudolph, Blackwell Companions to Art History (Oxford: Blackwell, 2006), 151–71.

12. Aliud est enim picturam adorare, aliud per picturae historiam quid sit adorandum addiscere. Nam quod legentibus scriptura, hoc idiotis praestat pictura cernentibus, quia in ipsa ignorantes uident quod sequi debeant, in ipsa legunt qui litteras nesciunt; unde praecipue gentibus pro lectione picture est. Quod magnopere a te, qui inter gentes habitas, attendi decuerat, ne dum recto zelo incaute succenderis, ferocibus animis scandalum generares. Frangi ergo non debuit quod non ad adorandum in ecclesiis sed ad instruendas solummodo mentes fuit nescientium collocatum; *Registrum epistularum*, ed. Dag Norberg (CCSL 140–140A) (Turnhout, 1982), 874; *The Letters of Gregory the Great*, trans. John R. C. Martyn, vol. 3 (Toronto, 2004), 744–46.

13. See Vincent Déroche, "La polémique anti-judaïque au VIe et au VIIe siècle un mémento inédit, les *Képhalaia*," *Travaux et Mémoires* 11 (1991): 275–311.

14. Kalman P. Bland, *The Artless Jew: Medieval and Modern Affirmation and Denials of the Visual* (Princeton, 2000); Henry N. Calman, *Jewish Images in the Christian Church* (Macon, 2000); Margaret Olin, *The Nation without Art: Examining Modern Discourses on Jewish Art* (Lincoln and London, 2001); Conrad Rudolph, "La resistenza all'arte nell'Occidentale," in *Arti e storia nel Medioevo*, ed. Enrico Castelnuovo and Giuseppe Sergi, vol. 3 (Turin, 2004), 49–84.

15. J. B. Mansi, ed., *Sacrorum Conciliorum nova et amplissima Collectio* (Florence, 1759), 11, cols. 921–1006.

16. Kathleen Corrigan, "The Witness of John the Baptist on an Early Byzantine Icon in Kiev," *Dumbarton Oaks Papers* 42 (1988): 1–11; George Nedungatt and Michael Featherstone, *The Council in Trullo Revisited* (Rome, 1995), 43–185.

17. Bernard's follower who wrote the *Pictor in Carmine* also allowed for the possibility at least of image-less churches when he conceded that "I did not think it would be easy to do away with the meaningless paintings in churches, especially cathedral and parish churches." See M. R. James, *Pictor in Carmine* (Oxford, 1951); Karl-August Wirth, ed., *Pictor in Carmine. Ein typologisches Handbuch aus der Zeit um 1200* (Berlin, 2006).

18. E [*missing*]ste vus le respuns saint gregorie a secundin le reclus/ //cum il demandout raison des/ // paintures. Altra cóse est aurier la painture/ e altra cose est par le historie de la painture ap[re]ndre/ quela cóse seit ad aurier · kar ico que la scripture aprestet/ as lisanz · icó aprestet la painture as ignoranz · kar an icele veient/ les ignoranz quet il deivent sivre · An icele lisent icels ki letres ne sevent · / ampur laquele cóse maismement la peinture est pur leceun as genz · / Laquele cóse tu q[u]i habites entra les genz deuses antendra · que tu n'angendrasses/ scandale de crueles curages dementiers que tu esbraseras nient cuintement/ par dreit amvidie · Geres nient ne deut aluiet [*scribal interlinear correction*] estra fruissiet icó que nient ne/ parmaint ad aurier an eglises · mais ad anstruire sulement les penses/ des nient savanz · e ampur icó que l'ancienetiet nient senz raisun cuman/dat les hystories estra depaint es honurables lius des sainz · se tu feisses/ amvidie par discrecion · senz dutance poeies salvablem[en]t purtenir les cóses/ que tu attendeies e nient dep[er]dra la cuileita folc · mais maisment ase[m]blier/ que le nient fraint num de pastur excellist · e nient an i oust la culpa del/ dep[er]dethur; http://www.abdn.ac.uk/stalbanspsalter/.

19. Paecht and Dodwell, *St. Albans Psalter*, 137–38.

20. I wish to thank Conrad Rudolph and Kathryn B. Gerry for discussing this issue with me. Bland, *Artless Jew*, 65. Meir of Rothenburg made a similar argument in the thirteenth century, when he argued that illuminations of birds and animals in Hebrew prayerbooks also risked diverting the "hearts" of those gazing at them away from God in heaven; see Bland, *Artless Jew*, 50, and Kalman P. Bland, "Defending, Enjoying, and Regulating the Visual," in *Judaism in Practice from the Middle Ages through the Early Modern Period*, ed. Lawrence Fine (Princeton, 2001), 281–97; Katrin Kogman-Appel, "Christianity, Idolatry, and the Question of Jewish Figural Painting in the Middle Ages," *Speculum* 84 (2009): 73–107.

21. ut ipse psalmista q[ui] studuit in sapientia & sonuit tale[m] divinitate[m] sit p[ro]-tra[c]tus] in specie / regi[s] & honorifice posit[us] ita in medio hoc .B. & teneat cythara[m] sua[m] in manu dextr[a] cont[ra] pect[us]. & suu[m] psalt[er]iu[m] i[n] / manu sinistra i[n] q[uo] sc[ri]bat[ur] beata annunciatio. Na[m] in illo s[an]c[t]o studio nob[is] notificavit via[m] salutis & n[ost]r[u]m rede[m]ptorem. / q[ui] nos illuminat & s[an]c[t]am eccl[es]ia[m] edificat. Michi visu[m] [est] q[uo]d sonus sue cythare significat voce[m] s[an]c[t]e eccl[es-]ie & suus lib[er] / que[m] habuit in magna dilectione significat sapienta[m] p[ro]phetie & illa[m] divina[m] p[re]dictione[m]. & id[e]o spirituales amant / psalteriu[m] & cupiunt sua[m] divina[m] doctrina[m]. id[e]o q[ui]a dulcedine[m] inserit cordib[us] eo[rum]; http://www.abdn.ac.uk/stalbanspsalter/.

22. Haney, *St. Albans Psalter.*

23. Kathryn Gerry, "Alexis Quire."

24. Gilbert Dagron, "Judaïser," *Travaux et Mémoires* 11 (1991): 359–80. In Rome, the church of SS. Cosma e Damiano with its rich mosaic decoration may be an early example of supersession; see John Osborne, "The Jerusalem Temple Treasure and the Church of Santi Cosma e Damiano in Rome," *Papers of the British School at Rome* 76 (2008): 173–81.

25. See Jean-Pierre Caillet, "La reappropriation du prophetisme," in *Le monde de la Bible* (Paris, 2000), 48–53.

26. *Rationale*, Book 3, chap. 11; Timothy M. Thibodeau, trans., *The Rationale divinorum officiorum of William Durand of Mende: A New Translation of the Prologue and Book One* (New York, 2007), 33.

27. Joachim Gaehde, "Le miniature," in *Bibbia di San Paolo fuori le mura* (Rome, 1993), 244.

28. Yolanta Załuska, *Manuscrits enluminées de Dijon* (Paris, 1991), 71–74; Walter Cahn, *Romanesque Manuscripts: The Twelfth Century* (London, 1996), 2:79- 80; William J. Travis, "Daniel in the Lions' Den: Problems in the Iconography of a Cistercian Manuscript Dijon, Bibliothèque Municipale, MS 132," *Arte medievale*, 2nd ser., 14 (2000): 49–71; *La France romane au temps des premiers Capétiens (987–1152)* (Paris, 2005), 231–32.

29. On the interplay of matter and image, see Herbert L. Kessler, " 'Hoc visibile imaginatum figurat illud invisibile verum:' Imagining God in Pictures of Christ," in *Seeing the Invisible in Late Antiquity and the Early Middle Ages: Papers from "Verbal and Pictorial Representations of the Invisible 400 to 1000" (Utrecht, 11–13 December 2003)*, ed. Giselle De Nie, Karl F. Morrison, and Marco Mostert (Turnhout, 2005), 293–328.

30. Herbert L. Kessler, "The Function of *Vitrum Vestitum* and the Use of *Materia Saphirorum* in Suger's St. Denis," in *L'Image. Fonctions et usages des images dans l'occident medieval*, ed. J. Baschet and J.-C. Schmitt (Paris, 1996), 179–203 (reprinted in Herbert L. Kessler, *Seeing Medieval Art: Picturing God's Invisibility in Medieval Art* [Philadelphia, 2000], 190–205).

31. The idea of such "personation" "sounding through" (from *per sonare*) may have originated in Carolingian art; it is evident in the Touronian Bibles, which seem to have inspired Suger. But the idea also had earlier precedents; in Cassiodorus's Commentary on Psalms in Durham, for instance, David is pictured with Christ's features and is shown victorious over the demons, pictured beneath his feet as a two-headed rod.

32. A. F. Kendrick, *Catalogue of Textiles from Burying Gounds in Egypt* (London, 1922), 3:65–66; Volker Illgen, *Zweifarbige reservetechnisch eingefärbte Leinstoffe mit grossfigurigen biblischen Darstellungen aus Ägypten* (Mainz, 1968), 43–46; Kessler, *Seeing Medieval Art*, 46, fig. 2.12.

33. Travis, "Daniel in the Lions' Den," 59.

34. *Les arts au Moyen Age* (Paris, 1846), 246–50; Robert Favreau, "La 'Table d'or' de la cathédrale de Sens," *Bulletin de la Société des Fouilles Archéologiques et des Monuments Historiques de l'Yonne* 18 (2001): 1–12, and Favreau, "Controverses judéo-chrétiennes et iconographie. L'apport des inscriptions," *Comptes rendus de l'Académie des inscriptions et belles-lettres* (2001): 1269–1303.

35. Torrentes lapides amplector ut hostia fiam
    Sed ne deficiam sufficit una fides.

36. Certant Judaei tam scribae quam Pharisaei
    Doctores legis cum summi milite regis.

37. Non voluit vere nasci Deus ex muliere.

38. Qui cruce mortuus est non Deus esse potest.

39. In cruce damnatus Deus est ex virgine natus
    Haec lex testatur quae tibi stulte datur.

40. Inspirante Deo martyr concludit Hebraeo
    Finis adest legis dum deficit unction Regis.

41. See also David Nirenberg, "Christian Sovereignty and Jewish Flesh," in *Rethinking the Medieval Senses*, ed. Stephen Nichols, Andreas Kablitz, and Alison Calhoun (Baltimore, 2008), 154–85.

42. Inscriptions from Quodvultdeus and other anti-Jewish tracts were inscribed on pulpits in southern Italy; see Dorothy Glass, "Pseudo-Augustine, Prophets, and Pulpits in Campania," *Dumbarton Oaks Papers* 41 (1987): 215–26.

43. Bland, *Artless Jew*.

44. Quem notat esse loco pictura superficialis
Qui loca cuncta replet, non est tamen ipse localis.

45. Bland, *Artless Jew*.

46. Stephen Gero, "Hypatius of Ephesus on the Cult of Images," in *Christianity, Judaism and Other Greco-Roman Cults: Studies for Morton Smith at Sixty* (Leiden, 1975), 2:208–16.

47. Mansi, *Sacrorum Conciliorum nova*, vol. 16, cols. 388–404. See Charles Barber, *Figure and Likeness: On the Limits of Representation in Byzantine Iconoclasm* (Princeton, 2002), 17–23.

48. Sirarpie der Nersessian, "Une apologie des images du septième siècle," *Byzantion* 17 (1944–45): 58–87; A. B. Schmidt, "Gab es einen armenischen Ikonoklasm? Rekonstruktion eines Dokuments der kaukasisch-albanischen Theologiegeschichte," in *Das Frankfurter Konzil von 794. Kristallisationspunkt karolingischer Kultur* (Mainz, 1997), 2:947–64.

49. Suzy Dufrenne, "Une illustration 'historique' inconnue du psautier du Mont-Athos, Pantokrator 61," *Cahiers archéologiques* 15 (1965): 83–95; and the very important book by Kathleen Corrigan, *Visual Polemics in the Ninth-Century Byzantine Psalters* (Cambridge, 1992), 34.

50. Déroche, "Polémique anti-judaïque," 292; see also Eva Frojmovic, "Messianic Politics in Re-Christianized Spain: Images of the Sanctuary in Hebrew Bible Manuscripts," in *Imagining the Self, Imagining the Other: Visual Representation and Jewish-Christian Dynamics in the Middle Ages and Early Modern Period*, ed. E. Frojmovic (Leiden, 2002), 91–128.

51. Herbert L. Kessler, "Medieval Art as Argument," in *Iconography at the Crossroads*, ed. B. Cassidy (Princeton, 1993), 59–70; Annemarie Weyl Carr, "Leo of Chalcedon and the Icons," in *Byzantine East, Latin West: Art Historical Studies in Honor of Kurt Weitzmann* (Princeton, 1995), 579–84; Charles Barber, *Contesting the Logic of Painting: Art and Understanding in Eleventh-Century Byzantium* (Leiden, 2007).

52. Thomas Mathews, "The Epigrams of Leo Sacellarios and an Exegetical Approach to the Miniatures of Vat. Reg. gr. 1," *Orientalia Christiana Periodica* 43 (1977): 94–133; *Die Bibel des Leo Patricius, Altes Testament, Reg. gr. I B entstanden im 10. Jahrhundert in Konstantinopel*, ed. S. Dufrenne and P. Canart (Zurich, 1988); Bissera Pentcheva, "Räumliche und akustische Präsenz in byzantinischen Epigrammen: Der Fall der Limburger Staurothek," in *Die kulturhistorische Bedeutung byzantinischer Epigramme*, ed. Wolfram Hörandner and Andreas Rhoby (Vienna, 2008), 75–83.

53. Herbert L. Kessler, "Through the Temple Veil: the Holy Image in Judaism and Christianity," *Kairos. Zeitschrift für Religionswissenschaft und Theologie* 32/33 (1990/1991): 53–77 (reprinted in Herbert L. Kessler, *Studies in Pictorial Narrative* [London, 1994], 49–73); Kurt Weitzmann and Massimo Bernabò, *The Byzantine Octateuchs* (Princeton, 1999), vol. 1, 228–29, and vol. 2, figs. 1163–64.

54. Kessler, *Spiritual Seeing*, 5–8, 31–32, 47–48; Massimo Bernabò, *Il fisologo di Smirne. Le miniature del perduto codice B. 8 della Biblioteca della Scuola Evangelica di Smirne* (Florence, 1998).

55. Elizabeth Cropper, "On Beautiful Women, Parmigianino, Petrarchismo, and the Vernacular Style," *Art Bulletin* 58 (1976): 374–94.

56. See Jeffrey F. Hamburger, "Body vs. Book: The Trope of Visibility in Images of Christian-Jewish Polemic," in *Ästhetik des Unsichtbaren. Bildtheorie und Bildgebrauch in der Vormoderne*, ed. David Ganz and Thomas Lentes (Berlin, 2004), 110–45.

57. *De templo*, 2, *Opera*, part 2 (CCSL, 119A), ed. David Hurst (Turnhout, 1969), 212–13; Homily 1, 13; *Opera*, part 3/4 (Turnhout, 1955), 93; see Paul Meyvaert, "Bede and the Church

     HERBERT L. KESSLER

Paintings at Wearmouth-Jarrow," *Anglo-Saxon England* 8 (1979): 63–78; Lawrence Duggan, "Was Art Really the 'Book of the Illiterate'?" *Word and Image* 5 (1989): 227–51.

58. Karl F. Morrison, *Conversion and Text: The Cases of Augustine of Hippo, Herman-Judah, and Constantine Tsatsos* (Charlottesville and London, 1992); Jean-Claude Schmitt, *La conversion d'Hermann le Juif. Autobiographie, histoire et fiction* (Paris, 2003).

59. *Liber bellorum domini*, chap. 30, 1, 133–43; Guillaume de Bourges, *Livre des guerres du Seigneur*, ed. and trans. Gilbert Dahan (Paris, 1981), 222–27.

60. See Thomas E. A. Dale, "Introduction," in *Shaping Sacred Space and Institutional Identity in Romanesque Mural Painting: Essays in Honour of Otto Demus*, ed. Thomas E.A. Dale with John Mitchell (London, 2004), 1–32.

61. "The opening of the sixth seal refers to the rejection of the Jews and the calling of the gentiles. And Christ gave birth to the destruction of the Jews and the election of the gentiles. 'The was a great earthquake.' In this place, the earth signifies the Jews, [for] there was a great earthquake when these people were devastated by the Romans."

62. See Kessler, "Evil-Eye(ing)"; and Kessler, "Sanctifying Serpent. Crucifixion as Cure," in *Experiments in Empathy: Studies in Honor of Karl F. Morrison*, ed. Rudolph Bell and Karl F. Morrison (Turnhout, forthcoming).

63. Celia Chazelle, "An *Exemplum* of Humility: The Crucifixion Image in the Drogo Sacramentary," in *Reading Medieval Images*, 27–37; and Michele Bacci, "'Quel bello miracolo onde si fa la festa del santo Salvatore': studio sulle metamorfosi di una leggenda," in *Santa Croce e Santo Volto. Contributi allo studio dell'origine e della fortuna del culto del Salvatore (secoli IX–XV)*, ed. Gabriella Rossetti (Pisa, 2002), 7–86, and Bacci, "Nicodemo e il Volto Santo," in *Il Volto Santo in Europa*, ed. M. Ferrari and A. Meyer (Lucca, 2005), 15–37.

64. Translated into Latin by Anastasius Bibliothecarius, c. 873, the story entered such standard accounts as Durandus's *Rationale* (where it is reduced to a minimum), Voragine's *Golden Legend*, and the *Passio imaginis*.

65. Forme ligitur corporis Christi quantitate et qaulitate diligentissime denotata, liniamentis etiam mente descriptis; as reported in the Leobinus legend; see Gustav Schnürer and Joseph M. Ritz, *Sankt Kümmernis und Volto Santo. Studien und Bilder* (Düsseldorf, 1933), 122–34. See also Jean-Marie Sansterre, "L'image blessée, l'image souffrante," *Bulletin de l'Institut historique belge de Rome* 69 (1999): 113–30; Bacci, "'Quel bello miracolo'"; and Bacci, "Nicodemo e il Volto Santo."

66. Elizabeth C. Parker and Charles T. Little, *The Cloisters Cross: Its Art and Meaning* (New York, 1994).

67. Parker and Little, *Cloisters Cross*, 176–81.

68. Anne Prache, *Saint-Remi de Reims. L'oeuvre de Pierre de Celle et sa place dans l'architecture gothique* (Geneva, 1978); Madeline Harrison Caviness, *Sumptuous Arts at the Royal Abbeys in Reims and Braine. Ornatus elegentiae varietate stupendes* (Princeton, 1990). See Jean Leclercq, *La spiritualité de Pierre de Celle (1115–1183)* (Paris, 1946).

69. Caviness, *Sumptuous Arts*, 40.

70. Secundum carnis naturam in cruce pendebat, secundum divinitatis substantiam paradisum et regnum coeleste donabat; Letter 6. Already in the fifth century, Faustus of Riez had claimed that "he hanged on the cross according to his human nature, he gave us paradise and the celestial kingdom according to the divine substance."

71. See Ann Freeman and Paul Meyvaert, "The Meaning of Theodulf's Apse Mosaic at Germigny-des-Prés," *Gesta* 40 (2001): 125–39. Theodulf's was only a brief and unsuccessful skirmish in the battle against art, however; in his reply to the *Opus caroli*, Pope Hadrian evoked Gregory's letters and once again confirmed the ark and cherubim were soulless objects made by hand and graven; as God made them and was glorified by them, so have our

images been made through pictures according to the visions and revelations of the prophets;
See Alia Englen, "La difesa delle immagini intrapresa dalla chiesa di Roma nel IX secolo," in
Caelius I. Santa Maria in Domnica, San Tommaso in Formis e il Clivus Scauri (Rome 2003),
257–84.

72. See Conrad Rudolph, *The"things of greater importance": Bernard of Clairvaux's Apologia and the Medieval Attitude toward Art* (Philadelphia, 1990). In a discussion I had with
Rudolph in connection with this paper, he suggested that Bernard's reference to the "rite of
the Jews" was a rhetorical move to dismiss the commonplace claims about Jewish *vasa sacra*
so that he could focus on more original arguments.

73. Iam vero quia se imaginum inspectione salvandos credunt, sicut serpentis inspectione Israheliticus populus a serpentium morsibus sanabatur, si qua forte eis quaedam corporis
inclementia accesserit, recurrant ad imagines easque aspiciant, quatenus, dum illarum inspectione minime sanati fuerint, revertantur ad Dominum et per sanctorum intercessiones ab
eo sanitatem se accepturos credant, qui totius sanitatis et vitae est auctor (1.18); *Opus Caroli
regis contra synodum (Libri carolini)*, ed. Ann Freeman (MGH. Concilia, vol. 2, suppl. 1)
(Hannover, 1998), 191–92. See Reinhard Hoeps, *Aus dem Schatten des goldenen Kalbes. Skulptur in theologischer Perspektive* (Paderborn, 1999).

74. See Nirenberg, "Christian Sovereignty and Jewish Flesh."

75. PL 104.617; Laura Kendrick, *Animating the Letter: The Figurative Embodiment of Writing from Late Antiquity to the Renaissance* (New York, 1999). See William Diebold, "'Except I
shall see . . . I will not believe' (John 20: 25): Typology, Theology, and Historiography in an
Ottonian Ivory Diptych," in *Objects, Images, and the Word*, ed. Colum Hourihane (Princeton,
2003), 257–73.

76. Dum staret Moyses in petra, pretereuntis terga uidet, non ora Dei. Petra Christus: in
illa stat Moyses, cum gens Mosaica credit in istum. Non uidet ora Dei: presentem noscere
Christum noluit hic populus. Videt eius posterior: post mortem cognouit eum pars maxima
credens; A. B. Scott, Deirdre F. Baker, and A. G. Rigg, "The *Biblical Epigrams* of Hildebert of
Le Mans: A Critical Edition," *Mediaeval Studies* 47 (1985): 272–316 (quotation at 305).

77. Bland, *Artless Jew*, 138–39.

78. Debra Higgs Strickland, "The Jews, Leviticus, and the Unclean in Medieval English
Bestiaries," in *Beyond the Yellow Badge: Anti-Judaism and Antisemitism in Medieval and Early
Modern Visual Culture*, ed. Mitchell B. Merback (Leiden and Boston, 2007), 203–32; see also
the depiction in an eleventh-century missal in Basel (Diocesan Archives, Codex Gressly); Éric
Palazzo, "L'illustration du codex Gressly, missel bâlois du XIe siècle," *Histoire de l'art* 11
(1990): 15–22.

79. On the relationship of art and the Sacraments, see Caroline Bynum, "Seeing and
Seeing Beyond: The Mass of St. Gregory in the Fifteenth Century," in *The Mind's Eye: Art
and Theology in the Middle Ages*, ed. Jeffrey Hamburger and Anne-Marie Bouché (Princeton,
2005), 208–40; Bynum, *Wonderful Blood: Theology and Practice in Late Medieval Northern
Germany and Beyond* (Philadelphia, 2007); and David Nirenberg's contribution in Chapter 13.

80. Bacci, "'Quel bello miracolo,'" 18.

81. *Recrucifando a Cristo. Los judios de la Passio Imaginis en la isla de Mallorca* (Palma,
2009) and "Jews Desecrating a Crucifix: A *Passio Imaginis* Altarpiece in Mallorca," *Icono-
graphica* 8 (2009): 80–94. See also Jean-Claude Schmitt, "Cendrillon crucifiée, à propos du
Volto Santo du Lucques," in *Le corps des images. Essais sur la culture visuelle au Moyen Âge*
(Paris, 2002), 217–71.

82. See Corine Schleif, "Nicodemus and Sculptors: Self-Reflexivity in Works by Adam
Kraft and Tilman Riemenschneider," *Art Bulletin* 75 (1993): 599–626.

83. Also Saint-Denis.

84. Weyl Carr, "Leo of Chalcedon"; Barber, *Contesting the Logic of Painting*, 131–57.

85. See Kessler, "Medieval Art as Argument"; Barber, *Contesting the Logic of Painting*, 112.

86. PG 48, cols. 846–47.

87. See Conrad Rudolph, "Communal Identity and the Earliest Christian Legislation on Art: Canon 36 of the Synod of Elvira," in *Perspectives for an Architecture of Solitude: Essays on Cistercians, Art and Architecture in Honour of Peter Fergusson*, ed. Terryl N. Kinder (Turnhout, 2004), 1–7. Also Walahfrid Strabo: "The bronze serpent which Moses made by the Lord's command was not to be despised—in fact, when bites by real snakes were healed by gazing on the image of a snake, because the people (always prone to idolatry) worshipped it afterwards with a kind of superstitious awe, Hezekiah, a very devout king of Judah, is read to have destroyed it"; Alice L. Harting-Correa, trans., *Walahfrid Strabo's* Libellus de exordiis et incrementis quarundam in observationibus ecclesiasticis rerum (Leiden, 1996), 78–79.

88. Non posse quempiam spiritualia bella suscipere, nisi prius carnis edomuerit cupiditates. Non potest ad contemplandum Deum mens esse libera, quae desideriis hujus mundi et cupiditatibus inhiat. Neque enim alta conspicere poterit oculus quem pulvis claudit; *Sententiae*, Book 2, 41.1–2, ed. Pierre Cazier (Turnhout, 1998), 180.

89. Hinc etiam est quod serpentem eneum quem Moyses erexerat, Ezechias rex confregit, quia populis illi, contra legis preceptum, thuris adolebat incensum; *Rationale*, 1, chap. 3.3 p. 35.

90. On the complicated interpretation of the Golden Calf episode, see Bland, *Artless Jew*, 117–40 passim; also Nirenberg in Chapter 13.

91. Kathleen Kamerick, *Popular Piety and Art in the Late Middle Ages: Image Worship and Idolatry in England, 1350–1500* (New York, 2002).

92. È stata avuta da fanciulli et alter persone semplici che hanno sgraffiate le teste tutte e le bracia e quasi il resto della persona de'Giudei, come se cosi avessino vendicato l'ingiuruia del Nostro Signore contro di loro; *Le vite de' piú eccellenti pittori scultori e architettori* (Florence, 1971), 356. See Gil Bartholeyns, Pierre-Olivier Dittmar, and Vincent Jolivet, "Des raisons de détruire une image," *Images Revues* 2 (2005): 9.

93. Hermannus Quondam Judaeus, *Opusculum de Conversione Sua*, ed. Gerlinde Niemeyer (*MGH. Quellen zur Geistesgeschichte* 4) (Weimar, 1963). Morrison, *Conversion and Text*; Schmitt, *Conversion d'Hermann le Juif*.

94. Cum igitur Christianus adorat crucem, diuino religionis cultu adorat in cruce Christi passionem propter hominis a Deo assumpti in unitatem persone passionem.

95. Caviness, *Sumptuous Arts*, 44.

96. See Donal Cooper, "Projecting Presence: The Monumental Cross in the Italian Church Interior," in *Presence: The Inherence of the Protoype within Images and Other Objects* (Aldershot, 2006), 47–69.

97. Pereda, *Imágenes de la discordia*. Here it should be noted how often the authors of these treatises were themselves converts and, also, the converso context of much art.

98. Rudolf Pörtner, "Eine Sammlung lateinischer Gedichte in der Handschrift Wien ÖNB 806 aus dem 12. Jahrhundert" (Ph.D. diss., University of Tübingen, 1989), 400–403.

99. Ibid., 355–57.

100. Herbert L. Kessler, *Neither God nor Man: Words, Images, and the Medieval Anxiety about Art* (Freiburg im Breisgau, 2007).

101. Ubi studiosius omnia perlustrans, inter articiosas celaturarum ac picturarum varietates monstruosum quoddam ydolum video. Cerno siquidem unum eundemque hominem humilitatum et exaltatum, despectum et evectum, ingnominiosum et gloriosum, deorsum

miserabiliter in cruce pendentem, et sursum pictura mentiente venustissimum velut deificatum residentem; Hermannus Quondam Judaeus, *Opusculum de Conversione Sua*, ed. Niemeyer, p. 75, trans. in Morrison, *Conversion and Text*, 80.

102. "Contra iudaios hereticos et sarracenos qui dicuntur nos adorare idola"; Vatican, BAV, Cod. Reg. lat. 1578, fol. 46r; Kessler, *Neither God nor Man*, 16, 131.

103. See Eugene Vance, "Relics, Images, and the Mind of Guibert de Nogent," *Semiotica* 85 (1991): 335–56.

104. The need to engage Christ's two natures was made explicit by an inscription around Christ's mandorla on a tenth-century altar formerly in Xanten altar, which advanced the claim that what is seen in a material is only an indication, a sign:

> The material and this image show things doubly,
> The image renders the form of a man, the gold signifies his divinity.
> Res et imago duas fert ista notaque figures
> Effigiatus homo, Deus est signatus in auro.

See Herbert L. Kessler, "Image and Object: Christ's Dual Nature and the Crisis of Early Medieval Art," in *The Long Morning of Medieval Europe*, ed. M. McCormick and J. Davies (London, 2008), 291–319.

105. Pereda, *Imágenes de la discordia*, 84–85.

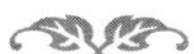

CHAPTER 4

Iudeus sacer:
Life, Law, and Identity in the "State of Exception" Called "Marian Miracle"

Francisco Prado-Vilar

There is so hot a summer in my bosom,
That all my bowels crumble up to dust:
I am a scribbled form, drawn with a pen
Upon a parchment, and against this fire
Do I shrink up.

—Shakespeare, *The Life and Death*
of King John, Act V, scene 7

In 1276, while traveling with his court in Northern Spain, King Alfonso X of Castile and León fell gravely ill in the city of Vitoria. For the past few years, he had been suffering from a chronic disease that subjected him to recurrent periods of intense pain and to a progressive physical deterioration. To add to his grief, the most recent bouts of the illness had come in the midst of a series of personal and political setbacks: the deaths of his eldest son and his youngest daughter, the invasion of the newly conquered territories of Southern Spain by North African troops, and the Papal rejection of his claims to the crown of the Holy Roman Empire. It was during his return to Castile from the disappointing meeting with Pope Gregory X at Beaucaire that put an end to his imperial dream, when, twice, illness pulled him close into the orbit of death, first in Montpellier and later in Vitoria.[1] A strong believer in science, as is attested by a lifetime of patronage of scientific studies, mostly Arabic treatises translated by

Jewish scholars, Alfonso could rest assured that this time he was surrounded by the best science could offer. Not only was he in the vicinity of a renowned center of medical learning such as Montpellier, but he also had by his side several of his trusted Jewish physicians, who often traveled with him fulfilling diplomatic duties.[2] Among them was, with all probability, his personal doctor Abraham Ibn Waqar, member of a prominent Jewish family of diplomats, courtiers, and physicians, who would remain in the king's service until his death, later to perform similar duties for his son Sancho IV. Another lifelong member of the king's intimate entourage was Yehuda Mosca (Yehuda ben Moshe ha-Kohen) who, back in 1250, had undertaken, at Alfonso's request when he was still a prince, the translation of the *Lapidary*, a book describing the magic properties of gems and stones and their healing qualities.[3] The prologue pays tribute to Alfonso's reliance on his Jewish physician for the procurement of knowledge: "He [Alfonso] obtained it in Toledo of a Jew who held it hidden, who neither wished to make use of it himself nor that any other should profit therefrom. And when he [Alfonso] had this book in his possession, he caused another Jew, who was his physician, to read it, and he was called Jehuda Mosca *el menor* and he was learned in the art of astrology and understood well both Arabic and Latin. And when through this Jew his physician he understood the value and great profit which was in the book, he commanded him to translate it from Arabic into the Castillian language."[4]

As Alfonso lay ill in Vitoria, a beautifully illuminated new edition of this book was under way at the royal *scriptorium* (Real Biblioteca del Monasterio de El Escorial, MS. H.I.15).[5] The two miniatures that illustrate the prologue present Alfonso as the inheritor and promoter of the natural philosophy of antiquity: juxtaposed to the portrait of the king receiving the book from his two translators, Yehuda Mosca and the cleric Garci Pérez, is a larger scene where Aristotle lectures to a gathering of scholars about the philosophy of divine emanation mentioned in the text (Figure 4.1).[6] Inside the codex, the knowledge of the workings of the natural world achieved by the ancients is transmitted to the present through the Castilian text, punctuated by miniatures in which the human body is viewed as an organism subject to dissection and study, in order to discern the effects of the physical laws of the universe in its inner operations. This is the case of the medallion that illustrates the section devoted to the so-called "*stone of man . . .*, which is formed in the bladder and the kidneys" (fol. 19r of MS. H.I.15), featuring the standard composition used throughout the manuscript, with a physician giving directions to his assistant to extract the stone at a specific moment of the astral calendar when its powers get activated (Figure 4.2). If properly obtained, ground into powder and administered over

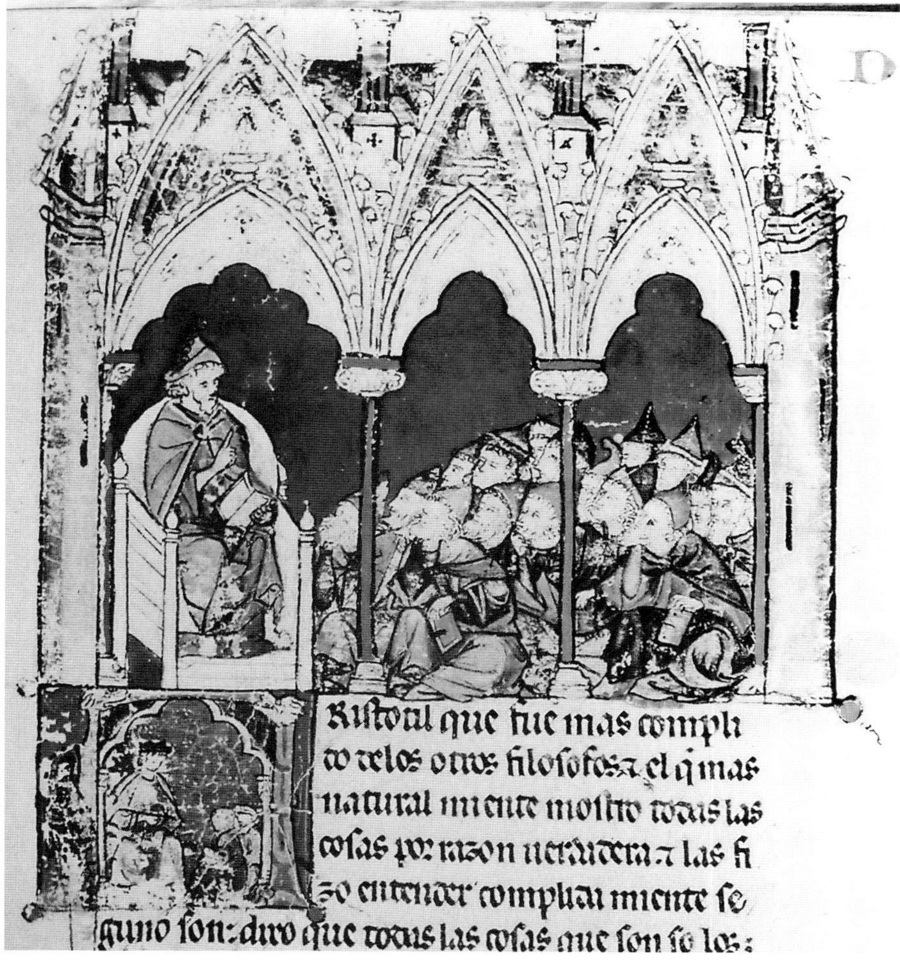

4.1. *Lapidary*, Escorial, Biblioteca del Real Monasterio, MS. H.I.15, fol. 1r. Photo courtesy Edilán.

time following the instructions given in the text, the "stone of man" may be transformed into a medicine to cure cataracts.

The Invisible Jew: Blind Spots in the Art Historical Record

At that dire moment in Vitoria, however, the king refused the certainties of science and the wonders of magic and felt compelled to appeal to a higher power, the Virgin Mary, to whom he professed a deep personal devotion. Indeed, years earlier he had pledged to leave his youthful folly behind in order to become her troubadour and had enlisted a host of Galician poets to compose songs in her honor, praising her virtues and recounting her miracles in the

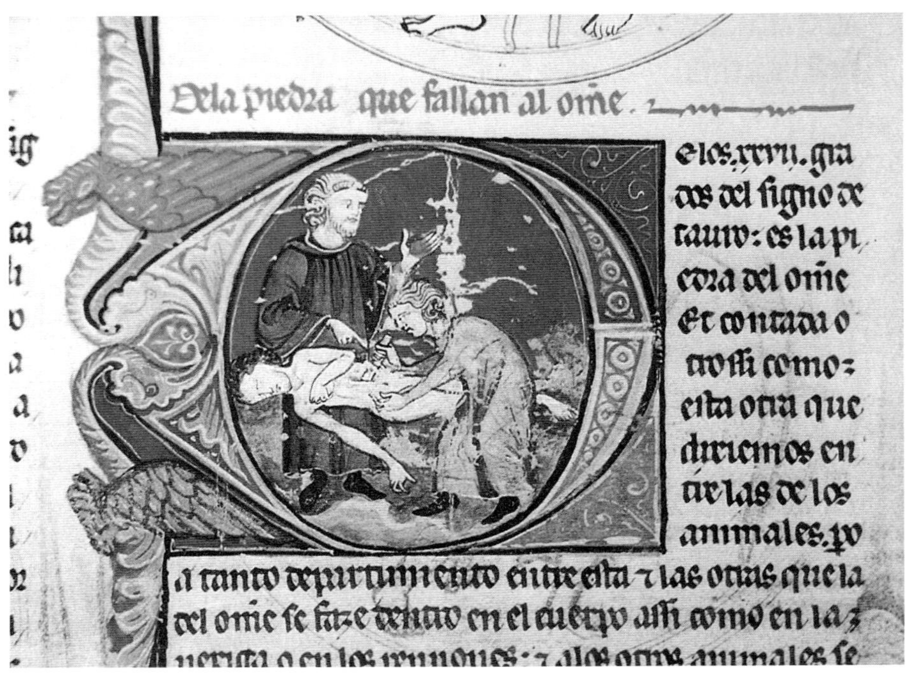

4.2. *Lapidary*, Escorial, Biblioteca del Real Monasterio, MS. H.I.15, fol. 19r. Photo courtesy Edilán.

language of courtly love. Around the time he fell ill in Vitoria, this collection of Marian songs, which came to be known as the *Cantigas de Santa Maria*, was still evolving, from an initial core of 200 songs, which had been probably completed by that time, to what would eventually expand to a total of 427 by the end of Alfonso's life nine years later.[7] According to Alfonso's own testimony, recorded in a song (cantiga 209) that was included and illustrated on fol. 119v of MS. B.R. 20—the last manuscript of the *Cantigas* to be undertaken—it was a book containing those canticles that saved him that day in Vitoria (Figure 4.3).[8] The images follow closely Alfonso's plaintive confession: "I shall tell you what happened to me while I lay in Vitoria, so ill that all believed I should die there and did not expect me to recover. . . . The doctors ordered hot cloths placed on me but I refused them and ordered, instead, that Her Book be brought to me [panels 2 and 3]. They placed it on me, and at once I lay in peace [panel 4]. The pain subsided completely, I felt very well and cried no more. I gave thanks to Her for it, because I know full well She was dismayed at my afflictions [panels 5 and 6]."[9]

With their characteristic documentary interest, and betraying a direct knowledge of the circles of the court, the *Cantigas* artists flesh out the story with

FRANCISCO PRADO-VILAR

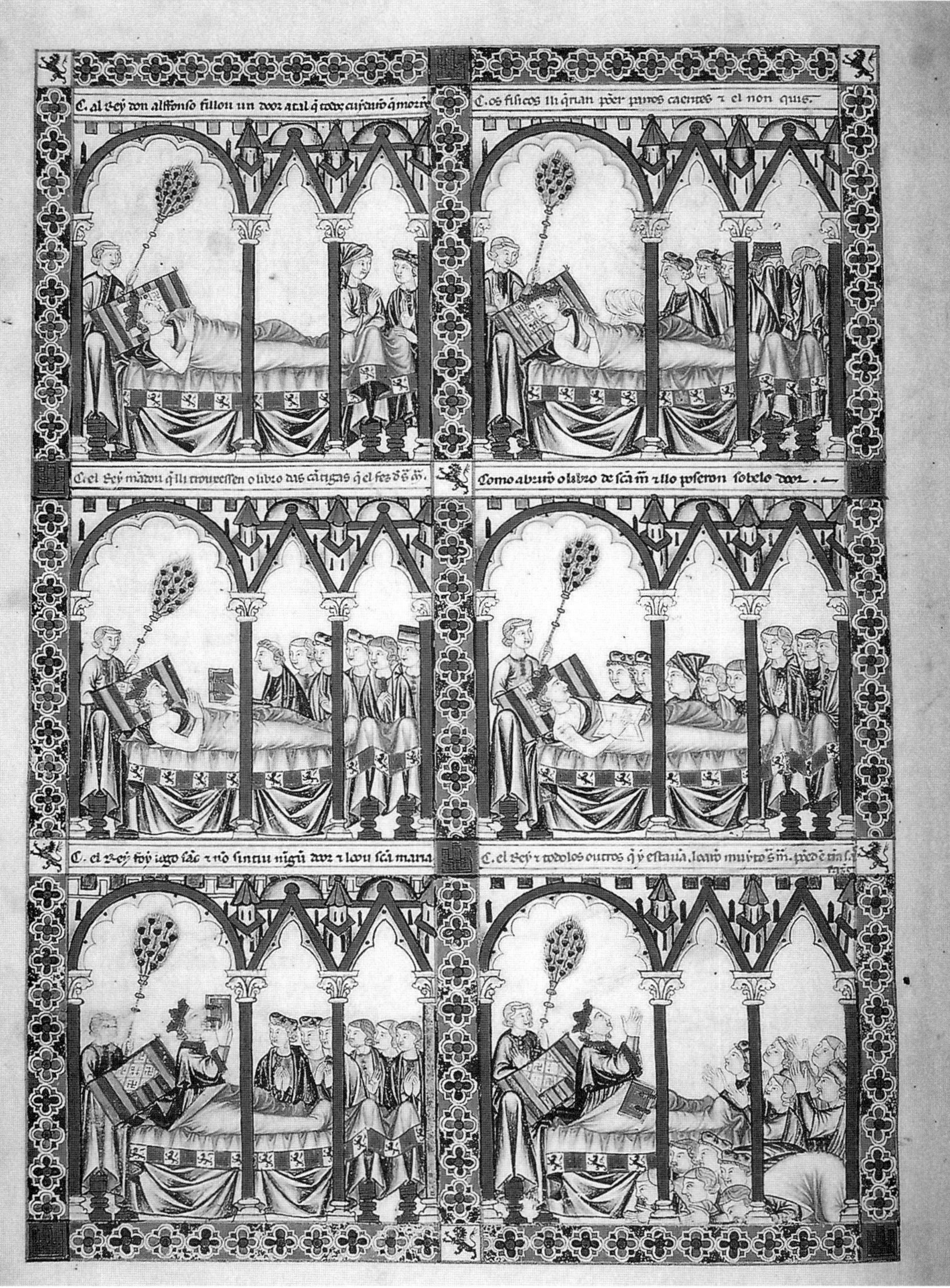

4.3. *Cantigas de Santa María*, Florence, Biblioteca Nazionale Centrale, MS. B.R. 20, fol. 119v. Photo courtesy Edilán.

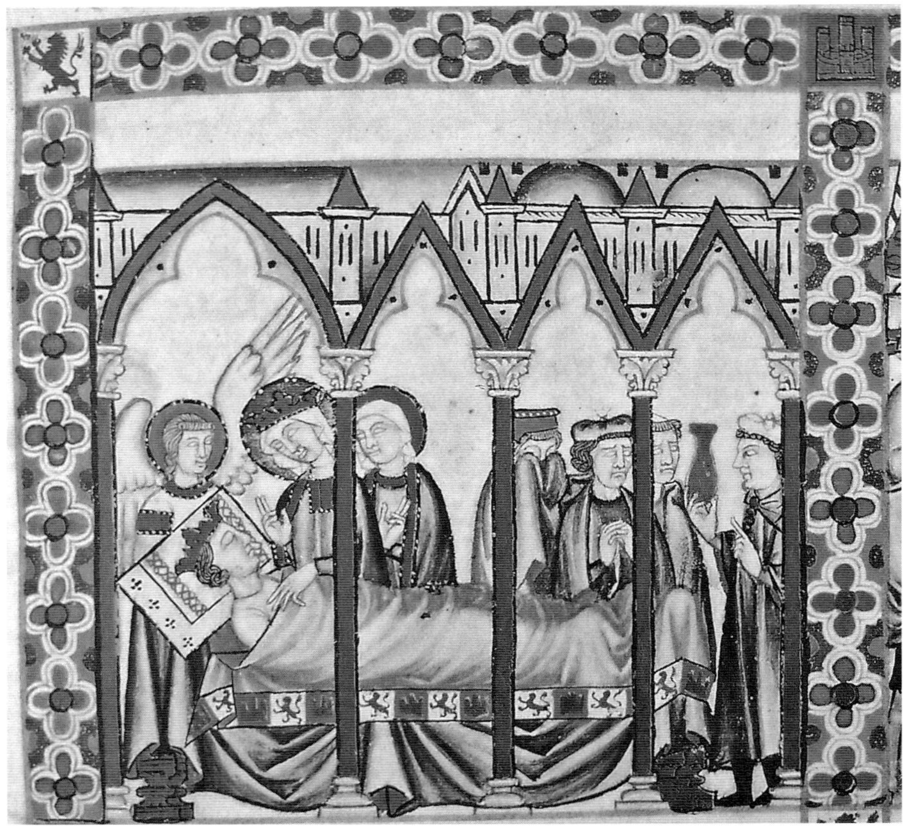

4.4. *Cantigas de Santa María*, Florence, Biblioteca Nazionale Centrale, MS. B.R. 20, fol. 92r. Photo courtesy Edilán.

substantial details that add new dimensions to its significance, thus managing to capture, in unexpected ways, the principal moral of the refrain: "He who denies God and His blessings commits a great error and is grievously in the wrong." A Jewish physician, not mentioned explicitly in the text, which only speaks generally of doctors, emerges as an unintended protagonist of the visual narrative. He appears in the first panel wearing the typical hooded cloak that distinguishes contemporary Jewish characters in the *Cantigas*, giving instructions to a courtier who is wearing a headgear similar to the ones worn by Christian doctors in the miniature that illustrates Alfonso's illness in Montpellier on fol. 92r of MS. B.R. 20 (Figure 4.4).[10] This Jewish physician appears prescribing the hot cloths that are to be administered to the king in the adjacent panel. His absence in this second scene reflects, with all probability, a specific regulation contained in the monumental law code promulgated by Alfonso, the *Siete Partidas*, according to which Christians were not allowed to take medicines prepared by Jews, although Jewish physicians could prescribe medication that Christians would then prepare.[11] The Jewish doctor is also absent, as might be expected, from the scene where a cleric presents the book of Holy Mary to Alfonso, but reappears again for the last time in the following panel where the miracle occurs. He is prominently displayed there as the silent central witness to the healing power of the Virgin. Thus this *cantiga,* which, in its literary version, is mainly a deeply felt personal testimony to the rewards of Marian devotion, is transformed into a subtle proselytizing *exemplum* of the protection extended by the Virgin to those who believe in her—a protection that reaches where human knowledge cannot. The Jewishness of the physician, rather than being marked primarily by his external features or his attire, becomes evident through his calculated appearances and disappearances on the parchment. Indeed, this is one of the invisible Jews of the *Cantiga*—a portrait of a character such as Abraham Ibn Waqar—those who shared with Alfonso some of his most private moments, and who, despite being extensively documented, are rarely seen by modern scholars.[12]

The Jews who are more clearly visible in the *Cantigas,* more readily susceptible to iconographic taxonomies, and have therefore attracted the most scholarly attention are those who conform to the antisemitic figural conventions so pervasive in thirteenth-century European art and literature.[13] In several miracles, Jews with crooked noses and terrifying grimaces play the typical roles of child murderers, greedy moneylenders, desecrators of Christian images, arrogant mockers, and so on. To the modern eye, the shocking effect of the accumulation of these images is somehow increased, in an anachronistic unconscious response, by the use of *swastikas* as decorative motif throughout the manuscript—a particularly startling vignette on fol. 39r of the *Códice rico* features a *swastika* ominously framing the head of a caricaturized Jew (Figure 4.5). These miniatures seem to bring the *Cantigas* close in spirit to another famous thirteenth-century work, the *Bible moralisée,* and to earlier popular collections of Marian miracles, such as Gautier de Coincy's *Les miracles de Nostre-Dame,* which the Alfonsine compilers probably used as one of their textual sources.[14] Indeed, the character of its sources is, in great measure, responsible for the appearance of standard anti-Jewish iconography in the *Cantigas.* Most of these images are located at the beginning of the collection precisely because Alfonsine compilers started by gathering stories from famous European vernacular and Latin collections of miracles and only later proceeded to incorporate miracles related to a specific Iberian context, including stories about Alfonso's own life and family history. The accumulation of anti-Jewish images at the beginning of the collection has, therefore, less to do with the implementation of a specific antisemitic agenda by Alfonso X and much to do with the specific genre to

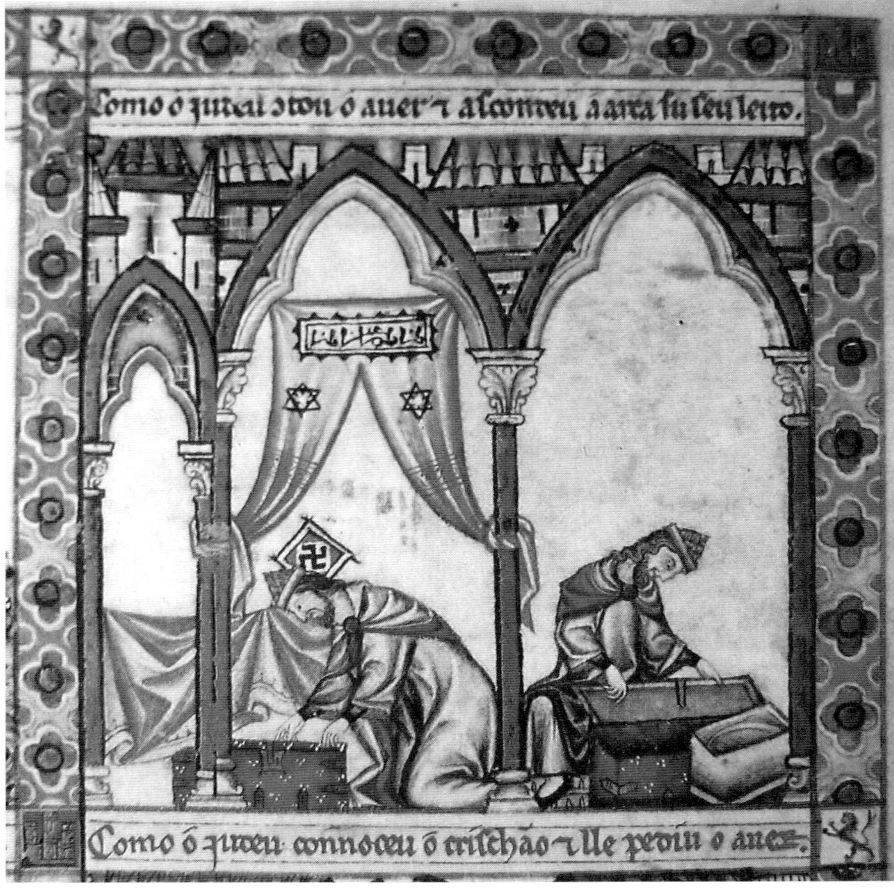

4.5. *Cantigas de Santa María*, Escorial, Biblioteca del Real Monasterio, MS. T.I.1, fol. 39r. Photo courtesy Edilán.

which the *Cantigas* collection belongs and the general design and evolution of the project.[15] An iconographic taxonomy of this kabuki theater of anti-Jewish masks, unmindful of the compositional rationale of the collection as a whole, of its gradual incorporation of clusters of textual sources, and of the sophisticated meanings encoded exclusively at the level of the visual narrative, has little to offer in the way of understanding the Jewish question in the *Cantigas*.

These patterns of misapprehension of the Alfonsine project help explain why an image that so profoundly encapsulates the unique complexity of this question in the *Cantigas* has completely escaped scholarly consideration (Figure 4.6): an intimate space inhabited by a monarch reminded of his mortality by illness, and reduced, by pain, to the confines of a bed and his own sentient body. There he holds onto a book that contains an alternative world where

     FRANCISCO PRADO-VILAR

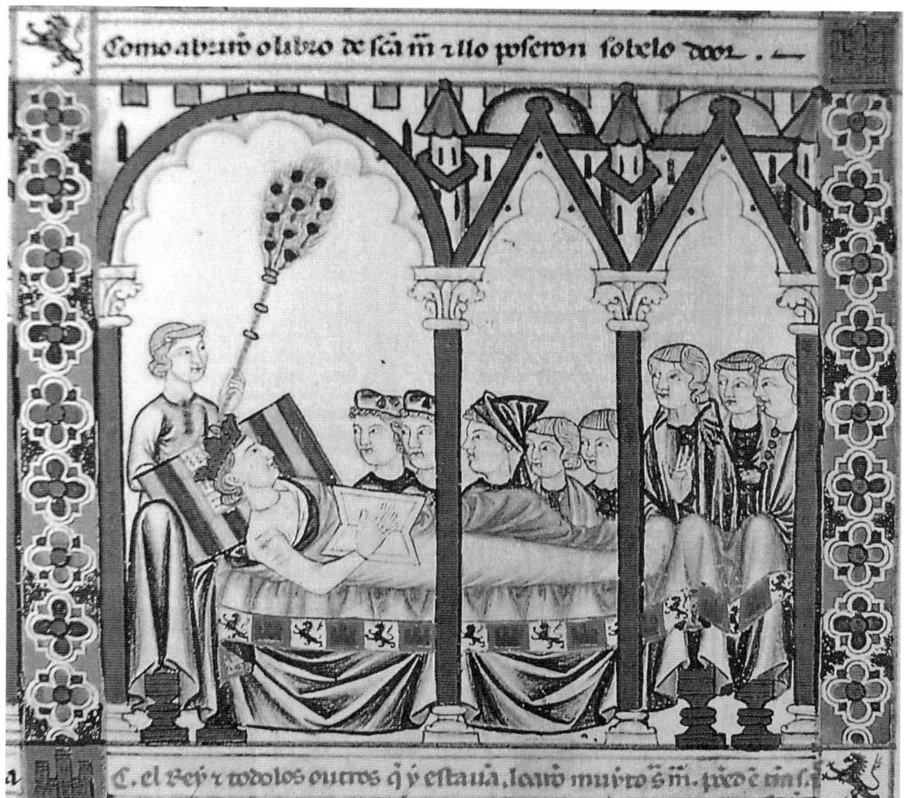

4.6. *Cantigas de Santa María*, Florence, Biblioteca Nazionale Centrale, MS. B.R. 20, fol. 119v. Photo courtesy Edilán.

illness is always cured and within which his emaciated body reemerges restored to its former plenitude on the surface of the vellum. Central to the constitution of this space of intimacy is a token of otherness, a Jewish physician, at once friend and foe, kin and stranger, the other within the self, who kneels gazing as a witness to the miraculous healing of his patron. The *punctum* of the miniature, and of the art of the *Cantigas* at large, lies in the dialectic modulations of meaning effected by the intercourse of these three bodies: the physical body of the king, the artistic *corpus* generated by his poetic voice and incarnated in parchment, and the body of the "other," which exists as an *extimate* presence in the visual *corpus* of the *Cantigas* (and inside the body of the nation that is figured within).[16] This image offers us a snapshot of a crucial moment in their interwoven vital trajectories: as the king became progressively weakened by illness and disillusioned with European politics, his attention shifted inward toward himself and his nation, and, progressively, compassion achieved an increasing centrality in both his piety and his political strategy of national formation. As a reflection of this, the *corpus* of the *Cantigas* grew more Iberian, personal, and "benign," bearing witness of permanent healing, a promise of earthly happiness and eternal bliss, and offering numerous testimonies of the possibilities of regeneration and acceptance for those "other" bodies that, by birth, religion, or deeds, had been excluded from that utopian Christian nation sheltered from pain, protected by the Virgin, and guided by her principal troubadour. We find, in conclusion, in this image, where the king-author and his Jewish subject meet at the creaturely level of their existence, the most fertile ground upon which to develop a complex and layered inquiry into the matter of Jewish representation in the *Cantigas*.

The Birth of *Iudeus Sacer*:
Bio-Theological Foundations of Conversion

Conversion is the kernel and central theme of the collection, both as personal improvement toward the fulfillment of a true Christian life, following Alfonso's own example, and as the embracing of the Christian faith by those outside it, exemplified in myriad stories that culminate with the baptism of members of religious minorities.[17] In radical contrast with other projects of social control and national formation such as the *Bible moralisée*, the *Cantigas* places an emphasis on healing, well-being, and happiness in the here and now, rather than on enforcing dogmatic orthodoxy or focusing on the promise of eternal salvation. In doing so, it promotes religious conversion as a way to provide entrance into a community that is defined primarily as a biopolitical space—a nation whose membership gives priority for the protection of the life of its citizens in their status as biological entities. This biopolitical strategy was specially directed to Muslim and Jewish women and their offspring, with the objective that a generational replacement could bring about the complete absorption of the religious minorities of the newly conquered territories. Accordingly, miracle stories of conversion often involve issues regarding procreation and the well-being of children. The protagonist of cantiga 89, for instance, is a Jewish woman who experienced problems during her pregnancy and was "abandoned in her great pain, in despair of living, for no medicine would help her" (Figure 4.7). Thanks to the Virgin, as we see on fol. 131r of the *Códice rico*, she was able to give birth and "all her body was restored to health." To the horror of the other Jewish women, who denounced her calling her "heretic, apostate and Christian convert," the Jewess decided, as the *cantiga* says, "to wait no longer for the Messiah" and received baptism alongside her son and daughter.

This biopolitical strategy of conversion had important theological ramifications, for it consciously exploited the biological underpinnings of the Marian cult, both in the context of an emotional piety, that is, in her condition as a

FRANCISCO PRADO-VILAR

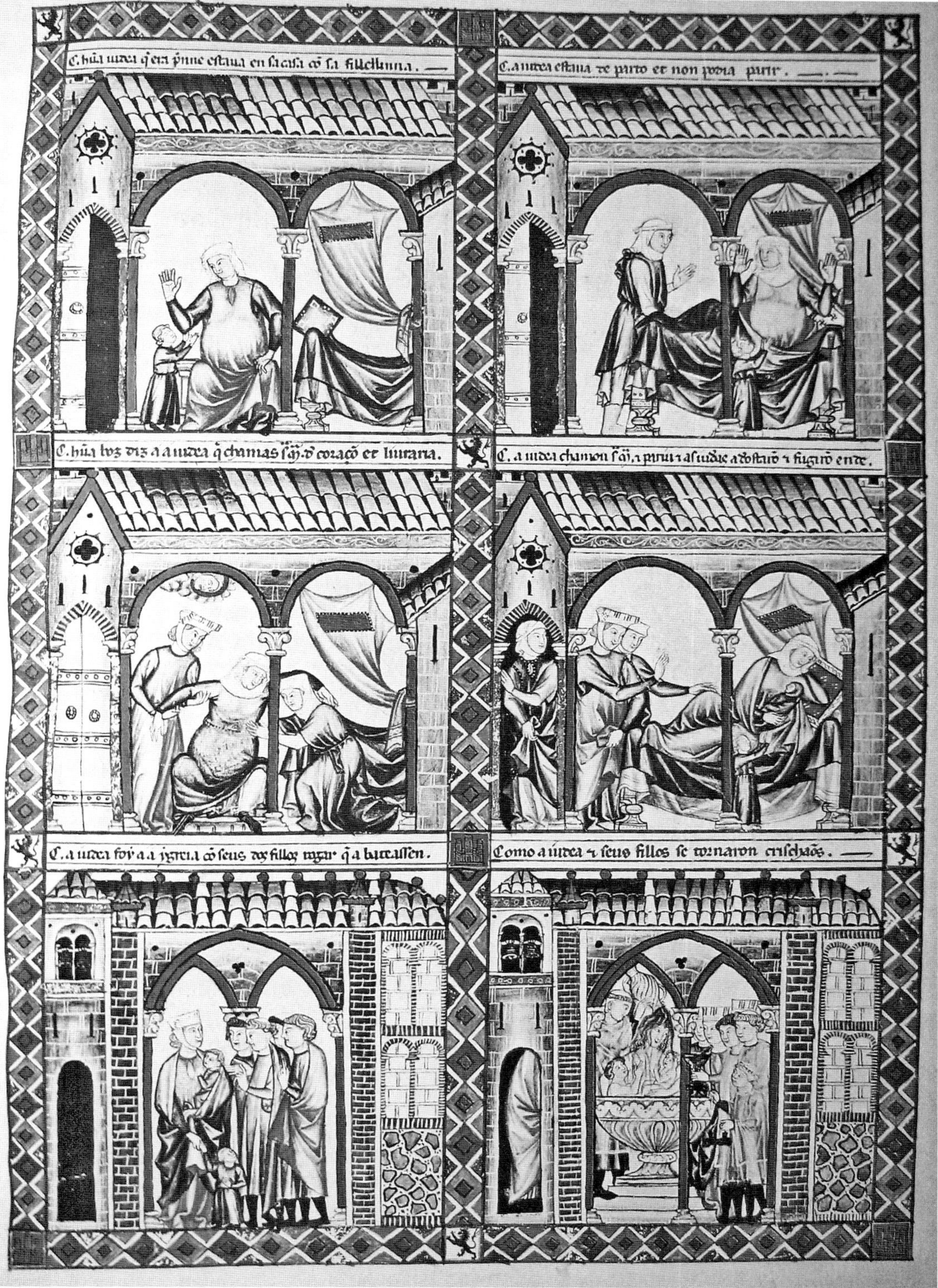

4.7. *Cantigas de Santa María*, Escorial, Biblioteca del Real Monasterio, MS. T.I.1, fol. 131r. Photo courtesy Edilán.

woman and a mother, and in the context of religious dogma, compelling Muslims and Jews to rethink the figure of Mary as the vessel for the materialization of God by engaging them in questioning the presuppositions of their own faiths as to how the divinity reveals itself in the world. The former is reflected in some miracles in which Muslim women and their children are likened to images of Mary and child, such as the ones represented on fol. 6r of MS. B.R. 20 asking for help at the top of a burning tower.[18] It is on account of this resemblance that the Muslim woman is rescued by the Virgin and compassionately embraced by Christians. Reciprocally, Muslim men are compelled to develop emotional bonds with images of the Virgin by relating them to their own intimate experiences of familial love—such is the case of the Moor represented on fol. 68v of the *Códice rico*, who gazes at an icon of the Virgin while his wife nurtures their child mirroring Mary's maternal disposition.[19] On the dogmatic side of this equation, the revered status of Mary in the Qur'an, which reaffirms both her virginity and the holiness of Jesus, was consciously highlighted in the *Cantigas* to present Mary as a sacred figure who could be embraced by Muslims within the acceptable paradigms of their popular piety where, miracle-working holy women fulfilled a role not unlike that of the Virgin in the stories. In sum, the collection sought to establish a common ground beyond dogmatic differences by underscoring the Virgin's role as a healer and a mother for all who believe in her. Alfonso deployed this biopolitical model to provide a unifying thread weaving together the different social, religious, and ethnic strands of the national identity he was striving to forge.

In the following, I explore a different development of the bio-theology of the *Cantigas* as it pertains to the conversion of the Jews. Unlike the Muslim case, where Alfonso's strategy could build on the holy status of Mary in the Qur'an, Judaism negated the bio-theological central mystery of the Christian dogma, the Incarnation, where Mary's sacredness was grounded. Interestingly, as we see in the examination of two representative examples that involve the conversion of Jewish children, the Incarnation provides a model to "imagine" the possibility of a complete spiritual and physical transformation of the Jewish body into a Christian subject—a new subject who, like Jesus, emerges from the womb of a Jewish woman, the Virgin Mary. The analysis of the genealogy and identity of this ideal Jewish convert promoted in the *Cantigas*, which I shall call *iudeus sacer*, will help illuminate the important place of the Alfonsine project in the history of Jewish representation in the Middle Ages.

The seminal rift between the two religions is the subject of cantiga 108, illustrated on fol. 155v of the *Códice rico*, which combines a theological discussion on the Incarnation and a tale of conversion centered on the metamorphosing body a Jewish child (Figure 4.8).[20] The story opens with an argument

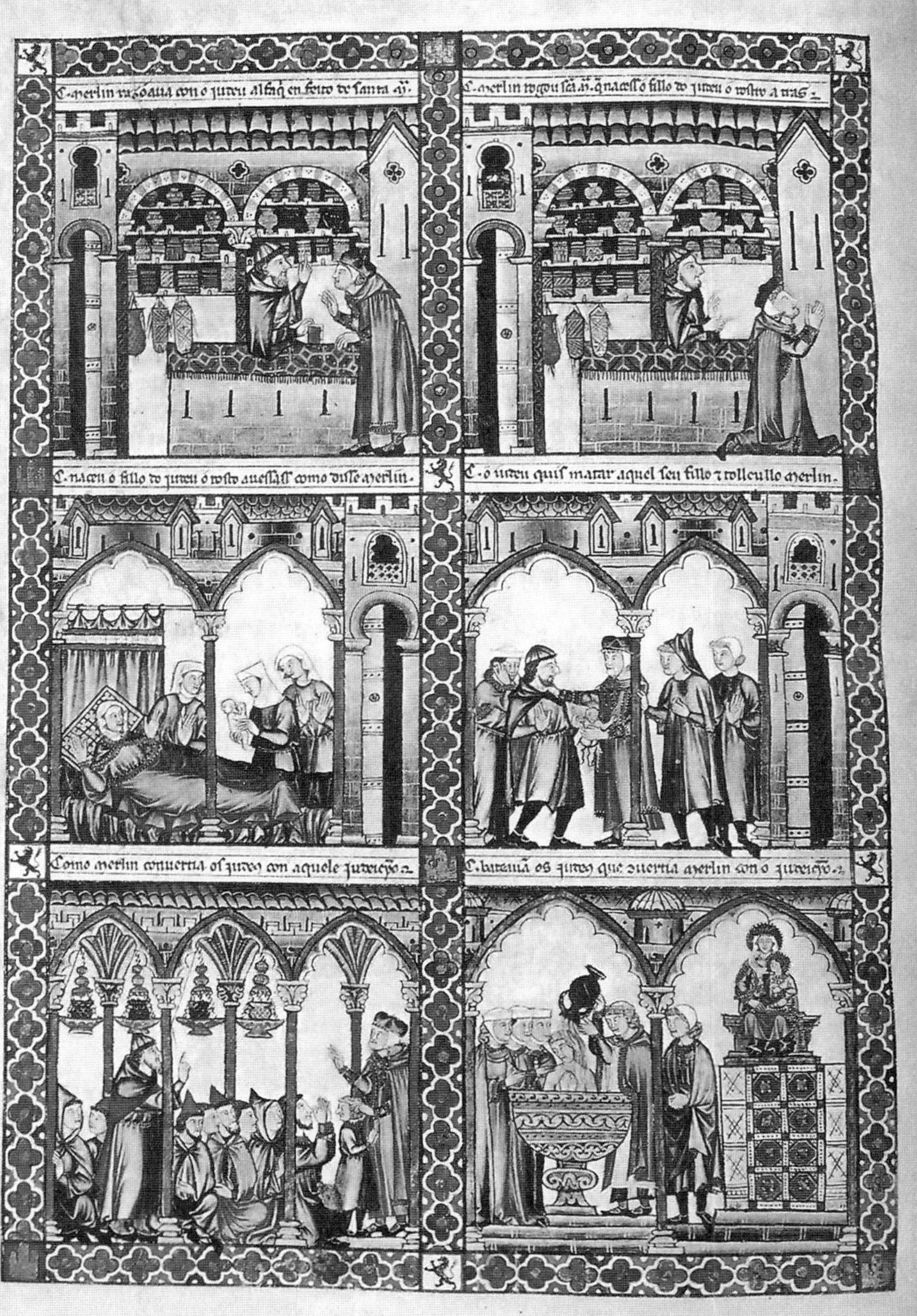

4.8. *Cantigas de Santa María*, Escorial, Biblioteca del Real Monasterio, MS. T.I.1, fol. 155v. Photo courtesy Edilán.

between Merlin and a Jewish sage from Scotland, named Caiphas, who force-fully argues against the possibility of the Incarnation, saying that God cannot be contained in the womb of a woman. To punish the Jew for his heretic stubbornness, Merlin requests that the Virgin cause the son that his wife is expecting to be born with his head facing backward. When the father sees the baby bearing a physical sign of his own error, he tries to kill him, but Merlin saves him, later to use him as an example "to convert Jews in order to lead them from their erroneous beliefs." The miniatures expand on the terse outlines of the story by presenting the Jewish sage as an *alfaquim* (physician) who sells pharmaceutical products at a street shop whose architecture evocatively relocates the story to an Iberian context. In the first panel, he argues with Merlin while he (the sage) holds a book and points to one of the containers displayed on the shelves—a beautiful visual metaphor illustrating his main argument against the Incarnation when he says of Mary's womb: "God could never enter into such a place, it stands to reason, for how could He Who contains so many things be contained."[21] In the subsequent panels, the story develops in charming detail, moving from a domestic space of femininity where the birth takes place, through the threshold of the house where the baby is rescued from the hands of his enraged father, to a synagogue where a diverse group of Jews listens to Merlin's cautionary tale—one of them, exhibiting the caricaturized features used to represent the father, confronts Merlin, while others, recalling the *invisible Jew* of the Vitoria miracle, both in countenance and attire, appear more receptive to his message.[22] Fundamental to the meaning of the story is the final scene where the Jewish boy is being baptized in the presence of a group of women—an exclusive creation of the illuminators, with no narrative support in the text of the *cantiga*, which simply concludes with Merlin using the boy to preach conversion. This scene adds one last crucial chapter to the story of the boy: the miraculous restoration of his body through the waters of baptism, surrounded by the Jewish women who attended his birth who now reappear as witnesses of his rebirth to Christianity.[23]

By concluding the story with the scene of the boy emerging to his new Christian life from the baptismal font, the illuminators shrewdly recall the metaphor of the container used by the father to deny the possibility of the Incarnation. Christian exegesis offers numerous comparisons between the birth of Christ from Mary's womb and the spiritual rebirth of Christians in baptism. Leo the Great, for instance, develops this analogy in his Christmas homilies (*In Nativitate Domini IV*): "And for every man coming to a rebirth, the water of baptism is an image of the virginal womb whereby the same Holy Spirit who also impregnated the Virgin [likewise] impregnates the font; just as the sacred conception casts out sin in that place, so here mystic ablution takes it away."[24]

In the section devoted to baptism in one of the editions of Alfonso X's law code *Siete Partidas* (Partida I, Tit. IV, law XVII), we find a suggestive passage expanding on this analogy, underscoring the creation of new lineage under the grace of God: "With the holy water, the sacred font becomes pregnant with a new uncorrupted creature. Therefore those who enter in it will be remade as part of a celestial lineage. So the baptismal font, which is like a mother, produces children under the grace of that lineage."[25] In conclusion, in their departure from the text, the illuminators have transformed the boy, who in the literary version of this *cantiga* is just a pawn in a cautionary tale addressed to Jews, into the real protagonist of the story, offering us the edifying tale of how he was saved from his father's murderous rage by Christian intervention and finally cleansed from his tainted heritage through baptism.

The image of the Jewish boy being reborn into Christianity from a container that symbolizes Mary's womb becomes the most startling iconographic creation of another story retold in *cantiga* 4 and illustrated on fol. 9v of the *Códice rico* (Figure 4.9), which also centers on the theme of the murderous Jewish father. A widely disseminated miracle in the Marian repertoire, this is the tale of the son of a Jewish glassmaker who is accustomed to attending a school with Christian children and "won such favor with the other boys with whom he studied that he was accepted into their group."[26] On Easter Sunday, having ventured into a church where his friends were to participate in the Eucharist, the boy was transfixed by the beauty of the image of the Virgin, who miraculously "stretched out Her hand to him and gave him the communion, which tasted sweeter than honey." When the child told his parents what had happened, the enraged father shoved him into the oven used for making glass. Alerted by the mother's cries of despair, a crowd entered the house to find the boy alive inside the oven, sheltered from the fire by the Virgin. The story ends with the baptism of mother and child and the punishment of the father, who was burned in the fiery furnace. Unlike cantiga 108, where, as we have seen, the baptism of the Jewish boy is not mentioned in the text but is prominently featured in the illuminations, in this *cantiga*, the baptism of Jewish mother and child is referred to in the text but absent from the visual narrative, which culminates, instead, with the burning of the father. This ostensible absence seems surprising if we take into account that the staging of baptism is one of the most recurrent images in stories of conversion throughout the *Cantigas*. However, the absence is only apparent because the miraculous rebirth of the Jewish boy to Christianity is still centrally displayed in an image that constitutes the metaphorical equivalent of the scene of baptism in *cantiga* 108. Panel 5 offers us the vivid illustration of the moment in which the Jewish boy is being pulled out of the oven, emerging from the womb of the Virgin, to be embraced by the Christian community. The

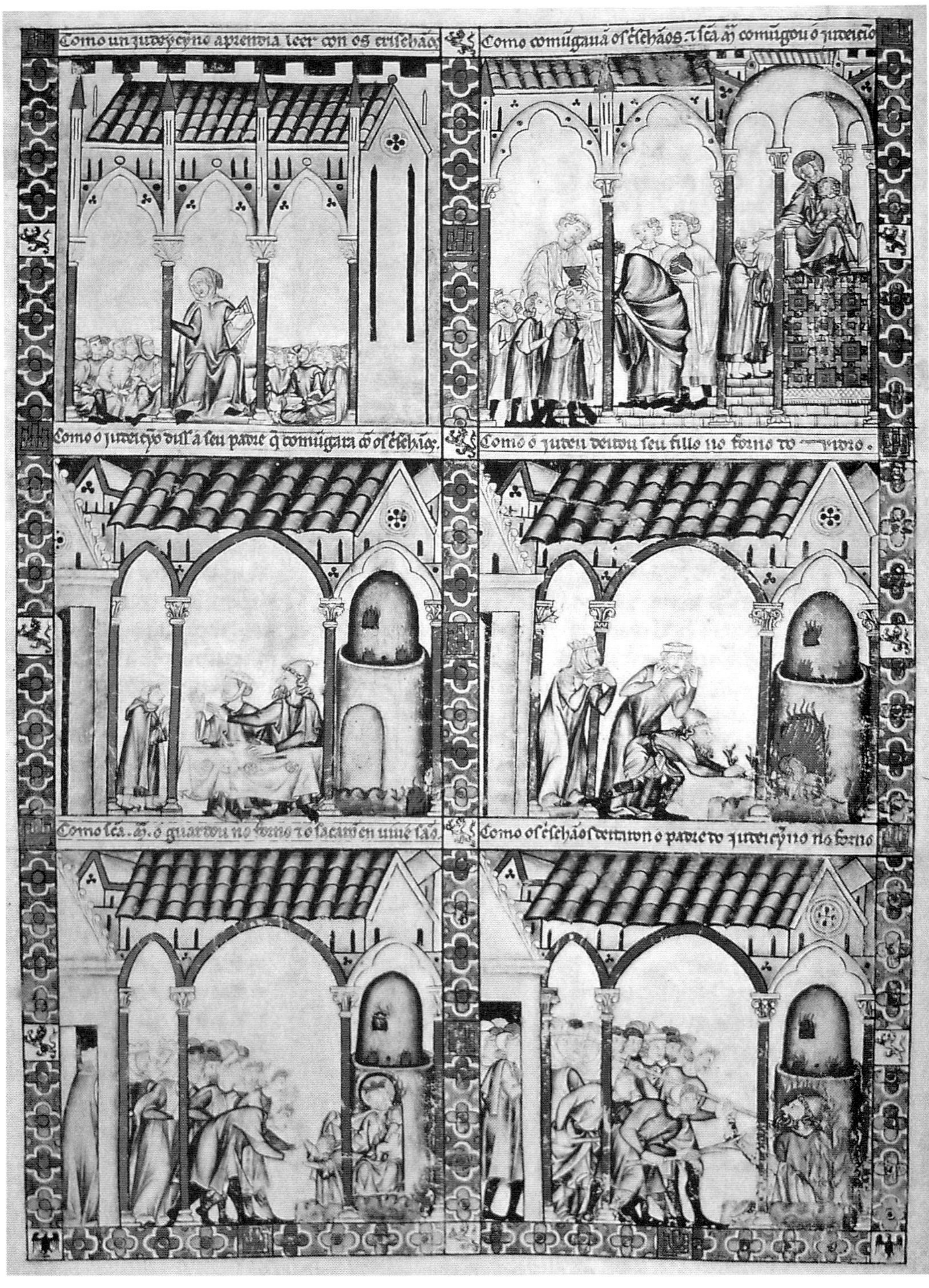

4.9. *Cantigas de Santa María*, Escorial, Biblioteca del Real Monasterio, MS. T.I.1, fol. 9v. Photo courtesy Edilán.

glassblowing oven where the boy's Christian identity "crystallizes" comes to symbolize, like the baptismal font in *cantiga* 108, Mary's womb—the sacred container where he is remade and restored to life in the image of Jesus. Medieval exegesis and iconography furnish numerous examples of the use of the image of the hearth oven as a symbol of Mary's womb. Relevant to our present discussion are the miniatures illustrating Leviticus 2:4 and its exegetical commentary in the Toledo *Bible moralisée* (Cathedral of Toledo, MS. 1, fol. 53v)—a manuscript that was in Alfonso's possession (Figure 4.10).[27] A roundel featuring a group of Jews placing sacrificial loaves into an oven—similar in shape to the one that appears in the *Cantigas*—illustrates the biblical passage, while the exegetical commentary is illustrated below by an "Annunciation" interpolated with the figure of Jesus being held between Gabriel and Mary. The captions explain the pairing: "The sons of Israel made bread, put it in the oven, took it out and offer it to the Lord / This signifies that God placed his son in the virginal womb; and when they offered the bread signifies that Jesus was offered to the temple by his parents."[28] The image in the *Cantigas* merges the two roundels from the *Bible moralisée*, showing the Virgin holding Jesus inside the oven as she begets the Jewish boy to life.

Like the image of the boy in the baptismal font, which was added by the illuminators in *cantiga* 108 in order to reframe the theme of the story, the scene of the boy emerging from the oven similarly allows us to realize that what is fundamentally at stake in *cantiga* 4 is not the explicit theme of the Eucharist as a sacrament but, rather, its core meaning in the context of the transformative bio-theology of the Incarnation, that is, its potential as a mechanism to "imagine" and promote the conversion of Jewish bodies following the type of Jesus himself, born from the womb of a Jewish woman. To be sure, the child's partaking of the body of Christ in the communion early in the story, that is, his incorporation of Jesus, prepares the way for his own corporeal transformation, renewal, and rebirth to Christianity. This Christomimetic symbolism is reinforced in the text of the *cantiga* where we are informed that the boy was called Abel, a reference to Christ's own biblical forerunner in Genesis, killed by Cain, who is, in turn, a type for the wandering Jew in medieval antisemitic literature.[29] The story's outcome, brilliantly visualized by the pairing of the last two panels where the oven becomes the site for both the rebirth of the child and the demise of the father, underscores the contrast between what I call *iudeus sacer*, the Jew excluded from his community and reborn to a new life out of the womb of the Virgin, and the Jewish father, condemned to death for his stubborn attachment to the law. I shall briefly address the question of the genealogy and identity of this modality of Jewish convert that is called into being under the exceptional

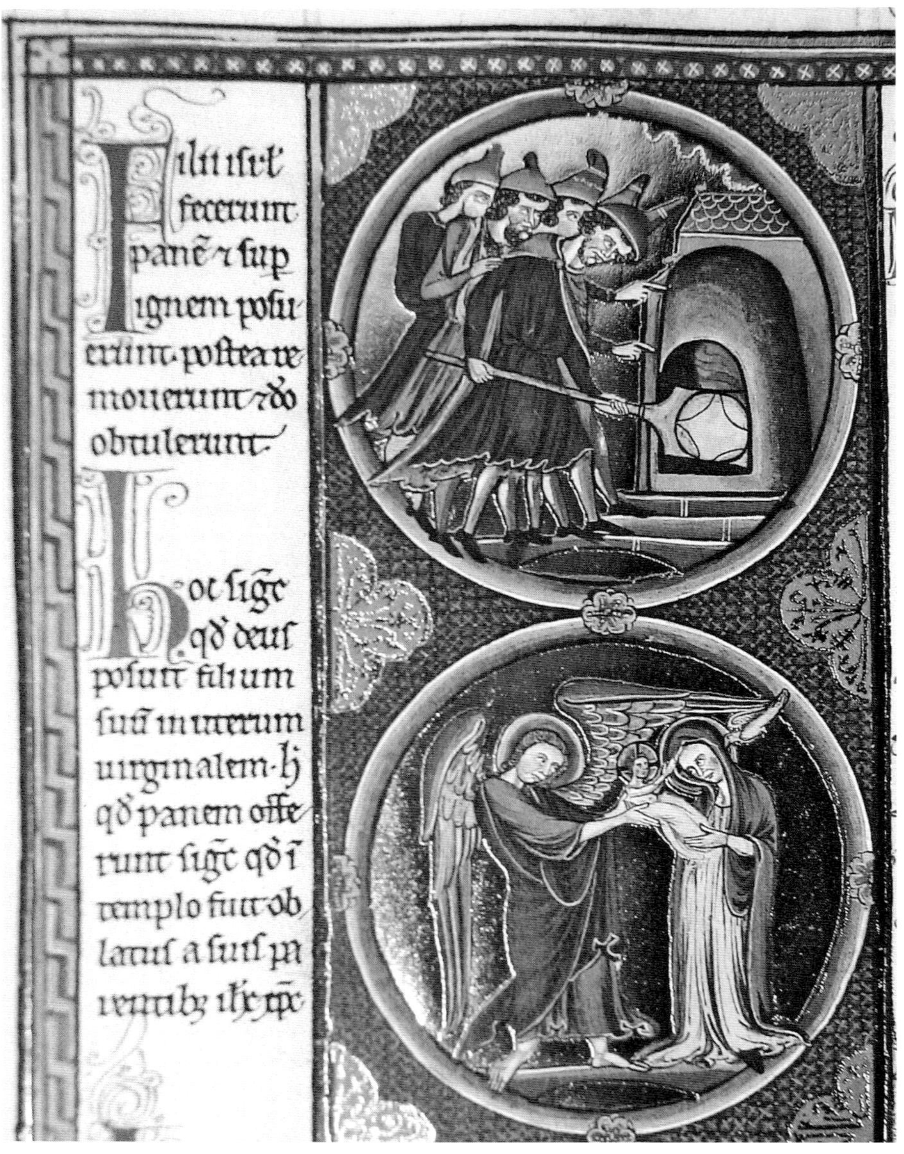

4.10. *Bible moralisée*, Toledo, Cathedral of Toledo, MS. 1, fol. 53v. Photo courtesy Moleiro.

circumstances of the miracle in the *Cantigas*, via a detour into the critical discourse inspired by Giorgio Agamben's inquiry into the biopolitical foundations of sovereignty.[30] This will allow us to frame more clearly the historical relevance of this modality of Jewish convert and situate it within a larger cultural framework.

   FRANCISCO PRADO-VILAR

From the point of view of the Jewish father, the miracle (the boy born with his head backward in *cantiga* 108 and the boy who takes communion from the hand of the Virgin in *cantiga* 4) triggers the state of exception that allows him to suspend the juridical order and reduce his son to the status of *iudeus sacer*, susceptible to be killed with impunity, outside penal law or ritual sacrifice. With his caricaturized features, the Jewish father is, from the Christian perspective, the ultimate embodiment of the law, while the boy is the ultimate form of bare life, effectively *abandoned* by the father and pushed toward a threshold of indistinction, neither Jew nor Christian. As Agamben put it: "He who has been banned is not, in fact, simply set outside the law and made indifferent to it, but rather *abandoned* by it, that is, exposed and threatened on the threshold in which life and law, outside and inside, become indistinguishable."[31] It is critical to understand the ambiguous status into which the Jewish boy is thrown in order to discern more clearly the social and religions implications of the subsequent mode of conversion he will undergo. Abandoned by the father, stripped of his legal status and religious identity, the Jewish boy becomes malleable to change. Indeed, it is in his condition as *iudeus sacer*, that is, in his reduction to bare life, that the Jewish boy becomes susceptible to enter, through the transformative bio-theology of the Incarnation, into the Christian community. As I formulate it here, the term *iudeus sacer*, with its double meaning of excluded and sacred, aims to capture the dialectical status of this figure, which stands at the biological, social, and religious threshold of Jewish and Christian identities. From the point of view of the father/Jewish law, he is *sacer* (accursed) in its negative sense as a figure of exclusion, while from the point of view of the mother/Mary/Christianity, he is *sacer* (sacred) in the positive sense as a sacredly begotten figure. The image of the Jewish boy coming out of the oven/womb into the Christian community dramatizes the transition between *iudeus sacer* in its negative sense and *iudeus sacer* in its positive sense—a transition that is embedded in this new subject's identity as a dynamic reversibility, that is, a constant dialectical movement from one sense of the term to the other. *Iudeus sacer* is a pure figure of potentiality because it is permanently suspended in that unresolved dialectical reversibility at the threshold of Jewish and Christian identities—a dialectical bipolarity that will determine, as we will see, its fleeting historical existence beyond the parchment page.

Creatures of Parchment: The King, the Jew, and the Codex

The figure of *iudeus sacer* portrayed in these illuminations reflects Alfonso X's ideal conception of the converted Jew and finds its existence only in the context of the utopian nation represented in the *Cantigas*. It emerges from the "state of exception" called Marian miracle and exists exclusively on the surface of the parchment. Unlike this ideal *iudeus sacer*, born out of a complete process of corporeal and religious regeneration through the bio-theology of the Incarnation, real Jewish converts (*conversos*) in Castilian society will endure very different conditions, carrying the stains of their heritage inscribed in their bodies. As we leave the thirteenth century and the world of Alfonso X behind, the ideal convert espoused in the *Cantigas* will be further away from actual materialization. "Many Christians," concludes David Nirenberg in his study of the situation brought about by the wave of attacks on Jews and mass conversions of the fourteenth and fifteenth centuries, "considered conversions a disaster that threatened the spiritual health of the entire Christian community. The converts and their descendants were now seen as insincere Christians, as clandestine Jews, or even as hybrid monsters, neither Jew nor Christian. . . . Some of them went as far as to see this insincerity as a product of nature. Baptism could not alter the fact that Jews' blood was corrupted by millennia of mixture and debasement, indelibly saturated with a hatred of everything Christian."[32] Unlike in the fluid world opened up by the state of exception inaugurated by the miracles of the *Cantigas*, blood and lineage became unshakable anchors of identity.[33] However, in the midst of this hardening of social and religious boundaries, we can still detect traces of the genetic constituents of the ideal *iudeus sacer* of Alfonso's project. Indeed, among the arguments brandished by converts against those who attacked them was that the blood of Jesus and Mary ran through their veins.[34] For instance, one of those *conversos* named Aldonza Romeu proudly responded to a stalker, saying that "we come from a better lineage than you do, for we descend from the lineage of the Virgin Mary and you descend from the lineage of the gentiles."[35] In conclusion, the dialectical bipolarity inscribed at a biological level in the identity of *iudeus sacer*, which is portrayed as a positive potential for complete regeneration in the *Cantigas*, will be experienced as a trauma in the actual stage of Castilian society.

The historical drama of Jewish conversion sketched in this discussion is fundamentally played out at the creaturely level. Indeed, it is when we move from the realm of allegory to the realm of creaturality that we can begin to comprehend the matter of Jewish representation in the *Cantigas*—a mode of representation that problematizes the very biological foundations of the issue of Jewish identity in Gothic art. J. L. Lupton's evocative analysis of the concept of *creatura* helps define more clearly the differences I have been drawing between the standard mode of representation of Jews as it appears in works such as the *Bible moralisée*, which is largely anchored in the concept of *figura*,

   FRANCISCO PRADO-VILAR

and the *iudeus sacer* of the *Cantigas,* which contains the essential bio-theological mobility of *creatura*:

> What is a creature? Derived from the future-active participle of the Latin verb *creare* ("to create"), *creature* indicates a made or fashioned thing but with the sense of continued or potential process, action, or emergence built into the future thrust of its active verbal form. Its tense forever imperfect, *creatura* resembles those parallel constructions *natura* and *figura,* in which the determinations conferred by nativity and facticity are nonetheless opened to the possibility of further metamorphosis by the forward drive of the suffix *-ura* ("that which is about to occur"). The *creatura* is a thing always in the process of undergoing creation; the creature is actively passive or, better, passionate, perpetually becoming created, subject to transformation at the behest of the arbitrary commands of an Other. The creature presents above all a theological conceptualization of natural phenomena.[36]

It will not be necessary to discuss in detail here the well-known use of "figura" as an operative principle for the generation of iconographic meaning in the visual apparatus of the *Bible moralisée,* which responds to the typological structure of medieval exegesis—a specular system in which *figurae* from the Old and the New Testaments and historical events are typologically related in form and meaning.[37] As opposed to the textual symbolic specularity of the *Bible moralisée,* the *Cantigas* constitutes an open performative text that connects to perceptual reality through a theatrical conception of mimesis. Consequently, in the signifying system of the *Cantigas,* symbolic and allegorical elements are almost banished from the visual language or realigned into modes of representation that aim at establishing a direct relation to the way meaning is produced in the theater of life. Therefore, while in the *Bible moralisée* characters occupy a fixed symbolic place within the larger system of Christian cosmology—they are *figurae* stating an eternal moment of being—the performative imagery of the *Cantigas* dramatizes the experience of characters undergoing processes of becoming—they are *creaturae* thrown miraculously into the mechanisms of divine remaking. These distinctions underscore some aspects of the "modernity" of the visual language of the *Cantigas* in the context of Gothic art. As I have pointed out elsewhere: "This modernity lies in a radical transformation of Gothic visual language through the redefinition of its central mechanism of visual signification: analogy. Unlike the codified typological structure of the *Bible moralisée,* the *Cantigas* detextualizes the operative principles of analogy and relocates them in the phenomenological domain of vision."[38] Parallel to the detextualization of analogy and its relocation in the domain of vision is the process of detextualization of *figura* and its transformation into *creatura*, that is, the mobilization of traditional symbolic iconographic forms into the domain of creaturality. As Santner has pointed out in his brilliant formulation of this concept, in words that can be adapted to the terms of the present discussion: "What I am calling creaturely life is the life that is, so to speak, called into being, *ex-cited*, by exposure to the peculiar 'creativity' associated with this threshold of law and nonlaw."[39] This threshold, as we have seen, defines/is the space opened up by the "state of exception" called Marian miracle, and it is there where the matter of Jewish representation is played out in the *Cantigas*.

Both these processes, which are essential to the representation of Jews in the *Cantigas*—the detextualizaton of analogy and the transition from *figura* to *creatura* as operative principle in the unfolding of the semiotic structure of the illuminations—appear paradigmatically dramatized in the miniature I have singled out at the beginning of this essay (Figure 4.6). In this scene, the figure of the Jew, being completely absent from the text of the *cantiga*, belongs exclusively to the performative level of the visual narrative. It is in this extratextual performative dimension where the illuminators choose to stage the Jew's process of conversion, presented here as the result of an intimate emotional interaction that occurs in the domain of vision. The object of the Jew's gaze is not Alfonso in his symbolic *figura* as a king but, rather, his dramatic persona at the creaturely level of his existence, reduced to the bareness of his biological life by illness. This empathetic encounter and the resulting miraculous conversion take place at the level of creaturely life, a bio-theological threshold where the Virgin operates as the transformative mechanism for the complete regeneration of the Jew and his conversion into *iudeus sacer*—a creature that was to be condemned to dwell perpetually in the realm of the potential, remaining just a scribbled form, drawn with a pen upon a parchment inside the codex of the *Cantigas* and ultimately consumed in the fires of intolerance.

NOTES

1. For the historical background of these events, see J. F. O'Callaghan, *Alfonso X and the Cantigas de Santa María: A Poetic Biography* (Leiden: Brill, 1998), 126–51. For a diagnosis of Alfonso's illness, using documentary and forensic evidence, see M. Presilla, "The Image of Death and Political Ideology in the *Cantigas de Santa María*," in *Studies on the Cantigas de Santa María*, ed. I. J. Katz and J. E. Keller (Madison: Hispanic Seminary of Medieval Studies, 1987), 403–57, esp. 436–39, where this scholar argues that Alfonso probably suffered from a squamous cell carcinoma of the maxillary antrum—a slow-growing cancer that had a disfiguring effect on his face, causing, among other things, the protrusion of the eyeball due to the pressure from the accumulation of liquid in the sinus, partial deafness, and unilateral facial paralysis. She interprets the monarch's miraculous cures as episodes of remission, which are consistent with the prognosis of this disease—patients may live for periods of up to seven

     FRANCISCO PRADO-VILAR

years without therapy. For an account of Alfonso's imperial quest, see C. J. Socarras, *Alfonso X of Castile: A Study on Imperialistic Frustration* (Barcelona: Ediciones Hispam, 1976).

2. For Jewish officials at the court of Alfonso X, see Yitzhak Baer, *A History of the Jews in Christian Spain*, 2 vols. (Philadelphia: Jewish Publication Society of America, 1961), vol. 1, 120–29.

3. For an introduction to the figure of Yehuda and his corpus of scientific translations, see N. Roth, "Jewish Collaborators in Alfonso's Scientific Work," in *Emperor of Culture: Alfonso X the Learned of Castile and His Thirteenth-Century Renaissance*, ed. R. I. Burns (Philadelphia: University of Pennsylvania Press, 1990), 59–71, esp. 60–66. For a more extensive study of this character, see G. Hilty, *El libro Conplido en los Iudizios de las Estrellas. Partes 6 a 8* (Zaragoza: Instituto de Estudios Islámicos y del Oriente Próximo, 2005).

4. English translation in Evelyn Procter, 'The Scientific Works of the Court of Alfonso X of Castile: The King and His Collaborators," *Modern Language Review* 40 (1945): 12–29, esp. 19.

5. The facsimile edition is Alfonso X el Sabio, *El primer Lapidario de Alfonso X el Sabio. Ms. h.I.15 de la Biblioteca de El Escorial* (Madrid: Edilán, 1982). For a study of the illuminations, see A. Domínguez Rodríguez, *Astrología y arte en el Lapidario de Alfonso X el Sabio* (Madrid: Edilán, 1984).

6. For an extended study of the theory of divine emanation as an unifying principle informing the epistemology and praxis of the power of images reflected in the ambitious editorial projects carried out by the royal *scriptoria* in the last decade of Alfonso's life, ranging from the *Cantigas de Santa María,* to the illuminated lapidaries, astromagical, and astrological manuscripts, see F. Prado-Vilar, "Sombras en el Palacio de las Horas: Arte, Magia, Ciencia y la Búsqueda de la Felicidad," in *Alfonso X el Sabio,* ed. I. G. Bango Torviso (Murcia: Caja de Ahorros del Mediterráneo, 2009), 448–55

7. For an introduction to the manuscripts of the *Cantigas* and basic questions of dating, structure, and authorship, see O'Callaghan, *Alfonso X and the Cantigas,* 1–13. For a recent study of the original locations and historical fortune of the manuscripts, see L. Fernández Fernández, "Cantigas de Santa María: fortuna de sus manuscritos," *Alcanate* 6 (2009): 323–48, where this scholar has conducted important historical and codicological research of the large corpus of Alfonsine manuscripts. Her dissertation "Los manuscritos científicos del *scriptorium* de Alfonso X: estudio codicológico y artístico", presented at the Universidad Complutense in Madrid in March 2010, sheds new light on the intricacies of the Alfonsine workshops.

8. This manuscript, now in Florence (Biblioteca Nazionale Centrale, MS. Banco Rari 20), was left unfinished at the king's death. It was conceived as the second volume of a single fully illustrated luxury edition of the *Cantigas* produced between 1275 and 1284, whose first volume is MS. T.I.1 of the Biblioteca del Real Monasterio de El Escorial, commonly known as the *Códice Rico.* Both are available in facsimile editions: Alfonso X el Sabio, *Cantigas de Santa María. Edición* Alfonso X el Sabio, *Cantigas de Santa María. Edición facsímil del Códice T.I.1 de la Biblioteca de San Lorenzo de El Escorial. Siglo XIII,* 2 vols. (Madrid: Edilán, 1979); and Alfonso X el Sabio, *Cantigas de Santa María. Edición facsímil del códice B.R. 20 de la Biblioteca Centrale de Florencia, siglo XIII,* 2 vols. (Madrid: Edilán, 1989).

9. The standard edition of the *Cantigas* is W. Mettmann, *Cantigas de Santa María,* 3 vols. (Madrid: Castalia, 1986–89). This and subsequent English quotations are taken, with minor adjustments, from the prose translation by K. Kulp-Hill in *Songs of Holy Mary of Alfonso X, the Wise* (Tempe: Arizona Center for Medieval and Renaissance Studies, 2000), 251.

10. The scene of the Montpellier illness belongs to the illustrations of cantiga 235, which covers more extensively events from the crucial period from 1269 to 1278—a decade that was

punctuated, as mentioned above, by physical and psychological pain, personal loss, and political betrayal. For the historical circumstances surrounding this cantiga, see R. P. Kinkade, "Alfonso X, *Cantiga* 235, and the Events of 1269–1278," *Speculum* 67.2 (1992): 284–323.

11. "We prohibit any Christian from receiving medicines or cathartics made by a Jew, although he may obtain it on the advice of a knowledgeable Jew, as long as it is prepared by a Christian fully aware of its contents" (Partida VII, Tit. XXIV, law 8), see D. E. Carpenter, *Alfonso X and the Jews: An Edition of and Commentary on Siete Partidas 7.24 "De los judíos"* (Berkeley: University of California Press, 1986), 34. For an English translation of the *Siete Partidas*, see S. Parsons Scott, trans., *Las siete partidas*, ed. Robert I. Burns, 5 vols. (Philadelphia: University of Pennsylvania Press, 2001).

12. Abraham Ibn Waqar became personal physician and friend of Alfonso's son, Sancho IV, and, according to Don Juan Manuel, was present at his deathbed; see Don Juan Manuel, "Tratado sobre las armas," in *Biblioteca de autores españoles* (Madrid: M. Rivadeneyra, 1846–80), series 1, vol. 51, p. 262; and A. Giménez Soler, *Don Juan Manuel, biografía y estudio crítico* (Zaragoza: Tip. La Academia, 1932), 688. The scene of Abraham Ibn Waqar by the deathbed of Sancho IV constitutes an evocative historico-literary parallel for the intimate relation between Alfonso and the Jewish physician represented in the Vitoria miniatures.

13. The basic general study of the Jews in the *Cantigas* is A. I. Bagby, "The Jew in the *Cantigas* of Alfonso X, el Sabio," *Speculum* 46 (1971): 670–88, whose views regarding the levels of antisemitism displayed in the miniatures should be balanced by those of V. Hatton and A. Mackay, "Anti-Semitism in the *Cantigas de Santa Maria*," *Bulletin of Hispanic Studies* 61 (1983): 189–99. Subsequent studies up to the present add practically nothing of substance to the debate and are, for the most part, characterized by contextualization and taxonomy. In this category, among the most recent are H. Salvador Martínez, *La convivencia en la España del siglo XIII. Perspectivas alfonsíes* (Madrid: Ediciones Polifemo, 2006), 233–39; P. Rodríguez Barral, "La dialéctica texto-imágen a propósito de la representación del judío en las *Cantigas de Santa María* de Alfonso X," *Anuario de Estudios Medievales (AEM)* 37.1 (2007): 213–43; P. K. Klein, "Moros y judíos en las 'Cantigas' de Alfonso el Sabio: Imágenes de conflictos distintos," in *El Legado de al-Andalus. Simposio Internacional: El arte andalusí en los reinos de León y Castilla durante la Edad Media* (Valladolid: Fundación del Patrimonio Histórico de Castilla y León, 2007), 341–64; and P. K. Klein, "Der Ausdruck unterscheidlicher Konflikte in der Darstellung der Juden und Mauren in den 'Cantigas' Alfons des Weisen von Kastilien und León," in *Bereit zum Konflikt: Strategien und Medien der Konflikterzeugung und Konfliktbewältigung im europäischen Mittelalter*, ed. O. Auge, F. Biermann, M. Müller, and D. Schultze (Osfildern: Thorbecke Vlg., 2008), 67–86. My 2005 article "The Gothic Anamorphic Gaze: Regarding the Worth of Others," in *Under the Influence: Questioning the Comparative in Medieval Castile*, ed. C. Robinson and L. Rouhi (Leiden: E. J. Brill, 2005), 67–100, was partly directed as a theoretical intervention to break with this succession of derivative studies and underscore the necessity to develop a sophisticated epistemology of the visual that captures the meanings generated at the points of disjunction between text and image. That article, whose general implications for the study of these issues, and other more general questions of representation in medieval art, are yet to be fully explored, provides the background for my present inquiry.

14. Gautier de Coincy's *Les miracles de Nostre-Dame* is notoriously vicious in its attacks on Jews, even within the standards of a traditionally anti-Jewish genre such as Marian miracle collections; see M. Rubin, *Gentile Tales: The Narrative Assault on Late Medieval Jews* (New Haven, Conn.: Yale University Press, 1999). For the *Bible moralisée*, see Sara Lipton, *Images of Intolerance: The Representation of Jews and Judaism in the Bible moralisée* (Berkeley: University of California Press, 1999).

15. Another structural reason for the accumulation of anti-Jewish stories at the beginning of the collection is related to its authorial genealogy. The manuscript opens with Alfonso's exhortation to troubadours to imitate his example and put their poetic gifts in the service of the Virgin, the only lady who never disavows her suitors. This is followed by a *cantiga de loor* (song of praise) celebrating the seven virtues of Mary as a preamble to the first narrative *cantiga* proper, which is dedicated to the life of Ildefonsus of Toledo—the seventh-century bishop of the Spanish Visigothic church who wrote the famous treatise *De perpetua virginitate Mariae contra tres infideles*, defending the virginity of Mary against two heretics (Jovianus and Helvidius) and a Jew. For being Alfonso's namesake and a doctor of the Spanish church, Ildefonsus's story provides the appropriate opening to the collection, offering the historical antecedent, model, and parallel for Alfonso's new pious poetic persona. After this miracle, and for the sake of thematic unity continuing with the subject of Ildefonsus's treatise, the compilers clustered some of the most famous Marian miracles related to Jews who negate the virginity of Mary: the popular Marian miracle of the story of Theophilus; the story of the Jew who killed a child because he sang the *Gaudeo maria* in honor of the Virgin; and the story of the Jew who killed his son because he participated in the Eucharist. The miracle of Theophilus has been recently studied by P. Patton in an article where the author, reflecting a tendency that has become endemic to the academic industry generated around the *Cantigas,* tries to stake out claims to originality in the "discovery" of the differences between text and image, even if pursued therein in rather simplistic terms, by selectively overlooking previous literature in which those issues have been treated at length from a more challenging theoretical perspective; P. Patton, "Constructing the Inimical Jew in the *Cantigas de Santa María*: Theophilus's Magician in Text and Image," in *Beyond the Yellow Badge: Anti-Judaism and Antisemitism in Medieval and Early Modern Visual Culture*, ed. M. B. Merback (Leiden: E. J. Brill, 2008), 233–56.

16. For the adaptation of *extimacy*, a notion originating in Lacanian psychoanalysis, as a critical term whose semantic field helps describe the complex dynamics of identity and alterity generated at the fissures between the textual and the visual in the *Cantigas,* see Prado-Vilar, "The Gothic Anamorphic Gaze," 69–70.

17. In what follows, I provide an overview of examples relating conversions of Muslims, which I have discussed more extensively in "The Gothic Anamorphic Gaze."

18. Illustration in ibid., fig. 4.

19. Illustration in ibid., figs. 1 and 2.

20. For the textual sources and background for this *cantiga,* see D. E. Carpenter, "A Sorcerer Defends the Virgin: Merlin in the *Cantigas de Santa Maria*," *Bulletin of the Cantigueiros de Santa Maria* 5 (1993): 3–24. The Jew's contentions against the Incarnation reflect actual arguments developed in the context of Christian-Jewish polemics; see D. J. Lasker, *Jewish Philosophical Polemics against Christianity in the Middle Ages* (New York: Ktav, 1977), 105–34.

21. The analysis of this miniature by a deft student of Gothic art, Sara Lipton, in "Where Are the Gothic Jewish Women? On the Non-iconography of the Jewess in the *Cantigas de Santa María*," *Jewish History* 22 (2008): 139–77, is, however, symptomatic of the dangers of trying to approach the art of the *Cantigas* by applying paradigms developed for the study of Northern manuscript illumination. Her long discussion of the symbolic disjuncture of the architectural setting in relation to the figures of the Jew and Merlin, and of the textual and visual precedents and parallels for the nose and hat of the former, shows a semiotic anxiety that is completely alien to the artistic sensibility and intentions of the illuminators of the *Cantigas.* In fact, in this miniature, they are just quite naturalistically representing a typical Spanish thirteenth-century parish church viewed from its southern flank. From left to right

we see the western façade with its portal and tower, followed by a nave whose exterior wall carries an arcade opening onto the street to provide space for stores, and finally ending with a view of its eastern chapel adorned with a polylobed window and covered by a gabled roof. It is not at the level of iconographic symbolism but at the level of theatrical performance, where we find the real genius of the *Cantigas* illuminators and the essential key to the meaning of the scene, and of the miracle at large, that is, the fact that the Jew is pointing to a container. By overlooking this essential aspect and focusing, instead, on cosmetic elements, Lipton's article shows how a problem of method and cultural decontextualization can radically flatten the relevance of the art of the *Cantigas* and reduce it to just another footnote in the homogenizing discourse of Gothic Jewish iconography.

22. Lipton rightly observes that caricaturized Jewish men in the *Cantigas* represent "a biblical or talmudic law that is antiquated, rigid, and unforgiving" as opposed to "Alfonso's merciful, penitential, Marian Christian ideal" ("Where Are the Gothic Jewish Women?," 151).

23. Lipton misses the point of this last panel when she affirms that the person being baptized is the mother of the Jewish boy or one of her "sister Jewish women." She argues that "the convert's face and hair mark her as a female, as does the fact that women stand sponsor for the conversion" ("Where Are the Gothic Jewish Women?," 152 and n. 54). However, the convert's hair and face are more similar to those of the other two male characters in the miniature (the priest and his attendant) than to the women. The convert is, in fact, the blond Jewish boy whose trials and tribulations we have followed in the previous three panels, where he is represented in different phases of his "growth" toward Christianity, from baby to small child to young neophyte in the last scene.

24. Cited in P. A. Underwood, "The Fountain of Life in Manuscripts of the Gospel," *Dumbarton Oaks Papers* 5 (1950): 41–138, esp. 63. These analogies are treated at length in W. M. Bedard, "The Font as Mother or as Womb of the Church," in *The Symbolism of the Baptismal Font in Early Christian Thought* (Washington, D.C.: Catholic University of America Press, 1951), 17–36.

25. For this text, which is absent from the English translation of the *Siete Partidas* cited above, see *Las Siete Partidas del Rey Don Alfonso el Sabio* (Madrid, 1807), 1:66. I am grateful to Rocío Sánchez Ameijeiras for calling my attention to this passage. For the iconography and promotion of baptism in thirteenth-century Gothic monumental portals, see R. Sánchez Ameijeiras, "The Faces of the Voice: Aesthetic Notions and Artistic Practice in 13th-century Gothic," in *Gothic Art and Thought in the Middle Ages: A Conference in Honor of Willibald Sauerländer*, ed. C. Hourihane (Princeton, N.J.: Index of Christian Art, forthcoming).

26. Rubin discusses different versions of this miracle and its illustrations in *Gentile Tales*, 7–28.

27. The first documentary mention of the *Cantigas* occurs in Alfonso's last testament, issued in January 1284. Together with the *Cantigas* manuscripts, Alfonso catalogues, among his most precious possessions, a three-volume illuminated Bible that had been presented to him by his cousin, the King of France, Louis IX. With all certainty, this corresponds to the *Bible moralisée* produced in Paris between 1226 and 1234 and now preserved in the Cathedral of Toledo (MSS. 1–3). See M. González Jiménez, "La Biblia de San Luis en el Testamento de Alfonso X el Sabio de Castilla," in *Biblia de San Luis: Catedral Primada de Toledo* (Barcelona: Moleiro, 2004), 39–58. For an edition of Alfonso's testament, see M. González Jiménez, *Diplomatario Andaluz* (Seville: Caja de Huelva y Sevilla, 1991), 560. For the Toledo *Bible moralisée*, see J. Lowden, *The Making of the Bibles moralisées*, vol. 1 (Philadelphia: University of Pennsylvania Press, 2000), 95–137. The facsimile edition is *Biblia de San Luis*, 3 vols. (Barcelona: Moleiro, 2000–2002).

28. "Filii Israel fecerunt panem et super ignem pusuerunt, postea removerunt et Deo obtulerunt / Hoc significat quod Deus posuit Filium suum in uterum virginalem; hoc quod

panem offerunt significat quod in templo fuit oblatus a suis parentibus Ihesu Christus." For brief analysis of the illustration of this passage in the Oxford *Bible moralisée* and a general discussion of the symbolism of the hearth oven in medieval art, see C. Ferguson O'Meara, "'In the Hearth of the Virginal Womb': The Iconography of the Holocaust in Late Medieval Art," *Art Bulletin* 63.1 (1981): 75–88, esp. 79.

29. See R. Mellinkoff, *The Mark of Cain* (Eugene, Ore.: Wipf and Stock, 2003).

30. Agamben's historico-philosophical inquiry into the relation between life and sovereignty has been very influential in the last decade, opening up a theoretical environment for a fruitful interdisciplinary dialogue around concepts such as *homo sacer*, biopolitics, state of exception, and so on. Agamben takes as his starting point the Roman legal figure of the *homo sacer*, which designates a person who can be killed with impunity but cannot be sacrificed in a religious ritual. The *homo sacer* represents the ultimate form of bare life because it occupies a space of indistinction where human life is devoid of rights or legal protection and is, therefore, subject to the unlimited exertion of power. Following Carl Schmitt, Agamben points out that sovereign power is fundamentally defined by the capacity to create and structure these spaces of indistinction, that is, the capacity to strip human life of its legal rights and reduce it to bare life. The primary mechanism used by sovereign power to create these spaces of indistinction is the state of exception, which effectively brings about a "legal" suspension of the law; see G. Agamben, *Homo Sacer: Sovereign Power and Bare Life*, trans. D. Heller-Roazen (Stanford: Stanford University Press, 1998); and Agamben, *State of Exception*, trans. K. Attell (Chicago: University of Chicago Press, 2005). It is not the purpose of this paper to discuss Agamben's work in depth nor do I intend strictly to anchor my use of the critical terminology I draw from it to the specific meaning it acquires in the context of his philosophical project. I consider that the disadvantages that some readers, expecting a tighter theoretical alignment, might find in this adaptation, are far outweighed by its hermeneutic value for this particular study, allowing me to articulate fundamental aspects of the representation of the Jews in the *Cantigas*, which would otherwise remain absent from the historical record. In the same vein, I also refer to the analogy famously drawn by Carl Schmitt between the notion of state of exception and the theological notion of the miracle, as part of his well-known thesis that political concepts are "secularized" theological ideas. Schmitt's analogy has been recently put in a larger ethico-political perspective by E. Santner, "Miracles Happen: Benjamin, Rosenzweig, Freud, and the Matter of the Neighbor," in *The Neighbor, Three Inquiries in Political Theology*, ed. S. Zizek, E. Santner, and K. Reinhard (Chicago: University of Chicago Press, 2005), 76–133.

31. Agamben, *Homo Sacer*, 28.

32. D. Nirenberg, "Conversion, Sex, and Segregation: Jews and Christians in Medieval Spain," *American Historical Review* 107.4 (2002): 1065–93, esp. 1078.

33. Nirenberg describes the historical process by which mass conversions produced a destabilization of traditional categories of religious identity and, as a result, there emerged a new emphasis on lineage and genealogy, which came to function as a "newly meaningful way of thinking about religious identity amongst Christians and Jews alike"; see D. Nirenberg, "Mass Conversion and Genealogical Mentalities: Jews and Christians in Fifteenth-Century Spain," *Past and Present* 174.1 (2002): 3–41, esp. 6.

34. Ibid., 31.

35. Cited in ibid., 32.

36. J. L. Lupton, "Creature Caliban," *Shakespeare Quarterly* 51.1 (2000): 1–23, esp. 1.

37. For the concept of *figura*, see E. Auerbach, "Figura," in *Scenes from the Drama of European Literature* (Manchester: Manchester University Press, 1984), 11–78. For these issues in the *Bible moralisée*, see M. Camille, "The Book of Signs: Writing and Visual Difference in

Gothic Manuscript Illumination," *Word & Image* 1.2 (1985): 133–48; and Camille, "Visual Signs of the Sacred Page: Books in the *Bible moralisée*," *Word & Image* 5 (1989): 111–30.

38. Prado-Vilar, "The Gothic Anamorphic Gaze," 99.

39. E. L. Santner, *On Creaturely Life: Rilke, Benjamin, Sebald* (Chicago: University of Chicago Press, 2006), 15.

CHAPTER 5

Abraham Circumcises Himself:
A Scene at the Endgame of Jewish
Utility to Christian Art

Marcia Kupfer

If one were to schematize the historical relationship between Judaism and Christianity in the form of an Abelardian exercise in *Sic et Non*, the following two perspectives might be set in contention. On the one hand, it can be said that Christianity succeeded by virtue of orchestrating a hostile takeover of its parent religion. To quote Susannah Heschel:

> In the domain of religion, Christianity colonized Judaism theologically, taking over its central theological concepts of the Messiah, eschatology, apocalypticism, election, and Israel, as well as its scriptures, its prophets, and even its God, and denying the continued validity of those ideas for Judaism. Indeed, no other major world religion has colonized the central religious teachings and scriptures of another faith and then denied the continued validity of the other, insisting that is own interpretations are exclusive truth. . . . In colonizing Judaism, Christianity was unable to erase it; Judaism is taken within, becoming the unwilling presence inside the Christian realm, a presence that is deeply troubling and gives rise to a variety of strategies within Christian theology to contain, redefine, and finally, exorcise that presence.[1]

On the other hand, it can also be asserted in counterpoint to this account of usurpation that rabbinic Judaism and Christianity, both offspring of ancient

Israelite religion, were largely co-constructed in parallel during several centuries following the destruction of the Second Temple.[2] Co-optation and neutralization did not proceed in one direction only. Positing ongoing sibling rivalry in the medieval period, Israel Jacob Yuval (among others) argues that Judaism continued to develop its identity through reciprocal negation and selective appropriation of its antagonistic other.[3] Christianity, its hegemony assured, set the agenda, however, while Judaism reacted. Jewish engagement with medieval Christianity—the minority's unavoidable acculturation to the majority environment—ultimately produced a shared ritual "language" operating within a common framework of sacred time and space.[4]

My purpose here is not the dialectical resolution of the colonialist and dialogic paradigms, nor do I aim to delineate their complementarity. Clearly, they each obtain given certain parameters and in their respective spheres of application. Rather, I wish to tack between these two paradigms as I consider at one end of the spectrum the Jew's involuntary utility to medieval Christian art and, at the other, artistic interaction across religious lines.[5]

My investigation juxtaposes material from late fourteenth-century France and fifteenth-century Spain, societies that, however different their histories, each stood at a crossroads with respect to the place accorded to Jews. Charles V of France, while still dauphin and regent, had by 1359 reversed decades of royal policy in order to readmit Jews to the crown territories. His decision is conventionally attributed to the need for cash to ransom his father, Jean le Bon, taken prisoner by the English at the battle of Poitiers in September 1356; the king returned from captivity on October 25, 1360. Religious privileges negotiated by the dauphin, subsequently confirmed by Jean le Bon in March 1361, and renewed again during Charles's own reign (1364–80) guaranteed the basics of Jewish life, though communities were minuscule in comparison with those before the expulsion of 1306.[6] In the Spanish kingdoms, Jewish communities decimated by the pogroms of 1391 and the Tortosa Disputation of 1413–14 began a modest recovery thanks to a reversal of political fortune.[7] The demise of the anti-Jewish triumvirate Fernando I of Aragon (died 1416), his compatriot Pope Benedict XIII (deposed 1417), and not least St. Vincent Ferrer (died 1419), together with the election of Pope Martin V, allowed new rulers—Alfonso IV in Aragon and on his majority in 1420 the Castilian king Juan II—to revert to a tradition of limited toleration and protection.

It was Augustine of Hippo who had long before articulated the theological rationale governing the status of Jews in Christian polities.[8] Likening the Jews to librarians, slaves who carry the schoolboy's books, or desks on which books rest, Augustine characterized the Jews as antique witnesses to the truth of the scriptural foundations of Christianity. He advocated sufferance of their continued existence and religious practice provided that the church benefits from their custodial and testimonial functions. Ecclesiastical forbearance of the Jews, conditional upon their degradation and subjugation, safeguarded their legal presence in Christendom. In both the French and Spanish arenas, the attempted return to the old Augustinian order coincided with a cultural undertaking that heralded and legitimated it.[9] At the very outset, the highest-ranking Christian patrons compelled Jews either to finance (in France) or actually produce (in Spain) sumptuously illustrated, vernacular bibles. By recruiting Hebrew Scripture and, with it, rabbinic patrimony to trumpet affirmation of Christian truth, rulers sought not merely to enhance their stature but also vindicate their reliance on and protection of Jews.

The French Bible of Jean de Sy (from c. 1361) and the Castilian Alba Bible (1422–31) staged Augustine's repeated characterization of the Jews as book-bearers for Christian masters. Part 1 of my study traces the contours of a distinctive tradition of ritual humiliation to which both bibles belonged. What makes Alba especially intriguing is the unique record it preserves of how a rabbi coped with his prescribed role in the commission. It is against the norm of Jewish servitude to the enterprise of Christian art that, in part 2, I explore the rabbi's creative engagement with iconography supplied by the Franciscan censor under whose direction he labored. The exceedingly rare scene of Abraham's circumcision, found exclusively in Christian productions like the Jean de Sy Bible, inspired in Alba a midrashic and kabbalistic response. The concluding section considers the Jewish dimension of the Alba Bible through the prism of its sponsors' Christian goals.

The Jews' Obligation

A single manuscript in Paris, itself unfinished and fragmentary, is all that survives of the ambitious, multi-volume Bible of Jean de Sy (BnF, MS fr 15397).[10] Jean le Bon had initiated the project before his misadventure at Poitiers, commissioning from the Dominican Jean de Sy a vernacular translation of scripture replete with extensive gloss. Composition of the text was well underway by 1355 and 1356, dates indicated in the commentary on two successive folios of the fair copy. Presumably the king's captivity interrupted progress on the manuscript, illustrated only as far as the first six gatherings with many of some forty scenes left merely sketched.

The project must have recommenced after Jean's return, however, for in his 1373 inventory of books in Charles V's library at the Louvre Gilles Malet mentioned two volumes as well as an additional sixty-two unbound quires. The 1373 inventory survives in a paper copy executed by Jean Blanchet for the Chambre des comptes in November 1380 (shortly after Charles's death). Blanchet concurrently prepared a second copy in the form of a parchment scroll for the personal possession of Charles VI, which he delivered to the new king along with the library keys.[11] The scroll includes a phrase, appended to the entry on the unbound quires, revealing that writing had continued at the expense of the Jews.[12] Notwithstanding the bible's commission a few years before the repatriation of the Jews (and its eventual completion more than twenty years after their expulsion), the remark indicates that Jean le Bon or, more probably, Charles V, architect of the policy, had associated renewed production with their recent arrival. The requirement that the Jews subsidize the bible demonstrated their compliance with the Augustinian bargain: insofar as they performed their service to the sacred page, they merited royal toleration. The same argument in defense of Charles's Jewish policy found literary expression in *Le songe du vergier*, written by an anonymous court official first in Latin between 1374 and 1376 and translated into French in 1378.[13]

The Jews' obligation with respect to the Bible of Jean de Sy sheds light, I believe, on the Alba Bible. The powerful Luis de Guzmán, grand master of the military order of Calatrava, commanded Rabbi Moses Arragel of Guadalajara to produce this richly illustrated, Castilian translation of Hebrew Scripture. Between prefatory scenes of Guzmán commissioning and ceremoniously receiving the work (Figures 5.1, 5.2), the image of Arragel touching the feet of Juan II (Figure 5.3) frames the project as a service to the kingdom of Castile.

Sonia Fellous—whose monumental study of the Spanish manuscript makes possible any insight I might contribute—no doubt rightly connects the impulse behind the commission to changes in royal and papal policy that, from the early 1420s, revitalized devastated Jewish communities.[14] It is her characterization of the project's underlying motivation and ostensive function that I would modify. She takes the work to "symbolize the hope of national reconciliation which still animated certain Jews and Christians seventy years before the expulsion."[15] Such an assessment is consistent with the master narrative into which, as Eleazar Gutwirth notes, the Alba Bible has been routinely folded ever since Américo Castro, in 1923, made it the foundation of what he would later famously call *convivencia*.[16] Thus the deluxe 1992 facsimile edition of the manuscript celebrates the work as an abortive attempt to renew the ideals of tolerance, pluralism, and multiculturalism eclipsed in the aftermath of 1391 and finally snuffed out with the expulsion.[17] I propose a more sober reading, one that has the advantage of eliminating the paradox troubling to Gutwirth, that the cornerstone of Castro's *convivencia* appears during the very period in which the model falls apart.[18] In my view, *convivencia*, however construed, is not the relevant

    MARCIA KUPFER

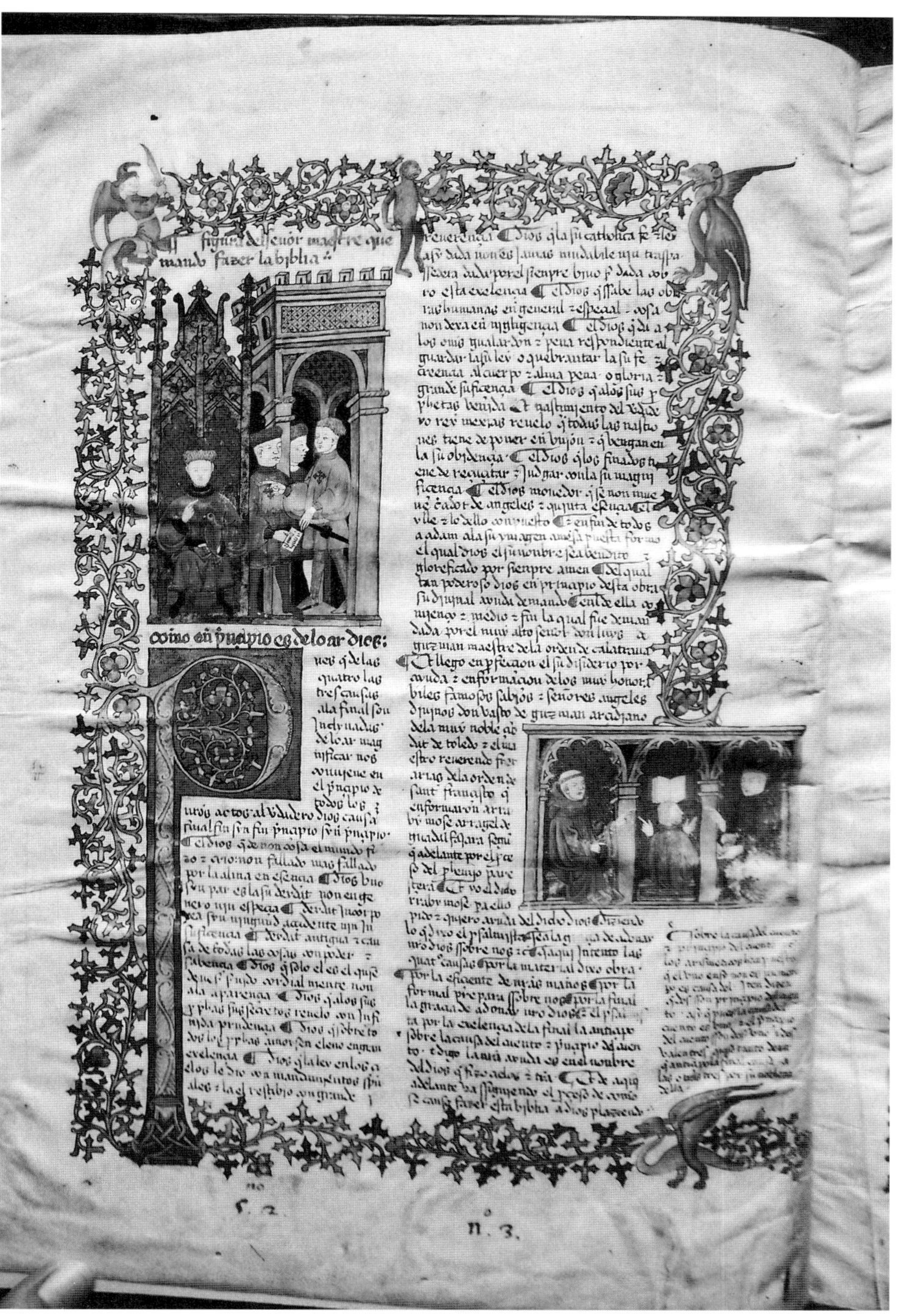

5.1. Alba Bible (Madrid, Palacio de Liria, library of the Duke of Alba, cat. no. 399), 1422–31/33, fol. 1v: Luis de Guzmán sending his letter of commission to Moses Arragel; the rabbi at work between his censors, the Dominican Johan of Zamora and the Franciscan Arias de Enzinas. Photo courtesy Felipe Pereda.

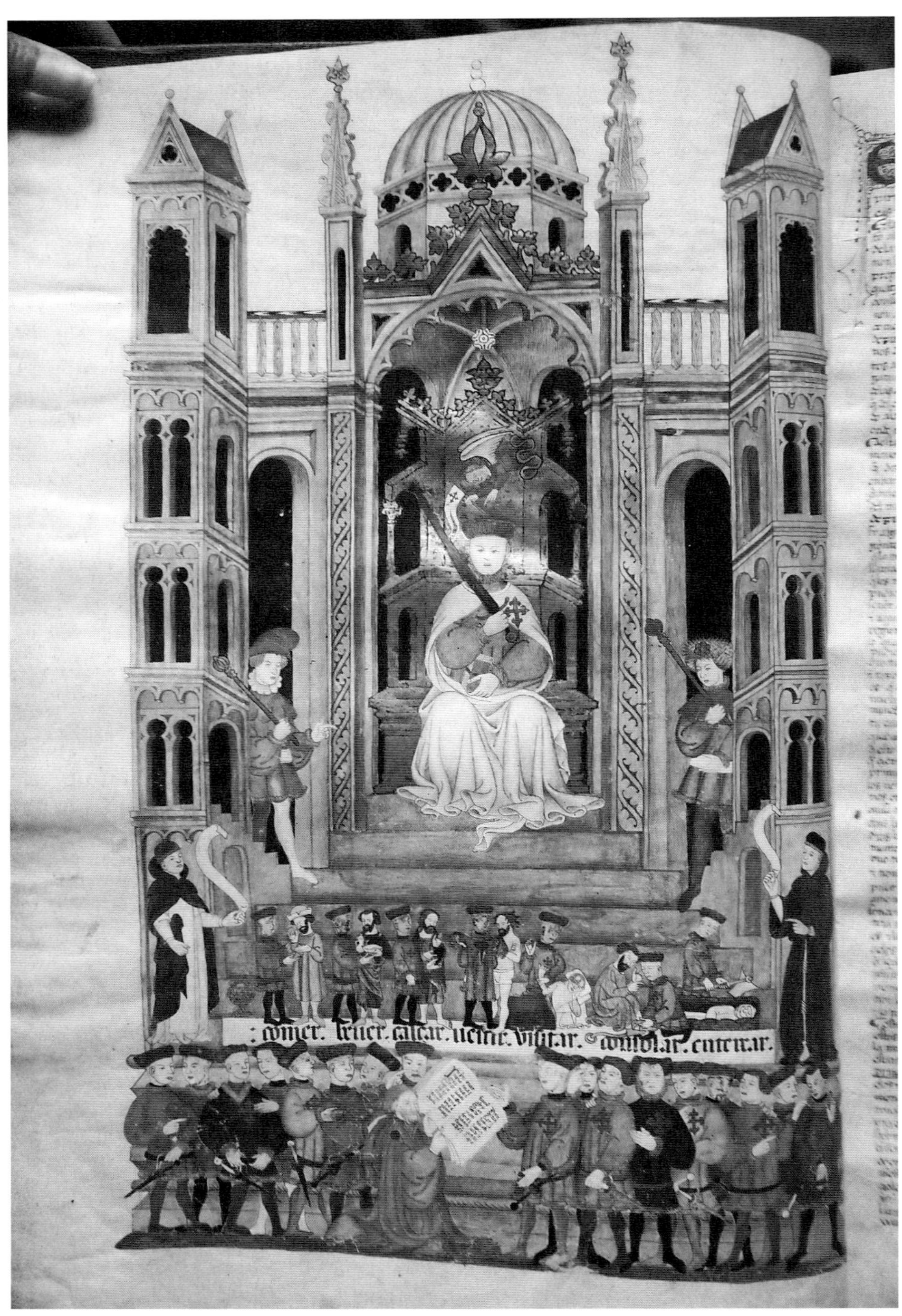

5.2. Alba Bible, fol. 25v: Rabbi Moses Arragel's presentation of the commissioned manuscript to Luis de Guzmán, grand master of the military order of Calatrava. Photo courtesy Felipe Pereda.

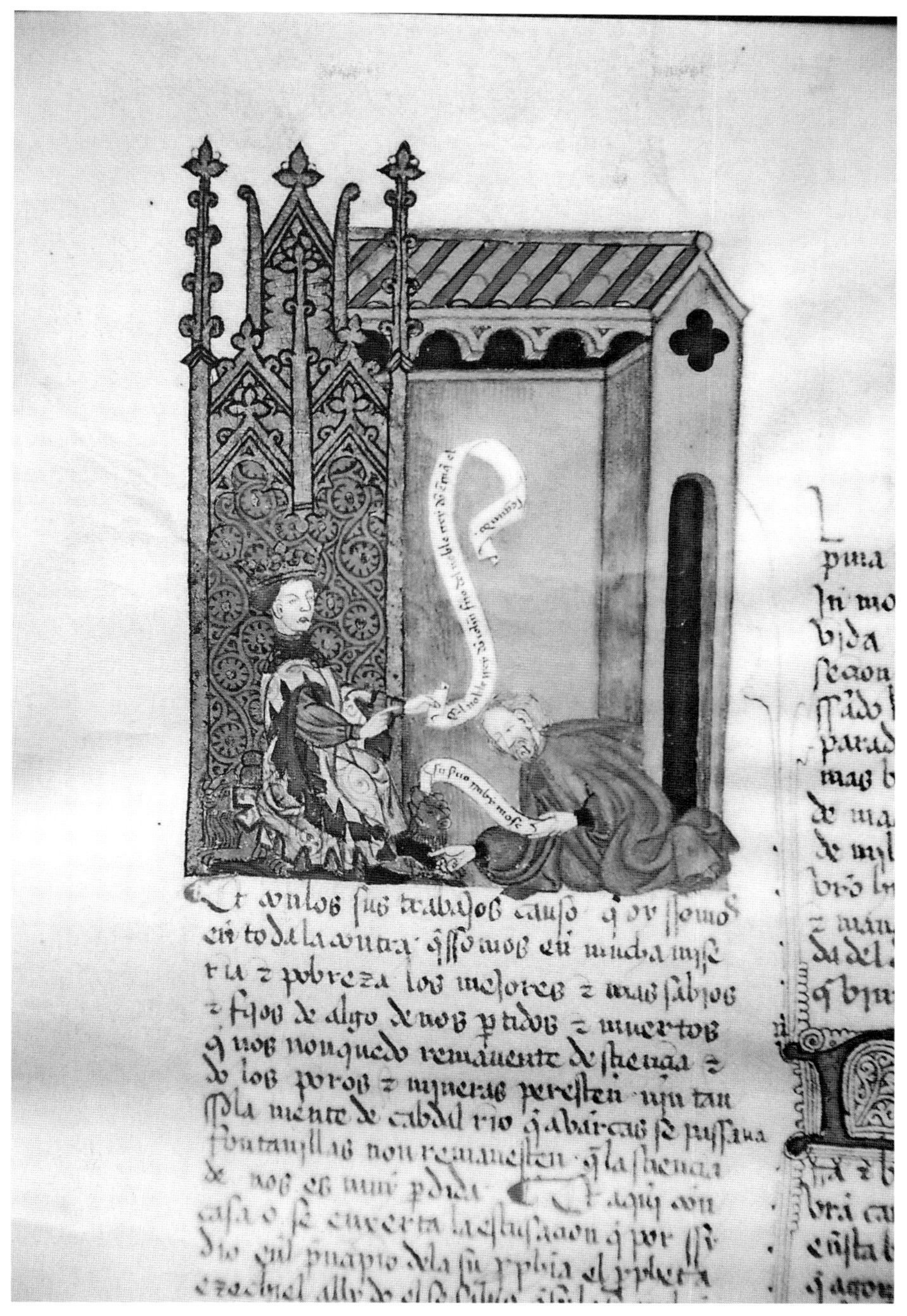

5.3. Alba Bible, fol. 11r: Arragel touching the feet of King Juan II of Castile. Photo courtesy Felipe Pereda.

explanatory framework for the bible's origin.[19] Rather, the commission symbolized, and advertised, Jewish subservience to Christian overlords in strict accordance with the Augustinian doctrine of witness, which it could therefore assert as grounds for détente. I am here building on a point advanced in studies by David Nirenberg and Mark Meyerson, namely that Christian toleration of Jews demanded the visible delineation of their subaltern status in the social hierarchy.[20]

An epistolary exchange between the Christian patron, his intermediaries, and the rabbi, copied into the opening folios of the manuscript (2r–12r), lays out the terms of the commission.[21] Luis de Guzmán, apprised that Arragel had recently settled in his town of Maqueda, welcomed his new vassal and invited the esteemed rabbi to produce a glossed and illustrated bible. The patron here explicitly invoked a theme that can only be inferred in the case of the Bible of Jean de Sy: new arrival, albeit to an established community, triggered the request for a vernacular edition of scripture. Arragel at first demurred, not least because he wanted to avoid having anything to do with the depiction of God in human form. As he well knew, images of Christ were typically retrojected into the "Old Testament." The grand master nevertheless ordered him to begin without delay.

Guzmán's initial letter makes clear that he had already discussed the project with church notables whom he appointed to supervise the effort. The ecclesiastically balanced committee of censors included the archdeacon of nearby Toledo, the superior of the city's Franciscan convent, and a Dominican from the University of Salamanca. The Franciscan, Arias de Enzinas, served as the rabbi's principal interlocutor. Friar Arias, in his letter to Arragel, stipulated that the gloss must include the opinions of modern rabbis neglected by Nicholas of Lyra and, wherever instructed, the exegeses of church doctors.[22] To be precise, Arragel could freely expound on those passages for which Arias did not supply Christian commentary. Echoing the critique of Nicholas by the bishop of Burgos Pablo de Santa Maria (formerly Solomon Halevi, the converted rabbi), Arias's insistence on including the moderns goes to the very heart of the commission.[23] The more comprehensive the rabbinic corpus made available to the church, the greater the hermeneutic and polemical arsenal with which to refute and convert the Jews. The stronger the Christian recuperation of Hebrew exegesis, the more thorough the dispossession of the Jews of their own scriptural heritage. This colonizing agenda had underwritten the trajectory of Christian Hebraism since the mid-twelfth century, governing intensive scrutiny of postbiblical texts (notably Talmud and Kabbalah) and animating, during the fifteenth, missionary and humanist interest in Hebrew materials.[24] On this score, the Alba Bible is no exception.

In each of his two letters, Luis de Guzmán promised the rabbi that he would be handsomely rewarded for his efforts: an annual salary would be forthcoming and his expenses reimbursed.[25] But statements made by both Arragel and Arias on the occasion of the finished bible's public presentation at the Franciscan convent suggest otherwise (fols. 20r–25r). Arragel hoped he would at last be repaid the one thousand *doblas* that he had personally spent on the project over the years.[26] This considerable sum must refer only to the cost of materials and aspects of production that Arragel subcontracted; it in no way covered his own labor as translator/glossator and likely also as scribe, a task he probably shared with his son.[27] Arias, too, acknowledged that compensation had been, and would continue to be, withheld: should the rabbi's work be accepted after the manuscript's careful examination, then he would be worthy of remuneration and the grand master would be so informed.[28] How did Arragel raise the funds to subsidize the decade-long project or find support for time consecrated to it? It seems likely that the Jewish community was obliged to support his effort, in which case the Alba Bible was no less a collective levy on the Jewish community than the Bible of Jean de Sy.

For the rabbi's text to pass ecclesiastical scrutiny, his translation had to take into account the authority accorded to the Vulgate, and his commentary had to incorporate the typologies worked out by the church fathers. The resultant effect fooled the editor of the 1918 and 1920 Roxburghe Club facsimiles of the Alba Bible. Antonio Paz y Melia wondered at the extent to which the Jew's docility led him to declare opinions dictated by his censors, at times speaking in his own voice as a Catholic, for glosses of a "repugnant obscenity" prove that he had been afforded great liberty.[29] The study by Moshe Lazar in the scholarly volume accompanying the 1992 facsimile, not to mention Fellous's 2001 mono-graph, has definitively laid the old charge of Arragel's complacency to rest. In fact, Arragel refused to compromise his self-identification as a Jew. Throughout he repeatedly professed the thirteen articles of faith as codified by Maimonides and sung communally in *piyyutim* such as *Yigdal 'Elohim Ḥai*, the internal rhyme of which he emulated in Spanish prose.[30] Far from acquiescing to the agenda of the bible's sponsors, Arragel took intellectual ownership of the project.

How, then, did the rabbi maintain his religious dignity even as he was required to make public concession to the hegemonic discourse of Christianity? I propose an answer based on James C. Scott's theory of "hidden transcripts."[31] The term encompasses the speech acts and nondiscursive behavior through which subalterns resist their domination. Their expression of a dissonant cul-ture can freely take place only "offstage." Arragel nevertheless maneuvered tex-tually in a manner that brings to mind practices of disguise whereby the

subjugated artfully infiltrate their cause into the public "transcript," the record
that reflects and preserves the officially sanctioned hierarchy. Thanks to ambiguity, indirection, evasion, and dissemblance—the ruses of the trickster typically celebrated in folktales—the powerful either do not discern the message
voiced at their expense or, alternatively, must tacitly concede some ground for
its delivery. The challenge to power can be obfuscated through private insider
language, or framed in terms of the values that the elites advance to justify their
rule; it can be dissipated by low-key gestures or shielded behind double-entendre
and even parodied self-caricature. Arragel's performance in the Alba Bible
belongs to a genre that Daniel Boyarin has wittily called "Brer Rabbi."[32]

Polemic, Rabbi Moses knew, would be futile and self-defeating. But diplo-
macy he could turn to his own advantage. He cleverly finessed discrepancies
between the Hebrew original and Jerome's Latin, giving priority to the former
even as he might draw on the latter to enhance the literary qualities of the
Castilian.[33] Among the classic negotiating strategies he deployed was linguistic
equivocation—contriving a formulation acceptable to opposing sides because
each could read it differently. To assist in this task, he provided a glossary (fols.
15v–19v) through which he appropriated and defused Christian vocabulary.[34] As
Fellous rightly observes, the cumulative effect of recuperating Christian terminology for Jewish purposes is a coded text. For example, Arragel defangs the
adjective "catholic," reviled, he admits, by Jews, so that it means no more than
"perfect, accomplished"; thereafter the phrase *santa fe catolica* consistently designates the Law of Moses, which Israel received on Sinai and to which the other
nations will convert when the Messiah son of David comes.[35] Considering that
the tradition of Christian exegesis familiar to Arragel relentlessly represented its
faith community as *verus Israel*, one has to admire the irony (not to mention
chutzpah) in the return favor.

Not only did Arragel control an impressive array of rabbinic materials. He
systematically placed Jewish exposition on equal footing with the requisite
Christian readings by appealing to the need to explicate straightforwardly the
divergence between the two faith traditions. Cross-references, too, became a
tool for elaborating a Jewish line of interpretation, which if fragmented and
dispersed might more easily elude the censors.[36] Finally, he purposively introduced the word *nascion* in selected contexts, drawing on its newly acquired legal
connotations, to characterize the Jewish people in exile.[37] In the end, Arragel
achieved, to quote Moshe Lazar, "the single most important Bible in any vernacular language produced in the Middle Ages," that is to say, "what could be
termed an 'ecumenical translation and interpretation' of the Hebrew Scriptures"; at the same time, Alba is also "the most Jewish rabbinical Bible in any
vernacular language."[38]

     MARCIA KUPFER

The combination of deference and oblique, understated defiance through which Arragel accomplished this feat comes sharply into focus at the close of his prolegomena, where he sets forth his working method and explains how readers should approach the work (fols. 14v–15).[39] Although Guzmán personally commissioned the bible, Arragel assumes—or at least proceeds by imagining—a wider audience that would comprise Jews as well as Christians. Explicitly addressing his coreligionists, he appeals for their understanding just as he appeals to his patrons for theirs. Thus, concerning passages on which Hebrew and Latin commentators do not conflict, his gloss will reflect the consensus and can be accepted equally by members of the two "nations." In cases where discord exists, he will identify the respective viewpoints. Arragel's next move, however, is key. He admits that he may have at times inadvertently forgotten to signal whether an opinion belongs to one side or the other (there are, after all, some 6,300 glosses by Lazar's count).[40] Consequently, whenever a Christian finds that the gloss contradicts the tenets of his faith, let him take it as a Jewish opinion expressed not to challenge his belief but rather simply to inform; similarly, whenever a Jew finds that the gloss contradicts the tenets of his faith, let him take it as an opinion not of a rabbi but of the Roman church derived from materials given to him by Arias. Neither Christian nor Jew should be misled into error on his account, nor hurl accusations of heresy against his work. "And as I did not but report or bring to mind [various interpretations], it leaves free anyone to believe, argue and defend his own law as much as he can."[41]

For all Arragel's effort to arrive at a text acceptable to both Christians and Jews, for all that he decries mutual misunderstanding to be the source of conflict and violence, it would be a serious mistake to construe the Alba Bible as a model of ecumenicism *avant la lettre*. The rabbi, for his part, was not remotely concerned to invent common religious ground between Christians and Jews, nor bridge the divide between the two faiths by harmonizing them. Quite the contrary, he underscored fundamental and irreconcilable differences, and, insofar as he could manage diplomatically, insisted they be respected absolutely. The Jew has his own creed, Israel its own sacred law—holy and perfect (i.e., catholic) in every respect. As for Luis de Guzmán and Friar Arias, their brief was to enforce the Jews' compliance with the "rules" governing Christian toleration of their communities. Arragel's assertion of his religious beliefs must have only confirmed to them that the rabbi indeed merited the labor imposed on him under the terms of the Augustinian contract. Chides Arias (fol. 12r), "so hardened a Jew you want to be that you do not want to ask the painters to depict the figure of God in the miniatures."[42]

How does Alba's illustration enter into this battleground of dissonant intentionalities, entrenched positions, and competing claims to revealed truth? To what extent do the miniatures—numbering some 324 scenes—ameliorate or exacerbate tension between Christian patronage and Jewish production? Arragel had objected to having any share in the making of anthropomorphic images of God on the grounds that he would thereby be sinning against his law (fols. 9r, v).[43] Grasping for a less parochial rationale with which to disqualify himself from Guzmán's commission, he further professed ignorance about how to go about the illustration altogether (*yo non sse cosa en el ystoriar*). Not to worry, Arias responded (fols. 12r, v). The Franciscan himself would designate the episodes to be depicted, for which the rabbi need only reserve sufficient space. (N.B. Arias thus implicitly acknowledged that Arragel would not only be responsible for authoring translation and commentary, but would also be involved in mise-en-page and scribal routines.) Master painters from Toledo would dispatch the illustration by referring to Arias's written remarks and by consulting a bible, now lost, from the Cathedral sacristy "que es muy bien ystoriada." The manuscript as actually realized, however, belies the simplicity of Arias's prospective solution. The epistolary front matter to the contrary, Arragel no more entirely avoided involvement in *ystoriar* than Guzmán fulfilled all his promises of financial support.

Fellous correlates the intervention of different teams of artists with a programmatic shift roughly halfway through the manuscript, the biblical books mostly following the traditional Hebrew order.[44] Through 2 Kings (ending fol. 264v), literalist illustration predominates, whether in the form of historical narrative or ritual description, despite scattered Christian imagery. Beginning with Isaiah (fol. 265r), Christological interpretation becomes more concentrated and gains the upper hand. Yet painstaking iconographic analysis reveals throughout—even in the most blatantly Christian scenes—a wealth of details derived from rabbinic materials and synagogue liturgy. Neither the manuscript text available to the artists nor recourse to pictorial models that already incorporated Hebrew sources can fully account for such extensive mediation of Jewish traditions.[45] Fellous draws the conclusion, now the scholarly consensus, that Moses Arragel indeed advised the illuminators, be they Jews or Christians.

Scholars who have emphasized the Jewish dimension of the bible have tended to downplay the impact of its Christian imagery.[46] To be sure, most scenes do respect the literal sense of Hebrew Scripture or otherwise purvey rabbinic exegesis (some two-thirds according to Fellous's calculus). But Arragel's clerical supervisors nonetheless wielded the pictorial medium so as to curtail, inhibit, and disrupt Jewish interpretive agency. Images of Christ constitute the irreducible nub of the commission (Figure 5.4). There is no getting around the fact that the depiction of an incarnate God, anathema to Arragel, was nothing short of a theological imperative to Arias. Centuries of Christian image

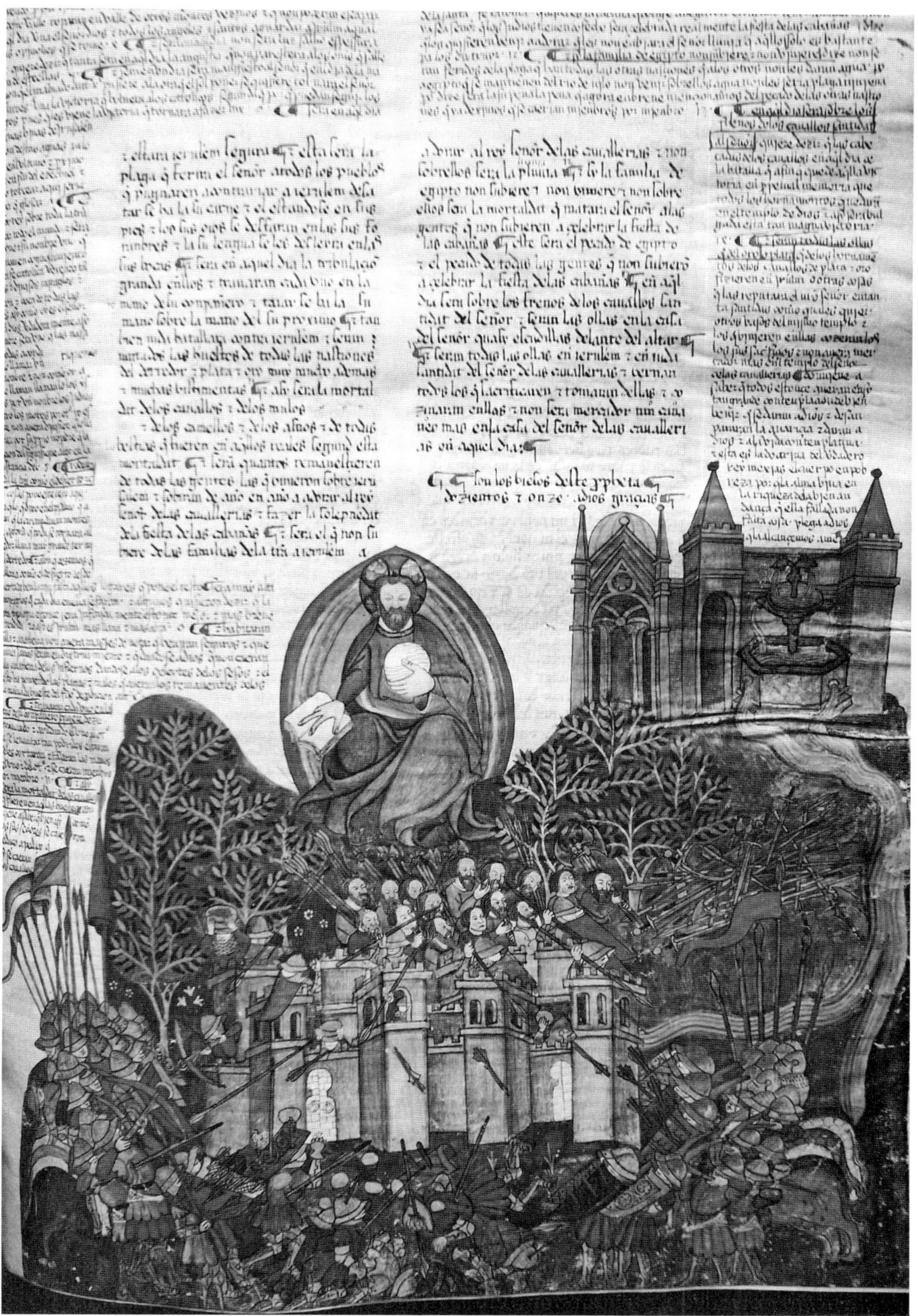

5.4. Alba Bible, fol. 368r: Jerusalem attacked by the nations. Photo courtesy Felipe Pereda.

theory rooted in the Incarnation (which Arragel summarily rehearses to rebut) had effectively turned the pictorial figuration of God into proof of doctrine.[47] What the rabbi could not countenance he was obliged to co-produce.

For a commission so elaborately documented that its initiation, terms of execution, and defense constitute a gateway into the finished work, its utter nonreception is stunning. The colophon (fol. 513v) records the completion of the bible proper at Maqueda on June 2, 1430, at a time when the grand master was in the midst of raising troops to wage war against the kings of Aragon and Navarre.[48] The bible's public presentation took place at the Franciscan convent in Toledo in November of 1430 or 1433; in any case, Luis de Guzmán did not attend.[49] Moreover, the manuscript seems never to have reached Guzmán or his family.[50] Was the grand master too distracted by political turmoil and his military responsibilities to collect the volume? Had he lost interest in the project? Whatever the reasons, Arragel's manuscript had no readership apart from the censors in whose possession it seems to have remained.[51] Mention of it surfaces in the archives of the Inquisition in 1622, in an account of its loan between members of different religious orders.[52]

The fiction of the presentation miniature can nevertheless tell us a great deal about the Augustinian *raison d'être* for the enterprise. Writing for Charles V, the author of the *Songe du vergier* had claimed that "the Jews are profitable to us like those who serve us because they carry the books through which our faith is proved. . . . Our books are held up by them. How better to convince them than through their own books."[53] Alba's presentation miniature might as well be a literal illustration of these words. Surrounded by peers of the Calatrava order, Arragel lifts up the open bible, his very body conformed to a pulpit in order to support the heavy tome. On the lowest step of the grand master's Solomonic throne, knights perform works of mercy to five thickly bearded, long-haired men (in *comer, bever, calçar, vestir, consolar*), the first of whom also wears a hat. By contrast, a bedridden man is clean-shaven and shorn (*visitar*), and the corpse, prepared for burial, is wrapped in a shroud (*enterrar*). In fact, the recipients of Calatrava charity represent Jews won over by proofs from "their own books." The absence of the red badge, in salient contrast with Arragel below (and throughout), signals that they have embarked on the path to baptism, if not already emerged from the waters.[54] The sequence moves from the retention to the shedding of externals that physically mark Jewish identity. The Christian grooming *in extremis* suggests quite plainly the death of the Jew; now, at last, his assimilation into the social body is complete.

The presentation miniature, then, subsumes the commission's place in a policy of toleration geared to advancing the Jews' conversion, itself a work of mercy directed at the soul. (Note that "to convert," like the depicted action "to

    MARCIA KUPFER

console," figures among the "spiritual," as opposed to the "corporeal," works of mercy.) Beginning in the 1430s, conversos would no longer be able so easily to dispose of their former Jewish identity; by 1449, it would run indelibly in the blood.[55] The image stands as an extraordinary record of a narrow historical window during which it was possible to proclaim Luis de Guzmán a wise ruler by virtue of his approach to his Jewish subjects. He mines them for the Hebrew underpinnings of Christian truth even as he leads them into the church.

By the same token, the miniature's conversion program brings to the light of day the "hidden transcript" in Arragel's poignant address to readers of both "nations" at the close of his prolegomenon (fols. 14v–15r). Hardly unaware of, or indifferent to, his patron's interest in converting his coreligionists, the rabbi proactively defends against missionary strategies on behalf of which he knows he has been set up. He tells Jewish readers to discount any of his own glosses (in the vernacular, after all) that contradict Hebrew authorities and implores them not to abandon their ancestral faith.[56] Moreover, anticipating the blandishments that Christianity but fulfils and perfects the law, that the convert therefore only gains while losing nothing, he offers a counterargument from the science of optics. He opens with a reference to Euclid and a marginal diagram illustrating how the eye processes visual rays to form a straight line, then makes the case that the "eyes of understanding" are best served by imitating the "material eyes."[57] To find the straight line, *la su rectalidat,* the carpenter must leave open one eye and close the other; opening both eyes he loses *lo derecho.* So, too, must readers exercise discernment when it comes to the glosses: one who does not follow the example of the carpenter cannot benefit from his reading. Arragel here warns against hermeneutic blur. In particular, the Jew must not succumb to the kind of misplaced typologizing that dooms the Christian reading of Hebrew Scripture; rather he should look through the eye of his own faith so that, like the straight beam of the visual ray itself, he keeps to *lo derecho,* the law.[58]

Picturing the Covenant

Despite reluctant concessions to Christian patronage, Rabbi Moses invested himself in the bible's pictorial illustration no less than in its text. Fellous goes well beyond earlier iconographic studies to apply to the miniatures the exegetical method that Arragel advocated for his glosses.[59] Just as the commentary should be amenable to both Christian and Jew, each reading in accordance with his own faith, so also the images. Arragel's play on the optical metaphor urging Christian and Jew "to see" respectively supports Fellous's effort in this regard.

The above-mentioned images of Christ nevertheless set limits to semiotic parallelism. I return to this issue below, but first I extend the principle to a miniature that Fellous excludes from multivalent interpretation.

The scene of Abraham circumcising himself, placed at the end of Genesis 17, shows the patriarch kneeling between two trees, his tunic lifted to expose a gigantesque penis (Figure 5.5). He grasps his member with one hand and cuts with the other so that a massive torrent of blood as well as lesser streams and droplets spill onto the ground.[60] Fellous connects the depiction of Abraham's enlarged organ to the word *grovieso* that Arragel uses throughout the chapter for foreskin. Yet she considers the image too grotesque, crude, and violent to have positive religious connotations (for either faith). Reflecting the Christian view of circumcision as barbaric, she concludes, the miniature serves up anti-Jewish caricature—hence the monstrous dimensions of the prepuce and gushing of blood. Against the derogatory representation of the Abrahamic covenant, presumably at the insistence of his supervisors, Arragel would have been powerless to interfere.[61]

The anti-Jewish angle seems odd, however, in light of the broader significance that Fellous would also attach to the Genesis scene with respect to the commission's underlying goal. The illustration for chapter 17, she suggests, provided an iconographic opportunity to follow through on the patrons' express wish that "Jews and Christians coexist on a ground of religious understanding."[62] Why else, she wonders, was Ishmael's circumcision left out of the pictorial record? Her answer: the elision deflected attention from the relationship between Judaism and Islam—joint descent from Abraham according to the flesh and concomitant ritual marking of male genitalia—at a time when Guzmán was campaigning against Muslims in the south. But if the motivation behind the scene was bilateral Christian-Jewish reconciliation at Muslim expense, why the caricature?

The pictorial conception and interpretive potential of the image can be better understood by returning to the dialogic paradigm. Christianity and Judaism radically diverged on the fundamental matter of religious initiation, baptism versus circumcision.[63] Still, the rival faiths each came to frame their respective, mutually antagonistic approaches through a common ritual "language" of blood symbolism and sacramental efficacy.[64] The salvific power of Christ's blood shed on the cross guarantees the spiritual remaking of the person in baptism; the theme of sacrificial blood as the source of divine grace is so pervasive in Christian theology and cult practice as to obviate further comment. Less generally well known is that from c. 800 rabbinic sources and Jewish custom began strongly to associate circumcision blood with atonement, sacrifice, and redemption.[65] By c. 1300, belief in the spiritually transformative nature of the covenantal

MARCIA KUPFER

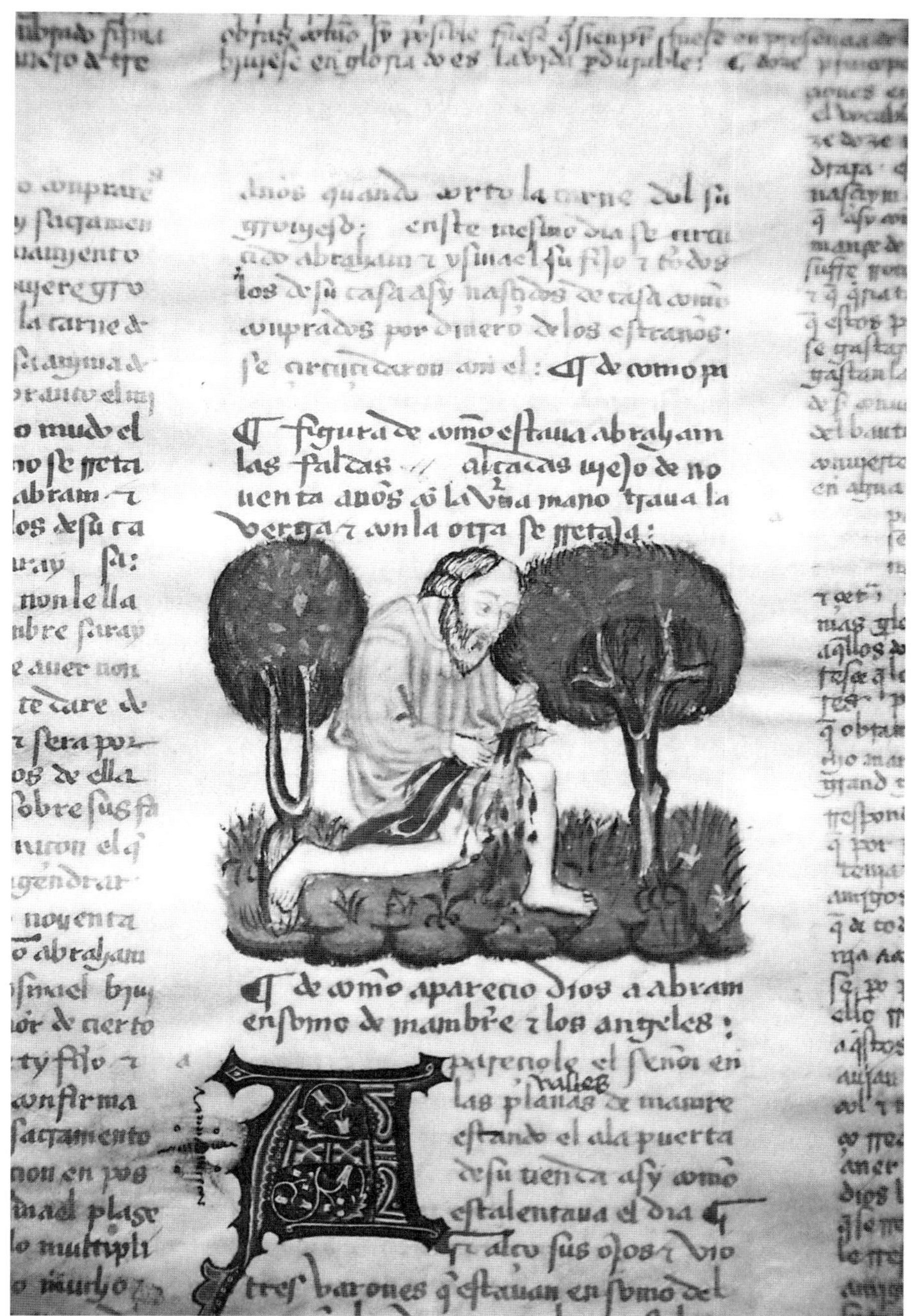

5.5. Alba Bible, fol. 37r: Abraham circumcises himself. Photo courtesy Felipe Pereda.

act had received sublime, esoteric expression in that most famous enterprise of Castilian kabbalists, the Zohar.[66]

Whereas modern viewers may react squeamishly to Alba's bloody circumcision scene, the Bible's fifteenth-century readers, Jews and Christians alike, were culturally conditioned to equate certain bloods with life, rebirth, and purification.[67] As for the emphasis on the phallus, far from being a point of ridicule, it introduces symbolism dependent on the zoharic universe. True, Christian culture denigrated the Jewish male, regarding him as castrated and feminized even unto menstruation.[68] But long before Arragel, Kabbalah enshrined in the Zohar had retorted by elevating the circumcised phallus into more than just a badge of honor.[69] It became a cosmic pillar supporting all creation, the link between heaven and earth, and the corona, physically inscribed with the divine name, the fleshly locus of the *tsaddiq*'s vision of God.[70] The Abraham image in Alba in fact thoroughly Judaizes what was an exclusively Christian iconography.[71] The episode, I will show, must have been depicted in the lost bible from Toledo Cathedral to which Arias referred. At the same time, the pictorial formulation in Alba capitalizes on equivocal symbols that permit Christian readings, *in bono et in malo*, for only thus hidden—"under cover" in plain sight, as it were— could Jewish praise, indeed celebration, of circumcision infiltrate the "public transcript" of Guzmán's commission.

Although nowhere articulated in Arragel's gloss on Genesis 17, the medieval Jewish theology of blood surely informs Alba's depiction of the prototypical circumcision. According to a midrash on the trials of Abraham in the *Pirqei de Rabbi Eliezer* (chap. 29), the patriarch's circumcision coincided with the date of Yom Kippur. The enduring sight of his circumcision blood annually induces God to forgive the collective sins of the Jewish people on that holiest of days. Abraham's blood permanently soaked the very ground where later the Temple altar stood, from which flowed the sacrificial blood of sin-offerings. The commingling of the two bloods concords with God's twofold pronouncement in Ezekiel 16:6: "I said unto thee: In thy blood, live."

> Know that on the Day of Atonement Abraham our father was circumcised. Every year the Holy One, blessed be He, sees the blood of our father Abraham's circumcision, and He forgives all the sins of Israel, as it is said, "For on this day shall atonement be made for you, to cleanse you" (Lev. 16:30). In that place where Abraham was circumcised and his blood remained, there the altar was built, and therefore, "And all the blood thereof shall he pour out at the base of the altar" (Lev. 4:30). (It, i.e., scripture, says also), "I said unto thee, In thy blood, live: yea, I said unto thee, In thy blood, live" (Ezek. 16:6).[72]

MARCIA KUPFER

For Arragel and the Jewish reader he had in mind, the image in Alba would not only have resonated with Israel's yearly cycle of atonement, purification, and renewal in the present. And it would not only have pointed back in time to the glory days of the Temple service, when Israel worshipped God in the Promised Land. It would have also pointed forward to messianic deliverance. As the midrash goes on to explain: "The Holy One, blessed be He, said: By the merit of the blood of the covenant of circumcision and the blood of the Paschal lamb ye shall be redeemed from Egypt, and by the merit of the covenant of circumcision and by the merit of the covenant of the Passover in the future ye shall be redeemed at the end of the fourth kingdom."[73] The fourth kingdom (cf. Dan. 2:40, 7:23) in rabbinic tradition most often stood for Rome, i.e., Christianity.[74] Insofar as the image spurs the viewer to recollect the midrash, it proclaims that at the threshold to the end time, when the evil empire falls, the covenant of circumcision will merit Israel's salvation in God's eyes.

Significantly, Arragel acknowledges the salvific power of circumcision blood not in his gloss on Genesis 17, but in his gloss on Zechariah 9:11 (fol. 368v), "As for you also, because of the blood of your covenant I send forth your prisoners out of the pit wherein is no water." The Roman church, he observes, applies this verse to Jesus Christ and the blood of his Passion, which saves the damned from hell; the Jews, however, say it means that they are saved by the blood of their circumcision. Already in the thirteenth century, Jewish polemicists of the Franco-German sphere had deployed the verse to argue that circumcision blood, superior to Christian sacramental waters, nullifies forced baptism.[75] The image of Abraham's circumcision implies pictorially what Arragel could not say explicitly. Channeling the eschatological lesson of the midrash to contemporary concerns, it addresses the newly baptized Jews whom Arragel's Christian patrons had depicted in the presentation miniature and the prospective converts whom the commission was designed to harvest. The blood of the covenant redeems even those who had succumbed to conversionary pressures if only they would heed the words of Zechariah 9:12 as Arragel had glossed them in code, "Return to the stronghold of *la santa fe catolica*," that is, the Law of Moses.

The author of the *Pirqei*, invoking Ezekiel, brings two bloods to bear on each other, that of circumcision and that of animal sacrifice (Temple altar, paschal lamb). The Alba miniature visually delineates two bloods, but inflects the doubling in accordance with rabbinic tradition that links the covenant of circumcision with the covenant of Sinai, when Moses splashed sacrificial blood at the altar and on the people (Exod. 24:6, 8).[76] While the knife cut into the penis unleashes streams and large droplets of blood, which fall to the ground, a pool of the same blood red pigment collects between Abraham's right knife-bearing hand and his right leg. Rather than fall across the leg onto the ground, this mass stains the hem of Abraham's tunic. It corresponds to the explication of Exodus 24:8 by the eleventh-century Tunisian rabbi Hananel ben Hushiel as embedded in the widely circulated Torah commentary of the Saragossan Bahya ben Asher (1255–1340): "He [Moses] sprinkled the blood on them in order to enable them to enter the covenant with God by means of blood. The bloodstain which remained on each of their garments was called *'adi*, 'jewel, ornament,' as this stain was a sign of distinction and honour for them. It served as testimony that they had entered into a covenant with the Lord."[77] Thus the image of Abraham circumcising himself adumbrates the moment when God cut [*karat*] the covenant of blood with the people, after they had collectively acclaimed, "All that the Lord has spoken will we do, and obey" (Exod. 24:7).

The commentary to which the image refers contains a warning, however: "Why did God employ blood as the instrument by means of which He made the covenant with the people? It was a hint that as long as the Israelites were to be loyal to the covenant and they would observe the commandments all well and good; if they were to fail to do so, God would permit their blood to their adversaries."[78] These cautionary words might well have struck Arragel as especially relevant to his own generation, which had seen the pogroms of 1391 and the Tortosa Disputation. The transfer of the stained garment into the scene of Abraham's circumcision nevertheless pictorially softens the threat of divine judgment. The Alba miniature follows Bahya's own exegesis of Genesis 17:13, which, explicitly citing the *Pirqei*, maintains that Abraham's bloodshed moves God to grant atonement for the patriarch's descendants.[79] Circumcision, avers Bahya, "will be the instrument saving Jews from *Gehinom* and its fires," precisely the point Arragel recalls in his gloss on Zechariah 9:11.

The covenantal significance of the depicted act extends to the scene's arboreal landscaping. By Levitical injunction (19:23), new plantings are considered uncircumcised (*'orlah*). The law of *'orlah* with respect to fruit trees grounds the explanation in the *Pirqei* for Isaac's election as the son to and through whom the covenant is transmitted. Pursuing the theme of blood and sacrifice, the midrash exemplifies the law by focusing on a single type of fruit-producing tree to which it applies, the grape vine. Thus before Abraham's circumcision, "the fruit which he produced"—i.e., Ishmael—"was disqualified from the altar; but when he was circumcised, the fruit was good . . . chosen to be put upon the altar like wine for a libation."[80] Written in the land of Israel in the late eighth century, the *Pirqei*, as well as reiterations of the midrash by the thirteenth-century Spanish kabbalists, may well have had Islam in their line of polemical fire.[81] But by Arragel's day, the vanishing power of Muslims in the Iberian Peninsula would have made the relevant target less Islam than Pauline readings of Genesis 17. For the answer to the question as to why Isaac, not Ishmael, is the son of the covenant has nothing to do with the status of their mothers, slave or free (Gal. 4:21–31). Rather, it has to do with the state of perfection that circumcision conferred on Abraham. Contra Paul, and the Christian exegetical edifice later constructed on his apostolic authority, the covenant of circumcision did not externally betoken a prior inner condition—Abraham's faith—by virtue of which some disembodied spiritual paternity could be universalized. No, God commanded Abraham to circumcise himself so that his sanctified member could then engender the heir and eventually the people destined for His law.[82]

Arragel's gloss on Genesis 17:1–13 reports, but can only weakly and back-handedly undercut, the canonical supersessionist line that the censors imposed on him. In contrast to the more equivocal tone of the gloss, the image—*when tied to the midrash and its reception in rabbinic exegesis*—vigorously rejects Christian claims. It replies to the charge that God has vacated His covenant of circumcision and the election of the Jewish people with a behind-the-back pictorial thumb of the nose tantamount, dare I suggest, to "giving the finger." But the scene more than defends against Christian theological assault. Refracting the *Pirqei* through a kabbalistic prism, it positively affirms the ongoing power of the covenant, renewed in perpetuity with each Jewish male.

The corpus of gloss in the Alba Bible attests to Arragel's familiarity with the Zohar, though he used kabbalistic vocabulary sparingly and fleetingly, without elaboration.[83] While commenting, for example, on the Melchizedek episode (Gen. 14:18–21), he mentions in passing the ten *sefirot* (*x çaphirot*), defining the divine gradations—for Christian consumption—as *una manera de dominaçiones e archangeles*.[84] The Zohar absorbed the theology of circumcision blood from the *Pirqei*, which it transposes into another key altogether: "The child that is circumcised is linked to the *Shekhinah*, who is a door to all the celestial crowns, a door that is linked to the holy name. The blood that comes from the child is preserved before the Holy One, blessed be He. And when judgments are aroused in the world, the Holy One, blessed be He, looks at the blood, and saves the world. . . . It is because of this blood that the world is perfumed with Love and all the worlds survive" (3:13b–14a).[85] Whereas in the midrash, Abraham's circumcision blood moves God to forgiveness on Yom Kippur, in Kabbalah the circumcision blood of every son of Israel mitigates judgment via the operation of the *sefirot*.

What makes the Zohar relevant to Alba's circumcision miniatures, however, is that the kabbalistic understanding of the covenant has pictorial repercussions apart from the blood. How not to see in the columnar enormity of Abraham's penis a visual metaphor for the ninth *sefirah*, Yesod (Foundation), symbolized by the covenant of circumcision? Equated with the phallus in the body of *Adam Kadmon*, or primordial man, *Yesod* concentrates in itself the totality of the divine energies from the upper gradations and is their conduit to the tenth, the feminine *Shekhinah*.[86] Abraham, the zoharic axis mundi and atlante figure par excellence, performs the function of *Yesod* at the moment of circumcision. He is the originary *tsaddiq*, the exemplum of all the righteous, about whom scripture says, "The righteous one is an everlasting foundation" (Prov. 10:25, *Ve-tsaddiq yesod olam*, the very passage Bahya cites to introduce his kabbalistic interpretation of Genesis 17:13), and about whom the Zohar repeatedly says, "The righteous one is the foundation of the world" (1:93a).[87] To take one passage from the Zohar's commentary on Genesis 17: "Come and see: Once Abraham was circumcised, he abandoned the foreskin and entered the sacred covenant, crowned with the sacred corona, entering the covenant upon which the world stands. Then the world was erected for his sake" (1:91b).[88]

The organ's magisterial display in the miniature corresponds to its significance as fleshly "standard bearer" of the most sacred of divine names, YHVH, in which the entire Torah is encapsulated. A nexus of midrashic and kabbalistic associations might well have allowed Arragel's imagined Jewish reader mentally to "see" in Abraham's bloodied phallus something of the red battle-standard waving from the javelin (a phallic symbol) carried by Joshua in his assault of Ai (Figure 5.6). Across the unfurled banner are written in Hebrew the divine name *Shaddai*, its Vulgate translation "Omnipotens," and the word Tetragrammaton. The Zohar's commentary on Genesis 17 relays an early medieval midrash (*Tanḥuma, Tsav* 14) according to which circumcision seals into the male organ the holy letter yod, last in the name *Shaddai*.[89] God calls himself by this name when, in Genesis 17:1, he commands Abraham to "walk in My presence and be perfect." Elliot Wolfson has traced how Castilian Kabbalah subsumed the older midrashic interpretation into its amplification of another tradition, Ashkenazi in origin, according to which the *yod* stands for the first letter in YHVH. With the act of circumcision, to quote Wolfson, "the bodily limb itself becomes the bearer of the divine letter and thus the eternal sign of the covenant between God and Israel."[90]

The scene's verdant setting assumes new meaning in relation to zoharic re-weavings of older midrashic traditions. The association in the *Pirqei* between Abraham's circumcision and the law concerning the pruning of fruit trees recurs in the Zohar (1:97a, b) to different effect. The cutting of foreskin and of branches is referred, through wordplay on a verse in the Song of Songs (2:12), to the springtime of the world, to the cycle of creation (divine emanation), fall (withdrawal of the divine presence) and regeneration.[91] Adam arrived, "everything" bloomed, but with his sin the ground was cursed; Noah arrived, but with his drunkenness "the powers of earth" likewise disappeared. Then Abraham came: "As soon as Abraham arrived in the world, immediately the blossoms

MARCIA KUPFER

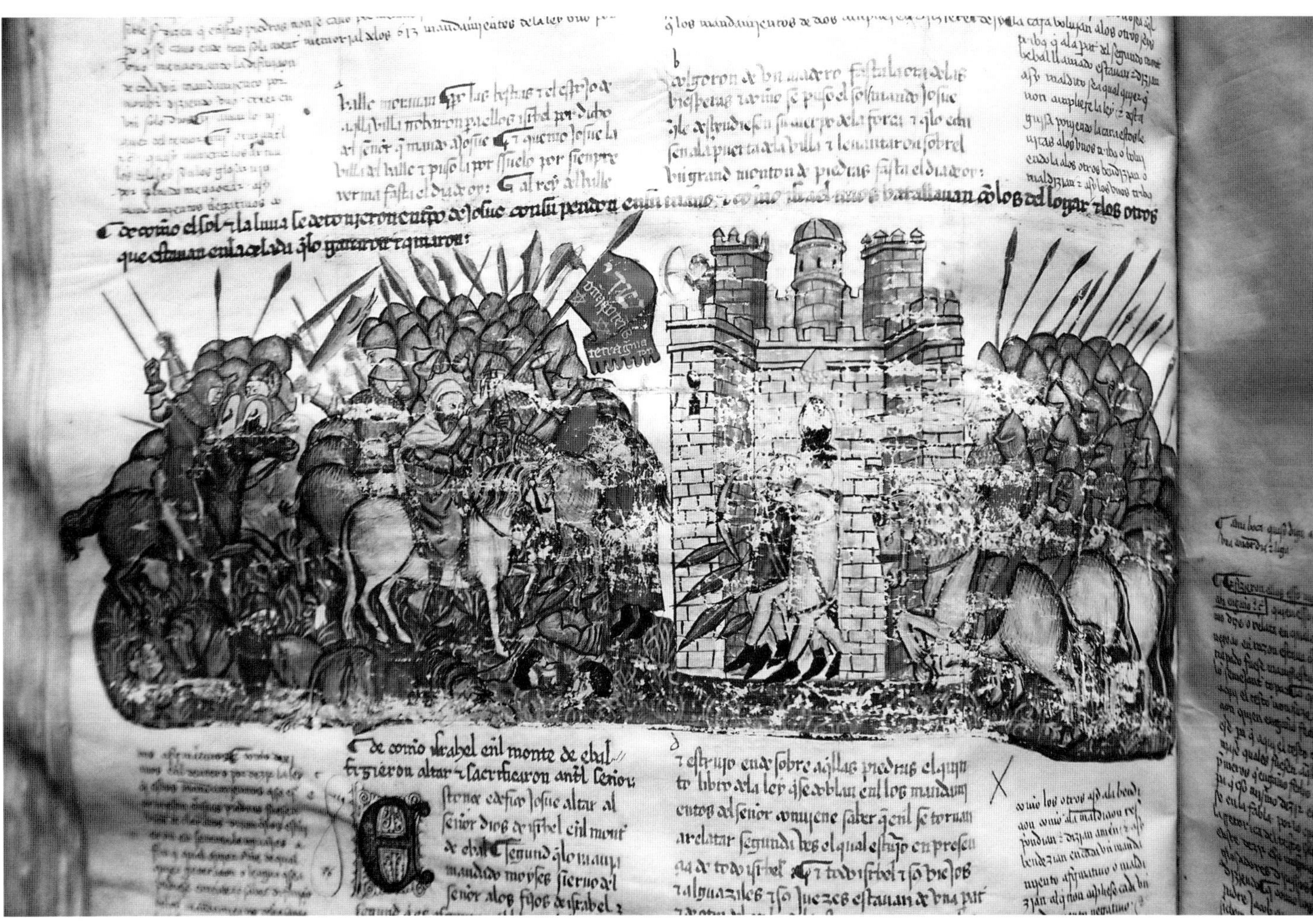

5.6. Alba Bible, fol. 170r: Joshua leads the assault on Ai (Joshua 8:16–19). Photo courtesy Felipe Pereda.

appeared on the earth—all powers of earth were arrayed and revealed. The time of pruning has arrived—when the blessed Holy One told him to circumcise himself. The moment that the covenant manifested in Abraham through circumcision, this entire verse was fulfilled, the world was firmly established, and the word of the blessed Holy One was openly revealed, as is written: 'YHVH appeared to him' (Gen. 18:1)."[92] Note the three white flowers at the lower right of the miniature. The image visually integrates the moment of Abraham's "arrival in the world" when "blossoms appeared on earth" with his circumcision (*milah*), when God's word (*millah*) was revealed in him. Just as the passage declares that Abraham, not Jesus, realized the incarnation of the divine word,[93] so the image implies that Abraham's blood, not Jesus', rectifies Adam's sin.

Like the white blossoms, the dark green sprouts have a textual correlate in the Zohar's treatment of Genesis 17. The lush ground vegetation evokes the symbolism of the land divinely planted, with all its Edenic resonance, as Israel's inheritance.[94] Paradise is a traditional metaphor for the world to come, onto which the Zohar superimposes the higher world that is coming, i.e., perpetually unfolding, through the *sefirot*.[95] Circumcision, as the inscription of the divine name on the body, is the prerequisite for coming into this inheritance.[96] At the same time, the zoharic commentary (1:93b) reworks the promise of Eden deferred into the *tsaddiq*'s vision of God in the flesh. Circumcision, Wolfson stresses, creates the space in which the vision itself transpires.[97]

The Alba scene shows the patriarch enjoying a plenary vision of the *Shekhinah*. The Zohar represents this mystical experience through the eroticized language of sexual intercourse, which is most definitely implicated in the miniature's visual emphasis on the erect penis. Prior to circumcision, Abraham's experience of God was limited to the lowest gradation. When the covenant manifested itself in him, he became identified with *Yesod*, the phallus being "the knot in which all the upper grades are united."[98] At that instant, the feminine hypostasis of the divine changed too so as also to comprise all the higher grades. Abraham thus experienced union with the *Shekhinah* in the fullness of her glory. The originary circumcision, in other words, culminated in cosmic orgasm. The blood in the image conceivably doubles for semen; recall that, according to medieval physiology, semen is "cooked" blood.[99] In any event, Kabbalah identifies the *Shekhinah* with the corona; conversely, Abraham's rapt gaze upon the exposed tip of his member is therefore tantamount to his vision of the *Shekhinah*.[100]

Abraham's circumcision is the template for that of every Jewish male, which results in the same orgasmic response in the sefirotic realm. The flow of circumcision blood unleashes the love that tempers "judgments aroused in the world"

MARCIA KUPFER

(as in Zohar 3:13b-14a, cited above). Initiation of individuals into the covenantal community typologically circles back upon the model, referred liturgically to the corporate body of the entire nation: gazing every Yom Kippur upon Abraham's circumcision blood where the Temple altar stood, God annuls the severity of the divine decree for all Israel.

Not only does the scene's paradisial ambiance and phallic energy suggest an unfolding visionary experience; but the Alba miniature also follows zoharic time in conflating Abraham's circumcision with God's appearance to him at Mamre. The relationship between image and text on the page explicitly links the fulfillment of the covenantal act to God's self-revelation. The miniature is set directly above the rubricated title to Genesis 18 announcing God's theophany to Abraham at Mamre: *de commo aparecio dios a abram en somo de mamre & los angeles*. In fact, it articulates the juncture between two Torah lections, at once closing *Lekh Lekha* ("Go you forth," Gen. 12:1–17:27) and opening *Va-Yera* ("He appeared," Gen. 18:1–22:24). The scene, its parallel streams of blood aligned with the words "aparecio dios," echoes the zoharic linkage between circumcision and the vision of the divine. Earlier midrashic texts had established Abraham's circumcision as the cause of the divine appearance at Mamre.[101] The Zohar, however, compresses, even collapses, the succession of the two scripturally discrete events, forging them into a conceptual unity: the progression from circumcision to vision of God occurs in a single revelatory moment. The Alba Bible omits a separate miniature for Genesis 18, bypassing the depiction of the three angelic visitors who, in Christian tradition, designate the Trinity. Programmatically, then, the one scene does double duty in illustrating both the circumcision and the theophany consequent upon the covenantal act. On this reading, the trees can be conflated with the terebinths of Mamre.

The image admits the learned Jew to the inner kernel of scripture, barring Christian access beyond the outer husk. Arragel thereby respected the zoharic principle, itself anchored in talmudic dictum, that only the circumcised may penetrate the sacred bride of Torah.[102] Although Fellous may have overlooked the multiple layers of Jewish meaning to which the Abraham scene gives rise, the miniature confirms yet again a point she repeatedly demonstrates throughout her study of the Alba Bible. Only Arragel's personal direction can account for the iconography of this image. Friar Arias proposed at the outset of the project that the painters consult an illustrated bible from Toledo Cathedral and that he provide them with written instructions concerning the illustration of the manuscript at hand. I would venture to speculate that, contrary to the Franciscan's modus operandi and in deliberate tension with it, Rabbi Moses orally conveyed his ideas on iconography to the illustrators in their shop.

Alerted to the susceptibility of the circumcision miniature to a Jewish reading, the foreskin removed from our eyes, we can better assess its dialogic interaction with Christian art. The miniature painters of the Alba Bible were not working in an art-historical vacuum. The iconographic tradition on which the episode stands sheds light on how particular deviations in Alba could convey a Jewish message even as they did so in terms also open to Christian interpretation. With some ad hoc compositional adjustment, an already available scheme could be sufficiently saturated with pictorial cues for an erudite Jewish reader to deploy an ingrained hermeneutic repertory. In approximating what the process of adaptation entailed, merely to emphasize the negation of Christian iconography would be reductive. A full and proper appreciation requires us to bear in mind that modifications presuppose a prior phase during which a Christian image creatively engaged the rabbi's attention, stimulating him to reflect on the interpretive resources of his own tradition. Jewish meaning is thus constructed around, or rather in conversation with, a Christian core.

Variously conceived, the scene of Abraham's circumcision appears in a mere handful of extant manuscripts—among which is the Bible of Jean de Sy (Figure 5.7). The works are of widely scattered geographic origin and date from the late twelfth century to the turn of the fifteenth.[103] The six-member set comprises only biblical paraphrases or picture cycles, suggesting that the bible to which Arias referred also illustrated Genesis 17 with a circumcision scene. Arragel would then have told illustrators only how to revise it. This set can be slightly extended by taking into account two cases in which Genesis 17 is illustrated without actually showing Abraham's own circumcision.[104] Whatever their differences, all the comparanda depict Abraham receiving the command of circumcision. In the atrium of S. Marco, the series of cupola scenes corresponding to Genesis 17 opens with Abraham addressed by God in the form of a hand emerging from concentric arcs of the starry sky. This mode of representing the deity, an archaism taken over from the Early Christian model, is not replicated elsewhere. Christ himself usually addresses the patriarch[105] or issues the command.[106] In the Bible of Jean de Sy, however, an angel, standing in for the deity, relays the message and supervises the operation.

Why this variation in the French example? The angelic figure, appearing as a protagonist with Abraham in the immediately preceding image of the altar at Hebron (Gen. 12:18, fol. 19r) and again, multiplied by three, in the visitation at Mamre (fol. 24v), creates visual connectivity within the pictorial narrative. More pointedly, though, the angel in the circumcision episode relates to the gloss, which states categorically that "the apparition of God was by an angel who took the semblance of a man and spoke as God, just as the legate speaks as the pope and the parliament speaks as the king."[107] In introducing angelic mediation,

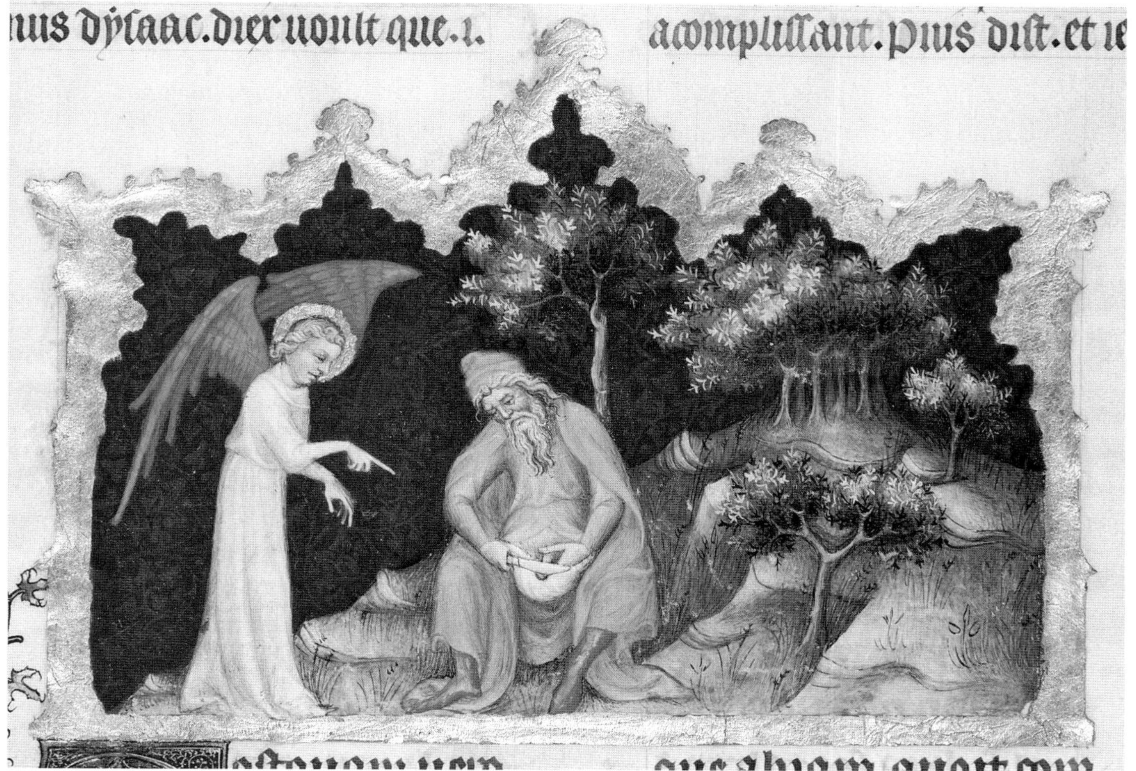

5.7. Bible of Jean de Sy (Paris, BnF, MS fr 15397), c. 1355, fol. 22v: Abraham circumcises himself. Paint added 1380s. Photo by permission of Bibliothèque nationale de France.

Jean de Sy accomplishes two moves with one stroke. First he devalues circumcision by denying the patriarch's direct encounter with God on the model of Paul (Gal. 3:19), who says the law was "enacted on account of transgressions, being delivered [merely] by angels through a mediator [Moses]."[108] Second, by comparing the annunciation of Isaac's birth with that of Christ's, he looks forward (as per the concluding phrase of Gal. 3:19) to the arrival of the offspring according to the promise (i.e., Christ, Gal. 3:16), through whom the gentiles spiritually trace their descent from Abraham.[109]

Jean de Sy did not, so far as I am aware, derive his exegetical strategy from commentaries on Genesis 17. Rather, I suspect that the French translator/glossator may have been responding to, and critiquing, the received iconography of Christ's appearance in the scene. The gloss elsewhere reveals that he did have before him a pictorial exemplar: several passages expound on images for which space was reserved but which were not executed.[110] If the Dominican saw fit to revise an iconographic scheme to bring it into line with his scholastic outlook, how much more must Arragel have wished to cast the foundational moment of Israel's election in Jewish terms. Alba uniquely eliminates any pictorial reference to the manner of God's verbal communication with Abraham, thereby avoiding both the anthropomorphic figuration of the deity, i.e., an image of Christ, and Paul's denigration of the law.

Whereas visualizing the transmission of the covenant is the Christian iconographic rule from which Alba departs, all illustrations of Genesis 17 selectively portray the ritual's implementation. The S. Marco sequence proceeds from Abraham's conversation with God to his circumcising of Ishmael and announcing the impending procedure to the males of his household. The Velislav Bible similarly skips the patriarch's circumcision, but moves to a scene of infant circumcision. The Padua Bible devotes a separate scene to Abraham's circumcision (Figure 5.8), which it follows with one for Ishmael and all the men on the next page. In the Egerton Genesis, a single scene satisfies the scriptural directives concerning Abraham, Ishmael, and the men. More often than not, Abraham is shown to circumcise himself,[111] though in a couple of examples he undergoes the procedure performed by others.[112] Remarkably, most of the comparanda either eliminate bloodletting or minimize it.[113] Still, a sacrificial aspect may be acknowledged: Abraham reclines on an altar in the prefatory biblical cycle of the *Omne Bonum*, where the episode is juxtaposed with the Binding of Isaac; at S. Marco, a chalice-like vessel holds Ishmael's circumcision blood and recurs in the scene of Isaac's circumcision on the west lunette.

Alba comes closest in certain respects to the depictions in the Jean de Sy and Padua Bibles. Both the French and Spanish examples isolate the action of Abraham circumcising himself in a luxuriant landscape. Padua, placing the scene against the backdrop of a wooden shed, prefers a domestic setting; a fruit tree, tellingly, nevertheless rises in the distance. Here, Abraham's blood does play an active role, trickling to the ground as in Alba, although the flow is not nearly as copious (the second Padua scene of collective circumcision is bloodier, however). Katrin Kogman-Appel and Sarit Shalev-Eyni have identified midrashic elements in some of Padua's miniatures in their respective attempts to assess the relationship between pictorial cycles in fourteenth-century Sephardic haggadot and Christian models from a north Italian orbit.[114] Shalev-Eyni has suggested that midrashic references in the Padua Bible are sufficiently extensive and particular to warrant the hypothesis that its makers consulted a Jewish advisor, a hypothesis she supports by analogy with the Alba Bible.[115] Might the Padua scene of Abraham's circumcision reflect awareness of the midrash in the *Pirqei* in which blood and the law of *'orlah* come into play? Whatever the answer, Kogman-Appel's perceptive observation concerning the comparative treatment of a different midrashic motif (marking the doorposts with the blood

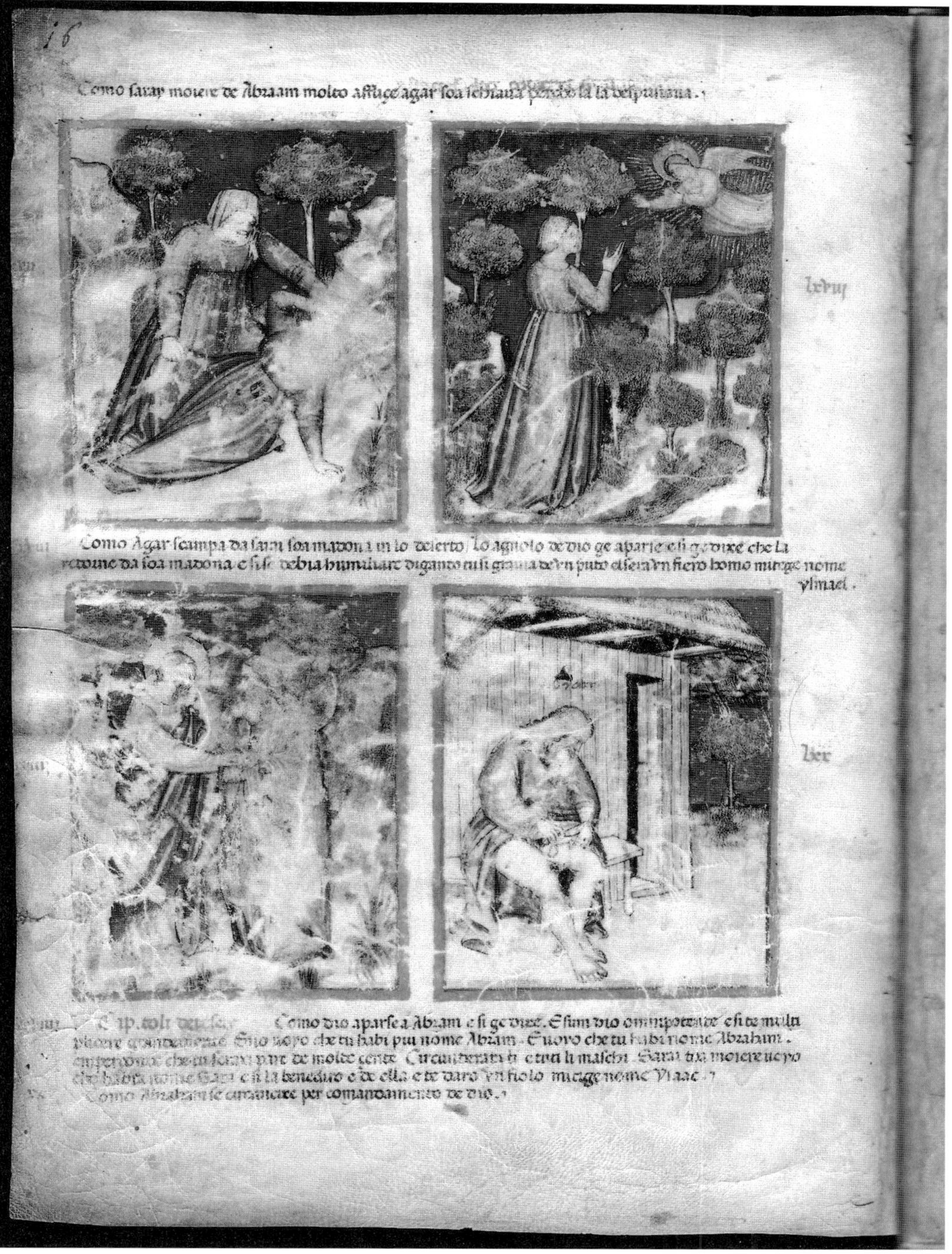

5.8. Padua Bible (Rovigo, Biblioteca dell'Accademia dei Concordi, MS 212), c. 1400, fol. 9v: conclusion of the story of Hagar (top pair of scenes); God in the person of Christ speaks with Abraham, and Abraham circumcises himself (bottom). Photo by permission of Accademia dei Concordi.

of the paschal lamb, Exod. 12:21–28) in Padua and two haggadot applies equally well to the present case: even if the Alba scene of Abraham circumcising himself were inspired by a Christian image that already contained midrashic insertions, Arragel "must have been aware of its midrashic background. Not only that, he emphasized it."[116]

Christian depictions of Abraham's circumcision may not only feature an arboreal landscape and bloodletting, but also focus on the sexual organ. Padua is modest in this regard, but the scenes in the Millstatt Genesis and, to a much greater degree, the Jean de Sy Bible and Egerton Genesis emphasize the genitalia. Yet phallic display in Alba eclipses by far that in any other example. Authors of a recent monograph on the Egerton Genesis characterize "the circumcision scene as an almost grotesquely comic interlude."[117] Although the pictorial tenor of the Egerton scene strikes me as entirely consistent with the work's expressive intensification of the biblical story throughout, the example suggests that genital articulation, even bordering on ribaldry (if that is what it is), could have already been an iconographic component of Alba's model. Arragel had only to ask the artist to augment Abraham's anatomy along with the flow of blood and add the stain on the tunic.

It is not the soteriology on which it is predicated that ultimately distinguishes visual comprehension of Alba's Abraham scene along either Jewish or Christian lines: in both traditions, blood saves. Rather, it is the parochial content through which the soteriology operates: *whose* blood? Christians could construe the image typologically; prompted by gloss emanating from Arragel's censors, they could visually extrapolate an associative chain leading from the blood of Christ's sacrifice, spilled first in his own infant circumcision and then in his Passion, to the baptism of the faithful.

To be sure, the discourse on circumcision, and therefore the Abraham scene in Alba, engaged a range of meanings particular to the Spanish context. The foreskin had long marked Christian difference vis-à-vis Muslims and Jews, not the other way around. By the time the Alba Bible was underway, however, Christian hegemony in the peninsula had reduced the circumcised penis to stigmatizing the otherness of the Jew; in the fifteenth century, the literary mocking of circumcision had a single, obvious referent.[118] Might not a Christian artist or viewer therefore be expected to disparage the enlarged, bloodied organ, to read the Alba scene derisively as castration? Still, I would invoke Scott's study to argue that pictorial excess qualifies as a technique with which Arragel could protectively disguise his "hidden transcript." Through subalterns' own exaggeration of their prescribed roles—the slave's vocal lean into his "Yes, Massa," the prisoner's comedic pantomime of his inability to outrun his guards during a jailhouse race—they might stage, if only fleetingly and subtly, a challenge to the power-holder's fantasy of absolute domination.[119]

Lost Causes

Much as I might like the principles of equivocation governing Arragel's text to have consistently prevailed with respect to miniatures throughout the work, this is not the case. What about miniatures where the figure of Christ himself directs the action or dominates a unified pictorial field (Figure 5.4)? Fellous's argument that even here Christian and Jew can read each in accordance with his own law rings hollow.[120] The unambiguous Christian sign trumps any esoteric Jewish contribution, whatever it may be, subsuming it within the visual hierarchy proper to the image. Pictorial integrity goes to reinforce the dictum that the New Dispensation fulfills and supplants the Old. Arragel in his commentary might chafe hard against the pictorial grain as he tries to compensate for the iconography. But between words and image there is no contest. Hard though he might look through the one open eye of his faith, Arragel's imagined Jewish reader could not avoid seeing in such miniatures the subjugation of his tradition, worked over until it conforms to the Christian vision of his erasure. Indeed, grasping the Jewish intention of surrounding gloss and caption strengthens the pictorial force of the supersessionist message all the more.

Focus on how Arragel confounded his sponsors' desire for a univocal monument to Christian truth should not blind us to their effective deployment of images to manage, in turn, his deft circumventions. Even as, on my reading, the Abraham miniature bolsters the case that Fellous makes for Arragel's subversive approach to the project, still, numerous others thwarted his efforts. The rabbi resisted as best he could the humiliation that the commission was designed, as ritual, to entail. But, needless to say, he could hardly sabotage the power relations of which the Bible was the official "transcript." As Scott reminds us, ruling groups always suspect subalterns of duplicity and subterfuge, to which the latter are inevitably constrained by the mere fact of their domination.[121] Over and above the multiple rounds of scrutiny to which the censors subjected Arragel's text, the pictorial program guaranteed that, notwithstanding a surreptitious attempt on his part to undermine the aims of the commission, the Christian sign system would claim the work for the hegemonic religion. Thus duly subordinated to a Christian agenda, the iconographic accumulation of midrashic, ritual, and kabbalistic references could, in the end, be arrayed like spoils.

The bible's sponsors may have hoped and believed that Jewish references could be marshaled to show potential or recent converts that cleaving to *verus Israel* entailed no loss, only gain. The fate of the manuscript suggests, however, that Christian apprehensions may not have been easily allayed. While we, following Fellous, may marvel at the sheer richness of a pictorial syncretism not seen since late antiquity, the bible's immediate audience may have feared a corrosive hybridity. The commission of 1422 sought to accommodate an attenuated, depleted Jewish presence within the classic Augustinian framework, but it also defied the massive cultural investment of the previous two decades in enforcing religious boundaries as a means to preserve Christian identity.[122] The work's consignment to oblivion on the heels of its public presentation in 1430/33 foreshadows the impending tide of misgiving about the logic of conversion. Could the rabbinic patrimony that Arragel had made available really be recuperated for the *santa fe catolica*? Did the Jew's baptism really end the menace of his corrupting influence? Even the presentation miniature itself equivocates in this regard. The image allows for conversion, a theologically necessary position after all, but shows that the Jew is successfully incorporated into Christian society only at his death. Within a generation of the bible's nonreception, the Alboraique—a composite creature so monstrous it exceeds any phantasm of the Romanesque imagination—incarnated the converso's ontological predicament.[123]

Abelard's *Sic et Non* suggested the rhetorical framework through which I have straddled the historiographies of Christian co-optation and Jewish acculturation. But by the 1450s in Spain, neither the absolute hegemony of Christianity nor the total acquiescence of baptized former Jews could quell an anxiety of immutable essence that centuries earlier had haunted his arch-nemesis Bernard of Clairvaux. The Cistercian monk had adamantly rejected, and agitated against, the legitimacy of a pope on the grounds of the man's descent, three generations removed, from a convert.[124] Perhaps Bernard's celebrated diatribe against the hybrid in pictorial art, unsettled by his own admission of irresistible fascination for the beauty in its contradictions, captures something of the response to the Alba Bible on the part of those who suppressed it.[125]

NOTES

A Franklin Research Grant from the American Philosophical Society allowed me to complete the research for this essay. I am especially grateful to Katrin Kogman-Appel, Pamela Patton, and Elliott R. Wolfson for their comments on an earlier draft. During presentations at the Ben Gurion University of the Negev, the Medieval and Early Modern Studies Institute at the George Washington University, and the University of Pittsburgh, scholars shared insights that I incorporated wherever possible. Felipe Pereda deserves my special thanks for helping me make it through the rough terrain of Christian-Jewish interaction in fifteenth-century Spain.

1. Susannah Heschel, "Christ's Passion: Homoeroticism and the Origins of Christianity," in *Mel Gibson's Bible*, ed. Timothy K. Beal and Tod Linafelt (Chicago, 2006), 99–119, esp. 100.

     MARCIA KUPFER

2. See, for example, two works by Daniel Boyarin: *Dying for God: Martyrdom and the Making of Christianity and Judaism* (Stanford, 1999), and *Border Lines: The Partition of Judaeo-Christianity* (Philadelphia, 2004).

3. Israel Jacob Yuval, *Two Nations in Your Womb: Perceptions of Jews and Christians in Late Antiquity and the Middle Ages*, trans. Barbara Harshav and Jonathan Chipman (Berkeley, 2006), esp. 20–30. See, however, Susan Einbinder's review, *Speculum* 82, no. 3 (2007): 780–81, critiquing the author's lack of attention to asymmetries in power relations.

4. I use the term "acculturation" to mean the premodern (inward) process of cultural reworking, as opposed to the modern (outward) process of assimilation or secularization, distinctions drawn by Ivan G. Marcus, *Rituals of Childhood: Jewish Acculturation in Medieval Europe* (New Haven, 1996), 11–12.

5. For a fine study of such interaction, with a brief overview of recent scholarship on the question, see Eva Frojmovic, "Jewish Scribes and Christian Illuminators. Interstitial Encounters and Cultural Negotiation," in *Between Judaism and Christianity: Art Historical Essays in Honor of Elisheva (Elisabeth) Revel-Naher*, ed. Katrin Kogman-Appel and Mati Meyer (Leiden, 2009), 281–308. I regret that my essay, already finalized at the time Frojmovic's appeared, could not more fully incorporate her insights. Especially relevant is her observation, 290–92, that even where Jews most forcefully countered Christian appropriation of traditional Jewish imagery, not to mention where they creatively transformed Christian modes of representation, the artistic processes entailed "hybridity and cultural negotiation rather than separation"; my statement above regarding unavoidable acculturation and the production of a shared ritual language aims at a similar point.

6. Roger Kohn, *Les juifs de la France du Nord dans la seconde moitié du XIV siècle* (Louvain, 1988), 3–18, 25–26, 284; Roger Kohn, "Les juifs en France du Nord dans la seconde moitié du XIVe siècle: un état de la question," in *L'explusion des juifs de France, 1394*, ed. Gilbert Dahan (Paris, 2004), 13–29, esp. 22–23, 27. The edicts of Jean le Bon are published in *Ordonnances des roys de France de la troisième race*, 21 vols. (Paris, 1723–1849), 3:467–81.

7. Among the many well-known histories of Spanish Jewry, see most recently Mark D. Meyerson, *A Jewish Renaissance in Fifteenth-Century Spain* (Princeton, 2004), esp. 65–69.

8. Jeremy Cohen, *Living Letters of the Law: Ideas of the Jew in Medieval Christianity* (Berkeley, 1999), 19–65.

9. For France, see my "'. . . lectres . . . plus vrayes': Hebrew Script and Jewish Witness in the Mandeville Manuscript of Charles V (1371)," *Speculum* 83, no. 1 (2008): 58–111.

10. Supporting references for this and the next paragraph can be found in ibid., 106–9.

11. Léopold Delisle, *Recherches sur la Librairie de Charles V, Roi de France, 1337–1380*, 2 vols. (Paris, 1907; reprint, Amsterdam, 1967), 1:23–35, esp. 23–27 and 2:8–9, nos. 32–33. See Yann Potin, "A la recherche de la librairie du Louvre: le témoignage de manuscrit français 2700," *Gazette du livre médiéval* 34 (1999): 25–36, esp. 30, on the function of the parchment scroll. I thank Claire Sherman for this reference.

12. Soixante et deux caiers de la Bible que commença maistre Jehan de Sy, et laquelle faisoit translater le roy Jehan dont Diex ait l'arme; que on a fait escripre aus despenz des Juyfs (Delisle, *Recherches*, 2: 8–9, no. 32).

13. Kupfer, "'. . . lectres . . . plus vrayes,'" 90–91; see also n. 53 below.

14. Sonia Fellous, *Histoire de la Bible de Moïse Arragel. Quand un rabbin interprète la Bible pour les chrétiens* (Paris, 2001), 47–49, 64, 74, 83, 85; for a summary of her arguments, see, more recently, Fellous, "Les rois et la royauté dans la biblia de Alba," *Jewish History* 21 (2007): 69–95, esp 69–74.

15. Fellous, *Histoire*, 51. Or take the statement, 25, "Ce projet humaniste avant l'heure confiait au rabbin la realization d'une traduction qui rapproche juifs et chrétiens autour de l'Ancien Testament." This argument is reiterated in her 2007 article (per n. 14), 73, 74.

16. Eleazar Gutwirth, "The Transmission of Rabbi Moses Arragel: Maqueda, Paris, London," *Sefarad* 63, no. 1 (2003): 69–87, esp. 70, 79–80. Américo Castro, "La biblia de la casa de Alba," *El Sol*, Madrid, January 26, 1923, reprinted in *De la España que aún no conocía*, 2 vols. (Barcelona, 1990), 2:339–44.

17. *La Biblia de Alba: An Illustrated Manuscript Bible in Castilian*, 2 vols. (Madrid, 1992). Throughout, I follow the foliation in this facsimile.

18. Gutwirth, "The Politics of the Hyphen: Mediating Hispano-Jewish Cultures Today," *Jewish Quarterly Review*, n.s. 91, nos. 3–4 (2001): 395–409.

19. Thomas Glick, "Convivencia: An Introductory Note," in *Convivencia: Jews, Muslims, and Christians in Medieval Spain*, ed. Vivian B. Mann, Thomas Glick, and Jerrilynn D. Dodds (New York, 1992), 1–9; and in the same volume, Benjamin R. Gampel, "Jews, Christians, and Muslims in Medieval Iberia: Convivencia through the Eyes of Sephardic Jews," 11–38.

20. David Nirenberg, *Communities of Violence: Persecution of Minorities in the Middle Ages* (Princeton, 1996), 200–230, esp. 229; Mark D. Meyerson, *Jews in an Iberian Frontier Kingdom: Society, Economy, and Politics in Morvedre, 1248–1391* (Leiden, 2004), 6–7, 57–97.

21. Like Fellous, I shall have to cite the text as transcribed in *Biblia (Antiguo Testamento). Traducida del hebreo al castellano por Rabi Mose Arragel de Guadalfajara (1422–1433?) y publicada por el Duque de Berwick y de Alba*, ed. Antonio Paz y Melia, 2 vols. (Madrid, 1920; hereafter cited as Paz y Melia); an English edition, i.e., with Paz y Melia's introduction in translation, was published in 1918. These will be superseded by the forthcoming two-volume critical edition by Moshe Lazar. I am indebted to Professor Lazar for sending me selected pages prior to its publication. For the letters exchanged between the parties, see Paz y Melia, 1:1–15; Fellous, *Histoire*, 23–25, 75–6, 86–87, 90, 97–99.

22. Fellous, *Histoire*, 80, 99, 165, 349.

23. Ibid., 347.

24. For recent discussions, with bibliography, see the essays collected in *Hebraica Veritas? Christian Hebraists and the Study of Judaism in Early Modern Europe*, ed. Allison P. Coudert and Jeffrey S. Shoulson (Philadelphia, 2004); Deborah L. Goodwin, "Take Hold of the Robe of a Jew": *Herbert of Bosham's Christian Hebraism* (Leiden, 2006), 94–127, 231–34; Sean Eisen Murphy, "Concern about Judaizing in Academic Treatises on the Law, c. 1130–c.1230," *Speculum* 82, no. 3 (2007): 560–94; Deeana Copeland Klepper, *The Insight of Unbelievers: Nicholas of Lyra and Christian Reading of Jewish Text in the Later Middle Ages* (Philadelphia, 2007); Bernard McGinn, "Cabalists and Christians: Reflections on Cabala in Medieval and Renaissance Thought," in *Jewish Christians and Christian Jews from the Renaissance to the Enlightenment*, ed. R. H. Popkin and G. M. Weiner (Dordrecht, 1994), 11–34; Harvey J. Hames, *The Art of Conversion: Christianity and Kabbalah in the Thirteenth Century* (Leiden, 2000).

25. Fellous, *Histoire*, 23–24, 97–99 n236.

26. Arragel requests reimbursement in the last sentence of his presentation speech, fol. 24v; Paz y Melia, 1:34. Moshe Lazar, "Moses Arragel as Translator and Commentator," in *Biblia de Alba*, 2:157–200, esp. 171.

27. The implementation of Hebrew scribal practices to write the Latin characters of the Castilian text proves that Jews penned the text. Additional evidence strongly suggests that Moses Arragel himself together with his son carried out the work. See Fellous, *Histoire*, 110–15, 348–49.

28. Paz y Melia, 1:35; Lazar, "Moses Arragel," 171; Fellous, *Histoire*, 78–79.

29. Paz y Melia, 1:xviii.

30. Lazar, "Moses Arragel," 162, 168–70; Fellous, *Histoire*, 79.

31. James C. Scott, *Domination and the Arts of Resistance: Hidden Transcripts* (New Haven, 1990, hereafter cited as Scott). I draw mostly from 136–82, esp. 136–40, 152–54, and

    MARCIA KUPFER

162–66, including n. 70. For discussion of Jewish resistance to and subversion of Christian culture in art made for internal Jewish consumption, see the groundbreaking studies by Marc Michael Epstein, *Dreams of Subversion in Medieval Jewish Art and Literature* (University Park, Pa., 1997), and *Imagining the Self, Imagining the Other: Visual Representation and Jewish Christian Dynamics in the Middle Ages and Modern Period*, ed. Eva Frojmovic (Leiden, 2002). More recent work along these lines includes Frojmovic, "Reframing Gender in Medieval Jewish Images of Circumcision," in *Framing the Family: Narrative and Representation in the Medieval and Early Modern Periods*, ed. Rosalynn Voaden and Diane Wolfthal (Tempe, Ariz., 2005), 221–43; Frojmovic, "Jewish Scribes and Christian Illuminators," and Katrin Kogman-Appel, *Illuminated Haggadot from Medieval Spain: Biblical Imagery and the Passover Holiday* (University Park, Pa., 2006). I found Scott's model particularly useful in dealing with the quite different scenario, not addressed in the aforementioned literature, of a work compelled from a Jew and intended by its Christian sponsors to serve the official agenda of the dominant religion.

32. Daniel Boyarin, "The Talmud Meets Church History," reprinted in *Sparks of the Logos: Essays in Rabbinic Hermeneutics* (Leiden, 2003), 246–84, esp. 263, 268; Boyarin, *Dying for God*, 42–66.

33. Fellous, *Histoire*, 128–47.

34. Paz y Melia, 1:21–27; Lazar, "Moses Arragel," 166–68, 195–96.

35. Fellous, *Histoire*, 82, 93–97, 149–53.

36. Ibid., 225–26.

37. Ibid., 92.

38. Quotes from Lazar, "Moses Arragel," 157, 165, 162.

39. Paz y Melia, 1:18–20; Lazar, "Moses Arragel," 165; Fellous, *Histoire*, 76–77.

40. Lazar, "Moses Arragel," 157.

41. Ibid., 165; Paz y Melia, 1:19.

42. Fellous, *Histoire*, 101; Paz y Melia, 1:15: E pues tan enduresçido judio queredes seer, en non menos querer mandar a los pintores en las ystorias poner figura en Dios. . . .

43. Paz y Melia, 1:10–11; Fellous, *Histoire*, 100n246.

44. There are some differences in ketuvim. Fellous, *Histoire*, 109; Lazar, "Moses Arragel," 199.

45. Fellous, *Histoire*, 119–23, 231–40, 245–343. Kogman-Appel, *Illuminated Haggadot*, 264n167 and 247n80, notes the minimal relationship between the Alba miniatures and the pictorial cycles in haggadot from Aragon and Catalonia. Motifs inspired by Hebrew textual sources had already entered the repertory of Spanish Christian art: Cain killing Abel with a bite to the neck, as told uniquely in the Zohar, appears both in Alba and in one of the late fourteenth-century reliefs of the choir screen of Toledo Cathedral.

46. Thus Lazar, "Moses Arragel," 162, considers Alba a "Spanish-Jewish rabbinical Bible draped in some Christian garments. . . . The Christian component, which might seem from a superficial and cursory consultation of the very dense manuscript, to be quite dominant in some passages, can be seen after careful study, to be marginal at most." Conversely, earlier scholars who emphasized the Christian traditions informing the Bible's pictorial program deny that Arragel would have had anything to do with the images, notably Joseph Gutmann, in a review of Carl-Otto Nordström, *The Duke of Alba's Castilian Bible: A Study of the Rabbinical Features of the Miniatures* (Uppsala, 1967), *Art Bulletin* 51, no. 1 (1969): 91–96.

47. See Herbert L. Kessler, "'Thou Shalt Paint the Likeness of Christ Himself': The Mosaic Prohibition as Provocation for Christian Images," in *Spiritual Seeing: Picturing God's Invisibility in Medieval Art* (Philadelphia, 2000), 29–52.

48. Fellous, *Histoire*, 65.

49. The prefatory matter (fols. 1v–25r) concludes with the speeches delivered at the Franciscan convent on that occasion and with a notice about the timeframe for committee review. Blank spaces were left to fill in the exact date of the presentation, Sunday ____ November 143__. Arias states that examination commenced on Monday November 6 *del dicho año*, and was to last until ____ June 143__. Lazar, "Moses Arragel," 171, and Fellous, *Histoire*, 78–79, 102, 114, 356, differ on how to fill in the blanks. Based on his understanding of the transcription of the prefatory quires and a speedy review process, Lazar constructs the following sequence: the presentation took place on November 5, 1430, the review began on November 6 and concluded in June 1431. He fits Arragel's complaint about having spent eleven years on the project (fol. 20v) into this schema: Arragel began work in early May 1422, so June 1431 is one month into the eleventh year. For Fellous, collective scrutiny probably began in November 1430, with the phrase "of the same year" referring to the year of the bible's completion, but the presentation itself occurred in 1433 following Arragel's eleven years. Guzmán's absence at the presentation can be inferred from Arragel's and Arias's speeches.

50. Fellous, *Histoire*, 357, notes that the manuscript is not attested in the estates of the grand master, his wife, or his heirs.

51. For manuscript evidence of censors' intervention during and after production, see Fellous, *Histoire*, 84–85, 101–2; Lazar, "Moses Arragel," 171.

52. Lazar, "Moses Arragel," 158; Fellous, *Histoire*, 115–16, 357.

53. *Le songe du vergier*, ed. Marion Schnerb-Lièvre, 2 vols. (Paris, 1982), 1:355–62, esp. 1:362.

54. Wallace S. Lipton, in "Anti-Iconic Preliminaries to the 'Biblia de Alba,'" *Romance Philology* 23, no. 1 (1969): 17–38, 25, identified these figures as Jews, but, taken in by the fiction spun by the work, he misreads the image: thus, n. 16, "Can removal of a Jew's beard only in (final) illness and death betray a discreet hope to convert him before the grave in this otherwise remarkably fraternal portrayal . . .?" I owe my alternative reading to discussants at a conference at Ben Gurion University (May 2008) where I presented a version of this paper. Shulamit Laderman emphasized the absence of the red Jew's badge, leading Katrin Kogman-Appel to propose identifying the figures as converts.

55. David Nirenberg, "Poetics and Politics in an Age of Mass Conversion," in *Cultures of Conversion*, ed. Jan N. Bremmer et al. (Louvain, 2006), 31–51, and below, nn. 118, 122.

56. Paz y Melia, 1:19.

57. Ibid. The line on Euclid and explanation keyed to the marginal diagram open the fourth and penultimate chapter of the prologue.

58. Seeing straight as a metaphor for correctly understanding and following the Torah is admonished in the Talmud tractate Berakoth 17a, where it is incorporated into a blessing recited upon leaving school or the study hall. I will take up the hermeneutic and polemical implications of Arragel's optical analogy in a future publication.

59. The most important forerunner to Fellous is Nordström, *The Duke of Alba's Castilian Bible*. Although some of Nordström's ideas no longer enjoy wide support (i.e., the underlying continuity since antiquity of lost Jewish models), and despite the errors enumerated by Gutmann (see above, n. 46), the book nevertheless remains an invaluable resource.

60. The caption above the image: Figura de como estava Abraham las faldas alçadas viejo de novento años con la una mano trava la verga e con la otra se rretaja.

61. Fellous, *Histoire*, 315 and esp. 327. She likewise qualifies as anti-Jewish caricature the bloody scene of Joshua circumcising the Israelites, their foreskins piled high (Josh. 5:2–3). I interpret the Joshua scene, however, as yet another instance in which Jewish celebration of circumcision clandestinely infiltrates the official Christian "transcript" of the Alba commission. A more extensive discussion of the Abraham and Joshua scenes than I can undertake here will have to await a future publication.

62. Fellous, *Histoire*, 327, under fig. 205.

63. For an overview of this topic, with bibliography, see Shaye J. D. Cohen, *Why Aren't Jewish Women Circumcised? Gender and Covenant in Judaism* (Berkeley, 2005), 68–108.

64. David Biale, *Blood and Belief: The Circulation of a Symbol between Jews and Christians* (Berkeley, 2007), 7, 44–122. On ways in which medieval Jewish images of circumcision (Isaac's, and Eliezer's by Zipporah) emphasized its sacrificial and salvific dimensions, see Frojmovic, "Reframing Gender in Medieval Jewish Images of Circumcision," esp. 222, 233–34, 240, 243.

65. For a debate on the developmental trajectory prior to c. 800, see Lawrence A. Hoffman, *Covenant of Blood: Circumcision and Gender in Rabbinic Judaism* (Chicago, 1996), 100–110; Cohen, *Why Aren't Jewish Women Circumcised*, 3–54, esp. 28–43; and Biale, *Blood and Belief*, 69–73.

66. Cohen, *Why Aren't Jewish Women Circumcised*, 43–45.

67. Caroline Walker Bynum, *Wonderful Blood: Theology and Practice in Late Medieval Northern Germany and Beyond* (Philadelphia, 2007).

68. Cohen, *Why Aren't Jewish Women Circumcised*, 163.

69. Arguably the Zohar is itself informed on many counts by the Christianity that it clandestinely attacks. See Yehuda Liebes, "Christian Influences on the Zohar," reprinted in *Studies in the Zohar*, trans. Arnold Schwartz et al. (Albany, 1993), 139–61, 228–44. For a succinct overview of the complex relationship between the Zohar and Christianity, see Arthur Green, *A Guide to the Zohar* (Stanford, 2004), 86–98, 140–44. On anti-Christian (and anti-Islamic) polemics within the Zohar, see Elliot R. Wolfson, *Venturing Beyond: Law and Morality in Kabbalistic Mysticism* (Oxford, 2006), 129–85, esp. 135–42 for imagery comparing "the children of Edom" (Christians) to menstruating women.

70. Green, *Guide*, 147–50. Elliot Wolfson, "Circumcision and the Divine Name: A Study in the Transmission of Esoteric Doctrine," *Jewish Quarterly Review* n.s. 78, nos. 1–2 (1987): 77–112; Wolfson, "Circumcision, Vision of God and Textual Interpretation: From Midrashic Trope to Mystical Symbol," *History of Religions* 27, no. 2 (1987), 189–215; Wolfson, *Through a Speculum That Shines: Vision and Imagination in Medieval Jewish Mysticism* (Princeton, 1994), 326–92; Gershom Scholem, *On the Mystical Shape of the Godhead: Basic Concepts in Kabbalah*, trans. Joachim Neugroschel, ed. Jonathan Chipman (New York, 1991), 88–139; Moshe Idel, *Ascensions on High in Jewish Mysticism: Pillars, Lines, Ladders* (Budapest and New York, 2005), esp. pp. 73–142.

71. On the long history of this process in Jewish art, see the bibliography provided in n. 31 above.

72. *Pirke de Rabbi Eliezer (The chapters of Rabbi Eliezer the Great) According to the Text of the Manuscript Belonging to Abraham Epstein of Vienna*, ed. and trans. Gerald Friedlander, 2nd ed. (New York, 1965), 204. I have modified the last line of the Friedlander translation in accordance with Cohen, *Why Aren't Jewish Women Circumcised*, 31. For a discussion of this passage from the Pirqei, see Biale, *Blood and Belief*, 71–72; on the verse from Ezekiel, see ibid., 34.

73. *Pirke* (Friedlander), 210.

74. Louis Ginzberg, *Legends of the Jews*, 2nd ed., 2 vols. (Philadelphia, 2003), 1:196n83.

75. Biale, *Blood and Belief*, 96–97.

76. Ibid., 73, 96–97.

77. *Midrash Rabbeinu Bachya: Torah Commentary by Rabbi Bachya ben Asher*, trans. Eliyahu Munk, 7 vols., 2nd ed. (Jerusalem, 2003), 4:1204; for the Hebrew text, see the edition of C. B. Chavel, *Rabbenu Bahya on the Torah*, 3 vols. (Jerusalem, 1968), 2:252–3. I am indebted to Joseph Galron-Goldschläger, Hebraica and Jewish Studies Librarian at the Ohio State

University, for his help in finding these sources. Biale, *Blood and Belief*, 93–94, discusses Hananel's explication of Exod. 24:8.

78. *Midrash Rabbeinu Bachya*, 4:1204

79. Munk, *Midrash Rabbeinu Bachya*, 1:266–69; Chavel, *Rabbenu Bahya on the Torah*, 1:160–62.

80. *Pirke* (Friedlander), 207.

81. See Wolfson, *Venturing Beyond*, 155–65, on the depiction of Islam in Spanish Kabbalah.

82. Daniel Boyarin, "'This We Know to Be the Carnal Israel': Circumcision and the Erotic Life of God and Israel," *Critical Inquiry* 18, no. 3 (1992): 474–505, esp. 482–83, 485–91.

83. Lazar, "Moses Arragel," 159.

84. Fellous, *Histoire*, 171, 194, 321–23, 305; for the quoted passage, 140–41n338; in Paz y Melia, 1:123–24.

85. *The Wisdom of the Zohar: An Anthology of Texts*, 3 vols., ed. Isaiah Tishby, trans. David Goldstein (Oxford, 1989), 3:1181. On the Zohar and the Pirqei, see Cohen, *Why Aren't Jewish Women Circumcised*, 30.

86. Wolfson, "Circumcision and the Divine Name," 101, 109.

87. *The Zohar* (Pritzker Edition), trans. and commentary by Daniel C. Matt (Stanford, 2004), 2:86 and n. 657. All subsequent citations from the text refer to volume and page number in this edition.

88. *Zohar*, 2:74–75.

89. 1:95a, b in *Zohar*, 2:103–4.

90. Wolfson, "Circumcision and the Divine Name," 77–112, quote from 112.

91. *Zohar*, 2:116: The word "appeared" in Gen. 18:1 ("The Lord appeared to him by the terebinths of Mamre") is the trigger for the citation of Song of Songs 2:12, in which, per editor's n. 1, the Hebrew word for singing (zamir) also means pruning.

92. *Zohar*, 2:117–18.

93. Wolfson, *Venturing Beyond*, 151–54.

94. *Zohar*, 2:79–90, esp. 85–86 for 1:93a.

95. Ibid., 2:81–82n629; on the symbolism of Eden, see also Arthur Green's introduction to the edition, 1:lxxiii.

96. See the discussion of *Midrash Tanḥuma*, Tsav 14, in Wolfson, "Circumcision and the Divine Name," 78–80; Jonathan Boyarin and Daniel Boyarin, "Self-Exposure as Theory: The Double Mark of the Male Jew," in *Rhetorics of Self-Making*, ed. Debbora Battaglia (Berkeley, 1995), 16–42, esp. 24. This midrashic tradition is incorporated in the commentary on Genesis 17 in *Zohar*, 2:103–4 and 104n794.

97. Wolfson, "Circumcision, Vision of God," 206; Wolfson, "Beautiful Maiden without Eyes: *Peshat* and *Sod* in Zoharic Hermeneutics," in *The Midrashic Imagination: Jewish Exegesis, Thought, and History*, ed. Michael Fishbane (Albany, 1993), 155–203, esp. 175–76.

98. Wolfson, "Circumcision, Vision of God," 201–2.

99. On semen as blood, see, e.g., Danielle Jacquart and Claude Thomasset, *Sexuality and Medicine in the Middle Ages* (Princeton, 1988), 54, 60.

100. On the identification of the Shekhinah with the corona, see Elliot R. Wolfson, "Crossing Gender Boundaries in Kabblistic Ritual and Myth," in *Circle in the Square: Studies in the Use of Gender in Kabbalistic Symbolism* (Albany, 1995), 79–121, esp. 88, 107; Wolfson, *Through a Speculum That Shines*, 336–45, 357–68.

101. Wolfson, "Circumcision, Vision of God," 189–215, esp. 192–98.

102. Ibid., 207–15; Wolfson, "Circumcision and the Divine Name," 100–106; Wolfson, "Beautiful Maiden without Eyes," esp. 169–70 and 185–86.

103. Apart from the Alba and Jean de Sy Bibles, the list includes the Millstatt Genesis (*Millstätter Genesis und Physiologus Handschrift. Vollständige Facsimileausgabe der Sammelhandschrift 6/19 des Geschichtsvereines für Kärnten im Kärtner Landesarchiv, Klagenfurt*, 2 vols. [Graz, 1967]); the Egerton Genesis (Mary Coker Joslin and Carolyn Coker Joslin Watson, *The Egerton Genesis* [London, 2001]); the biblical cycle prefacing the *Omne Bonum* (Lucy Freeman Sandler, *Omne Bonum: A Fourteenth-Century Encyclopedia of Universal Knowledge*, 2 vols. [London, 1996]); and the Padua Bible (Gianfranco Folena e Gian Lorenzo Mellini, *Bibbia Istoriata Padovana dell fine del trecento* [Venice, 1962]; Susan MacMillan Arensberg, "The Padua Bible and the Late Medieval Biblical Picture Book" [Ph.D. diss., Johns Hopkins University, 1986]; "Bibbia istoriata padovana," in *La miniatura a padova dal medioevo al settecento*, exhibition catalogue [Modena, 1999], 161–73).

104. The mosaics of the Abraham cupola in the atrium of S. Marco, Venice; and the Velislav Bible (*Velislai Biblia picta*, ed. Karel Stejskal, 2 vols. [Prague, 1970]). On the relationship of members of the extended set to the Cotton Genesis, see Kurt Weitzmann and Herbert L. Kessler, *The Cotton Genesis: British Library Codex Cotton Oho B. VI* (Princeton, 1986), esp. 18–26, 78–79, and John Lowden, "Concerning the Cotton Genesis and Other Illustrated Manuscripts of Genesis," *Gesta* 31, no. 1 (1992): 40–53.

105. Millstatt, Egerton, Padua, and Velislav

106. *Omne Bonum.*

107. Fol. 22v, col. A: . . . ceste apparicion de dieu fu par .i. angre. qui auoit pris la semblance dun homme. et parloit comme diex si comme le legat parle comme le pape. et parlement parle comme Roy.

108. On Paul's invocation of angelic delivery to degrade the law, see Ithamar Gruenwald, "Midrash and the 'Midrashic Condition': Preliminary Considerations," in *The Midrashic Imagination*, 6–22, esp. 17–18. Note also Acts 7:53, where the martyr Stephen rebukes the Jews "who received the Law as an ordinance of angels."

109. Fol. 22v, col A, continuing from n. 107 above: et pource que il creust nier a sa promesse de ysaac qui sensuit il li dist que il estoit diex tout puissant si comme gabriel dist a la vierge marie. ou premier chapitre. s. luc. toute parole ne sera mie impossible devant dieu. . . .

110. For examples, see Deslisle, *Recherches* (as in n. 11), 1:406–7.

111. Millstatt, Jean de Sy, and Padua as well as in Alba

112. Egerton; *Omne Bonum*, where the male and female figures, respectively, wielding the knife and holding the patriarch's legs, recur exactly in the scene of infant circumcision set within the historiated initial C for the encyclopedia entry *Circumcisio* (fol. 269r); see Sandler, *Omne Bonum*, 1:103, 2:105.

113. Eliminated in Millstatt, Jean de Sy, Velislav, *Omne Bonum*. In Egerton, the only blood depicted—in the basin below Abraham—is barely noticeable. The discussion of the scene by Joslin and Watson, *Egerton Genesis*, 83, needs some fine tuning. Contrary to their description, the knives in the scene are not bloody. And they have misread the image in the Millstatt Genesis, which depicts two successive phases in the narrative, Abraham receiving the divine command and then carrying it out. He raises a knife with one hand and with the other holds his penis.

114. Kogman-Appel, *Illuminated Haggadot*, 92–94, 123–31, 164–65; Sarit Shalev-Eyni, "The Antecedents of the Padua Bible and Its Parallels in Spain," *Arte Medievale* 4, no. 2 (2005), 83–94.

115. Shalev-Eyni, "Antecedents," 90–91.

116. Kogman-Appel, *Illuminated Haggadot*, 165.

117. Joslin and Watson, *Egerton Genesis*, p. 83.

118. David Nirenberg, "Figures of Thought and Figures of Flesh: 'Jews' and 'Judaism' in Late-Medieval Spanish Poetry and Politics," *Speculum* 81, no. 2 (2006): 398–426, esp. 402–5.

119. Scott, *Domination and the Arts of Resistance*, 139–40.

120. See Fellous, *Histoire*, 283–86, on miniatures illustrating the prophecies of Ezekiel 38–39 (fol. 342r) and Zechariah 14 (fol. 368r), 288–327, for other examples.

121. Scott, *Domination and the Arts of Resistance*, 35: "The white slave master is always wary of being put on by his slaves; an eighteenth-century Japanese landlord can wonder, 'Does anyone lie as much as a peasant?' What is notable here, I believe, is not that the dominant should assume that wily subordinates will try to get around them. To believe that is not to be paranoid; it is merely to perceive reality. They attribute such behavior, however, not to the effect of arbitrary power but rather to the inborn characteristics of the subordinate group itself."

122. Discussed in a series of articles by David Nirenberg, "El concepto de la raza en la España medieval," *Edad Media* 3 (2000): 39–60; "Mass Conversion and Genealogical Mentalities: Jews and Christians in Fifteenth-Century Spain," *Past and Present* 174 (2002): 3–41; "Conversion, Sex and Segregation: Jews and Christians in Medieval Spain," *American Historical Review* 107 (2002): 1065–93; "Enmity and Assimilation: Jews, Christians, and Converts in Medieval Spain," *Common Knowledge* 9, 1 (2003): 137–55.

123. Moshe Lazar, "Anti-Jewish and Anti-Converso Propaganda: Confutatio libri Talmud and Alboraique," in *The Jews of Spain and the Expulsion of 1492*, ed. Moshe Lazar and Stephen Haliczer (Lancaster, Calif., 1997), 153–236.

124. Jonathan Elukin, "From Jew to Christian? Conversion and Immutability in Medieval Europe," in *Varieties of Religious Conversion in the Middle Ages*, ed. James Muldoon (Gainesville, Fla., 1997), 171–90, esp. 183–84. For a larger discussion of immutability as an ontological problem in Bernard's thought, see Caroline Walker Bynum, "Monsters, Medians, and Marvelous Mixtures: Hybrids in the Spirituality of Bernard of Clairvaux," in *Metamorphosis and Identity* (New York, 2001), 113–62.

125. *Apologia ad Guillelmum Abbatem* 12, 29 in Conrad Rudolph, *The "Things of Greater Importance": Bernard of Clairvaux's Apologia and the Medieval Attitude toward Art* (Philadelphia, 1990), 282–83.

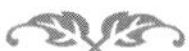

CHAPTER 6

Frau Venus, the Eucharist,
and the Jews of Landshut

Achim Timmermann

In an article published a number of years ago in the journal *Gesta,* I examined the image of the Living Cross, without doubt one of the most violent anti-Jewish Crucifixion allegories of the later Middle Ages.[1] In most of the forty or so surviving examples, as at St. Francis at Poniky in Slovakia (Figure 6.1),[2] four hands, gesturing or holding objects, grow from the arms of the cross to which Christ has been nailed. The hands at the top and bottom of the vertical stem unlock the gate of heaven and obliterate hell or Purgatory, respectively, while the horizontal crossbar—known as the *patibulum*—generates two hands that pass judgment on the personifications of Ecclesia and Synagoga riding or standing beneath them. Usually the dexter hand crowns or blesses the church, while that on Christ's sinister side, wielding sword, dagger, or arrow, stabs the head, neck, or breast of Synagoga, not only keeping her at bay but completely annihilating her. In my study, I paid particular attention to the action of the left hand, delivering the fatal blow to Synagoga. I argued that beyond mercilessly allegorizing the redundancy of the Old Law, this iconography lends itself to specific historical readings, as it glosses on contemporary events, narratives, and anxieties. I thus contended that the Living Cross punishes Synagoga and her followers, the Jews, and as such may be read as a polemical inversion of contemporary stories of purported Jewish abuse, especially those of Eucharist desecration and ritual murder, recently explored in a series of thought-provoking studies by Miri Rubin, Ronnie Po-chia Hsia, and Wolfgang Treue.[3] In the image, the roles of subject and object, of perpetrator and victim, become reversed. I

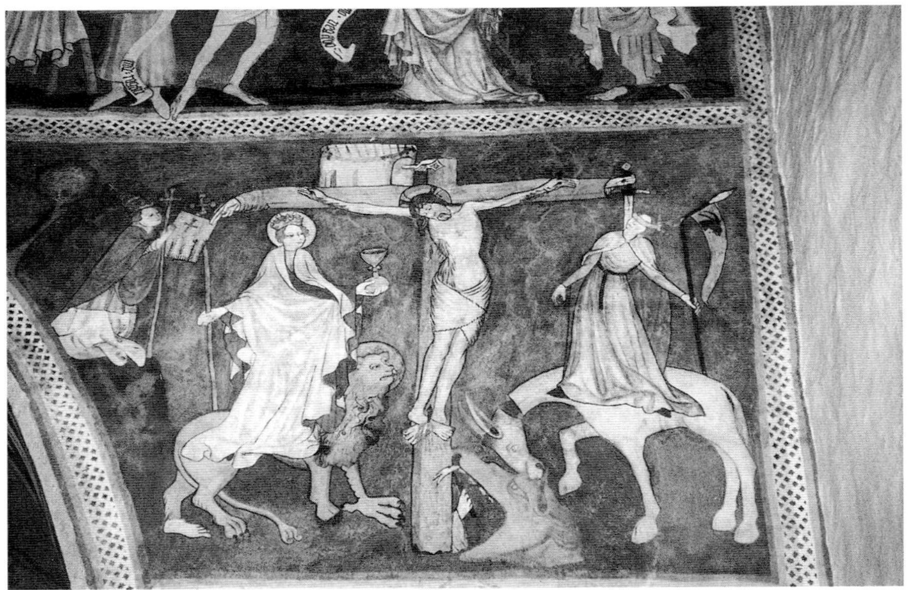

6.1. Poniky, St. Francis, Living Cross, 1415. Photo: Achim Timmermann.

also advanced the argument that the development of this iconography needs to be understood in the broader context of the fifteenth-century church reform and its anti-heretical propaganda, which often accused the Jews of collusion with heretics, the Bohemian Hussites in particular. It seemed significant to me that the image appeared at precisely the time when the Roman church was threatened by fragmentation, from within and without. In view of the Living Cross at Poniky, dating to 1415, I reasoned that the incorporation of the figure of a pope to the left of Ecclesia can be read as a contemporary conciliarist statement about the concord of the papal church under the banner of the sacrament, while defeated Synagoga on the left side of Christ symbolized and subsumed in herself at once Jews, Hussites, and other perceived foes of the church.

I wish here to return to the image of the Living Cross, focusing on one specific example, which adorns the tympanum of the west portal of St. Martin's church at Landshut, Lower Bavaria (Figures 6.2, 6.3).[4] The Landshut Living Cross is unusual for two reasons: not only is it the sole surviving sculptural adaptation of this iconography from before the Protestant Reformation,[5] the representation also substitutes the traditional figure of Ecclesia personified with that of a priest celebrating Mass before his congregation. What partly prompted me to undertake this study was an entry in a recent exhibition catalogue that, based on a number of older, local publications not known to me before, convincingly argued that the traditional dating of the tympanum to 1432—which I

          ACHIM TIMMERMANN

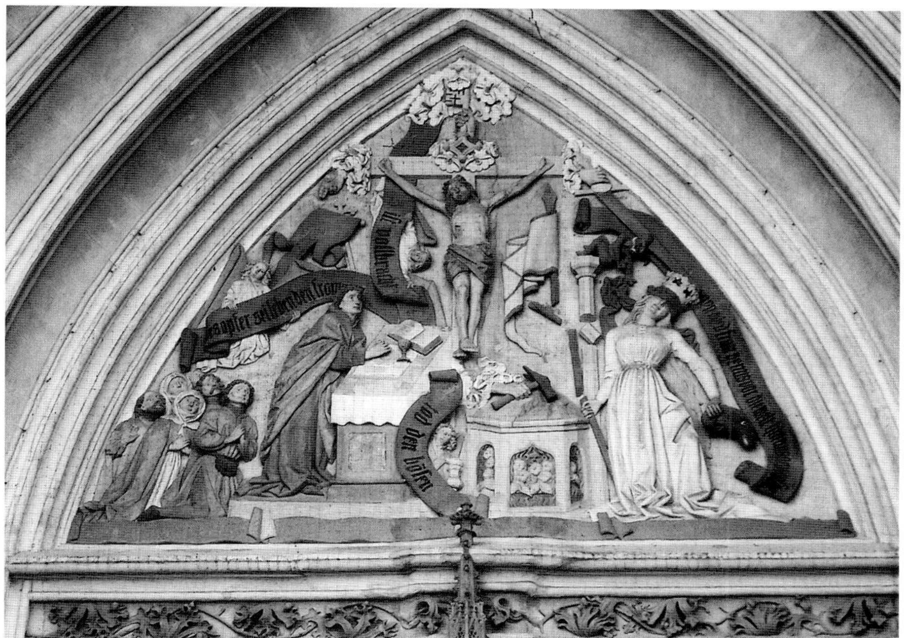

6.2. Landshut, St. Martin, Living Cross, 1452. Photo: Achim Timmermann.

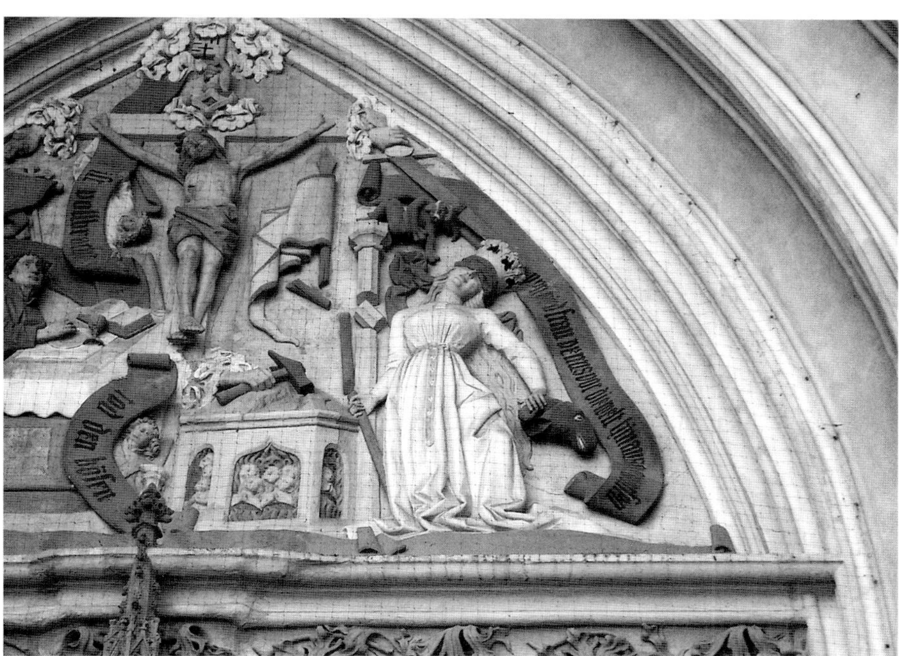

6.3. Landshut, St. Martin, Living Cross, detail of Synagoga. Photo: Achim Timmermann.

had assumed to be accurate in my *Gesta* article[6]—is in fact erroneous, and that the correct date of this ensemble must in fact be 1452.[7] This redating in turn allows for the Living Cross tympanum to be considered in the context of a series of dramatic events that culminated in the expulsion of Landshut's Jews in 1450, and in the appropriation of their synagogue for Christian use in 1452.

Before turning to the image, we need to recapitulate briefly the argument for its re-dating, and look at its location within the urban fabric of Landshut itself. Measuring about thirteen by eleven feet, the Living Cross extends above the west door of the parish church of St. Martin's, a vast hall church begun c. 1385 by Hans von Burghausen, and completed, save for the upper parts of the colossal west tower, by the latter's nephew, Hans Stethaimer, who died in 1461.[8] Dendrochronological research has confirmed that the foundations for the 440-foot tower—incidentally the tallest brick spire in the world[9]—were not laid until 1444 to 1445, which strongly suggests that the date we find inscribed in Arabic numerals on a scroll below the tympanum—1432—and which numerous scholars including myself have so far relied on to date the Living Cross, is in fact incorrect.[10] It is certainly conceivable that the date was deliberately falsified to mark the tower as the achievement of St. Martin's *first* architect, Hans von Burghausen, who died in 1432, though it is equally possible that the inscription was accidentally altered during a post-medieval restoration of the portal, for instance in the wake of the Swedish occupation of Landshut in 1634, which had caused considerable damage to the church.[11] At any rate, it can safely be assumed that given the fact that work on the western tower did not commence until the mid-1440s, the inscription must be read as 1452 rather than 1432. This re-dating is corroborated by the tympanum figures themselves, whose powerful plasticity stands in marked contrast to the lyricism of the *Weicher Stil* or Soft Style, exemplified by the high altar of St. Martin's, which dates to the mid-1420s, and which is introduced toward the end of this essay (Figure 6.7).

St. Martin's church itself faces the main thoroughfare of Landshut, the so-called Altstadt, which bisects the western half of the city in a north-south direction. On a hill to the south of the Martinskirche rises Castle Trausnitz, during the high and later Middle Ages the principal residence of the dukes of Bavaria-Wittelsbach, who will play a significant role in my argument. To the southwest, neatly wedged between church and castle, is the so-called Dreifaltigkeitsplatz,[12] whose position roughly marks the extent of the former Jewish quarter, also known as "unter den Juden."[13] Founded during the thirteenth century (perhaps as early as 1204, concurrently with the foundation of the Landshut itself), the *Judenviertel* was one of the largest and most prosperous in Bavaria; by the mid-fifteenth century, its four or five hundred inhabitants made up about a tenth of the overall population of the city. At the heart of the religious, cultural, and

   ACHIM TIMMERMANN

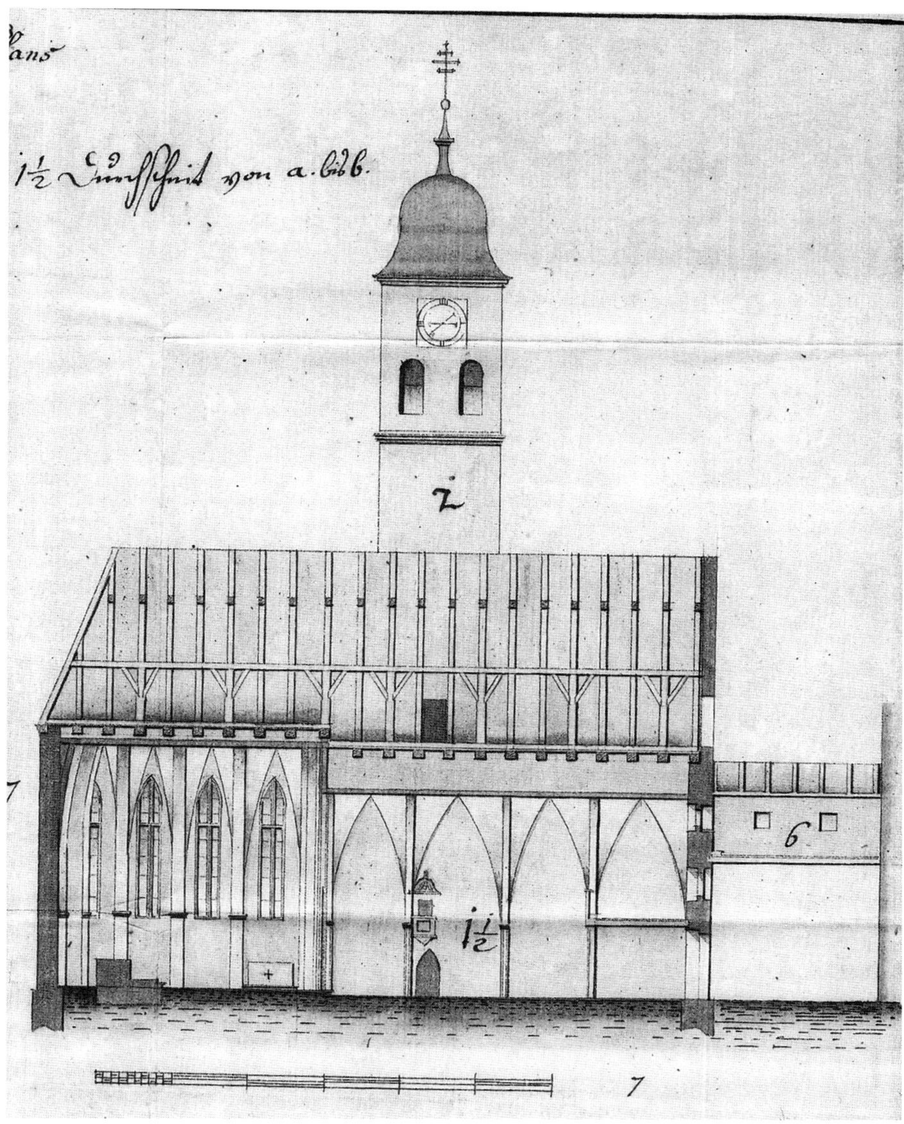

6.4. Joseph Huber, longitudinal section of Landshut's synagogue, c. 1807 (Landshut, Stadtarchiv). Photo courtesy Stadtarchiv.

social life of Landshut's Jews was the synagogue, also known locally as the *Judenschule* (or simply *Schul*), which stood in a walled enclosure at the eastern extremity of "unter den Juden" (Figure 6.4). The building that served the religious needs of Landshut's Jews around the time of their expulsion was probably of mid-fourteenth century origin, though it is likely that it rose on the foundations of an earlier predecessor.[14] Other important public edifices or institutions essential to Jewish life and ritual included the so-called *Trukchhaus* or butcher's shop, the bakery or *Backhaus*, in which the *mazzoth* were prepared, the *mikwe* (locally referred to simply as the "hole" or *Loch*), a fountain with a cistern, as well as the cemetery. Archaeological research carried out during the 1980s suggests that the *Backhaus* and *Trukchhaus* stood in closest proximity to the synagogue, respectively occupying positions at or around the site of the extant ducal granary, the Herzogkasten (1468–70), and in the center of what is now the Dreifaltigkeitsplatz. Anyone entering or exiting the Jewish quarter at the southern end of the city walls would have done so through the Neues Judentor or New Jew's Gate, sometimes also called the Münchnertor, demolished in 1874.[15]

The Living Cross

Activated through Christ's mortal agonies—graphically represented here by his taut, drawn-out corpus—the cross generates four hands, which, growing from sleeve-like clouds at the end of each cross arm, bring about mankind's Salvation through various tools and gestures (Figure 6.2). Replacing the traditional titulus, the hand sprouting from the top of the upright cross bar thus inserts a large golden key into a crumpled cloud, which either represents or obscures the entrance to the Heavenly City. At the lower end of the vertical stem a second hand, now wielding a hammer, cracks open the dome-shaped roof of Purgatory, a polygonal theater of fiery horror, in which grimacing devils preside over the inaudible laments of the poor souls. As the hammer smashes this blazing habitat, a small vested angel, holding a jug of water and a loaf of bread, promises temporary relief, if not from searing pain then at least from thirst and hunger.[16] His charitable gesture is echoed by St. Martin on the trumeau below, who divides his cloak to clothe a crippled beggar.[17] Whether the angel was meant to be an occasional visitor or a permanent presence is open to conjecture; while some theologians such as the twelfth-century mystic Elizabeth of Schönau maintained that such merciful angels called on the imprisoned souls only twice a year, specifically on the feast day of St. Michael and on All Souls Day, other writers, including the fourteenth-century Franciscan Marquard of Lindau, argued for their continuous presence in or near Limbo.[18]

While the upright stem of the Landshut Cross transports the viewer from Purgatory into Heaven, from harrowing atonement to blissful subsumation in God, the *patibulum* passes inexorable judgment on the New and Old Law (as well as their adherents), and in doing so once more transforms into a vector between the opposite states of pertinence, and complete and utter redundancy. While Judaism assumes the traditional guise of Synagoga, its nemesis, the

ACHIM TIMMERMANN

church, is allegorized not as the typical female personification of Ecclesia, but as a priest celebrating Mass before a congregation.

We consider both allegories in sequence, beginning with that of the church, which is, not in the least surprisingly, blessed by the dexter hand of the *patibulum*. Its main protagonist is an almost life-sized priest, dressed in alb and chasuble, and clearly marked by the bannered cross-staff above him as Ecclesia's lawful representative. As he expectantly raises his gaze toward, though not at, the suffering Savior, his hands almost mechanically perform the *fractio panis* at a perspectively tilted altar strewn with the paraphernalia of Mass—an open missal, a white corporal, a silver paten, and—conspicuously located near Christ's side wound—a golden chalice. On the floor behind him kneel his parishioners, at once generic members of the *corpus mysticum*, and decorously though not unfashionably dressed burghers of mid-fifteenth-century Landshut. Hovering above this ritual scene are two vested angels, whose unwieldy, flapping banderoles announce that "this sacrifice shall give life to the just, and death to the wicked" ("das opfer sei leben den frommen, tod den bösen").[19] The inscription appears deliberately ambiguous, as "opfer" can refer to both Christ's historical sacrifice on the cross, which is accompanied here by a scroll inscribed with the words of John 19:30, "It is accomplished" ("es ist vollbracht"), and the timeless reenactment of that sacrifice in the sacrament of the Eucharist. In this context I once more wish to draw attention to the edifice of Purgatory at the base of the cross, with its imprisoned souls, and to the small angel with the water jug, who, upon second glance, appears to have crawled out of the altar at which the priest breaks the bread. At Landshut, it seems the fate of the poor souls is positively affected by both the continuous hammering of the cross hand, a metaphor for Limbo's ultimate redundancy, and the priest's action at the high altar, the *fractio panis* into three pieces—a ritual division that according to Berthold of Regensburg signifies the three parts of the *corpus mysticum*, namely those who live on earth, those who are in heaven, and those who dwell in Purgatory.[20] This interpretation, which effectively transforms the *Armeseelen* into active participants of the eucharistic ceremony, also appears to have left its mark on the Landshut tympanum, where the poor souls devoutly clasp their hands in prayer and eagerly turn their heads toward the high altar and its angelic messenger.

While portrayals of Purgatory can be found in other versions of the Living Cross, for instance at Lindar in Istria, where the souls are entrapped in a giant wooden vat (c. 1430–40),[21] the combination of Limbo with a scene of Mass *substituting* the traditional figure of Ecclesia is unique to Landshut. Possible iconographical sources for this specific choice include representations of so-called *Armeseelenmessen*, Poor Souls' Masses, as shown, for instance, in a stained glass window in the Collegiate Church of Niederhaslach, Alsace,[22] and the imagery of the *Gregorsmesse* or Gregorymass, by the mid-fifteenth century still a relatively recent pictorial invention.[23] In one of the earliest printed Gregorymasses, a German single-leaf woodcut of c. 1460, cords transmit the beneficial effects of Gregory's vision into the blazing pit of Purgatory (Washington, National Gallery of Art).[24] Just why the Landshut sculptors and their iconographical advisors sought to adjust their Living Cross to incorporate this type of imagery is suggested below.

For the time being, however, I return to the tympanum itself and focus on the figure of Synagoga, who meets her violent end below the sinister side of Christ (Figure 6.3). Wearing a tight-fitting, belted robe that highlights her feminine forms, almost to the point of caricature, and trailing a cascade of disheveled blond hair, Synagoga is the embodiment of gendered, sexualized carnality, and as such the scandalous antithesis to the miraculous enfleshment of the *logos* celebrated on the other side of the cross. Yet this alluring seductress crumbles before the beholder's gaze, as her lower body, obscured by myriad edgy folds, appears to dissolve into the ground, and as her bannered lance, held too close to the numinous body of the Crucified, suddenly snaps into splinters. To precipitate her fall, an executioner's sword, swung by the left hand of the *patibulum*, simultaneously lashes at her crown and at a horned idol falling from a column beside her. As Synagoga and her grotesque companion lose their balance and topple toward the edge of the pictorial field, a banderole unfurls and ominously declares "Now Frau Venus will be cast from this world" ("Nun wird Frau Venus vor die Welt hinausgeworfen"). The designation "Frau Venus" may at first seem surprising—if not entirely inaccurate—though the term aptly encapsulates and invokes those vices that Landshut's Synagoga is most associated with, that is unbridled sexual passion, *luxuria*, and idol worship, *idolatria*.[25] In the following I wish to concentrate on the significance and implications of the latter part of the inscription—Frau Venus, it will be remembered, *is to be driven from this world*.

The Jews of Landshut

On October 5, 1450, Duke Ludwig IX of Bavaria-Landshut, also known as the Rich (reg. 1450–79), ordered the arrest of every Jew in his far-flung south German territories.[26] Having only just succeeded his father, Heinrich (who died July 29, 1450), the detention of his Jewish subjects was Ludwig's first political act.[27] The Jewish men were imprisoned in the so-called *Schergenstube*, the civic jail, while their women and children were held captive in the synagogue, located on the east side of the present Dreifaltigkeitsplatz. Ludwig then commanded the

ACHIM TIMMERMANN

confiscation of all Jewish property. Furthermore, in order to secure their release from prison, Landshut's Jews were made to pay the enormous sum of 25,000 gulden Rhenish. Once the last gulden had been received by the Duke's treasurer, the Jews were given three days either to leave the city or to accept baptism and conversion.[28] Most chose exile, leaving Landshut through the Neues Judentor, and soon all physical traces of their former presence in the city, including the *mikwe*, bakery, and cistern, were obliterated.[29] Only the synagogue escaped complete destruction. On the orders of Duke Ludwig, it was converted into a church dedicated to the Holy Trinity (*Dreifaltigkeit*) and consecrated with great pomp on November 19, 1452. The conversion involved the transformation of the main body of the synagogue into a nave, and, more important, the addition of a new, luminously glazed choir,[30] erected to the plans of the then-architect of St. Martin's, Hans Stethaimer. An approximate idea of the appearance of Ludwig's Dreifaltigkeitskirche can be gleaned from Jakob Sandtner's famous model of Landshut, made in 1571 and now preserved in the Bayerisches National-almuseum, Munich,[31] and from a cross-section drawn by the court architect Joseph Huber just before the demolition of this church in 1807 (Figure 6.4).[32]

Even before these violent and catastrophic events unfolded between 1450 and 1452, the situation of Landshut's Jews had become increasingly precarious. In 1449, a year prior to their expulsion, they were thus faced with accusations of Host desecration and ritual infanticide, both from an itinerant Fransciscan named Heinrich Feichtwanger, who preached before great crowds in St. Martin's church,[33] and from the Dominican inquisitor Heinrich Kalteisen, who in a letter addressed to Ludwig's father, Duke Heinrich, spoke with great gusto of the "Jewish need for Christian blood."[34] While Ludwig's motives for the banishment of the Jews and the confiscation of their possessions were probably entirely financial, he did not hesitate to justify his actions with similar arguments of alleged Jewish crimes. Writing in 1461 to Emperor Frederick III, he thus maintained that he had ordered the banishment "because the Jews had brutally tortured the holy sacrament" ("das sy sich am heyligen sacrament gröblich verwürchet [. . .] haben").[35] Still further in this correspondence, he accused the Jews of "illegally procuring and grossly desecrating the venerable sacrament of our dear body of Christ" ("das die judischait mit dem wirdigen sakrament unseres lieben fronleichnam etwas ain grossen frävel und hanndl begangen hieten").[36] To a modern reader, the vagueness and mechanical nature of these charges are truly remarkable, particularly as Bavaria's list of ostensible Host desecration cases was notoriously long, even by the mid-fifteenth century.[37] Clearly, to Ludwig and most of his contemporaries, the mere invocation of this arch-narrative of Jewish abuse appeared entirely sufficient to silence all critics.

It is my contention that the Living Cross of St. Martin's glosses the events of 1449 to 1452 in three significant ways (again, the correct dating of the image to 1452 ought to be kept in mind here). First, the dislodging of Synagoga and the accompanying text "Now Frau Venus will be cast from this world" commemorates the banishment of Landshut's Jewish community in 1450, though the future tense of the inscription and the phrase "vor die Welt" promise what can only be described as the global erasure of the Jews and their religion. While Synagoga's position below the sinister side of Christ tallies with the traditional right-left dialectics of images of the Living Cross (and similar such Crucifixion allegories),[38] the fact that she *sinks toward* the former Jewish quarter and its converted synagogue, located just two hundred yards due south, would not have been lost on the contemporary viewer. Furthermore, as is suggested in Figure 6.5, her fall *away* from the body of Christ established a vector toward Neues Judentor at the southern end of the present Dreifaltigkeitsplatz—the starting point of the Jewish exodus in November 1450. The photograph in Figure 6.5 was taken from directly below the figure of Synagoga; it shows the ducal granary (the large building in the left middle ground), the Dreifaltigkeitsplatz and—at the end of the thoroughfare—a yellow house that was built on the site of the Judentor, torn down in 1874. The same vector of sight and movement has been inscribed onto a modern map of Landshut's historic city center.

Second, the Living Cross celebrates the absolute victory of Ecclesia—here in the guise of an officiating priest—over Synagoga, and as such also reflects on the conversion of Landshut's former synagogue into the Dreifaltigkeitskirche, completed in 1452 (Figure 6.4). Of course, in the tympanum, Synagoga, with her idolatrous and wanton antics, has no use-value whatsoever and suffers total annihilation, while the fabric of the *Judenschule* was retained as the nave of the new church. But again, the right-left dichotomy of the image, with its sequence of eucharistic ceremony, crucifix, and Synagoga, encourages a topographical reading, as it would probably have echoed the divisions within the Dreifaltigkeitskirche itself. It is thus likely that Hans Stethaimer's lofty *schönn Korr* was initially separated from the only dimly lit synagogue-turned-nave by some kind of rood-screen surmounted by a cross or representation of Calvary. In the new Dreifaltigkeitskirche, this arrangement would have been invested with heightened significance: not only would the body of the crucified have divided clergy from laity, it would also have dramatized the total soteriological triumph of Ecclesia over Synagoga.

Third—and I have elaborated on this aspect in my *Gesta* article[39]—the Living Cross comments on the charges of Host desecration and ritual infanticide,

ACHIM TIMMERMANN

6.5. Landshut, view of the Dreifaltigkeitsplatz (the area of the former Jewish quarter), as seen from directly below the figure of Synagoga. Photo: Achim Timmermann.

levied against Landshut's Jews in 1449 and the following years. These accusations—and their pictorial reenactments, such as the famous Passu *Hostienfrevel* broadsheet of c. 1477[40]—helped construct an ethnography of Jewish abuse, in which the holy and innocent was defiled and profaned, and wickedly sacrificed, continuing the biblical Passion narrative to the present day. As the sacrament is victimized by the traditional enemies of the church, most often through piercing, cutting, or stabbing, the agonies of the body of Christ are perpetuated. Landshut's Living Cross—as well as the other examples of this imagery—effectively turn this narrative on its head. Miraculously activated by the Savior's self-immolation, the instrument of his torture and death becomes kineticized, and transforms itself into an inescapable, cross-shaped machinery of salvation and judgment. With the precision of an automaton that is both life-giving and lethal, the Living Cross transmutes the Eucharist from object into subject, the ritual murder weapon (such as knife or dagger) into an instrument of justice (here the sword of the executioner), and the eternal miscreant into the doomed and helpless victim of divinely sanctioned cruelty and bloodshed. In many cases, the pictorial violence against Synagoga matched the physical violence against the accused Jews; in Landshut, at least, the Jews escaped with their lives, if precious little else.

It will be recalled that in 1450 Duke Ludwig had his Jewish subjects expelled not only from his capital Landshut, but also from his other Bavarian territories. The question then arises whether images exist in other towns that retrospectively commemorate this banishment. A possible candidate is the vast Living Cross on the exterior of the choir of St. James in Wasserburg am Inn, about eighty miles due south of Landshut (Figure 6.6). Measuring about seventy-five square meters, the wall painting suffered numerous ill-advised restorations, and is therefore difficult to date with accuracy. Most scholars agree on a date of c. 1460–70, with which for the time being I concur.[41] In contrast to its counterpart at Landshut, Wasserburg's Living Cross features both Synagoga and Ecclesia as equestrian personifications, who face each other beneath the arms of the Crucified. Of particular note is the violent sinister cross hand, which buries its sword in Synagoga's skull. Perhaps the most important difference to Landshut is the antithetical pair of Eve, who harvests a skull from the Tree of Knowledge, and a Madonna of Mercy (here wrongly restored as a saintly bishop), who picks a small crucifix from a tree laden with eucharistic wafers.[42] How exactly this Living Cross may have functioned within the urban topography of Wasserburg is difficult to ascertain, at least for the moment, as the history of Wasserburg's Jews has largely remained unstudied—even the location of the former *Judenviertel* is not known.[43] Future research on the historical significance of the image

ACHIM TIMMERMANN

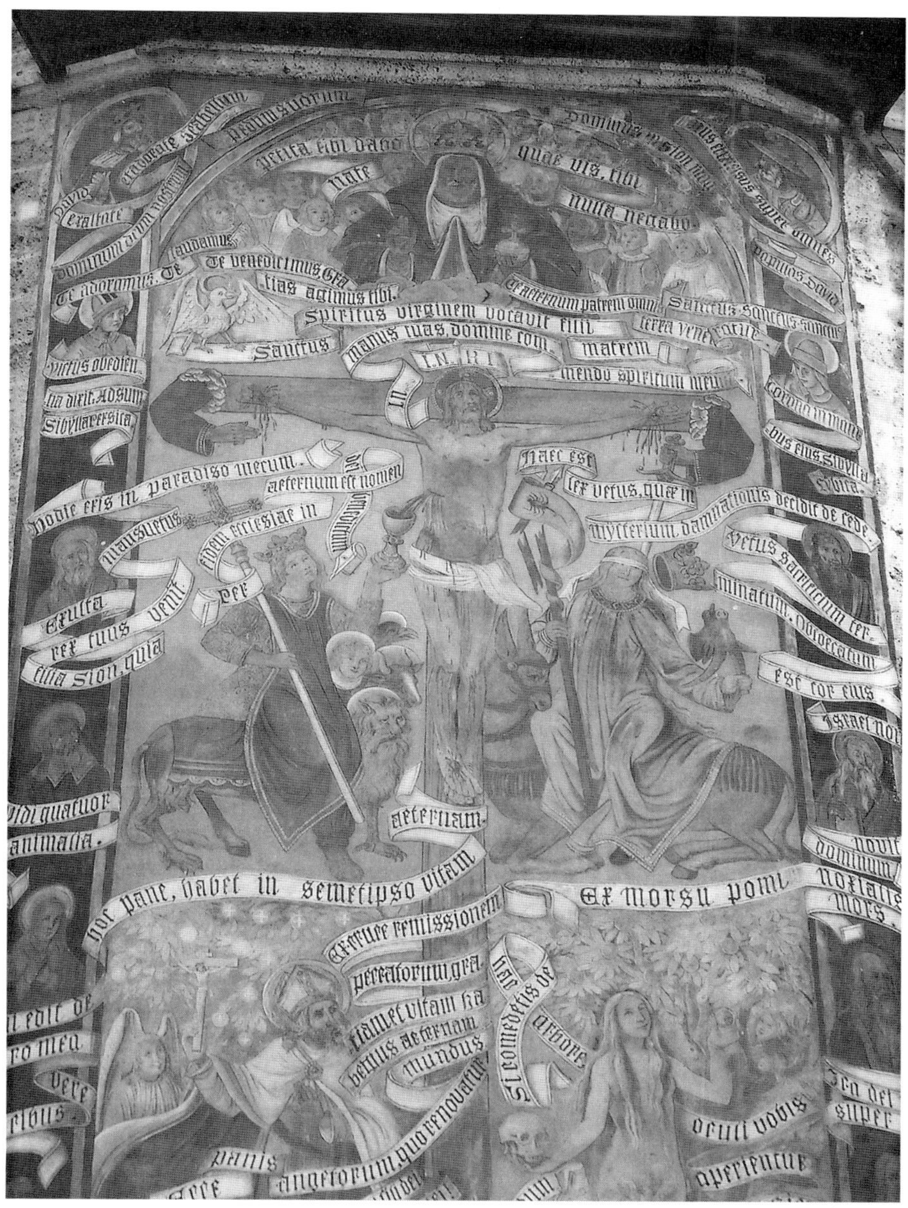

6.6. Wasserburg am Inn, St. James, Living Cross, c. 1460–70. Photo: Achim Timmermann.

will certainly have to address its sheer size and its visual accessibility on the exterior of the Jakobskirche.

The Eucharist

Finally I wish to turn to the figure of the priest, who performs the *fractio panis* before the *corpus mysticum*, a mixed congregation of devout parishioners and purgatorial dead. His actions undoubtedly serve to dramatize the demise of the Old Law and her followers: as he leans forward over the altar, breaking the body of Christ, Synagoga shrinks away, crumbling, her attributes exploding into fragments. But were such polemical considerations reason enough to necessitate his inclusion in the image? Or was this unusual iconographical intervention warranted by specific historical and/or topographical circumstances, as with the portrayal of Synagoga? The evidence for a specifically historical reading of the priest figure and the ritual he performs is unfortunately quickly exhausted. His decorous behavior toward the sacrament, which is witnessed by two groups of anxious, salvation-seeking spectators, and which directly and positively affects those trapped in Purgatory, certainly provides a role model for the proper handling and adoration of the body of Christ, and as such may have been intended as an antithetical reference to the Host desecration charge of 1449.

More mileage, it seems, can be gained from considering the priest's very position above the western portal, which provides access to the main vessel of the nave. A visitor passing through this portal will find him-or herself on the longitudinal axis of Hans von Burghausen's luminous hall church, with its soaring piers and billowing net vault, and, at the eastern end, diametrically opposite the Living Cross tympanum, its dramatic, forty-foot-high altarpiece retable of 1424 (Figure 6.7).[44] What sets this retable apart from others of its type is the fact that it incorporates on its central axis a polygonal, grilled receptacle for the reservation and visual adoration of the eucharistic Host, which could be physically accessed via a flight of stairs on the verso side. Such retables became *de rigeur* after the Council of Milan (1565),[45] though in the first half of the fifteenth century they were extremely rare, and almost exclusively relegated to monastic churches, a case in point being the so-called *Klarenretabel* from Cologne's Franciscan Convent of St. Clare, of c. 1345–50 (now in Cologne Cathedral).[46] Dating to the mid-1420s, the Landshut retable is the earliest such tabernacle altar to survive in a German parish church. What prompted the *fabrica* of St. Martin's to opt for this particular retable type at this early stage is open to conjecture. In tandem with its spectacular fusion of imagery, architecture, and sacrament shrine, it certainly offered numerous liturgical and paraliturgical advantages, as it combined the site of consecration and elevation with that of the *expositio et*

ACHIM TIMMERMANN

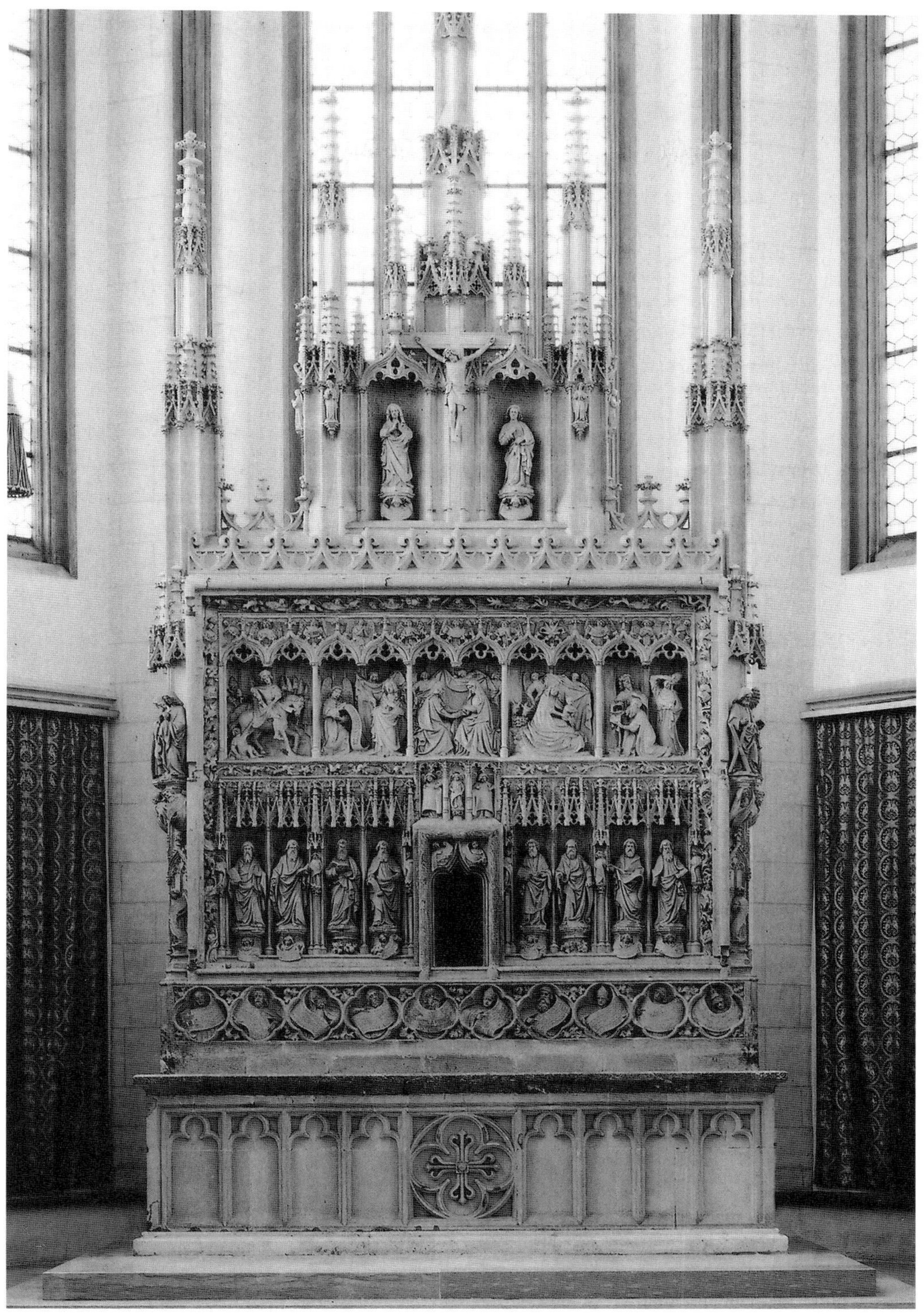

6.7. Landshut, St. Martin, tabernacle altar, c. 1424. Photo: Achim Timmermann.

adoratio sanctissimi, performed when no services took place. Its central and strictly frontal Host shrine also established a visual axis along which optical access to the eucharistic Christ was mediated.

This axis was perfectly aligned with the longitudinal axis of the church, and hence with the west portal and its surmounting Living Cross. In some ways, the officiating priest in the tympanum provided a pictorial prelude to a range of salvific rituals performed at Landshut's unique high altar, and as such marked the starting point of what may be termed "a symbolic axis of Redemption" through the entire length of St. Martin's church.

Ultimately, then, the Living Cross established not just one but two vectors of movement across the physical and temporal fabric of Landshut, the first suggested by Synagoga's inglorious fall, pointing toward the Dreifaltigkeitsplatz and the Neues Judentor (Figure 6.5), the second implied by the priest and his expectant congregation, aimed toward St. Martin's high altar, the residence of the eucharistic God (Figure 6.7). In soteriological terms, of course, both vectors extend beyond the microcosm of fifteenth-century Landshut, beyond the thresholds of tabernacle door and city gate. To Ecclesia's followers, the Living Cross thus promises an easy upward transition from Purgatory to the Heavenly City, while Synagoga, "vor die Welt hinausgeworfen," faces global exile.

NOTES

1. Achim Timmermann, "The Avenging Crucifix: Some Observations on the Iconography of the Living Cross," *Gesta* 40 (2001), 141–60. The only monographic study on the Living Cross remains Robert Füglister, *Das Lebende Kreuz: Ikonographisch-ikonologische Untersuchung der Herkunft und Entwicklung einer spätmittelalterlichen Bildidee und ihrer Verwurzelung im Wort* (Einsiedeln: Benziger, 1964). While Füglister's analysis is rooted in textual sources, such as the patristic writings and the staurological exegesis of Otfried von Weißenburg and Rupert of Deutz, my own investigation explores the Living Cross in its late medieval iconographical and historical context.

2. For the image at Poniky, see now esp. Dušan Buran, "Az Eleven kereszt és Szent Gergely miséje: Kontinuitás vagy konkurencia?," *Különlenyomat a Muvészettörténeti Értesíto* 51 (2002), 1–15 passim; Dušan Buran, *Studien zur Wandmalerei um 1400 in der Slowakei: Die Pfarrkirche St. Jakob in Leutschau und die Pfarrkirche St. Franziskus in Poniky* (Weimar: Böhlau, 2002), 143–53; Dušan Buran, "Vel'ká západná schizma, pápežká propaganda a umenie okolo roku 1400: K počiatkom ikonografie tzv. Živého kríža," in *Umenie Slovenska—jeho historické funkcie,* ed. Ivan Gerát and Tomáš Surý (Bratislava: Petrus, 1999), 53–59. See also Timmermann, "The Avenging Crucifix," 141, 145, 152, and 157n5 (with older bibliography).

3. For the tale of host desecration, see Miri Rubin, *Gentile Tales: The Narrative Assault on Late Medieval Jews* (New Haven, Conn.: Yale University Press, 1999). For the narrative of ritual murder, see Ronnie Po-chia Hsia, *The Myth of Ritual Murder: Jews and Magic in Reformation Germany* (New Haven, Conn.: Yale University Press, 1988); Ronnie Po-chia Hsia, *Trent 1475: Stories of a Ritual Murder Trial* (New Haven, Conn.: Yale University Press, 1992); Wolfgang Treue, *Der Trienter Judenprozeß: Voraussetzungen—Abläufe—Auswirkungen (Forschungen zur Geschichte der Juden, Abteilung A. 4)* (Hannover: Hahn, 1996). Further literature on both narratives is given in Timmermann, "The Avenging Crucifix," 159nn41–42.

　　　　　　　ACHIM TIMMERMANN

4. Previous discussions of this image include the following: *Vor Leinberger: Landshuter Skulptur im Zeitalter der Reichen Herzöge, 1393–1503*, exhibition catalogue, 2 vols., ed. Franz Niehoff (Schriften aus den Museen der Stadt Landshut, 10) (Landshut: Museen der Stadt Landshut, 2001), 2, 310–14 no. 26; Volker Liedke, "Zur Baugeschichte der kath. Stadtpfarr- und Stiftskirche St. Martin und Kastulus sowie der Spitalkirche Heiliggeist in Landshut," *Ars Bavarica* 39–40 (1986), 1–98, at 55–56; Brigitte Kurmann-Schwarz, "Hauptwerke der mittelalterlichen Ausstattung," in *St. Martin zu Landshut*, ed. Alfred Fickel (Hans von Burghausen und seine Kirchen, 1) (Landshut: Trausnitz-Verlag, 1985), 53–99, at 92–95; Theo Herzog, "Die Baugeschichte des St. Martinsmünsters und anderer Landshuter Kirchen im Lichte der Jahrring-Chronologie," *Verhandlungen des Historischen Vereins für Niederbayern* 95 (1969), 36–52, at 40, 53; Theo Herzog, *Landshut im XIX. Jahrhundert* (Landshut: Stadtarchiv, 1969), 333; Füglister, *Das Lebende Kreuz*, 29–31; *Die Kunstdenkmäler von Niederbayern, XVI: Stadt Landshut mit Einschluß der Trausnitz*, ed. Felix Mader (Die Kunstdenkmäler von Bayern, 4: Regierungsbezirk Niederbayern) (Munich: Oldenbourg, 1927), 31.

5. The only other sculptural representation of the Living Cross is the now badly damaged epitaph of the Kerberow family (c. 1570) in the parish church of St. Nicholas in Brzeg (Brieg), Silesia. See Tadeusz Chrzanowski, *Rzeźba lat 1560–1650 na Ślasku opolskim* (Warsaw: Państwowe Wydawnictwo Naukowe, 1974), 52, 125. Cf. also Füglister, *Das Lebende Kreuz*, 76–77.

6. Timmermann, "The Avenging Crucifix," 154.

7. *Vor Leinberger*, 312.

8. For the architecture of St. Martin's, see Peter Kurmann, "Die Baugeschichte," in *St. Martin zu Landshut*, 19–53 (with further bibliography); cf. also John Wesley Cook, "St. Martin, Landshut and the Architecture of Hanns von Burghausen" (Ph.D. diss., Yale University, 1975). For a detailed account of the chronology of the church and its architects, see Volker Liedke, "Zur Baugeschichte der kath. Stadtpfarr- und Stiftskirche St. Martin und Kastulus sowie der Spitalkirche Heiliggeist in Landshut," *Ars Bavarica* 39–40 (1986), 1–98; see also Volker Liedke, "Hanns Purghauser, genannt Meister Hanns von Burghausen, sein Neffe Hanns Stethaimer und sein Sohn Stefan Purghauser: Die drei Baumeister an St. Martin in Landshut," *Ars Bavarica* 35–36 (1983–84), 1–70.

9. Robert Bork, *Great Spires: Skyscrapers of the New Jerusalem* (Kölner Architekturstudien, 76) (Cologne: Kunsthistorisches Institut, Abteilung Architekturgeschichte, 2003).

10. *Vor Leinberger*, 312.

11. That the west portal was indeed modified during the later seventeenth century is indicated by the two Baroque doors below the tympanum, which date to c. 1690 (*Vor Leinberger*, 312).

12. Adolf-Hitler-Platz between 1933 and 1945.

13. For Landshut's medieval Jewry and their quarter, see esp. Georg Spitzlberger, "Die Juden im mittelalterlichen Landshut," *Verhandlungen des Historischen Vereins für Niederbayern* 110–11 (1984–85), 165–238, on which the following account is based.

14. Spitzlberger, "Die Juden," 173–89, with a detailed discussion of the documentary and archaeological evidence for this building. For other late medieval synagogues in the German-speaking world, see Vivian B. Mann, "The Artistic Culture of the Prague Jewry," in *Prague: The Crown of Bohemia, 1347–1437*, exhibition catalogue, ed. Barbara Drake Boehm and Jiří Fajt (New York: Metropolitan Museum of Art, and New Haven, Conn.: Yale University Press, 2005), 83–89; Elmar Altwasser, "Die Erforschung von mittelalterlichen Synagogen in Hessen," *Zeitschrift für Archäologie des Mittelalters* 33 (2005), 63–67; Pia Heberer, "The Medieval Synagogue in Speyer: Historical Building Research and Reconstruction," in *The Jews of Europe in the Middle Ages*, exhibition catalogue (Speyer: Historisches Museum der Pfalz, 2004), 77–81; Otto Böcher, *Die Alte Synagoge in Worms am Rhein* (DKV-Kunstführer, 181)

(Munich and Berlin: Deutscher Kunstverlag, 2001); Silvia Codreanu-Windauer and Stefan Ebeling, "Die mittelalterliche Synagoge Regensburgs," in *Monumental: Festschrift für Michael Petzet zum 65. Geburtstag* (Munich: Bayerisches Landesamt für Denkmalpflege, 1998), 449–64; Heidrun Helgert, "Die spätmittelalterliche Synagoge in Wien," in *Papers of the 'Medieval Europe Brugge 1997' Conference, 4: Religion and Belief in Medieval Europe* (Zellik: Instituut vor het Archeologisch Patrimonium, 1997), 185–99; Wilhelm Volkert, "Die spätmittelalterliche Judengemeinde in Regensburg," in *Albrecht Altdorfer und seine Zeit: Vortragsreihe der Universität Regensburg* (Regensburg: MZ-Druck, 1981), 123–49. For medieval synagogues in general, see Richard Krautheimer, *Mittelalterliche Synagogen* (Berlin: Frankfurter Verlags-Anstalt, 1927); Lee I. Levine, ed., *Ancient Synagogues Revealed* (Jerusalem: Israel Exploration Society, 1982); and Hannelore Künzl, "Der Synagogenbau im Mittelalter," in *Die Architektur der Synagoge*, ed. Hans-Peter Schwarz (Stuttgart: Klett-Cotta, 1988).

15. For this structure, see esp. Spitzlberger, "Die Juden," 172–74, 210–11.

16. Similar charitable angels appear on the Epitaph of Werner II of Palant and his family (c. 1425), where they perform the Seven Works of Mercy (Aachen, Suermondt-Ludwig-Museum), and on the altarpiece of the Michaelskapelle at Niederolang in the Tyrol (c. 1525), where they feed the poor souls in Purgatory with hosts (Innsbruck, Tiroler Landesmuseum); cf. *Himmel, Hölle, Fegefeuer: Das Jenseits im Mittelalter*, exhibition catalogue, ed. Gesellschaft für das Schweizerische Landesmuseum (Zürich: Verlag Neue Zürcher Zeitung, 1994).

17. Like the tympanum and angel busts above it, the figure of St. Martin dates to 1452 (the eight jamb figures of the Evangelists and church Fathers were added to the portal program in c. 1480). See *Vor Leinberger*, 2, 310–14, no. 26, with fig. on 315.

18. Philipp Maria Halm, "Ikonographische Studien zum Armeseelen-Kultus," *Münchner Jahrbuch der bildenden Kunst* 12 (1921–22), 1–24, at 10.

19. Together with the other components of the image the inscriptions were repainted several times, and while their wording may have slightly changed over the centuries (all texts are now in modern German), there is no reason to assume that their overall textual program is not original.

20. Halm, "Ikonographische Studien," 10.

21. Füglister, *Das Lebende Kreuz*, 25–26, no. 3, with further literature and figure.

22. For the practice and imagery of Poor Souls' Masses, see Mitchell B. Merback, "Channels of Grace: Pilgrimage Architecture, Eucharistic Architecture, and Visions of Purgatory at the Host-Miracle Churches of Late Medieval Germany," in *Art and Architecture of Late Medieval Pilgrimage in Northern Europe and the British Isles*, ed. Sarah Blick and Rita Tekippe (Studies in Medieval and Reformation Traditions, CIV) (Leiden and Boston: Brill, 2005), 587–646, at 633–42, with further literature. For the Niederhaslach window, see Brigitte Kurmann-Schwarz, "Niederhaslach, les vitraux de l'église Saint-Florent," in *Strasbourg et Basse-Alsace: Congrès archéologique de France, 162e session 2004* (Paris: Société Française d'Archéologie, 2006), 91–101.

23. For this imagery, see now esp. Caroline Walker Bynum, "Seeing and Seeing Beyond: The Mass of St. Gregory in the Fifteenth Century," in *The Mind's Eye: Art and Theological Argument in the Middle Ages*, ed. Jeffrey F. Hamburger and Anne-Marie Bouché (Princeton, N.J.: Princeton University Press, 2006), 208–40. Two other recent studies on the Mass of St. Gregory are Esther Meier, *Die Gregorsmesse: Funktionen eines spätmittelalterlichen Bildtypus* (Cologne, Weimar, and Vienna: Böhlau, 2006), and Andreas Gormans and Thomas Lentes, *Das Bild der Erscheinung: Die Gregorsmesse im Mittelalter* (Kultbild: Visualität und Religion in der Vormoderne, 3) (Berlin: Reimer, 2007). But see also Karsten Kelberg, *Die Darstellung der Gregorsmesse in Deutschland* (dissertation, Münster, 1983), and *Die Messe Gregors des Grossen: Vision, Kunst, Realität*, ed. Uwe Westfehling, exhibition catalogue (Cologne: Schnütgen-Museum, 1982).

     ACHIM TIMMERMANN

24. *The Illustrated Bartsch, 165: German Single-Leaf Woodcuts before 1500*, ed. Richard S. Field (New York: Abaris Books, 1999), 145 (Schreiber 1487).

25. On the textual and visual correlation of Synagoga (and Judaism in general) with these and other vices, see esp. Sarah Lipton, *Images of Intolerance: The Representation of Jews and Judaism in the Bible moralisée* (Berkeley: University of California Press, 1999).

26. For a detailed account of the following events, see Josef Kirmeier, *Die Juden und andere Randgruppen: Zur Frage der Randständigkeit im mittelalterlichen Landshut* (Sonderveröffentlichung des Historischen Vereins für Niederbayern) (Landshut: Stadtarchiv, 1988), 128–43; cf. also Spitzlberger, "Die Juden," 228–31. For a contemporary description of the expulsion of Landshut's Jews, see *Die Chroniken der baierischen Städte: Regensburg. Landshut. Mühldorf. München*, ed. Historische Commission bei der Königlichen Academie der Wissenschaften (Die Chroniken der deutschen Städte vom 14. bis ins 16. Jahrhundert, 15) (Leipzig: S. Hirzel, 1878), 300–330. For the politics of Duke Ludwig in general, see Beatriz Ettelt-Schönewald, *Kanzlei, Rat und Regierung Herzog Ludwigs des Reichen von Bayern-Landshut (1450–1479)*, 2 vols. (Schriftenreihe zur bayerischen Landesgeschichte, 97/I) (Munich: C. H. Beck'sche Verlagsbuchhandlung, 1996).

27. For Duke Heinrich's own, arguably more tolerant attitude toward Landhut's Jews, see Raphael Straus, "Die Judenpolitik Herzog Heinrichs des Reichen von Landshut," *Zeitschrift für die Geschichte der Juden in Deutschland* 1 (1929), 96–118; see also Stephanie Rilling, "Studien zur Heinrich dem Reichen von Bayern-Landshut: Aspekte der Sanierung des Herzogtums Anfang bis Mitte des 15. Jahrhunderts," *Verrhandlungen des Historischen Vereins für Niederbayern* 116–17 (1990–99), 141–208, at 157–66; Spitzlberger, "Die Juden," 225–28.

28. For a prosopographical account of those Jews who agreed to be baptized, see Spitzlberger, "Die Juden," 231–34.

29. The *mikwe* was sold in 1453 and presumably demolished soon thereafter. The *Backhaus* and cistern were at the latest torn down during the 1460s to provide space for the still extant ducal granary, the Herzogkasten (Spitzlberger, "Die Juden," 189–90).

30. The contemporary *Ratschronik* speaks of "ain schönn Korr [. . .] verglaßen" (*Die Chroniken*, 303).

31. For Sandtner's model, which belongs to a series of similar such *maquettes* produced between 1568 and 1572 for Duke Albrecht V of Bavaria, see Alexander Freiherr von Reitzenstein, *Die alte bairische Stadt in den Modellen des Drechslermeisters Jakob Sandtner* (Munich: Callwey, 1967); see also Uta Lindgren, "Bayerische Stadtmodelle des 16. Jahrhunderts und die zeitgenössische Kartographie," *Zeitschrift für bayerische Landesgeschichte* 55 (1992), 647–58.

32. Now preserved in Landshut's civic archive (StA B 2/2086).

33. Feichtwanger could not have inveigled against the Jews for long. His sermons soon attracted the displeasure of Duke Heinrich, who subsequently had the preacher expelled from his Bavarian territories. On the whole affair, see esp. Spitzlberger, "Die Juden," 226–28; Kirmeier, *Die Juden*, 129–31.

34. "[. . .] das sie [i.e., the Jews] Cristenplüt bedürfen, das hat manger großer maister geschrieben" (HstA Munich; quote after Sptzlberger, "Die Juden," 227). Kalteisen's letter was written on the instigation of Pope Nicholas V, who was outraged at Duke Heinrich's treatment of Feichtwanger.

35. HstA Neuburger Copialbücher, XI, fol. 65. Quoted after Kirmeier, *Die Juden*, 129n35.

36. Ibid.

37. On late medieval host desecration charges levied against Bavaria's Jews, see esp. Merback, "Channels of Grace," passim.

38. On the symbolism of right and left in Crucifixion imagery and medieval art in general, see esp. Manfred Lurker, "Die Symbolbedeutung von Rechts und Links und ihr Niederschlag in der abendländisch-christlichen Kunst," *Symbolon*, n.s. 5 (1980), 95–128. See also Anna Esmeijer, *Divina Quaternitas: A Preliminary Study in the Method and Application of Visual Exegesis* (Amsterdam: Van Gorcum, 1978), 120–22. For the anthropology of right and left, see Rodney Needham, ed., *Right & Left: Essays on Dual Symbolic Classification* (Chicago: University of Chicago Press, 1973).

39. Timmermann, "The Avenging Crucifix."

40. Rubin, *Gentile Tales*, fig. 12.

41. Füglister, *Das Lebende Kreuz*, 49–53, no. 11, quoting older literature; Theodor Feulner, *Der sogenannte 'Lebensbaum' an der Außenwand des Chores von St. Jakob in Wasserburg am Inn: Kurzer Abriß seiner Geschichte und Versuch einer Deutung seines ikonographischen Programms* (Heimat am Inn, 2) (Wasserburg: Stadtarchiv, 1981), 13–15.

42. On this pairing of Eve and Mary, see esp. Ernst Guldan, *Eva und Maria: Eine Antithese als Bildmotiv* (Graz and Cologne: Böhlau, 1966), 136–41. See also Timmermann, "The Avenging Crucifix," 158n25, with further references.

43. The only publication on Wasserburg's Jewry is a worksheet addressed primarily to high school students, which presents the available data in a brief, chronological narrative (Ferdinand Steffan and Maximilian Armbruster, *Juden in Wasserburg: Quellen zur Geschichte des Judentums in Wasserburg und Umgebung* [Arbeitsblatt, Städtisches Museum Wasserburg am Inn] [Wasserburg: Städtisches Museum, 1999]).

44. The appearance of the retable has somewhat changed over the centuries. In the seventeenth century, it was physically absorbed by a colossal Baroque altarpiece of 1664, and, as a result, lost its original architectural crest and the two wooden and presumably painted shutters—shutters that would initially have turned the retable into a triptych. More alterations were undertaken in the nineteenth century, when, following its "rediscovery" in 1858 and the subsequent demolition of its Baroque envelope, the retable received its present pinnacle-pyramid and a series of neo-Gothic sculptural additions and replacements. Despite these changes, however, the work has retained most of its late medieval fabric, statuary, and decoration. For a detailed discussion of the retable, see esp. *Vor Leinberger*, 1, 256–71, nos. 17–18, with further literature and detailed illustrations. Cf. also Achim Timmermann, *Real Presence: Sacrament Houses and the Body of Christ, c. 1270–1600* (Architectura Medii Aevi, 4) (Brepols: Turnhout, 2009), chaps. 3 and 6.

45. Giovanni Domenico Mansi, *Sacrorum conciliorum nova et amplissima collectio*, 53 vols. (Florence, Vienna, and Paris, 1759–98), 34, col. 17: "Episcopus [i.e., Carlo Borromeo] diligentissime curet, ut in cathedrali, collegiatis, parochialibus & aliis quibusvis ecclesiis, ubi sacrosancta aucharistia [*sic*!] custodiri solet, vel debet, *in majori altari collocetur* [. . .]." My italics.

46. On this altarpiece, see Norbert Wolf, *Deutsche Schnitzretabel des 14. Jahrhunderts* (Berlin: Deutscher Verlag für Kunstwissenschaft, 2002), 84–94, with figs. and further literature.

CHAPTER 7

Jewish Carnality, Christian Guilt, and Eucharistic Peril in the Rotterdam-Berlin Altarpiece of the Holy Sacrament

Mitchell B. Merback

Like those powerhouses of Christian iconography, the Crucifixion of Christ and the Last Judgment, the biblical scene known as both the Lord's Supper (*Coena domini*) and the Last Supper has stood for centuries as a veritable emblem of Christianity's self-understanding. Even more than the sacrifice on Golgotha or the apocalyptic tribunal in heaven, the scene of bread-offering and blessing in the "upper room" (*cenaculum*) in Jerusalem, where Jesus and his disciples celebrated the Passover (Matt. 26:20–30; Mark 14:18–26; Luke 22:14–33; John 12–13), has signified universal Christian fellowship, community, and the sacerdotal claims of the institutional church. Last Supper imagery has therefore found a wide range of functional applications and interpretations, and it has come to allegorize a number of situated meanings, including Christianity's troubled relationship with Judaism. My broader aim in this article lies in discerning something of the Last Supper's polemical potential within the complex psychodynamics of this relationship. More specifically, I wish to inquire into one distinctive cultural situation in which the theme mobilized Christian loyalties against perceived "Jewish" and "judaizing" threats to the security and integrity of the Eucharistic Host. By placing quotation marks around *Jewish* and *judaizing* here I hope to make it clear that the principal targets of this polemic, in my view, were Christianity's own reifications—or "figures of thought," as David Nirenberg has put it[1]—of Judaism's challenge to the orthodox cult of the Eucharist, and the Jewish ritual interpretation of Passover as a commemorative meal.

The polemical energies of the Last Supper were decidedly reformist, not missionary.

It is well known that all three principal interpretations of the Gospel story—as the Institution of the Eucharist, as the Betrayal by Judas, and as the Communion of the Apostles—can be dated as far back as the sixth century. By the later Middle Ages, however, when the theme appeared most often in Passion cycles, it was the psychologically galvanizing moment of Jesus' revelation that he would be betrayed by one of his disciples (*unus vestrum*) that painters, sculptors, and printmakers were most keen on portraying.[2] Dramatic emphasis on the betrayal made the meal a farewell gathering before the Crucifixion, and found its sharpest expression in the so-called Communion of Judas, an image-trope powerful for the way it compounds the disciple's treachery with the travesty of a sacred ritual performed in bad faith. As scholars have shown repeatedly, that theme, with the red-haired Judas as its antagonist, intersects on several levels with the negative conception of Jews and Judaism endemic in Christian art, literature, and drama.[3] Arch-traitor of the Passion story, Judas has long embodied the reprobate status of Judaism: as ally of the Devil he exemplifies Jewish blindness, enmity, greed, and evil.

Yet the Last Supper is a far more nuanced and multifaceted touchstone of Christian aspiration than this, and its versatility stems first of all from the complex nature of the scriptural accounts themselves.[4] The same culture that elevated the Gospel story to a veritable *psychomachia* of Christian discipleship also turned it in the direction of doctrinal consensus-building. Thematizing the "Eucharistic words" spoken by Jesus in Matthew 26:26 as he blesses the bread—"Take, eat; this is my body"—and intoned by every priest who consecrates bread at the altar, a sacramental interpretation of the Last Supper found increasing currency in late medieval art. It credits Christ's ritual performance at the meal with inaugurating the priestly commemoration of his own sacrifice *sub gratia,* giving the rite of the Eucharist its biblical warrant and its clerical administrators their apostolic authority. More often than not, as Leo Steinberg rightly points out, late medieval and Renaissance artists were intent on visualizing the already "duplex nature" of the scriptural accounts.[5]

In the decades immediately preceding the Reformation, the sacramental interpretation of the Last Supper found special use as the central image of winged altarpieces (it would later come to dominate Lutheran altarpieces to the virtual exclusion of other themes).[6] Such "holy sacrament altarpieces" were typically commissioned by Corpus Christi confraternities as expressions of their civic and religious commitments. Dense in the heavily urbanized territories of the Low Countries and the larger cities of Germany, confraternities, with their elite membership, stood at the center of a new civic religion in the later Middle

Ages, and ranked high among those corporations whose godliness, beneficence, and stature within the sacred community found expression in high-profile altar-piece projects.[7] Although the pre-Reformation corpus surviving north and south of the Alps is small, within it we find considerable diversity and an exciting flexibility in iconographic design. The genre includes such well-known works as the Corpus Domini Altarpiece in Urbino, commissioned by that city's Brotherhood of the Sacrament in 1473 and featuring Joos van Ghent's *Communion of the Apostles* and a predella cycle of six scenes by Paolo Uccello; the altarpiece made for Lübeck's sacrament brotherhood around 1496, combining reliefs by Henning van der Heide and panels by Wilm Dedeke; and the retable long regarded as the fountainhead of this genre, the so-called Altarpiece of the Holy Sacrament by Dirc Bouts, executed for the Church of St. Peter's in Leuven between 1463 and 1467 (Figure 7.1).[8] In such monumental works, commonly made for endowed side-chapels where the mystery of the Eucharist was cele-brated, artists and their patrons drew upon the legitimating power of the Last Supper image "as the significant guarantee of the Eucharist's [biblical] founda-tion."[9] Their heyday across Europe came as part of the final consolidation of cultic, liturgical, and civic traditions around the Feast of Corpus Christi (insti-tuted in 1264 and confirmed as universal in 1311), and marks that historic con-vergence of civic patronage and artistic industry that made the altarpiece the preeminent vehicle for individual, family, and corporate forms of self-assertion.

To this constellation of factors driving the proliferation of holy sacrament altarpieces in the half-century before the Reformation, I propose adding one more: the widespread unease with the security, integrity, and inviolability of the Host as the living image of Christ's glorified body and the vehicle of his substan-tial presence (*praesentia realis*) on earth.[10] In the fifteenth century the body of God had many enemies, and there existed something like a *continuum* of threats to the purity and wholeness of the Eucharist. This continuum, as I am calling it, stretched between the Eucharistic sacrileges associated with unbelievers—heretics, witches, Jews—through the many unwitting abuses perpetrated by mis-guided or overzealous Christians—including priests themselves—to the problem of communion undertaken in a spiritually compromised state. Let us parse this within a relatively small space. A centuries-long tradition of Christian fantasy and legend concerning the ritual sacrileges committed against the Eucharist by unbelievers forms the bulwark of these perceptions. Such fantasies, as is well known, coalesced in one of premodern Europe's most virulent antise-mitic myths: the idea of the Host's sinister defilement by Jews. Along with the ritual murder myth and the blood libel charge, Host-abuse accusations were often (but not always) raised in connection with the springtime holiday of Passover (a fact whose ramifications for Last Supper imagery remain as yet

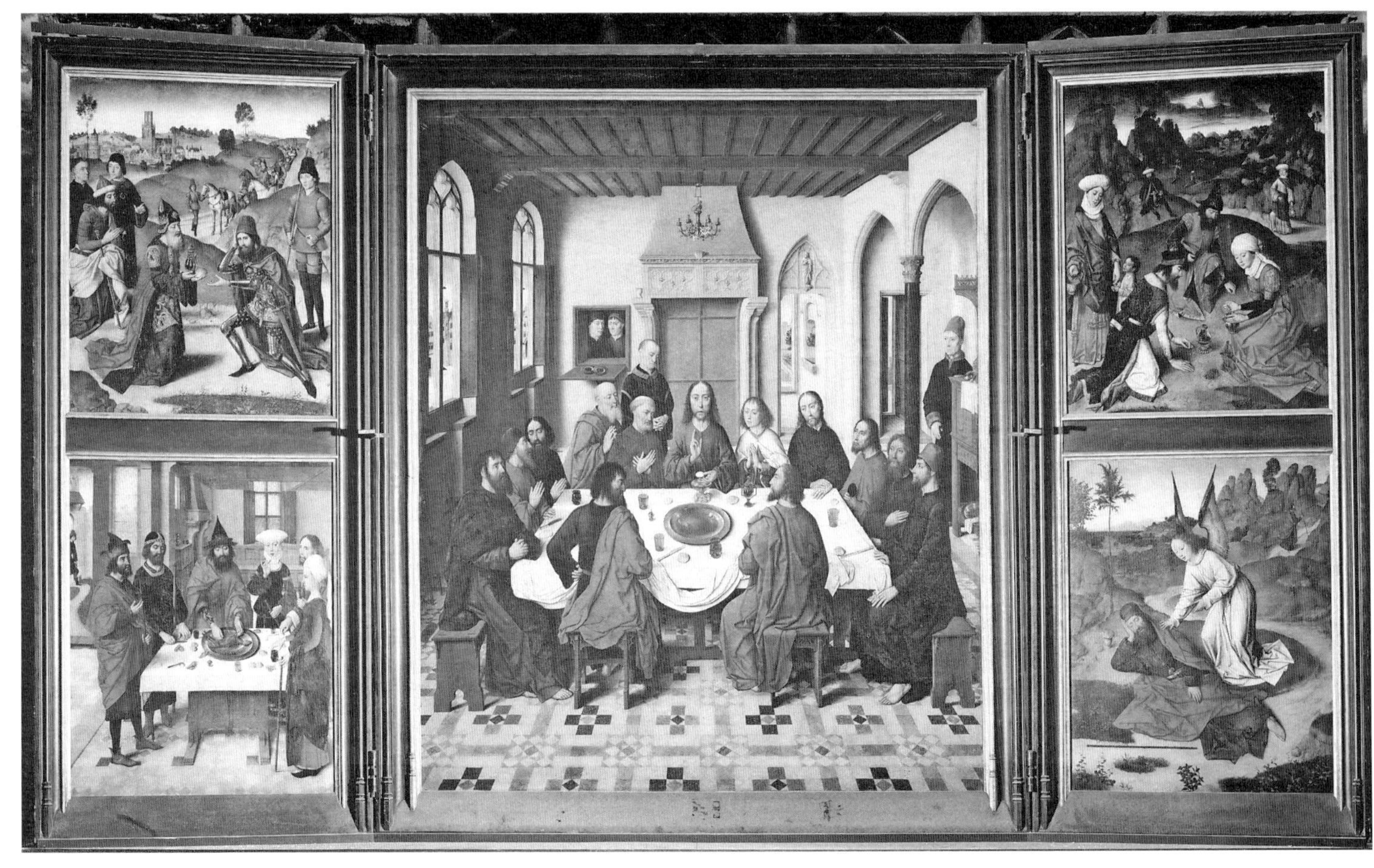

7.1. Dirc Bouts, *Altarpiece of the Holy Sacrament*, Leuven, Sint-Pieterskirk/Museum voor Kerlijke Kunst. Photo: Lessing/Art Resource, New York.

unexamined). Anxieties about Jewish aggression toward the Eucharist were magnified from the early fourteenth century, the heyday of Host-crime accusations and the bleeding Host (*Bluthostien*) cults that often followed in their wake.[11]

Christian perceptions of the distinct threat Jews posed to the Eucharist were thus naturalized by an expanding constellation of persecutory myths, accusations, rumors, and suspicions. Some of these may have been informed by a distant awareness of what the rabbis of Ashkenaz actually said about the Eucharist in the context of polemical disputes with Christian opponents, or defensive proclamations made under the pressure of specific Host-crime accusations or legal proceedings. An existing rabbinical critique of transubstantiation, elaborated in several important polemical works and distilled into a variety of abusive tropes—curses by any other name—were directed at the Eucharist.[12] To the extent that ordinary Christians could become at all aware of such adversarial Jewish positions on the Eucharist and its cult, they would surely have been subsumed within a preexisting mental category, shaped in advance by persecutory myths and biases. Nevertheless, as such, they would have been felt as part of the continuum of perils that Christ's sacramental body faced.

But the continuum also included—and here is the crucial point—the carnal and impure treatment of the sacramental body by *sinning Christians*. Christian and Jewish transgressions against the *corpus Christi* were always already mirror-images of one another, especially in the two centuries before the Reformation. Concerns about the "perils" (as churchmen called them, *pericula*) to which the ever-vulnerable Host was subject, already current in the thirteenth century, escalated among university and reform-minded theologians as the forms of the Eucharist's cultic veneration multiplied, exposing it to greater risk of accident, and to novel situations of abuse. Host miracles and their resulting cults—from the popular *Bluthostien* pilgrimages widely distributed through southern Germany, to relics like the Holy Host of Dijon, celebrated by Burgundian and French aristocrats in Dijon—exposed the Host, in the eyes of critics, to wanton idolatry, thus representing another kind of peril for the Eucharist and its orthodox conception. But the most immediate danger that sinning Christians posed to the sacramental body came from a willingness to receive that body in a spiritually unworthy state—a travestied form of discipleship theologians equated with responsibility for the death of Christ and linked to his "perpetual" suffering. Ready to receive the Lord's body and yet capable of defiling it with the very touch of his lips, Judas stood as its archetype, and hence served as the model of a threatening, magic-invested, embodied pollution that moved along the continuum of sin connecting Christians and Jews. In this capacity the image of the Communion of Judas became a negative exemplum of the first order, a mirror for penitential introspection available to every Christian who approached the altar.

The Rotterdam-Berlin Triptych

Preserved today in the Museum Boijmans van Beuningen in Rotterdam is a solitary altar panel, unsigned, measuring 98.5 by 91.5 centimeters (Figure 7.2).[13] Undoubtedly this was once the central panel of a triptych, dispersed and now lost, its wings bearing typological scenes designed to illuminate the prehistory of the Eucharist. For a time one of those wing panels, depicting the Passover feast of Exodus 12, survived in the Kaiser-Friedrich Museum in Berlin (present-day Bode Museum), though the work was destroyed in 1945 (Figure 7.3). That the two panels fit together in an ensemble is proven both by their matching vertical dimensions, and by the *trompe-l'oeil* column running the lengths of their adjacent sides. How the typological cycle was completed on the right wing panel, however, is a problem that remains unsolved. Comparison with a Last Supper triptych by the Master of the Legend of St. Catherine, a Flemish work made under the spell of Dirc Bouts's Leuven Altar and surviving today in Bruges (Bisschoppelijk Seminarie), strongly suggests that a scene of the Miraculous Feeding of Elijah by an angel once held the right-hand position.[14] At any rate, this typological conception places the Rotterdam-Berlin altar squarely within the family of Corpus Christi altarpieces. In contrast to the Leuven altar's scheme of stacked pairing of scenes on the wings, however, both interior wings of our dismembered triptych carried one scene only in its original state.

With its droll characterizations, its picaresque flair, its bright colors and drastic bird's-eye view, the ensemble was once regarded as a youthful work by the Swabian master Jörg Ratgeb, the eccentric creator of the *Herrenberg Altarpiece* (c. 1517), whose panels survive in Stuttgart with the painter's signature. This attribution is no longer tenable, despite several suggestive similarities with the Herrenberg *Last Supper*, which I must gloss over here.[15] Although no convincing named alternative to Ratgeb has yet been proposed, Julien Chapuis has made a good case for a south German origin on the basis of stylistic and technical factors, and this is the attribution I tentatively accept.[16] Suppositions about an early confraternal commission and context, though impossible to prove, have not been challenged, and I take it as a solid working premise that the triptych was made for a confraternal chapel, serving a function analogous to the one we can document for the Leuven altar.[17] Though reconstructing an original context is not my present goal, the presumption of a confraternal commission will, in the course of my discussion, find some significant support.

Whatever we may say about the lines of affiliation linking the Rotterdam-Berlin altar and its older Netherlandish cousin, the formal divergence is sharp

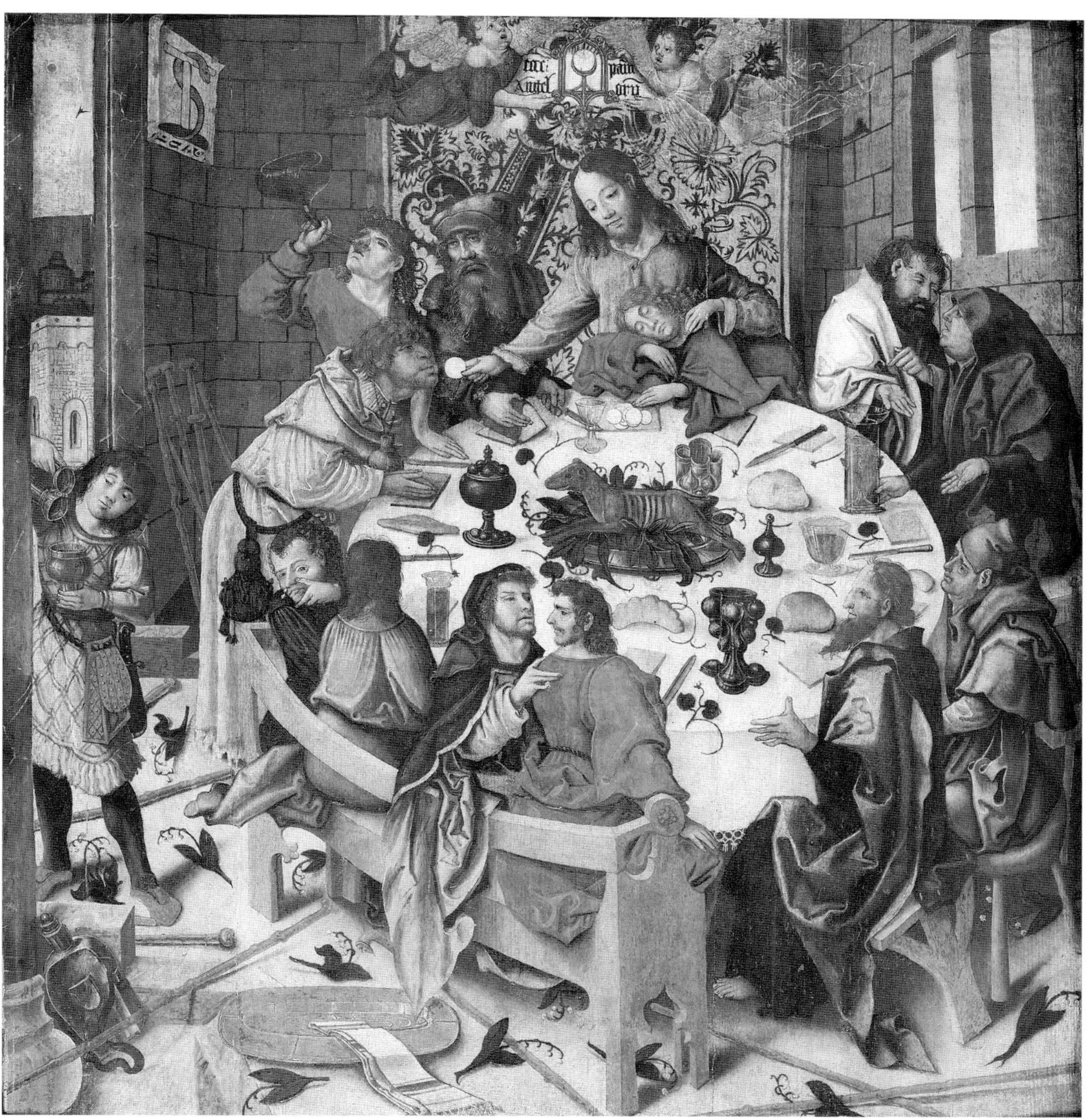

7.2. *Last Supper*, center panel of the *Rotterdam-Berlin Corpus Christi Altarpiece*, c. 1510. South German. Netherlands Institute for Cultural Heritage, Rijswijk/Amsterdam, on loan to Museum Boijmans Van Beuningen, Rotterdam.

and reveals much more than a difference in artistic skill and sensibility. Rather than arranging his figures around a square table, as Bouts had, and coordinating the ensemble with the architectonics of the room, the Rotterdam master winds his composition tight like a spring. Around a circular table the painter has arrayed a gallery of figures who react and respond to the event in different

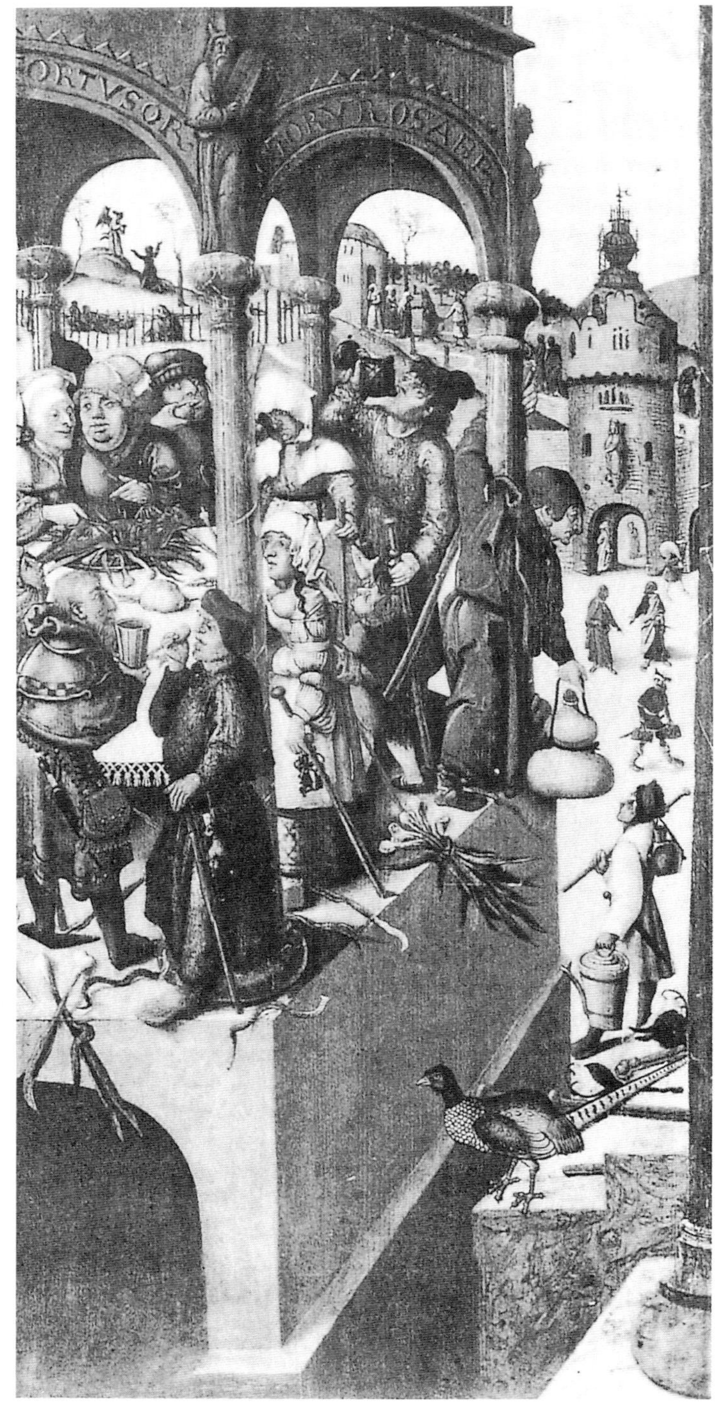

7.3. Israelite Passover, left wing of the *Rotterdam-Berlin Corpus Christi Altarpiece*, c. 1510. Presumably fir panel, 102 x 48.5 cm. Formerly in Berlin; now destroyed.

ways. A carnivalesque energy suffuses the visual field, activating even inanimate objects. Crystal beakers, gilt chalices, napkins, knives, and loaves of varying shapes bedeck the table; the floor is strewn with objects—travelers' staves dropped here and there, lilies of the valley belching out their apex stems of white, bell-shaped flowers,[18] and a gold basin conspicuously placed in the foreground. Half-filled with clear water and referring to the Washing of the Feet before the Last Supper (John 13:5),[19] the basin has, folded over its rim, a striped cloth resembling a Jewish prayer shawl, or *tallit* (minus the fringes that, according to Jewish law, are the essential elements). Such cloths are frequently seen in the sanctified domestic spaces of Netherlandish pictorial tradition, for example in the *cubiculum* of the Annunciation. Hardly disguised as symbols, they proclaim a sacerdotal significance for the scene but probably also counted in the minds of Christian viewers as an "authentic" detail of a Jewish interior.

Whereas Bouts strove for symmetry and equilibrium, then, the Rotterdam master has created a compact and busy clockwork of furniture, bodies, gestures and expressions, one that threatens at any moment to spin into disarray. Like the broken spokes of a wheel, the scattered staves on the ground rhyme with the radiating lines formed by the knives on the table, and reinforce the merry-go-round impression of the whole.[20] Even the air above is aflutter with movement. Two angels swoop down to juxtapose a monstrance and the sacred words embroidered on the baldachin behind Christ's head: *Ecce pani[s] Ange loru[m]*, they read, "Behold the Bread of Angels."

So the mood is one of agitation, and there is no repose for the viewer. Of course the painter's audience would have had no trouble grasping the source of the tumult, for a scandal has set the room abuzz. As Christ cradles his "beloved disciple" John in his lap, he extends an offering of the sacramental bread to the lips of another. Who among the twelve is the first to receive this blessing but the one most *unworthy* to receive it, Christian antisemitism's poster boy for Jewish deception and treachery, Judas Iscariot (Figure 7.4). Marked as the descendant of Cain by his bright yellow robes, and fitted out with the red hair and beard that made him, in Ruth Mellinkoff's words, a "paradigm of Jewish caricature,"[21] Judas in the Rotterdam panel clasps his hands in false piety while the money bag hangs heavy around his neck. Like his many artistic predecessors who drew on John 13 when staging the Communion of Judas, for example, Master Bertram of Minden, in the panel painted for a Passion altarpiece of around 1400 now in Hannover (Figure 7.5), the master of the Rotterdam-Berlin altar constructs his Judas through a surplus of negative signifiers.[22] In the *Herrenberg Altar* Ratgeb went even further and linked Judas's treachery and greed to a menacing Jewish carnality by depicting him with a visible erection, which he then closely juxtaposed with the gamblers' die.

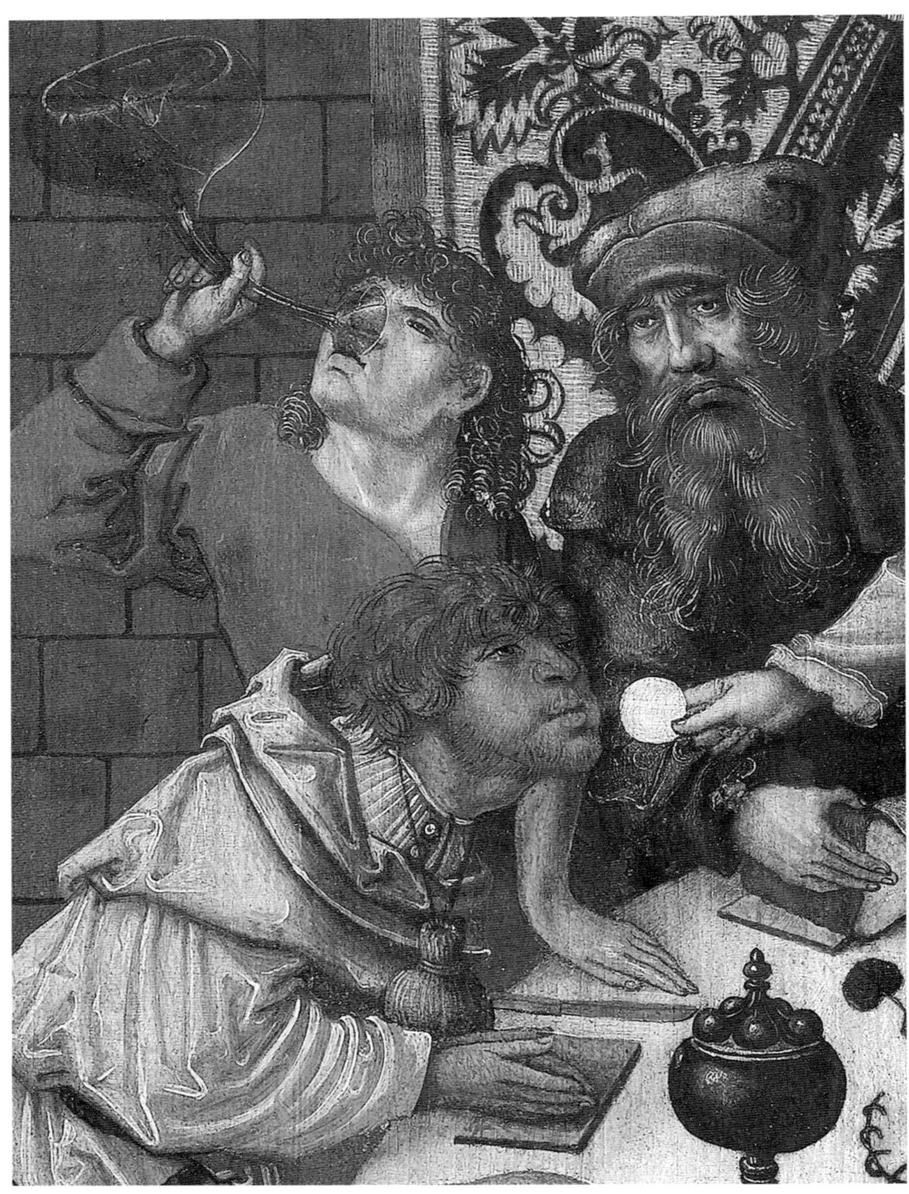

7.4. Detail of Judas from the *Rotterdam-Berlin Corpus Christi Altarpiece*. Netherlands Institute for Cultural Heritage, Rijswijk/Amsterdam, on loan to Museum Boijmans Van Beuningen, Rotterdam.

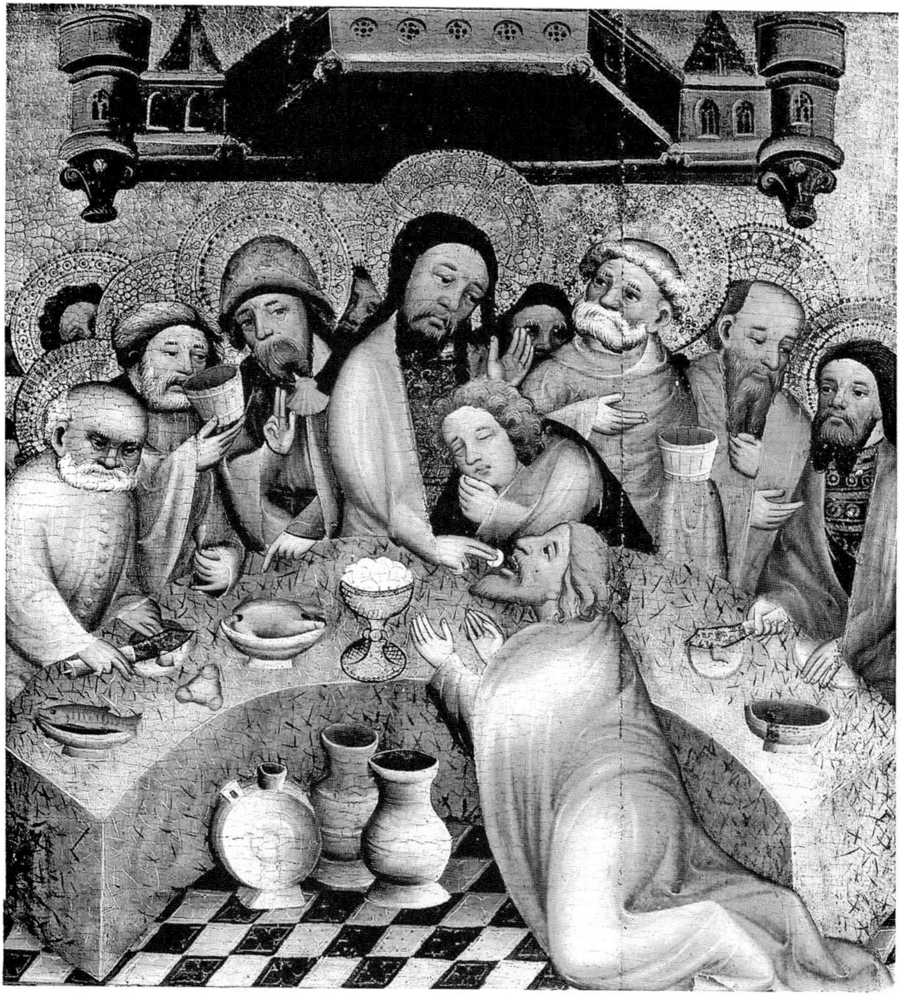

7.5. Master Bertram of Minden, *Last Supper,* from Passion Altar, c. 1400. Hanover, Niedersächsisches Landesmuseum, Landesgalerie.

It is not my intention here to recapitulate Judas's role in the iconography of antisemitism. But there is one visible sign of otherness in the Rotterdam panel worth pausing over. Medieval manuscript illuminators often showed the Devil—in the form of a black bird—entering Judas's mouth as he feeds falsely on the "morsel" Jesus has dipped into a dish (John 13:27).[23] Later artists more often dispensed with it, either as superstitious motif or as a distracting intrusion of the invisible into their artfully contrived real spaces. Navigating around this problem, the Rotterdam master depicts Judas leaning toward Jesus' outstretched hand from the left side of the table. Not yet opening his mouth, the traitor seems to sniff at the proffered host with an odd uncertainty, like an animal attracted by a scent, instinctively aloof, wary of a trap. One wonders if there is a half-hidden visual exegesis of that redolent admonition from Matthew 15: "Give not that which is holy unto dogs" (Matthew 15:26; cf. 7:6), a source text Kenneth Stow has recently linked to long-running Christian fears of Jewish aggression against the Eucharist, themselves rooted in biblical codes governing impure contact.[24] Through this motif the unholy menace to sacred bread, and thus the pure incarnate Christ, becomes visible as a product of human volition rather than the Devil's machinations. At the same time, however, Judas's bestial features, and his quasi-animalistic response to the heavenly bread, render that menace palpable as a sort of uncleanness, a pollution spread by an inhuman carnality. Inside a moment those defiling lips will touch God's most pure and holy body. How should the pious beholder respond?

Carnal and Spiritual Banquets

My hypothesis has been that the Christian beholder's response to Judas's unclean reception of the host, and the concomitant perception of a polluting Jewish carnality inside the picture, was shaped by an awareness that, outside the picture, there existed a continuum of threats to the purity of the Eucharist and the wholeness of God's body. From the vantage point of Eucharistic theology and practice, the Communion of Judas stood as the archetype of a special type of transgression, what churchmen called "unworthy reception." The notion is rooted in Paul's first letter to the Corinthians, chapter 11, which declares any sacramental communion undertaken without faith in the risen Christ to be a form of blood-guilt: "For as often as you shall eat this bread, and drink the chalice, you shall shew the death of the Lord, until he come. Therefore whosoever shall eat this bread, *or drink* the chalice of the Lord unworthily, shall be *guilty of the body* and of the blood of the Lord [and] eateth and drinketh judgment to himself, not discerning the body of the Lord" (1 Corinthians 11:26–29).

To fail to "discern the body of the Lord" and yet receive his sacramental body in a state of unworthiness anyway was an abomination, and in the view of some an outright desecration of the holy of holies itself, an act that rendered the communicant personally responsible for the death of the Lord.[25] As such, it called forth learned explanations of the conditions attending worthy reception. In the High Middle Ages concerns arising from moral theology—questions of individual conscience, intent, and merit—led scholastic theologians to refine the distinction. Petrus Comestor (c. 1100–1178), for example, argued that the good receive the sacrament "unto their salvation" while the evil receive it "to their damnation."[26]

     MITCHELL B. MERBACK

Such discussions embedded a particularly difficult problem of Eucharistic theory. Notions of the sacrament's unique ontology and efficacy had evolved during a long-running controversy within the church about the nature of Christ's Real Presence in the consecrated bread and wine. Even after the Fourth Lateran Council's ruling that belief in transubstantiation was incumbent upon all the faithful (1215), the matter remained unsettled. Between the major Dominican and Franciscan theologians who wrestled with the issue there was, generally speaking, agreement that Christ's glorified body was truly and "substantially" present in the host. Relying on Aristotelian terms, they understood that an invisible divine substance (*substantia*) lay objectively behind the visible appearances (*figurae*) of bread and wine, which were equally objective. But only the Franciscans conceived the Eucharist as a sign (*sacramentum*) of the glorified body, a conception that imposed limits on what kinds of sentient beings could receive sacramentally. Salvific benefits, their theory demanded, were available *only* to those capable of understanding and hence believing in what the sign signified. Where there is no faith or knowledge there can be no "sacramental eating," according to Alexander of Hales (d. 1245), only a kind of "carnal feeding" common to animals and infidels. Among other issues, this semiotics of substance seemed to solve the vexing problem of what happens to the body of Christ when the proverbial field mouse breaks into the tabernacle, nibbles the consecrated Host, and swallows. No salvific benefit came to the mouse, Franciscan theorists had to conclude. Among other demands, this theory categorically denied that Jews, Muslims, or pagans could receive sacramentally.[27]

Pastoral applications were never far from the minds of mendicants scholars, and the necessity of worthy reception was vigorously transmitted by preachers, confessors, and penitential manuals for the laity. Against the backdrop of these teachings, the "Jewish" Judas became a fearful and fascinating two-way mirror for every Christian sinner's requisite self-examination before communion. Both disciple and traitor, apostle and apostate, knowing and yet blind, Judas at the Last Supper presented to each Christian viewer a powerful foil for considering his or her own worthiness to eat sacramentally. Generations of researchers into the psychology of antisemitism have explained how conflicted guilt feelings among the Christian majority, laboring under their own penitential burdens and insecurities, could provoke feelings of outrage and hatred for the "Other."[28] It is not difficult to imagine how Judas the arch-traitor could function as a screen for conflicted (Christian) guilt-feelings, that is, one's sense of unworthiness in the face of God's infinite love. To avoid the sin of pride, Christians were urged to regard each sin as delivering Christ's body and soul up for the most grievous affliction, the pain caused by humanity's ingratitude. According to a liturgical trope first concretized in the words of the *Improperia,* the Savior's reproaches to the Jews on Good Friday, Christ suffers his Passion not once but perpetually; his perfect, innocent suffering continues because the work of redemption remains incomplete. With every new transgression Christ is not only denied and betrayed once more, his tender limbs are scourged bloody again, his wounds are reopened, his brain is again pierced by thorns, his face covered with spittle, his blood drained once more from his body. A fifteenth-century German hymn places so much of the burden on Christian shoulders it reads today as a modern plea for tolerance: "It is *our* great sin and grievous misdeeds that nailed Jesus the true Son of God to the Cross. For this reason we must not revile you, Poor Judah, and the host of Jews. The guilt is indeed *ours.*"[29] Nevertheless, as the fate of Ashkenazi Jewry in the fifteenth century shows, the trope of a "judaizing" rebellion against God did not exhaust itself in penitential catharsis, but made its way back to its original targets—the "mythical Jew" and his flesh and blood counterparts.

Such theories of guilt-displacement, its mechanisms and breakdowns, however generally valid, are not able to tell us which response to the Communion of Judas—recrimination of the Self or hatred of the Other—was dominant or more typical among this or that class of viewers. And in theory any representation of the theme, any vilifying portrayal of Judas, could condense these opposed meanings. But the master of the Rotterdam panel has given us several specific prompts to reflect on the contrast between sacramental eating and "carnal" feeding. To see this, let us return to the triptych and its imagery.

Again a comparison with the Leuven Sacrament Altar can take us straight to the heart of the matter. There, in the wing panel depicting the Passover of Exodus, the biblical Jews comport themselves with a dignified reserve and genteel poise that complements the ceremonial mood inside the *cenaculum*. By contrast, the Rotterdam Master's Passover feast transpires as a Rabelasian banquet of lust and gluttony (cf. Figure 7.3). Under an exotic pavilion adorned with an indecipherable "magic formula" carved over the arches[30] and simulated architectural sculpture—a horned Moses bearing the Tablets of the Law is depicted[31]—we find a disorderly gathering of busty wenches and guzzling knaves, all with traveler's staves in hand. Between two of them there is a child begging for food while a corpulent man feasts with his wife on the paschal lamb, splayed out on a platter. Bundles of what appear to be uprooted onions or garlic bulbs lie on the floor and spill onto the street below. All this takes place in a space that is both contiguous with the *cenaculum*—as the bifurcated column between the two panels attests—and isolated from it, shown by the dark gap between the two elevated buildings. Passing between the two spaces and pausing on the stairs facing the pavilion is a pheasant, which some scholars have seen as an attribute of Judas.[32] More important than any arcane meanings "hidden"

     MITCHELL B. MERBACK

behind the surface phenomena, however, is something plain for everybody to see: the fact that an ordered ritual meal, the Passover, taken in accordance with divine law, has degenerated into an eccentric comedy of gustatory pleasures. Why?

When Renaissance painters, north and south of the Alps, sought to convey the sinful carnality of the ancient Israelites, they often conjoined an orientalizing biblicism with contemporary peasant genre. We find this, for example, in Lucas van Leyden's famous *Dance around the Golden Calf* (c. 1530), now in the Rijksmuseum in Amsterdam. Here the swirling drapery of the dancers and the rampage of appetites satisfying themselves—both active discharges of bodily impulse—articulate a warning against the blind sensuality idolatry inspires. Although movements and gestures in the Rotterdam-Berlin altar's Passover scene are limited to the body's gastronomic self-servicing, one suspects that a similar aspersion is being cast over carnal Israel here, too.[33] Idolatrous Israelite feasting becomes an allegory and a type for the "carnal feeding" Alexander of Hales contrasted with the "sacramental eating" properly reserved for the Eucharist. Prefiguring the Lord's Supper in line with the typological standards established in such late medieval commentaries as the *Biblia pauperum* and the *Speculum humanae salvationis*,[34] the Rotterdam-Berlin altar's left wing seems to warn against the meal's abuse by those who would "fail to discern" its holiness. Sinners violate God's body with the polluting power of their own.

Apotropaic Signs

A curious critique of this kind of pollution is registered in the Rotterdam panel from the margins of the main event. One of the young apostles, seated on the left side of the table, turns away and raises his finger to his nose. Shooting a knowing glance at the viewer, he also shoots two globules of snot toward the floor (Figure 7.6). More than an inspired embellishment to the Gospel story, the gesture is not as idiosyncratic as it may first seem. Predating the Rotterdam panel are two appearances of a closely related motif: the first is a sheet printed around 1485 by the Dutch goldsmith and engraver, Master I. A. M. van Zwolle, in which an elderly apostle with a cleft beard and hood, sitting next to Judas, turns away while gripping his nose with thumb and index finger from above, his palm facing out—a gesture that not only calls attention to the money bag Judas clutches behind his back, but also engages the viewer in an odd game of peek-a-boo (Figure 7.7). It may well be that Master I. A. M.'s figure is not blowing but holding his nose; Eric Zafran has interpreted this as an explicitly antisemitic expression of disgust, the apostle's recoil from the so-called *foetor Judaicus,* the "goatlike" odor supposedly exuded by unbaptized Jews.[35] However, if one looks carefully, this

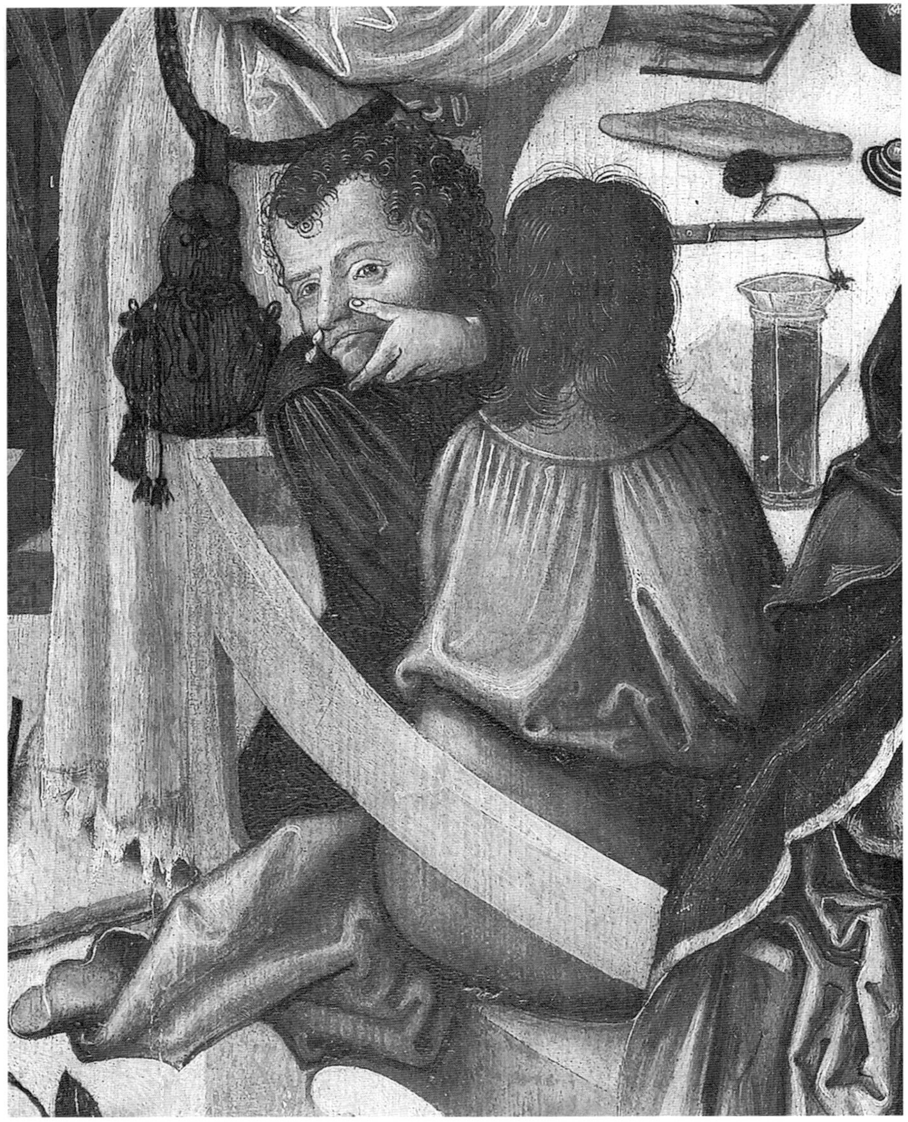

7.6. Detail of youthful apostle from the *Rotterdam-Berlin Corpus Christi Altarpiece*. Netherlands Institute for Cultural Heritage, Rijswijk/Amsterdam, on loan to Museum Boijmans Van Beuningen, Rotterdam.

same figure also seems to be holding open his opposite sleeve below his nose, suggesting that he may indeed be evacuating. Within a decade this motif, along with much else in the composition, was adapted for a *Last Supper* by Maestro Bartolomé, a Castilan painter who collaborated with Fernando Gallego (c. 1440–1507) on the great Cuidad Rodrigo Altarpiece, whose parts are now preserved in

MITCHELL B. MERBACK

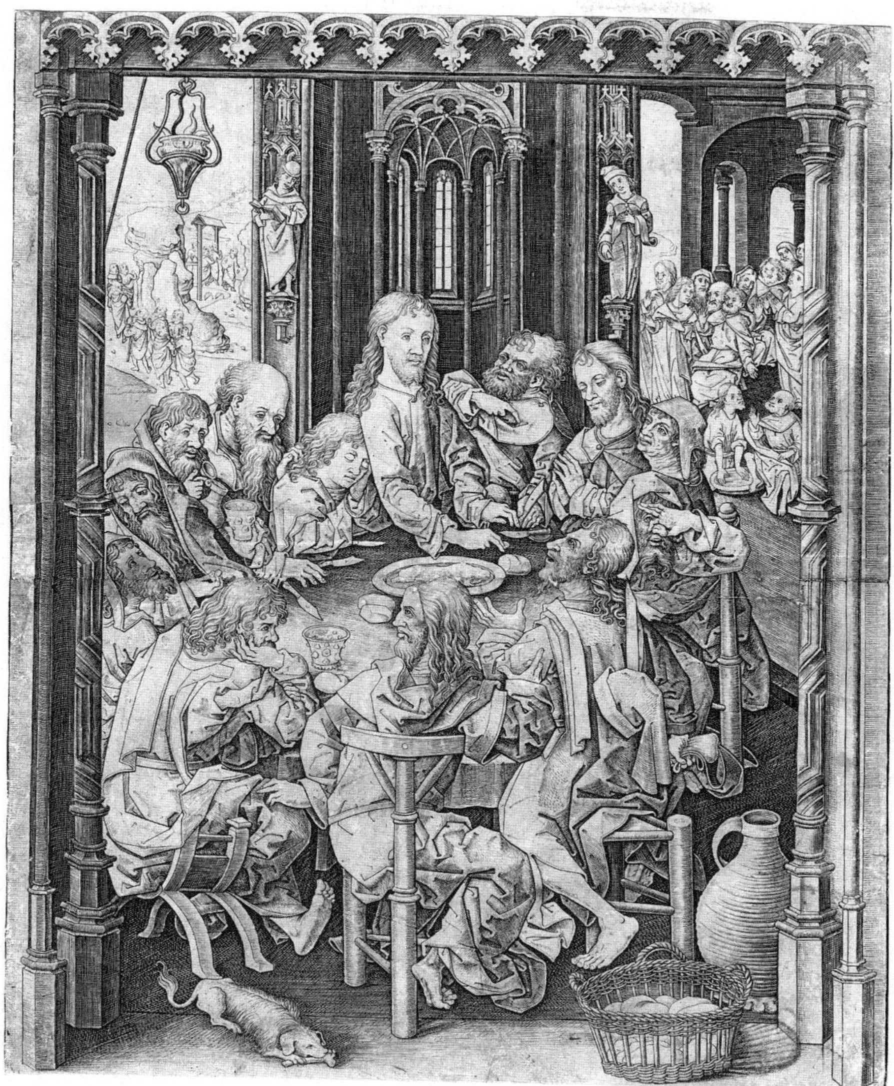

7.7. Master I. A. M. van Zwolle, *Last Supper*, c. 1485. Engraving, 33 x 26.8 cm. Photo © Trustees of the British Museum.

Tucson.[36] The close juxtaposition of Judas and the nose-blowing apostle on the right side of the table closely follows the Netherlandish precursor. In the Castilan work, however, the nose-clutching gesture admits far less ambiguity—the apostle is alerting the viewer that something is very rotten indeed. Finally, it bears mention that Jörg Ratgeb's Last Supper for the *Herrenberg Altar,* which postdates the Rotterdam panel, employs the motif in a version closer to that found in Rotterdam panel: more a blow than a pinch.

Resisting its burlesque quality, past scholars have interpreted the Rotterdam panel's motif in more serious terms: either as an expression of contempt or a cleansing of the body to gird it against sin.[37] These readings may be right, but from an anthropological point of view they are only half the picture. Bodily evacuations and effluvia were indeed regarded as impurities in premodern culture; but they were also seen, and valued, as counter-agents that could be aimed at sources of pollution as a way of neutralizing their power. Memorable for their frankness are the episodes Luther recounts in his *Tischreden*, when, for example, he mooned and farted at the Devil and—in a thinly disguised scatological tactic—threw black ink to drive away the foul intruder.[38] Shit may have been premodern culture's apotropaic substance par excellence, but its logic appears to extend to other bodily wastes. Performed for the approval of the implied viewer, the gesture takes its place within an economy of sanctity, pollution, and counter-magic that is, in one sense, circumscribed by the walls of the *cenaculum* and, in another, always threatening the space outside the picture, that is, the space of the chapel where the picture's viewer takes the Eucharist into his own mouth. Thus the apostolic nose-blow not only "expresses [the young apostle's] disapproval" for the traitor's defiling act—it throws down an apotropaic gauntlet, so to speak, against the pollution associated with unworthy, carnal, or "judaizing" receptions of the heavenly bread. It may well be that the viewer saw the counter-magical gesture affecting two targets simultaneously: Judas's sinful reception, and its Old Testament "type," the idolatrous feasting of the Israelites in the pavilion just outside the *cenaculum*.

Apotropaic magic of a different kind is evoked in the Rotterdam Last Supper, again, apparently, as a symbolic gloss on the potency and perils of sacramental reception. Affixed to the interior wall of the *cenaculum,* just inside the doorway where the water-pourer performs his task and leads us into the scene, is a sheet of paper or parchment bearing the figure of the brazen serpent from Numbers 21 (verses 4–9), coiling over a Tau-shaped cross (Figure 7.8). That the painter has contrived the sheet in the form of a hand-colored, single-sheet woodcut (*Bilderbogen*), a type of inexpensive devotional image often accompanied by indulgenced prayers and displayed in domestic spaces—a well-known instance is Petrus Christus's portrait of circa 1450, now in London, showing a young man at prayer—is significant, both for its anachronism and its hybridity. Rendered as an appurtenance of the biblical dining room, the sheet's visual emblem is captioned by large Hebraic letters that look as if they form some kind of acrostic. Now Hebrew letters, real and ersatz, were routinely employed by late medieval and Renaissance altar painters, often with no more profound an intention than to furnish an exotic, orientalizing design or to establish the biblical provenance of a particular figure, object, or scene. In other contexts

MITCHELL B. MERBACK

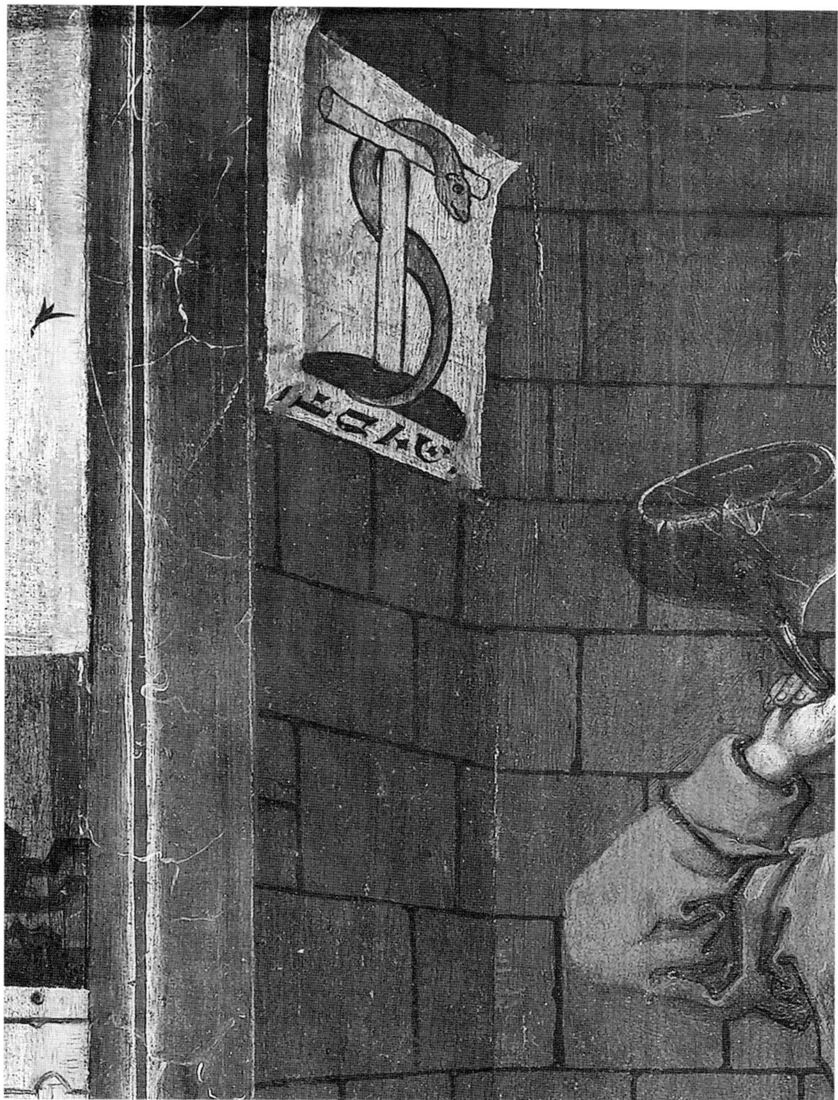

7.8. Detail of brazen serpent sheet from the *Rotterdam-Berlin Corpus Christi Altarpiece*. Netherlands Institute for Cultural Heritage, Rijswijk/Amsterdam, on loan to Museum Boijmans Van Beuningen, Rotterdam.

Christian artists took over Hebrew words and letters to stigmatize the bearer as "Jewish" or lend a mocking tone to a polemical image.[39] In still other contexts, it was the putative magical power of Hebrew script, corollary to the mystical formulas and "name-magic" that so intrigued hermeticists, that was being exploited.[40] Art historian Wilhelm Fraenger believed he could identify the Rotterdam panel's Hebrew inscription with the formula combining two of the three divine names, *tob elohim elyon* (Merciful is God the Most High), though this has since been disproven.[41] Without denying that the inscription might spark similar hopes of de-encryption in a learned medieval viewer, let us consider that the logic behind the *Bilderbogen*'s cross-cultural play of word and image lies elsewhere.

To Christian eyes the brazen serpent was an established *figura* for the Crucifixion, and here, as a "disguised symbol" among several up our eccentric painter's sleeve, it resonates with the trompe l'oeil statue of Moses on the left wing panel, visible among the architectural sculptures adorning the Passover pavilion. Conventional readings of the typological relationship between serpent and Savior hinged on long-standing ideas and cultic practices surrounding the healing power of the Cross, but in the biblical story the serpentine effigy is also a paradoxical invitation to idolatry. Recall the story from Numbers. Thirst and hunger afflicted the Israelites in the desert, and when they complained, doubting their deliverance, God sent "seraph serpents" to punish them. Moses, enlisted as intercessor, prayed until God commanded him to set up a bronze effigy of the self-same serpent, "mount it on a pole, and if anyone who has been bitten looks at it, he will recover" (21:8). Interpreted allegorically, the effigy becomes a type for the Crucified Redeemer who takes away the sins—the deadly poisons—of the world. "And as Moses lifted up the serpent in the desert," writes John (3:14–15), "so must the Son of man be lifted up. That whosoever believeth in him, may not perish; but may have life everlasting." Herbert Kessler has shown how theologians, building upon the patristic sources, invoked the allegory during the image-controversies of the eighth century as compelling proof of divine sanction in the legitimacy of images and, among Byzantine writers at least, the efficacy of icons.[42] Most agreed that the therapeutic efficacy of seeing the brazen serpent parallels the salvific power of gazing at the image of Christ on the Cross in the manner that Bishop Gerald I of Arras-Cambrai (1013–48) claimed. Gerald drew upon the biblical story precisely to demonstrate how, through the very sight (*respectum*) of the Crucified, we "are rid from our hearts of the venom of the ancient enemy."[43] Not surprising, a similar principle of homeopathic magic informed medieval Ashkenazi folk magic. Rabbi Judah ben Samuel of Regensburg (d. 1217), in whose name the *Sefer Hasidim* (Book of the Pious) was compiled shortly after his death, recommended the following precaution: "When a man finds himself among suspected poisoners and he is afraid they will tamper with his food or drink, he should procure a knife with a handle of snake bone, and stick it into the table. If there is any poison present the handle will quiver, for the snake is full of venom, and like attracts like."[44] Has the painter stuck the knife into the table on behalf of those who would protect the Lord's Supper against defilement and sacrilege, visually inoculating us, as it were, against "the venom of the ancient enemy"?

That the apotropaic token is presented as an image within the image is crucial, for the painter, relying on the means normally at his disposal as a professional maker of pictures, has employed a device normally considered beyond the means of Jews. In this connection it is interesting to note that, within the context of the medieval Jewish-Christian debate, the brazen serpent story cut two ways as a lesson in the divinely sanctioned use of images. *Sefer Milhamot ha-Shem* (The Book of the Wars of the Lord), a widely circulated treatise by Jacob ben Reuben (1136–80s), a polemicist writing from northern Spain, denounces the allegorical resemblance of serpent and savior in response to the charge that, when the Israelites erected the serpent, they did so in defiance of the Mosaic prohibition on images, thus proving their impious and idolatrous nature:[45] "Our blessed Creator never forbade the making of statues and images. He only forbade bowing down and worship." Glossing the larger passage Kalman Bland has concluded that, not only was Jacob ben Reuben concerned to show that Jews were "not forbidden to make all forms of art," as the Christian caricature would have it, but they could also "fully appreciate the healing power of legitimate visual images."[46]

Also indicative of the artist's intention to invest his hybrid artifact with amuletic properties is its placement on the doorpost of the room. Entertaining the conceit a bit further, we might venture to see the brazen serpent *Bilderbogen* as a fanciful kind of Jewish-Christian *mezuzah*. Traditionally *mezuzot* take the form of capsules containing a rectangular strip of parchment, inscribed with the verses taken from Deuteronomy 6 (verses 4–19) and 11 (13–20) and are affixed to doorposts and thresholds, both outside and inside the home. Whereas modern Jews typically place one upon only the doorjamb of a building's main entrance, medieval sources testify to the proliferation of *mezuzot* throughout domestic space. No less an authority than Rabbi Meir of Rothenburg boasted of having twenty-four of them.[47] Although its scriptural contents were prescribed by Jewish law, popular imagination and custom treated the *mezuzah* as an especially powerful kind of amulet, as Joshua Trachtenberg has demonstrated.[48] Its foremost function was apotropaic, and specifically anti-demonic.

Clearly, the brazen serpent sheet in the Rotterdam panel bears little resemblance to the *mezuzah*'s traditional form, and though Jewish amulets could be decorated with emblematic figures and symbols, none would have ever carried so blatantly idolatrous a form as a living serpent. Ironically, this may turn out to be the point. Accompanied by its ersatz Hebrew inscription, which surrounds the already salvific and potent *figura* of the brazen serpent with an inscrutable aura of magic, the *mezuzah* attains the paradoxical status of a "Jewish" amulet deployed against a "Jewish" source of pollution. Dangers both demonic and human are contained, allowing the communion that is not Judas's, the paschal meal that is no longer Jewish, to go forward in the spirit of the angelic injunction to "behold the heavenly bread." Communicants before the altar could confidently see Christ, eat Christ, and, in doing so, anticipate the messianic banquet of the eschatological future, the "third Pascha," as Origen called it, "celebrated among myriads of angels in the most perfect festivity."[49]

Piety, Security, and Access

Like the apostolic nose-blow, the counter-magical potential of the brazen serpent in the Rotterdam panel could be realized only once it became the object of a viewer's attention. Seeing evil being warded off and pollution neutralized must have given reassurance that it had been so, and can be so again, but also required participation, for present dangers demanded vigilance in protecting what was fragile, vulnerable, and most holy. Aside from clerical reformers, Corpus Christi confraternities were conspicuous as a group that invested itself in upholding the integrity and prestige of the altar sacrament as an object of cult. Foundation charters for these voluntary lay associations begin to enter the documentary record north and south of the Alps in the half-century following Pope Clement V's decree of 1311, which ordered that the feast (in French *Fête Dieu,* in German *Fronleichnamsfest*) promulgated by Urban IV in 1264 be adopted universally by the church.[50] Leuven's brotherhood, for example, was founded in 1432, a generation before the Bouts altar was commissioned. In large cities such as Cologne, where multiple brotherhoods existed for each of the major patrons, associations devoted to the sacrament ranked second only to those devoted to Mary.[51] Despite their ubiquity, however, it is hard to generalize about the activities or the religious views espoused by these groups, for they exhibited, according to Miri Rubin, a "variety of understandings and uses of the Eucharist" and engaged in a wide range of activities: taking the *viaticum* to the sick and dying, providing funerary services, commemorating and obtaining indulgences for the dead, organizing feasts and dinners, staging pageants and para-liturgical dramas around the Easter Sepulchre, providing for the safety and proper lighting of the Host wherever it was exposed or elevated, and taking part in processions on Corpus Christi itself.[52] In short, sacrament confraternities were "providers of essential personal, familial, religious, economic and political services [and] security in some essential areas of life."[53]

Securing salvific benefits for themselves through devotion to the Eucharist was, in the activities of these groups, inextricably tied to securing access to those benefits for others, both the living and the dead. Their commitment to

Eucharistic orthodoxy was part of a conservative religious and civic agenda; and from all appearances it was wedded to a militant protectiveness toward the Eucharist itself—its physical integrity and the protocols surrounding its ritual display, use, and administration. Brothers often served as assistants to the clergy in their administration of the sacrament, a fact that supports the identification of certain figures we see pictured inside the scene, as witnesses to the Last Supper, as confraternity members (four attending figures in the Leuven Altar have been so identified). Not all the surviving examples of Corpus Christi Altarpieces feature donors inside or outside the scene, however, and the faces assembled around the table in the Rotterdam panel do not, in my view, lend themselves very well to the game of identifying embedded portraits.

Regarding confraternal attitudes toward Jews, Judaism, and Jewish ritual, scholarship has little concrete to offer. As a placeholder for future research, it would be fair to say that confraternity members brought to their pious activities the attitudes of the civic elites from whose ranks they came: negative conceptions of the Jewish religion, grounded most likely in mendicant preaching and propaganda; a cautious credulity concerning reports of Jewish sacrilege, conspiracy, ritual murder, and the popular speculations such reports prompted; outward opposition toward Jewish economic privileges and usury; and a conviction about the alien status of Jews within the "well-ordered" Christian commune. Anxiety connected with these last two features of late medieval *bürgerliche* anti-Judaism would have dropped away, to be sure, once cities and territorial rulers opted to expel their Jewish populations, as happened in the Low Countries, and across the German empire, during the "long fifteenth century."[54]

Of the confraternal sacrament altarpieces that survive, it is perhaps surprising that only the one in Urbino (mentioned earlier) incorporates overt anti-Jewish imagery: the predella cycle with six scenes by Paolo Uccello, which gives an Italian version—based on French and English sources—of the stereotyped tale of Jewish Host-sacrilege.[55] It is striking that this should be the case in the one context—Renaissance Italy—where no Host-abuse accusations, and no persecutory episodes to which we might relate the cycle's imagery, are recorded.[56] In northern Europe, especially in Germany and the Netherlands, where Host-abuse affairs resulting in riots, arrests, executions, expulsions, miracle cults, and pilgrimages span the two centuries before the Reformation, the iconographic choices for Corpus Christ altarpieces were more conservative. Why? It may be that bleeding Host affairs of the kind that aroused worries among conservative reformers in the fourteenth century—for example, Korneuburg and Pulkau, both in Lower Austria, both of them exposed as frauds—and in the fifteenth century—most spectacularly at Wilsnack in Brandenburg—presented sacrament confraternities with the dilemma of measuring the benefits of cult expansion against the increased potential for idolatrous abuse of the Eucharist.[57] Such abuses, after all, played into the hands of critics on both sides of the religious divide, Christian and Jewish. The orthodox impulse behind the Leuven's Corpus Christi Brotherhood's aggressive slate of commissions for the Church of St. Peter—two major altarpieces with decorative covers (also by Bouts), a spectacular stone tabernacle—may well be understood as a response to the highly successful blood-host cult in Brussels, which formed in the wake of a religious riot and the expulsion of the Jewish community from Brabant, and centered upon a commemorative chapel built on the site of the destroyed synagogue. But further research is needed to test these connections.[58]

Conclusion

To venture that a Christian iconographic theme such as the Last Supper, in and of itself, harbors a hidden polemic against Judaism would be incautious at best, misleading and irresponsible at worst, since it is always the specific functional and ideological context in which an image appears that furnishes its antagonistic charge and grounds the circuitries of meaning. Nevertheless, as the preceding discussion has made clear, where context demanded a dramatization of his role as a "judaizing" threat and source of carnal pollution, it was the figure of the Jewish Judas that conducted the theme's polemical charge. That this was a polemic turned inward, however, a message of reform rather than mission, is critical to remember. I have argued that Judas's communion in the Rotterdam-Berlin Altar, the suspended moment before his impure contact with the pure and incorruptible body of Christ, fascinated and vexed its Christian audience precisely because it revealed just how narrow was the gap between two types of sacramental reception, one worthy, the other unworthy. The distance between was left to the beholder to negotiate for himself. To face down the "judaizing" impulses every sinning Christian harbored, to live *sub gratia* instead of *sub lege*, one had to reenact within oneself, as it were, the historic supersession of carnality by spirit. This manner of typological thinking found its visual analogy in the triptych's original design, with its pairing of Old and New Testament scenes. *Antitypos* supersedes *typos,* just as, in Thomas Aquinas's formulation, the truth dispels the shadows. But just as the shadow (*umbra*) remains unforgotten inside the image (*imago*) as the guarantee of its origins,[59] the specter of a Jewish carnality looms behind every act of sacramental eating, when the "heavenly bread" becomes identical with the vulnerable, suffering, bleeding flesh of the human Christ.

MITCHELL B. MERBACK

For the confraternity members who took communion against the backdrop of their altar's rhetoric of admonition of fellowship and betrayal, sanctity and defilement, the contrast between carnal and a spiritual receptions of the sacred bread would have recalled something rather specific in Paul's words to the Corinthians, something that speaks directly to this reformist impulse. Paul chastised those who, having arrived at the feast first, did not wait for the others, left others to go hungry, and, giving in to their factionalism, denied the communal *wholeness* of the meal. "Their selfish behaviour," explains theologian Geoffrey Wainwright in his gloss on this passage, "meant that they were turning the *Lord's* supper into their *own* supper . . . to eat and drink these [things] unworthily on account of being in a state of division . . . meant becoming guilty of the body and blood of the Lord."[60] Theology could content itself with solutions to the crisis provoked by every instance of unworthy reception, and liturgical innovations—the ciborium and tabernacle to contain the host, the pyx and paten which transported it, the candelabra illuminating it, even the *flabellum* used for shooing flies from its surface—might have promoted a sense of security against accidents, but at the same time such innovations could only press home the fact of the Host's fragile vulnerability. From their privileged position in their own chapel, lay members of Corpus Christi confraternities committed themselves to the pious mission of ensuring that the Lord's Supper remained the Lord's Supper—a universal supper, whole and undivided, untouched by accidents, unriven by dissensions within, nor threatened by aggressions coming from without.

By transforming the scene in the *cenaculum* into a virtual battlefield of apotropaic magic, the painted altarpiece may have worked to reassure its viewers that the pollution spread by unworthy reception might be counteracted, even eliminated. Thus, as every sinning Christian's dilemma before the receiving the Eucharist was replicated before the image of communion's origin, the image also betokened a displacement of that judaizing carnality so threatening to sacramental purity. *Manducatio per visum,* the ocular communion that enacted the promise of a wholly spiritual eating, may have distinguished Christian from Jew as effectively as the Christian monopoly on visual imagery itself—even as another type of threat, that of the "evil eye" (*oculus fascinus*), loomed up behind it.

NOTES

Help and encouragement in improving my arguments came, at various stages, from Herbert Kessler, David Nirenberg, Kalman Bland, and Jacqueline Jung and my co-participants in the Lavy Colloquium. A version of this chapter was delivered at Bar Ilan University in June 2008; I am grateful to Bracha Yaniv and the Department of Jewish Art for the invitation and lively discussions. Biblical passages in English are from the Douay-Rheims Catholic Bible (http://www.drbo.org) and, unless stated otherwise, all other translations are my own.

1. David Nirenberg, "Figures of Thought and Figures of Flesh: 'Jews' and 'Judaism' in Late Medieval Spanish Poetry and Politics," *Speculum* 81 (2006): 398–426, who poses the analytical difficulty of separating the historical realities of Jews, Judaism, and Jewish behavior from their figurations within Christian thought (in sources where they appear conflated). Recognizing the conceptual difficulties and the ideological entanglements obtaining in any such effort, I am perhaps more sanguine about the objective prospects.

2. On the iconography of the Last Supper, see Karl Künstle, *Ikonographie der Christlichen Kunst*, 2 vols. (Freiburg im Breisgau: Herder & Co., 1928), 413–25; Klaus Wessel, *Abendmahl und Apostelkommunion* (Recklinghausen: Aurel Bongers, 1964); Gertrud Schiller, *Iconography of Christian Art*, trans. Janet Seligman (Greenwich, Conn.: New York Graphic Society, 1971), 2:24–41; and the more focused studies cited below. Relevant Gospel texts are Matt. 26:20–30; Mark 14:18–26; Luke 22:14–33; and passages scattered through John 12–13.

3. Among others, Schiller, *Iconography*, 2:34–37; Ruth Mellinkoff, "Judas's Red Hair and the Jews," *Journal of Jewish Art* 9 (1982): 31–46; Hyam Maccoby, *Judas Iscariot and the Myth of Jewish Evil* (New York: Free Press, 1992); and Annette Weber, "The Hanged Judas of Freiburg Cathedral: Sources and Interpretations," in *Imagining the Self, Imagining the Other: Visual Representation and Jewish Christian Dynamics in the Middle Ages and Early Modern Period*, ed. Eva Frojmovic (Leiden: Brill, 2002), 165–88.

4. Each of the relevant synoptic gospel accounts—here as elsewhere, John is the exception—includes all three dramatic units: the revelation of betrayal, Jesus' *separate* blessings over the bread and the wine, and his injunction to the disciples to "do this in remembrance of me."

5. Leo Steinberg, *Leonardo's Incessant Last Supper* (New York: Zone Books, 2001), 40.

6. Joseph Leo Koerner, *The Reformation of the Image* (Chicago: University of Chicago Press, 2004), 321–29.

7. Anne-Laure Van Bruaene, "*In Principio Erat Verbum:* Drama, Devotion, Reformation and Urban Association in the Low Countries," in *Early Modern Confraternities in Europe and the Americas*, ed. Christopher Black and Pamela Gravestock (Aldershot: Ashgate, 2006), 64–80.

8. Fundamental for the Urbino Altar is Marilyn Aronberg Lavin, "The Altar of Corpus Domini in Urbino: Paolo Uccello, Joos van Ghent, Piera della Francesca," *Art Bulletin* 49, no. 1 (March 1967): 1–24; and for Lübeck, *Corpus der mittelalterlichen Holzskulptur und Tafelmalerei in Schleswig-Holstein, Band I: Hansestadt Lübeck, St. Annen-Museum*, ed. Uwe Albrecht (Kiel: Ludwig, 2005), 272–82 (cat. no. 86). Literature on the Bouts altar is expansive; the best recent treatment is Heike Schlie, *Bilder des Corpus Christi: Sakramentaler Realismus von Jan van Eyck bis Hieronymus Bosch* (Berlin: Gebr. Mann, 2002), 76–83. These and other examples are brought together comparatively in Barbara Welzel, *Abendsmahlaltäre vor der Reformation* (Berlin: Gebr. Mann, 1991).

9. Miri Rubin, *Corpus Christi: The Eucharist in Late Medieval Culture* (Cambridge: Cambridge University Press, 1991), 298.

10. Achim Timmermann posits the instrumental role of these same anxieties in the development of eucharistic *architecture* within the church in his forthcoming book, *Real Presence: Sacrament Houses and the Body of Christ, c. 1270–1600* (Turnhout: Brepols, 2009).

11. See my forthcoming *Pilgrimage and Pogrom: Myth, Memory and Visual Culture at the Host-Miracle Shrines of Germany and Austria.*

12. For examples and analysis, see Daniel J. Lasker, "Transubstantiation, Elijah's Chair, Plato, and the Jewish-Christian Debate," *Revue des Études juives* 143, nos. 1–2 (January–June 1984): 31–58; Daniel J. Lasker, "Popular Polemics and Philosophical Truth in the Medieval Jewish Critique of Christianity," *Journal of Jewish Thought and Philosophy* 8 (1999): 243–59;

and Miri Rubin, *Gentile Tales: The Narrative Assault on Late Medieval Jews* (New Haven and London: Yale University Press, 1999), 93–103.

13. Museum Boijmans Van Beuningen Rotterdam, inv. 2294. See Wilhelm Fraenger, *Jörg Ratgeb. Ein Maler und Märtyrer aus dem Bauernkrieg* (Dresden: Veb Verlag der Kunst, 1972), 62–65 (center panel) and 70–72 (wing panel); Welzel, *Abendmahlsaltäre*, 102–5 and 157 (catalogue); and Julien Chapuis, *Duitse en Franse schilderijen. Vijftiende en zestiende eeuw / German and French Paintings. Fifteenth and Sixteenth Centuries* (Rotterdam: Museum Boymans-van Beuningen, 1995), 44–53.

14. See Griet Steyaert, "The Last Supper by the Master of the Legend of St. Catherine," in *Bouts Studies: Proceedings of the International Colloquium (Leuven, 26–28 November 1998)*, ed. Bert Cardon et al. (Leuven: Uitgeverij Peeters, 2001), 259–71.

15. The attribution was first proposed by Betty Kurth (1924) and accepted by Otto Benesch (1927) and Max Friedländer (1930). Lisa de la Mare Farber, "Jerg Ratgeb and the Herrenberg Altarpiece" (Ph.D. diss., Princeton University, 1990), also accepts the attribution of the Rotterdam-Berlin panels to Ratgeb. But Barbara Welzel's attribution of the work to an unnamed "Antwerp Mannerist," which essentially updates H. Th. Musper's (1952–53) proposal of a Netherlandish origin, has likewise been dismantled (as Fraenger had already dismantled Musper's argument in 1972).

16. See Chapuis, *Duitse en Franse schilderijen*, 52–53, who bases his conclusions on stylistic parallels with south German limewood sculpture and the fact that the use of fir (as a support) rules out an Antwerp attribution, since oak was preferred in the Netherlands.

17. The altarpiece was designed to adorn the larger of the confraternity's two apsidal chapels in the northern ambulatory of St. Peter's; the Leuven brothers were also given space in the choir to construct a large sacrament tabernacle; see Schlie, *Bilder des Corpus Christi*.

18. Flowering stems of *convallaria majalis* have two large leaves and, between them, a raceme of between five and fifteen small, scented, bell-shaped flowers arrayed along the axis stem; like other flowers in the lily family, their biblical and folkloric associations are dense and hard to disentangle. A variety of legends, however, seem to agree on their apotropaic value. That their flowering cycle comes between late March and May, after which they are named, certainly gave rise to their association with the events of Holy Week.

19. Two other scenes, the Agony in the Garden and Christ Taking Leave of the Holy Women, appear in the background of the Passover wing panel.

20. Cf. Fraenger, *Jörg Ratgeb*, 63, who aptly compared the composition to a carousel.

21. Mellinkoff, "Judas's Red Hair," 40.

22. For an instance of an artist renouncing the conventions of defamatory physical features that dominated the imagery of Judas, see Jacqueline E. Jung, "The Passion, the Jews, and the Crisis of the Individual on the Naumburg West Choir Screen," in *Beyond the Yellow Badge: Anti-Judaism and Antisemitism in Medieval and Early Modern Visual Culture*, ed. Mitchell B. Merback (Leiden and Boston: Brill, 2008), 145–77.

23. Cf. the Last Supper from the thirteenth-century psalter in Melk (Melk Stiftsbibliothek, Ms. lat. 1903; formerly 1833; fol. 11v), repr. in Ruth Mellinkoff, *Outcasts: Signs of Otherness in Northern European Art of the Late Middle Ages*, 2 vols. (Berkeley: University of California Press, 1993), plate VII.4.

24. Kenneth Stow, *Jewish Dogs: An Image and Its Interpreters: Continuity in the Catholic-Jewish Encounter* (Stanford: Stanford University Press, 2006), esp. 133–57.

25. For the medieval background, see Rubin, *Corpus Christi*, 68–70; on the Pauline doctrine, see *First Corinthians: A New Translation with Introduction and Commentary*, trans. Joseph A. Fitzmyer (New Haven: Yale University Press, 2008), 445.

26. Discussed and quoted in Rubin, *Corpus Christi*, 65–66.

27. See Gary Macy, *The Banquet's Wisdom: A Short History of the Theologies of the Lord's Supper* (New York: Paulist Press, 1992), 109–12; also Rubin, *Corpus Christi,* 66–69.

28. On the dialectic of guilt and blame inspired by late medieval devotional art and literature, see Caroline Walker Bynum, "Violent Imagery in Late Medieval Piety," *Bulletin of the German Historical Institute* 30 (Spring 2002): 3–36; and my response in the same issue, "Reverberations of Guilt and Violence, Resonances of Peace," 37–50.

29. Quoted in Walter Gibson, "Imitatio Christi: The Passion Scenes of Hieronymus Bosch," *Simiolus* 6, no. 2 (1972): 83–93, here 83, with my emphases.

30. See Fraenger, *Jörg Ratgeb,* for the author's failed attempts to make sense of the inscription.

31. Bouts has painted a Moses statue in grisaille as a carved socle figure affixed to the traceried blind arch above the door, at the right rear of the room, a passage that leads past a laver in a niche to a garden outside; on its significance, see Aloys Butzkamm, *Bild und Frömmigkeit im 15. Jahrhundert. Der Sakramentsaltar von Dieric Bouts in der St.-Peters-Kirche zu Löwen* (Paderborn: Bonifatius, 1990), 93–101.

32. Chapuis, *Duitse en Franse schilderijen,* 51, who notes that a pheasant also walks along the rear window ledge in Ratgeb's Herrenberg *Last Supper,* though he offers no further references.

33. I refer to Augustine's characterization of Judaism as "carnal" against Christianity's spiritualization of the mind-body relationship; as discussed in Daniel Boyarin, *Carnal Israel: Reading Sex in Talmudic Culture* (Berkeley: University of California Press, 1993).

34. Whereas the *Biblia pauperum* offered only two types for the Last Supper, the *Speculum* expanded the selection to three. See Adrian Wilson and Joyce Lancaster Wilson, *A Medieval Mirror: Speculum humanae salvationis 1324–1500* (Berkeley: University of California Press, 1984).

35. Eric Zafran, "Saturn and the Jews," *Journal of the Warburg and Courtauld Institutes* 42 (1979): 18n19.

36. See *Fernando Gallego and His Workshop: The Altarpiece from Ciudad Rodrigo: Paintings from the Collection of the Arizona Museum of Art,* ed. Amanda W. Dotseth, Barbara C. Anderson, and Mark A. Roglán (Dallas: Meadows Museum, Southern Methodist University / Philip Wilson, 2008), 100 and 318–19 (cat. no. 19). Bartolomé's use of the motif, once attributed to Gallego, was kindly pointed out to me by Felipe Pereda.

37. For example, J. Forderer, "Ein Jugendwerk Jörg Ratgebs," *Tübinger Blätter* 22 (1931): 13–16, who also interprets the young man on the opposite side of Judas, shown guzzling from the gourd-shaped flask, along similar lines (15); and Bruno Bushart, "Jörg Ratgeb. Der Maler des Herrenberger Altars," reprinted in *Aus Schönbuch und Gäu, Heimatbeilage zum Böblinger Boten* (Böblingen, 1959), 3–17, at 14, which I have not been able to consult (noted in Chapuis, *Duitse en Franse schilderijen,* 143n11).

38. Luther's "sublimated anality" is memorably analyzed in Norman O. Brown, *Life against Death: The Psychoanalytic Meaning of History* (Middletown, Conn: Wesleyan University Press, 1959), 211.

39. The most accessible discussion of Hebrew inscriptions in medieval and Renaissance Christian art remains Mellinkoff, *Outcasts,* 1:97–98; but see also the more comprehensive list (containing 362 items) assembled by the Hebrew linguist Gad B. Sarfatti, "Hebrew Script in Western Visual Arts," *Italia: Studi e ricerche sulla storia, la cultura e la letteratura degli Ebrei d'Italia* 13–15 (2001): 451–547; and Sarfatti, "Addenda," *Italia* 16 (2004): 135–56. Exceptional among recent studies is Shalom Sabar, "Between Calvinists and Jews: Hebrew Script in Rembrandt's Art," in Merback, *Beyond the Yellow Badge,* 371–404, with relevant Hebrew literature cited.

     MITCHELL B. MERBACK

40. On the development of magical formulas (verbal and numerical), name-magic, and the perceptions surrounding these, see Joshua Trachtenberg, *Jewish Magic and Superstition: A Study in Folk Religion* (New York: Atheneum, 1982), 78–103.

41. Only Fraenger himself, to my knowledge, has expressed any confidence in this reading of the inscription, which he transliterates as *t'obh 'älohim äljon,* and translates as "Gnädig ist Gott der Höchste" (*Jörg Ratgeb,* 65). But the letters are not recognizable as Hebrew, as Chapuis, in consultation with Bernard Levinson of Indiana University, also confirmed (*Duitse en Franse schilderijen,* 143n2). Though the comparison is to my mind inconclusive, Fraenger claims that the same phrase, rendered in an Ashkenazic script in use since 1400, appears in the Circumcision panel Ratgeb composed for the *Herrenberg Altar,* inscribed upon the headscarf of the rabbi holding the Christ child; see his *Jörg Ratgeb,* Figure 99.

42. Theodulf of Orléans, the Carolingian author of the *Opus caroli* (c. 790), a treatise issued in response to the Second Council of Nicaea's rulings, devoted a full chapter to the brazen serpent; see Herbert L. Kessler, "A Sanctifying Serpent. Crucifix as Cure," in *Experiments in Empathy: Studies in Honor of Karl F. Morrison,* ed. Rudolph Bell and Karl F. Morrison (Turnhout: Brepols, forthcoming). My gratitude to the author for sharing his work with me prior to its publication.

43. From Gerard's account of the anti-heresy synod convened in Arras in January 1025, *Acta synodi Atrebetensis in Manichaeos,* quoted and discussed in Rachel Fulton, *From Judgment to Passion: Devotion to Christ and the Virgin Mary, 800–1200* (New York: Columbia University Press, 2002), 85.

44. Judah ben Samuel, *Sefer Hasidim—Das Buch der Frommen (nach der Rezension in Cod. de Rossi, No. 1133),* ed. Judah Wistinetzki, 2nd ed., with introduction by Jacob Freimann (Frankfurt: M. A. Vahrmann, 1924), 1471, quoted and discussed in Trachtenberg, *Jewish Magic,* 184. Apparently both Clement V and John XXII owned knives whose handles were made of serpents' horns.

45. On this theme in Jacob ben Reuben's work, see Kalman Bland, "Defending, Enjoying, and Regulating the Visual," in *Judaism in Practice: From the Middle Ages through the Early Modern Period,* ed. Lawrence Fine (Princeton: Princeton University Press, 2001), 281–97, esp. 290–91, kindly shared with me by its author. On the overall thematics of the treatise, see Robert Chazan, *Fashioning Jewish Identity in Medieval Western Christendom* (Cambridge: Cambridge University Press, 2004), 98–103. That the arguments of *Milhamot ha-Shem* against the New Testament struck Christian nerves can be seen in the extensive response given by Nicholas of Lyra (c. 1270–1349), who "vigorously rebutted" (Chazan, *Fashioning Jewish Identity,* 99n26) chapter 11 in his *Responsio ad quendam Iudaeum.*

46. Bland, "Defending, Enjoying, and Regulating," 283.

47. Trachtenberg, *Jewish Magic,* 146.

48. Ibid., 145–52.

49. Origen, *Commentary on the Gospel of John* 10, 18, sections 108–11; in Raniero Cantalamessa, ed., *Easter in the Early Church: An Anthology of Jewish and Early Christian Texts,* rev. ed., trans. James M. Quigley and Joseph T. Lienhard (Collegeville, Minn.: Liturgical Press, 1993), 54.

50. At present, appraisals of the role of medieval and early modern European confraternities as patrons of art is lopsided in favor of Italy; some tasks for future research are outlined in Barbara Wisch, "Incorporating Images: Some Themes and Tasks for Confraternity Studies and Early Modern Visual Culture," in Black and Gravestock, *Early Modern Confraternities,* 243–63.

51. In Cologne, for example, ten Corpus Christi brotherhoods were founded between the mid-fourteenth and mid-sixteenth centuries; see Klaus Militzer, ed., *Quellen zur Geschichte*

der Kölner Laienbruderschaften von 12. Jahrhundert bis 1562/63, 2 vols. (Düsseldorf: Droste, 1997), 1:xliv for the comparative table of patrons.

52. See Rubin, *Corpus Christi*, 233–43, though her focus is England.

53. Ibid., 233.

54. For the German expulsions, see the essays in Friedhelm Burgard, Alfred Haverkamp, and Gerd Mentgen, eds., *Judenvertreibungen in Mittelalter und früher Neuzeit* (Hannover: Hahnsche, 1999); for the Netherlands, consult B. M. J. Speet, "The Middle Ages," in *The History of the Jews in the Netherlands,* ed. J. C. H. Blom, R. F. Fuks-Mansfeld, and I. Schöffer; trans. Arnold J. Pomerans and Erica Pomerans (Oxford: Littman Library of Jewish Civilization, 2002), 13–43.

55. Also incorporating anti-Jewish legend material is the Corpus Christi Altar (c. 1415) from the monastery of San Bartholomé near Villahermosa del Rio (Valencia), in which a Last Supper is flanked by a six-scene sequence of the Paris Host-abuse narrative, among other themes; as far as can be ascertained, however, the work's commission did not involve a lay brotherhood. See Welzel, *Abendmahlsaltäre*, 71–74 and her figs. 2a–b.

56. This is perhaps owing to the ambivalent attitude of toleration the Montefeltre ducal house extended toward Urbino's Jews. See Dana E. Katz, "The Contours of Tolerance: Jews and the Corpus Domini Altarpiece in Urbino," *Art Bulletin* 85, no. 4 (December 2003): 646–61, at 646–47.

57. On frauds at German shrines, see esp. Friedrich Lotter, "Hostienfrevelvorwurf und Blutwunderfälschung bei den Judenverfolgungen von 1298 ('Rindfleisch') und 1336–1338 ('Armleder')," in *Fälschungen im Mittelalter, Teil V: Fingierte Briefe, Frömmigkeit und Fälschung, Realienfälschung* (Hannover: Hahnsche, 1988), 533–83, at 559 for Korneuburg. For the Pulkau case, see my "Fount of Mercy, City of Blood: Cultic Anti-Judaism and the Pulkau Passion Altarpiece," *Art Bulletin* 87, no. 4 (December 2005): 589–642, esp. 618–22. On the Wilsnack controversy, see Caroline Walker Bynum, *Wonderful Blood: Theology and Practice in Late Medieval Northern Germany and Beyond* (Philadelphia: University of Pennsylvania Press, 2007).

58. On the Brussels affair, see Luc Dequeker, *Het Sacrament van Mirakel: Jodenhaat in de Middeleeuwen* (Louvain: Davidfonds, 2000), esp. 21–50. The Holy Blood chapel in the Cathedral of St. Gudule's got its official start with an indulgence from Pope Eugenius IV in 1436, and eventually produced the richest reserve of visual artifacts associated with any single Host-abuse legend I know. For a survey of this material, see Eric M. Zafran, "The Iconography of Antisemitism: A Study of the Representation of the Jews in the Visual Arts of Europe 1400–1600" (Ph.D. diss., New York University; Ann Arbor, Mich.: University Microfilms, 1973), 155–67.

59. For a powerful account of typological consciousness, see Friedrich Ohly, "Typology as a Form of Historical Thought," in *Sensus Spiritualis: Studies in Medieval Significs and the Philology of Culture,* ed. Samuel P. Jaffe, trans. Kenneth J. Northcott (Chicago: University of Chicago Press, 2005), 31–67.

60. Geoffrey Wainwright, *Eucharist and Eschatology* (New York: Oxford University Press, 1981), 81.

MITCHELL B. MERBACK

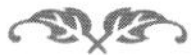

CHAPTER 8

The Ghetto and the Gaze
in Early Modern Venice

Dana E. Katz

In "A Scene from the Venice Ghetto," the twentieth-century poet Rainer Maria Rilke vividly describes the architectonics of Jewish life in Venice: "[The Venetians] reduced the area of the Ghetto . . ., so that its [Jewish] families . . . were forced to build their houses in the vertical dimension, one on the roof of another. And their city, which did not lie on the sea, grew slowly into the space of heaven as though it were another sea; and all around the square where the well was, buildings rose in dizzy perpendicularity like the walls of some giant's tower."[1] For Rilke, the tiny houses constituting the Venetian ghetto, "jammed in countless stories one on top of the other," created Babel-like towers that set the scene for future storytelling. Such tales, however, belong not to Rilke's twentieth century. The story of these multistoried buildings, which remain largely extant today, instead begins in the Renaissance.[2]

On March 29, 1516, the Venetian Senate ordered all Jews residing in the city to move behind the walls of the Ghetto Nuovo (Figure 8.1). The mandate stipulated that the Jews would be watched by six Christian guards twenty-four hours a day and locked into the ghetto at night behind two iron gates (Figure 8.2). The proclamation specifies: "To prevent the Jews from going about all night, provoking the greatest discontent and the deepest displeasure on the part of Jesus Christ, be it determined that . . . two doors shall be made. . . . These doors must be opened in the morning at the sound of the *marangona* [the bell rung at sunrise], and in the evening they shall be shut at the twenty-fourth hour [sunset] by four Christian guards. . . . If by chance any Jew is found by officials

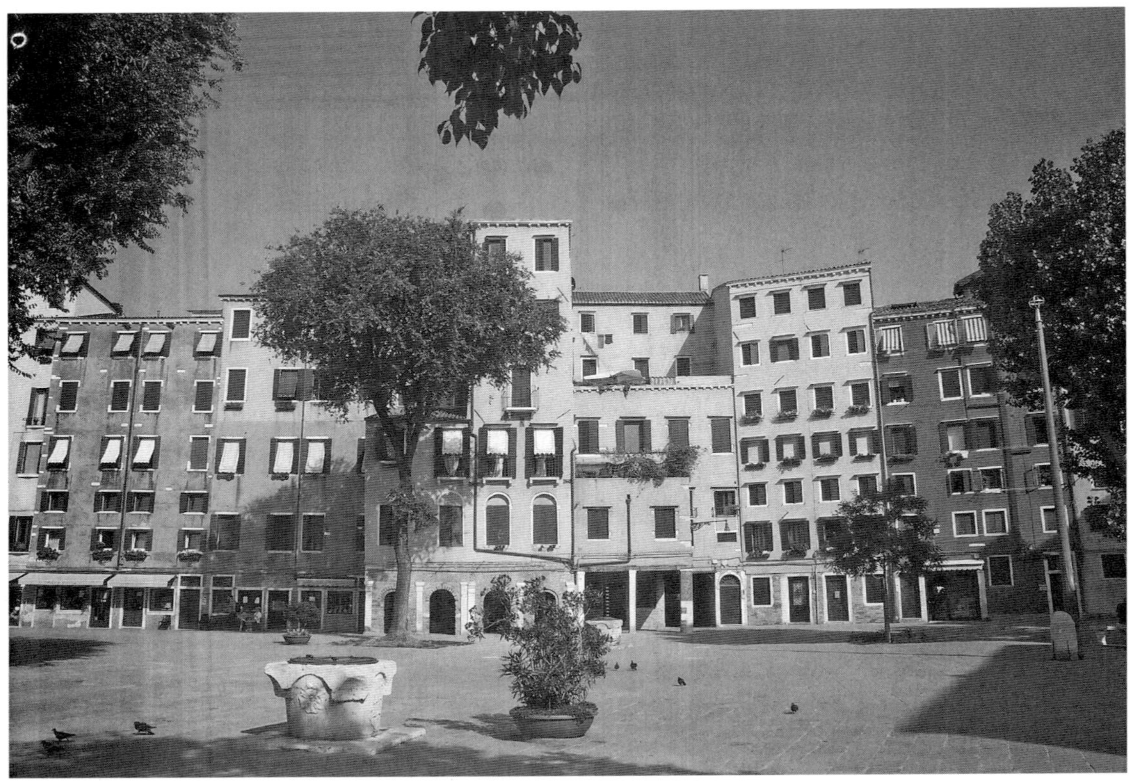

8.1. The Ghetto Nuovo, established in Venice in 1516. Photo: Dana E. Katz.

or public servants outside the Geto after the hours specified above, they shall be bound to arrest him at once for his disobedience."[3] The decree further mandated that the Jews, who would come to reside in the ghetto for nearly three hundred years, would be responsible for paying the salaries of their Christians guards, four of whom would live inside the ghetto and two would patrol the surrounding canals by boat.[4] Strategically situated on both sides of the ghetto walls, the guards would keep close watch on the Jews by day and by night. The principal motivation for the Jews' confinement was to enforce their separation from Christians after nightfall. The magistracy of the Cattaveri, charged with overseeing the affairs of the Jewish communities, established pecuniary fines for those Jews found outside the ghetto after hours. The penalty obliged the Jews to pay 100 lire for the first offense, 200 lire for the second, and 500 lire and two months in prison for the third.

The built environment of the Jewish ghetto (Figure 8.3) offers an extraordinary look at Renaissance urban planning, as the cityscape of Venice provides insight into the processes of ghettoization that partitioned a population and

     DANA E. KATZ

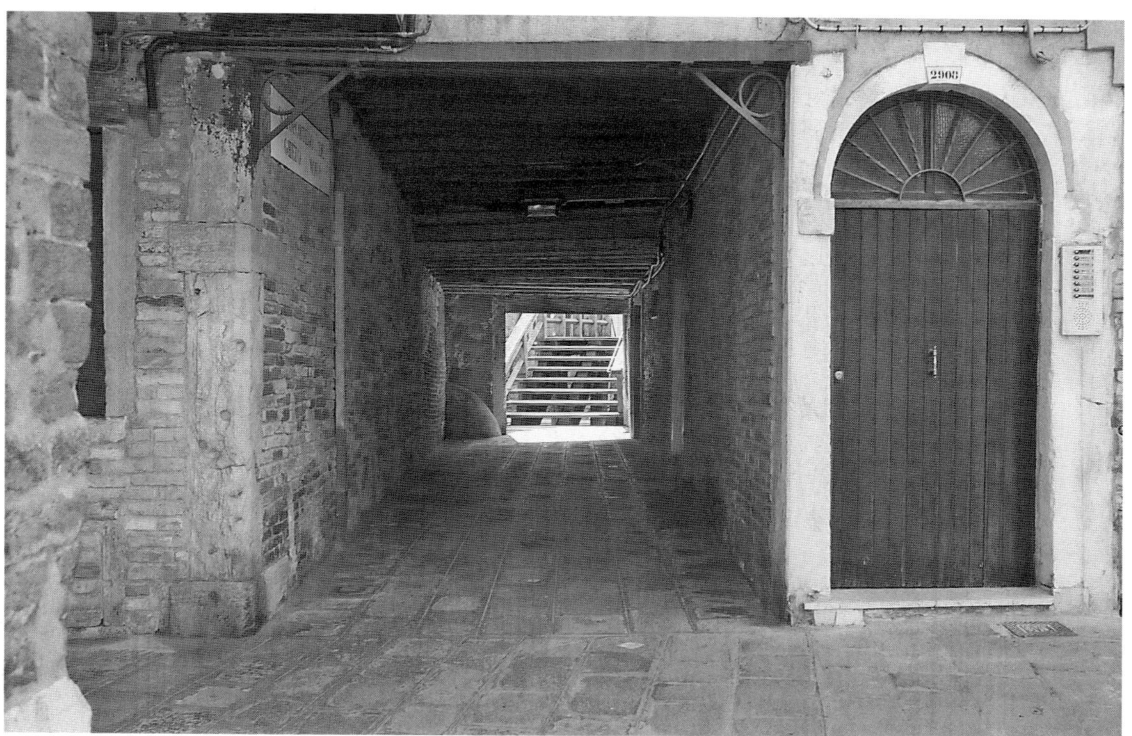

8.2. Former gated entrance to the Ghetto Nuovo, Venice. Photo: Dana E. Katz.

monitored the activities of Jews and Christians alike. The ghetto inscribed religious difference into the urban fabric of early modern Venice and in it prescribed a larger social order. The formation of the Venice ghetto offered an embodiment of the city's republican values. The construction of the ghetto complex perpetuated the mythologizing of Venice as the harmonious, stable, just, and tolerant republic, one that emanated from its walls a well-established political and social order.[5] Francesco Sansovino emphasized this toleration when writing in 1581 that Jews "prefer to live in Venice rather than in any other part of Italy. Since they are not subject to violence or tyranny here as they are elsewhere, . . . reposing in most singular peace, they enjoy this city almost like a true promised land."[6] As Sansovino suggests, the ghetto offered Jews the opportunity to settle in Venice without the fear of physical violence. Despite the Jews' constrained prosperity, the presence of the ghetto also served as a form of contestation that worked to counter Venice's controlled mythmaking. The distinctive architecture of the ghetto, established to provide physical form to the subordination of Jews and Judaism in Venice, paradoxically revealed through its protective walls and gates the spatial expression of Jewish agency. An era of

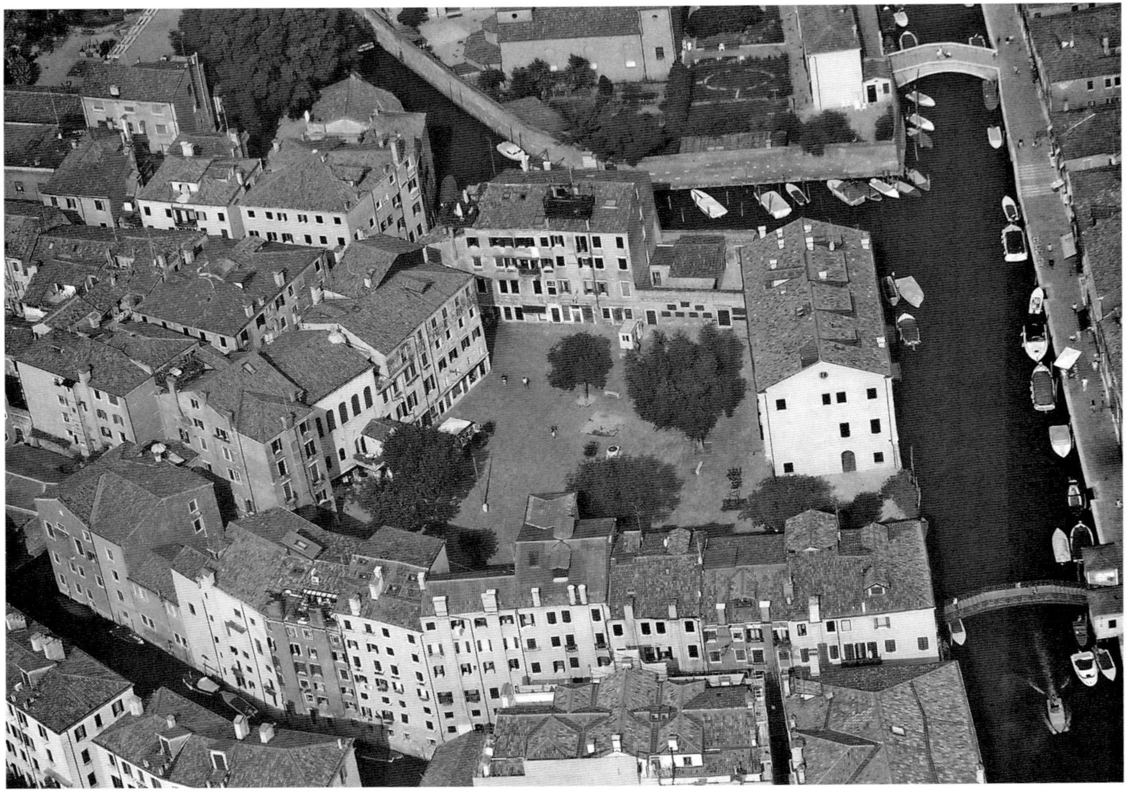

8.3. Aerial view of the Venetian ghetto complex. Photo courtesy Davide Calimani.

ghettoization began in 1516 when Venetians reduced Jews to objects of surveillance and supervision. For Venetians the Jews' social and religious marginality marked them as executors of a defiant, and at times perverse, will that required compulsory and confining accommodations. In other words, Venetian authorities forced Jews into the ghetto to survey their actions and interactions, to make the Jews objects of the Venetian gaze.[7] Yet Venetians were confronted with the reciprocity of that gaze when, as we will see, the Jews returned their look. Ghetto architecture, rising high above the horizon line, placed Jews in the position of urban onlookers whose viewing point did not necessarily degrade them to passive objects but rather animated the Jews' status as observing subjects. This essay studies the Jewish ghetto in Christian Venice through the archival voice of Venetian authorities, governmental and ecclesiastical. Through analyses of the Jews' vernacular spaces, I explore Renaissance conceptions of vision, space, and subjectivity for their fissures and discontinuities. Specifically, how did the confinement of Jews on the margins of Venice provoke a disordering of Venetian social order and symbolically transform Jewish aberrancy to agency?

 DANA E. KATZ

The Venetian ghetto changed the urban physiognomy of Venice when in 1516, as the Senate legislation details, Jews were "obliged to go at once to dwell together in the houses in the court within the Geto at San Hieronimo, where there is plenty of room for them to live."[8] The island of the Ghetto Nuovo in the parish of San Girolamo was a likely space for the ghetto because it was circumscribed on all sides by narrow canals and contained no churches or grand palaces. In this way, the Jews were physically relegated to the city margins on land that was not highly valued because of its distance from the Rialto and San Marco, nor was it inscribed with Christian iconography through prominent churches (Figure 8.4). The materials used in construction of the ghetto were of the poorest quality, and as a result restoration of the buildings was continually necessary.[9] Bricks were the principal building material used in the ghetto. Brick, together with a soft mortar of lime, could withstand the structural movement typical of Venice.[10] Istrian stone, a white limestone significantly lighter than marble, was used for the sills, gutters, and doorframes. To avoid excessive loads, Jews constructed all public stairways, ceilings, and partitions separating rooms of timber.[11] The ground floor of the ghetto housed the shops, stores, and lending institutions (Figure 8.5). To maximize space, this floor was often divided horizontally into two, creating an extra floor with ceilings just under six feet that could be used for storerooms, kitchens, or servant quarters (Figure 8.6).[12] Overcrowding, resulting from natural population growth and immigration, caused the Jews to expand their tenements vertically, constructing buildings up to nine stories around the central *campo* (public square). It is known from Jacopo de' Barbari's map of Venice, dated 1500, that the ghetto complex originally housed buildings of two stories (Figure 8.7).[13] Because the foundations were laid to support this original load, the multistory and multifamily structures were perpetually in danger of collapsing under the stress of the increased weight. The Jews built upward against the drag of gravity and the weakness of the soil they were forced to build upon.

The defectively designed and feebly constructed buildings of the ghetto complex on the city's periphery residentially and socially relegated the Jewish minority to the margins, creating a community in Venice defined spatially by its common belief in Christianity, and not through the diversity of its parts.[14] Jews were not the only social outgroups in Venice affected by the project of urban segregation. The ethnic landscape of the city included the strategic placement of Greeks, Turks, Germans, Albanians, Dalmatians, and Armenians, who preserved their own identities in separate districts of the city.[15] By granting different ethnic groups autonomous spaces, Venice presented itself in myth and practice as an equitably mapped republic. Neither persecuting nor banishing its minorities, Venetian civic ideology claimed to offer peace and security to various

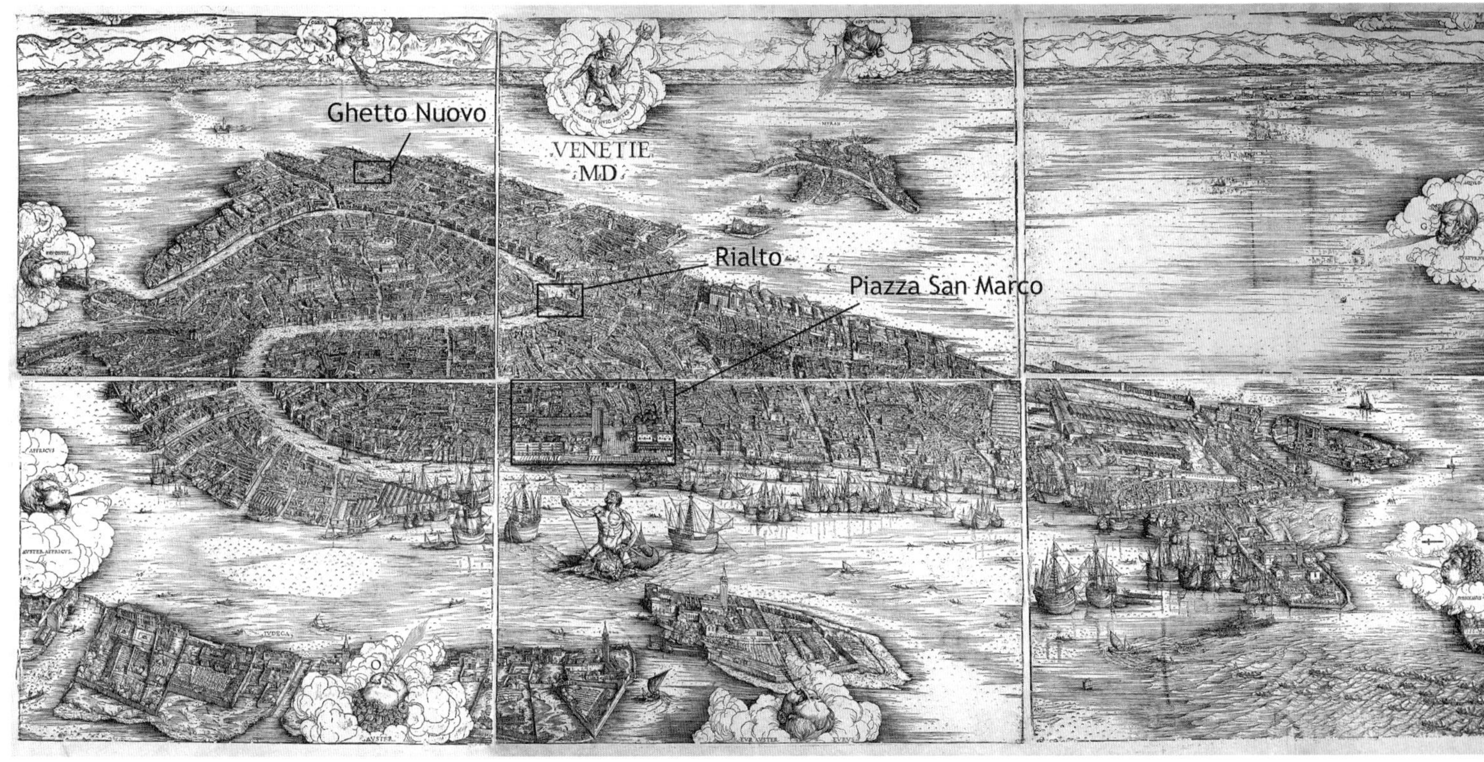

8.4. Jacopo de' Barbari, *Venetie*, 1500. Monument indications added to original by author. Photo courtesy Novacco Collection, The Newberry Library, Chicago.

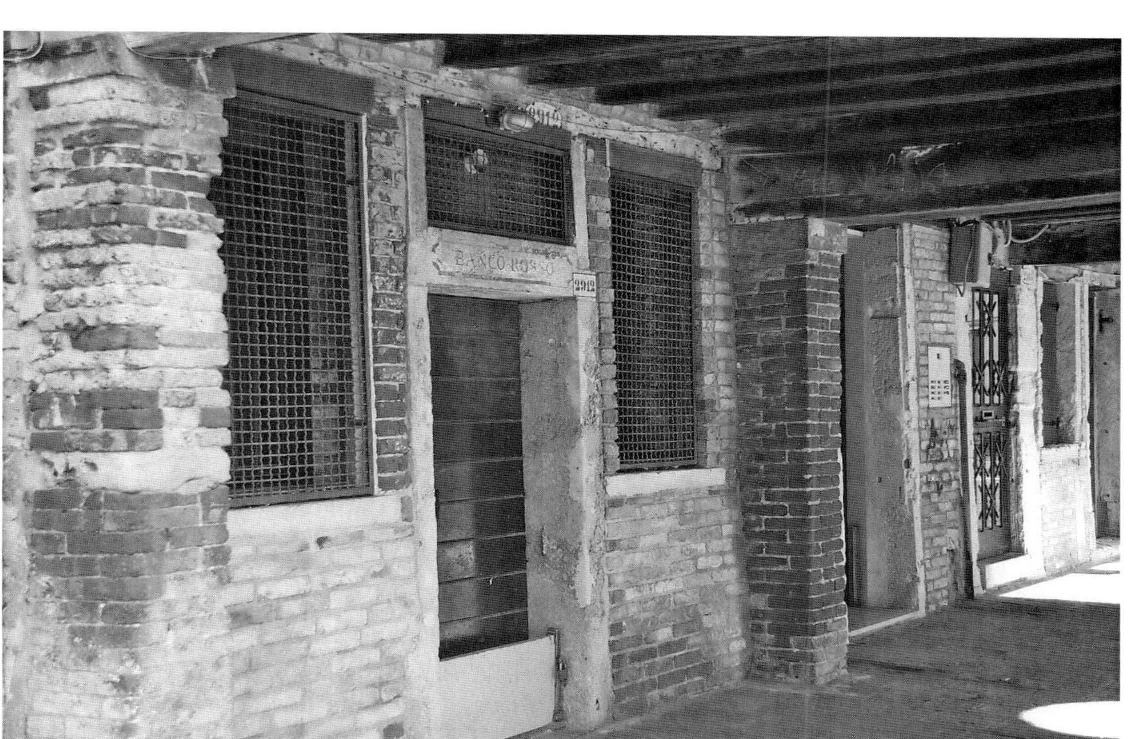

8.5. The Banco Rosso pawnshop in the Ghetto Nuovo, Venice. Photo: Dana E. Katz.

groups, cooperating politically and economically to form a perfect republic. The separation of foreigners into distinct ethnic enclaves became a physical expression of the republic's policy of tolerance. The early modern conception of tolerance, which circulated in the works of canon law and scholasticism, permitted Jews and other social outgroups to dwell among the communities in Latin Christendom provided their deviance proved no threat to Christianity. Tolerance offered limited social forbearance to Jews while opposing policies of expulsion and extermination.[16] In Venice the establishment of the ghetto gave urban form to Renaissance toleration, inviting Jews to the lagoon city with the penetration of regulatory restrictions permeating the details of everyday life.

Venice made segregation compulsory for many of its foreigners. For example, Venetian law penalized German merchants 50 ducats for taking lodging outside the German exchange house, known as the Fondaco dei Tedeschi.[17] Of all the foreigners residing in Venice, only the Jews and the Turks were locked up at night and patrolled. Venetians feared the presence of Turks both for their religious difference and the political puissance of the sultan. The confinement of Muslim Ottoman Turks in the Fondaco dei Turchi followed the model of

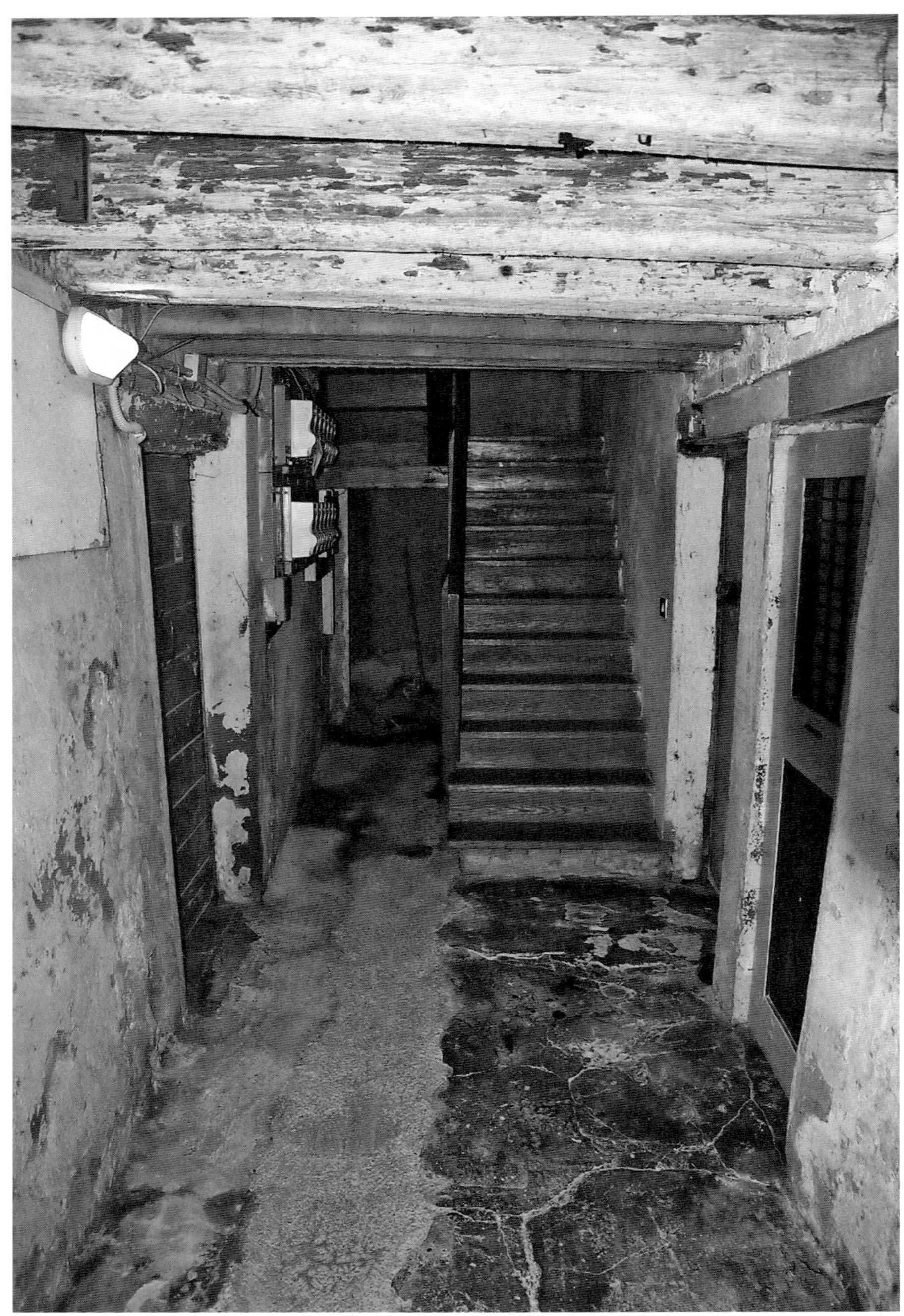

8.6. Stairwell in the Venetian ghetto complex demonstrating the narrow spaces. Photo: Dana E. Katz.

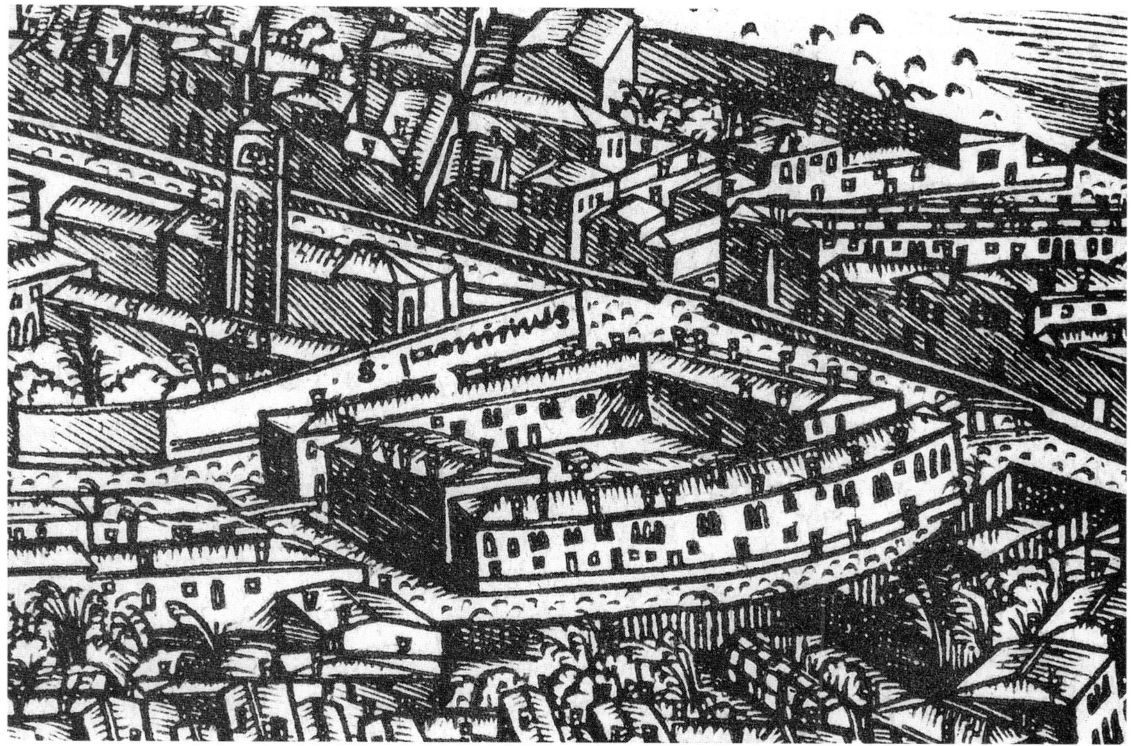

8.7. Detail of Jacopo de' Barbari, *Venetie*, 1500. Photo courtesy Novacco Collection, The Newberry Library, Chicago.

Jewish ghettoization. In 1621 the Venetian government required Turkish residence in an isolated area of the city, along the Grand Canal in the parish of San Giacomo dall'Orio, with house rules that mirrored those established in the early sixteenth century in the Jewish ghetto. The Cinque Savi alla Mercanzia (Board of Trade) mandated that the Turks, like the Jews, must have a guardian, who "shall be obliged to lock the doors, both to landward and to seaward, at dusk, and to open them again at sunrise, from the outside, with good and effective keys, which he must keep."[18] Whereas the Fondaco dei Turchi was a warehouse and living quarters for itinerant Turkish merchants traveling between the Ottoman Empire and their trading post in Venice, the ghetto housed families of Jews who settled permanently into the Christian cityscape of Venice. Segregation was not temporary for the Jews as it was for the Turks, but rather an ongoing condition of confinement and surveillance.

Renaissance architectural theorists, including Leon Battista Alberti, Serlio, and Palladio, treat the built environment as a space predicated on symmetry and uniformity, as such unity bespeaks a community governed by social order.

As historian Edward Muir states, the Neoplatonic dictum that outward beauty signifies inward virtue inspired humanist theorists to conjoin rationally ordered architecture with civic stability and harmony.[19] Alberti, for instance, in his *De re aedificatoria* of c. 1452, consigns the regularized and well-proportioned Florentine loggia to the elders of society, who, enjoying the salubrious air and protected from the heat of the central Italian sun, were to monitor and control the city's boisterous young men.[20] Here the Renaissance portico and its accompanying piazza serve as a site for social conviviality among the community's senior members, while also functioning didactically to teach proper civic comportment to the city's youth. In this mid-fifteenth-century architectural treatise, Alberti assigns the urban environment the powers of social control to promote civic order. Later commentators repeated the trends of this socioaesthetic assessment. In his mid-nineteenth-century *The Stones of Venice*, John Ruskin similarly invests the spatial expression of the Venetian Piazza with social resonance. Whatever might be said of his historicism, Ruskin presents architecture in this book as a system of beliefs for those who constructed its walls. Indeed, he describes the optical harmony of the long arms of colonnaded structures that flank the Piazza San Marco as a metaphor for the city's virtue and as a visual demonstration of the republic's stability (Figure 8.8). He writes: "for between those pillars [at the end of the Piazza] there opens a great light, and, in the midst of it, as we advance slowly, the vast tower of St. Mark seems to lift itself up visibly forth from the level field of chequered stones: and, on each side, the countless arches prolong themselves into ranged symmetry, as if the rugged and irregular houses that pressed together above us in the dark alley had been struck back into sudden obedience and lovely order."[21] The rhythmic design of Venetian architecture was a marker of civic pride in the early modern period, a source of admiration among the city's residents and tourists. If it is true that urban symmetry and harmony are associated with obedience and order, as Ruskin writes, and that the "stunning [Venetian] cityscape alone gave proof of a well-arranged political and social order," as Edward Muir describes in his study of Venetian historiography, then the opposite must also be true.[22] That is, the disharmonious, asymmetrical, unstable, and even dangerous Venetian ghetto can be interpreted as a subversion of Venice's political and social order. Thus the ghetto is not merely an embodiment of republican justice, but also a visual remonstration against the traditional "myth of Venice."

The irregular fenestration pattern, uneven building heights, and unsystematic projection of structures extending into the ghetto *campo* create a space visually charged with discord. Renaissance harmony and uniformity do not characterize these structures. Rather, the ghetto appears organic, evolving and growing (upward and outward) with the increasing demographic pressures of

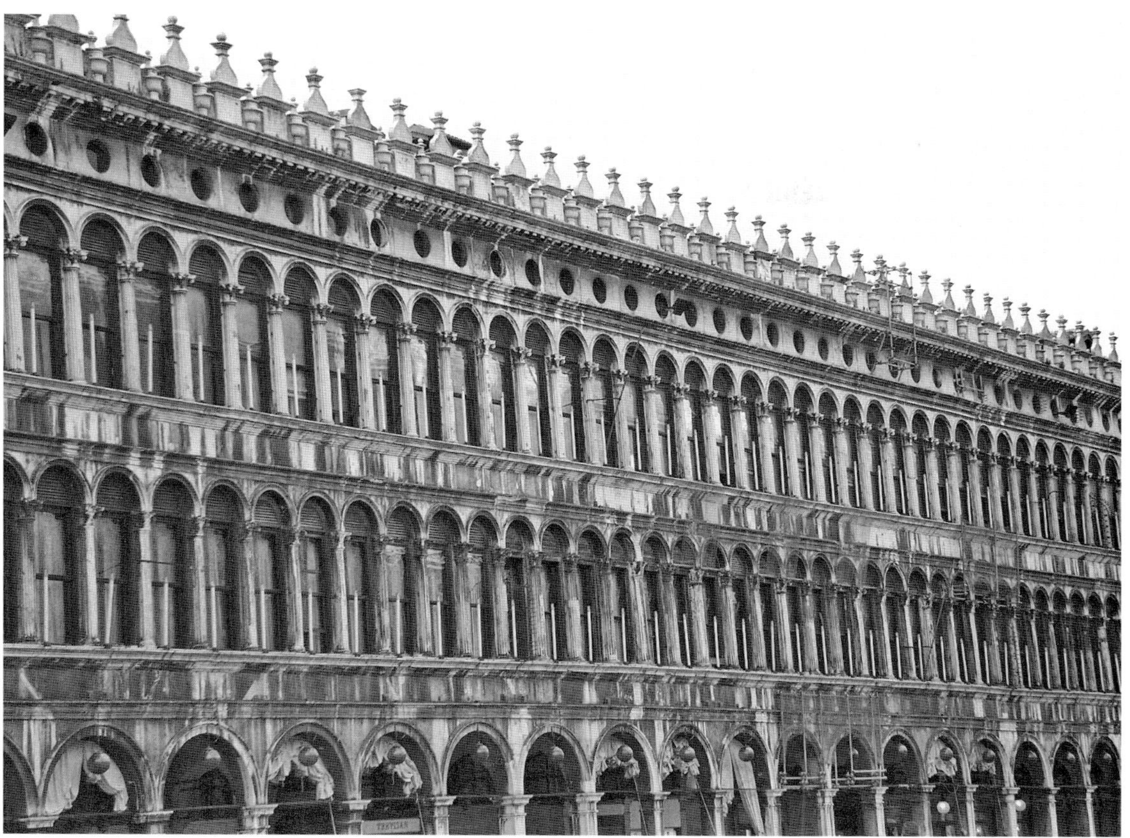

8.8. The Procuratie Vecchie, Piazza San Marco, Venice, begun c. 1500. Photo: Dana E. Katz.

its inhabitants. The exterior articulation of the buildings accentuates their pronounced verticality and demonstrates the axial social hierarchy of ghetto life with wealthier Jews residing on the upper floors because they were able to pay the city an annual tax for the privilege of adding balconies or rooftop belvederes to their apartments. The gables, terraces, and small domes that pepper the upper stories of the ghetto are therefore architectural signifiers of the affluence of certain Jews (Figure 8.9). Whereas the Christian patrician class resided on the *piano nobile,* or the second story of a residential palazzo, wealthy Jews instead chose to live on the higher floors. The way of life for the ghetto Jews, even those with significant financial means, did not parallel Christian life. For Jews to obtain more space, they climbed the long stairways to the top of their tenement buildings.

The geographic displacement of Jews into cramped quarters on the city's periphery redefined the external boundaries of social space in Venice. It is here

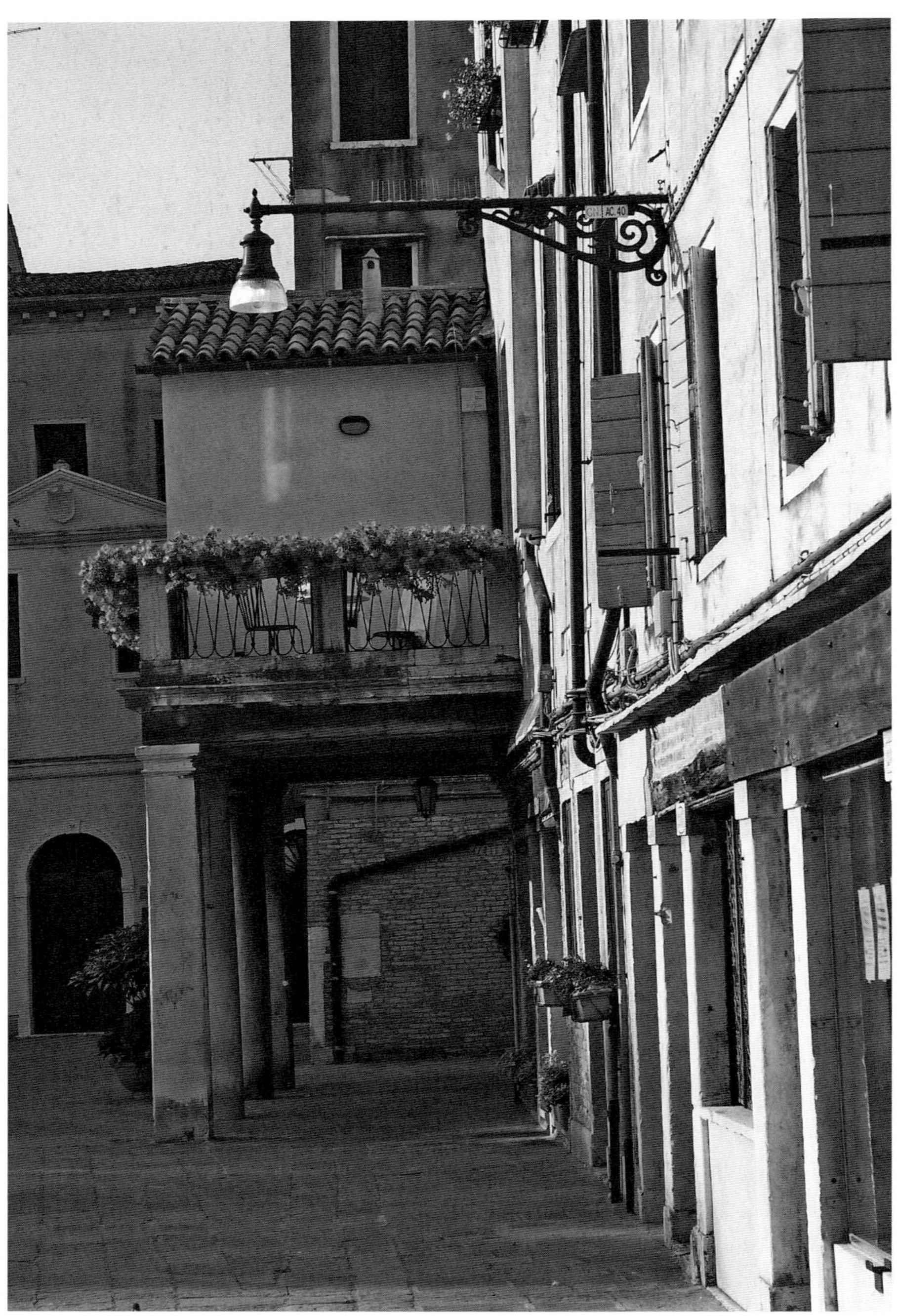

8.9. Terrace at the Ghetto Nuovo, Venice. Photo: Dana E. Katz.

on the isolated margins of the city where authorities monitored the activities of Jews as well as Christians. The seventeenth-century Venetian rabbi Leon Modena records in his autobiography (compiled between 1617 and 1648) the social interactions between Jews and Christians in the ghetto. His autobiography, *The Life of Judah,* describes the permeability of the ghetto walls during the daytime hours when the ghetto doors remained open: Jews ventured out to work, shop, gamble, visit Christian friends, and teach Christian children, while Christians entered the ghetto compound in search of loans and trade.[23] After nightfall, however, the Venetian government attempted to restrict social contact—specifically sexual contact—between Jews and their Christian counterparts.[24] On July 19, 1424, the government unanimously passed legislation that forbade sexual relations between Jewish men and Christian women. The penalty for such an act depended on the Christian woman's station. Venetian authorities fined Jews 500 lire and sentenced them to six months in jail when found with a prostitute from the Rialto. The pecuniary fine remained the same when a Jew had carnal relations with a Christian woman of higher social stature, additionally subjecting him to one year in prison. As Benjamin Ravid explains, the financial cost of sexual collusion between Jew and Christian was secondary to socioreligious considerations.[25] The nighttime lockdown of Jews acted to avert sexual forays *entre* Jew and Christian. The fortified and surveyed ghetto walls prevented midnight trysts turned transgressions, infidelities turned blasphemies. Architectural confinement controlled carnal lusts under the cover of darkness, thereby precluding the possibility of miscegenation.

The ghetto provided Venetians a visible space where Jews could submit to regulatory discipline. Ghetto surveillance, particularly at night, was central to Venetian urban life as it sought to prevent Jews from infiltrating society and causing nocturnal disorder.[26] Night during this period possessed an element of the horrific and the sublime; that is, the darkness of the night induced both demonic acts of violence and spiritual visions.[27] The nocturnal vignettes of Paolo Uccello's Corpus Domini predella of 1468, representing the desecration of the Eucharist, incorporate both aspects of night. The artist situates the Jew's bloody attempt to destroy the Host after nightfall. Here, darkness is made to reaffirm eucharistic truth and fortify Christian faith, while perpetuating the notion of the Jew as demonic.[28] Suspicions of Jewish nighttime violence were not unusual in the Renaissance. According to a ritual murder case in Trent in 1475, a guard testified that he heard a child (said to be the two-and-a-half-year-old Christian boy Simon Unferdorben) screaming from Samuel Ebreo's house at night.[29] The veil of darkness also incited Jews in sixteenth-century northern Italy to engage in the carnivalesque acts of dancing and gambling on the eve of a young Jewish boy's circumcision, fusing sacred ceremonies with profane nocturnal Jewish rituals.[30] Other Jewish rites were affected by the close of day. In Venice and other cities, including Ancona and Mantua, the establishment of the ghetto coffeehouse in the seventeenth century initiated a new form of piety inspired by the silence and isolation of the twilight hours.[31] Coffee and its capacity to instill wakefulness in those who imbibe it created an innovative form of nighttime male sociability and study outside the home that further perpetuated fears of Jewish violence. The strict nighttime curfew established in Venice for the ghetto inhabitants sought primarily to prevent such nocturnal abuses, thus assuaging Christian fears and Christ's discontentment.

When the government granted Jews, particularly doctors and merchants, privileges to stay outside the ghetto after hours, authorities stipulated that they were to avoid "forbidden" spaces, including brothels and the houses of respectable Christian women. The restrictions of the ghetto mirrors the Venetian regulation first established by the Fourth Lateran Council in 1215, mandating Jews to wear distinguishing garb. Both residential and sartorial restrictions visually differentiated Jew from Christian and controlled social intercourse. The indelible mark of difference blazoned on the body of Jews, the special colored Jewish head cover in Venice or the yellow badge in other Italian cities, denoted their nonnegotiable visual identity; Jews were to be "distinct and diversified from Christians in dress as they are in faith."[32] If the bright yellow and red head coverings served to identify and draw attention to the Jew within the Christian crowd in Venice, the ghetto, on the contrary, functioned to minimize the Jews' appearance by relegating them to compulsory residences on the city margins.[33] The ghetto compound made marginalization complete through the very visible positioning of Jews on the city's periphery, literally putting Jews in their place.

The principles of urban planning in the Venetian context emphasized social unity through the redistribution of urban space. Venice constructed difference in its urban form with ideological traces of otherness and inferiority mapped spatially onto the Venetian cityscape. Ghettoization thus became an early modern spatialization of power that evolved outside the ghetto by dominating (Christian) forces that sought to minimize the Jews' presence. Yet as Jews erected their irregular and attenuated apartments, the Jewish presence in Venice became more prominent—more visible—when the ghetto reached extraordinary heights. The elevation of these structures was even more exaggerated during the sixteenth century because there were fewer buildings in this area, which was dominated primarily by gardens and one- or two-story structures, as noted in Jacopo de' Barbari's map (Figure 8.7).[34] The Serenissima, the Most Serene Republic of Venice, subjected Jews to their cramped and confined conditions on the city's periphery to separate Jew from Christian and to minimize the Jewish presence. The conspicuousness of the buildings instead visualized, both

   DANA E. KATZ

physically and symbolically, the Jews' appearance. Architectural ideology indeed sought to control social difference through an elaborate configuration of spatial relations, defining Jew from Christian, center from periphery; nevertheless, the formation of the ghetto created a space in which Jews visually commanded a marked presence in Venice. Rather than forging a distinct binary between insiders and outsiders, the walls of the ghetto identified a liminal space within which things Jewish and things Christian continually commingled.

The ring of densely populated, elevated structures that constituted the ghetto became a highly dynamic housing environment that drew attention from afar. One example of the ghetto's urban attraction is noted in the writings of the English visitor, Thomas Coryat. In 1611 Coryat dedicated a lengthy portion of his travelogue to the "place where the whole fraternity of Jews dwelleth together, which is called the Ghetto, being an Iland: for it is inclosed round about with water."[35] *Coryat's Crudities* emphasizes the form and content of the ghetto through ethnographic examinations of Jews and their rituals. Coryat, for example, includes a rich discussion of the layout of the Venetian synagogues and their decor, while also reporting on a religious service in which a "Levite . . . pronounce[d] before the congregation not by a sober, distinct, and orderly reading, but by an exceeding loud yaling, undecent roaring, and as it were a beastly bellowing of it forth."[36] The Englishman's ghetto excursion elicited both fascination and frustration toward the "unchristian miscreants," ending with an altercation with a rabbi. Coryat's accounts provide a compelling look at the ghetto from the gaze of a Christian foreigner.[37] His travelogue defines the geographical identity of the ghetto by localizing the compound and its residents' cultural practices in Venice proper. The physical configuration of space as well as the social and ideological control of place converge in this early seventeenth-century account and demonstrate how the ghetto, from the eyes of an English tourist, operated as a marker of civic identity and social distinction.

In addition to providing the Jews of Venice a prominent visibility *in* the city, these structures offered them an ideal view *of* the city, as the tall tenements provided the Jews an unmediated view of their Christian neighbors.[38] Rilke's twentieth-century story of Venetian ghetto life describes the Jews' views of the Palazzo Foscari, a local church, the "silvery" seascape, and the "quivering" sky.[39] The Jewish inhabitants in Rilke's spiritual story ascend as high as the clouds with the increasing height of their homes on the ghetto's scarce ground. Although looking heavenward perhaps inspired the Jews' humility, their watchful gaze outside the ghetto compound represented to the Christian majority the Jews' temerity. Ghetto gazes that penetrated also alienated. As a result, Venetian magistrates during the Renaissance sought to control not only the Jews but also their ghetto vistas. In 1560 the Cinque Savi alla Mercanzia required Jews to obstruct their canal-side view outside the newly constructed buildings in the Ghetto Vecchio, an expansion to the original Ghetto Nuovo, by walling up windows, balconies, and doors to prevent ocular contact between Jew and Christian. Defining the forbidden views from the ghetto formed part of Venetian legislation with the founding of the Ghetto Vecchio in 1541 (Figure 8.10). The Venetian government prohibited the construction of balconies along the wall of the Ghetto Vecchio at Cannaregio without also installing iron grates on all the windows.[40] This act of fortification, though later rejected, sought literally to bar Jews entry into Christian spaces, for Christians remained on portions of the land adjoining the Ghetto Vecchio. Although the iron grates participated in a project of segregation, they did not neccesarily preclude visual access to the Christian world, as did the recommendations of 1560. In this later mandate, the Cinque Savi sought not only to close off windows, balconies, doors, and quays, but they also requested the erections of new unpunctured walls to ensure complete enclosure (Figure 8.11).[41]

Legislative exemptions at times deferred the reality of a completely sequestered windowless space, but the idea of an idealized geography that occluded Jewish vision lingered in the legislation. Such directives indicate that the Venetian government would not permit the Jews to experience the world outside the ghetto with autonomous eyes. The reciprocity of the urban gaze, the look and the look returned, engendered an encroachment of space explicitly identified as Christian that created an uneasy social instability. The establishment of the ghetto produced a space that visually defined the Jews' objecthood. Venetian authorities positioned Jews as objects on the periphery for continual observation. Built into this system of surveillance was the potential for Jews to conduct their own act of fenestral looking. This reciprocity of gazes and sight lines provoked social tensions precisely because Jews as objects, controlled and disciplined, transformed with their optical powers into subsidiary subjects. As Beatriz Colomina argues, "Architecture is not simply a platform that accommodates the viewing subject. It is a viewing mechanism that produces the subject. It precedes and frames its occupant."[42] The renegotiation of the Jews' visual access to Christians in the vicinity conveys the Venetian authorities' attempt to define the edges of urban space, to overcome the visual reciprocity, through the occluded views of the ghetto. Displaced within the controlling ghetto walls, the Jews were "caught in the act of seeing, entrapped in the very moment of control" that housed their illicit varieties of viewing.[43]

The Jewish ghetto was but one instance of religious architectural sequestering. The obstructed ghetto vistas are analogous structurally to those found in early modern convents. To protect the purity and moral virtue of female monastics and to enhance their spiritual education, the convent segregated religious

DANA E. KATZ

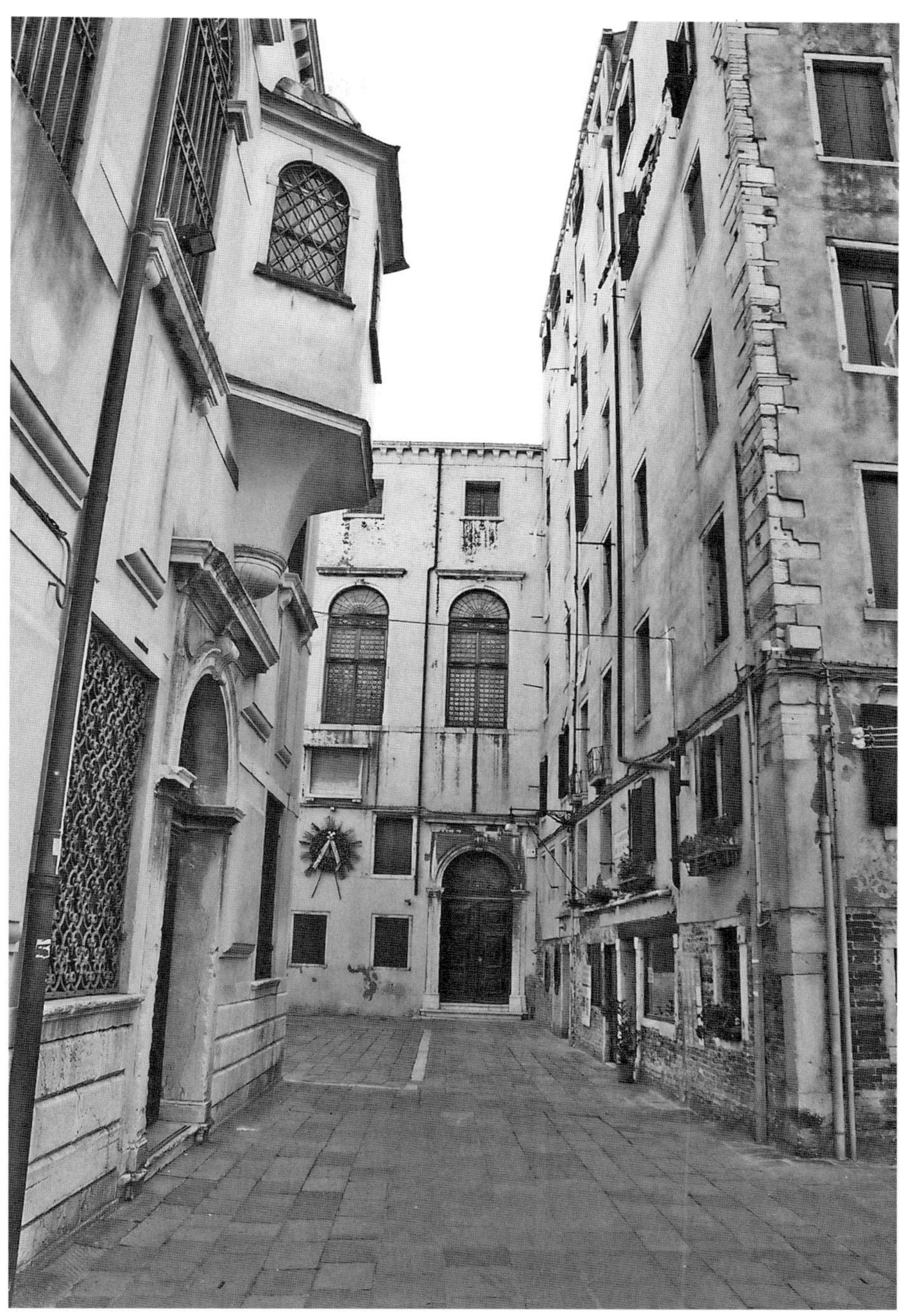

8.10. The Ghetto Vecchio, established in Venice in 1541. Photo: Dana E. Katz.

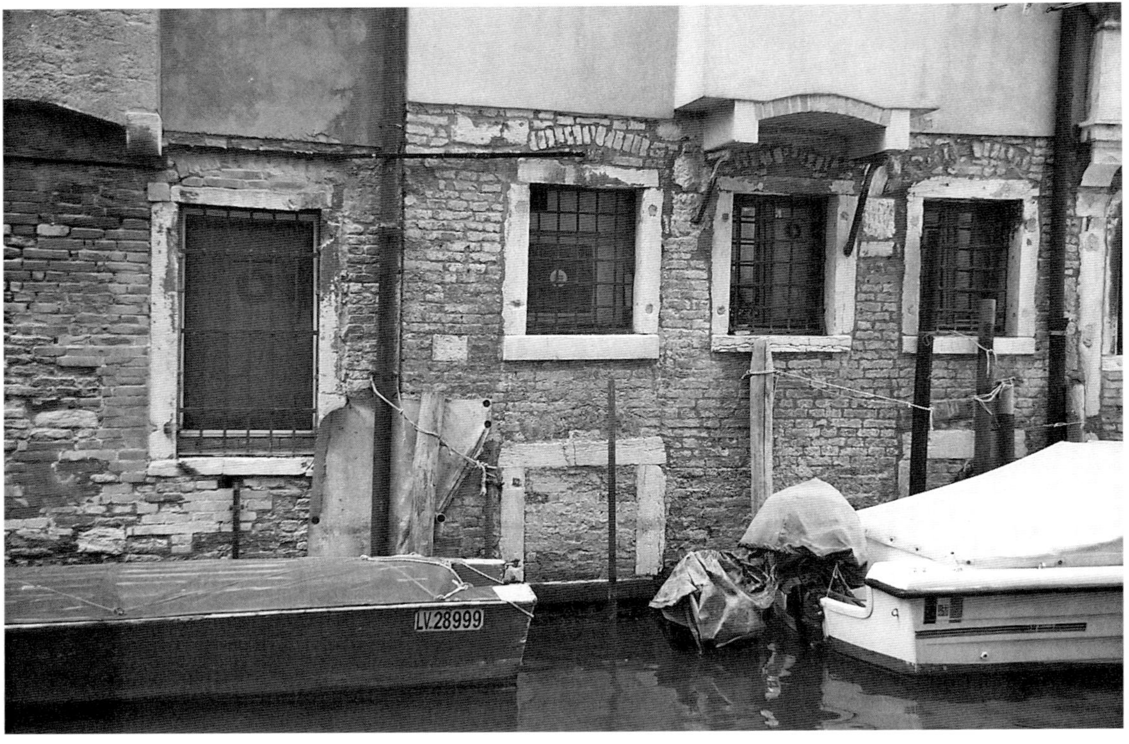

8.11. Bricked-up quays along the waterway at the Ghetto Nuovo. Photo: Dana E. Katz.

women from secular society within an architecture of *clausura*. The complete enclosure of nuns, advocated by the mid-sixteenth-century reforms of the Council of Trent (1545–63), sought to regulate monastic behavior through the built environment. Marilyn Dunn writes in her work on post-Tridentine convent architecture in early modern Rome that shaping the spiritual life of nuns required the erection of high walls that surrounded the convent complex to separate the sacred from the profane.[44] Problems arose when neighboring residents from nearby palaces or houses threatened the introverted conventual life with windows that overlooked the nuns' cloistered space and compromised the nuns' disciplined privacy. Dunn cites an example implicating the Dominican religious from the convent of Santa Caterina a Magnanapoli in Rome when they threw stones at the masons working on an addition to the Buzi family palace. Fearing the Buzi would disturb the nuns' strict *clausura* with potentially dangerous stares and horrible noises from their windows that looked out over the convent, the nuns petitioned Pope Alexander VII to have the work on the Buzi palazzo halted immediately. The pontiff rejected the Dominicans' written appeal, although other communities, including the Discalced Carmelites at

DANA E. KATZ

Santa Teresa, protected their cloistered sanctuary by purchasing the land adjacent to their convent.

Such monastic anecdotes related to conventual urbanism emphasize in this case the nuns' need for optical seclusion. In a cramped early modern city where space was difficult to find and building projects required vertical expansion, these cloistered nuns sought male authorization to protect their sanctified space and their moral virtue from the outside gaze. Here *clausura*, defined by a complex negotiation of male supervision residing beyond the convent, was a positive accomplishment, a spatially desirable ideal, safeguarded by the female monastics housed within. As recent scholarship on convent culture demonstrates, the cloistered confines of early modern nuns were not in fact impregnable.[45] Nuns fought to defend their visual presence not only by terminating urban building projects that overlooked their cloisters, but also by improving their views within the convent itself. Prelates and noblemen often governed the convent and designed its walls—adorned with iron grills and wooden shades covering windows and strong locks securing thick doors—to minimize contact between the nuns and outsiders. The strictures of *clausura* instituted a community of enclosure that nonetheless inspired some female monastics to pursue the convent's perforated points. Convent apertures, located at exposed places in the public church, sacristy, and garden, offered nuns a momentary look at men both clerical and lay performing duties related to the convent's spiritual and physical maintenance.[46] Despite ecclesiastical attempts to render female religious houses impenetrable with reinforced stone- and ironwork and enforced rules of isolation, nuns at times advocated for architectural alterations to their convents to enhance their views. For instance, in 1629 the abbess of San Francesco dell'Osservanza in Naples appealed to Cardinal Buoncompagno to increase the nuns' visual access to the convent church, among other sites.[47] After the Council of Trent, nuns no longer could enter conventual churches; instead, they watched the mass performed at a distance from screened clerestory windows. The nuns of San Francesco exemplify how early modern female monastics attempted to defend and expand their visual contact within the convent's interior and to exercise their cloistered powers of sight.

Both the sequestration of nuns and the ghettoization of Jews engender a relationship of power and discipline that expresses how a spatially confined subgroup articulates politics and ideology.[48] In both examples the gaze is spatially at play. As clerics feared the outsider's penetrating look on the virginal nun because it sought to sexualize her, so Venetians, at least in part, feared the sexuality of Jews and ghettoized them as a means of control. Such control was lost when Jews built their disproportionately tall tenements. The pronounced verticality of the ghetto structures became a prominent aspect of Venice's sky-line; its conspicuousness within the Venetian cityscape demonstrated its symbolic powers. "Command of the city was epitomized vertically," writes Helen Hills in her study of seventeenth-century Neapolitan convents.[49] Perhaps female monastics problematized the highly prized performance of seeing and being seen from their cloisters, but their quest to maintain visual dominance through the unrivaled elevation of their bell towers or unobstructed clerestory windows sought principally to heighten their spirituality rather than incorporate them within the larger secular society. Hills offers various examples whereby nuns from their convent belvederes refused a glimpse of the laity below during civic celebrations including Carnival. Invoking discourses of humility, the nuns protected themselves from the sights of the world around them.[50]

The spatial practices of early modern nuns, who repeatedly avoided their views from on high, differentiate the convent's claims to the urban fabric from that of the Venetian ghetto and its Jewish occupants. While female monastics often repudiated the panoramic view of the outside world and refused to return the look, Jews unequivocally directed their ocular attention to the world outside the ghetto. Such a distinction relates to conflicting conceptions of *clausura*. The convent walls that nourished nuns spiritually also barricaded them in. Post-Tridentine cloistration sought to seal off the nun permanently from societal contact. *Clausura* in the Jewish ghetto instead came with a key. The establishment of the Venetian ghetto endeavored to promote commercial interactions during the day when the ghetto remained opened and to prohibit sexual interrelations at night when guards closed the ghetto gates. Closure and aperture of the Venetian ghetto complex were inseparable and mutually constitutive conditions of confinement, interconnected categories essential to the stabilization of Venice's social geography and economic prosperity. In Venice the financial and residential needs of the city produced an anomalous place for the Jews within the Venetian skyline. Through the vertical ascendancy of the ghetto and its resultant rooftop vistas, the complex received power and recognition urbanistically, and from its heights sheds light on the new spatial relations built between Jews and Christians.

The Venice ghetto became an architectural apparatus predicated on confinement and surveillance in which spatial discourses of centrality and marginality, visibility and invisibility, were continuously negotiated. As such, the ghetto offers a compelling comparative to the modern conception of the Panopticon. The Panopticon, developed by Jeremy Bentham and recognized in the work of Michel Foucault, is an annular building of light-flooded cellblocks that surround an opaque central inspection tower.[51] Situated within the tower is an unseen supervisor who has constant visibility of the cells' occupants. The

D A N A   E .   K A T Z

arrangement offers the tower an axial visibility that conditions the occupants in their cells to monitor themselves for fear of the perpetual gaze of supervision. This built environment constructs a well-ordered mechanism of power that segregates, on the one hand, and disciplines, on the other. It is not my intention to align the complex institutional forms of disciplinary power in Bentham's blueprint for a Panopticon in the late eighteenth century to the establishment of the ghetto in cinquecento Venice, nor is it to question the historicity of the panoptical moment in the modern period. The Jewish ghetto in Venice was hardly an early modern precursor to Bentham's Panopticon. Rather, I am interested instead in the ways architectures of surveillance create social controls grounded in networks of stability and community that ensure the constant regulation of daily life. From the central tower in Bentham's design, the cellmates never exchanged gazes with their panoptical guard, who remained permanently out of sight. Similarly, the virginal nun in her conventual enclosures (and her male supervisors) sought an analogous system of invisibility to protect the nun "from her own (inappropriate) looking and especially from the looking of others."[52] The ghetto, however, offered a new architectonic system of visuality whereby the power of opticality resided with the marginalized Jews. The spatial disposition of early modern Venice included the hierarchical ordering of the city's architecture to isolate difference and map social order. While supervised enclosures secured the Jews' placement through urban policies of displacement, this contained world of protected topography was breached when Jews looked out from their windows. The ghetto, erected to spatialize alterity and mobilize walls through social denunciation, concomitantly transformed Jews to observing subjects.

The ghettoization of the Jews in Venice raises critical questions about how religious difference and agency came to dwell in early modern Venice, how Jews and Christians deployed the gaze in negotiating Venetian life. Ghettoization presented the Jews of Venice a structured visibility that allowed them access to a fluid exchange of gazes, that is, they could see and be seen, they could initiate the gaze and the look returned. The ghetto window consequently engendered a new form of social relations that provoked continual contestation and renegotiation. That the Serenissima sought to block the Jews' view from their windows and balconies suggests they attempted to impede the vertical prominence of the ghetto vistas and to deflect the Jews' powers of observation. Although deferment of such closure policies at times displaced this reality, the recurrent legislation to blockade architectural apertures corresponds to a vision of an idealized urban geography that inhibited the Jews' status as fully sighted onlookers. By rendering the Jews' gaze impotent, the government acted to control ocular tensions between Christians and Jews, whose invitation to dwell in the lagoon city did not extend as far as their lines of sight. Hills writes in the conventual context of Naples that "the struggle over the optics of power sheds light on how new urban spatial relationships were forged and on the nature of . . . power itself."[53] Given the ghetto's visibility within the Venetian skyline, the Jews acquired an agency from their elevated optical placement that provoked a disordering of the Venetian order of things.

Archival records support such a claim, as authorities such as the Venetian patriarch Lorenzo Priuli advocated for more rigorous enclosure regulations by blockading the dangerous views of the Jews.[54] In the late sixteenth century, allegations circulated that Jews had committed indecent acts before the windows of the ghetto facing the nunnery of San Geronimo. Priuli recommended that the Venetian Senate modify the windows such that only light could be transmitted—not the defiling look of the Jews.[55] Separating Jews, supposed Christ-killers, from nuns, brides of Christ, was especially important in early modern Venice, where post-Tridentine efforts to enclose the nuns within the confines of *clausura* did not prevent them from maintaining social, and at times sexual, relations with members of secular society.[56] For instance, convent *parlatori* (parlors) in Venice evolved as a salon space that offered monastic women limited contact with outside visitors. Furnished with an iron screen and an overseeing chaperone, conventual *parlatori* partitioned the sisters from their callers through a wall of window-like apertures. The permeability of *parlatori* made them highly regulated fenestral sites since they cultivated relations with people from all social backgrounds including, according to a document from 1625, a converted Jew named Moisé Coppio, who was found having "noisy," "licentious," and "scandalous" discussions with multiple nuns from the convent of Santa Maria Maddalena.[57]

As the respectable Christian woman, sacred and secular, required protection from the Jews and their gaze, so did the body of Christ as it passed in procession in the form of the Eucharist along the *fondamenta* (quay) of Cannaregio. According to Priuli and later a local parish priest, Jews would stand at their ghetto windows screaming insults and throwing trash at the sacrament on a daily basis. This problem continued until the early years of the seventeenth century when the Cinque Savi recommended placing iron railings over the Jews' windows. Through the senatorial directives to cover the exterior apertures of the ghetto complex, Venetian authorities sought to block the field of visibility, to blind the Jews' powers to opticality. The occlusion of ghetto windows blinding the Jews became an architectural metaphor for their rejection of Christ. The reprobate practices of Jews treated in the *adversus judaeos* tradition of the church fathers required Jewish blindness to define Christian identity and to make Jewish beliefs and rituals obsolete.[58] The conflicts over ghetto vistas in

Venice symbolize the ongoing contestation between Christian and Jew, between social order and disorder. Only the Jews' blindness could assure social order. Robert Bonfil writes, "The reception of Jews into Christian society was transformed by means of the ghetto from being exceptional and unnatural into being unexceptional and natural."[59] Here Bonfil insists that the formation of the ghetto paradoxically reintegrated Jews into Christian culture, thus colluding segregation with integration. While the ghetto complex was indeed incorporated within the larger civic context of Venice, its urban involvements never naturalized the Jewish presence in Christian Venice. The Jews' religious difference and, of course, their so-called usurious practices, which themselves were based on the invisibility of Jewish production that made money merely from the passage of time, promoted the ghetto's distinction.[60] The complex and its inhabitants always maintained a subordinated status, as the marginality conferred on the Jews created displacements physical and discursive. With the vertical expansion of the ghetto, the Jews' panoramic views polarized the community as such vistas remained intrinsically unnatural and juridically reprehensible. What remained at issue, and at stake, was the Jews' gaze. Although Christian guards were to patrol the ghetto twenty-four hours a day, it was the Jews from their windows and rooftop belvederes who possessed a room with a view—a view eventually obstructed to elude sight.

NOTES

I am grateful for support provided by the Gladys Krieble Delmas Foundation, the Michael E. and Carol S. Levine Foundation, the Renaissance Society of America, the Memorial Foundation for Jewish Culture, and Reed College. I began this research thanks in large part to the National Endowment for the Humanities Institute on "Venice, the Jews, and Italian Culture: Historical Eras and Cultural Representations." For their conversations and collaborations, I am deeply indebted to the Institute's participants and especially its organizers, Murray Baumgarten and Shaul Bassi. I am also thankful to the staff of the Archivio di Stato di Venezia, Dr. Norman and Marion Lavy, Herbert Kessler, David Nirenberg, Benjamin Ravid, Diane Wolfthal, Karen-edis Barzman, Kathryn Lofton, Erin Hazard, Lia Markey, Meredith Kennedy Ray, Guisela Latorre, Marina Del Negro Karem, E. J. Carter, and the anonymous readers of this volume.

1. Rainer Maria Rilke, "A Scene from the Venice Ghetto," in *Stories of God*, trans. Michael H. Kohn (Boston: Shambhala, 2003), 57; and Rilke, "Eine Szene aus dem Ghetto von Venedig," *Geschichten vom lieben Gott* (Wiesbaden: Insel, 1955), 94.

2. Since its erection, the ghetto complex in Venice has undergone continuous restoration programs. The interior spaces no longer resemble those of the sixteenth century, but the buildings' exterior with its irregular fenestration patterns and soaring heights is a distinguishing formal element dating to the early modern period.

3. Archivio di Stato di Venezia (ASV), Senato, terra, registro 19, fols. 78r–79r, March 29, 1516. See David Chambers and Brian Pullan, eds., *Venice: A Documentary History 1450–1630* (Oxford: Blackwell, 1992), 338–39. Despite the fact that Jews by law could not own real estate, the ghettoized Jews of Venice were able to secure a *jus gazaka*, a right of possession that was

tantamount to a permanent lease. The *jus gazaka* was a socially and ecclesiastically sanctioned contract that could be sold as well as passed by inheritance to younger generations of Jews. See, for example, Cecil Roth, *History of the Jews in Venice* (New York: Schocken, 1958), 109. On the complexities of property and possession related to ghetto real estate, see Ennio Concina, "Owners, Houses, Functions: New Research on the Origins of the Venetian Ghetto," *Mediterranean Historical Review* 6 (1991–92): 180–89; and Benjamin Ravid, "The Minotto Family and an Unapproved Construction Project in the Ghetto Vecchio of Venice, 1608–1609," in *Daniel Carpi Jubilee Volume* (Tel Aviv: Tel Aviv University, 1996), 91–108.

4. The Venetian government ultimately eliminated the boat patrol; nevertheless, Christian surveillance remained a permanent feature of ghetto life. Authorities posted four Christian guards in the ghetto complex twenty-four hours a day and required them to live within its walls without their families.

5. In 1364 the humanist Francesco Petrarch celebrated Venice as the ideal city: "The august city of Venice rejoices, the one home today of liberty, peace and justice, the one refuge of honorable men, the one port to which can repair the storm-tossed, tyrant-hounded craft of men who seek the good life. Venice—rich in gold but richer in fame, mighty in her resources but mightier in virtue, solidly built on marble but standing more solid on a foundation of civil concord, ringed with salt waters but more secure with the salt of good counsel!" Francesco Petrarch, *Letters*, trans. Morris Bishop (Bloomington: Indiana University Press, 1966), 234. On the myth of Venice and a rich bibliography related to Venetian mythmaking, see in particular Edward Muir, *Civic Ritual in Renaissance Venice* (Princeton, N.J.: Princeton University Press, 1981), 13–61; Edward Muir, "Images of Power: Art and Pageantry in Renaissance Venice," *American Historical Review* 84 (1979): 16–52; David Rosand, *The Myths of Venice: The Figuration of a State* (Chapel Hill: University of North Carolina Press, 2001); Iain Fenlon, *The Ceremonial City: History, Memory and Myth in Renaissance Venice* (New Haven, Conn.: Yale University Press, 2007); and Benjamin Ravid, "Between the Myth of Venice and the Lachrymose Conception of Jewish History" in *The Jews of Italy: Memory and Identity*, ed. Bernard Dov Cooperman and Barbara Garvin (Potomac: University Press of Maryland, 2000), 151–92; reprinted in *Studies on the Jews of Venice, 1382–1797* (Aldershot: Ashgate, 2003).

6. "Questi per il negotio, sono opulentissimi & ricchi, & dimorano più volentieri in Venetia che in altra parte d'Italia. Percioche non si usano loro violenze ne tirannidi come altrove, & sono sicuri in ogni occorrenza delle facultà loro, & conseguiscono giustitia contra qualunque si sia percioche riposandosi in singolarissima pace, godono questa patria quasi come vera terra di promissione." Francesco Sansovino, *Venetia, citta nobilissima et singolare, descritta in XIIII. libri* (Venice: Iacomo Sansovino, 1581), fol. 136v; and Patricia Fortini Brown, *Private Lives in Renaissance Venice: Art, Architecture, and the Family* (New Haven, Conn.: Yale University Press, 2004), 216.

7. On the subjectivity of the gaze, see Jacques Lacan, "Of the gaze as *Objet petit a*," in *The Four Fundamental Concepts of Psycho-Analysis*, ed. Jacques-Alain Miller, trans. Alan Sheridan (New York: W. W. Norton, 1978), 67–119. The Lacanian gaze is not the look we direct onto the world around us. Instead, it acknowledges the presence of an exterior eye looking back at us. In this essay, I pursue the idea of the gaze both in its formal aspects as applied to architecture and in its ideological structure as to define and redefine Jew and Christian, object and subject. Slavoj Žižek's study of pornography and perversion in popular culture informed this analysis in that he problematizes the antinomic relation of gaze and eye articulated by Lacan: "This antinomy of gaze and view is lost in pornography—why? . . . Contrary to the commonplace according to which, in pornography, the other (the person shown on the screen) is degraded to an object of our voyeuristic pleasure, we must stress that it is the spectator himself who effectively occupies the position of the object. The real

　　　　　DANA E. KATZ

subjects are the actors on the screen trying to rouse us sexually, while we, the spectators, are reduced to a paralyzed object-gaze." Slavoj Žižek, *Looking Awry: An Introduction to Jacques Lacan through Popular Culture* (Cambridge, Mass.: MIT Press, 1991), 110.

8. The Senate decree states, "Tuti li Zudei che de presenti se attrovano habitar in diverse contrade de questa cita nostra . . . siano tenuti & debino andar immediate ad habitar unidi in la corte de case che sono in Geto apresso San Hieronymo, loco capacissimo per sua habitacione." ASV, Senato, terra, registro 19, fol. 78r, March 29, 1516. See also Chambers and Pullan, *Venice: A Documentary History*, 338.

9. On the history of the Venetian ghetto, see Ennio Concina, Ugo Camerino, and Donatella Calabi, *La città degli ebrei: Il ghetto di Venezia, architettura e urbanistica* (Venezia: Albrizzi Editore, 1991). See also Donatella Calabi, "The 'City of Jews,'" in *The Jews of Early Modern Venice*, ed. Robert C. Davis and Benjamin Ravid (Baltimore: Johns Hopkins University Press, 2001), 31–49; Umberto Fortis, *The Ghetto on the Lagoon: A Guide to the History and Art of the Venetian Ghetto (1516–1797)*, trans. Roberto Matteoda (Venice: Storti Edizioni, 1988); Riccardo Calimani, *The Ghetto of Venice*, trans. Katherine Silberblatt Wolfthal (New York: M. Evans, 1987); Roberta Curiel and Bernard Dov Cooperman, *The Venetian Ghetto* (New York: Rizzoli, 1990); Richard Goy, *Venice: The City and Its Architecture* (London: Phaidon, 1997), esp. 86–93; Richard Sennett, *Flesh and Stone: The Body and the City in Western Civilization* (New York: W. W. Norton, 1994), 212–51; David Cassuto, "The Scuola Grande Tedesca in the Venice Ghetto," *Journal of Jewish Art* 3–4 (1977): 40–57; Francesca Brandes, ed., *Venice and Environs: Jewish Itineraries* (Venice: Marsilio, 1997); Annie Sacerdoti, *The Guide to Jewish Italy* (New York: Rizzoli, 2004); Vivian B. Mann, ed., *Gardens and Ghettos: The Art of Jewish Life in Italy* (Berkeley: University of California Press, 1989); and *Encyclopaedia Judaica* (New York: Macmillan, 1971), s.v. "Venice."

10. Goy, *Venice: The City and Its Architecture*, 46. For a history of architecture in Renaissance Venice, see such studies as Deborah Howard, *The Architectural History of Venice* (New Haven, Conn.: Yale University Press, 2002); Deborah Howard, *Venice and the East: The Impact of the Islamic World on Venetian Architecture, 1100–1500* (New Haven, Conn.: Yale University Press, 2000); Ennio Concina, *Storia dell'architettura di Venezia: Dal VII al XX secolo* (Milan: Electa, 1992); trans. Judith Landry as *A History of Venetian Architecture* (Cambridge: Cambridge University Press, 1998); Richard Goy, *Venetian Vernacular Architecture: Traditional Housing in the Venetian Lagoon* (Cambridge: Cambridge University Press, 1989); Ralph Lieberman, *Renaissance Architecture in Venice* (New York: Abbeville, 1982); and John McAndrew, *Venetian Architecture of the Early Renaissance* (Cambridge, Mass.: MIT Press, 1980).

11. Calimani, *The Ghetto of Venice*, 133. The most common types of wood used for the construction of Venetian buildings were larch, fir, and oak. At times, elm was also used. See Goy, *Venice: The City and Its Architecture*, 48.

12. Curiel and Cooperman, *The Venetian Ghetto*, 36.

13. For studies of Jacopo de' Barbari's map, see Juergen Schulz, "Jacopo de' Barbari's View of Venice: Map-Making, City Views, and Moralized Geography," *Art Bulletin* 60, no. 3 (September 1978): 425–74; and Bronwen Wilson, *The World in Venice: Print, the City, and Early Modern Identity* (Toronto: University of Toronto Press, 2005), 23–69.

14. On the aesthetics and social theories related to the Jewish ghettos in early modern Italy, see Stefanie B. Siegmund, *The Medici State and the Ghetto of Florence: The Construction of an Early Modern Jewish Community* (Stanford, Calif.: Stanford University Press, 2006); Kenneth R. Stow, *Theater of Acculturation: The Roman Ghetto in the Sixteenth Century* (Seattle: University of Washington Press, 2001); Stow, "Hatred of the Jews or Love of the Church: Papal Policy Toward the Jews in the Middle Ages," in *Antisemitism through the Ages*, ed.

Shmuel Almog, trans. Nathan H. Reisner (Oxford: Pergamon Press, 1988); Stow, "The Consciousness of Closure: Roman Jewry and Its *Ghet*," in *Essential Papers on Jewish Culture in Renaissance and Baroque Italy*, ed. David B. Ruderman (New York: New York University Press, 1992); Stow, "Sanctity and the Construction of Space: The Roman Ghetto as Sacred Space," in *Jewish Assimilation, Acculturation and Accommodation: Past Traditions, Current Issues and Future Prospects*, ed. Menachem Mor (Lanham, Md.: University Press of America, 1992); Stow, "Ethnic Rivalry or Melting Pot: The *Edot* in the Roman Ghetto," *Judaism* 41 (1992): 286–96; Stow, "A Tale of Uncertainties: Converts in the Roman Ghetto," in *Shlomo Simonsohn Jubilee Volume: Studies on the History of the Jews in the Middle Ages and Renaissance Period*, ed. Daniel Carpi et al. (Tel Aviv: Tel Aviv University, 1993); Stow, "Marriages Are Made in Heaven: Marriage and the Individual in the Roman Jewish Ghetto," *Renaissance Quarterly* 48, no. 3 (Autumn 1995): 445–91; Howard Adelman, "Jewish Women and Family Life," in *The Jews of Early Modern Venice*, ed. Robert C. Davis and Benjamin Ravid (Baltimore: Johns Hopkins University Press, 2001), 143–65; and Diane Wolfthal, *Picturing Yiddish: Gender, Identity, and Memory in the Illustrated Yiddish Books of Renaissance Italy* (Leiden: Brill, 2004). See also Maria Georgopoulou, "Mapping Religious and Ethnic Identities in the Venetian Colonial Empire," *Journal of Medieval and Early Modern Studies* 26, no. 3 (Fall 1996): 467–96.

15. Philippe de Commynes, the French ambassador who wrote a panegyric of Venice in the early sixteenth century, declared: "Most of the people [of Venice] are foreigners." See Frederic C. Lane, *Venice: A Maritime Republic* (Baltimore: John Hopkins University Press, 1973), 273. Regarding Venice's "Others," see Benjamin Ravid, "How 'Other' Really Was the Jewish Other? The Evidence from Venice," in *Acculturation and Its Discontents: The Italian Jewish Experience Between Exclusion and Inclusion*, ed. David N. Myers (Toronto: University of Toronto Press, 2008), 19–55.

16. On tolerance in the late medieval and early modern period, see Hans Oberdick, *Tolerance: Between Forbearance and Acceptance* (Lanham, Md.: Rowman and Littlefield, 2001); Cary J. Nederman, *Worlds of Difference: European Discourses of Toleration, c. 1100–c. 1550* (University Park: Penn State University Press, 2000); John Christian Laursen and Cary J. Nederman, eds., *Beyond the Persecuting Society: Religious Toleration before the Enlightenment*, (Philadelphia: University of Pennsylvania Press, 1998); István Bejczy, "*Tolerantia*: A Medieval Concept," *Journal of the History of Ideas* 58, no. 3 (July 1997): 365–84; Ole Peter Grell and Bob Scribner, eds., *Tolerance and Intolerance in the European Reformation*, (Cambridge: Cambridge University Press, 1996); and Dana E. Katz, *The Jew in the Art of the Italian Renaissance* (Philadelphia: University of Pennsylvania Press, 2008).

17. Regarding the house rules for Germans in the Fondaco dei Tedeschi, see Chambers and Pullan, *Venice: A Documentary History*, 328–30.

18. Ibid., 352. See also Benjamin Ravid, "From Geographical Realia to Historiographical Symbol: The Odyssey of the Word *Ghetto*," in *Essential Papers on Jewish Culture in Renaissance and Baroque Italy*, ed. David B. Ruderman (New York: New York University Press, 1992), 380–81.

19. Muir, *Civic Ritual in Renaissance Venice*, 15.

20. Alberti writes, "The presence of an elegant portico, under which the elders may [stroll] or sit, take a nap or negotiate business, will be an undoubted ornament to both crossroad and forum. Furthermore, the presence of the elders will restrain the youth, as they play and sport in the open, and curb any misbehavior or buffoonery resulting from the immaturity of their years." Leon Battista Alberti, *On the Art of Building in Ten Books*, trans. Joseph Rykwert, Neil Leach, and Robert Tavernor (Cambridge, Mass.: MIT Press, 1988), 263. See also Sharon T. Strocchia, "Theaters of Everyday Life," in *Renaissance Florence: A Social*

　　　　　　　　　　　　　DANA E. KATZ

History, ed. Roger J. Crum and John T. Paoletti (Cambridge: Cambridge University Press, 2006), 67; and Gene Brucker, *Renaissance Florence* (Berkeley: University of California Press, 1969), 43.

21. John Ruskin, *The Stones of Venice,* vol. 1 (London: George Allen, Sunnyside, Orpington, 1896), 101.

22. Muir, *Civic Ritual in Renaissance Venice,* 15.

23. Mark R. Cohen, *The Autobiography of a Seventeenth-Century Venetian Rabbi: Leon Modena's Life of Judah* (Princeton, N.J.: Princeton University Press, 1988), 5–6.

24. Fear of the Jews' sexuality permeated early modern Europe. According to Christian theologians and anatomists, the sexual dangers of Jews derived from their distinct biology. For instance, Jewish women were thought to have enhanced libidos that triggered their uncontrollable attraction to Christian men, whereas the unusual sexual proclivities of Jewish men stemmed from the belief that they menstruate. See Irven M. Resnick, "Medieval Roots of the Myth of Jewish Male Menses," *Harvard Theological Review* 93 (2000): 241–63; David S. Katz, "Shylock's Gender: Jewish Male Menstruation in Early Modern England," *Review of English Studies* 50 (1999): 440–62; and Willis Johnson, "The Myth of Jewish Male Menses," *Journal of Medieval History* 24 (1998): 273–95. See also Amy Neff and Anne Derbes, "'This Unnatural Flow': Bleeding Demons in the *Supplicationes variae,* the Arena Chapel, and Notre-Dame des Fontaines, La Brigue," in *Anathmata Eortia: Studies in Honor of Thomas F. Mathews,* ed. J. Alchermes, H. Evans, and T. Thomas (Mainz: von Zabern, forthcoming). I would very much like to thank Amy Neff and Anne Derbes for sharing their forthcoming essay with me.

25. In 1443 the Senate revisited the punishment for Jewish men found guilty of having sexual intercourse with Christian women. Benjamin Ravid explains, "To prevent relations with Christian women, the fine was increased from five hundred lire to five hundred ducats, an increase of 620%, and the jail sentence extended from one year to two." The Avogadori di Comun also penalized more severely Christian men who had sexual relations with Jewish women. Benjamin Ravid, "The Legal Status of the Jew in Venice to 1509," in *Proceedings of the American Academy for Jewish Research* (Jerusalem: Ben-Zvi Printing Enterprises, 1987), 185–87.

26. The Signori di Notte was a Venetian magistracy established to provide public security through nighttime patrol. See Elisabeth Pavan, "Recherches sur la nuit venitienne à la fin du Moyen Age," *Journal of Medieval History* 7 (December 1981): 339–56. The archival documents in the Archivio di Stato di Venezia related to the civil and criminal branches of the Signori di Notte indicate no significant Jewish nocturnal activity during the early modern period. Although the Jews did not commit numerous crimes, their nocturnal presence remained a cause for fear in the Christian consciousness.

27. On night in the medieval and early modern periods, see A. Roger Ekirch, *At Day's Close: Night in Times Past* (New York: W. W. Norton, 2005); Bryan D. Palmer, *Cultures of Darkness: Night Travels in the Histories of Transgression* (New York: Monthly Review Press, 2000); Jean Verdon, *La nuit au Moyen Age* (Paris: Perrin, 1994); and Jean Verdon, "Recherches sur la société religieuse et la nuit au Moyen Age," in *Les prélats, l'Église et la société, XIe-XVe siècles: Hommage à Bernard Guillemain,* ed. Françoise Bériac (Bordeaux: Université Michel de Montaigne, 1994), 327–36. See also Craig Koslofsky, "Princes of Darkness: The Night at Court, 1650–1750," *Journal of Modern History* 79, no. 2 (June 2007): 235–73; and Craig Koslofsky, "Court Culture and Street Lighting in Seventeenth-Century Europe," *Journal of Urban History,* 28, no. 6 (2002): 743–68.

28. On the presence of Jews in Uccello's Corpus Domini predella, see Marilyn Aronberg Lavin, "The Altar of Corpus Domini in Urbino: Paolo Uccello, Joos Van Ghent, Piero della

Francesca," *Art Bulletin* 49, no. 1 (1967): 1–24; Catherine Gallagher and Stephen Greenblatt, *Practicing New Historicism* (Chicago: University of Chicago Press, 2000), 75–109; Dana E. Katz, "The Contours of Tolerance: Jews and the Corpus Domini Altarpiece in Urbino," *Art Bulletin* 85, no. 4 (December 2003): 646–61; and Katz, *The Jew in the Art of the Italian Renaissance*, 16–39.

29. Regarding the alleged ritual murder of Simon of Trent, see R. Po-chia Hsia, *The Myth of Ritual Murder: Jews and Magic in Reformation Germany* (New Haven, Conn.: Yale University Press, 1988); R. Po-chia Hsia, *Trent 1475: Stories of a Ritual Murder Trial* (New Haven, Conn.: Yale University Press, 1992); Wolfgang Treue, *Der Trienter Judenprozeß: Voraussetzungen, Abläufe, Auswirkungen, 1475–1588* (Hannover: Hahnsche Buchhandlung, 1996); Anna Esposito and Diego Quaglioni, *Processi contro gli ebrei di Trento (1475–1478): I processi del 1475* (Padova: CEDAM, 1990); Iginio Rogger and Marco Bellabarba, eds., *Il principe vescovo Johannes Hinderbach (1465–1486) fra tardo Medioevo e Umanesimo* (Bologna: Edizioni Dehoniane, 1992); Gianni Gentilini, *Pasqua 1475: Antiguidaismo e lotta alle eresie, il caso di Simonino* (Milan: Medusa, 2007); and Katz, *The Jew in the Art of the Italian Renaissance*, 119–57.

30. Elliott Horowitz, "The Eve of the Circumcision: A Chapter in the History of Jewish Nightlife," *Journal of Social History* 23, no. 1 (Autumn 1989): 45–69.

31. Elliott Horowitz, "Coffee, Coffeehouses, and the Nocturnal Rituals of Early Modern Jewry," *AJS Review* 14, no. 1 (Spring 1989): 17–46.

32. ". . . li Zudei, che habiteno in questa sua cita, et tutto el dominio, siano distincti et diversificati da li Christiani cossi in habito come sono in la fede." Archivio di Stato di Mantova, Archivio Gonzaga, busta 2038–39, fascicolo 9, fol. 2v. Canon 68 of the Fourth Lateran Council (1215) records the first church law obliging Jews to wear distinguishing garb: "In certain provinces of the church, divergence in clothing distinguishes Jews from Christians and Saracens from Christians; however in certain [provinces], there has arisen such confusion that no differences are discernible. Thus, it sometimes happens that by mistake Christians mingle with Jewish or Saracen women, and Jews and Saracens with Christian women. Therefore, lest they, under the cover of error, find an excuse for the grave sin of such mingling, we decree that these people [Jews and Saracens] of either sex and in all Christian lands and at all times be readily distinguishable from others by the quality of their clothing. Indeed, this very legislation is decreed for them [the Jews] also by Moses." Robert Chazan, *Medieval Stereotypes and Modern Antisemitism* (Berkeley: University of California Press, 1997), 100.

33. On the sartorial restrictions placed on the Jews of Venice, see Benjamin Ravid, "From Yellow to Red: On the Distinguishing Head-covering of the Jews of Venice," *Jewish History* 6, nos. 1–2 (March 1992): 179–210; reprinted in *Studies on the Jews of Venice, 1382–1797* (Aldershot: Ashgate, 2003). On dress and social marginalization, see also Diane Owen Hughes, "Distinguishing Signs: Ear-Rings, Jews and Franciscan Rhetoric in the Italian Renaissance City," *Past and Present* 112 (August 1986): 3–59; and Sara Lipton, *Images of Intolerance: The Representation of Jews and Judaism in the "Bible moralisée"* (Berkeley: University of California Press, 1999), esp. 15–19.

34. Concerning the Venetian garden, see, for example, John Dixon Hunt, "The Garden in the City of Venice: Epitome of State and Site," *Studies in the History of Gardens and Designed Landscapes* 19, no. 1 (January–March 1999): 46–59.

35. Thomas Coryat, *Coryat's Crudities* (Glasgow: James MacLehose, 1905), 370.

36. Ibid., 371.

37. On the ghetto and the foreign gaze, see Benjamin Ravid, "Christian Travelers in the Ghetto of Venice: Some Preliminary Observations," in *Studies on the Jews of Venice, 1382–1797* (Aldershot: Ashgate, 2003), 111–50; and Calabi, "The 'City of Jews,' " 45–48.

38. For the architectural history of viewing in medieval Italy, see Marvin Trachtenberg, *Dominion of the Eye: Urbanism, Art, and Power in Early Modern Florence* (Cambridge: Cambridge University of Press, 1997). See also Renzo Dubbini, *Geography of the Gaze in Early Modern Europe,* trans. Lydia G. Cochrane (Chicago: University of Chicago Press, 2002).

39. Rilke, "A Scene from the Venice Ghetto," 58–60; and Rilke, "Eine Szene aus dem Ghetto von Venedig," 95–97.

40. Benjamin Ravid, "Curfew Time in the Ghetto of Venice," in *Medieval and Renaissance Venice,* ed. Ellen E. Kittell and Thomas F. Madden (Urbana: University of Illinois Press, 1999), 257–59; and Ravid, "New Light on the Ghetti of Venice," in *Shlomo Simonsohn Jubilee Volume: Studies on the History of the Jews in the Middle Ages and Renaissance Period,* ed. Daniel Carpi et al. (Tel Aviv: Tel Aviv University, 1993), esp. 155–58. See also Carla Boccato, "Processi ad ebrei nell'archivio degli uffical al Cattaver a Venezia," *Rassegna mensile di Israel* 41 (1975): 166–68.

41. ASV, Inquisitorato alle Arti, busta 102. See also Ravid, "Curfew Time in the Ghetto of Venice," 257–59; and Ravid, "New Light on the Ghetti of Venice," 155–58.

42. Beatriz Colomina, "The Split Wall: Domestic Voyeurism," in *Sexuality and Space,* ed. Beatriz Colomina (New York: Princeton Architectural Press, 1992), 83.

43. Ibid., 82.

44. Marilyn Dunn, "Spaces Shaped for Spiritual Perfection: Convent Architecture and Nuns in Early Modern Rome," in *Architecture and the Politics of Gender in Early Modern Europe,* ed. Helen Hills (Aldershot: Ashgate, 2003), 151–76.

45. Anne Jacobson Schutte, "The Permeable Cloister?," in *Arcangela Tarabotti: A Literary Nun in Baroque Venice,* ed. Elissa B. Weaver (Ravenna: Longo, 2006), 19–36; Helen Hills, *Invisible City: The Architecture of Devotion in Seventeenth-Century Neapolitan Convents* (New York: Oxford University Press, 2004); Gianna Pomata and Gabriella Zarri, eds., *I monasteri femminili come centri di cultura fra Rinascimento e Barocco* (Rome: Edizioni di Storia e Letteratura, 2005); Gabriella Zarri, "Venetian Convents and Civic Ritual," in *Arcangela Tarabotti: A Literary Nun in Baroque Venice,* ed. Elissa B. Weaver (Ravenna: Longo, 2006), 37–56; and Meredith K. Ray, "Letters and Lace: Arcangela Tarabotti and Convent Culture in *Seicento* Venice," in *Early Modern Women and Transnational Communities of Letters,* ed. Julie D. Campbell and Anne R. Larsen (Farnham, U.K.: Ashgate, 2009), 45–73.

46. See Schutte, "The Permeable Cloister?," 23–24.

47. Hills, *The Invisible City,* 146–47.

48. Women regularly entered the convent under duress for familial and economic reasons, despite conciliar decrees proscribing forced monachization. Jews similarly entered the ghetto unwillingly, yet in this case with senatorial directives mandating compulsory confinement for all coreligionists. Many Jewish families left Venice in 1516 for fear of insufficient space. The wealthy moneylender Asher Meshullam, known as Anselmo dal Banco, instead offered the Venetian government 2,000 ducats (in vain) for the privilege of remaining in his house outside ghetto walls.

49. Hills, *Invisible City,* 121.

50. Ibid., 122–23.

51. Jeremy Bentham, *The Panopticon Writings,* ed. Miran Božovič (London: Verso, 1995); and Michel Foucault, *Discipline and Punish: The Birth of the Prison,* trans. Alan Sheridan (New York: Vintage Books, 1979), esp. 195–228.

52. Hills, *Invisible City,* 145.

53. Ibid., 137.

54. For Patriarch Lorenzo Priuli and his memorandum on Jews as *nemici domestici,* see ASV, Senato, terra, filza 141 (m.v.), January 30, 1596. See also Ravid, "Curfew Time in the

Ghetto of Venice," 257–59; and Brian Pullan, *Rich and Poor in Renaissance Venice: The Social Institutions of a Catholic State, to 1620* (Cambridge, Mass.: Harvard University Press, 1971), 557–58.

55. The document specifies, "haver consideratione a quella parte dal Ghetto, che risguarda il monasterio delle monache di S. Gironimo perche vi sono alcune finestre che predominano tutto l'horto delle monache, et da quelle gli hebrei parlano et usano atti molti indecenti, onde quelle finestre sara bene redurle solamente a luce in modo che non habbiano prospetto nel monasterio." ASV, Senato, terra, filza 141 (m.v.), January 30, 1596.

56. Jutta Gisela Sperling, *Convents and the Body Politic in Late Renaissance Venice* (Chicago: University of Chicago Press, 1999), 158. See also Mary Laven, *Virgins of Venice: Broken Vows and Cloistered Lives in the Renaissance Convent* (New York: Viking, 2002).

57. Sperling, *Convents and the Body Politic in Late Renaissance Venice*, 158.

58. See Rosemary Radford Ruether, "The *Adversus Judaeos* Tradition in the Church Fathers: The Exegesis of Christian Anti-Judaism," in *Essential Papers on Judaism and Christianity in Conflict: From Late Antiquity to the Reformation*, ed. Jeremy Cohen (New York: New York University Press, 1991), 174–89.

59. Robert Bonfil, "Change in the Cultural Patterns of a Jewish Society in Crisis: Italian Jewry at the Close of the Sixteenth Century," in *Essential Papers on Jewish Culture in Renaissance and Baroque Italy*, ed. David B. Ruderman (New York: New York University Press, 1992), 410.

60. On usury, see Jacques Le Goff, *Your Money or Your Life: Economy and Religion in the Middle Ages* (New York: Zone Books, 1988); Benjamin Nelson, *Idea of Usury: From Tribal Brotherhood to Universal Otherhood* (Princeton, N.J.: Princeton University Press, 1949); John Noonan, *The Scholastic Analysis of Usury* (Cambridge, Mass.: Harvard University Press, 1957); Robert Bonfil, *Jewish Life in Renaissance Italy*, trans. Anthony Oldcorn (Berkeley: University of California Press, 1994), 79–98; R. Po-chia Hsia, "The Usurious Jew: Economic Structure and Religious Representations in an Anti-Semitic Discourse," in *In and Out of the Ghetto: Jewish-Gentile Relations in Late Medieval and Early Modern Germany*, ed. R. Po-chia Hsia and Hartmut Lehmann (Cambridge: Cambridge University Press, 1995), 161–76; Joel Kaye, *Economy and Nature in the Fourteenth Century: Money, Market Exchange, and the Emergence of Scientific Thought* (Cambridge: Cambridge University Press, 1998), esp. 79–115; and Maristella Botticini, "A Tale of 'Benevolent' Governments: Private Credit Markets, Public Finance, and the Role of Jewish Lenders in Medieval and Renaissance Italy," *Journal of Economic History* 60, no. 1 (March 2000): 164–89.

DANA E. KATZ

CHAPTER 9

Through a Glass Darkly:
Paths to Salvation in Spanish Painting
at the Outset of the Inquisition

Felipe Pereda

Estos religiosos a quienes fue dado este cargo, como quier
que primero con dulces amonestaciones e después con agras
reprehensiones, trabajaron por reducir a estos que
judaizaban, pero aprovechó poco, porque su pertinacia fue
una ceguedat tan necia e una inorancia tan ciega, que como
quier que negaban e encubrían su yerro, pero secretamente
tornaban a recaer en él, e facer e guardar sus ritos judaicos.
—Hernando del Pulgar (d. c. 1493)[1]

According to the chronicles, when the court arrived at Seville in the summer of 1478, King Ferdinand of Aragon and Queen Isabella of Castile were extremely disappointed to find that the local community of *conversos* (many of whom had been baptized after the antisemitic riots of mid-century) had no shame in exhibiting their unbroken fidelity to the Mosaic religion they were supposed to have abandoned. As a result, the monarchs decided to organize an evangelizing crusade that is usually considered to be an essential episode in the genesis of the modern Inquisition, and whose first tribunal began to function in the same town only three years later.

From this moment on we know very little, except that a missionary campaign was entrusted to Seville's archbishop, Pedro González de Mendoza, and the Queen's confessor, Fray Hernando de Talavera. Mendoza and Talavera tried not only to redirect the converts' erratic religiosity, but also to force the important community of converted Jews to exhibit outward and explicit signs of their faithful incorporation in the Church.

Images were more than mere instruments of this missionary strategy. In the following months, after the resistance of some of the *conversos* to these disciplinary measures, the increasing importance of sacred images in private and public devotion was the subject of a polemic with the religious authorities. In this chapter I reconstruct not only the role images may have played in this socioreligious development but also how they may have shaped a new theoretical discourse; finally I suggest how this process could be related to a specific stylistic development in early modern Sevillian painting.

The missionary campaign of Mendoza and Talavera that began in 1478 included a significant piece of ecclesiastical legislation on the confessional use of images. That same year an edict was published that obliged all of the converted population to keep religious images in their houses. Thanks to Hernando de Talavera's careful documentation, we have the original wording of this order: "And because it is reasonable that the houses of faithful Christians should [honor] the memory of the passion of Our Lord Jesus Christ and of his blessed Mother, we desire and declare that every Christian should have at home the painted image of the cross where Christ was sacrificed and some painted images of the Virgin and other saints that would provoke the inhabitants, arousing them to devotion."[2]

To my knowledge there are no parallels in early modern Europe[3] for this politicization of religious imagery. It is certainly not a coincidence that just a few months after the edict was announced, a drastic reconfiguration of the local painters' market was begun. In September 1480, new civic *Ordenanzas*—new regulations governing the local workshops—were issued. Presented by two local painters, Juan Sánchez de Castro and Juan Sánchez de San Román, the new regulations attempted to impose order on a barely organized market that comprised at least twenty-eight different workshops. The primary objective of these *Ordenanzas* was to introduce a new system that would control both the quality and the style of every picture produced in the local workshops. As a consequence, from this point painters and their products were to be put under the control of local inspectors (*veedores*). Moreover, painters would be allowed to work only in the genre in which they had been examined—from decoration, or gilding, to the category that required the highest degree of skill, that of the *imagineros*, or "painters of figures."[4]

A Reformed Style

Apart from some general references to their iconography, we know nothing of the images that were to be kept in *conversos*' households. As for media, the edict of 1478 mentions "painted images," but it is more likely that prints were produced to fulfill this requirement. Even so, we do have some early panel paintings from the same masters who implemented the market reform. While few examples survive from the last years of the fifteenth century, it can be said that the first documented panel paintings show a progressive assimilation of the northern Netherlandish influence—both technically and stylistically, marked by an increasing naturalism seen, for example, in the introduction of cast shadows and landscapes.

By the end of the century, when the market reform had been accomplished, a more distinct way of painting—an "indigenous" trend, as the connoisseur Chandler Post called it—was in evidence.[5] And it is here that we find for the first time the renowned mastery in the rendering of full-sized single figures. The paradox is that while this new "style" of painting is more elegant, complex, and, in a way, sophisticated, it is at the same time a step backward in time, a recovery of what were by then old pictorial referents. The result is somehow old-fashioned: it looks anachronistic.[6] In these panels landscapes either disappear or are reduced to planar, tapestry-like backgrounds, or often they are replaced by highly elaborated gilding. Surface predominates over space to the point that geometrical floor designs are shown with complete disregard of perspective laws.

This new pictorial strategy is best represented by Juan Sánchez de San Román's "Man of Sorrows," a *Varón de Dolores* or *Schmerzensmann* (Figure 9.1).[7] This painting has been deemed a leading exponent of the reform movement, and we know from documents that Juan Sánchez de San Román was an avid promoter of the new inspectors' system, for whose adoption he had lobbied the ecclesiastical authorities.

The panel represents what at that time was popularly believed to be the exact form in which Christ appeared to Pope Gregory during mass: the paradoxical image of Christ alive, though already sacrificed; dead, but still suffering.[8] The painting is small, just over thirteen inches high (forty centimeters), and retains its original frame, indicating that it was not meant to be part of an altarpiece. It is probably one of those private images that Seville's citizens had been told to keep in their households, although this one would certainly have belonged to a member of the social elite—someone who could afford such a refined and expensive object. The most astonishing characteristic of this work, as of many contemporary products of Sevillian workshops, is the peculiar balance it strikes between the new possibilities offered by northern European panel painters and the strictures of its cultic function. However strong its emotional content, however detailed and convincing the rendering of the figure's anatomy, the picture follows the conventions of cult images as sacred images.

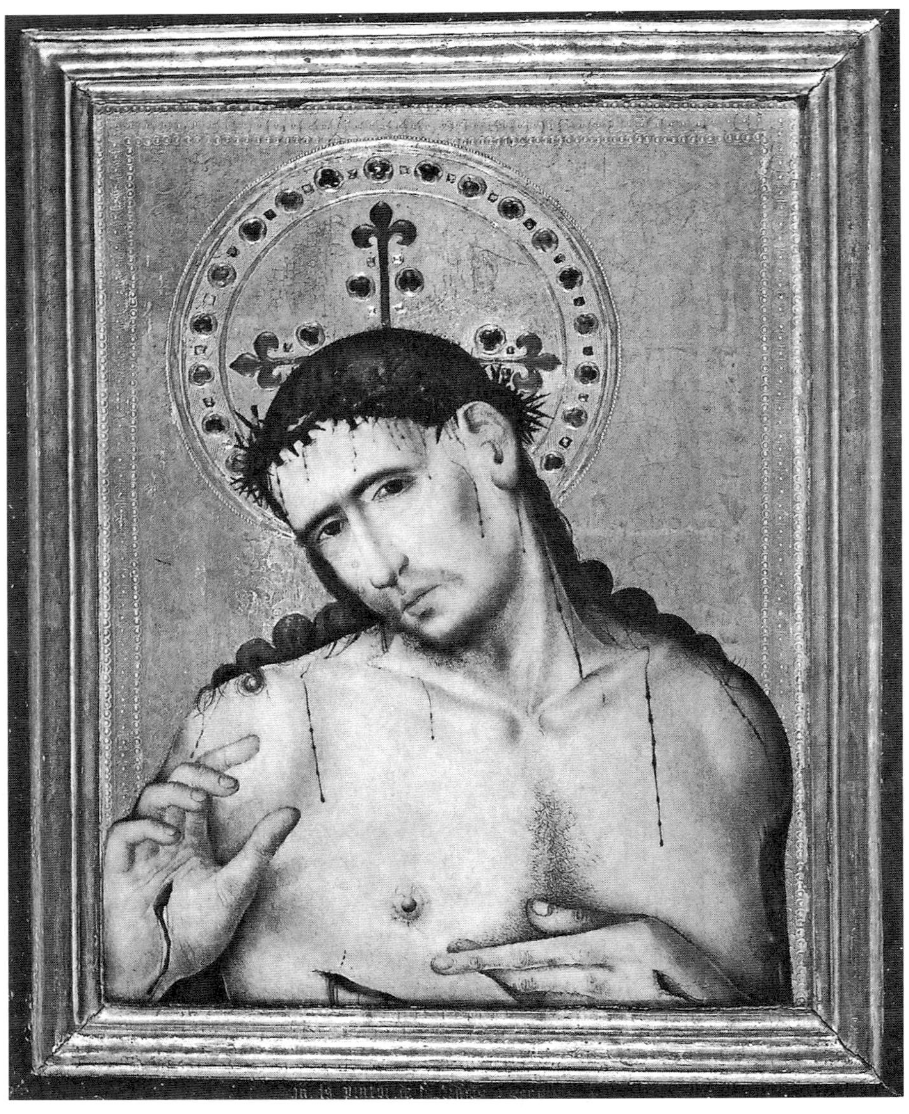

9.1. Juan Sánchez de San Román, *Cristo Varón de Dolores*. Oil on panel. Museo Nacional del Prado, Madrid. Photo: Museo Nacional del Prado.

On one hand, the painter has conceived the image as a fiction, a portable object mounted inside a frame. Through this window- or mirror-like border, the figure stares directly at the viewer. While his left hand calls our attention to the open wound in his side, his right arm begins to unfold as if his fingers were just touching the border where the painted fiction meets the real, physical space of the beholder. The painter has even adopted the convention of signing the painting at the bottom, clearly distinguishing two different levels of representation—

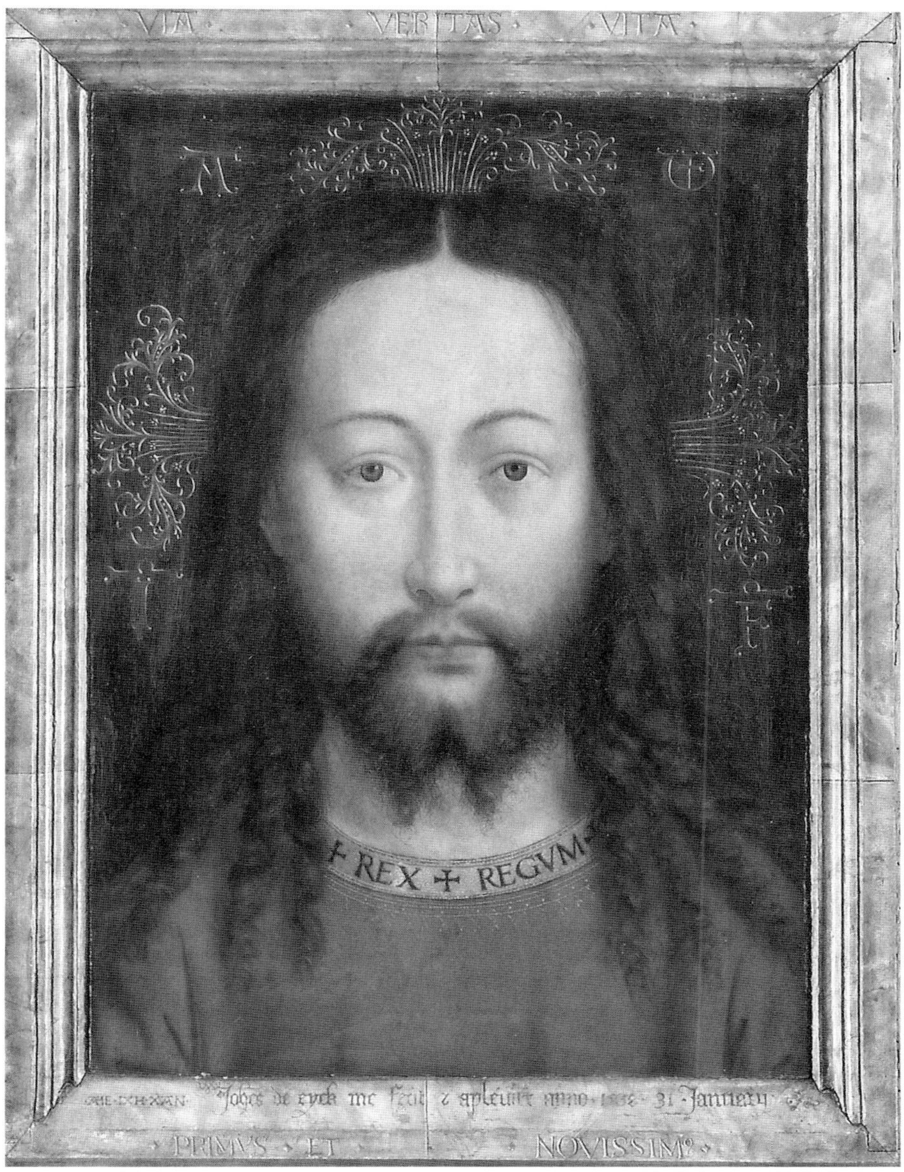

9.2. School of Jan Van Eyck, *Portrait of Christ*, 1438. Oil on panel. Berlin, Staatliche Museen zu Berlin, Gemäldegalerie, Inv. 528. Photo courtesy Jörg P. Anders.

illusion and reality—in a way previously unknown in Spain but which he could have seen in early modern Flemish imports, such as Van Eyck's head of Christ (Berlin), a panel we know was in Castile at the time (Figure 9.2).[9]

On the other hand, while the painting evinces most of the qualities necessary for modern naturalism, it lacks one of the main conditions: depth.[10] This absence is a hallmark of sacred icons or image-relics. A comparison with one of the most charismatic images of the time in Andalusia, the Veronica kept in the Cathedral of Jaén (an icon recorded only after the 1450s, which was thought to be the original cloth on which Christ had imprinted his face),[11] shows a similar super-imposition of Christ's body upon a gilded and decorated background. It seems clear that this numinous effect was precisely what Juan Sánchez de San Román was looking for (Figure 9.3).

The strengthening of the painting's planarity, however, doesn't work against the figure's realism but suggests a physical intimacy that reinforces the sense of empathic dialogue with the beholder. And this sort of paradoxical balance is to be found not only in Castile; in the years around the close of the century we find it in northern as well as southern Europe.[12] However, certain circumstances make the Andalusian case quite unique. First, in Seville, this approach was much more than episodic: it gave birth to an important stylistic stream that developed in small devotional paintings and also in altarpieces or *retablos*; second, it extended its notable heritage well into the baroque era. In fact, this same strategic balance between illusionism and planarity can be traced in some of the most "Spanish-style" images of the Sevillian School of painting well into the seventeenth century.[13]

The peculiar equidistance between illusionism and iconicity in Juan Sánchez de San Román's panel makes it impossible to decide whether this panel should be regarded as a devotional or as a cult image.[14] Here both categories have been conflated. I would like to point out that the reason our painting does not fit into the historiographic narrative moving from an era of cult (*Kultbild*) to an era of art (*Kunstbild*)[15] is that, at the end of the fifteenth century, religious painting in Seville was subject to a particular tension that forced this evolution in a very specific direction. As I try to show, socioreligious circumstances provide solid evidence why painters would have tried to incorporate a new form of imported naturalism without breaking with the received template of medieval cult images.

The first evidence of this comes from how the painting itself was received, based on the testimony of a *converso* in a document that was, not surprisingly, a result of the missionary campaign that had begun in 1478. We know that the censorship rules and official prescriptions promulgated by the religious authorities were strongly contested. One converted Jew, probably a priest (which we can infer from his good knowledge of Christian scriptures and teachings—a situation that was fairly common, as we will see) wrote a provocative pamphlet that began to circulate in Seville in manuscript form.[16]

The anonymous document itself has been lost, but its contents are known through the mediation of Fray Hernando de Talavera, who was commanded to

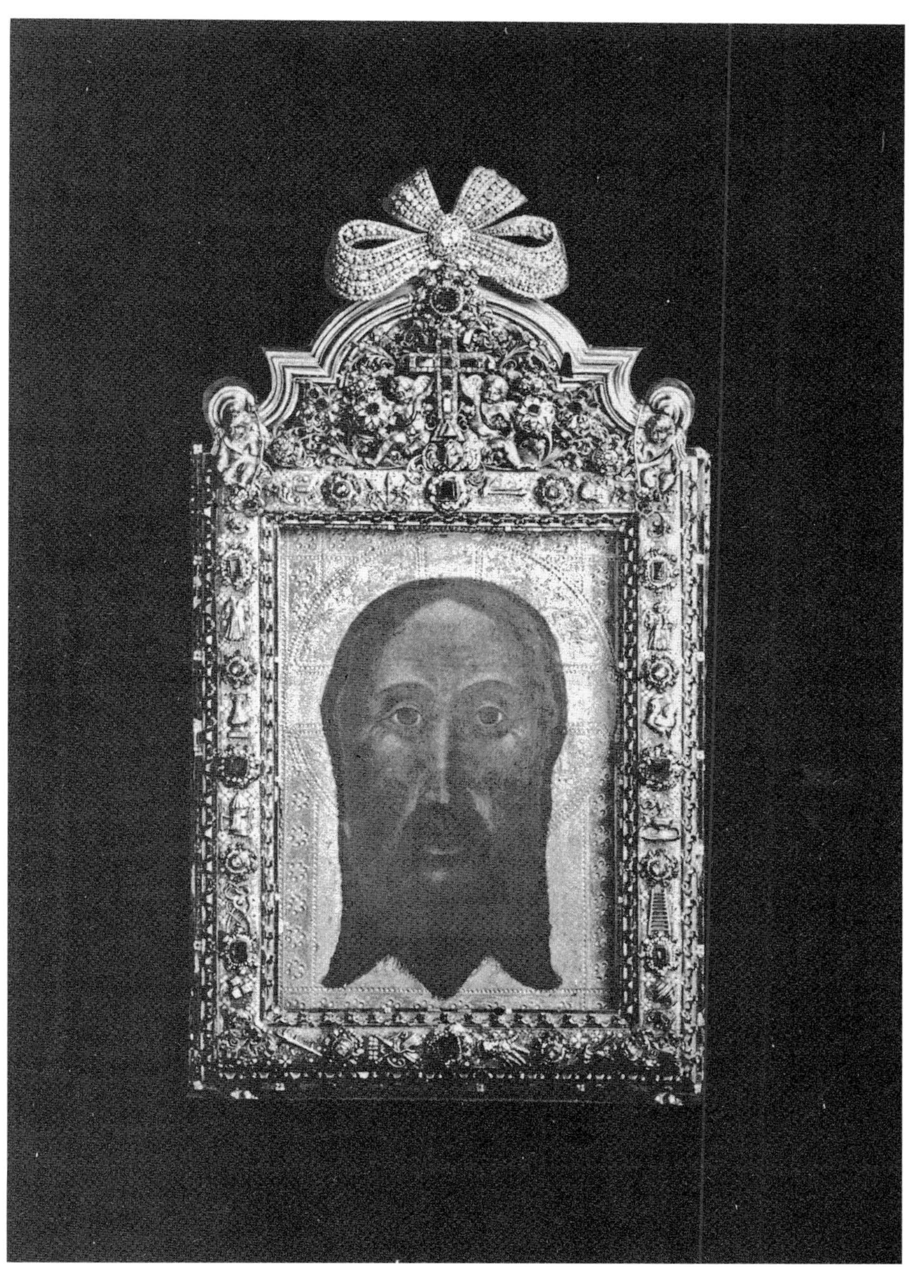

9.3. *Santo Rostro*, Cathedral of Jaén. Photo: Felipe Pereda.

counteract the priest's obtrusive arguments, summing up the controversy in an apologetic treatise called the *Católica Impugnación* that appeared immediately on the heels of the pamphlet. (The fact that Talavera was also of *converso* lineage should be kept in mind when reading both his translation of his opponent's opinions as well as his own arguments.)[17]

According to Talavera, the anonymous pamphlet was a tough critique of the direction that local religious behavior had been taking. It seems the pamphlet considered the unaccomplished history of salvation in continuity with and not departing from rabbinic teachings. This *converso* urged his Christian neighbors not to "contaminate [themselves]" with idols, nor fall into homosexual fornication—two faults that, according to the Acts of the Apostles (Acts 15), were the vices that gentiles had to abandon before qualifying for baptism.[18] The author's arguments should not be considered evidence of apostasy, nor of crypto-Judaism, but the expression of a desire to overcome the opposition of the Old versus the New Law—of Judaism versus Christianity. From this point of view, all religious Christian behavior that violated the Deuteronomic prescriptions, beginning with the proliferation of sacred images, was a departure from law into evil.

As far as we know, no specific images were mentioned in the pamphlet, the author's critique being more general than concrete. But he did refer to one particular image indirectly. We know from the detailed record of his intellectual adversary, the Queen's confessor, that one of the main targets of attack in the diatribe was the idolatrous belief that "old" images had more power—more *virtue* is the precise word that he seems to have used—than new ones.[19] This was clearly a frontal attack on one of the most adored images of Seville, the *Virgen de la Antigua* or Virgin of the Old [Cathedral], a mid-fourteenth-century mural Hodegetria painted on a pillar of the old mosque, where it was supposed to have resisted the attacks of the Moors until the final conquest of Seville in 1248 (Figure 9.4).[20] At the end of the fifteenth century this venerable icon was kept in a rich new chapel where the queen had revered it daily during her stay in Seville.

More specifically, with regard to illusionism in painting, this is what the new Christian priest had to say, according to Talavera:

> Thinks this idiot that there is some great inconvenience in preferring to pray in front of images that are better-made and more ornamented? But there is not, and there's no fault in it, because we [i.e., the good Christians] don't do so thinking that the more beautiful image has any more virtue than the others, but because our intellect naturally enjoys more what better fits its object; and if the purpose of images is to represent what they represent, the better they do it, the more pleasure they

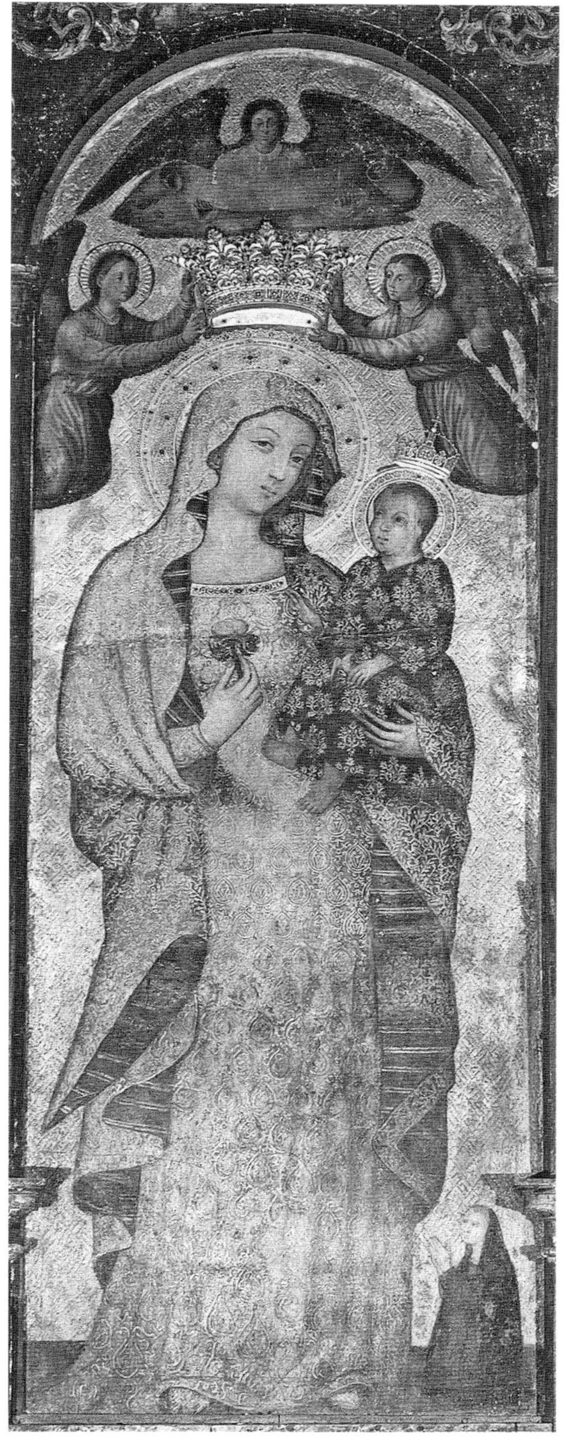

9.4. Virgen "de la Antigua." Chapel of La Antigua, Cathedral of Seville. Photo: Felipe Pereda.

provide, just as anyone who wants to see himself in a mirror will try to find the one that makes him look better.

This idiot also finds it unseemly when people say that images cry, or that they laugh, or that they sweat. And he's right to say that there is often some fraud here, and that there are many opportunists involved in such things. But it is certainly possible for an image to laugh, and to cry, to sweat, and to talk, and even to move, and to make present what's absent—but only if we understand all these things in the correct way.[21]

It would be misleading simply to interpret the two positions as representing two completely opposite attitudes about images. As is evident from the last paragraph, Fray Hernando was forced to admit that many abuses were being committed with religious images. In fact, throughout the *Católica Impugnación* the Friar's defense of images was insistently based on their convenient use as *biblia illiterati* or for their devotional utility; while he admitted their cult value only within the strict limits described in scholastic theology, he dismissed as hearsay the excesses of popular and local devotion.[22]

At the same time, both contenders had to deal with the increasing power of religious icons. When we read Hernando's response to the pamphlet, it is not difficult to think of the "Man of Sorrows" we examined earlier. As his text proves, at least for *this* convert, the new illusionism recently introduced in the town did not detract from the cultic function of images. On the contrary, it was illusionism, the almost *trompe-l'oeil* capacity of images to compete with real life, that sparked the confusion between the material sign and its sacred referent, blurring the difference between the two and thereby seducing beholders into a kind of idolatry. It could be argued that Talavera and his opponent were referring to two different kinds of illusions: one psychological (the anonymous *converso*), and the other stylistic (the Friar)—the new Christian priest thinking more of iconic Byzantine-like images such as the Hodegetria *Virgen* in the cathedral, and Talavera of the new northern-style novelties. But both concepts of illusionism are closely related—in the texts and, as we have seen from our analysis of the "Man of Sorrows," in contemporary painting.

Toward a Social History of Sevillian Icons

The problem with images, however, was certainly not merely a problem of style. Put another way, formal issues cannot be separated from the cultural utility of images. There are two operative levels: one the public sphere and the other the private. I will begin with the latter. As we have already seen, one of the main prescriptions enforced in Seville was to compel all citizens (new as well as old

Christians) to have images at home. Before the end of the fifteenth century,[23] domestic images were apparently still rare in Castile, and that makes the edict all the more significant. Also, its impact on the population seems especially relevant when thinking of converted Jews, a community that grew after 1492, when those who had not already converted were given the choice of abandoning their creed or leaving the country.

At that point the Inquisition had been hard at work in Seville for ten years. And we know that because of the failure of the authorities to manage the heterodox religiosity of the local population, the difficulty of policing the *conversos'* private behavior, and the pronounced resistance of some of them—including the anonymous author of the incendiary pamphlet—the Monarchs had established the first Inquisition Tribunal in Seville in 1480. Unfortunately, local trial transcripts or registers from these early years have not come down to us, but we can compare records from other contemporary Inquisition courts in Castile, such as those in Toledo or Cuenca.

As these documents show, from a very early date—actually as soon as the Inquisitional machine began to run—accusations about the misuse of images became common. This material follows quite a fixed pattern, so I mention only a few examples. Many of them refer to someone who had been surprised by an unexpected visitor while praying at home "as the Jews do." Seemingly insignificant external evidence could lead to tragic consequences: personal mannerisms, such as praying standing up facing a wall, or, of course, the spoken language used, and, in a more undisputed way, whether images were present in the room where the accused had been reported to be praying.

This last was the case for a certain Cristobal de Atienza in 1485. One of his neighbors testified that he had seen Cristobal "praying in a corner, facing the wall, [with no images there] or anything else."[24] Later the accused argued that he did have a small crucifix in his room, but it had gone unnoticed by his neighbor because that fellow already had "bad thoughts about him."

A similar case is that of the wealthy Isabel de los Olivos. This time it was a housemaid who accused the woman and her husband, saying that in the palace where they lived, where her mistress read and prayed, there were "no images of Our Lord, neither of the Virgin Mary, or of any other saint."[25]

In other cases it was the Inquisitor who would ask, after hearing testimony, if there were any images inside the room, thereby spontaneously broaching the subject and setting up an argument for suspicion. Such was the case of Isabel de Setién, who denounced her neighbor on that basis. Having testified about the strange way her neighbor prayed, she was asked if "there were images in that [i.e., his] room."[26]

From such a stage in the public's imagination, to consider the absence of images a sign of heterodoxy was a very short leap, and people were quick to make it. Already in 1484, only two years after the Inquisition began, one Donosa Ruiz, resident of Teruel, was brought before the Tribunal because she "never had, nor has at home [at the moment] an oratory of the Virgin Mary or Jesus Christ or the saints, such as Christians usually have to pray in front of."[27] At Marina González's trial in 1494, one of her prosecutors declared that "in order to show more openly her heresy, she did not have at home any image, or any saint, nor a sign of the cross, or any other Christian sign, because she did not consider herself to be a Christian."[28]

It is understandable that many *conversos* (whether faithful or false, sincere or just struggling for survival) would have begun to introduce images in their houses despite their personal reluctance. But that only opened a new host of potential accusations—from lack of care or inappropriate handling to more serious (but in many cases completely false) charges of ritual profanation.[29] To cite only one example among many, in Toledo in 1485 a Jewish woman was imprisoned because an image of Christ had been seen lying on the floor of her dormitory at the foot of her bed, and because she had it thrown into a latrine.[30]

As a consequence, in the last years of the century, religious images became an inevitable source of conflict for converted Jews. Whether *conversos* kept them or not, images were in the process of being reckoned an exterior sign (*señal* is the precise word sometimes used) of the uncontaminated blood of the old Christians, and therefore an instrument of exclusion. This sense is extraordinarily explicit in the testimony of a baptized Jewish bookseller named Luis García but known to his neighbors as "Abraham." Someone had heard him say that "he did not want to have and would not allow in his house any image of the Lord, our Mother the Virgin Mary, or the Saints, finding all this ridiculous." In the course of his trial, García used several testimonies to prove that he was a faithful Christian, observing the offices of the mass and performing his duties like any other citizen in the town. But when he was asked why he kept no images in his house, he found himself in trouble. At last he confessed that many years earlier, when he was first married, he had bought an image of the Pietà (*Quinta Angustia*) for his new house, but then, "hearing the things and dangers that happened to the new converts who kept images in their houses, and the testimonies of those who accused them for whipping them and vexing them in so many ways, I preferred to throw them out rather than fall victim to the false testimony that a housemaid might have brought against me."[31] García's apprehensions echo a real case that happened in Zaragoza between 1483 and 1484, when a whole group of the converted from the powerful family of the Cavallería were prosecuted on the charge of ritual profanation of a wooden crucifix in a private dwelling. The sole testimony came from a priest who claimed to be a twelve-year-old when those events took place, saying that he had seen how several people performed a play in which a figure of Christ was judged, found guilty, whipped, and finally thrown into the fire.[32]

But "Abraham" García's story does not end here; he was sent to jail and his trial continued. He shared a cell with several other accused, and in this cell an image of the Virgin and a crucifix hung on the wall. Called to testify against García, one of his cellmates said that all the prisoners would kneel and pray twice a day in front of these images—but not the bookseller. When asked why, he answered that a cell was not a proper place to pray to an image. Images were to be worshipped inside temples, not around latrines. Such filthy places, so García argued, were unworthy and therefore unfit for the display of sacred images.

García's position on the suitability of the devotional environment was not limited to him or his circumstances in the Toledo jail. The concepts of idolatry, filth, and pollution also arise in many other contexts, beginning with the anonymous Sevillian author of the pamphlet who (as we have already seen) expressly connected idolatry with homosexual intercourse. And this association can also be observed through analysis of the ritual structure of iconoclastic attacks on religious images.[33] To illustrate this point, a final example comes from a priest seized in 1486 in southern Castile on the charge of crypto-Judaism.[34] The priest had assaulted an image placed on the street—a common location for images in late medieval towns, where the boundaries between the sacred and the profane where sometimes hardly distinguishable.[35] This case is especially interesting because the protagonist perfectly represents the persona of the anonymous author of the Sevillian pamphlet: both were learned priests, both were former Jews, and both considered themselves to be good Christians.

The priest, named Andrés González, always passed on his daily walk in Calatrava (Ciudad Real) an image of Christ "drawn in the same form as he [Christ] appeared to Saint Gregory." The image was therefore a Man of Sorrows, probably similar to the *Varón de Dolores* (the Spanish term for the type) painted by Juan Sánchez de San Román. The type of image chosen for the priest's desecration is also significant because it was one of those late medieval images that were privileged with indulgences, which made them, at least in a certain way, interactive.[36] González's assault was, therefore, not only against images as a representation of the divine based on an intellectual prejudice, but also against the role images played as religious mediations in the global economy of salvation.

According to his testimony, the priest would often stop and urinate at the feet of this image. What's more, he once even tried to remove the image with a rod, beating it until he was exhausted. This testimony came not from the pressure of interrogation but from the accused's voluntary confession. This was certainly not a case of crypto-Judaism; as he himself admitted, the reason for his assault was that he found the place indecorous.

Andrés González's statement may be highlighted with the help of the "Sevillian affair." Public images had also been a key point of argument between Fray Hernando de Talavera and the Sevillian *converso*. An entire chapter of the *Catolica Impugnación* was devoted to defending the Christian custom of locating sacred images in "filthy" places such as street corners, public markets, or the portals of buildings; and while he admitted that some of these places might not be appropriate, the Friar rationalized such public placement of images on the basis of their prophylactic powers.[37] In this context the priest's assault on the image of the Man of Sorrows can be interpreted as a "paradoxical desecration," an agonic act of protest against the ubiquity of images in public urban spaces.[38]

From Devotion to Theory

So far we have been moving from social history to art history and back again in order to understand the very complicated and multifaceted Sevillian context in which images were created and used. For a deeper understanding of the circumstances, and to establish a correlation between the religious/social conflict and a specific development in imagery, we must introduce another element: the theological writings on image-worship.

Image-worship had been a controversial issue in the late Middle Ages in Iberia; it was slow to blossom in Castile until the beginning of the fifteenth century, but by the 1450s the practice had grown so important that it appeared as an almost inevitable topic in the treatises *adversus iudeos*. There was much discussion about images whenever and wherever they were contested, and this discussion prompted Christians to reflect on how images characterized them as a discrete social group. This process of self-reflection should be studied as a dynamic development that transcends static evidence. It is also relevant for this study that the literature is far from homogeneous. Especially in the case of images, the surviving texts vary greatly, in both form and content, primarily according to whether the author was an "old Christian" (*cristiano viejo*) or a converted Jew, and ranging from positive enthusiasm toward images as cult objects to a modest defense of their value as memory-aids for *illiterati*.

Among these treatises, there is one very specific text whose ideological influence on the Inquisitorial discourse can hardly be overestimated. Haim Beinart described Fray Alonso de Espina, author of the *Fortalitium Fidei* or "The Fortress of Faith," as the "father of the rigorous and hard attitude on

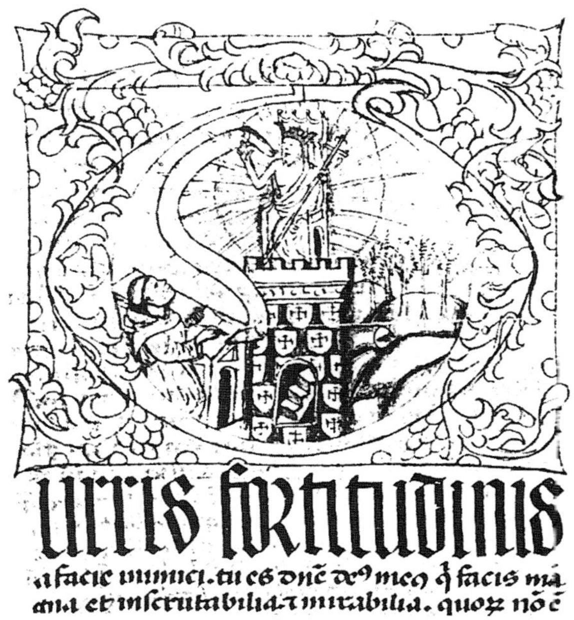

9.5. Fray Alonso de Espina, "Fortalitium Fidei" (illustrator unknown). Biblioteca Capitular de la Catedral del Burgo de Osma (Soria), Ms. 154. Photo courtesy Carlos Espí Forcen.

heresy prosecution" and considered his work "[a] catechism of hate towards Jews" (Figure 9.5).[39] Although images have hardly been considered in relation to Spanish apologetics, Fray Alonso devoted a whole chapter to this topic in the *Fortalitium*; he also brought this subject to bear on other occasions when accusations of idolatry had to be contested. In contrast to other authors who assign to images a much more routine role, Espina placed images at the heart of his spiritual economy.

Unlike any of his predecessors, Fray Alonso in the "Fortress of Faith" does not treat images as a discrete subject. On the contrary, he deals globally with accusations of idolatry, defending first the adoration Christians profess to the Eucharist and then the adoration of images. It is clear that he linked these acts of devotion because he believed the problem of cult, or worship, could not be analyzed independently, and that both images and Eucharist were part of one and the same complex system of mediations established through the incarnation. In theological terms we would say that Espina's effort was to show how images were part of an economy of grace, even an "economy of the visible,"[40] and therefore much more than just vicarious substitutes of the Word for the unlettered. For this reason, his arguments would be better characterized as a clear step toward the "sacramentalization" of images, which Ernst Kitzinger described as a sort of "re-enactment" of the Incarnation.[41]

Espina remarked that the highest form of worship, the *adoratio* or *latria*, should be directed both to the Eucharist and to images of Christ.[42] Although often contested, this position spread widely among fifteenth-century theologians. While the adoration of the Eucharist was considered to be obligatory at least since the Lateran Council of 1215,[43] the highest form of image-worship (adoration or *latria*) had been reserved by Thomas Aquinas for crucifixes alone, relying on a psychological (or, we might say, *semiotic*) argument that regarded the sensible image as a medium that enabled direct communication between the referent and the soul of the observer who stood before it. According to Aquinas, worship could be directed either toward the image as a material object or as a sign of something different from itself; consequently, crucifixes were to be adored only *qua* representations, only "insofar" as they referred to Christ himself but, at the same time, with the same quality of cult as their *Urbilder*.[44]

However intellectually subtle Aquinas's explanation, the Angelic Doctor was solving an ancient problem but creating a new one: if images are only material "signs," are they not at the same time related to the other sacraments institutionally and functionally, and therefore deserving of the same external forms of reverence?[45] Espina pushed this contradiction forward.

Espina despised those who, like the nominalist philosopher Robert Holkot, had argued against Aquinas's image-worship theories (and this opposition was very much alive in the mid-fifteenth century).[46] He intended to show that images—or at least certain christological images—could also be related to the sacraments from a structural point of view. In so doing Espina departed from Saint Paul's metaphor of Christ as the "image of the invisible God" (Colossians 1, 15) in order to show how images could partake of sacramental grace. To validate his proposition he collected several examples in which Christ had manifested himself through images, in pictures as well as sculptures. Just as God's image had been manifested in Christ, reasoned Espina, so had Christ manifested himself in history through material representations.

The Friar took his examples from different sources: some came from John of Damascus, the *De fide Orthodoxa* (the legend of Abgar's portrait of Christ); others were selected from popular oral culture, such as his references to the Veronica or to the portraits attributed to Saint Luke that were to be seen in Rome;[47] the rest came from The Golden Legend, a book rich in antisemitic legends that featured images as protagonists.[48]

If the first group proved Jesus' personal approval of the devotional use of images, the second concerned their theological status. Interestingly, the last group of examples was introduced not as a general vindication of images but in the chapter where Espina defends the Eucharist against the Jews' attacks on the impossibility of transubstantiation, citing examples provided by images as a way to explain how this miracle could happen (Figure 9.6). This equation of Eucharist and images (or images and Eucharist) has to be understood both ways, for it was not only images that could explicate transubstantiation but the sacramental reality that communion was "visually ingested." In fact, in late fifteenth-century Castile, avoiding eye contact with the Host during the rite of its elevation was a common accusation against *conversos*. In 1487 a Hieronimyte monk from the monastery of Lupiana was accused of not looking at the Host during consecration and, more curious, of holding it inclined over his head in such a way that the faithful could not clearly see it—thereby precluding their fall into idolatry.[49]

On the basis of such accounts, it is hardly surprising that when Espina explains how the wafer becomes Christ's body without this metamorphosis being literally visible, he considers images as examples. Out of twelve cases Espina collected to show that the Eucharist had manifested its virtue when attacked or profaned,[50] three used images as examples; while being desecrated, all these images had given outward signs of holding a personal *virtus* or of being animated, especially bleeding.[51] These included icons from Constantinople in Emperor Constantine's time, and also the famous case of the Beirut Christ, a legend about the crucifix carved by the mythical Nicodemus.[52] The Beirut legend held that the figure of Christ actually bled from its wound when a group of Jews performed a satirical pantomime of Christ's death, using the wooden crucifix as victim.

These stories have left scant evidence in Spanish visual culture.[53] But they certainly influenced how paintings and sculptures were perceived—sometimes with dramatic consequences. It can hardly be a coincidence, for example, that the ritual profanation of a crucifix in Zaragoza in 1484 (when different members of a family were said to have been surprised while whipping a crucifix) is an exact representation of what Espina had described only a few years before. Some of these episodes have been taken as historical fact, but it is much more likely that most of them only represent an increasing paranoia about *conversos'* presumed iconoclastic desecrations.

As these anecdotes became folklore, the authority and "virtue" of old images was reinforced. This was undoubtedly the case with the uncertain but probably Rhenish origin of "Cristo de Burgos" (Figure 9.7), which could be the most important sacred image in Castile after the fifteenth century.[54] Although at least a century older, this Crucifix is first recorded in 1465 in Castile when a Bohemian nobleman and his steward traveling through Spain were told about its miraculous powers.[55] At the middle of the century Burgos still had an important Jewish community. Gabriel Tetzel remarked how Christians, Jews, and Moors

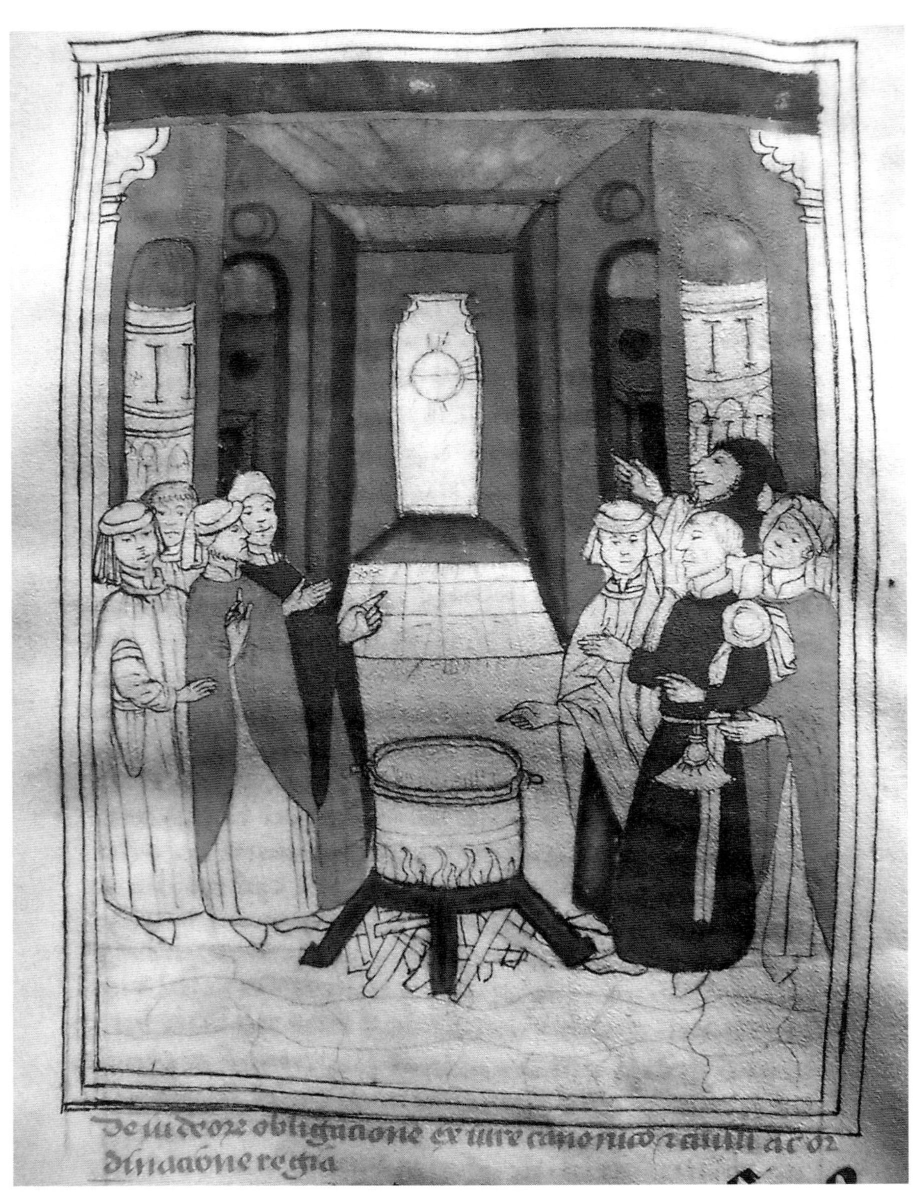

9.6. "Miracle of the Host," in Fray Alonso de Espina, "Fortalitium Fidei" (illustrator unknown). Biblioteca Capitular de la Catedral del Burgo de Osma (Soria), Ms. 154 f. 108r. Photo courtesy Carlos Espí Forcen.

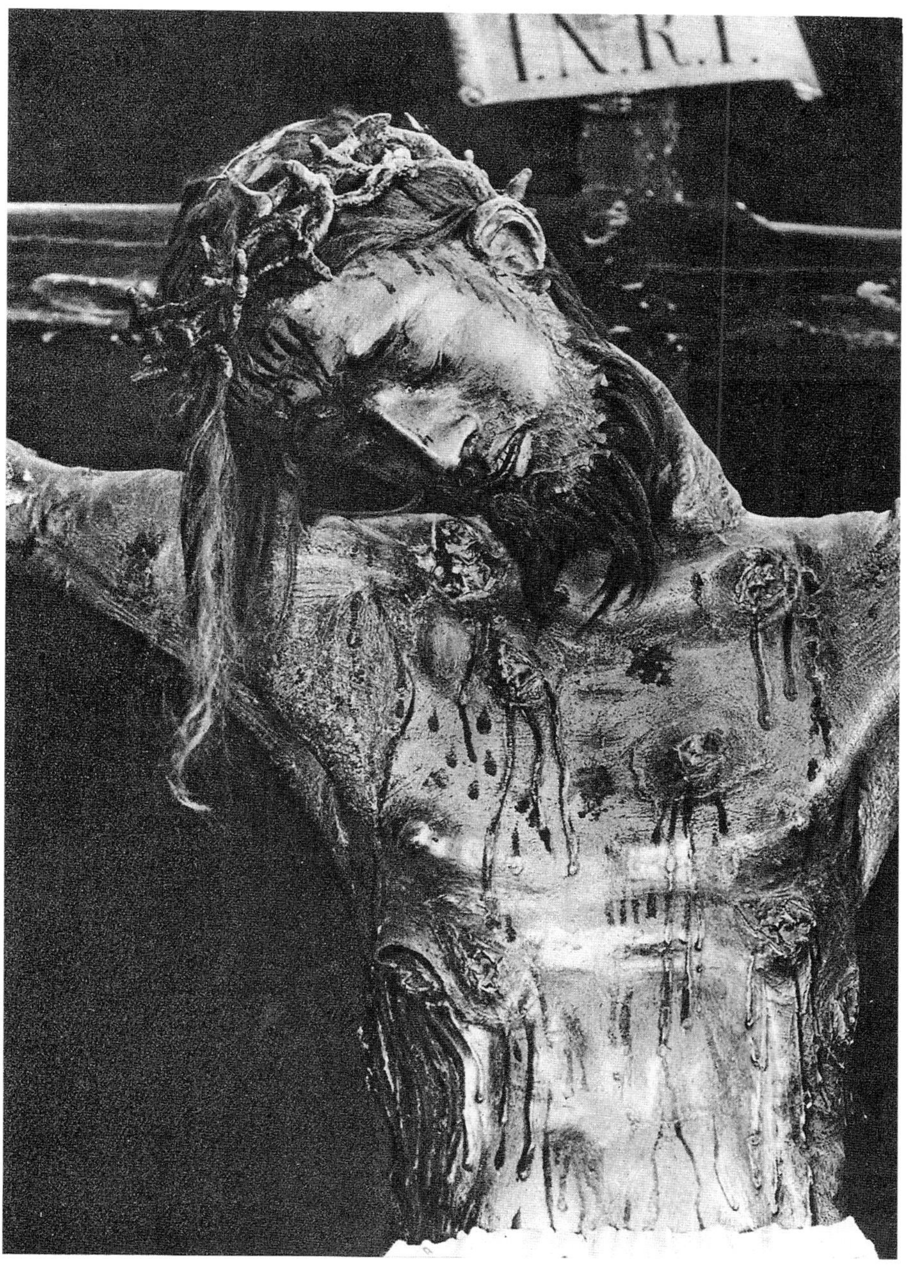

9.7. "Cristo de Burgos," Burgos Cathedral. Photo from José Ortiz Echagüe, *España Mística* (Madrid: Mayfe, 1943).

(*Heiden*) lived peacefully in town under the tolerant government of the local authorities who "let each person believe in his own faith."[56] At the monastery of St. Augustine where the image was kept, visitors could attend two miraculous healings. Inquiries about the origin of the image were answered with the story that it had arrived from the sea and had been made by Christ's disciple, Nicodemus. The two preeminent qualities associated with the Beirut Crucifix— antiquity (heritage) and power to miraculously heal—developed in a peculiar way when transplanted to the specific context of Iberia.

Especially significant for our present argument is Tetzel's note that the miraculous nature of this crucifix was first recognized by the *converso* bishop of Burgos, Pablo de Santa María (c. 1350/55–1435),[57] one of the most important biblical authorities of the late Middle Ages (who was formerly Selemó Ha-Leví but better known as *Paulus Burguensis*). The image would therefore have had the support of the Bishop and would have exercised an important effect at least on members of his family who had not converted.

The case of the Cristo de Burgos is most important, because Pablo de Santa María exemplifies an intellectual attitude toward images contrary to that of Fray Espina. In his widely read *Scrutinium scripturarum* (1434), composed after his conversion,[58] the former rabbi remained on the defensive, leaving the problem of image-worship in the background and emphasizing instead the use of images as memory-aids or instruments to excite devotion:

> The prohibition is not superfluous to the making of sculptures, because one who makes a sculpture and adores it is breaking two different precepts, but if he adores images already made, but he did not make them, then he is breaking only one command. Nevertheless, he who makes [an image], but does not adore it, nor makes it with the intention of being adored, is breaking no precept at all. And so you have here the clear sense of these prohibitions, so that you cannot accuse us any more of disobedience. Because we usually make figures and images in our oratories not for them to be adored or to venerate them like Gods, but only for the use of those, especially the unlettered, to remember the heroic deeds and virtuous actions of the saints, and be moved spiritually in the adoration of God, and the imitation of the Saints.[59]

Santa María was not alone in undermining the cult value of images. The same approach is to be found in most of the *converso* writings about images in the second half of the fifteenth century, from Pedro de Cavalleria's *Zelus Christi contra iudaeos* (1450)[60] to the *Dialogus Ecclesiae et Synagoge* that Gonzalo García de Santa María published in Zaragoza in 1488.[61] If the former exalted the

   FELIPE PEREDA

importance of images (*litterae figurales*) for their power to make accessible the sacred stories for those unable to read, the latter defended their power to spark emotion: "For we don't use images to be adored, but to remember God's goodness, and to excite our passions [*affectus*], because through sight the hearts of men are very much excited. And, therefore, we often stare with our eyes, so that through images men can be brought to mourning and weeping."[62]

Ironically, both Pedro de Cavallería and Alfonso Garcia de Santa María were involved in a case of alleged ritual profanation of an image in Zaragoza at the end of the century.[63] Both had written enthusiastically about the devotional function of images, and both placed the power of images to excite emotions at the core of their defense of figurative representations. It would be impossible and probably misleading to construct a coherent *converso* attitude toward images, given the scarce but also contradictory documents available. At the same time, the surviving texts show that in Castile images were approached from very different theological sensibilities, and that confrontations about the "proper" use of images dramatize those different perspectives. In this context, the strong claim for the cult function of images made by Fray Alonso de Espina is in many ways exceptional. Contrary to other authorities, and in a mode that was to remain almost canonical after the Inquisition had been established, Espina put forward a theory of the image that could be said to address a "sacramental gaze."[64] But this experience involved more than just a psychological dimension—as has been traditionally emphasized for late medieval imagery; at the same time, it implied a sociological one. The act of perception certainly had to do with what people sought to achieve *from* looking, but also with what people were socially expected to do *when* looking—that is, the specific environment in which images were confronted and the public respect to be shown. The evidence of the Inquisition documents we have analyzed here proves that the newly enforced devotional protocols of the last two decades of the fifteenth century had a demonstrable effect on the public and private behavior of the converted minorities.

We observed early in this chapter that the "cultic" value and function of images were not independent of a manifest trend in contemporary stylistic development—at least as far as we can tell on the basis of the Sevillian work that survives. If painters working in Seville in the years immediately after the new regulations reformed the studios were quick to adopt northern novelties, their efforts were simultaneously counterbalanced by an interest in preserving the dignity that characterized the old, charismatic medieval models. A perfect illustration of this confluence of stylistic trends, I would suggest, is Sánchez de San Román's "Man of Sorrows," a picture believed to represent the true form in which Christ had shown himself to Saint Gregory. For this panel employs pictorial devices intended to make images empathically effective, while preserving the *decorum* associated with sacred ancient icons.

NOTES

This chapter summarizes the first chapter of my book, *Las imágenes de la discordia. Política y poética de la imagen sagrada en la España del '400* (Madrid, 2007). I thank Thomas Grizzard for editing the text.

1. H. del Pulgar, *Crónica de los Reyes Católicos* (Madrid, 1943), I, 335.

2. "Iten, porque es cosa razonable que las casas de los fieles cristianos sean munidas y guardadas de la memoria de la passión de nuestro Redentor Jesucristo y de su bendita Madre, queremos y ordenamos que cada fiel cristiano tenga en la casa de su morada alguna imagen pintada de la cruz, en que nuestro Señor Jesucristo padeció, y algunas imágenes pintadas de nuestra Señora o de algunos santos o santas, que provoquen y despierten a los que allí moran a devoción." Hernando de Talavera, *Católica Impugnación,* ed. F. Márquez and F. Martín Hernández (Barcelona, 1961), 186.

3. This legal document, which would certainly have had a big impact on local workshops' production, has gone unnoticed in art historical analyses of the period.

4. "Petición presentada en el Cabildo de Sevilla, el 18 de Septiembre de 1480" (Actas Capitulares del Arch. Municipal de Sevilla 45–47), in J. Gestoso y Pérez, *Ensayo de un diccionario de artífices que florecen en Sevilla durante el siglo XIII al XVIII,* 3 vols. (Sevilla, 1899). Now in C. Rallo Grus, *Aportaciones a la técnica y estilística de la pintura mural en Castilla a final de la Edad Media. Tradición e influencia islámica* (Madrid, 2002), 451–52.

5. C. R. Post, *A History of Spanish Painting, V: The Hispano-Flemish Style in Andalucía* (Cambridge, Mass., 1934), 3–59.

6. On the complex issue of anachronism and early modern painting, see A. Nagel and C. S. Wood, "Interventions: Toward a New Model of Renaissance Anachronism," *Art Bulletin* 87, no. 5 (2005), 403–15, and the subsequent responses.

7. On this panel, see J. M. Serrera, "Un Cristo Varón de Dolores de Juan Sánchez de San Román, Juan Sánchez II, en el Prado," *Boletín del Museo del Prado* 23 (1987), 75–84.

8. The topic has a vast bibliography. See now A. Gormans and T. Lentes, eds., *Das Bild der Erscheinung. Die Gregorsmesse im Mittelalter,* Kultbild. Visualität und Religion in der Vormoderne, 3 (Berlin, 2007).

9. F. Pereda, "'Eyes that they should not see, and ears that they should not hear': Literal Sense and Spiritual Vision in the 'Fountain of Life,'" in *To Tell, Think and Experience Religious Images in the Early Modern Period* (Leuven, in press).

10. Cf. H. Grootenboer, "The Invisibility of Depth," in *The Rhetoric of Perspective: Realism and Illusionism in Seventeenth-Century Dutch Still-Life Painting* (Chicago and London, 2005), 21–59.

11. Although the legend suggests much greater antiquity, this icon is first mentioned in 1453. See M. López Pérez, *El Santo Rostro de Jaén* (Córdoba, 1995).

12. For an overview, see M. Ainsworth, "À la façon grèce: The Encounter of Northern Renaissance Artists with Byzantine Icons," in *Byzantium: Faith and Power (1261–1557)*, Metropolitan Museum of Art (New Haven and London, 2004), 545–55.

13. I am thinking here, for example, of the different versions Francisco de Zurbarán made of the *Veronica*.

14. For a distinction between the two from the standpoint of Catholic theology, see R. Guardini, *Kultbild und Andachtsbild* (Würzburg, 1939). For a historical narrative of this evolution, see H. Belting, *Das Bild und sein Publikum im Mittelalter. Form und Funktion früher*

FELIPE PEREDA

Bildtafeln der Passion (1981; 2nd ed., Berlin, 1995). On the general difficulty of defining the distinction between devotional and cult images, see D. Freedberg, "Holy Images and Other Images," in *The Art of Interpreting*, ed. S. Scott (Philadelphia, 1992), 69–80.

15. Cf. H. Belting, *Likeness and Presence: A History of the Image before the Era of Art* (Chicago, 1994).

16. The text itself has been lost, but its content is well preserved in the response written by Fray Hernando de Talavera, *Católica Impugnación*, ed. F. Márquez (Barcelona, 1961).

17. The best biography is still that in F. Márquez Villanueva, *Investigaciones sobre Juan Álvarez Gato. contribución al conocimiento de la literatura castellana del siglo XV* (Madrid, 1974), 104–54. In 1506, Talavera would be tried for "Judaizing" along with several members of his family. Due to Julius II's intervention he was finally absolved: T. Herrero del Collado, "El proceso inquisitorial por delito de herejía contra Hernando de Talavera," *Anuario de Historia del Derecho Español* 39 (1969), 671–706.

18. "Y entonces terminaron allí, San Pedro y Santiago, esta cuestión, declarando . . . que no debían guardar la ley de Moisén, ni tampoco las ceremonias gentílicas, más que se abstuviesen de comer las cosas que eran sacrificadas a los ídolos, y de la fornicación. . . . [Talavera's response:] Así que parece claramente que allí no fueron defendidas las imágenes ni aún el pecado contra natura, salvo si este necio malicioso llama a la fornicación pecado contra natura, como es verdad que Aristóteles la ha por tal, hablando en su Económica." *Católica Impugnación*, 188.

19. "También ha por yerro este necarrión y burla de ello que digamos santa María la antigua y santa María la nueva, etc. Verdad es que no tiene más *virtud* la imagen vieja que la nueva; ni aún tampoco la iglesia, si ambas son bendecidas o consagradas; mas puede el pueblo cristiano tener más afección y más devoción de obtener oraciones y sacrificios a nuestro Señor ante la imagen antigua o en la iglesia vieja, porque allí han sido muchas veces oídas sus oraciones y han sido consolados de nuestro Señor y librados de sus necesidades y tribulaciones. Lo cual no tienen así experimentado ante la imagen moza, o en la iglesia nueva." Ibid., 197.

20. For a hypothetical reconstruction of this image's origins, see *Las imágenes de la discordia*, 145–81.

21. "Piensa este necarrión que es grande inconveniente escoger de hacer nuestra oración ante las imágenes mejor pintadas y más adornadas, mas no es inconveniente ni yerro alguno, porque esto no se hace creyendo que aquella imagen, mejor pintada, tenga más virtud que las otras, más porque naturalmente huelga nuestro entendimiento en lo mejor y más apto y, como todo el bien que la imagen tiene, cualquier que ella sea, consista en representar bien aquello que representa, cuanto mejor lo hace, tanto más aplace, como los que se miran en espejo quieren y escojen aquel que hace mejor cara; y cuanto el libro es de mejor letra, tanto más agrada. También ha este necio por inconveniente, que se diga que la imagen ríe y que llora y que suda. Verdad es que puede haber y de hecho hay en esto muchas burlas y mucho sacadinero, pero es bien posible que ría y llore y sude y hable, que es más, y se mueva y se absente presente, entendiéndolo todo esto sanament[e]." *Católica Impugnación*, 189.

22. "La Iglesia no adora a aquellas imágenes, agora sean de pincel, agora de bulto, quier sean de palo, quier de piedra, quier de algún metal, ni adoran las personas, que por esas son ideadas, imaginadas y representadas, como las adoraban los paganos idólatras y necios gentiles [but] tenemos y honramos las imágenes porque nos reducen a la memoria y nos representan a aquelllas personas y cosas, cuyas imaginaciones son, y nos recuerdan de ellas." Ibid., 138–39.

23. Unfortunately, no statistical study is available. Comparative studies for Valencia, however, show that private images began to appear on the Iberian peninsula only after the

middle of the fifteenth century. Writing in Castile ca. 1315, Martín Pérez could even warn against those who thought that keeping images in a private oratory was sinful: *Libro de las Confesiones. Una radiografía de la sociedad medieval,* ed. M. N. Sánchez (Madrid, 2002), 40.

24. Archivo Histórico Nacional, Inquisición legajo [henceforth AHN, Inq. Leg.]130, 2: "Puede aver quatro años poco mas o menos que este testigo fue a casa del dicho d de acosta a pedille una escriptura como escribano de la dicha villa e este t[estig]o subio por una escalera a un entresuelo del dicho d de acosta e estaban alli el dicho d de acosta y el dicho gonzalo de acosta su padre en pie bueltos hazia la pared y no vido ymagen este t en la pared. . . . Preguntado si en aquel tiempo si entro en los dichos palaçios de dia e si vido puesta en la pared alguna ymagen, o colgada en algun paramento, o paño, dijo que este testigo [que] entro en los dichos palaçios algunas vezes de dia pero que no se acordaba de aver visto en ellas ymagen ninguna."

25. H. Beinart, *Records of the Trials of the Spanish Inquisition in Ciudad Real, II: The Trials of 1494–1512 in Toledo* (Jerusalem, 1977), 539.

26. AHN, Inq., Leg. 150, 3 [Toledo, January 9,1500].

27. "Nunca tuvo ni tiene ni costumbró tener en su casa oratorio de la Virgen María ni de Jhu. Xristo, ni de sus santos, segunt que xristianos costumbran tener e delant de los quales fazen oración." B. Llorca, "La Inquisición española y los conversos judíos y marranos," *Sefarad* 8 (1942), 357–89.

28. "Et por mostrar mejor su herejía no tenía en su casa imagen ni figura de santo, ni de santa alguna, ni la señal de la cruz, ni otra señal de christiano, porque no se tenía por tal." Beinart, *Records of the Trials of the Spanish Inquisition in Ciudad Real, II,* 12.

29. There is, however, an important literature that admits as historical most reports of rituals or satirical pantomimes that included the desecration of images. See most recently D. M. Gitlitz, *Secreto y engaño. La religión de los criptojudíos* (Valladolid, 2003), 167. Elsewhere Gitlitz discusses this more extensively: "Las presuntas profanaciones judías del ritual cristiano en el decreto de expulsion," in *Judíos. Sefarditas. Conversos. La expulsión de 1492 y sus consecuencias,* ed. Á. Alcalá (Valladolid, 1995), 150–69. See also, although with a wider perspective, M. Alpert, "Did Spanish Crypto-Jews Desecrate Christian Images and Why? The Case of the *Cristo de la Paciencia (1629–32),* the *Romance* of 1717 and the Events of November 1714 in the *Calle del Lobo,*" in *Faith and Fanaticism: Religious Fervour in Early Modern Spain,* ed. L. Twomey (Ashgate, 1997), 85–94.

30. AHN, Inq., Leg. 183, 787. Cf. F. Baer, *Die Juden in christlichen Spanien. II. Kastilien/ Inquisitionsakten* (Berlin, 1936), 448.

31. AHN, Inq., Leg. 150, 9: "Oyendo las cosas y peligros que se syguían a los nuevamente convertidos de tener ymágines en sus casas y los testimonios que les levantaban diziendo que açotavan las ymágines y otros vituperios que cree que les levantan, ovo por bien de sufrir antes de no tener ymagen en su casa que no estar atado a un falso testimonio que una moça le quisiese levantar." His wife's testimony followed: mejor tenía que dijesen que no tenía ninguna imagen en su casa, que no que dijesen lo que avían dicho de aquel que disen que tenía las imágenes adonde tenía el baçín."

32. F. Baer, *Die Juden in christlichen Spanien. II. Kastilien/Inquisitionsakten* (Berlin, 1936), 464–65. Y. Baer, *Historia de los Judíos de la España Cristiana* (1945; reprint, Barcelona, 1998), 807–17. And now A. Y. D'Abrera, *The Tribunal of Zaragoza and Crypto-Judaism 1484–1515* (Brepols, 2008), 185–87.

33. Cf. N. Z. Davis, "The Rites of Violence," in *Society and Culture in Early Modern France* (1965; reprint, Oxford, 2004), 152–87.

34. AHN, Inq. Leg. 153, 7, f. 6: "Digo mi culpa e acúsome dello. Otrosy digo mi culpa que viviendo en una casa entre çerca de la cárçel del rey a un rincón detrás de la puerta al

unbral de arriba estaba debujado un cruçifijo en sy como aparesçio a san gregorio e muchas vezes viniendo por de andar por la villa vertia aguas en aquel rincon, por mi poca fe fazía aquel denuesto. Otrosí digo mi culpa que un día tomé una vara por le quitar de tan desonesto lugar, e prové arrancar el yeso o cal en que estava debujado, e di çiertos golpes por lo quitar e non pude, digo dello mi culpa que lo fazía con poca fe por lo quitar de allí denostando a quien allí lo debujó, digo mi culpa dello."

35. Cf. E. Muir, "The Virgin on the Street Corner: The Place of the Sacred in Italian Cities," in *Religion and Culture in the Renaissance and Reformation*, ed. S. Ozment (Kirksville, Mo., l989), 25–40; M. Camille, "Signs on Medieval Street Corners," in *Die Strasse. Zur Funktion und Rezeption öffentlichen Raums im späten Mittelalter* (Vienna, 2001), 91–117.

36. In this precise case, 11,000 years of purgatory for every "Our Father". See more recently C. W. Bynum, "Seeing and Seeing Beyond: The Mass of St. Gregory in the Fifteenth Century," in *The Mind's Eye: Art and Theological Argument in the Middle Ages*, ed. Jeffrey F. Hamburger and Anne-Marie Bouché (Princeton, 2006), 208–40; H. Scalie, "Erscheinung und Bildvorstellung im Spätmittelalterlichen Kulturtransfer: Die Rezeption der Imago Pietatis als Selbstoffenbarung Christi in Rom," in *Das Bild der Erscheinung. Die Gregorsmesse im Mittelalter*, Kultbild. Visualität und Religion in der Vormoderne, 3, ed. A. Gormans and T. Lentes (Berlin, 2007), 58–121; C. Hecht, "Von der Imago Pietatis zur Gregormesse. Ikonographie der Eucharistie vom Hohen Mittelalter bis zur Epoche der Humanismus," *Römisches Jahrbuch der Bibliotheca Hertziana* 36 (2005), 9–44.

37. *Católica Impugnación*, chap. 57, 197–200.

38. It is interesting to compare this case with contemporary cases documented in Italy, in which Jews where punished for removing images from private dwellings, even if they had previously acquired a license from the local Christian authorities. See M. Luzzati, "Ebrei, chiesa locale, 'principe' e popolo: due episodi di distruzione di immagini sacre alla fine del Quattrocento," *Quaderini Storici* 54, no. 3 (1983), 847–77. In contrast, the case of the spontaneous desecration of several public religious images in Florence in the 1490s, as recently analyzed by Dana E. Katz, was not perpetrated by a local Jew but by a certain Sephardic Jew named Bartolomeo de Cases, who had probably been expelled from the Iberian peninsula in 1492: see "The Jew, the Madonna, and the Mob in Republican Florence," in *The Jew in the Art of the Italian Renaissance* (Philadelphia, 2008), 99–109.

39. H. Beinart, *Los conversos ante el Tribunal de la Inquisición* (Barcelona, 1983), 19–20. For Espina, see B. Netanyahu, "Alonso de Espina: Was He a New Christian?," *Proceedings of the American Academy for Jewish Research* 43 (1976), 107–65, where he corrects the mistaken assumption that Espina belonged to a *converso* family. A. Meyuhas Ginio, *De bello iudaeorum. Fray Alonso de Espina y su Fortalitium Fidei*, Fontes Iudaeorum Regni Castellae 8 (Salamanca, 1998); Ginio, *La fortresse de la foi. La vision du monde d'Alonso de Espina, moine espagnol (?–1466)* (Paris, 1998); S. McMichael, *Was Jesus of Nazareth the Messiah? Alphonso de Espina's Argument against the Jews in the Fortalitium Fidei (c. 1464)* (Atlanta, 1994).

40. M.- J. Mondzain, *Image, Icône, Économie. Les sources byzantines de l'imaginaire contemporain* (Paris, 1996).

41. E. Kitzinger, "The Cult of Images in the Age before Iconoclasm," *Dumbarton Oaks Papers* 8 (1954), 85–150.

42. "Circa vero ymaginum venerationem dicitur quod Christi ymago et crux et alie sanctorum ymagines dupliciter possunt considerari. Uno modo ut sunt ymagines dei aut virginis marie sev sanctorum, deum vel virginem mariam aut aliquem sanctorum representantes. Secundario ut sunt quedam res puta aurum et argentum lignum sive lapis, et illo secundo modo considerando nulla veneratio eis exhiberi debet immo crimen ydolatrie incurrere, qui ut sunt solum res quedam ipsas veneraretur. Alio modo possunt considerari ut representant

Ihesum Christum aut virginem maria*m* sev sanctos paradisi et sic utiq*ue* venerari debe*nt* etia*m* eade*m* veneratio*ne* qua ymaginatu*m* veneratur et ita crux Christi et eius ymago venerari debet adoratione latrie ymago autem virgi*nis* marie alioru*m*que sanctorum venerari debe*nt* veneratione dulie q*uia* tot*us* honor refertur ad p*ro*totypum i*d est,* ad exe*m*plar sev ymagina-tum et hec est opinio Thome in iii sententiarum distinctione ii." *Fortalitium Fidei* (1487), f. m ii r–v.

43. So believed, for example, by Lucas Tudensis, *Adversus Albigensium errores Libri III* (Ingolstadt, 1612), 144, written ca. 1230.

44. T. Aquinas, *Summa Theologiae,* III, q. 25, a. 3.

45. E. Bevan, *Holy Images: An Inquiry into Idolatry and Image-Worship in Ancient Pagan-ism and in Christianity* (London, 1940), 150–58; J. Wirth, "Structures et fonctions de l'image chez Saint Thomas d'Aquin," in *L'Image. Fonctions et usages des images dans l'Occident médié-val,* Cahiers du Léopard d'Or, ed. J. Baschet and J.-C. Schmitt (Paris, 1996), 56. See also J. C. Schmitt, "De Nicée à Thomas d'Aquin: l'émancipation de l'image religieuse en Occident," in *Le corps des images. Essais sur la culture visuelle au Moyen Âge* (Paris, 2002), 63–95. For an overview, J. Wirth, "Faut-il adorer les images? La théorie du culte des images jusqu'au concile de Trente," in *Iconoclasme. Vie et mort de l'image médiévale* (Zurich, 2001), 28–37.

46. J. Wirth, "Théorie et pratique de l'image Sainte á la veille de la réforme," *Biblio-thèque d'Humanisme et Renaissance* 48, no. 2 (1986), 319–58; Wirth, "La critique scolastique de la théorie thomiste de l'image," in *Crises de l'image religieuse/Krisen religiöser Kunst,* ed. O. Christin and D. Gamboni, Éditions de la Maison des sciences de l'homme Paris (Paris, 1999), 93–109.

47. The bibliography on this topic is quite extensive. For the revival of both legends at the end of the Middle Ages, see H. L. Kessler and G. Wolf, eds., *The Holy Face and the Paradox of Representation* (Bologna, 1998); G. Wolf, *Schleier und Spiegel. Traditionen des Christusbildes und die Bildkonzepte der Renaissance* (Munich, 2002).

48. These legends were collected by Iacopo della Voragine, *Legenda Aurea,* and they are reproduced in the chapter corresponding to the Feast of the Triumph of the Cross. See L. Kretzenbacher, *Das verletzte Kultbild. Voraussetzungen, Zeitschichten und Aussagewandel eines abendländischen Legendentypus* (Munich, 1977), 58–85.

49. AHN, Inq. Leg. 137, 22 [1487–91]. For similar cases in the Hieronimyte order, to which Fray Hernando de Talavera belonged, see G. D. Starr-LeBeau, *In the Shadow of the Virgin: Inquisitors, Friars and Conversos in Guadalupe, Spain* (Princeton, 2003), 200–223; S. Pastore, "Nascita e fortuna di una leggenda antigiudaica: Fray García de Zapata e gli inizi dell'Inquisizione di Toledo," in *Le Inquisizioni cristiane e gli ebrei. Atti dei convegni lincei* (Rome, 2003), 65–104.

50. For legends of desecration of the Eucharist, see M. Rubin, *Gentile Tales: The Narra-tive Assault on Late Medieval Jews* (Philadelphia, 2004); on Espina, see 46–47.

51. "De sanguine et aqua que exierunt de latere imaginis xpi quod lancea iudei aperuer-unt et quomodo suppositum vas fuit impletum. Quartum mirabile accidit circa annum domini septuagesimumoctavum imperante Constantino quinto qui fuit lxv romanorum imperator, et sedente in cathedra petri paulo primo. Tunc enim in syria civitate herito [*sic*] quidam christianus sub annua pensione hospicium habens ymaginem domini crucifixi contra lectuli faciem parieti afflixerat et ibi orationes suas continuo faciebat. Post annum vero aliam domum locavit et imaginem ibidem ex oblivione reliquit, quidam autem iudeus predictam domum conduxit et die quadam unum de suis contribulibus ad convivium invitavit. Inter epulas autem ille qui invitatus fuerat casu circunspiciens imaginem infixam parieti intuetur, et in illum que se invitavit ira fremens cur imaginem ihesu nazareni tenere audebat commi-natur. Ille autem cum predicta imaginem adhuc non vidisset sacramentis quibus poterat

affirmabat quod illam de qua dicebat imaginem penitus ignorabat. Tunc ille placatum se simulans valefecit et ad principem sue gentis abiens iudeum illum de eo quod viderat accusavit. Iudei ergo congregati ad domum eius conveniunt et visa imagine illum contumeliis diris afflixerunt et extra synagogam semiviuum eiiciunt imaginem vero pedibus conculcantes cuncta in ea dominice passionis obprobia renovarunt. Cum vero latus lancea perforassent pertinus sanguis et aqua ubertim exivit et suppositum vas implevit stupefacti iudei sanguinem illum ad synagogas detulerunt et omnes infirmi ex ipso inuncti pertinus curabantur. Tunc iudei episcopo terre omnia per ordinem narraverunt et baptismatum et fidem xpi unanimiter susceperunt." *Fortalitium Fidei* (1487).

52. E. von Dobschütz, *Christusbilder. Untersuchungen zur christlichen Legende, Texte und Untersuchungen zur Geschichte der altchristlichen Literatur*, 18 (Leipzig, 1899), 280–83**; Sansterre, J.-M., "L'image blesée, l'image souffrante: quelques récits de miracles entre Orient et Occident (VIᵉ–XIIᵉ siècle)," in *Les images dans les sociétés médiévales: Pour une histoire comparé, Bulletin de l'Institut Historique Belge de Rome*, 69 (Rome, 1999), 113–30; M. Bacci, "Quel bello miracolo onde si fa la festa del santo Salvatore: studio sulle metamorfosi di una leggenda," in *Santa Croce e Santo Volto. Contributi allo studio dell'origine e della fortuna del culto del Salvatore (secoli IX–XV)*, ed. G. Rossetti (Pisa, 2002), 7–86.

53. The only Spanish representation of the Beirut crucifix episode is to be found in a Mallorca altarpiece (Felanitx) of the first half of the fifteenth century. See, more recently, C. Espí, *Recrucificando a Cristo. Los judíos de la Passio Imaginis en la isla de Mallorca* (Mallorca, 2009); J. Molina, "La imagen y su contexto. Perfiles de la iconografía antijudía en la España medieval," in *Els jueus a la Girona medieval* (Girona, 2008), 29–82. Medieval representations of Host desecration are frequent in Catalonia, but not in Castile. See Rodríguez Barral, "Eucaristía y antisemitismo en la plástica gótica hispana," *Boletín del Museo e Instituto Camón Aznar* 98 (2006), 279–347.

54. I am currently preparing an extensive work on the history of this image, for which no previous study is available.

55. This according to the testimony of the traveler Leo von Rozmital, *Des böhmischen Herrn Leo's von Rožmital, Ritter-, Hof-und Pilger-Reise durch die Abendlände 1465–1467* (Stuttgart, 1843), 65–67, 167–68.

56. "In seiner stat [the Count of Haro's town of Burgos], auch an seinem hof sein Christen, Heiden, Juden. Jeden lässt er in seinem gelauben beleiben. *Der graf ist ein Crist genant, aber man weiss nit, welches gelauben er ist.*" Ibid., 167.

57. F. Cantera Burgos, *Alvar García de Santa María. Historia de la judería de Burgos y de sus conversos más egregios* (Madrid, 1952), is the most complete biography.

58. G. L. Jones, "Paul of Burgos and the *Adversus Iudaeos* Tradition," *Henoch* 21 (1999), 313–29. The book had several incunabular editions (Strassbourg, 1470; Rome, 1470; Mantua, 1475; Mainz, 1471 and 1478, etc.). I quote from Mainz, 1471.

59. "Non est superflua illa prohibitione de factione sculptilium quia qui fac sculptile et illud adorat est transgressor duorum preceptorum, si autem adorat sculptilia iam facta qua ipse non fecit est transgressor unius precepti tantummodo. Qui autem facit et non adorat nec cum intentione adorandi hoc facit non est transgressor alicuius precepti et sic habes planum sensum harum prohibitionum ex quo non potes nos arguere de earum transgressione. Simulacra enim et ymagines qua conmuniter fiunt in orationis nostris non adorantur neque coluntur ut deus secundum fiunt principaliter ad hoc ut homines praesertim simplices ad memoriam reducant gesta sev facta sanctorum virtuosa sev meritoria, ut inde excitentur ad laudem dei et ad eorum imitationem." *Scrutinium Scripturarum*, fols. 86–86v.

60. P. Cavallería, *Tractatus Zelus Christi contra Iudaeos, sarracenos et infideles* (Venice, 1592).

61. M. Orfali, "El 'Diálogus pro Ecclesia contra Synagogam': un tratado anónimo de polémica antijudía," *Hispania* 54 (1994), 679–732. Published by Gonzalo García de Santa María as *incerto autore,* its author was the converted Teobald de Sezanne, a Dominican friar but also a former Parisian rabbi, c. 1238–45.

62. "Eccle. O lupa fantastica tibi ad memoriam revoco quod dicitur in vulgari proverbio. Credit inesse capro vitium quod habet caper in se. . . . Nos ymagines non ponimus pro adoratione sed pro beneficiorum dei rememoratione et affectione excitatione, quia per visum, multum excitantur corda hominum. Unde videmus saepe ad oculum quia per inspectione ymaginum homines ad gemitas et lacrimas provocateur." *Dialogus Ecclesiae et Synagoge,* fol. viv.

63. For a possible explanation, see *Las imágenes de la discordia,* 98–109.

64. R. Scribner, "Popular Piety and Modes of Visual Perception in Late-Medieval and Reformation Germany," *Journal of Religious History* 15 (1989), 448–69; "Das Visuelle in der Volksfrömmigkeit," in *Bilder und Bildersturm im Spätmittelalter und in der frühen Neuzeit,* Wolfenbütteler Forschungen, Band 46 (Wiesbaden, 1990), 9–20. For a revision of the term, see, more recently, T. Lentes, "As Far as the Eye Can See: Rituals of Gazing in the Late Middle Ages," in *The Mind's Eye: Art and Theological Argument in the Middle Ages* (Princeton, 2006), 360–73.

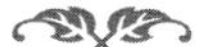

CHAPTER 10

Renaissance Naturalism and the Jewish Bible: Ferrara, Brescia, Bergamo, 1520–1540

Stephen J. Campbell

The confrontation of Synagoga and Ecclesia, a theme recurrent in Northern European art from the thirteenth to the fifteenth centuries, makes a rare and belated Italian appearance in Ferrara in 1523: Garofalo's colossal *Allegory of the Old and the New Testaments*, painted for the refectory of the Augustinian Hermits at S. Andrea, Ferrara, is perhaps the most extreme and forthright statement of Christian anti-Judaism to be produced in Italy, and not least because of its scale and its considerable celebrity (Figure 10.1).[1] Vasari, who somewhat disingenuously described it as "many figures . . . bringing the Old Testament into accord with the New," hailed it as a work of "beautiful and fantastic invention."[2] As an imaginative and technical achievement, it is indeed unsurpassed in Garofalo's work: the surreal horror of its impact results from the combination of a Raphaelesque elevated naturalism, transposed into the rich color of the Ferrarese school, with diagrammatic abstraction. There is also an element of the monstrous, a breach of the codes of naturalism in order to mark the work as *figura* in Augustinian terms, and perhaps also with the resonance that monstrosity (as portent or "showing") would have had in a period of eschatological anxiety.[3] The towering cross, with its strangely bloodless Christ, marks a kind of axis—effectively a historical and confessional divide—that separates Jew from Christian. The cross itself has become a living, hybrid being, sprouting three pairs of human arms. One set of limbs brandishes the papal keys of heaven and hell, and a crown for the regal figure of Ecclesia who is enthroned on the symbols of the Evangelists. Another pair of arms holds the lance of Longinus,

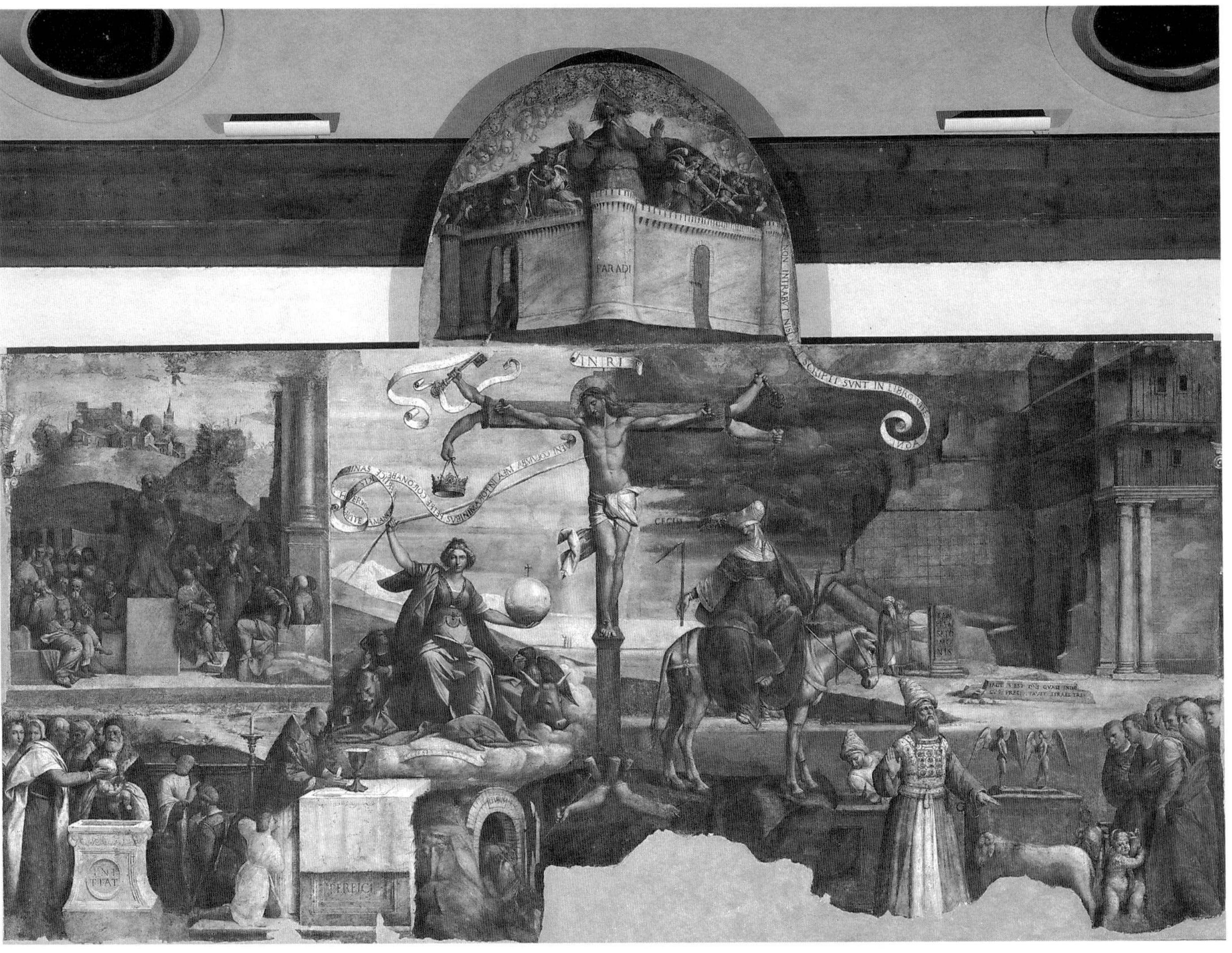

10.1. Garofalo, *Allegory of the Law and the Gospels*, 1523. Ferrara, Pinacoteca. Photo: Alinari/Art Resource, New York.

which is plunged into the heart of Synagoga, a blindfolded and apparently horned woman who rides an ass below the cross, her head framed with the legend CAECID[ITAS]. MOSTRI: "blindness of the monster." Another inscription originally in the lunette above Synagoga paraphrased the text of Isaiah 1:13: "Bring no more vain offerings; incense is an abomination to me. Even though you make many prayers, I will not listen: your hands are full of blood." The ruins of the TEMPLUM SALAMONIS appear nearby; on the same side are the High Priest who turns his back on the cross, along with the horned altar, the Ark of the Covenant, the sacrificial animals, and a naked male child.

Far more than is the case in any earlier representation of the Synagoga/Ecclesia theme, or the variant known as "the Avenging Crucifix" represented here, there seems to be an almost structural and systematic displacement of sacrificial violence from the body of Christ to the enemies of the faith. There is no issue of blood from Christ's side, but rather a silken cord that binds him to the enactment of Penance in a performance of the sacraments to the right: Christian identity and orthodoxy of observance, defined in relation to Christianity's perennial antagonist, is of paramount concern to Garofalo and his Augustinian audience. In addition to the brutal dispatching of a blinded Synagoga, a phalanx of warrior angels in the castle of Paradisum above shoots arrows in the direction of the Jewish assembly. Such a ritualized transformation and redirection of violence will support a number of mutually compatible readings: first, it is an instance of the ritual use of violence against a scapegoat other employed by premodern (and later) Christians in the interests of communal self-definition.[4] Second, to turn to a recent study of the fresco by Dana Katz, it might be seen as an instance of the force of visual representation in rendering acts of surrogate violence, especially in a city whose ruling dynasty long observed a policy of toleration toward the Jews.[5] It could even allow Duke Alfonso d'Este or his chief minister Antonio Costabili (directly involved in the commission) to observe a longstanding and generally popular policy of protecting and encouraging Jewish banking interests while posing at least symbolically as a promoter of Christian orthodoxy.

And that takes us to the heart of the matter: for how was it possible to define, let alone to paint, Christian orthodoxy in 1523? What were the limits of Catholic orthodox beliefs as distinct from new confessional formulations coming from Wittenberg and elsewhere, which challenged the Roman church on the willfulness and inconsistency of its traditions, its errancy from scripture, and the spirit of the early church? And what single representation could possibly do justice to a disquieting variance in Catholic tradition on matters such as the Eucharist, on faith and good works, on penance and salvation? The sharply drawn lines between Synagogue and Ecclesia as we see them in Garofalo's fresco had the certain advantage of allowing Christianity to be defined through confrontation with what it was *not*.[6] Certainly, the fresco bears traces of the historical Jewish community of Ferrara as it appeared to Christian eyes: for instance, the rain of arrows from heaven is normally a sign of plague in Renaissance art. A contemporary viewer might have referred this motif to an outbreak of plague among the Jews of Ferrara in March 1523. "The Jews easily succumb to plague because of their commerce and their avidity for gain," remarked the chronicler Zerbinati.[7] But Jews are more important here as a means of articulating *Christian* identity.

Jews and Judaism, especially (but not exclusively) in the stereotypes of Christian art, offered a means of thinking about norms and boundaries, especially when these needed to be clarified with some urgency. The figurative status of Judaism, a defeated theology, would prove particularly productive in the confessional crisis of the decades before the Council of Trent, and not just among Catholics. In the 1520s, the ultimate target of Garofalo's violently polemical fresco could very well have been the followers of Luther. The news that the 1522–23 smashing of religious images of Wittenberg involved the participation of members of Luther's own Augustinian order would have alarmed, if it did not actually fragment, the Augustinian communities of Italy, like Sant'Andrea in Ferrara.[8] The ruins of the Temple of Solomon, with its vast expanses of blank wall unadorned by images, would have evoked the activity of the iconoclastic and "judaizing" evangelicals.

Correspondingly, the typological opposition of Synagogue and Ecclesia would, within only a few years, also serve the ends of Lutheran self-definition. The resemblances between Garofalo's image of militant Catholicism and Lucas Cranach's *Allegory of the Law and the Gospels* is perhaps not so surprising given their joint roots in Augustinian theology.[9] But while such parallelism between Catholic and Protestant visual polemics will have other later manifestations, Catholic artists will find other uses for typology: the diagrammatic, unrelenting clarity of Garofalo's *Allegory* will not be repeated.

There is a possibility that such imagery may have begun to look "too Lutheran" by the following decade, although such a response cannot be documented. A more likely reason for its lack of an afterlife might be that such imagery of violent intolerance and scapegoatism could have been associated with religious extremism, social fragmentation, and disorder. Before 1523, a symbolic treatment of the Crucifixion such as Garofalo's would have offered a rationalization of the passion and its sacramental significance; the blood that flows is the sign of Christ's union with his church in the Eucharist. Yet the imagery of flowing blood was a dangerously productive symbol, and increasingly a matter of jurisdictional concern on the part of ecclesiastical authority.[10]

STEPHEN J. CAMPBELL

It epitomized a Catholicism of the periphery, as that was imagined to undermine the control of the center: we might think of the copious streaming blood of mystical passion cults with their bleeding Hosts, fantasies of profanation, murderous outbreaks of anti-Jewish violence. Such popular devotional phenomena entailed threats to civil order and clerical authority that the church, both administratively and theologically, was trying to contain and bring under control. Schematic forms of visual propaganda such as those employed here by Garofalo were a passing phase, a testimony not only to a confessional crisis but to a crisis in the representation of doctrine.[11]

I introduce Garofalo's fresco here as an early example of art responding to the imperative of reform. We will see that Catholicism continues to visualize Judaism in order to affirm points of doctrine challenged by the Reformers, clarifying these anew for a Catholic laity, and serving in crucial ways to organize artistic and theological thinking about the status of representation and truth in Christian art. Yet henceforth this typological tendency will manifest a strange and unexpected complicity with new forms of representational naturalism that seem, at first glance, opposed to the diagrammatic tenor of allegorical propaganda.[12]

From the 1520s onward—in other words, well before the 1563 Tridentine ruling on religious images—there are few signs that Christian art was something that itself needed to be reformed.[13] The concern was rather with the category "art" and its adaptability to the urgencies of the religious crisis. What role could art and artists have in the promotion of institutional reform, the clarification of doctrine, and the affirmation of ecclesiastical authority in the face of challenges and contention from within and without the church? The turning point occurs at mid-century, with the attacks on Michelangelo's *Last Judgment*. Up until that point, artists mostly served the cause of Catholic orthodoxy by taking their cue from Raphael, Titian, Leonardo, and Michelangelo—the influential leaders of the *maniera moderna*. The question of art and reform before the crisis of the *Last Judgment* is less about the reform of art itself than about testing the possibilities of the *maniera moderna* to serve the ends of doctrinal reform. The result was a culture of artistic experiment in which artists (such as Lotto, Parmigianino, Michelangelo, Titian) led the way, rethinking the conditions for making altarpieces, sacred narratives, and devotional images. Only with the controversies around the *Last Judgment* do we encounter the rise of a prescriptive theory of art written by clerics such as Giovan Andrea Gilio (1568), Johannes Molanus (1570), and Gabriele Paleotti (1582), and clear instances of art being instrumentalized and normalized in the interests of propagating doctrine.[14]

By the 1520s, a rapid recent transformation in the professionalization of artists had led to the widespread sense that there was something called "art," which might have aims of its own, even as artists continued to fulfill all the traditional tasks assigned to them. Painting, sculpture, and architecture were assuming a strongly institutional profile and were associated with a broadening field of discourse in which practitioners and amateurs participated. The liveliness of this culture was manifest in a plethora of publications, in informal associations of artists, poets, and patrons, and finally, from the 1560s, through incorporated academies of art.[15] Art was widely understood, for instance, not as mimetic representation, but in terms of its fictive character, as the outcome of a process of invention characteristic of poetry. Painting was not just to be the act of picturing or illustrating but as a particular discursivity manifest in the systematic imitation of other art, the pursuit of ideal beauty, and a self-conscious command of the resources of style. These were all at the basis of what can be called "artistic interest"—art as a distinct and privileged form of image production, that asks to be regarded as a distinct and privileged form of visual culture.[16]

In Italy, the pre-Tridentine concern with images is a concern with the exploitation of artistic practice as a living and changing tradition: it is not an attempt to subordinate or even to reform the tradition itself. Garofalo and other Northern Italians whose work we will examine would have seen little tension between being a "modern painter" and responding to the new doctrinal and devotional imperatives. Art was a powerful instrument, not yet a suspect, error-prone practice that required monitoring and regulation. Thus painters like Savoldo, Lotto, Moretto, and Romanino could aim to represent doctrine as credible visual fact, within the realm of sensory experience, and to describe the realm of sensory experience, even the world of the everyday, in ways that made it theologically significant. I would now like to consider some early instances of pre-Tridentine art that pursues what can be described as a Catholic reformist objective, and thus pursues a highly inventive idiom of visualizing doctrine in ways that also entailed a critical adaptation of the modern manner.

My examples are drawn from cities in what has been called the "double-periphery" of the Veneto and Lombardy.[17] Although close to Milan, Bergamo and Brescia were outposts of the Venetian territorial state. The intermittent suspension of Venetian rule during the traumatic years 1509 to 1520, with waves of occupation by French or imperial forces, gave rise to a new assertiveness and independence at the level of culture. It is from about 1520 that the emergence of a self-consciously modern and independent artistic culture is manifest in both cities. The prolific output of the Brescians Girolamo Romanino (c. 1484–c. 1559) and Alessandro Bonvicino, known as Moretto (c. 1498–1554), occurs in tandem with a strong Catholic evangelical current.[18] An upsurge in the market for religious art, and the sweeping reorganization of the religious life of the

   STEPHEN J. CAMPBELL

laity, are both signs of a preoccupation with the reconstitution of the city as a
Christian community, reborn after the horrors of the Italian wars and able to
negotiate an identity at least symbolically distinct from the Venetian territorial
state. With secular clergy in a state of disarray until the reforms of the 1550s,
and with the office of archbishop operating mainly as a source of patronage and
political advancement for the ruling Venetian patriciate, the wave of revitalized
confraternal activity was the official and approved face of an organic civic and
religious movement.[19]

In Brescia, the years after the Sack of 1512 saw an extraordinary wave of
confraternity organization centered on devotion to the Eucharist in particular.
By mid-century, nearly every church had a Blessed Sacrament altar and sometimes also a *scuola* dedicated to the adoration of the mystical body of Christ.[20]
A number of recent studies have shown that preoccupations with Christian
identity and community centered on eucharistic devotion were accompanied by
a concern with social homogeneity and by hostility toward imagined adversaries
and outsiders, chiefly the Jews.[21] Brescia's large Jewish population had been
targeted in the 1490s when Observant friars like Bernardino da Feltre preached
the establishment of Christian loan banks; the Republic of Venice, however, like
the rulers of Ferrara, refused to countenance the expulsion or harassment of
Jewish communities in subject cities.[22] Although anti-Judaism manifested itself
in sermons and other public discourse, Brescia continued to be the home of a
Jewish community. The very distinctive representation of Jewish biblical subjects in Brescian religious art, to be considered below, might be considered as a
response to this fact: it was a way of assigning the Jews a meaning, and hence a
place.

In Brescia, the catalyst for a new religious art centered on the Eucharist was
Titian's monumental altarpiece of the *Resurrection of Christ with Saints Sebas-
tian, Nazarius and Celsus*, installed in 1522 in the Church of SS. Nazaro e Celso
(Figure 10.2). The work was for a Brescian prelate, Altobello Averoldi (portrayed
kneeling in the left hand panel), who had spent most of his career at the Papal
Court and in Venice. Such a commission is clearly to be seen as a declaration
of cultural identification with Venice, and a pointed turning away from the
older Lombard tradition of the local painters Vincenzo Foppa, Vincenzo Civerchio, and the Milanese Bernardino Zenale.[23] Not only is the painting a virtuoso
display of qualities associated with the Venetian modern manner: an atmo-
spheric nocturnal landscape with varied lighting effects, an emotionally charged
energy in the figures—Titian also conspicuously "romanized" his style, with
conspicuous citations of Michelangelo's *Slaves* and the Belvedere *Laocoon*. The
appeal to Rome also gives the work the character of a manifesto, as if seeking a
more universal status in order to set the terms for modern painting in Brescia

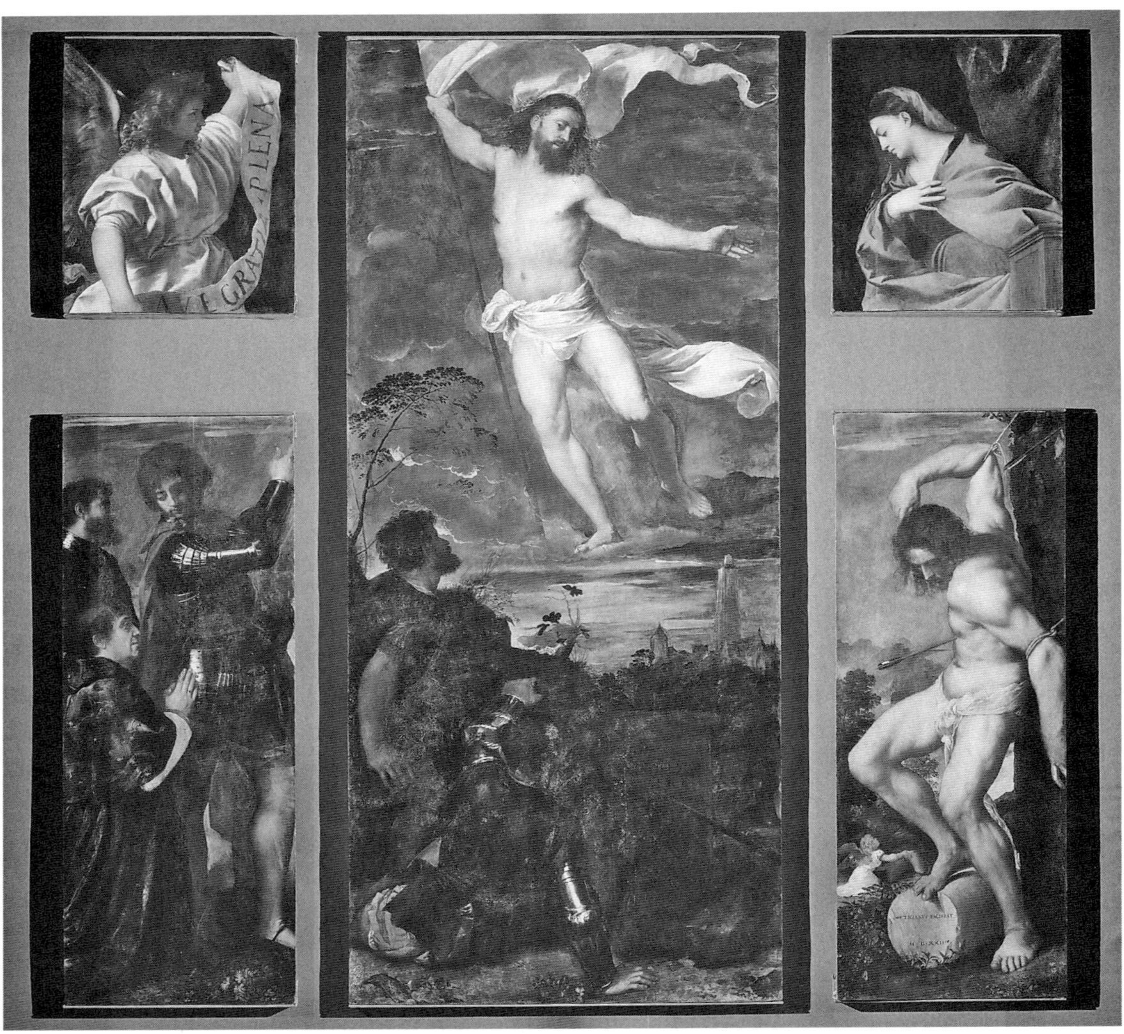

10.2. Titian, *Resurrection*, 1521 (Averoldi Altarpiece). Brescia, San Nazaro e Celso.
Photo: Scala/Art Resource, New York.

and throughout the *terraferma*. However, while Brescian painters clearly paid close attention to Titian's altarpiece, borrowing from it in their own works, their reaction was anything but complacent. In many respects they could be said to have resisted it, and such resistance can be seen most deliberately in works that have the Eucharist and the body of Christ as their subject. Romanino, a Brescian contemporary of Titian with a distinguished body of work in centers such as Padua, Milan, and Cremona, challenged Titian in his own deliberately primitive treatment of the *Resurrection* in the rural church of Capriolo outside Brescia (1523–25; Figure 10.3).[24] The coarse, squinting figure of Christ,

STEPHEN J. CAMPBELL

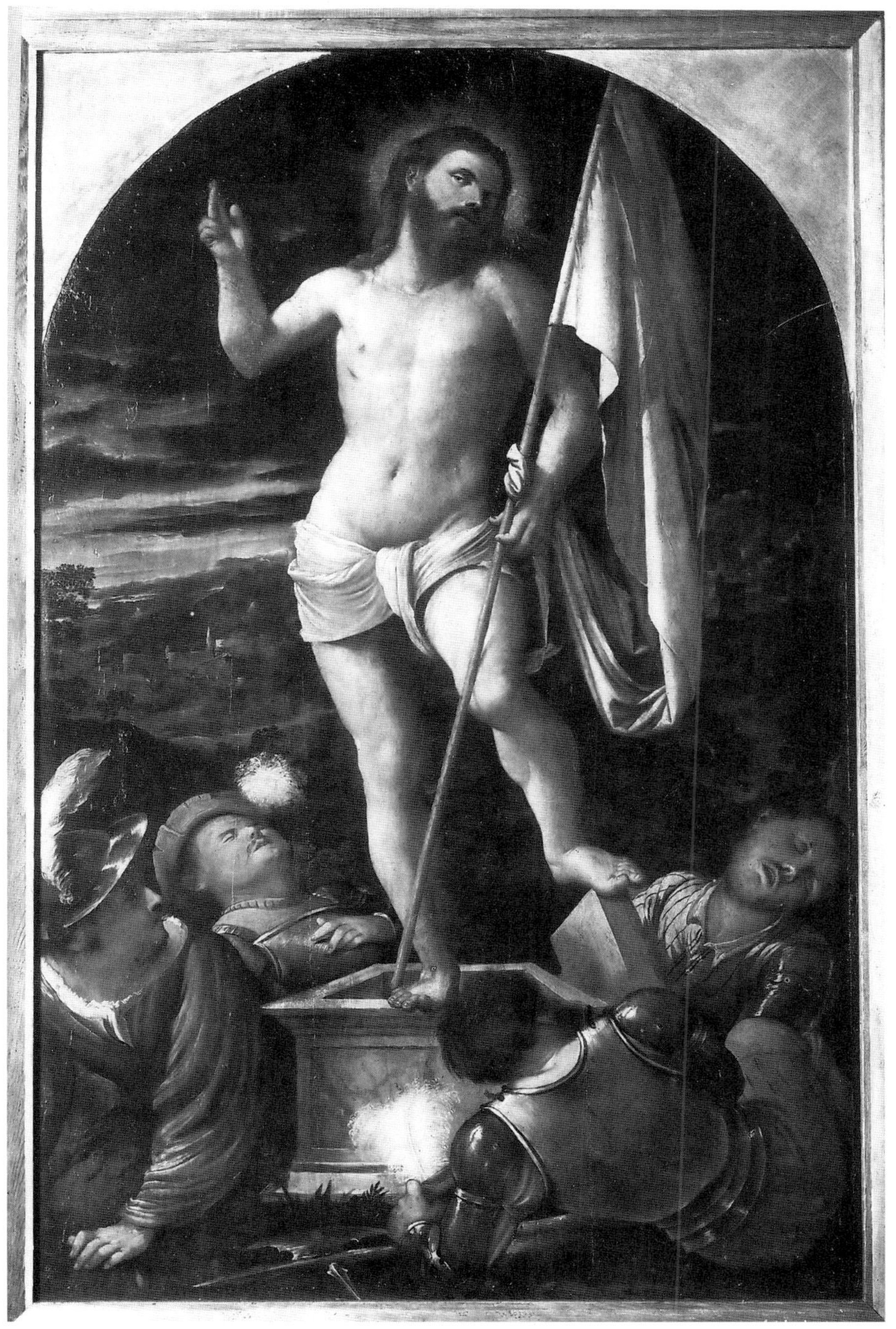

10.3. Romanino, *Resurrection*, c. 1525. Parish church, Capriolo (Brescia). Photo courtesy Delegato vescovile per i Beni Culturali di Brescia.

who stands squarely on the edge of the sarcophagus rather than soaring through the air, is like a caricature of Titian's ephebic figure. Romanino's rendering of the stocky, moon-faced soldiers flouts the idealizing proportions of Roman art, just as the wayward recession of the tomb proclaims an indifference to perspective.

Close in date, Romanino produced an altarpiece for the sacrament altar of Santa Maria in Calchera in Brescia, which by conspicuously raising the question of artistic models can also be seen as a polemical refusal of Titian (Figure 10.4). The subject of the altarpiece, *The Mass of St. Apollonius*, is the very sacrament enacted daily in front of it: in this case it is performed by a saintly bishop from Brescia's early Christian past, with assistance from the martyr saints Giovita and Faustinus.[25]

It is almost certainly the case that the choice of subject and Romanino's treatment of it was determined by an ever-widening controversy about the nature of the mass and the sacrament of the altar during the 1520s. There is a particular insistence on the use of correct forms and apparatus: the celebrant holds the paten with Hosts in his left hand while striking his breast with his right, thus signaling that he is uttering the words "Ecce Agnus Dei, ecce qui tollit peccata mundi." The servers hold the thurible and the chalice for the ablutio oris, while the altar is outfitted with candles, cloths, and an altarpiece (in Nuremberg in 1525, a church ordinance ordered the removal of "vestments, altarcloths, silver and gold vessels, and lights").[26] Moreover, the question of images and their liturgical function is addressed by Romanino's inclusion of a painted altarpiece of the *Pietà*. The unusual depiction of an altarpiece within an altarpiece suggests not only the legitimacy but even the necessity of the image on the altar: the depicted painting also demonstrates that the function of such images is to underscore the significance (even ontological status) of the Eucharist itself—the Eucharist *is* the body of Christ.[27] Romanino also incorporates the authority of older images without himself resorting to archaism: the painting on the altar is modeled on a work by an older Brescian painter, Vincenzo Civerchio, painted around 1508 for the church of Sant'Alessandro (and probably itself modeled on a lost *Lamentation* by Foppa from around 1498). The most striking invocation of artistic authority, however, is the stylistic reference to a contemporary artist who is pointedly not Titian, nor any other of the progressive artists of the modern manner: instead the figure of the saint recapitulates the *maniera devota* of Perugino, only recently deceased in 1523. Perugino's considerable reputation around 1500 had a long afterlife, despite (according to Vasari) his eclipse by his own follower Raphael and the derision of Michelangelo and the younger generation of Florentine artists: his works could be seen at Venice, Pavia, and Cremona.[28] Romanino's Saint Apollonius seems particularly close to the

STEPHEN J. CAMPBELL

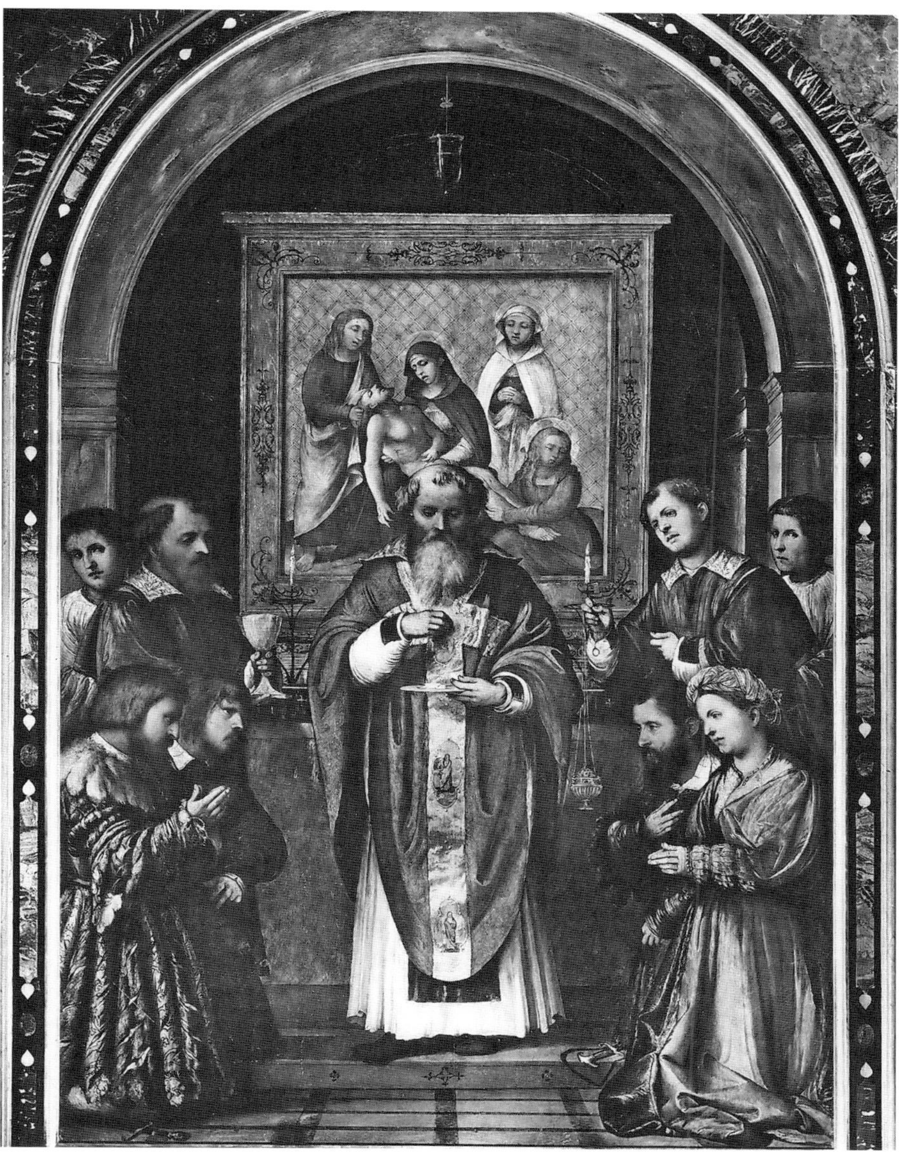

10.4. Romanino, *Mass of St. Apollonius*, c. 1525. Brescia, S. Maria in Calchera. Photo: Alinari/Art Resource, New York.

bearded figure of St. John the Evangelist in Perugino's 1494 altarpiece for the Cremonese church of Sant'Agostino, which Romanino could have studied when working at Cremona only a few years before (and is even closer to the figure of the Jewish high priest in the Perugia *Marriage of the Virgin* [Figure 10.5]). Perugino would have provided an *alternative* version of the modern manner to the classicism of Raphael and Titian, one valorized—as Vasari disparagingly

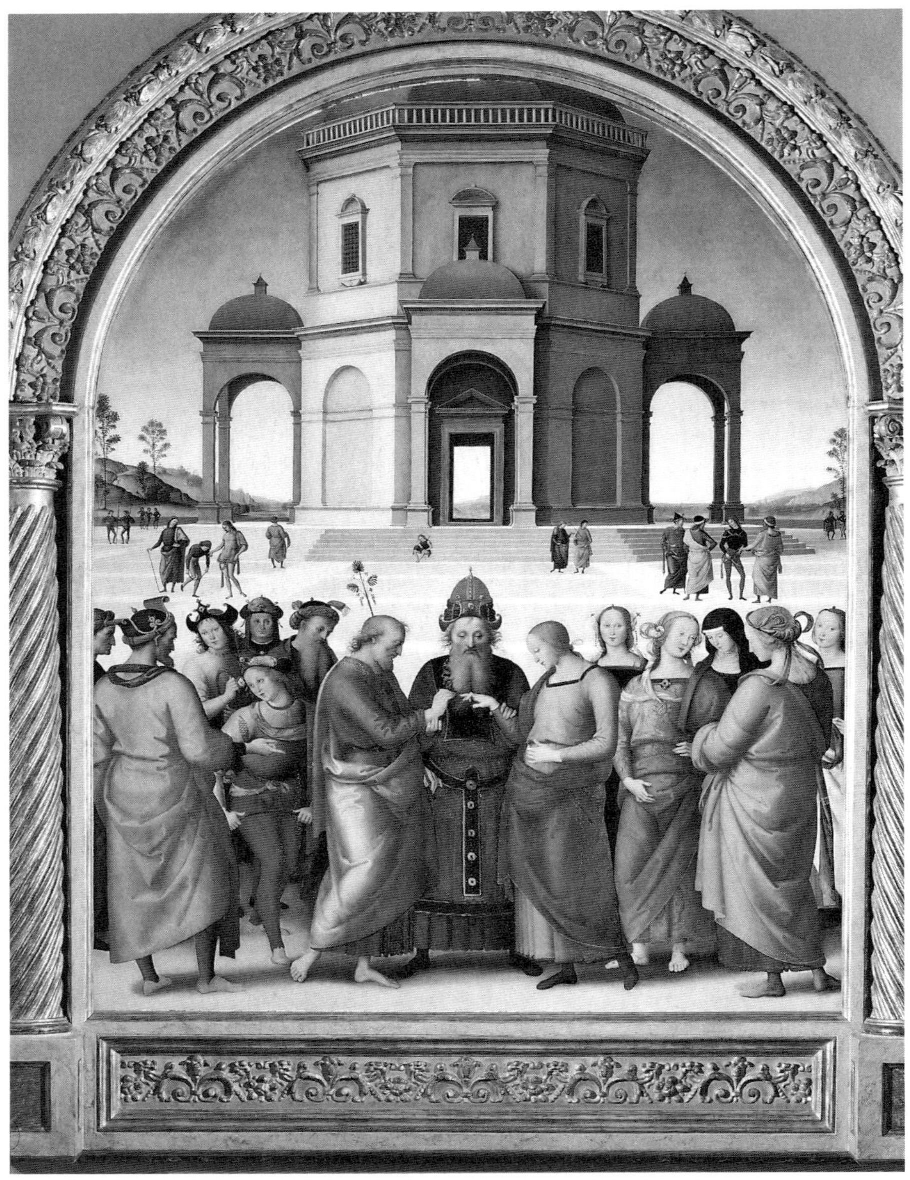

10.5. Perugino, *Marriage of the Virgin*, 1504. Caen, Musée des Beaux-Arts. Photo: Erich Lessing/Art Resource, New York.

noted—for its devout characteristics of pious simplicity, contemplative serenity, and ritualistic repetition as opposed to poetic imitation.[29]

The "sacred naturalism" of Perugino acquires an extraordinary importance in the depiction of eucharistic subjects, since, as we will see, the naturalism it connotes will come to stand for nothing less than a property of the Eucharist

   STEPHEN J. CAMPBELL

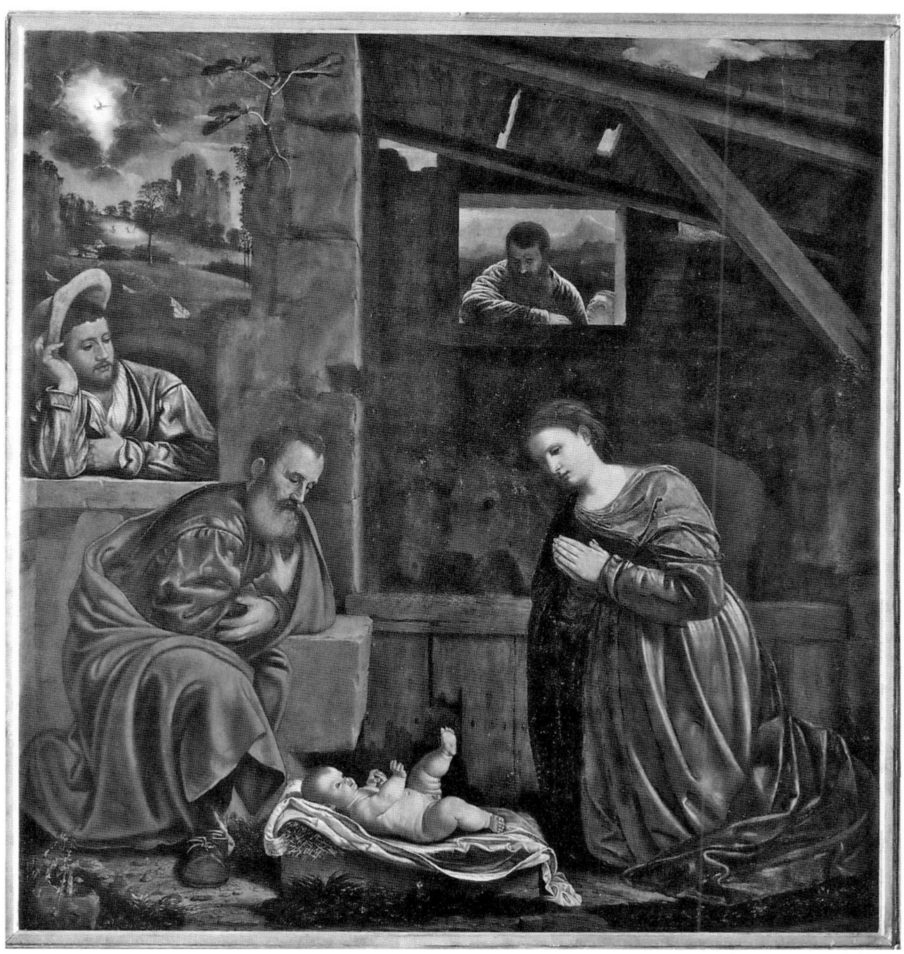

10.6. Girolamo Savoldo, *Adoration of the Shepherds*, 1530. Brescia, Pinacoteca Tosio Martinengo. Photo: Scala/Art Resource, New York.

itself. Not much more than a decade later, around 1540, Girolamo Savoldo painted a *Nativity* for the Bargnani chapel in the Brescian church of San Barnaba that suggests an even more explicit analogy between pictorial and eucharistic "realism" (Figure 10.6).[30] Savoldo was a native Brescian who had worked in Milan and in Rome but by this time was mainly based in Venice (where he produced a variation of this composition for the church of San Giobbe; a third version was made for a Franciscan church at Terlizzi in Apulia). For this sole surviving commission for his hometown, he consciously localized his approach, producing a work which seeks to recognize and to extend a particular tradition of the image in Brescia, and to respond to the artistic requirements that were upheld by the leading artists of the city. The artist based his composition on a

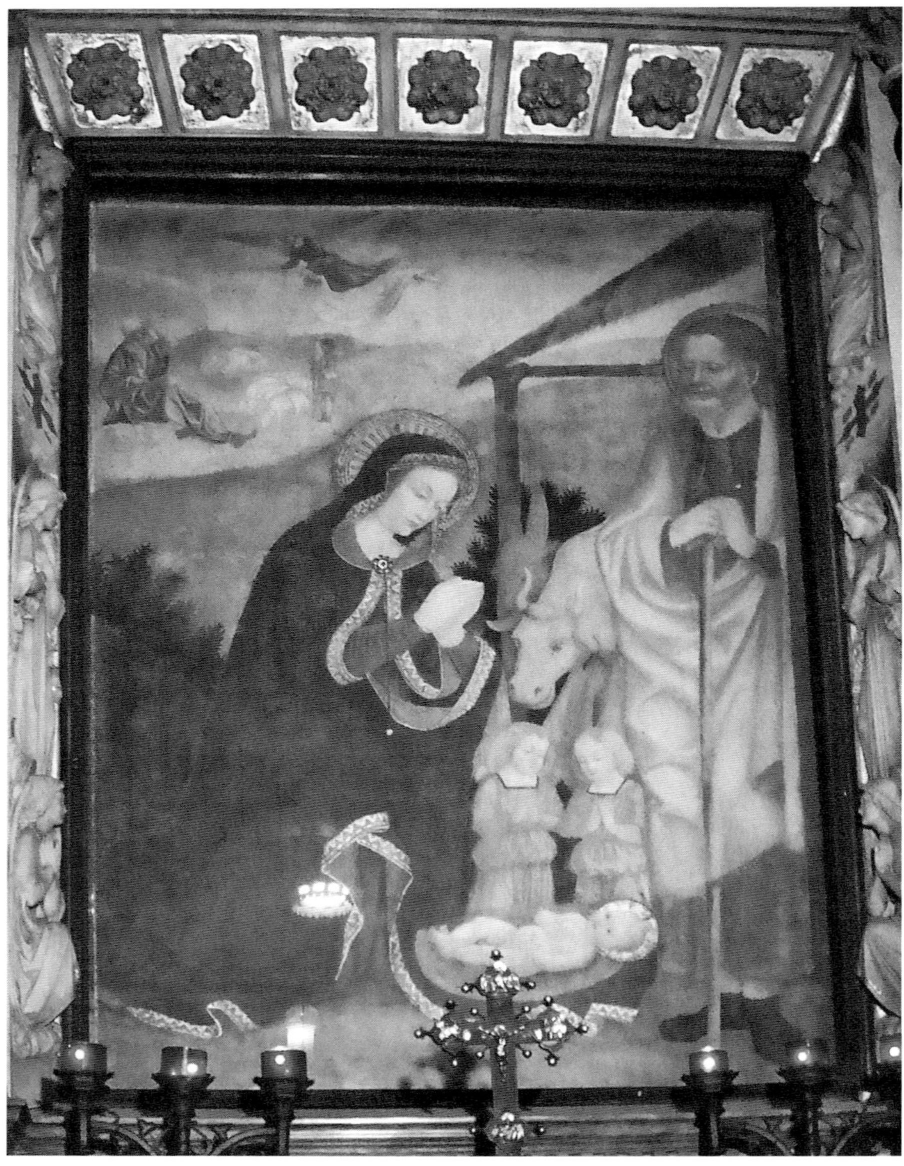

10.7. *Adoration of the Child,* c. 1440. Brescia, S. Maria delle Grazie. Photo courtesy Delegato vescovile per i Beni Culturali di Brescia.

fifteenth-century fresco of the *Nativity* (Figure 10.7) that had started to perform miraculous cures in May 1526, when first the Virgin and then the child, followed by St. Joseph and the angels, were seen to open their eyes and move their limbs. The fresco was detached and moved to its present location in the Brescian church of Santa Maria delle Grazie in 1539—a date corresponding closely with

STEPHEN J. CAMPBELL

the putative date of Savoldo's altarpiece.[31] Savoldo has transposed and adapted not only the figures of Christ and the Virgin, but also the stable with its square window and—in a disposition particularly faithful to the original—the head of the ass. His most substantial modifications are to the figures of St. Joseph, who kneels in adoration instead of standing, and the addition of the witnessing figures of two shepherds. These figures are symptomatic of new devotional interests on the part of Savoldo's clientele, which may have included the patron Bartolomeo Bargnani. The latter, in a will made as far back as 1513 (and thus long before the Grazie image had achieved its cult status), had specified the inclusion of Joseph along with the Virgin, the infant and the manger. Later records show that the Bargnani altar bore a dedication to St. Joseph, and Savoldo's two derivative versions were similarly intended for St. Joseph altars.[32] The Venetian patron Pietro Contarini, whose will of 1527 mentions four paintings by Savoldo, composed a poem entitled *Christologos Peregrinorum*, in which four Venetian pilgrims travel to the Holy Land and, in the guise of shepherds, participate as witnesses in the Nativity of Christ.[33] In designing an image that responded to the new importance of St. Joseph and the shepherds, Savoldo seems to have taken the initiative of basing his design on an older image that had assumed extraordinary prominence in the years that had elapsed since the altarpiece was endowed.

Most remarkable, however, is Savoldo's reconceptualization of the pictorial codes through which the divine or the miraculous are manifest to human vision in the older image. Instead of the aureole of light surrounding the Christ child in the earlier image, his gleaming skin is now offset by a kind of negative halo produced as if accidentally by the decay of wooden planks in the structure behind him. Other signs of the supernatural are present in the form of angels, but these have now migrated to the background where they constitute a remote prelude to the foreground scene—the Annunciation to the Shepherds. But supernatural effulgence is now only a supplement or foil for an emphatically material and everyday manifestation of the divine: as the shepherds regard the Christ child through frames and across parapets, it is impressed upon us in our parallel condition as viewers of the painting that the divine does indeed exist in the realm of facts accessible to human vision. This is the case even if we perceive it through the mediation of frames and thresholds that mark off the domain of the sacred but do not disrupt its continuity with the world from which we regard it. I will again refer to this style of handling religious subjects as "sacred naturalism"; it is distinguished not simply by fidelity to natural appearances, but by hierarchically ordered degrees of reality within the pictorial field itself. It is as if that which we, like the shepherds, perceive just beyond the frame is the most "real" of all—the incarnate body of Christ.

The incarnate body of Christ is central to a conception of pictorial representation that seeks to correspond as fully as possible to its object. This is because Christ's body is already manifest in the world as both sign and referent: it is both representation and real presence.[34] Such a concern with the hyper-real nature of Christ's body and its eucharistic hypostasis informs another Eucharist-themed image by Romanino painted in the early 1520s for the prominent Blessed Sacrament Confraternity of S. Giovanni Evangelista (Figure 10.8).[35] In this formidable and ambitious work, Romanino depicts a range of representatives of the clergy and religious orders, together with sumptuously attired members of the laity (in all probability standing for the confraternity itself) witnessing the Eucharist manifesting itself as a radiant child. Attempts have been made to identify the scene with one of a number of "Host miracles" from Northern Italy in the proceeding decades, which saw a noteworthy proliferation of bleeding Hosts and manifestations of the Christ child in the altar sacrament. It seems, however, that Romanino has deliberately created a generic representation. In fact, it is questionable that he intended to refer to a Host miracle as distinct from a didactic representation of that aspect of the Eucharist which such miracles served to clarify: to affirm the ontological peculiarity of eucharistic presence, the fact that the Eucharist *is* the body of Christ. Host miracles, however, were becoming ever more controversial by the 1520s, a point of tension between the religious life of the periphery and the authority of the center that sought to test and challenge the validity of such miracles. It seems more likely that what we are seeing here is an institutional maneuver where forms of sensational mysticism identified with popular devotion—and perhaps also, in a local context, with women—have been appropriated, contained, and made to serve the ends of doctrinal didacticism. Women are particularly prominent here among the laity, and it is clear that their understanding of the Eucharist is being monitored by members of the clergy.

The painting works to clarify and to simplify an increasingly anxious theological argument about the nature of eucharistic presence, with its fraught distinctions of "substance" and "accident." By activating a long-established tradition on the efficacy of "ocular communion"—the belief, ultimately overruled by Trent, that seeing the Host was equivalent to receiving it orally—it allays fears about communion as cannibalism.[36] But there is also an artistic investment: for Romanino, and for his contemporaries, the Eucharist is the ideal, if ultimately unobtainable, model of representing Christ's body.

The Host has come to life, and this representation-made-presence has become the center of a richly characterized portrait-like visualization of clerics and confraternity members, adults and children, and all the ephemera of costume. Through the manifestation of Christ as real presence, it is as if the world

STEPHEN J. CAMPBELL

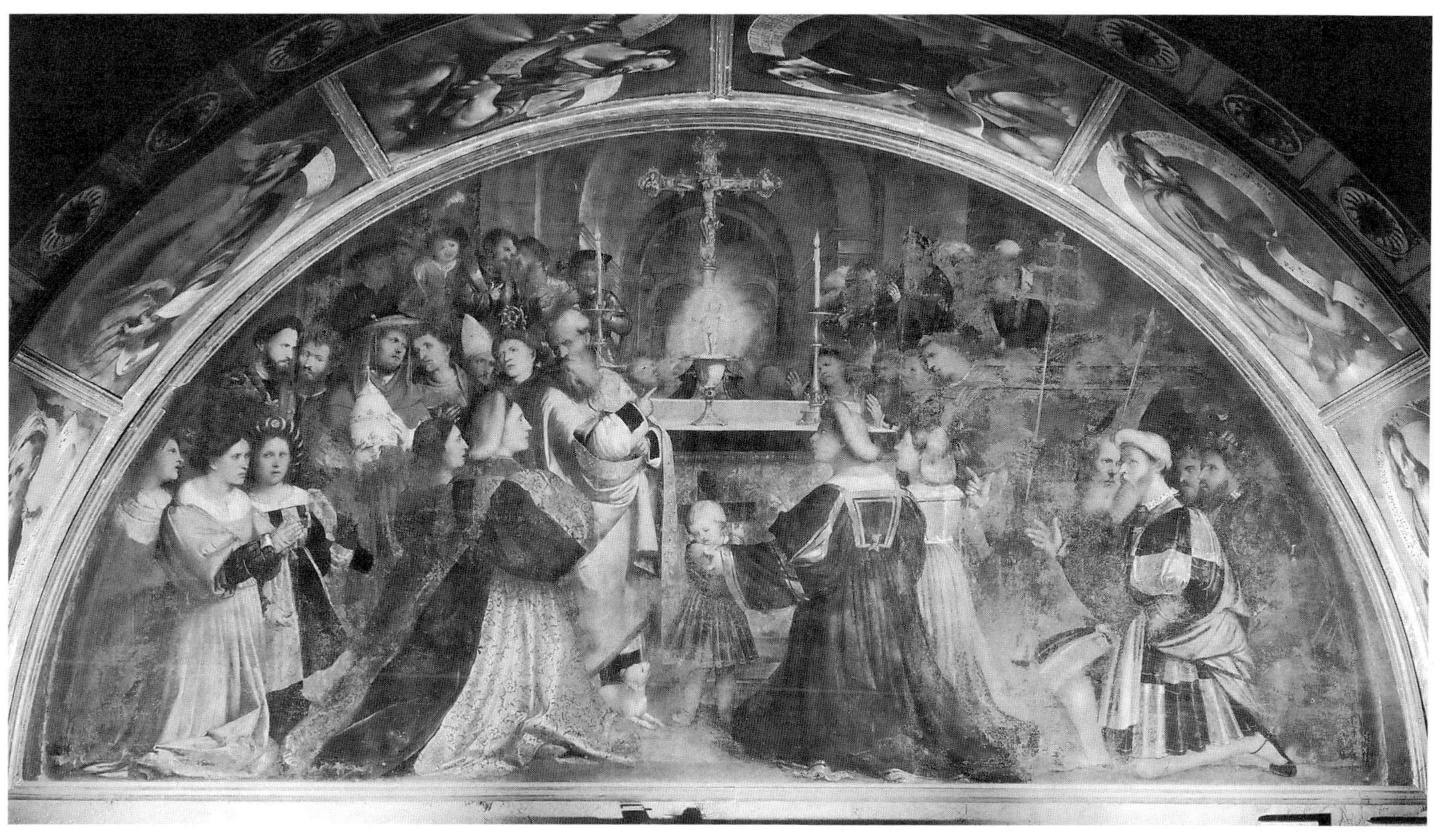

10.8. Romanino, *Adoration of the Eucharist*, 1522. Brescia, San Giovanni Evangelista. Photo: Scala/Art Resource, New York.

itself has become visible. On the axis of crucifix, infant, and chalice appears a red cross on the altar frontal. Juxtaposed with the red cross is a small boy, a nameless member of the cluster of laity before the altar. His appearance on axis with the child in the Host directs us to consider what the two infants have in common—we are asked to associate and compare them in their shared identity as children. At the same time, the boy's non-identity with the child in the Host is proclaimed through his childish preoccupation with a small white dog: his mother seeks to divert his attention toward the miracle. This is an anecdotal and even sentimental detail, but it is also more than that. The world of contemporary life, of the normative and the everyday, forms an *antitype* for the world of the miraculous and the exceptional. It can at best constitute a pointer or metaphor (children in their innocence are "like" Christ and thus "like" the Eucharist) for that which is in no sense a metaphor, but the thing itself. Metaphor, in other words, provides an antitype for that which is much more than a metaphor. The identity of the Eucharist with Christ's incarnate body and his sacrificial form is thus underscored by a *figura* that underscores identity by counterposing non-identity.

A link is being established here between the representation of the Eucharist and naturalistic elements that will later be associated with "genre" painting. Correspondingly, the imagery of the Eucharist becomes at once a place of iconographic experiment as well as epistemological inquiry. In a series of eucharistic projects undertaken over a twenty-year period, between 1520 and the early 1540s, Romanino and his Brescian colleagues worked out the principles of what I have been calling "sacred naturalism." This was first and foremost a mode of visualizing sacred subjects, especially narratives, in terms of the particularity and the concreteness of the everyday. But it is also a mode that is conceived in a dialectical relation to what these artists understood to be the "modern manner," following the practice of Florentine and Venetian artists in the wake of Raphael and Titian. The modern manner is itself already characterized by naturalism but defined in a century of art theory from Alberti to Paolo Pino through the model of poetic invention.[37] Such a conception of painting, which was perhaps most influentially embraced by the later Raphael and by Titian in the 1520s, is manifest in the practice of imitation (that is, conspicuous reference to other works of art), the conception of artistic subjects in terms of literary genres, the use of figures such as allegory or personification, and by a sensuous idealism that seems to call forth an affective response from the beholder.[38] The Brescian mimetic mode of *sacred naturalism*, on the other hand, aspires to free itself of these obvious tropes of artfulness (this is why, in the *Mass of Saint Apollonius*, Romanino turned to Perugino). But this is more than an opposition between

STEPHEN J. CAMPBELL

poetic fiction on one hand and unvarnished truth on the other. Operating in this hierarchy of naturalisms,

1. Eucharist
2. mimesis
3. imitation

is the ideal of the Eucharist as a supreme mode of representation with a unique purchase on the real: it is the sign that is consubstantial with what it represents. The mimetic mode of sacred naturalism seeks to occupy a kind of second rung in this hierarchy, between the "ultra-true" Eucharist on one hand and the fictive or poetic mode on the other.

Sacred Naturalism can only exist in a system of differences; it needs to be confronted and offset by that which is less sacred and less natural. This is where, as we shall see, the modern manner of Venice and Rome comes to have a place; and, as we will also see, so does the imagery of the Jewish Bible. Romanino's *Adoration of the Eucharist* forms part of a commission that the artist, alongside his colleague the painter Moretto, received in 1521 for the decoration of the Chapel of the Most Holy Sacrament in the Augustinian church of S. Giovanni Evangelista.[39] The chapel's altarpiece, a *Lamentation* by the Milanese Bernardino Zenale, had already been in place for more than ten years. The sparse documentation reveals that Moretto's *Last Supper* was complete by 1524, and it has generally been supposed that the facing lunette by Romanino depicting the *Adoration of the Eucharist* was completed around the same time, along with two groups of six prophets, one group assigned to each artist, for the intrados of the arch framing each lunette. The four canvasses that each artist painted to go on the walls below the lunettes were added at least twenty years later.[40]

Moretto's *Last Supper*, which faces Romanino's lunette on the opposite wall of the chapel, clarifies the significance of the *Adoration of the Host* (Figure 10.9). It is also a polemical revision of a now canonical model, the Milanese fresco by Leonardo, toward the ends of doctrinal clarity and representational naturalism. By moving Judas to his traditional place in the foreground and reinstating John and Peter as central protagonists on either side of Christ, Moretto revises Leonardo's narrative so that the emphasis is now on the institution of the Eucharist rather than the announcement of the impending betrayal—he retains Leonardo's alignment of Christ's hands with the bread and wine. The perplexity of the apostles, whose thoughts are on Christ's "hard saying" rather than on the accusation of betrayal, is extended to the beholder, whose attention and concentration are solicited by the apostle who looks out of the painting and into the chapel. But note how Moretto also insists on the particular, the local, and the

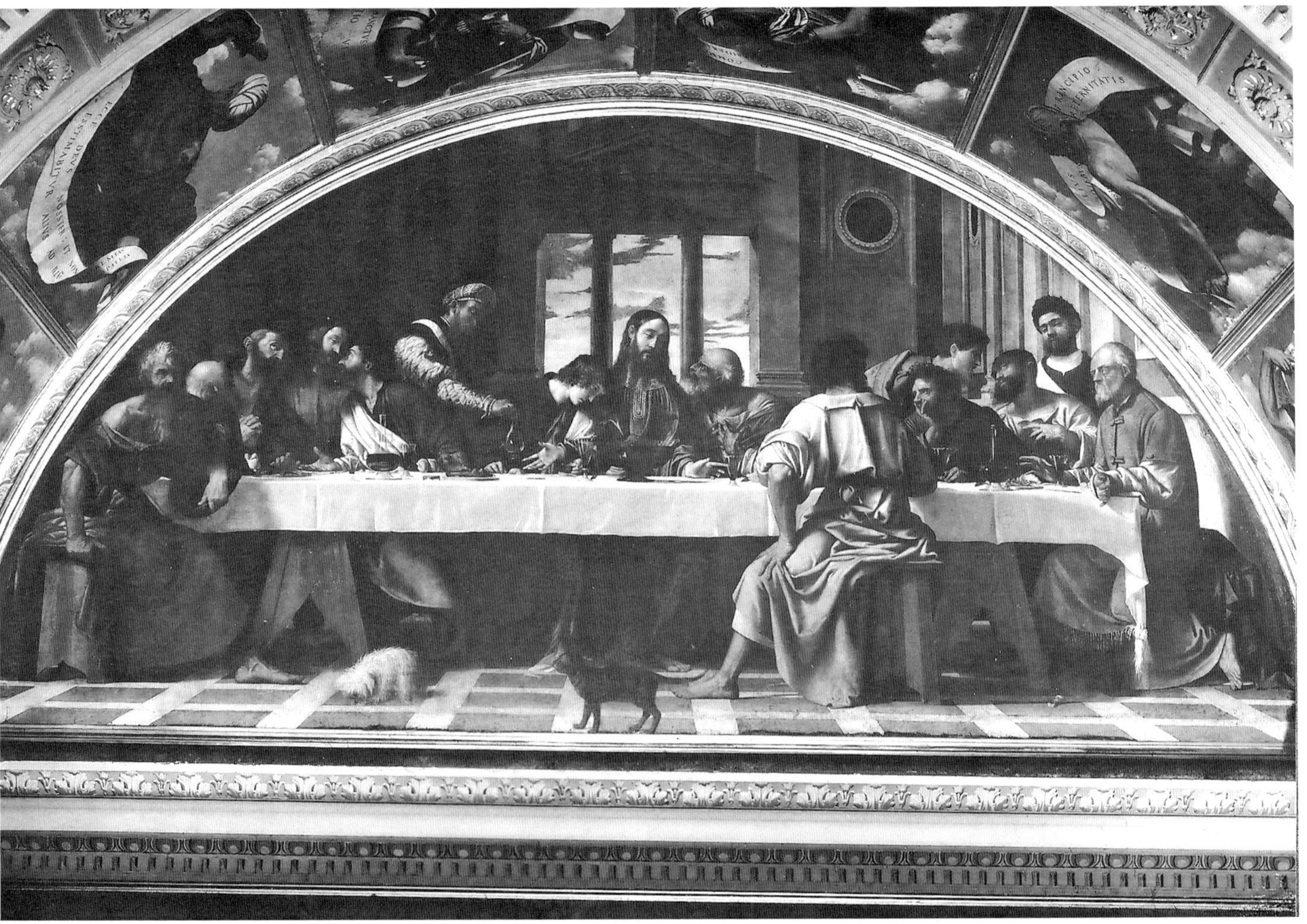

10.9. Moretto, *Last Supper*. Brescia, San Giovanni Evangelista. Photo: Alinari/Art Resource, New York.

idiosyncratic in ways that Leonardo never would—the ogival cusps of the table leg, the red and green stripes on the chairs, the livery and Brescian *berrette* of the two servants,[41] the striped cat and the long haired dog—all these connote the world of the everyday in which the miraculous—right now—is immanent.

The main narrative canvasses are organized according to a typological program that, apart from well-known examples like the Sistine Chapel in Rome, was relatively rare in Italian Renaissance art by the early sixteenth century. In addition to the *Last Supper*, Moretto's two later narrative canvasses are Old Testament antitypes of the Eucharist: *The Gathering of Manna, Elijah in the Desert*. The links between Moretto's *Last Supper* and Romanino's *Miracle*, and between these paintings and Zenale's altarpiece, are of a different order. The relations between the Eucharist, the dead Christ, and the person of Christ at the Last Supper are not figurative but actual. Christ living, Christ dead, and the eucharistic Host all ask to be recognized as the *same* body.

Elijah and the Angel (Figure 10.10) and *The Gathering of the Manna* (Figure 10.11) have been seen as instances of a preoccupation with central Italian mannerism by Moretto around 1540, when he is presumed to have seen the works by Salviati and Vasari in Venice.[42] But Moretto had other reasons to direct his beholders to the practice of imitation among contemporary artists of the modern manner. *Elijah* is an essay in the *maniera* of Raphael or Giulio Romano; Elijah sprawled in sleep is modeled on the figure of a melancholy river god from a print by the Master of the Die, designed by an artist close to Giulio.[43] The angel, more reminiscent of Parmigianino, embodies a canon of ideal beauty typical of the Roman school but otherwise foreign to Moretto's art. The extraordinary *Gathering of the Manna* is dominated by another such figure, the statuesque matron in the turning pose holding the tablet with the scriptural source: Exodus 16. Were the text not there, the viewer might be hard put to identify Moses and Aaron, who are almost lost in the teeming crowd, eclipsed by the striking ascendency of the everyday and the domestic, the domain of women and infants. Closely akin to the foreground mother is the vase bearer seen from the back at the extreme left, who relates directly to a source in Parmigianino's Steccata frescoes in Parma, just recently completed in 1539. The male figure on the opposite side who directly engages the viewer would be a direct quotation of the Raphael/Marcantonio *Judgment of Paris* print were it not for an aggressive cropping of the figure that strikes through his body, and his grinning expression, as if canceling them (Figure 10.12). Such a gesture points to a strong degree of self-consciousness about the practice of imitation, making visible the procedures of expropriation and dismembering, but above all it gives the borrowing of canonical sources a playful and even subversive character. The game-like character is here underscored by the children fighting over the tambourine in

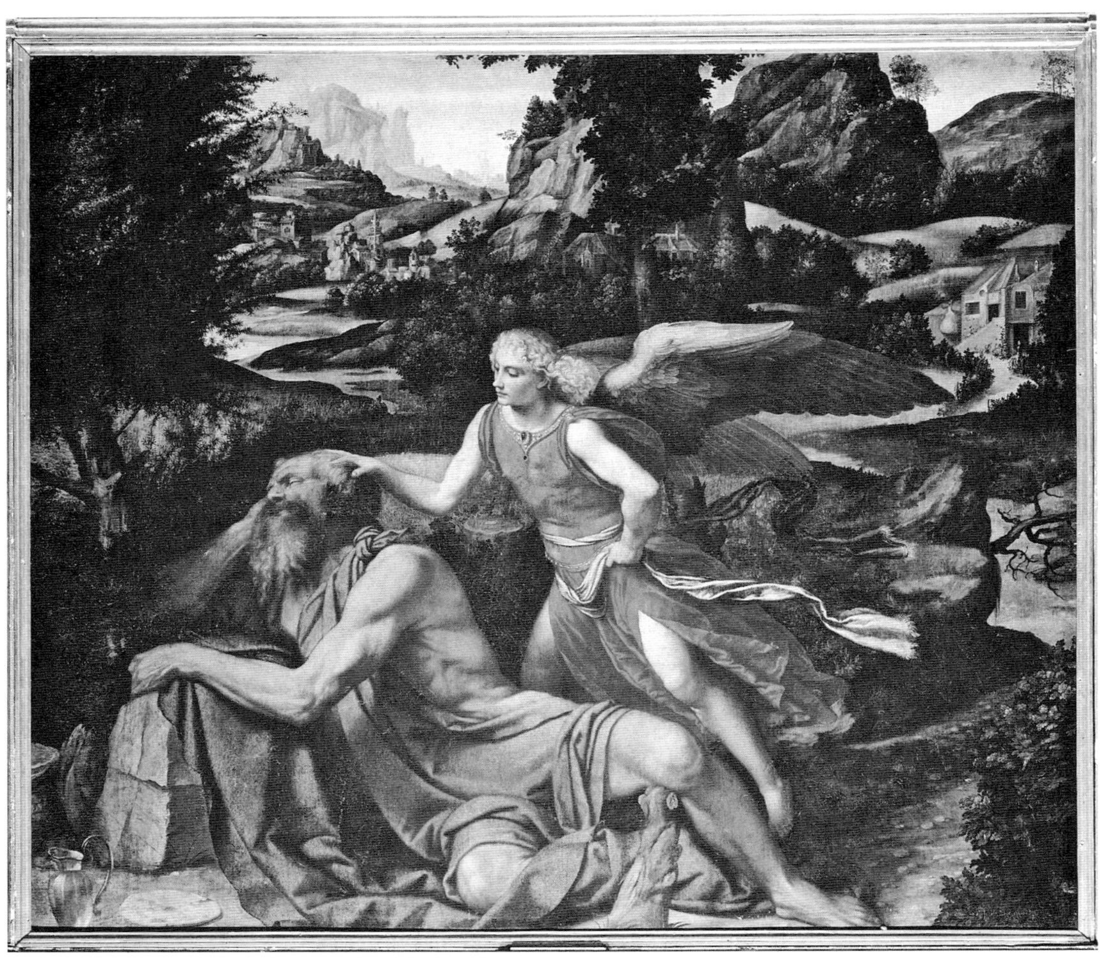

10.10. Moretto, *Elijah and the Angel*, c. 1540. Brescia, San Giovanni Evangelista. Photo: Scala/Art Resource, New York.

the foreground and by a monkey whose demeanor echoes that of the grinning man. In compositional terms this is an avant-garde experiment that has little to do with the grand style of narrative painting in Rome or Venice: not only are figures cropped, but anonymous figures in the crowd are given priority over historical protagonists. It also proclaims a naturalism that is invested in the anecdotal and the marginal—but it is still at one remove from a purer non-allusive naturalism.

The overall effect is to focus on the principle of mediation: the conspicuous incorporation of artistic sources points to the fact that these naturalistic and

STEPHEN J. CAMPBELL

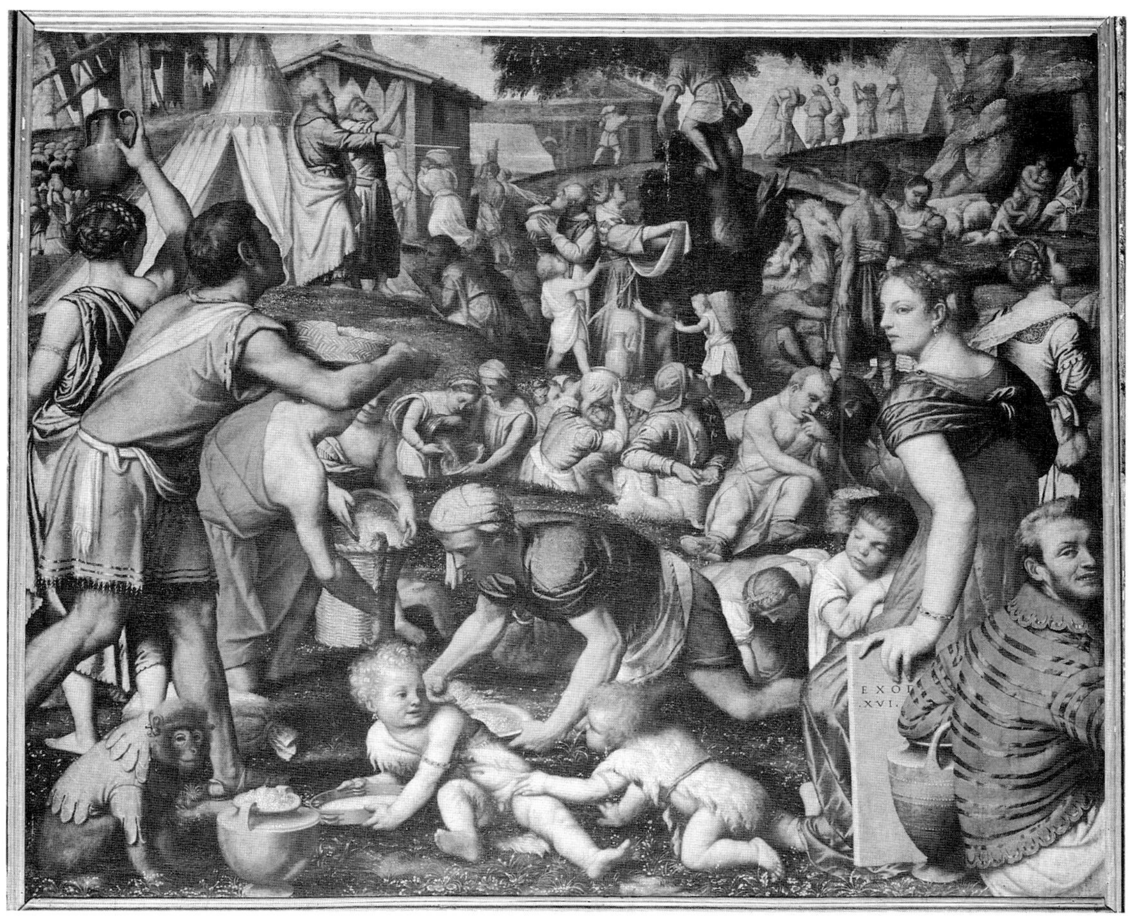

10.11. Moretto, *The Gathering of the Manna*, c. 1540. Brescia, San Giovanni Evangelista. Photo: Scala/Art Resource, New York.

historical scenes are themselves to be regarded as *figurae*, transmissions of the truth but not the truth in itself. However fundamental might appear the material and bodily domain of eating, its principle validity is to point to the spiritual sustenance of the Eucharist, whose devotees as portrayed in Romanino's *Adoration* seem to consume with their gaze rather than through physical eating. In *Gathering of Manna*, the sprawling, disunified composition of bodies preoccupied by their physical needs is the antitype of Romanino's work, where disparate bodies assume a unified, symmetrical ritual formation around the mystical body of Christ. Moretto's naturalism here, then, is a kind of ironic naturalism— ironic in the sense of being allegorical as well as including a sense of parody. And it is confronted by Romanino's ponderous and grave *Feast in the House of*

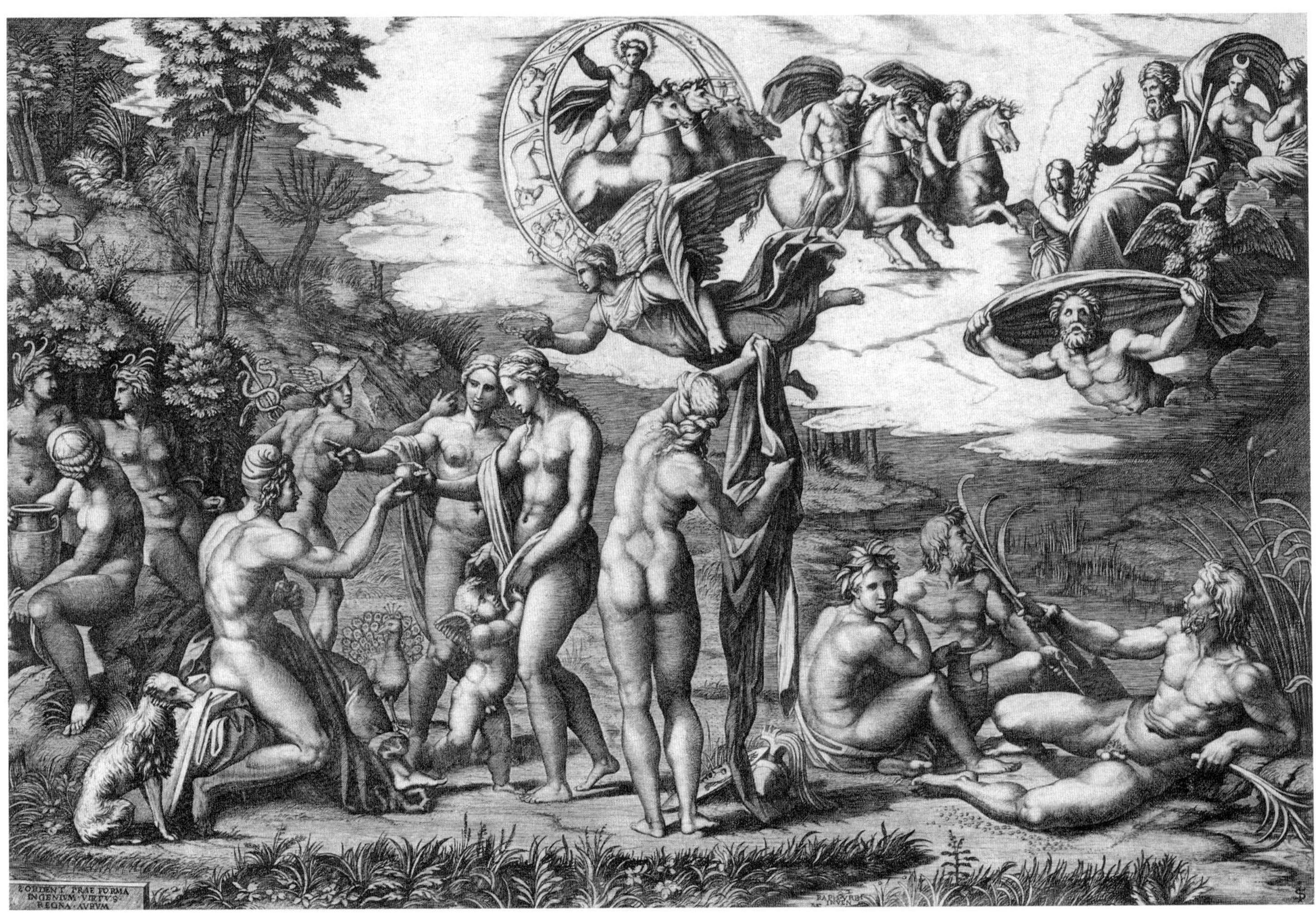

10.12. Marcantonio Raimondi after Raphael, *The Judgment of Paris*. Photo © The Metropolitan Museum of Art/Art Resource, New York.

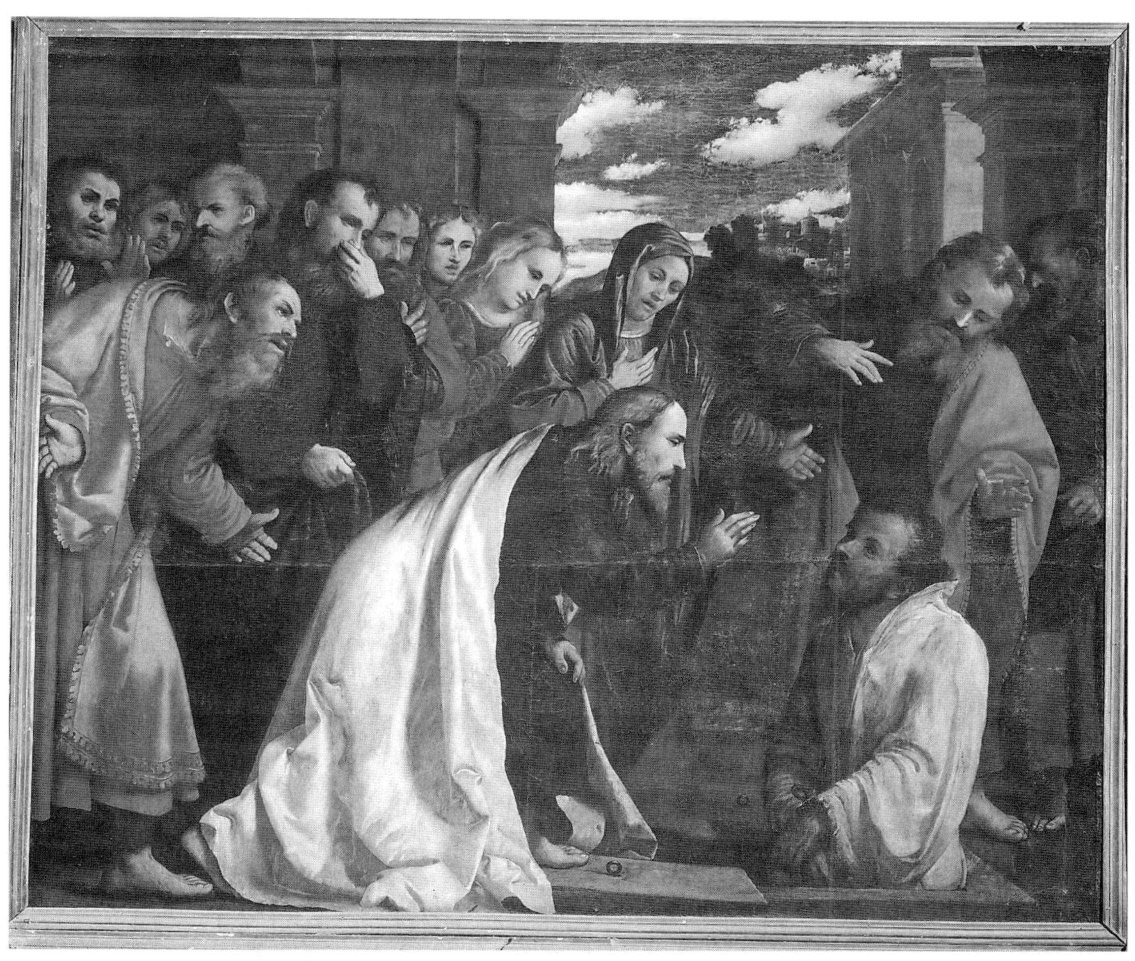

10.13. Romanino, *Raising of Lazarus*, c. 1540. Brescia, San Giovanni Evangelista. Photo: Scala/Art Resource, New York.

Levi and *Raising of Lazarus* (Figure 10.13). These, by contrast, are works of "sacred naturalism" that conspicuously avoid the mediations of metaphor, allegory, or the citation of other art. The only correspondence with other images to be remarked on here is the strange conformity between the figure of Christ in one painting with that of the Magdalene in the other (there is no priority as to who conforms to whom). The theme is Christ's operation in the everyday world, where he performs with the same miraculous efficacy that is claimed for the Eucharist—the resurrection of the dead and the forgiveness of sins. The divine, clasped here by Mary Magdalene, is represented as present and accessible, not remote and ineffable. This is painting that seeks to place the sacred in the realm of immediate experience, the tactile as well as the visible.

Moretto also completed a second set of canvasses for another eucharistic chapel, this time in the cathedral of Brescia and completed in two documented campaigns: in 1531–34 and 1551–54.[44] The program is similar to that of S. Giovanni Evangelista, with the difference that Old Testament antitypes of the Eucharist now appear without corresponding episodes from the Gospel and the Christian era. It is as if the Eucharist itself has displaced the intermediate and problematic stage of "sacred naturalism." The Gospels are designated instead by portraits of the Evangelists. By 1534, Moretto had produced the *St. Luke* and the *St. Matthew*, figures of startling physicality and presence, and also of quiet, concentrated self-absorption, the inspiration for which has sometimes been ascribed to Moretto's contact with Savoldo in Milan in 1530. Rather different in tenor, however, is the Old Testament scene of *Elijah and the Angel* (Figure 10.14). Although its conception as a nocturne also evokes the painting of Savoldo, Moretto's characterization of its protagonist indicates that he conceived the prophet as a humiliated antitype of the Evangelists. Elijah is sprawled unconscious on the ground in a moonlit landscape, while an angel descends from above bearing flatbread and a flask of water. The "earthy" quality is reinforced by elements in the background landscape, among which appears a man fishing and another who urinates against a rock.

The motif, which seems worlds away from Tridentine standards of decorum, recalls a contemporary *intarsia* designed by Lorenzo Lotto for Santa Maria Maggiore in Bergamo that Moretto certainly knew, since, following Lotto's own recommendation, the Brescian artists worked briefly on the same project in 1528 (Figure 10.15).[45] One of the *intarsie* shows the Jewish heroine Judith leaving the encampment of the Philistines, at the edge of which soldiers engage in even more graphic acts of bodily elimination.

To dwell momentarily on the Bergamo *intarsias*: their most extraordinary implication is that orders of reality and of representation are conceived as layered. The series of Old Testament histories form a kind of *parerga* or typological frame in the choir of the church, suggesting that they ultimately function as *figurae* pointing to the true reality of Christ in the Eucharist. The Old Testament scenes are each provided with an *intarsia* cover presenting a hieroglyphic "translation" of each biblical scene, basically a visual rebus incorporating metonymic abbreviations and moralizations.[46] In a decade when reformers demanded a new attentiveness to the literal truth of scripture and for the dissemination of the word of God in the vernacular, the cycle presents a rejoinder, insisting on the nontransparency of the Biblical text: reading the Old Testament is upheld as a process of deciphering enigmas and mysteriously figured truths. For, especially in the case of Old Testament histories, the literal and the factual is always figurative, or rather prefigurative. Lotto's Old Testament narratives make the point

STEPHEN J. CAMPBELL

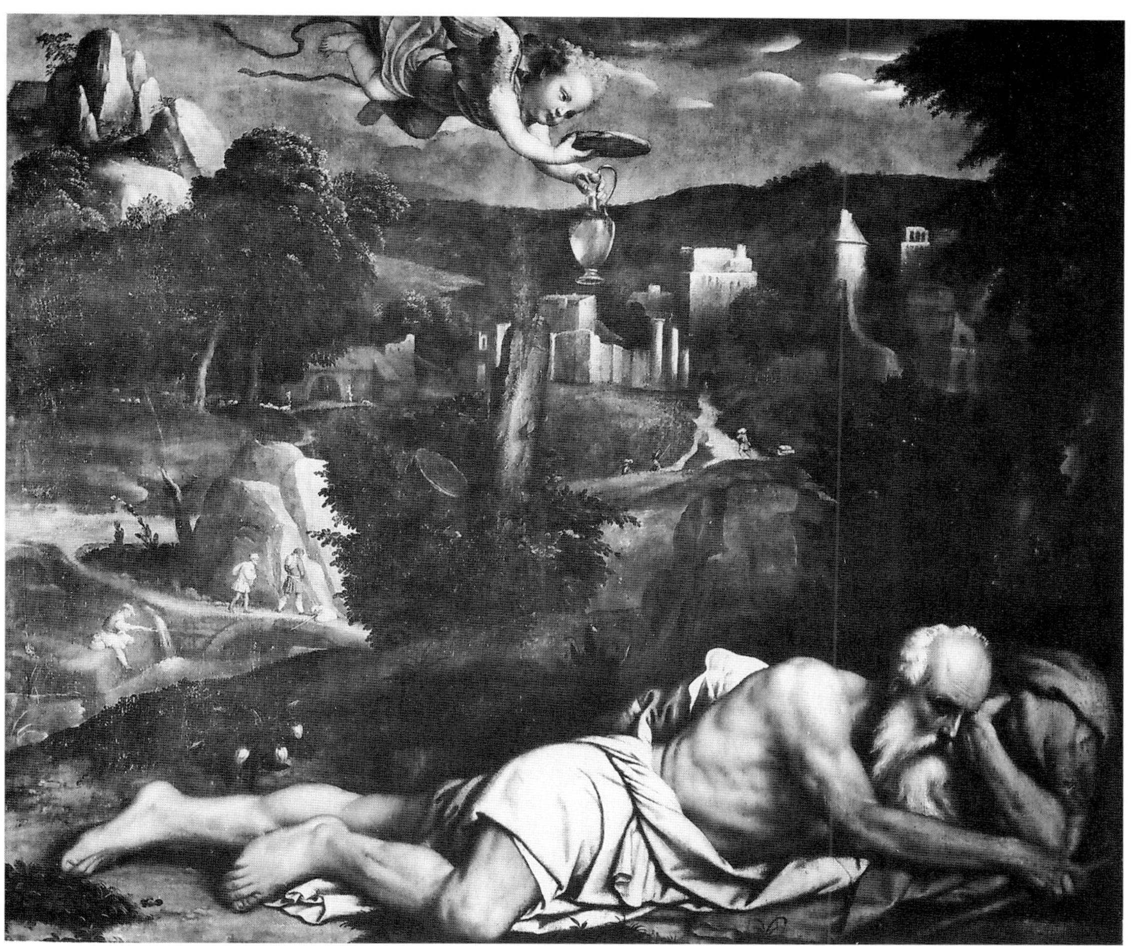

10.14. Moretto, *Elijah and the Angel*, 1531–34. Brescia, Duomo Vecchio. Photo: Alinari/ Art Resource, New York.

all the more forcibly by being conceived in a mode of manifesto-like naturalism, with an emphasis on materiality and carnality, even a level of frankness about the body in all its coarser aspects. (In so doing, it also effectively brings us to the world of the macaronic or the grotesque comic naturalism of Teofilo Folengo and Rabelais).

But even the fabric of everyday reality is only a figure or a sign for an ultimate reality, which is the union of sacrament with Christ's body and the church itself. Lotto insists on this through alerting the viewer to the fallibility and the limited nature of the perspective effects demonstrated with such celebrated virtuosity throughout the *intarsie*. The hieroglyphic imagery of the covers constantly draws upon the motif of the eye, along with spectacles, blindfolds,

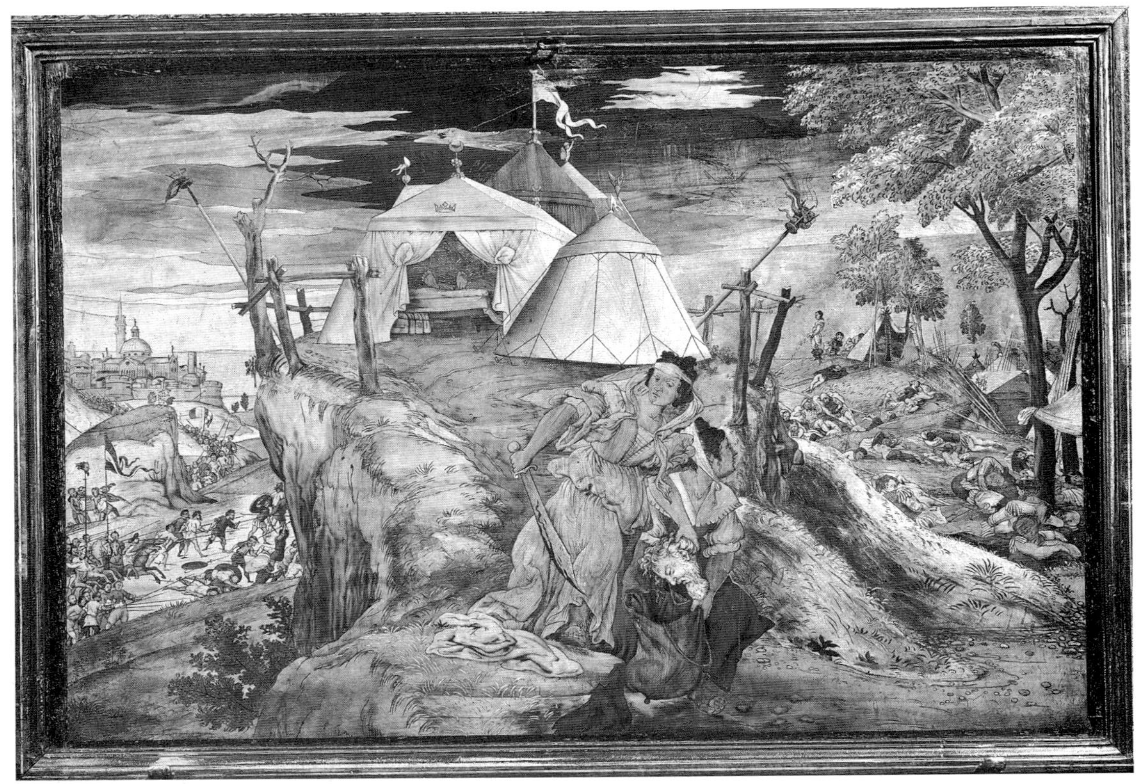

10.15. After Lorenzo Lotto, *Judith Leaving the Philistine Camp*, c. 1530. Bergamo, S. Maria Maggiore Photo © DeA Picture Library/Art Resource, New York.

and peacock tails. Thus they offer a moralization on the limits of carnal vision, underscoring the limited perspective afforded by human (or Jewish) history, as well as the perils attending on an overreliance on the sense of sight—fascination and idolatry, where surfaces are taken for ultimate truth or ultimate good. The paradoxical claim is that even while Old Testament history is the sphere of the literal, the carnal, and the real, all of this is redeemed by its figurative status, as antitypes for the sacraments instituted by Christ—penance, remission of sins, Eucharist.

In his later paintings for the chapel in the Duomo of Brescia, which again depict Old Testament prefigurations of the Eucharist, Moretto more emphatically incorporates elements of the grotesque and parodies of the Roman-Venetian style. The *Sacrifice of Isaac* most explicitly lays bare a tendency to associate Jewish history with the principle of mediation.[47] Here, the servants who dominate the foreground of the lunette are river gods from the Raphael/Marcantonio

STEPHEN J. CAMPBELL

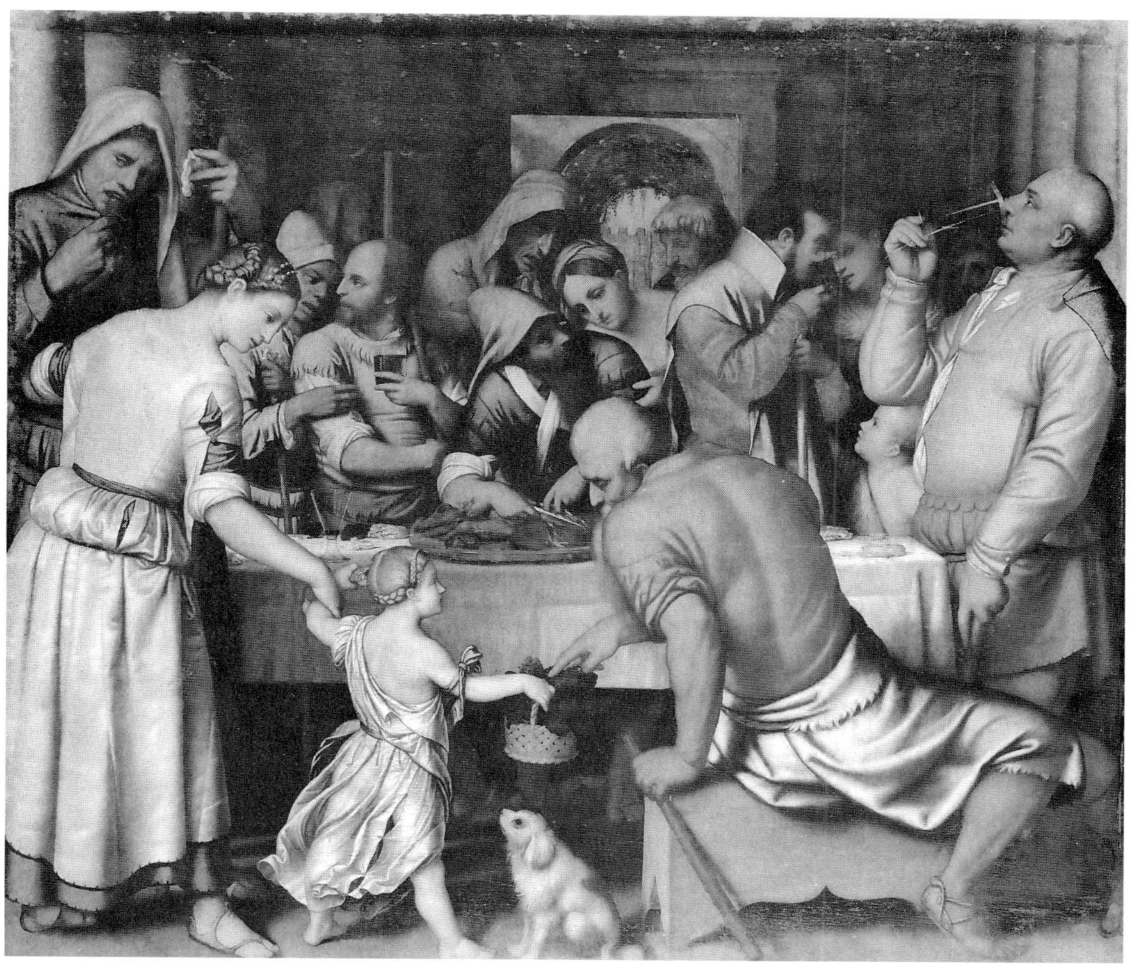

10.16. Moretto, *Feast of the Paschal Lamb*, 1554. Brescia, Duomo Vecchio. Photo courtesy Delegato vescovile per i Beni Culturali di Brescia.

Judgment of Paris masquerading in peasant dress. Were it not for its original context, the *Feast of the Paschal Lamb* (Figure 10.16) would be recognized as an essay in pure genre, with its unidealized everyday human types indulging in eating and drinking: it is through an extravagant allusion to the high style—a citation of the *Bed of Polycleitos* in the figure of the old man with his shoulders turned toward the picture plane—that alerts us to the possibility of another order of significance. *Abraham and Melchizedek* appears as a kind of carnivalesque orientalism, where the grinning dwarf once again indicates that the solemn mysteries of the Eucharist are being signaled in their opposite. Moretto, in fact, seems precociously close to the language of genre painting as it was then emerging in the art of Northern Europe; not until the 1580s, however, with the market scenes of Vincenzo Campi, do we find comparable Italian depictions of food sellers, kitchens, feasting, drinking, and music making.[48] Moretto's work, in other words, raises questions about the degree to which the emergence of "genre" corresponds to a secularizing tendency in art, as distinct from a mode of organizing experience—artistic and social—which is grounded in the reading of scripture. Scripture, that which is fetishized by anti-catholic reformists, is associated with a range of apparently disparate phenomena: the literal, the physical, the natural—and "the Jewish." The task of the Catholic artist/exegete is to reveal the always provisional and referential nature of the apparently literal, by inflecting his representations with the tropes of *style*. In his portrayal of Jewish history in terms of the raw physicality of landscape and the body, Moretto anticipates the rustic Bible scenes painted by Jacopo Bassano two decades later. In *The Journey of Jacob* (now in Venice, Palazzo Ducale), often regarded as a kind of pastoral nocturne, only the appearance of a camel among the other beasts indicates that we are not (or not only) looking at a depiction of contemporary shepherds of the Terraferma: as are the beleaguered and landless rural poor of the late 1500s, so (the image implies) were the chosen people before the time of the new covenant. The important shift in Bassano's work, made for a collector's studiolo rather than a chapel, is that the antitype of Jewish history is not the Eucharist, but the contemporary agrarian world.[49]

All this is to say that the style of *imitazione*—of Titian, Raphael, and Parmigianino—has been invested with apparently paradoxical associations: it designates the domain of the bodily and the sensual, while at the same time being encompassed by a representational mode based on the poetical refinements of metaphor and allusion. It is associated at once with the domain of the secular and the profane, and these in turn are presented as the hallmarks of Judaism, in accordance with a characterization of Judaism characteristic of Augustinian thought. The Jews are those who embrace the carnal and the literal, refusing the figurative import not only of their own scriptures but of their very historical existence in the world.[50]

The "judaization" of a representational mode associated with the most privileged sites of artistic production in Italy has several very interesting artistic implications. One of them is a subversion of the mode itself, to provide a foil for a mode of ideal naturalism that the painters of Brescia can claim as their own. Moretto will go on to produce definitive instances of that mode in later works like the *Feast in the House of Levi* for Santa Maria in Calchera (1550), which has been proclaimed as a major antecedent of Caravaggio's art. The corollary, however, is that painting can now be seen in terms of distinct modes of representation. Another consequence, I would propose, is the invention of a new kind of painting that is truly "profane" in its orientation, and truly poetic in its ability to construct meaning from a combination of naturalism, citation, and allegory. A self-referential mode of painting emerges that has as its goal the visualization of the word as much as of the world, and with a profound grasp of both their tension and their interdependency. In other words, naturalistic genre painting has its roots in the inversion of the high style; this inversion may also arise from concerns with Christian identity as those are manifest in art. Later in the century, the Carracci would model their manifesto-like *Butcher Shop* on a Marco Dente print after Raphael showing a scene of Old Testament sacrifice.[51] With such examples, any claim that the rise of genre painting in Italy is a proclamation of the new autonomy of art requires serious qualification.

By way of a coda, I want to illustrate another way in which modes of representation adhere to articulations of difference grounded in the Jewish and the Christian. Romanino was one of several artists who painted in the Palazzo Magno at Trent in the 1530s.[52] Here, we have a striking instance of how the various modes of secular painting work together to articulate the nature of profane space. Profane space is characterized by a playful hybridity, a pleasurable collision of a number of non-sacred idioms, of genre-like themes with mythology and history. Outside the prince bishop's chapel, the limit of sacred space is established by a fresco decoration with pagan gods. We encounter intrusions of the everyday: allegories of Prodigality and Avarice accompanied by a scene of a courtier paying two workmen. In Romanino's loggia we find a strange collision of things that are defined through their difference from sacred art: realism or "genre" painting and mythology—fat fleshy comic gods are present along with groups of musicians and a series of tragic heroines.

Elsewhere, we find frescoes by Romanino that actually have been hailed as the beginnings of genre painting in Italy. The *Castragatti* ("Cat Castrator") supposedly based on a painting later attributed to Giorgione by Ridolfi, constitutes a rather strange and discomforting beginning for genre.[53] It is an extraordinarily extreme instance of genre painting defined in terms of that which does not belong elsewhere. Yet the coexistence of violence with humor may be read in an ironic register, as a cue to a figurative or even typological purpose. Even scenes of the everyday may, like Lotto's intarsia covers and the intarsias themselves, be pointing us elsewhere: on one hand, to a cultural obsession with marking ethnic and religious others through violence, and on the other, trying to contain the socially disruptive potential of that violence. Already sinister in its bid to be pleasing, it becomes even more so when we recognize what it parodies: images of the *Martyrdom of Simon of Trent*. The *Castragatti* thus mediates a recently invented devotional subject that originated here, in the city of Trent, in 1475. The torture of the helpless animal surrounded by grinning figures recalls exactly similar outrages allegedly perpetrated on the infant Simon of

Trent by members of the local Jewish community, subsequently exterminated in its entirety. The subject had taken on a life of its own, not only in the region of Trent but, with particular intensity, in the towns of the Valcamonica near Brescia where Romanino and Moretto frequently worked. In one mural painting (c. 1500), in the parish church of San Martino at Cerveno, Simon's martyrdom is placed in an explicit typological relationship with Christ's Crucifixion.[54] For Romanino at Palazzo Magno, however, *The Martyrdom of Simon of Trent* has, like the Eucharist, become a ground of reference for new pictorial kinds far removed in spirit and in tone. In this case, the typological element of grotesque realism, any reference it might bear to "sacred history," seems ironic and jarring in character. It acknowledges and commemorates an event, yet offers a disclaimer on the truth of that event, distancing itself from its violence and disorder through the low comedy of the everyday.

NOTES

1. The discussion of Garofalo's fresco presented here recapitulates some material from the conclusion of my essay "The Conflicted Representation of Judaism in Italian Renaissance Representations of Christ's Life and Passion," in *The Passion Story: From Visual Representation to Social Drama* (University Park: Penn State University Press, 2008), 67–91.

2. "Finalmente lavorò a fresco nel refettorio di Santo Andrea, con bella e capricicciosa invenzione, molte figure, che accordano le cose del vecchio Testamento col nuovo." *Le opere di Giorgio Vasari*, ed. Gaetano Milanesi, 7 vols. (1906; reprint, Florence: Sansoni,1981), 6:466.

3. Ottavia Niccoli, *Prophecy and People in Renaissance Italy*, trans. Lydia G. Cochrane (Princeton, N.J.: Princeton University Press, 1990).

4. Analyzed by David Nirenberg, *Communities of Violence: Persecution of Minorities in the Middle Ages* (Princeton, N.J.: Princeton University Press, 1996).

5. Dana E. Katz, *The Jew in the Art of the Italian Renaissance* (Philadelphia: University of Pennsylvania Press, 2008), 69–99.

6. In his study of earlier representations of the "Avenging Crucifix," Achim Timmermann has observed that its fifteenth-century appearances signal a crisis in Christian identity, when the universal church is threatened with fragmentation through heresy and schism. Judaism may not be the sole target or even the principal one: it may stand for other more current and pressing threats to Christendom, such as the Hussite movement, which was sometimes regarded as being supported by the Jews. "The Avenging Crucifix: Some Observations on the Iconography of the Living Cross," *Gesta* 40 (2001), 141–60.

7. Giovanni Maria Zerbinati, *Croniche di Ferrara, 1500–1527*, ed. Giuseppina Maria Muzzarelli (Ferrara: Deputazione provinciale ferrarese di storia patria, , 1989), 157: "Gli hebrei facilmente infetano di peste per lo comercio et avidità del guadagno."

8. It was in Ferrara in 1523 that the Augustinian Andrea Bauria composed his *Apostolice potestatis defensio . . . in Lutherum*. See Eugenio Riccòmini, *Affreschi Ferraresi Restaurati ed Acquisizioni per la Pinacoteca Nazionale di Ferrara* (Bologna: Edizioni Alfa, 1973), 33. Baura had earlier preached against the papacy and was held to be a Lutheran; for a recent discussion on Baura with bibliography on Luther's followers among the Augustinians of Italy, see Niccoli, *Prophecy and People*, 89–91, 105–8.

     STEPHEN J. CAMPBELL

9. On Cranach's *Allegory of the Law and the Gospels,* see Joseph Leo Koerner, *The Moment of Self-Portraiture in German Renaissance Art* (Chicago: University of Chicago Press, 1993), 379–83.

10. Caroline Walker Bynum, *Wonderful Blood: Theology and Practice in Late Medieval Northern Germany and Beyond* (Philadelphia: University of Pennsylvania Press, 2007), esp. 85–112.

11. Sacred allegory makes some return in the later sixteenth century in allegories of the rosary; otherwise, Counter Reformation theorists of art tended to be highly critical of the use of allegory by artists, who had to take pains that historical truth, that is, scripture, would be distinguishable from poetic fiction. On the controversy with regard to allegorical imagery in religious art, see Charles Dempsey, "Mythic Inventions in Counter-Reformation Painting," in *Rome and the Renaissance: The City and the Myth,* ed. Paul A. Ramsay (Binghamton, N.Y.: Center for Medieval and Renaissance Studies, 1982), 55–75.

12. On typological imagery and scriptural exegesis, see Beryl Smalley, *The Study of the Bible in the Middle Ages* (Oxford: Blackwell 1952); Kathleen Biddick, *The Typological Imaginary: Circumcision, Technology, History* (Philadelphia: University of Pennsylvania Press, 2003); Sara Lipton, *Images of Intolerance: The Representation of Jews and Judaism in the Bible Moralisée* (Berkeley: University of California Press, 1999); Christopher Hughes, "Typology and its Uses in the Moralized Bible," in *The Mind's Eye: Art and Theological Argument in the Middle Ages,* ed. Jeffrey F. Hamburger and Anne-Marie Bouché (Princeton, N.J.: Princeton University Press, 2005), 133–51.

13. The case of the Dominican Girolamo Savonarola has been much debated as an instance of a "proto-reformation" call for the reform of Christian art. Jill Burke, *Changing Patrons: Social Identity and the Visual Arts in Renaissance Florence* (University Park: Penn State University Press, 2004), 155–187, has pointed out that much of the friar's preaching on the errors of artists and patrons is both "steeped in a Christian discourse about images that is centuries old" and framed by a broader polemical concern about the correct use of wealth. Artists like Lorenzo Lotto have also been discussed as responding to the religious crises of the 1520s onward, but their reaction can only be meaningfully discussed at the level of content: there is no overt concern with the reform of art (encompassing style and artistic invention) as such. For a critical reassessment of scholarly debates on Lotto's religious heterodoxy, see Massimo Firpo, *Artisti, gioiellieri, eretici: il mondo di Lorenzo Lotto tra Riforma e Controriforma* (Rome: Laterza, 2001). For an argument linking debates about Catholic orthodoxy with the experimental art of Rosso and Parmigianino and the emergence of new forms such as the statue altar, see Alexander Nagel, "Experiments in Art and Reform in Italy in the Early Sixteenth Century," in *The Pontificate of Clement VII: History, Politics, Culture,* ed. Sheryl Reiss and Kenneth Gouwens (Burlington: Ashgate, 2005), but the attempt to see such experiments as a proto-Tridentine "reform" of art (as distinct from a confidence in its possibilities) requires further debate and inquiry.

14. The standard works on Counter Reformation art theory and practice are Paolo Prodi, *Ricerca sulla teorica delle arti figurative nella Riforma Cattolica* (1962; rev. ed., Bologna: Nuova Alfa, 1984), and Federico Zeri, *Pittura e Controriforma: L'arte senza tempo di Scipione da Gaeta* (Turin: Einaudi, 1957). On the creation of a Catholic visual culture, see Gauvin A. Bailey, *Between Renaissance and Baroque: Jesuit Art in Rome, 1565–1610* (Toronto: University of Toronto Press, 2003); Pamela Jones, "Art Theory as Ideology: Gabriele Paleotti's Hierarchical Notion of Painting's Universality and Reception," in *Reframing the Renaissance: Visual Culture in Europe and Latin America, 1450–1650,* ed. Clare Farago (New Haven, Conn.: Yale University Press, 1995), 127–323; Michele Di Monte, "Immagini, devozione e pubblico: sul problema dell'interpretazione della pittura religiosa del Cinquecento," *Venezia Cinquecento* 8 (1998), 5–51.

15. On the "discourse of workshops," see David Summers, *Michelangelo and the Language of Art* (Princeton, N.J.: Princeton University Press, 1981); on workshop culture and academic institutionalization, see Karin-edis Barzman, *The Florentine Academy and the Early Modern State: The Discipline of Disegno* (Cambridge: Cambridge University Press, 2000).

16. Among the Lutherans, the rapid creation of a new evangelical visual culture has been widely held to have been formulated programmatically at the expense of artistic interest. This view has been most recently espoused by Joseph Leo Koerner in *The Reformation of the Image* (Chicago: University of Chicago Press, 2004), which recognizes a distinction between art and visual culture, and addresses the systematic ideological reduction of the former to the latter.

17. On the critical potential of art from outside the major centers, the *perferia*, see Enrico Castelnuovo and Carlo Ginzburg, "Centro e periferia," *Storia dell'arte italiana*, ed. Giovanni Previtali, pt. 1, vol. 1 (Turin: Einaudi, 1979), 287–352; English edition, "Centre and Periphery," in *History of Italian Art*, trans. Ellen Bianchini and Claire Dorey, 2 vols. (Cambridge: Polity Press, 1994), 2:29–113. Double-periphery designates a zone of artistic production located between two major centers, in this case the neighboring Lombard metropolis of Milan and the more distant but politically dominant Venice, capital of the state to which the Lombard city of Brescia belonged.

18. On Catholic evangelism in Brescia after the Sack, see most recently the essays in the catalogue *Aspirazioni e Devozioni. Brescia nel Cinquecento tra Preghiera e Eresia*, ed. Ennio Ferraglio (Milan: Mondadori Electa, 2006); see also Antonio Cistellini, "La vita religiosa nei secoli XV e XVI," in *Storia di Brescia*, ed. Giovanni Treccani degli Alfieri (Bologna: Morcelliana, 1963), 399–473. Also useful is Querciolo Mazzonis, *Spirituality, Gender and the Self in Renaissance Italy: Angela Merici and the Company of St. Ursula (1474–1540)* (Washington, D.C.: Catholic University of America Press, 2007). For a comprehensive discussion of painters and their relation to the religious culture of the laity, see Valerio Guazzoni, *Moretto: Il tema sacro* (Brescia: Grafo, 1981). For a recent survey of artistic patronage in Brescia in the 1500s, see Andrea Bayer, "Bergamo and Brescia," in *Venice and the Veneto*, ed. Peter Humfrey (Cambridge: Cambridge University Press, 2007), esp. 306–26. On Moretto and Benedictine reform, see Gabriele Neher, "Moretto and the Congregation of S. Giorgio in Alga 1540–1550: Fashioning the Visual Identity of a Religious Congregation," in *Fashioning Identities in Renaissance Art* (London: Ashgate, 2000), 131–49.

19. On the Brescian clergy before Trent, see Cistellini, "La vita religiosa," 437–47.

20. On the Scuole del Sacramento in Brescia, see Guazzoni, *Moretto*, 19–29, and Daniele Montanari, *Disciplinamento in terra veneta: La diocesi di Brescia nella seconda metà del XVI secolo* (Bologna: Il Mulino, 1987), 209–16.

21. For instance, Miri Rubin, *Gentile Tales: The Narrative Assault on Late Medieval Jews* (New Haven, Conn.: Yale University Press, 1999); Mitchell Merback, "Fount of Mercy, City of Blood: Cultic Anti-Judaism and the Pulkau Passion Altarpiece," *Art Bulletin* 87 (2005), 589–642.

22. Fabio Glissenti, *Gli Ebrei nel Bresciano al Tempo della Dominazione Veneta* (Brescia: Tipografia F. Apollonio, 1890); Dominique Rigaux, "Antijudaïsme per l'Image: L'iconographie de Simon de Trente dans la Région de Brescia," in *Politique et Religion dans le Judaïsme Ancien et Médiéval: Interventions au Colloque des 8 et 9 Décembre 1987*, ed. Daniel Tollet (Paris: Desclée, 1989), 309–18. In 1505, the Dominican Order who defended their right to lavish honoraria for funeral services were accused of making common cause with the Jews of the city, at a time when Franciscans (who joined in the opposition to the Dominicans) were pressing for their expulsion. See *Vainglorious Death: A Funerary Fracas in Renaissance Brescia*, ed. Stephen Bowd (Tempe: Arizona Center for Medieval and Renaissance Studies, 2006), xxii–xxiii, xxviii–xxix, lxiii, 7, 27, 87.

STEPHEN J. CAMPBELL

23. See Giovanni Agosti, "Sui gusti di Altobello Averoldi," in *Il polittico Averoldi di Tiziano restaurato*, ed. Elena Lucchesi Ragni and Giovanni Agosti (Brescia: Grafo, 1991), 55–80.

24. See the entry by Stefania Buganza in the exhibition catalogue *Romanino: Un pittore in rivolta nel Rinascimento italiano* (Milan: Silvana, 2006), 146–48; on Romanino's relationship to Titian, see the essay by Alessandro Nova in the same catalogue, "Centro, periferia, Provincia: Tiziano e Romanino," 48–68.

25. Buganza in *Romanino*, 132–34.

26. Lee Palmer Wandel, *The Eucharist in the Reformation: Incarnation and Liturgy* (Cambridge: Cambridge University Press, 2006), 126. On eucharistic imagery in the Veneto during the 1500s, see Maurice Cope, *The Venetian Chapel of the Sacrament in the Sixteenth Century* (New York: Garland, 1979).

27. Although there is a possible equivocation here—the Eucharist "stands for the body of Christ"/ "is the body of Christ," which an image is not called upon to resolve. The equivocation was at the heart of passionate controversies concerning the Eucharist already by the eve of the Reformation; see Wandel, *Eucharist in the Reformation*. It seems unlikely that Romanino would have known the one comparable representation of an altarpiece-within-an-altarpiece, the *Miracle of Galla Placidia* painted by Niccolo Rondinelli around 1505 for S. Giovanni Evangelista, Ravenna (now Milan, Brera).

28. On the decline in Perugino's reputation before and after his death, see Jonathan K. Nelson, "La disgrazia di Pietro: L'importanza della pala della Santissima Annunziata nelle Vita del Perugino del Vasari," in *Pietro Vannucci: Il Perugino*, ed. Laura Teza (Perugia: Volumnia, 2004); Michelle O'Malley, "Quality and the Pressures of Reputation: Rethinking Perugino," *Art Bulletin* 89 (2007), 676–96; Alessandro Marabottini, "Aspetti della fortuna e sfortuna di Perugino nella pittura e nella teoria artistica dal Cinquecento all'Ottocento," in *Perugino: Il Divin Pittore*, exhibition catalogue, ed. Vittoria Garibaldi and Francesco Federico Mancini (Milan: Silvana, 2004), 387–401.

29. For remarks on Perugino and the *maniera devota*, see Charles Dempsey, "Introduction," in *Drawing Relationships in Northern Italian Renaissance Art: Patronage and Theories of Invention* ed Giancarla Periti (London: Ashgate, 2004), 3–4. Romanino's interest in the art of Perugino does not seem to have lasted beyond the *Mass of St. Apollonius*. About a decade later, c. 1535, he reworked the composition in a confraternal banner for the church of Saints Faustino and Giovita, where he has clearly moved beyond any reference to Perugino, or indeed to any artistic forebear other than his own earlier work. The three saints now dominate the composition; St. Apollonius, who looks upward at a heavenly apparition of the Eucharist, is more markedly a figure of mid-cinquecento painting. The altarpiece behind him is largely obscured apart from two angels who, with a pictorial wit characteristic of Romanino, also can be read as heavenly attendants on Apollonius himself. The other side of the banner is a more decorous reworking of the Capriolo *Resurrection*, where Christ levitates placidly against a dawn sky turbulent with clouds.

30. On Savoldo's altarpiece and the version in San Giobbe, proposing a date of 1540 for both (the version in Venice allegedly once bore this date), see the entries by Pier Vigilio Begni Redona in *Giovanni Gerolamo Savoldo tra Foppa, Giorgione e Caravaggio*, exhibition catalogue (Milan: Electa, 1990), 109–15; also Carolyn C. Wilson, *St. Joseph in Italian Renaissance Art and Society: New Directions and Interpretation* (Philadelphia: St. Joseph's University Press, 2001), 33–34, and the entry by Beverly L. Brown in *Renaissance Venice and the North: Crosscurrents in the Time of Bellini, Dürer and Titian*, ed. Bernard Aikema and Beverly L. Brown (New York: Rizzoli, 2000), 474.

31. On the miraculous image, see D. Paolo Guerrini, *Il Santuario di S. Maria delle Grazie: Cenni di storia e d'arte* (Brescia: Scuola Tipografica di Maria Immacolata, 1923), 104–7.

32. Wilson, *St. Joseph*, 33–34.

33. For the will and an account of the *Christologos Peregrinorum,* see *Giovanni Gerolamo Savoldo,* 320. See also Bernard Aikema, "Savoldo, la Città di Dio e il pellegrinagio della vita," *Venezia Cinquecento* 3 (1993), 99–120.

34. On eucharistic hermeneutics, see Wandel, *Eucharist in the Reformation,* esp. 14–45, 208–55; also David Aers, "New Historicism and the Eucharist," *Journal of Medieval and Early Modern Studies* 33 (2003), 241–59. On the Eucharist as representational model, see Regina Stefaniak, "Replicating Mysteries of the Passion: Rosso's *Dead Christ with Angels,*" *Renaissance Quarterly* 45 (1992), 677–738.

35. For an excellent treatment of the chapel, addressing the records of the commission, the iconography, and the theological context, see Barbara Maria Savy, "*Manducatio per visum. Temi Eucaristici nella pittura di Romanino e Moretto,*" *Pittura del Rinascimento nell'Italia Settentrionale, Quaderni* 2 (Cittadella: Bertoncello Artigrafiche, 2006).

36. On ocular communion, see Édouard Dumoutet, *Le désir de voir l'hostie et les origines de la dévotion au Saint-Sacrement* (Paris: Beauchesne,1926); Bynum, "Seeing and Seeing Beyond: The Mass of St. Gregory in the Fifteenth Century," in *The Mind's Eye: Art and Theology in the Middle Ages,* ed. Anne-Marie Bouché and Jeffrey Hamburger (Princeton, N.J.: Princeton University Press, 2005), 208–40. In her comprehensive treatment of the role of Augustinian theology in the formulation of the chapel's program, Savy, *Manducatio per visum,* 39–51, has regarded Romanino's lunette as fundamental to the meaning of the entire complex. While the Old Testament scenes deal with food that is physically consumed, the comportment of the figures in the lunette who gaze in reverence and awe at the sacrament suggests a higher kind of reception, a *manducatio per visum* or "feeding through the eyes," in Augustine's words. Here, the visible character of the Host in its elevation before the people, its presentation in monstrances, is an expression of its efficacy, which is not to be limited by its original character as food. Conversely, simply eating the host has no salvific benefit without the faith that is here manifest in the gaze that reveres and acknowledges the host's divinity.

37. In his *Dialogo di Pittura* of 1538, Savoldo's pupil Paolo Pino declared, "La pittura e poesia, cioè invenzione." *Trattati d'arte del Cinquecento,* ed. Paola Barocchi, 3 vols. (Bari: Laterza, 1960), 1:115. For a comprehensive recent treatment of Titian's self-conscious practice of poetic painting, see Una Roman d'Elia, *The Poetics of Titian's Religious Paintings* (Cambridge: Cambridge University Press, 2005).

38. For useful considerations on Raphael as a poetic painter, see Kurt Badt, "Raphael's Incendio del Borgo," *Journal of the Warburg and Courtauld Institutes* 22 (1959), 35–59; also Kim Butler, "Reddita lux est: Raphael and the Pursuit of Eloquence in Leonine Rome," in *Artists at Court: Image Making and Identity 1300–1550,* ed. Stephen J. Campbell (Boston: Isabella Stewart Gardner Museum, 2004), 138–48.

39. Pier Virgilio Begni Redona, entry in *Alessandro Bonvicino Il Moretto* (Bologna: Nuova Alfa, 1988), 186–93; Savy, *Manducatio per visum*; Giovanni Testori, *Romanino e Moretto alla Cappella del Sacramento* (Brescia: Grafo, 1975); entries by Luigi Samoggia in *Mistero e immagine: l'Eucaristia nell'arte dal XVI al XVIII secolo,* ed. Salvatore Baviera and Jadranka Bentini (Milan: Electa: 1997), 96–100.

40. Alessandro Ballarin, "La Cappella del Sacramento in San Giovanni Evangelista a Brescia," in *La 'Salome' del Romanino ed altri studi sulla pittura bresciana del Cinquecento,* ed. Barbara Maria Savy, *Pittura del Rinascimento nell'Italia Settentrionale* 9 (Cittadella: Bertoncello Artigrafiche, 2002), 151–87.

41. On Brescian headgear, see Nicholas Penny, *The Sixteenth Century Italian Paintings,* vol. 1: *Paintings from Bergamo, Brescia and Cremona* (London: National Gallery Company, 2004), 154.

   STEPHEN J. CAMPBELL

42. Ballarin, "La Cappella del Sacramento"; Chiara Parisio, "Alcune indicazioni sulle fonti figurative del Moretto," in *Alessandro Bonvicino Il Moretto* (Bologna: Nuova Alfa, 1988), 273–79.

43. Parisio, "Alcune indicazioni," 277.

44. Savy, *Manducatio per visum*, 31–38, 105–15.

45. The connection is noted by Savy, "*Manducatio per visum*," 36; on the Bergamo *intarsia*, see Francesca Cortesi Bosco, *Il coro intarsiato di Lotto e Capoferri per Santa Maria Maggiore in Bergamo*, 2 vols. (Milan: Silvana, 1987); for documentation on Moretto's involvement, see references in *Alessandro Bonvicino il Moretto*, 292.

46. Diana Galis, "Concealed Wisdom: Renaissance Hieroglyphic and Lorenzo Lotto's Bergamo *Intarsie*," *Art Bulletin* 62 (1980), 363–75.

47. For an illustration, see *Alessandro Bonvicino il Moretto*, 103, and Savy, *Manducatio per visum*, fig. 34.

48. On Italian "genre" pictures, see Sheila McTighe, "Food and the Body in Italian Genre Painting c. 1580: Campi, Passarotti, and Carracci," *Art Bulletin* 86 (2004), 301–23; Stefania Mason, "Low Life and Landcape: *Minor pictura* in Sixteenth Century Venice," in *Renaissance Venice and the North*, 558–613.

49. Interestingly, the owner of the work, Giacomo Contarini, seems to have followed a typological impulse by exhibiting the work with a Veronese *Rape of Europa*, and ensuring in his will that that the works would be kept together in posterity. The juxtaposition invites reflection on the analogy and differences between two modes of pictorial and discursive representation, one denoting the "scriptural" and the other "the poetic." For a reading of the *Journey of Jacob* that attempts to take account of the simultaneity of scriptural reference and contemporary sociological fact (in 1648 Carlo Ridolfi asserted that the painting depicted the nocturnal "transit of the shepherds" on newly enclosed land near Bassana di Grappa), see Paolo Berdini, *The Religious Art of Jacopo Bassano: Painting as Visual Exegesis* (Cambridge: Cambridge University Press, 1997), 83–87.

50. For a recent study of Christian conceptions of the carnality of Judaism, see Sara Lipton, "The Temple Is My Body: Gender, Carnality and Synagoga in the Bible Moralisée," in *Imagining the Self, Imagining the Other: Visual Representation and Jewish-Christian Dynamics in the Middle Ages and Early Modern Period*, ed. Eva Frojmovic (Leiden: Brill, 2002), 129–63.

51. Noted by John Rupert Martin, "The Butcher's Shop of the Carracci," *Art Bulletin* 45 (1963), 263–66.

52. On the Romanino frescoes in Palazzo Magno at Trent, see the essays in *Romanino: Un pittore in rivolta*, 221–70 and 362–68. On contemporary responses to the problem of decorum in the frescoes, see Thomas Frangenberg, "Decorum in the Magno Palazzo in Trent," *Renaissance Studies* 7 (1993), 352–77.

53. Carlo Ridolfi, *Le meraviglie dell'arte*, 2 vols. (Venice, 1648), 1:129; for an illustration and discussion, see Francesca de Gramatica, "Un 'palazzo piacevole,' i 'gran progenitori,' e le giovani bagnanti: note sulla pittura profana di Romanino al Buonconsiglio," in *Romanino: Un pittore in rivolta*, 242–58, quotation at 245.

54. On the Cerveno mural and other images of Simon in the region of Brescia, see Katz, *The Jew in the Art of the Italian Renaissance*, 142–57.

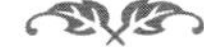

CHAPTER 11

Poussin's Useless Treasures

Richard Neer

For the Augenblicks: Richard, Irene, and Eva

In the spring of 1647, Nicolas Poussin was hard at work on a set of seven pictures illustrating the holy sacraments of the Catholic church. He had already completed one full set for his chief supporter in Rome, the antiquarian Cassiano dal Pozzo. But then his French patron, Paul Fréart de Chantelou, had jealously demanded copies for himself—and Poussin had adroitly parlayed the request into an entirely new commission: not mere copies of the dal Pozzo series, but seven original paintings.[1] This second set of *Sacraments* would turn out to be the capstone of his career. Yet the work was long in completion, and Chantelou was demanding. *Baptism*, completed in 1646, was judged a disappointment. So when, on June 3, 1647, Poussin wrote to inform his patron that *Penance* was ready for crating, he took care to underscore the "loving diligence" with which he had executed the work (Figure 11.1).[2] He even made a stab at humor: "I am now sending you the *penance* I have made; I do not know if it will be enough to erase the blame for past faults."[3] He had been working up the picture for three years.

In both the series for Chantelou and the earlier one for dal Pozzo, Poussin illustrated most of the sacraments with biblical exempla. *Penance*, in each case, shows Christ's dinner at the house of Simon the Pharisee (Luke 7:36–39): "And one of the Pharisees desired him that he would eat with him. And he went into the Pharisee's house, and sat down to meat. And, behold, a woman in the city, which was a sinner, when she knew that Jesus sat at meat in the Pharisee's

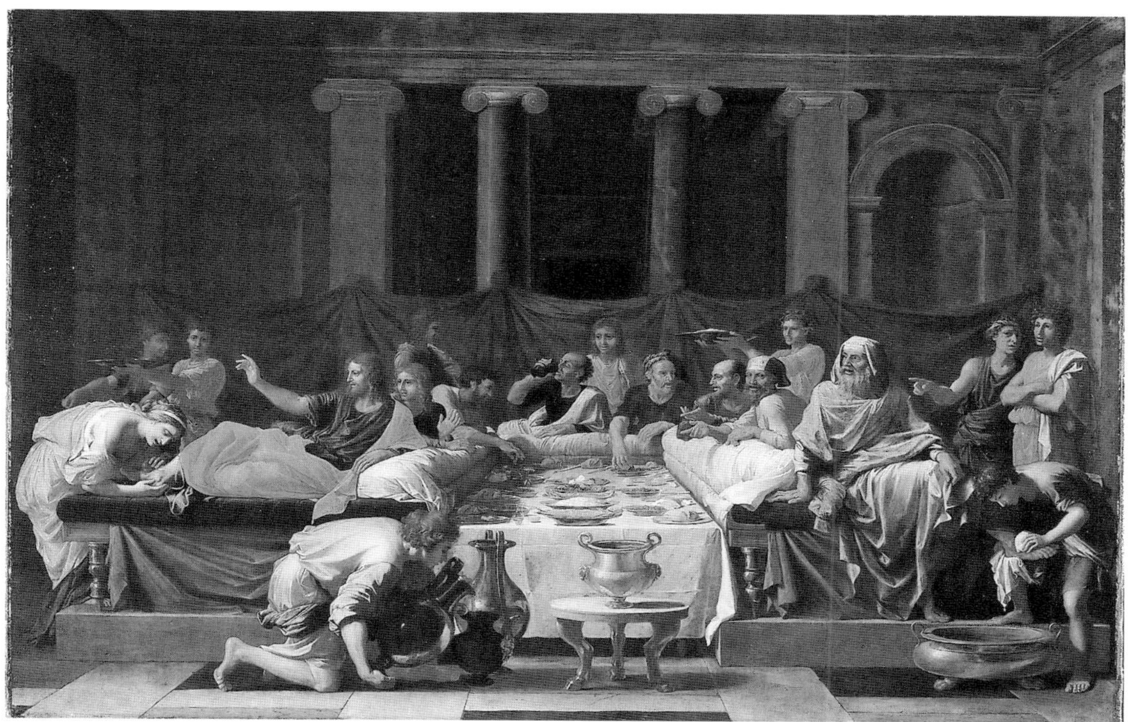

11.1. Nicolas Poussin, *Penance*, 1647. Duke of Sutherland Collection, on loan to National Gallery of Scotland, Edinbugh. Used by kind permission.

house, brought an alabaster box of ointment, and stood at his feet behind him weeping, and began to wash his feet with tears, and did wipe them with the hairs of her head, and kissed his feet, and anointed them with the ointment." Poussin set this story in a Roman-style dining room. He put a lot of effort into ensuring the correctness of period detail.[4] What sort of *triclinia* should be used? How should they be arranged? How should the guests be seated? Poussin was, however, willing to jettison accuracy when the situation demanded. For example, his source for Roman dining customs, the *De arte gymnastica* of Girolamo Mercuriale (Venice, 1601), dictated that the host should sit at center; Poussin placed Simon the Pharisee at right, directly opposite Christ, in order to produce a bilateral contrast between Jew and messiah.[5] One consequence of this arrangement is that the penitent Magdalene is at the extreme left of the picture; Simon's startled gaze runs the full length of the canvas to reach her. The picture's chief dramatic action is not Mary's act of contrition but Simon's reaction to it, as described in Luke 7:39: "And the Pharisee, who had invited him, seeing it, spoke within himself, saying: This man, if he were a prophet, would know surely who and what manner of woman this is that toucheth him, that she is a sinner."

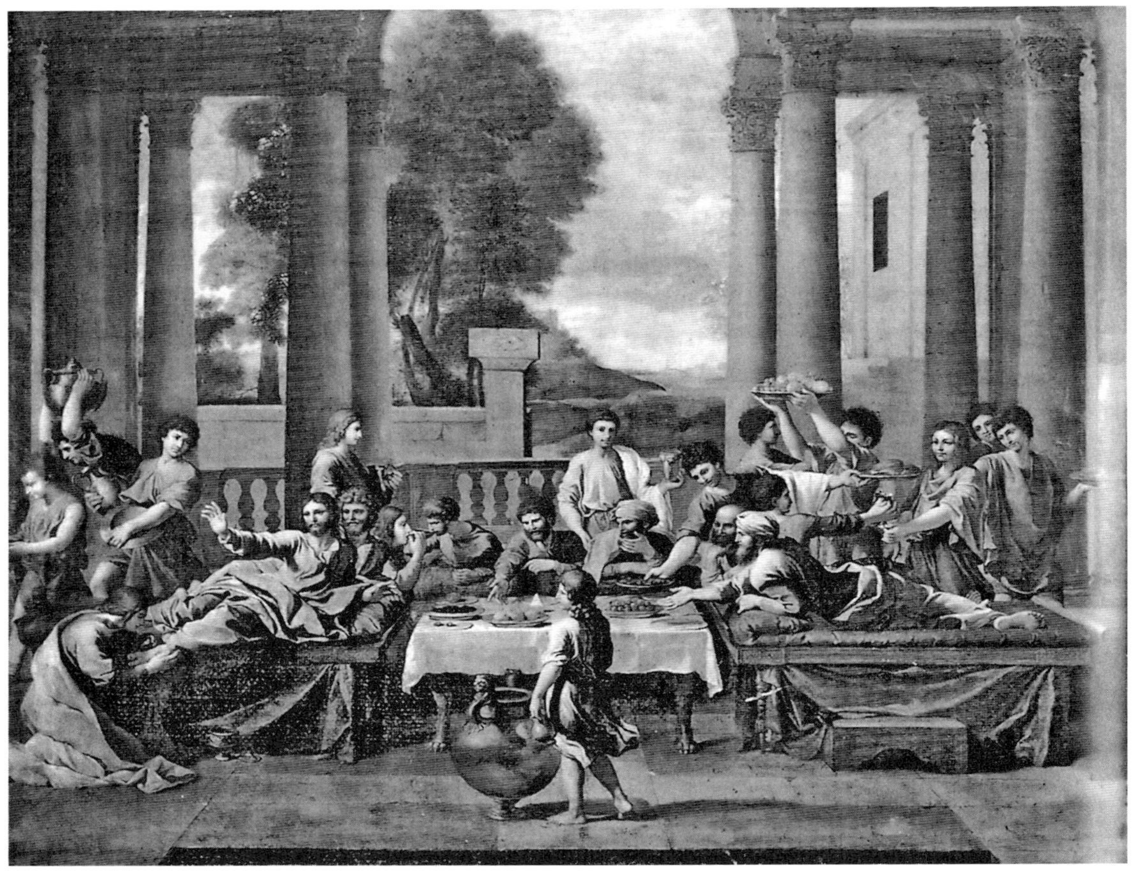

11.2. Anonymous, after Nicolas Poussin, *Penance*, original c. 1636–40. Present location unknown. Photo after von Henneberg, 1987.

Here, to borrow Jean Starobinski's description of Corneille, "vision is the real point at which the action culminates."[6] For Poussin, the story of Christ's visit to the house of Simon was as much about visual recognition, its stakes and vicissitudes, as it was about penance.

It is useful, in this regard, to compare the picture for Chantelou with the earlier version for Cassiano dal Pozzo (destroyed by fire in 1816 but known through copies).[7] In the earlier version, a pillar at center bore a carved emblem: an open hand with an eye staring from its palm (Figure 11.2).[8] As Jean Badouin glossed this *manu oculata* in his *Recueil d'Emblèmes divers* (1638–39), it conveys the principle that "one must, so to speak, touch what people report with one's finger, before believing in it."[9] Blazoned on the Pharisee's house, it provides a key to his action and, by extension, to the underlying *pensée* of the picture as a whole.[10] Essentially contradicting the Pauline definition of faith as "the evidence

RICHARD NEER

of things not seen" (Heb. 11:1), the emblem suggests the literalism of Pharisaic vision, its failure to see with *les yeux de la foi*, the eyes of faith, to recognize the Word in the flesh.

Although Poussin omitted the emblem from the version for Chantelou, he compensated by altering the costume of the Pharisees. Instead of generic Oriental garb, complete with turbans, they now wear carefully researched rabbinical attire. Elizabeth Cropper and Charles Dempsey have drawn attention to the inscribed bands over their foreheads.[11] These bands seem intended to represent phylacteries or *tefillin*, which Poussin (like some other gentile artists) has confused with the *tallit*, or prayer scarf. The inscriptions themselves, however, are not those that belong inside a phylactery. Instead, Poussin has taken the opportunity to blazon a motto across the Pharisee's brow. The text, as Cropper and Dempsey were the first to observe, is a subtly modified version of Psalm 25:15. Where the Bible reads, "Mine eyes are ever toward the Lord," the headbands say, "Mine eyes are ever toward *the letter of the Law of* the Lord." The result may be bad Hebrew but it usefully glosses Simon's action. "His blind faith in the written law renders him unable to recognize the Lord, even with eyes turned full upon him; and this in its turn renders even more poignant Poussin's representation of the acknowledgment of Christ by a simple woman from the city, the penitent Magdalene."[12] The Hebrew text, in other words, serves the same function as the emblem in the earlier version: it is a cipher-key to the picture's *pensée*.

The change from emblem to inscription had two consequences. First, it explicitly judaized Simon's failure of vision. In the first version, the generic emblem and Oriental attire entailed no explicit connection to Judaism per se. Confession and penance were topics of fierce debate between Catholics and Protestants in the seventeenth century, and one might argue that the dal Pozzo picture merely used Simon to figure the "heretical" denial of the sacrament by the Calvinists and Lutherans.[13] With the version for Chantelou, however, Judaism itself is inescapably at issue. The messiah's presence contravenes more than the conventional wisdom of emblem-books; it overthrows the Wisdom of the Jews.

Second, the change from emblem to inscription made the picture significantly more obscure. Who, after all, could be expected to understand the text on Simon's brow? Certainly not Poussin himself; he must have had help from one of the scholars in his Roman milieu in order to compose and transcribe this modified line from the twenty-fifth psalm.[14] In general, the ability to read Hebrew was quite rare in France.[15] It could even be suspect: François Béroalde de Verville tells a story of a man who brought a Hebrew book to church for a prank; although by his own admission he could read the words "no better than a monkey," he left it in his pew to be discovered by a canon, who, equally illiterate, promptly denounced him as a magician.[16] Just so, Poussin's friend Gabriel Naudé complained, "Someone who understands Hebrew well is taken for a Jew or a *marrano*; and those who study mathematics or the less commonplace sciences are suspected of being enchanters or magicians."[17] "Almost all the syllables of this language, and the punctuation marks as well, are admirable mysteries [*mystères admirables*]," wrote the historian Léonard Bertaut in 1662.[18] A passage from Corneille's *Le Menteur* (1644) dramatizes the situation. The lying Dorante claims to know how to make a powder that can resurrect the dead; asked to reveal the recipe, he replies: "I would give it to you, just to make you happy, but the secret consists of a few words of Hebrew which are so hard to pronounce that, for you, they would be but useless treasures."[19] Hebrew contains the secret of defeating death, but nobody can read it. Just so, Poussin's text—a spell of sorts for unlocking the meaning of the picture—will have been for Chantelou a "useless treasure." All the more puzzling, therefore, that the artist should have told his patron, "The subject is represented in such a way that it seems to me that there is no need for interpretation provided only that one has read the Evangelist."[20] The effort that Poussin must have expended to obtain and transcribe the text, not to mention its importance to the picture, makes this statement puzzling.

What is going on here? Why present one's patron with a text he cannot read, a key that itself requires decryption? Having done so, why disavow the picture's complexity? These circumstantial questions give rise to more important ones about the picture itself. For reading, and the failure to read, are central to the narrative action: the chief drama, again, is Simon's failure properly to recognize the Saviour, hence to read the prophecies of His coming. But the Hebrew text makes reading a problem for the beholder as well. What, then, is the relationship between the gaze of the Pharisee, and that of the picture's own spectators? And why should Hebrew writing, specifically, be the way to figure this crux? To answer such questions requires an account of early modern concepts of the image and its relation to the written word, and of the role of Judaism—a certain idea of Judaism—in articulating and stabilizing such concepts.

There were few Jews in France in Poussin's day.[21] Expelled in 1394, they had begun to trickle back during the sixteenth century. Bordeaux was an important center for refugee *marranos* from Spain and Portugal (including Montaigne's family on his mother's side), as was Rouen; Avignon was home to remnants of "the Pope's Jews"; Metz had a small but growing community.[22] But the Bourbon kings maintained an official proscription on Judaism; France was in this respect far stricter than England, the Netherlands, or Italy. For most French

RICHARD NEER

people, Jews were literally a "people of the book," known through literary representations and sermonizing. Cardinal de Richelieu was an avid collector of Hebrew manuscripts, which were hard to come by, and printed books in Hebrew could be purchased in Paris at the shop of an oddly named Rabbi L'Abbé.[23] As for Jewish learning, savants like Marin Mersenne and Blaise Pascal were familiar with talmudic and kabbalistic scholarship, and Maimonides remained a basic authority on questions of idolatry.[24] Yet, as we have seen, few people could actually read such texts in the original. Although Hebrew was taught at Port-Royal, even Pascal would have relied on translations.[25] In 1640, there were already efforts underway in London to establish a College devoted to Judaic scholarship, but the idea would have been unthinkable in France.[26] As a result, most French people—even educated ones—were ignorant of the realities of Jewish life. In 1637, the Venetian rabbi Leon da Modena published the first account of Jewish customs by a professing Jew for a gentile audience, under the title *Historia de' riti ebrei*; although it appeared in English by 1650, a French translation would have to wait until 1674.[27] Poussin's confusion in the matter of phylacteries was, in this respect, par for the course.

Untrammeled by facts, the French imagination was free to make of Judaism what it wished. In particular, it used Judaism as a way to think figurality and literalism. The guiding assumption, rooted in the Pauline epistles, was that the Old Testament was a cipher or, in Augustine's phrase, "a promise in figure."[28] Erich Auerbach, in a classic study, has shown how *figura* evolved in Late Antiquity from a rhetorical term for allusive discourse to a mode of reading that saw the Old Testament as a "pure phenomenal prophecy," every episode a prefiguration of salvation to come. "Figural interpretation establishes a connection between two events or persons, the first of which signifies not only itself but also the second, while the second encompasses or fulfills the first."[29] Moses, for instance, was an *umbra* (shadow) or *figura* (figure) of Christ; the manna prefigured the eucharistic host, the brazen serpent prefigured the Crucifixion, just as Jewish circumcision prefigured Pauline "circumcision of the heart." Such interpretations in no way entailed that the Old Testament be merely an allegorical conceit. On the contrary, scriptural narratives were historically accurate in every particular; not so much the biblical text, but the very history of the world, was prophetic. Just as God was a real presence in the eucharistic Host even as the Host remained bread, so figural significance inhered in a biblical text that remained historically true.[30]

Judaism was a requisite foil to this figural or typological mode of reading. Where a radical allegoresis might deny the historical truth of the Old Testament narratives, hence the reality of Jewish history, Jews themselves were taken to embody the opposite error: literalism. As Augustine put it, they "accepted the law in a carnal sense and did not understand its earthly promises as types [*figures*] of heavenly things."[31] They attended only to the letter, not the spirit, of the Old Testament; and "the letter killeth" (2 Cor. 3:6). This view remained current in the seventeenth century.[32] Perhaps the only things on which Jesuits, Gallicans, and Jansenists could agree were that the Old Testament was figural, and that Jews were blind, carnal literalists. On the Jesuit side, authors like Juan Marquez, Antoine Girard, and Louis Richeome were firmly committed to typology and, by extension, to the notion of Judaic blindness.[33] Here is Richeome in a contemporary English translation: "The ancient Iewes could not write more clearly of the Figure of our Truth amongst the Shadowes of their Law: and he, that seeth not this Truth, brightly shining in the Sacrifice of the Law of Grace, is blinde at noone-day, and worse than a Iew."[34] At the opposite end of the political and theological spectrum, similar themes figure prominently in the writings of the Port-Royal scholars. As Pascal put it in a letter to Mlle de Roannez (October 1656):

> For there are two perfect meanings, the literal and the mystical; and the Jews stopping at the one do not even think there is another and do not dream of searching for it. Just so the impious, on seeing natural effects, attribute them to nature without thinking that there is another author. And just as the Jews, on seeing a perfect man in Jesus Christ, did not think of seeking another nature in Him ("We did not think it was he," as, again, Isaiah put it), even so the heretics, on seeing the perfect appearance of the bread, do not think to seek another substance in it. All things cover up some mystery; all things are veils which cover God. Christians should recognize Him in everything.[35]

The figurality of the Old Testament, and the Jews' blindness to it—hence to Christ's true nature—were commonplaces. Richelieu subscribed to a version of this thesis, and the only difference between Pascal and his Jesuit nemeses in this regard was the severity with which the Jews were to be condemned for their obstinacy in misreading.

As Auerbach observed, figuralism tended to obscure the specifically Jewish character of the Old Testament.[36] Indeed, prior to the emergence of historical criticism in the later seventeenth century, the Old Testament was not available as a specifically *Jewish* text: what Pascal called *la perpetuité de la foi* subsumed it under a Christian reading.[37] This fact explains the availability of Old Testament narratives as exemplars in French discourse.[38] Moses, for instance, was the paradigmatic lawgiver for both Richelieu and the Parlement de Paris; David was the exemplary opponent of tyranny for both monarchists and rebels.[39] Such references were varied and opportunistic, but they all assumed a non-Jewish Old Testament. When partisans of the Prince de Condé called him David to Mazarin's Goliath, for instance, the point was not that he was Judaic but that he was an underdog. In short, the Old Testament as such was not necessarily associated with Judaism, but a particular way of reading it certainly was.

But Jews were also understood to possess wisdom, albeit of a suspect type. Kabbalah was a source of fascination and contributed to the association of Judaism and sorcery. As Poussin's acquaintance Georges de Scudéry put it:

> As one can draw from the ingrate viper a powerful medicine . . . just so . . . the prudent reader . . . takes good from evil, light from shadow; sees the snare and avoids it wisely; and follows the main road to proceed securely. . . . With little effort one can follow the trails of the curious and wise kabbalists: to pass after them along these winding paths, and distinguish clarity from the Hebrew shadows. Everything the rabbis have written on the sublime, on the legitimate power of the great name of God, on the mysterious art of sacred numbers, and the occult power of images of them, in short, all the wisdom of ancient Judea, which she claims comes to her from the eternal Idea, which she claims to withdraw from the heavenly treasure-house, is to be found in these writings which we still preserve.[40]

In its mingled admiration and suspicion of Jewish lore, this text is typical of the period. For present purposes, the importance of kabbalism is that it stood as the antithesis of carnal literalism: it was rampant figurality, a cryptographic reading gone to a dangerous or ridiculous extreme.

In short, two tendencies dominated French representations of Jews and Judaism in Poussin's day. On the one hand, Judaism was a way to think about tropes. The Old Testament was "a promise in figure," with the corollary that the Jews were blind to this figurality. On the other, the Old Testament was exemplary, with the corollary that its narratives and heroes had no specifically Jewish character at all. These tendencies were symmetrical, in that each laid particular emphasis on paradigmatic relations. The former read the Old Testament as the base material sign of Christian truth, while the latter took the Old Testament itself as paradigmatic without reference to local (that is, Jewish) context. Each wound up effacing the Jewish specificity of the narrative. As a result, Judaism was less a matter of thematics or semiotics than of rhetoric and reading. Moses and the Old Testament were not inherently Jewish, but had to be judaized if and when the need arose. Conversely, particular modes of reading—or, more accurately, particular travesties—could be "Jewish" regardless of circumstances.

Although working in Rome, where Judaism was legal and the ghetto well organized, Poussin adhered to many of these views. He was very much alive, for instance, to the figural or typological connotations of the Old Testament.[41] A good illustration of his general attitude is the frontispiece he designed for the *Biblia Sacra* of 1642 (Figure 11.3). Engraved by Claude Mellan, it replaces the traditional allegories of Church and Synagogue with emblematic figures of Poussin's own devising. He identified them in a letter of 3 August: at left is History, at right Prophecy.[42] The latter is swathed in veils and holds a sphinx. Her veils represent the figural language of the Old Testament, as in 2 Corinthians 3:13–16 ("But even until this day, when Moses is read, the veil is upon their heart," etc.) or Pascal's sixteenth Provincial Letter ("Of Jesus Christ the Jews possessed only figures and veils, such as the manna and the paschal lamb").[43] The sphinx, Poussin says, stands for "Enigmatic Things," *Choses Énigmatiques* (for the Jesuit Juan Marquez, it represented *Figura*).[44] So total is Poussin's identification of the Old Testament with figural language that he can substitute for synagogue the personification of a rhetorical mode.[45]

Returning to the picture, Cropper and Dempsey have already shown that Poussin's Simon is a stock figure of Jewish carnality. Yet the cipher-key on his brow stresses that this literalism is, specifically, an attachment to the carnality of the text, as opposed to the evidence of the eyes: "Mine eyes are ever toward *the letter of the Law of* the Lord." Simon attends to letters—he reads—when he should simply be "turning his eyes" toward Christ. To make this point, Poussin asks his audience to read words they cannot understand. It is, of course, perfectly possible to appreciate *Penance* without reading the Hebrew inscription; people have been doing it for hundreds of years. But the words are clearly important, given the effort that went into producing them. Poussin must have been counting on someone, at some point, actually reading the inscription—otherwise, why bother? Insofar as he knew that his audience could not read Hebrew, he must have expected people to get the meaning at second hand (much as Poussin himself must have found someone to help him produce the text in the first place). Such ostentatious erudition was the artist's stock in trade. But, exactly because of its subtle modification of the biblical text, this inscription cannot be dismissed as mere pedantry. While Cropper and Dempsey showed that the text glosses the narrative action and reveals the metaphysical stakes of Simon's gaze, its decipherment is equally important. The text is about reading, but its own reading is also at issue.

What matters, in short, is not just the content of the Hebrew inscription, but also its form and, by extension, its address to beholders. These beholders—

RICHARD NEER

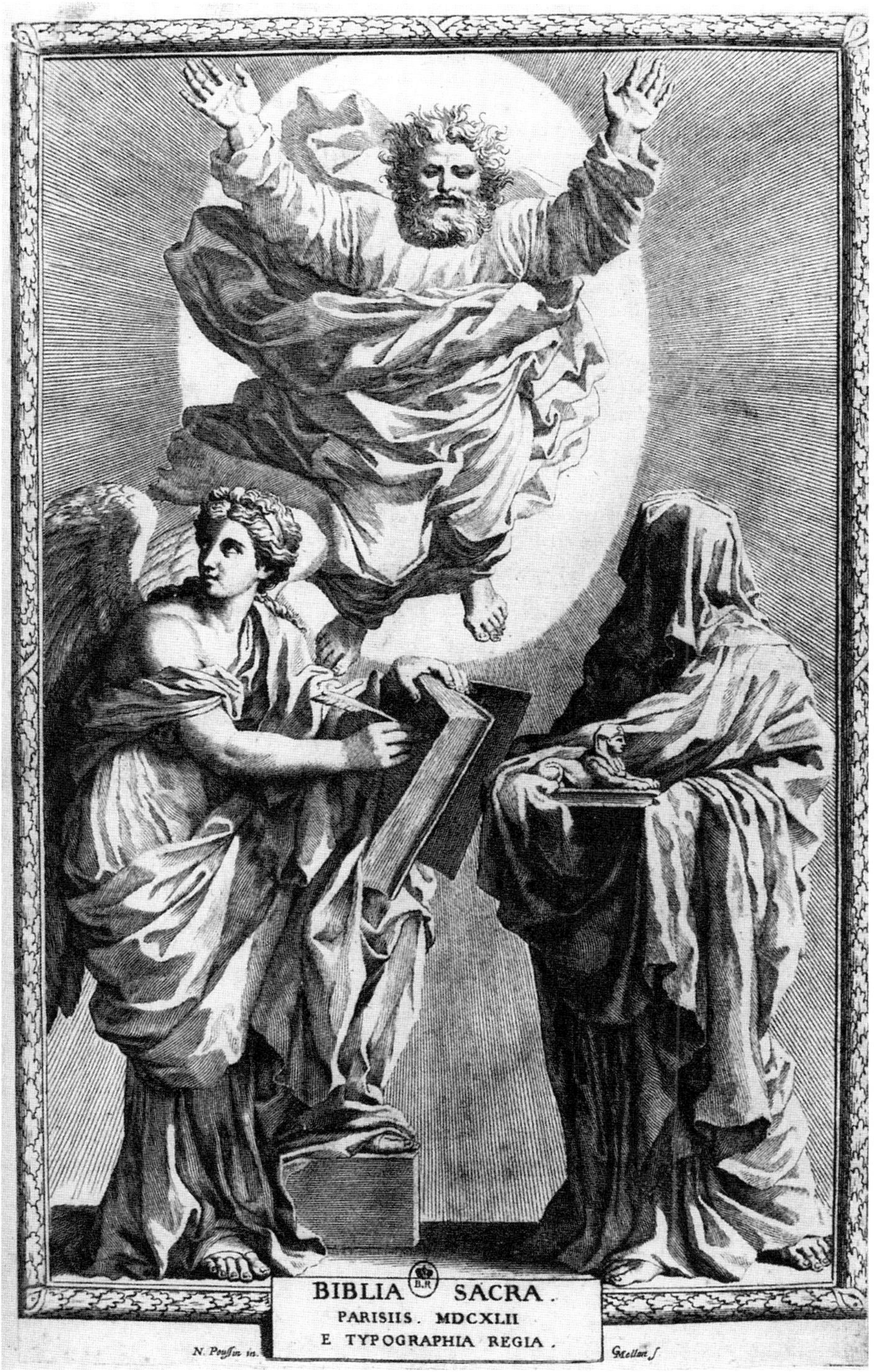

11.3. Nicolas Poussin (engraved by Claude Mellan), frontispiece to *Biblia Sacra* (Paris, 1641). Photo courtesy Epstein Archive, University of Chicago.

people like Chantelou, educated but unable to read Hebrew—are in a position symmetrical to that of Simon himself. Unlike the Pharisee, all such beholders will immediately recognize Christ. But the text is a different matter. Confronted with unreadable characters, "the letter of the Law of the Lord," most French people would have had to take their meaning at the word of others. They would have had to see with the eye of faith. In this way, the predicament of the narrative's main figure—Simon—reiterates that of the beholder of the narrative itself. *Penance* is an allegory or dramatization of its own beholding. The Pharisee cannot "read" the scene that unfolds before his eyes; if he could do so, if he could see as the Magdalene does, he would recognize the Savior come into his house. Just so, the beholder (in theory) cannot read the line of Hebrew. Simon stands to Christ, the "image of the invisible God," *imago Dei invisibilis* (Col. 1:15), as the beholder stands to the Hebrew word, the "letter of the Law of the Lord." Simon's reaction is disbelief. That of the beholder, who cannot make sense of the Hebrew line, is (must be) faith—and submission to the authority of the learned.

The picture establishes a hierarchy of text and image. Chantelou, or any other beholder illiterate in Hebrew, cannot be said actually to *read* the Pharisaic text at all; he merely *sees* it, learns from another the meaning of the *chose énigmatique*. The Hebrew characters are also depictions, part of the furniture of the tableau. It is as pictures of characters, rather than as words to be read, that they function for those who cannot understand them; they are, literally, "scripture for the unlettered." Even for the literate, however, simply reading the text would not suffice. Taken at face value, *à la lettre*, the words assert the importance of the letter of the Law. In their narrative and pictorial context, however, they admonish the opposite. We should *not* fix our eyes upon the letter of the Law but, like the Magdalene, should see Christ in our midst, "in the spirit, and not in the letter" (Rom. 2:29). The picture contravenes the text, the Image contravenes the Word—which is, of course, exactly what this picture is all about.[46]

The result, however, is not a simple negation of the text. "Do we then make void the Law through faith?" asks St. Paul (Rom. 3:31). "God forbid: yea, we establish the Law." Following Simon's gaze across the canvas, the eye scans from right to left. A number of Poussin's compositions share this leftward movement (e.g., *The Death of Sapphira, Christ and the Woman Taken in Adultery, The Golden Calf*). In this case, however, the organization has special significance, for the composition and indeed the very style actually evolve as the eye proceeds. Everything flattens. The right side, where Simon sits, is cluttered, the figures posed at angles to the picture plane; a foot basin in the foreground establishes the spatial relations clearly, while a deep niche opens into the background. At left, by contrast, the foreground is blank, the niche is lost in shadow; the main

RICHARD NEER

figures are in profile with crisp silhouettes, and the black oblong of Christ's couch sounds the dominant note. Between the two, the principle of isocephaly keeps the diners' heads on a single row, producing a frieze-effect that counteracts the perspectival recession at center. At the same time, Poussin introduces several archaisms of style on the left side of the canvas, including yellow-gold highlights on Christ's tunic—a late Gothic technique.[47] Christ's pose, meanwhile, derives from ancient Greek banquet reliefs. In sum, the left is relatively flat, relatively hieratic, more in the manner of a quattrocento altarpiece than a post-Renaissance easel picture. By comparison with the twisting, dramatic figures at right, Christ and the Magdalene are close to being symbols. They are fully realized images, but they are like letters. The assimilation of painted figures to written ones was dear to Poussin. As he would remark in conversation with André Félibien the following year, "Just as the twenty-four letters of the alphabet serve to form our words and express our thoughts, so do the lineaments of the human body serve to express the various passions of the soul in order to make appear on the outside what one has in the mind."[48] On offer, however, is not a simple antithesis but, rather, a chiasm. For the deeper side, the spatially realized side, is the side of Simon the Pharisee, the side of the letter of the Law of the Lord, the side of script; while the flatter side, the alphabetic side, is that of Christ, the "image of the invisible God."

The cumulative result may be seen as a pictorial alternative to the Hebrew text. *Penance* is a set of characters to be scanned from right to left, like a line of Hebrew. It is legible, however, not as letters but as images comprehensible to anyone with eyes to see—"provided only that one has read the Evangelist." A line of text, that is, for Gentile eyes. The unreadable Hebrew script thus functions as the model for a composition that, in its narrative and in its programmatic opposition of word and image, seems the very negation of "the letter of the Law of the Lord." Which is to say, the text is, exactly, "a promise in figure," redeemed through integration into a picture of redemption.

By way of contrast, Simon Vouet's altarpiece in St. Merri in Paris treats its Hebrew text in a very different manner (Figure 11.4). It dates to 1647, hence is one of Vouet's last works (he died the following year).[49] Here four saints and two prisoners adore the Holy Name of God, which appears above them in radiance. Overlapping bodies and sharply receding architecture produce a congested semi-circle of pictorial space in the picture's lower half. As often in Counter Reformation altarpieces, a figure at lower right extends an arm in the direction of the beholder while looking at a miraculous vision in the upper part of the frame. Here, a blue-clad prisoner and a saint in a bishop's cassock perform the function: they reach out in our direction, connecting the depicted

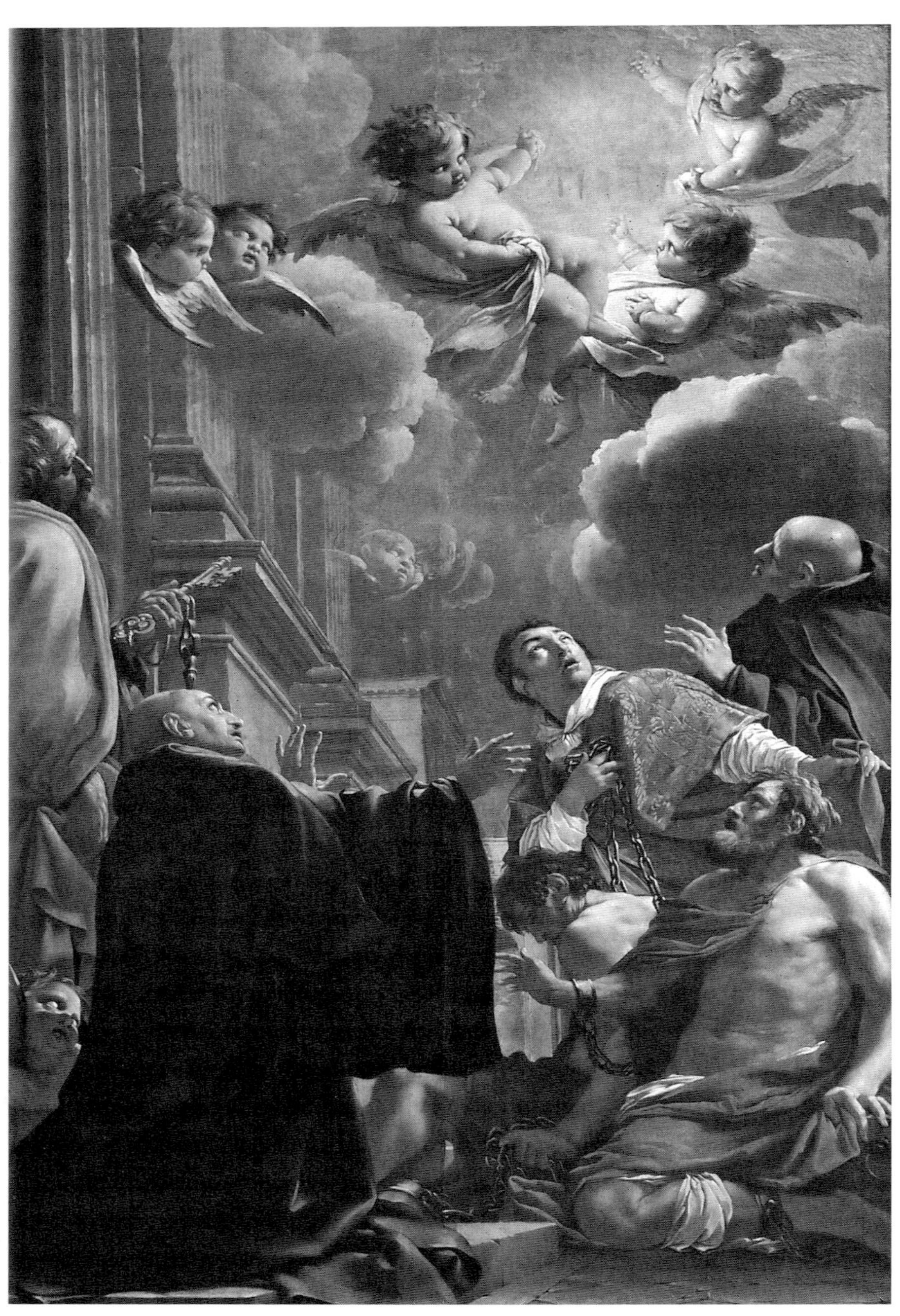

11.4. Simon Vouet, *Adoration of the Holy Name* (1647). Paris, St. Merri. Photo: Scala/
White Images/Art Resource, New York.

world with our own. At left, on the other hand, heavy robes of black and gold block access to the foreground. The lower half of the picture thus establishes a discrete spatial zone, screened from the beholder while yet giving access. In the register immediately above are five putti against a flat gold background. Their placement describes a sagging arc that reiterates the arrangement of the mortals at ground level, but with fewer spatial cues. Color links the groups as well. Over the gold-clad saint at left is a blond putto; over the black-clad saint is a black-haired one. Over the saint in rose and gold is blond putto with a pink sash; over the blue-clad prisoners, a blue-clad putto; over the black saint in the background, a dark putto with a grey sash. In this way, the Vouet establishes a connection between the mortals and the putti, even as the picture becomes relatively flat and ethereal as the eye moves upward. The climax is the Holy Name itself: יהוה. Thus the contemplative beholder progresses from the real, lived space of the church into the congested pictorial space of the picture's lower half, to the related but relatively flat zone of the putti, to the frankly two-dimensional text of the Name. Like his rival Poussin, in other words, Vouet manipulates space to make the object of veneration into something relatively two-dimensional and script-like. But where Poussin knit this device into an elaborate dialectic of word and image, Judaic and Christian, Vouet gives a straightforward teleology—from the lived space of the beholder to the flat text of the Tetragrammaton. In so doing, he recuperates the Hebrew as object of Christian meditation, much as a figural reading of the Old Testament might do.

But Poussin's own intricacies were not lost on contemporaries. In 1656, his old friend Philippe de Champaigne painted the story of Christ and Simon for the refectory of Val-de-Grâce (Figure 11.5).[50] This picture has been the subject of important discussions by Claude Gandelmann and Louis Marin.[51] It contains numerous details characteristic of Champaigne—the grid-like creases on the table cloth, the open curtain in the background, the pellucid spatial construction, the emphasis on reflections and glitter, the pastel tones. Yet it owes so much to Poussin that it seems fair to call it a response to the *Penance* for Chantelou.[52] The basic compositions are closely similar. In a 1668 *conférence* on Poussin's *Eliezer and Rebecca*, Champaigne would seem almost willfully to misread his former colleague and friend; here, however, he was a remarkably sympathetic interpreter.[53] Gone are Poussin's left-to-right movement, the archaisms and the all-important phylactery. Instead, Champaigne provides a strongly centralized composition, illustrating a slightly later moment in the story, when Christ turns to the Pharisee, saying "Dost thou see this woman?" (Luke 7:44). There is, however, a Hebrew text embroidered on the hem of the Pharisee's garment and on his prayer shawl. Three sections are visible, all from the opening of the Decalogue as it appears in Exodus 20 and Deuteronomy 6. On the veil is

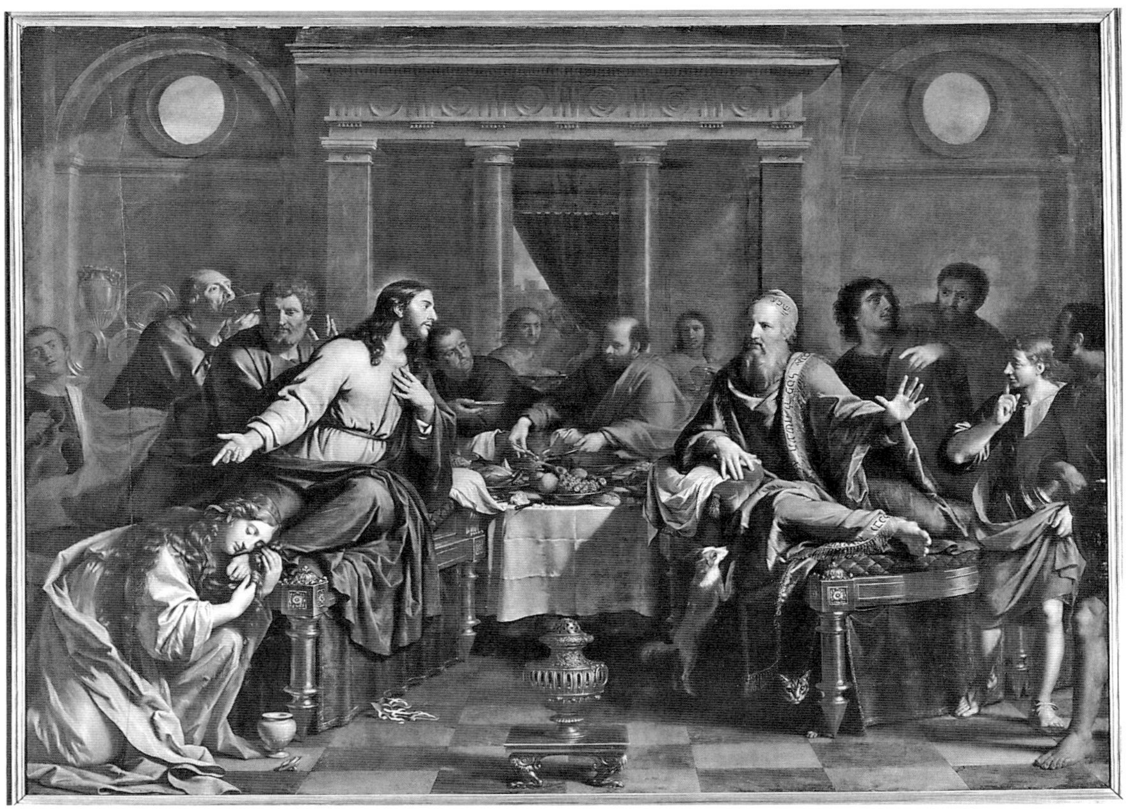

11.5. Philippe de Champaigne, *Christ at the House of Simon the Pharisee* (1656). Nantes. Photo: Réunion des Musées Nationaux/Art Resource, New York.

Shema Yisrael, "Hear, O Israel," and on the mantle the first commandment according to the conventional numeration of the day: "I am the LORD thy God, which brought thee out of the land of Egypt, from the house of bondage. Thou shalt have none other gods before me. Thou shalt not make thee any graven image."[54] Champaigne follows Poussin in seeing the meal at the house of Simon as a narrative centrally concerned with images and their relation to texts. But where Poussin emphasized the ethical and ethnic stakes of recognition and reading in the field of vision, Champaigne is more concerned with semantics. Perhaps because he was painting for a royal convent, and deeply involved personally with the Jansenists of Port-Royal (where Hebrew was taught), he seems to have taken some familiarity with Hebrew for granted. Instead of trading on the sheer obscurity of the text, at any rate, he plays a sort of game with the written words themselves. He hides certain key words in the folds of the Pharisee's garment, including "I am" and "Thou shalt have none other gods before me." God's statement of his own being is hidden in Simon's costume:

RICHARD NEER

he is the *Deus absconditus*, the Hidden God (Isa. 45:15), the *verbum absconditum*, the Hidden Word (Job 4:14), literally obscured behind the Pharisaic "veil." As with Poussin, painting *makes visible* this aspect of the text, this aspect of a specifically Hebrew Bible, hence this aspect of Judaism: its carnality. "Thou that abhorrest idols, dost thou commit sacrilege?" (Rom. 2:21). But, to repeat, the central difference between the two painters concerns, precisely, the comprehensibility of Hebrew. For Poussin, legibility as such is at stake; for Champaigne, the legibility of the text is not at issue so much as the visibility or occlusion of particular characters. In the one case, Judaism articulates a principle of utter inscrutability that painting, uniquely, can render visible; it is a differential element that organizes the picture from its spatial layout on upward. In the other, the inscribed letter of the Law is important as such, for it is only through attention to those letters—those *Hebrew* letters—that one can see the very occlusion of God's being, the hiddenness of the *Dieu caché*.

Poussin reverted to many of these themes with *Christ and the Woman Taken in Adultery*, painted in 1653 for the landscape architect André Le Nôtre (Figure 11.6).[55] The picture shares a number of features with the *Penance* of 1647. Like its predecessor, it articulates a narrative of feminine penance, a Hebrew text, and larger issues of legibility and vision. Even the composition bears a structural resemblance to *Penance*: two foreground groups flanking a perspectival recession at center, with the action consisting of a movement right-to-left parallel to the picture plane. Poussin was in the habit of repeating and revising compositions over many years, returning doggedly to certain themes and narratives; Le Nôtre's painting may be another instance of this tendency.[56] Like Champaigne's painting for Val-de-Grâce, albeit in a more oblique fashion, it extends and clarifies the themes of the 1647 *Penance*. In this case, Poussin has discarded antiquarian mise-en-scène in favor of a spare, theatrical setting, "Classical" more in organization than in any use of period detail.[57] In Bellori's words, it expresses Christ's judgment "with a great sense of painting."[58]

The Gospel source (John 8:2–11) is worth quoting in full:

> And early in the morning he came again into the temple, and all the people came unto him; and he sat down, and taught them. And the scribes and Pharisees brought unto him a woman taken in adultery; and when they had set her in their midst, they said unto him, Master, this woman was taken in adultery, in the very act. Now Moses in the law commanded us, that such should be stoned: but what sayest thou? This they said, tempting him, that they might have to accuse him. But Jesus stooped down, and with his finger wrote on the ground, as though he heard them not. So when they continued asking him, he lifted up

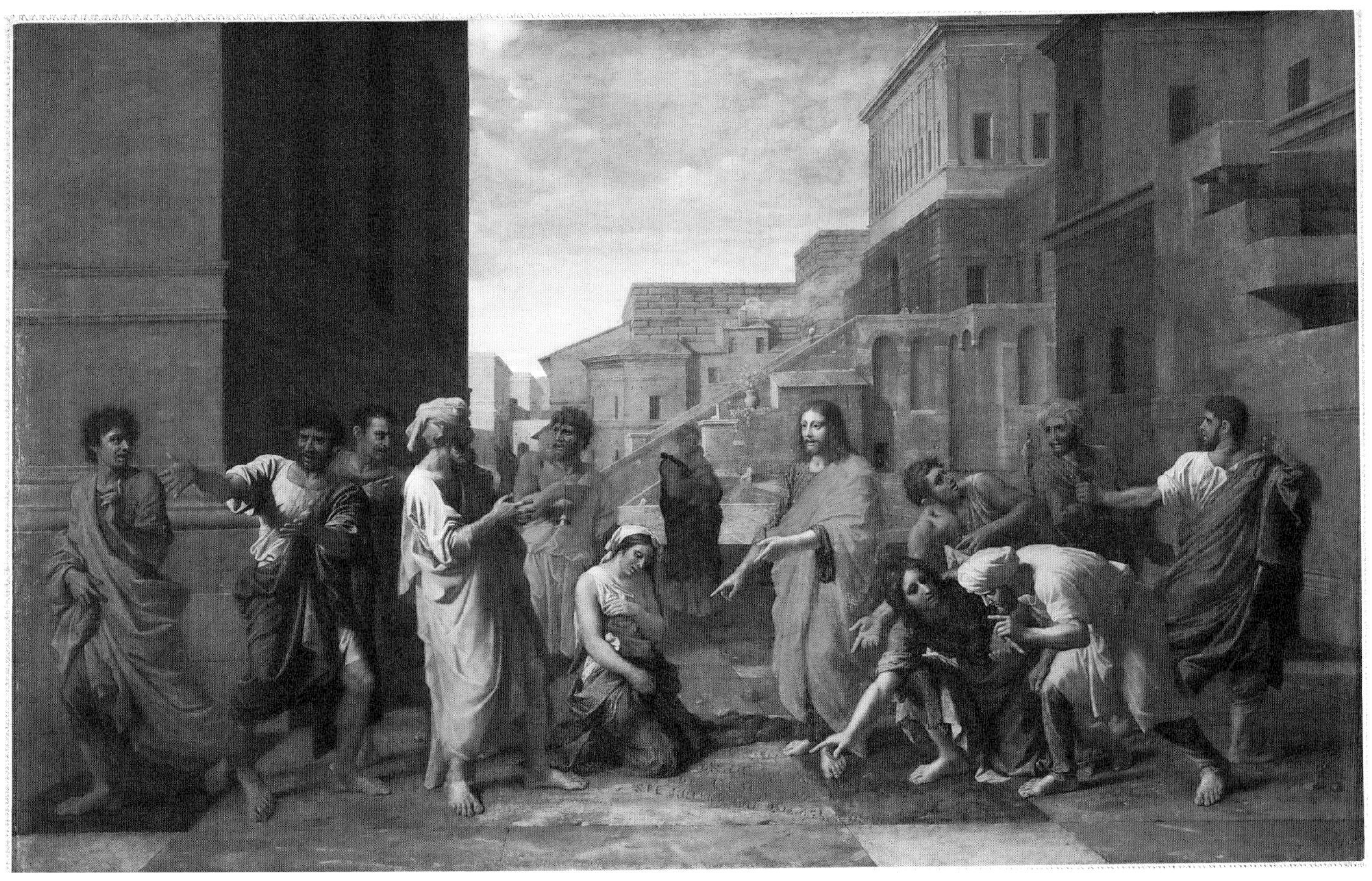

11.6. Nicolas Poussin, *Christ and the Woman Taken in Adultery*, 1653. Paris, Louvre 7282. Photo: Erich Lessing/Art Resource, New York.

himself, and said unto them, He that is without sin among you, let him
first cast a stone at her. And again he stooped down, and wrote on the
ground. And they which heard it, being convicted by their own conscience, went out one by one, beginning at the eldest, even unto the last:
and Jesus was left alone, and the woman standing in the midst. When
Jesus had lifted up himself, and saw none but the woman, he said unto
her, Woman, where are those thine accusers? hath no man condemned
thee? She said, No man, Lord. And Jesus said unto her, Neither do I
condemn thee: go, and sin no more.

Poussin here combines several episodes from the Gospel narrative in a single
Augenblick. In John, the Pharisees first dispute with Christ, then he stoops to
write, stands, and stoops again; the Pharisees depart with Christ still on the
ground; he then rises and addresses the sinner. Poussin shows all these episodes
simultaneously. Some Pharisees are arguing, some leaving, some examining the
writing in the dust; Christ, meanwhile, is gesturing to the woman. Such depar-
tures from narrative sequence were not unusual in Poussin's work, and they
caused much consternation in the academic debates of the 1660s.[59] Critics
deplored the seeming illogic of Poussin's temporal condensations, their violation of the protocols of history painting. As one viewer—often thought to be
Philippe de Champaigne—complained of *The Israelites Receiving Manna*, Poussin had shown the manna falling even as the Israelites were awake and harvest-
ing it, "*ce qui est contre le texte de l'Ecriture.*"[60] Charles Le Brun defended
Poussin by arguing that painting is condemned to show a single moment, lacking literature's resource of temporal duration. Poussin, he suggested, was motivated by a higher truth: what mattered was not temporal unity, or the accurate
representation of single moment, but the communication of a narrative's deeper
significance. "These different states and these diverse actions took the place, for
him, of discourse or words as means to convey his thought."[61] Although the
picture presupposes familiarity with the Gospel narrative, it corresponds to no
specific moment in the narrative discourse. It is, rather, a meditation on the
narrative, a *pensée* in paint, with various episodes (*péripéties*) distributed over
the canvas in juxtaposition.

Something similar is going on in the organization of space. On the one
hand, Poussin alludes to a quintessentially durational art: theater. His *péripéties*
occur as if on a stage, with strongly foreshortened "wings" and an architectural
backdrop.[62] The result is a disjunction between the figures and their setting.
While Poussin's organization of the "actors" decomposes narrative time into
the simultaneous presentation of multiple instants, his organization of the "set"
asserts coherence and consistency while evoking the orderly narrative sequence
of Classical theater. But there is more to the matter. Counteracting the perspectival recession of the architecture are certain features that tend to *flatten* the

composition. Three strong diagonals run from upper right to lower left: the pointing arm of a Pharisee, the pointing arm of Christ, and the stairway in the furthest distance. Arrayed in parallel, the three lines suggest a single plane surface and reduce the sense of depth; the line of the stairway, in particular, carries through into the arms of the two Pharisees behind the adulteress, thereby knitting the foreground into the background (and conversely). Chromatic affinities complement these lines and further bind together the near and the far: a Madonna-like woman in the shadows and Christ out front wear matching blue and red combinations.[63] Tethering the two is the only pavement line to run all the way from foreground to background; Christ and the Marian woman toe the same line, walk the same tightrope. This line establishes spatial relations on the ground, but it also lies perpendicular both to the pointing arms in the foreground and to the stairway in the distance. Depth, consequently, is always in danger of collapsing into pattern work. To see the arms, stairway, and pavement as a series of right angles on the plane surface of the canvas is to bracket the very spatial relations that it is the job of the pavement line to establish.

In short, just as the painting both asserts and negates distinctions of narrative time, so it asserts and negates relations of foreground and background. There is an established sequence of events, but they are presented in and through simultaneity; there are determinate relations of foreground and background, but they are presented in and through planarity. The picture reads both as perfectly ordinary history painting and as a sort of diagram or a page of text.[64] As if to signal the importance of such organizing structures, one wall of the Temple is still under construction, exposing its very armature to view.

It is by means of this oddly duplex system that Poussin revisits *Penance*. The Pharisees do not wear phylacteries, nor even "correct" attire; they resemble in this regard their counterparts in the picture for dal Pozzo. But they remain addicts of the letter, for the group at right is puzzling over the odd Hebrew inscription that Christ has written in the dust (Figure 11.7). The Gospel does not say what these words were. According to Church tradition, *primo scripsit, postea protulit*, "First he wrote, then he attested."[65] On this view, the words spelled out the dictum, "He that is without sin among you, let him first cast a stone at her." Quite a few early modern artists included the Latin version of Christ's dictum in their renderings of this scene; others employed mere scratches, or omitted the writing entirely.[66] In Poussin's case, it is often assumed that the words in the sand follow precedent in spelling out the words of Christ.[67] Yet the idea is implausible (would Poussin have gone to the trouble to obtain a Hebrew translation of the Greek or Latin New Testament?) and, indeed, untenable. The inscription is almost, but not quite, illegible, yet it is possible to spell out the first word. It is אנכי, "I am," as in, "I am the LORD thy God, which

    RICHARD NEER

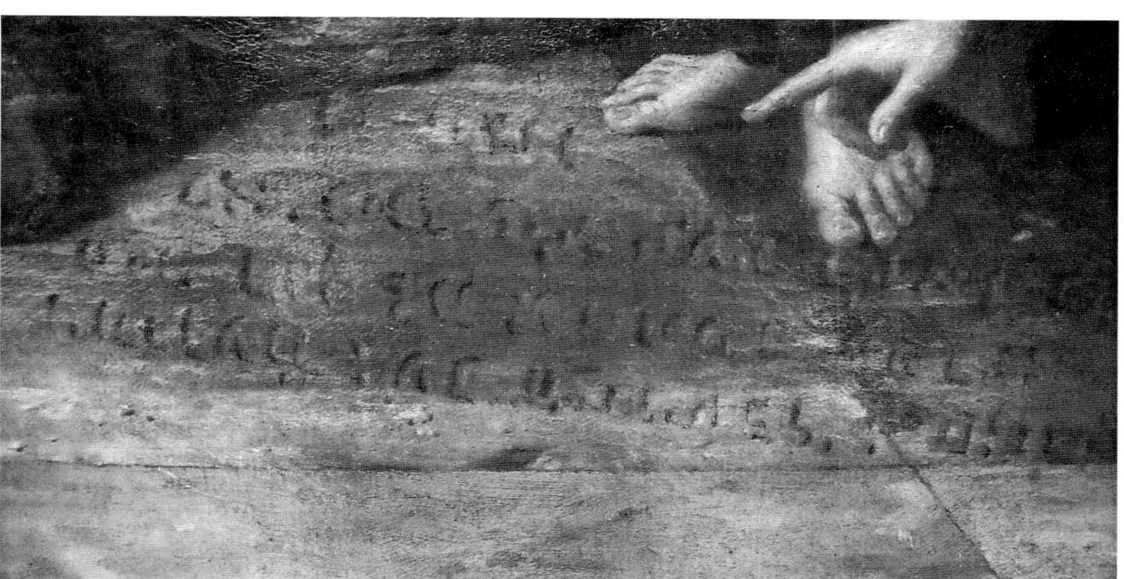

11.7. Detail of Nicolas Poussin, *Christ and the Woman Taken in Adultery*: the writing in the dust. Photo: Richard Neer.

brought thee out of the land of Egypt . . ." (Ex. 20: 2). This word is the very one conspicuous in its absence from Philippe de Champaigne's picture for Val-de-Grâce. In Poussin's case, however, the text quickly peters out into barely legible characters: not quite Hebrew, but a sort of *hébraïsant* scrawl.

It is possible to spend a long time looking at this inscription. An informal survey of scholars at the University of Chicago, all versed in Hebrew, suggests that the inscription is at once enticing and frustrating, not quite nonsensical enough for immediate dismissal, nor sufficiently cogent actually to yield a reading. Instead, *"mystère admirable,"* it invites hours of fruitless headscratching. The beholder, in this situation, winds up in much the same situation as the Pharisees in the picture: pointing, puzzling, and conversing. Which is surely to the point: as in the 1647 *Penance*, the Pharisaic dilemma becomes the beholder's own.[68] It is as though Poussin had combined that painting with *The Arcadian Shepherds* to produce a narrative of reading in a Christian, as opposed to a pagan, context. In this case, however, although the text states the existence of God, it remains otherwise a cipher. A literate informant will not help.[69]

Once again, the distinction of word and image is at stake. For just as the Pharisees point at the ambiguous text, so Christ points to the adulteress. The symmetrical gestures suggest comparability, even root affinity, between the two: the adulteress is, in some way, like the Hebrew lines. Indeed, the pointing hands and rigid arms suggest nothing so much as *yadayim,* "hands," the hand-shaped pointers used for reading the Torah (Figure 11.8).[70] But if the woman is a text of sorts, still she has a figural meaning that painting is uniquely positioned to show. Even as Christ points to her, there intervenes between them the distant woman holding an infant. The position of her arms mimics, in reverse, that of the adulteress; where the one holds a child, the other hugs herself in sorrow. The red and blue costume assimilates her to Christ, but also to any number of High Renaissance Madonnas (Raphael's Sistine or Small Cowper Madonnas, for instance). Exceeding the letter of the Gospel text, this Marian image is not really part of the narrative; the Virgin appears, literally, from amid the shadows (*umbrae*) of the Temple.[71] Christ points to her figure even as he points to the adulteress—points, that is, to two things simultaneously. Poussin had used this device elsewhere, notably in the closely related *Death of Sapphira*: Peter strikes Sapphira dead with a gesture for failing to tithe, and as he does so he points simultaneously to a tiny figure in the background who gives alms to a beggar (Figure 11.9).

In *Christ and the Woman Taken in Adultery*, this *making visible* of a double ostentation is a pictorial equivalent to figuralism. In pointing to the adulteress in forgiveness, Christ points to the Virgin, hence to the age of grace and charity that she brought forth. As the *Glossa Ordinaria* put it, "The woman taken in adultery signifies the Synagogue, which according to the tradition of the Fathers adulterated the law of Moses."[72] So she does here, in her affinity with the Hebrew line that so exercises the Pharisees. Yet Poussin reveals the mystic or figural meaning of this "text," its redemption in Christ's forgiveness.

Crucially, however, this simultaneity is visible only in and through a suspension of the picture's spatial organization. As we have seen, the composition combines two spatial logics. In the theatrical or scenographic mode of the stage-set, the Marian figure is in the distance, far behind Christ and the adulteress; he does not point *at* her but *before* her. Yet the mode of the *pensée* and the *péripétie*, the perpendicular and the plane, tells a different story. Here the canvas becomes an array of episodes in juxtaposition; seen in this manner—seen "flat"—Christ does point to the Madonna (or, more specifically, the hem of her garment). It is exactly when the canvas is seen like a page of text, as a plane surface and not an open window, that the figural meaning becomes apparent.

Where the 1647 *Penance* had contrasted depth of field on the right with flatness on the left, here the entire picture is at once recessive and planar. This disjunction is that between a literal reading and a figural one, between seeing Christ as pointing at an adulterous woman and seeing him as pointing at a figure of grace and charity. "Read the story *and* the picture," said Poussin to Chantelou of *The Israelites Receiving Manna*.[73] The advice holds good in this

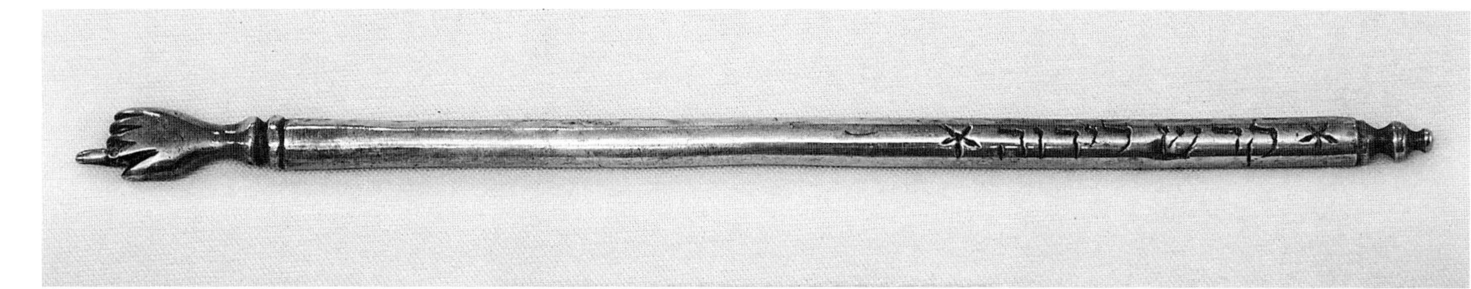

11.8. Torah pointer (*yad*), Ferrara, mid-fifteenth century. Silver. Jerusalem, U. Nahon Museum of Italian Jewish Art. Photo reproduced by courtesy U. Nahon Museum of Italian Jewish Art, Jerusalem.

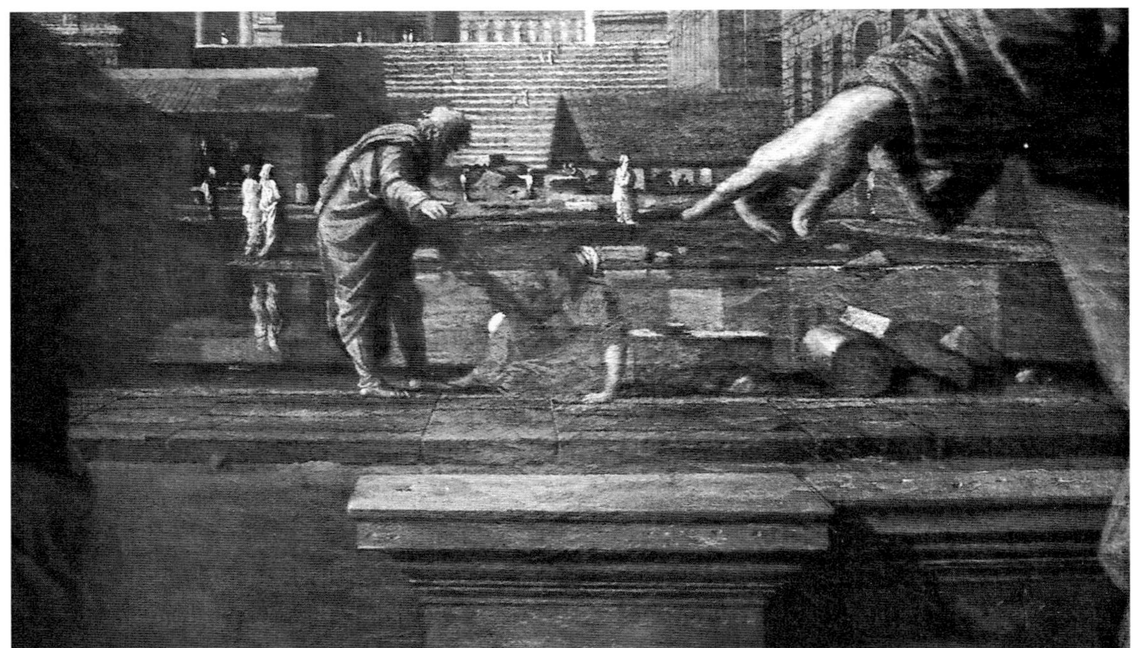

11.9. Nicolas Poussin, *The Death of Saphira*, c. 1652 (detail). Paris, Louvre inv. 7286.
Photo: Richard Neer.

case; story (the space of diegesis) and picture (the space of *péripétie* and *pensée*)
both claim attention.

The Hebrew text in the dust, meanwhile, is illegible due in part to its integration into the space of the narrative. It is subordinate to the spatial and discursive
regime of scenographia. Relative to the beholder, it is upside-down; placement
on the receding pavement distorts it further. Even if the words made sense
(which they do not), they would be hard to read; one must lean forward and
peer at the vertical canvas just as the Pharisees stoop and peer at the horizontal
ground. Neither point of view yields a cogent meaning; the text remains one of
Poussin's "Enigmatic Things," *Choses Énigmatiques.* The upshot, however, is
that the Hebrew lines are flat within the scenographic or narrative space—flat
for the Pharisees—but distorted and strongly recessive for the picture's
beholder, that is, for us. They are thus antithetical to the Madonna figure, who
establishes the middle distance within the scenographia, yet is nonetheless an
object of Christ's gesture for a beholder with eyes to see. The lines exist only
within the space of the narrative, while the pair of the adulteress and the
Madonna work simultaneously in flatness and in depth. The Hebrew, that is,
exists only in a carnal, literalist mode that sees the narrative but not its deeper
significance. As in *Penance,* the Pharisees keep their eyes turned toward the

letter; but in this case, the letter is all but void of meaning, stating the Lord's "I am" but little more.

With this picture, Poussin decomposes the spatial and temporal regimes of classical painting: narrative sequence becomes the simultaneous presentation of *péripéties*, scenographia becomes the flatness of a page. Yet the result of these internal disjunctions is anything but subversive or paradoxical. Academic cavils notwithstanding, the picture has always been perfectly comprehensible. Even the text is not "austerely" nonsensical, to use the terms of contemporary American philosophy; it is not patent gibberish, but composed of meaningful characters that occasionally cohere into words and even statements ("I am").[74] So far from undoing the protocols of classical history painting (God forbid!), the picture takes them as its very ground ("yea, we establish the Law"). Poussin establishes precise conditions of intelligibility. It is necessary, first, to "read the Evangelist," for without background familiarity with the Gospel story his pictorial discourse will not be comprehensible; will not, in fact, be recognizable as a temporal *decomposition* at all. Just so, it is necessary to accept the conventions of perspectival recession in order to recognize the background Madonna as a *figural* counterpart to the adulteress. Seeing the collapse into flatness as, precisely, a *collapse*, as a pictorial *figura*, presupposes the normative value of pictorial depth. Beholders can and do establish logical relations, as Le Brun would have insisted. They establish them on the negative, as those rules, that Law, which Poussin has contravened—hence, by the logic of this picture, redeemed. As Christ redeemed the adulteress, that is, the Synagogue.

Poussin, in short, is trafficking in the ineffable. He establishes a transcendent perspective from which sense and nonsense are clearly distinct. For one sort of viewer—someone like Simon in *Penance*, or Philippe de Champaigne when he complained about *The Israelites Receiving Manna*—the picture is a kind of nonsense, a contravention of Scripture and of the rules of history painting. For another, however, it is exactly the violation of those rules that reveals the ineffable conditions of sense under the New Covenant. For present purposes, the crucial point is that the paradigm for this act of discrimination is the recognition of a *Hebrew* text as what might nowadays be called "substantial nonsense" relative to the Christian, iconic *péripétie*. The Hebrew lines literally ground the picture. They instantiate the standing conventions of intelligibility in history painting: ordered, sequential progression (one letter after another, follow them with a finger or a *yad*) and perspectival recession (marking out the pavement). But their significance only becomes visible in the recognition that their true meaning lies in Christ's gesture, in attending to Christ's gesture at the expense of the words on the ground.

In this way, Hebrew becomes a way to think history painting's grounding laws of space, time, and legibility, laws that Poussin states precisely in order to transcend them in his figural juxtapositions. The picture is not gibberish to just the extent, in just the same way, that the Hebrew text is not: its substance becomes visible within a matrix of figuralism. It is, of course, absolutely necessary that the words be in Hebrew if they are to fit into the narrative of charity and redemption on offer. That, indeed, is the special usefulness of Hebrew to this picture: as the figure of a set of rules, a law, a covenant, which is essential and yet transcended; which is revealed as essential in the moment of its transcendence in Christ. What might look like incoherence or paradox turns out to be redemption. An uncharitable viewer might call it *mauvaise foi*.

NOTES

I am deeply grateful to David Nirenberg, Uri Shachar, Joel Snyder, David Stern, and Josef Stern for help with Hebrew. Thanks are due as well to Eric Driscoll, Jaś Elsner, and Aden Kumler. All translations are my own unless otherwise noted; all errors are my own in any case.

1. For a recent discussion of this episode, see M. Franken, "'Pour mon honneur et pour vostre contentement': Nicolas Poussin, Paul Fréart de Chantelou and the Making and Collecting of Copies," in *The Learned Eye: Regarding Art, Theory, and the Artist's Reputation*, ed. M. van den Doel and E. van de Wetering (Amsterdam, 2005), 181–89.

2. J. Thuillier, *Nicolas Poussin* (Paris, 1994), no. 162.

3. C. Jouanny, ed., *Correspondance de Nicolas Poussin publiée d'après les originaux* (Paris, 1911), 356: "Je vous enuoye maintenant la penitense. que jei fette Je ne sey si elle suffira pour effacer la coulpe des fautes passées." On Poussin's correspondence with Chantelou, see H. Raben, "'An oracle of painting': Re-reading Poussin's Letters," *Simiolus* 30 (2003): 34–53; P. Mason, "The Letters as Deferred Presence: Nicolas Poussin to Paul Fréart de Chantelou, 28 April 1639," in *Cultural Exchange in Early Modern Europe: Correspondence and Cultural Exchange in Europe, 1400–1700*, ed. F. Bethencourt and F. Egmond (Cambridge, 2006–7); and especially O. Ranum, "Servitude and Friendship in the Letters of Poussin and Chantelou, with a Weak Coda on Chantelou as an Art Critic," http://www.ranumspanat.com/Poussin_Chantelou.htm (accessed December 12, 2008).

4. On Poussin's *Sacraments* generally, see W. Löhneysen, "Die ikonigraphischen und geistesgeschichtlichen Voraussetzung des 'sieben Sakramente' der Nicolas Poussin," *Zeitschrift für Religions und Geistesgeschichte* 4 (1952): 133–50; C. Thompson, *Poussin's Seven Sacraments in Edinburgh* (Glasgow, 1980); M. Bruhn, *Die beiden Fassungen der "Sieben Sakramente" von Nicolas Poussin* (Hamburg, 1992) (non vidi); P. Rosenberg, ed., *Nicolas Poussin 1594–1665* (Paris, 1994), 240–52, 312–38; E. Cropper and C. Dempsey, *Nicolas Poussin: Friendship and the Love of Painting* (Baltimore, 1996), 109–44; T. Green, *Nicolas Poussin Paints the Seven Sacraments Twice* (Watchet, England, 2000).

5. Green, *Seven Sacraments*, 269. On the question of Poussin's erudition and visual sources, see E. Wilberding, "History and Prophecy: Selected Problems in the Religious Paintings of Nicolas Poussin" (Ph.D. diss., New York University, 1997), 159–85. Wilberding shows convincingly that the general composition derived from J. Prado and J. B. Villalpando, *In Ezechielem Explanationes et Apparatus Vrbis, ac templi Hierosolymitani. Commentariis et Imaginibvs Illvstratvs* (Rome, 1596–1605).

  RICHARD NEER

6. Quotation from J. Starobinksi, *L'Œil vivant. Corneille, Racine, La Bruyère, Rousseau, Stendhal* (Paris, 1961), 44.

7. Thuillier, *Nicolas Poussin*, no. 124.

8. The emblem appears on a recently discovered copy (J. von Henneberg, "Poussin's *Penance*: A New Reading," *Storia dell'arte* 61 [1987]: 229–39 and fig. 3; Rosenberg, *Nicolas Poussin*, 245 no. 65a), but not on a copy in Rome (Rosenberg, *Nicolas Poussin*, 245 no. 65). On the emblem, its role in the painting—arguing that it was a feature of the lost original—see M. Stanic, "Le mode énigmatique dans l'art de Poussin," in *Poussin et Rome*, ed. O. Bonfait (Rome, 1996), 93–118, at 98–100. On the role of emblems in religious art of the period, see M. Fumaroli, *L'École du silence. Le sentiment des images au XVIIe siècle* (Paris, 1998), 236–37.

9. Quoted in Stanic, "Le mode énigmatique," 99 and n. 22, where the emblem and its significance receive detailed discussion.

10. For Poussin's use of the term *pensée*, see *inter alia* Jouanny, *Correspondance*, 376.

11. Cropper and Dempsey, *Nicolas Poussin*, 116–17 and n. 18. The text is absent from the engraving in Prado and Villalpando, *In Ezechielem Explanationes* (Wilberding, *History and Prophecy*, 182).

12. Cropper and Dempsey, *Nicolas Poussin*, 117.

13. On the importance of the debate over penance to seventeenth-century art, see E. Mâle, *L'art religieux d'après le Concile de Trente. Étude sur l'iconographie de la fin du XVIe siècle, du XVIIe, du XVIIIe siècle. Italie—France—Espagne—Flandres* (Paris, 1932), 65–72. With reference to Poussin's picture specifically, see von Henneberg, "Poussin's *Penance*."

14. A likely candidate (as noted in Wilberding, *History and Prophecy*, 183) is the hebraicist and botanist Giovanni Batista Ferrari, a friend and sometime patron of Poussin from the circle of Cassiano dal Pozzo. On Ferrari, see D. Freedberg, "From Hebrew and Gardens to Oranges and Lemons," in *Cassiano dal Pozzo. Atti del Seminario internazionale di Studi. Napoli, 18–19 dicembre 1987*, ed. F. Solinas (Rome, 1989), 37–72; D. Freedberg, *The Eye of the Lynx: Galileo, His Friends, and the Beginning of Modern Natural History* (Chicago, 2002), 38–57.

15. On French collections of Hebrew manuscripts, see M. Garel, *D'une main forte. Manuscrits hébreux des collections françaises* (Paris, 1991).

16. F. Béroalde de Verville, *Le Moyen de Parvenir* (Paris, 1879 [1610]), 122: "Je lisois ne plus ne moins qu'un singe."

17. G. Naudé, *Apologie pour tous les grand hommes qui ont esté accusez de magie* (Paris, 1669), 25: "Celuy qui entendoit mieux la langue hebraïque estoit pris pour juif ou maran; et ceux qui recherchoient les mathematiques et sciences moins communes, soupçonnez comme enchanteurs et magiciens, quoy que ce fust une pure calomnie."

18. L. Bertaut, *L'illustre Orbandale, ou L'histoire ancienne et moderne de la ville et cité de Chalon-sur-Saône, enrichie de plusieurs recherches curieuses et divisée en éloges. Tome I* (Paris, 1662), 15: "Cette langue . . . de qui quasi toutes les syllables, & mesme tous les ponctes, sont des mysteres admirable."

19. Pierre Corneille, *Le Menteur* IV.iii.1195–98: "Je te le donnerois, et tu serois heureux; / mais le secret consiste en quelques mots hébreux, / qui tous à prononcer sont si fort difficiles, / que ce seroient pour toi des trésors inutiles."

20. Jouanny, *Correspondance*, 356: "Le subiec est représenté en manière quil me semble quil n'a besoin d'interprète poureu seullement que l'on aye leu l'euangille."

21. For overviews of the history of Jews in France during the earlier seventeenth century, see R. Mousnier, *The Institutions of France under the Absolute Monarchy, 1598–1789* (Chicago, 1979), 413–28; B. Bedos-Rezak, "Tolérance et raison d'État," in *L'État baroque. Regards sur la pensée politique de la France du premier XVIIe siècle*, ed. H. Méchoulian (Paris, 1985), 143–87.

More recently, see D. L. Graizbord, "Becoming Jewish in Early Modern France: Documents on Jewish Community-Building in Seventeenth-Century Bayonne and Peyrehorade," *Journal of Social History* 40 (2006): 147–80.

22. Cf. F. Garasse, *La doctrine cvrievse des beavx esprits de ce temps, ou, Pretendvs tells* (Paris 1623), 273 ("les juifs qui sont aujourd'huy à Rome, à Mets, en Avignon").

23. See, e.g., M. Mersenne, *L'impiété des deistes, athées et libertins de ce genre* (Paris, 1624), 140–69. On the development of Mersenne's thought, see D. Garber, "On the Frontlines of the Scientific Revolution: How Mersenne Learned to Love Galileo," *Perspectives on Science* 12 (2004): 135–62. For Rabbi L'Abbé, see G. Simpliste, *Rymaille sur les plus célèbres bibliotières de Paris* (Paris, 1649), 4: "Le Hebreu est chez Rabbi L'Abbé, / Et tout L'Arabe chez le Bé."

24. On the importance of Maimonides, see G. Stroumsa, "John Spencer and the Roots of Idolatry," *History of Religions* 41 (2001): 1–23, at 14–18. For an overview of *hébraïsant* scholarship in the seventeenth century, see S. Kessler-Mesguich, "Les hébraïsants chrétiens," in *Le Grand siècle et la Bible*, ed. J-R. Armogathe (Paris, 1989), 83–95; also S. Burnett, *From Christian Hebraism to Jewish Studies: Johannes Buxtorf (1564–1629) and Hebrew Learning in the Seventeenth Century* (Leiden, 1996). For the sixteenth century, see I. Zinguer, *L'Hébreu au temps de la Renaissance* (Leiden, 1992).

25. E.g., G. Postel, *Le thrésor des propheties de l'univers*, ed. F. Secret (The Hague, 1969); G. Postel, *Le candelabre de Moses*, ed. F. Secret (The Hague, 1971).

26. R. Popkin, "The First College of Jewish Studies," *Revue des études juives* 143 (1984): 351–64.

27. The 1684 translation has been reprinted as L. Modena, *Les Juifs présentés aux chrétiens: cérémonies et coutumes qui s'observent aujourd'hui parmi les Juifs* (Paris, 1998).

28. Augustine, *Serm.* 4.8, quoted in E. Auerbach, *Scenes from the Drama of European Literature* (Minneapolis, 1984), 41. For Paul, see 1 Cor. 10:6, 11, and 15:21; Gal. 4:21–31; Col. 2:16–17; Rom 5:12, Heb. 9:11.

29. Auerbach, *Scenes*, 11–78 (quotations at 39, 53).

30. Ibid., 31.

31. Augustine, *de Civ.* 20.28, quoted and translated in Auerbach, *Scenes*, 40–41. On Auerbach and Judaism, see J. Porter, "Erich Auerbach and the Judaizing of Philology," *Critical Inquiry* 35 (2008): 115–47.

32. R. Popkin, "The Third Force in Seventeenth-Century Philosophy: Scepticism, Biblical Prophecy and Science," *Nouvelles de la Republique de Lettres* 3 (1983): 35–63; H. Savon, "Le Figurisme et la 'Tradition des Pères,'" in Armogathe, ed., *Le Grand siècle et la Bible*. In French drama, see E. Marks, *Marrano as Metaphor: The Jewish Presence in French Writing* (New York, 1996), 21–42.

33. On Marquez, see L. Pericolo, *Philippe de Champaigne* (Tournoi, 2002), 160–65. On Richeome, see J. Vanuxem, "Les *Tableaux sacrées* de Richeome et l'iconographie de l'Eucharistie chez Poussin," in *Nicolas Poussin*, ed. A. Chastel (Paris, 1960), 151–62; von Henneberg, "Poussin's *Penance*"; F. Siguret, "La triple peinture des *Tableaux sacrés* du Père Richeome," in *Inventaire, Lecture, Invention. Mélanges de critique et d'histoire littéraires offerts à Bernard Beugnot*, ed. J. Martel and R. Melançan (Montreal, 1999), 195–210; F. Cousinié, *Le peintre chrétien. Théories de l'image religieuse dans la France du XVIIe siècle* (Paris, 2000); C. Hughes, "*Embarras* and *Disconvenance* in Poussin's Rebecca and Eliezer at the Well," *Art History* 24 (2001): 493–519. On Girard, see Cousinié, *Le peintre chrétien*, 65–67. On Poussin and the Jesuits, see P. Santucci, *Poussin: tradizione ermetica e classicism gesuita* (Salerno, 1985).

34. L. Richeome, *Holy Pictures of the Mysticall Figures of the Most Holy Sacrifice and Sacrament of the Eucharist* (London, 1619), 160.

35. B. Pascal, *Œuvres complètes II*, ed. M. Le Guern (Paris, 2000), 30–31. The same sentiment appears in the sixteenth Provincial Letter and numerous *Pensées*. Compare also A.

Arnauld, *De la Frequente Communion* (Paris, 1643), 100: "The Jews believe themselves devout observers of God's law in observing some of its precepts according to the letter which kills, and not according to the spirit which gives life" ("Les juifs se croyoient tres-religieux observateurs de la loy de Dieu, en observant quelques-uns de ses preceptes, selon la lettre qui tuë, et non selon l'esprit qui donne la vie"); also: "It is pharisaic to attend to exteriors before attending to what's inside" ("c'est estre pharisien que d'examiner le dehors, avant que d'avoir examiné le dedans") (Arnauld, *De la Frequente Communion*, 169).

36. Auerbach, *Scenes*, 52–53.

37. On *la perpertuité de la foi*, see J. Miel, *Pascal and Theology* (Baltimore, 1969), 152. For the emergence of the concept of religious difference, with particular reference to idolatry, see Stroumsa, "Roots of Idolatry."

38. On the rhetoric of exemplarity, see J. D. Lyons, ed., *Exemplum: The Rhetoric of Example in Early Modern France and Italy* (Princeton, 1989). On biblical themes in French tragedy, especially Garnier's *Les Juifves* (1583), see Marks, *Marrano as Metaphor*, 21–42; C. Mazouer, "Théâtre et religion dans la seconde moitié du XVIe siècle (1550–1610)," *French Studies* 60 (2006): 295–304.

39. Regarding Moses: Gabriel Naudé and Louis Machon both invoked him as an exemplary statesman in works commissioned by Richelieu (P. S. Donaldson, *Machiavelli and Mystery of State* [Cambridge, 1988], 171–72, 193–94), while at the opposite end of the spectrum Pomponne II de Bellièvre, president of the Parlement de Paris, regarded him as the lawgiver par excellence and collected pictures of him by Philippe de Champaigne and Poussin. Regarding David: when, in 1617, Louis XIII staged a *coup d'état* by assassinating Concino Concini, he was promptly hailed as a new David who had defeated a tyrannical Goliath (A. L. Moote, *Louis XIII, the Just* [Berkeley, 1991], 95–96); just over thirty years later, when the Prince de Condé led a rebellion against Louis XIV and Mazarin, he too became a David. The great rebellion, the Fronde or "slingshot," was named for David's weapon, while Abraham Bosse's print of *David and Goliath* (1651) gave the former the features of Condé, the latter those of Mazarin.

40. G. Scudéry, *Alaric, ou, Rome vaincue: poëme heroïque* (Paris, 1654), 194–95: "Car comme on peut tirer de l'ingrate vipere, un remede puissant . . . le lecteur prudent . . . tire le bien du mal; de l'ombre la lumiere; voit le piege tendu; l'esvite sagement; et suit le grand chemin pour aller seurement. Icy des curieux et sçavans cabalistes, avec peu de travail on peut suivre les pistes: traverser apres eux ces sentiers escartez; et des obscurs hebreux demesler les clartez. Tout ce que les rabins ont escrit de sublime; et du grand nom de Dieu la force legitime; et des nombres sacrez l'art tout misterieux; et l'occulte pouvoir des images des cieux; enfin tout le sçavoir de l'antique Judée, qu'elle dit luy venir de l'eternelle idée; qu'elle pretend tirer du celeste thresor; se trouve en ces escrits que l'on conserve encor." On Scudéry and Poussin, see J. Unglaub, *Poussin and the Poetics of Painting: Pictorial Narrative and the Legacy of Tasso* (New York, 2006), 179.

41. W. Sauerländer, *Geschichte der Kunst—Gegenwart der Kritik* (Cologne, 1999), 90–116; K. Krause, "Die Kamele Eliezers und die Elephanten des Porus. Typologie und 'Parallele' in Historien von Nicolas Poussin, Sebastien Bourdon und Charles Le Brun," *Marburger Jahrbuch für Kunstwissenschaft* 24 (1997): 213–30; Hughes, "*Embarras* and *Disconvenance*."

42. Jouanny, *Correspondance*, 87–88. See O. Bätschmann, *Nicolas Poussin: Dialectics of Painting* (London, 1990), 58.

43. Pascal, *Œuvres II*, 771: "Les juifs n'ont possédé de Jésus-Christ que les figures et les voiles, comme était la manne et l'agneau pascal." On the image of the veil, see P. Hadot, *The Veil of Isis: An Essay on the History of the Idea of Nature* (Cambridge, 2006); also Fumaroli, *L'École du silence*, 242–43.

44. Poussin, in Jouanny, *Correspondance*, 87; Marquez, quoted in Pericolo, *Philippe de Champaigne*, 160.

45. Also by Mellan, but without evident input from Poussin, is the frontispiece to a Greek New Testament (1642). An angel incises a Greek text onto a pyramid; it translates as "Law of Love on Mount Zion." Supporting the pyramid is a cubic base, which bears in a relief a Classical figure with winged sandals incising a Hebrew text; it translates as "Law of Fear on Mount Sinai." Although intended for an erudite audience, the iconography is fairly straightforward and even a Hebrew-less reader could likely get the gist. For the print, see H. T. Goldfarb, *Richelieu: Art and Power* (Montréal, Cologne, and Ghent, 2002), 187, no. 77.

46. For the distinction between a "'theopoetics' of the image" and its opposition the "vanity of words," in Poussin and his Roman milieu, see Fumaroli, *L'École du silence*, 188–231, esp. 194–96.

47. I owe this last observation to Green, *Seven Sacraments*, 271–72, but have confirmed it through autopsy. It is most apparent if one compares the highlights on Christ's right arm to those on blue-clad figures elsewhere in the picture, notably St. John immediately to Christ's left, or the drinking man at center. Those on Christ are yellow-gold; those on the others are pale blue-white. On archaism in Poussin, see T. Olson, *Poussin and France* (New Haven, 2002), 156–59.

48. Félibien, quoted in Thuillier, *Nicolas Poussin*, 163: "De mesme que les 24 lettres de l'alfabet servent à former nos parolles et exprimer nos pensées, de mesme les lineamens du corps humain à exprimer les diverses passions de l'ame pour faire paroistre au dehors ce que l'on a dans l'esprit."

49. For the date, see J. Thuillier, B. Brejon de Lavergnée, and D. Lavalle, *Vouet* (Paris, 1990), 351.

50. Musée des Beaux-Arts, Nantes inv. D-982–2-1P. B. Dorival, *Philippe de Champaigne, 1602–1674: la vie, l'œuvre, et le catalogue raisonné de l' œuvre II* (Paris, 1976), 34–35, no. 53.

51. C. Gandelman, *Le regard dans le texte. Image et écriture du Quattrocento au XXe siècle* (Paris, 1986), 106–12; L. Marin, *Philippe de Champaigne ou la présence cachée* (Paris, 1995), 335–50; see also Pericolo, *Philippe de Champaigne*, 280–82.

52. On the relation between the two, see B. Dorival, "Poussin et Philippe de Champaigne," in Chastel, *Nicolas Poussin*, 64–68.

53. J. Lichtenstein and C. Michel, eds., *Conférences de l'Académie royale de Peinture et de Sculpture, I* (Paris, 2006), 196–205.

54. On the representation of the Ten Commandments in early modern art, see O. Christin, *Les yeux pour le croire. Les Dix Commandements en images, XVe–XVIIe siècle* (Paris, 2003).

55. Paris, Louvre 7282. Rosenberg, *Nicolas Poussin*, no. 214, with earlier bibliography; Thuillier, *Nicolas Poussin*, no. 207. See also S. Germer, ed., *Vies de Poussin. Bellori, Félibien, Passeri, Sandrart* (Paris, 1994), 102, 195.

56. Cf. P. Joch, *Methode und Inhalt: Momente von künstlerischer Selbstreferenze im Werk von Nicolas Poussin* (Hamburg, 2003).

57. Cf. Thuillier, *Nicolas Poussin*, 38.

58. Germer, *Vies de Poussin*, 102. "Avec un grand sens de la peinture."

59. Superbly discussed in J. Thuillier, "Temps et tableau: la théorie des 'péripéties' dans la peinture française du XVIIe siècle," in *Stil und Überlieferung in der Kunst des Abendlandes. Aktes des 21, Internationalen Kongresses für Kunstgeschichte in Bonn 1964* (Berlin 1967), 3:191–206. See also L. Marin, *To Destroy Painting* (Chicago, 1995), 41–44; L. Marin, *Sublime Poussin* (Stanford, 1999), 5–28; Unglaub, *Poussin and the Poetics of Painting*, 157–97, esp. 178–85; J. Jurt, "Die Debatte um die Zeitlichkeit der *Académie Royale de Peinture* am Beispiel von Poussins *Mannalese*," in *Zeitlichkeit in Text und Bild*, ed. F. Sick and C. Schöch (Heidelberg,

     RICHARD NEER

2007), 337–47. For Le Brun on the *The Israelites Receiving Manna,* see Lichtenstein and Michel, *Conférences,* 171–74.

60. Lichtenstein and Michel, *Conférences,* 171.

61. Ibid., 172: "Ces différents états et ces diverses actions lui tenant lieu de discours et de paroles pour faire entendre sa pensée."

62. On Poussin's scenographia, see F. Siguret, *L'Œil surpis. Perception et représentation dans la première moitié du XVIIe siècle,* 2nd ed. (Paris, 1993), 161–71. On the theater mentioned at the 1667 *conférence,* see Lichtenstein and Michel, *Conférences,* 173.

63. It is sometimes suggested, plausibly enough, that this distant woman with child represents the offended wife, whose husband the adulteress has seduced. Yet it is not clear from the Gospel whether or not the adulteress has been with a married man. A related figure appears in Tintoretto's version of the scene in the Palazzo Barberini (Wilberding, *History and Prophecy,* 333).

64. On picture and diagram in Poussin, see R. Neer, "Poussin and the Ethics of Imitation," *Memoirs of the American Academy in Rome* 51–52 (2006–7): 298–344.

65. J. Dadré and J. Cuilly, eds., *Bibliorum sacrorum cum glossa ordinaria* (Venice, 1603), 5:1154. Various other theories of what Jesus wrote naturally abound in medieval and early modern commentaries. Since Poussin's text is illegible, it is fruitless to speculate as to which theory, if any, he favored. Not only does the picture itself offer no support for any particular account, but it suggests that the whole question is misguided: had Poussin wished to take a position on this question, he could easily have done so by writing the appropriate words.

66. Iconographic tradition frequently omits the writing, as in Jerome Nadal's *Evangelicae Historiae Imagines* of 1593 (see J. MacDonnell, *Gospel Illustrations: A Reproduction of the 153 Images Taken from Jerome Nadal's 1595 Book* Adnotationes et Meditationes in Evangelia [Fairfield, Conn., 1998]). Alternately, it replaces the writing with chicken scratches: see A. Osiander, *Harmoniae Euangelicae libri quator* (Antwerp, 1540); or Rembrandt, on whom see M. Podro, "Rembrandt's Woman Taken in Adultery," *Journal of the Warburg and Courtauld Institutes* 50 [1987]). Or the text simply repeats Christ's injunction, "Let you who are without sin cast the first stone": see P. Bruegel the Elder's version in the Courtauld, 1563; or J. Taylor, *Antiquitates Christianae, or, The History of the Life and Death of the Holy Jesus* (London, 1678).

67. See, for instance, K. Oberhuber, "Raphaël et Poussin," in Bonfait, *Poussin et Rome,* 73, and the Louvre's website, http://cartelen.louvre.fr/cartelen/visite?srv = car_not_frame& idNotice = 2130 (accessed December 12, 2008): "Les Pharisiens déchiffrant les mots tracés par le Christ sur le sol: 'Que celui d'entre vous qui est sans péché lui jette la première pierre.'"

68. Marc Fumaroli arrives at a similar conclusion by a different route when he remarks, "It is as though the painter wanted to establish, between his canvas and the spectator's eye, that type of mute, meditatative *sacra conversazione* which is the very subject of *Christ and the Woman Taken in Adultery*—as opposed to the hasty, frivolous or pretentious 'reading' which the Pharisees make of this dialogue between God and the sinner." Fumaroli, *L'École du silence,* 225.

69. There is some precedent for this conceit in an illustration to the same passage in John by Heinrich Vogtherr for the 1547 edition of Erasmus' New Testament. In that instance the Hebrew text seems to read something like *caas miadi,* "anger of my hand," but while the letters themselves are clear, their sense is not.

70. On the history of the Torah pointer, see N. Feuchtwanger-Sarig, "Chanting to the Hand: Some Preliminary Observations on the Origins of the Torah Pointer," *Studia Rosenthalia* 37 (2004): 3–35. The earliest known hand-shaped example, illustrated here, comes from Ferrara and dates to the late fifteenth century. Other examples are known from seventeenth-century Rome. I am grateful to David and Josef Stern for directing me to this article.

71. As Bätschmann puts its, she appears "almost as a moralistic allusion." Bätschmann, *Nicolas Poussin,* 81–82.

72. Dadré and Cuilly, *Bibliorum sacrorum,* 5:1153.

73. Jouanny, *Correspondances,* 21 (April 28, 1639): "Lisés l'istoire et le tableau."

74. The discussion of nonsense and ineffability here and in what follows derives from a reading of J. Conant, "Mild Mono-Wittgensteinianism," in *Wittgenstein and the Moral Life: Essays in Honor of Cora Diamond,* ed. A. Crary (Cambridge, 2007), especially 42–47.

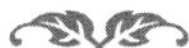

CHAPTER 12

Eugène Delacroix's Jewish Wedding
and the Medium of Painting

Ralph Ubl

The white wall in the center of Eugène Delacroix's *A Jewish Wedding in Morocco* (Figure 12.1) has always struck me as a color field announcing what modernist painting would be. Emerging from an exuberant surrounding of purple, green, red, and orange, it addresses us as forcefully as a figure or a gaze, although it is neither. The critical engagement with modernism has produced a set of categories, such as opticality, thickness, and facingness, which could be implemented to analyze this effect.[1] In proceeding this way, one would be continuing a tradition initiated by writers such as Charles Baudelaire, Paul Signac, Julius Meier-Graefe, or René Huyghe, who placed Delacroix firmly in the history of modernism (Huyghe actually compared the white wall in *A Jewish Wedding* with Mondrian).[2]

But since the publication of Huyghe's monumental *Delacroix* in 1963, art history has of course become highly suspicious of ignoring the specificities of historical and ideological context, and this suspicion is particularly pertinent in the case of Orientalist paintings. With the ascendancy of postcolonial studies, Delacroix's Orientalism has mainly been interpreted as a documentary and imaginary contribution to French colonialism. There is indeed undeniable evidence supporting this claim. Even before he made the trip to Morocco, his art was richly nourished by fantasies of oriental despotism and violence.[3] The journey itself, accomplished in the first half of 1832, was sponsored by the French government as a measure to secure its new colonial possessions in Algeria. Art

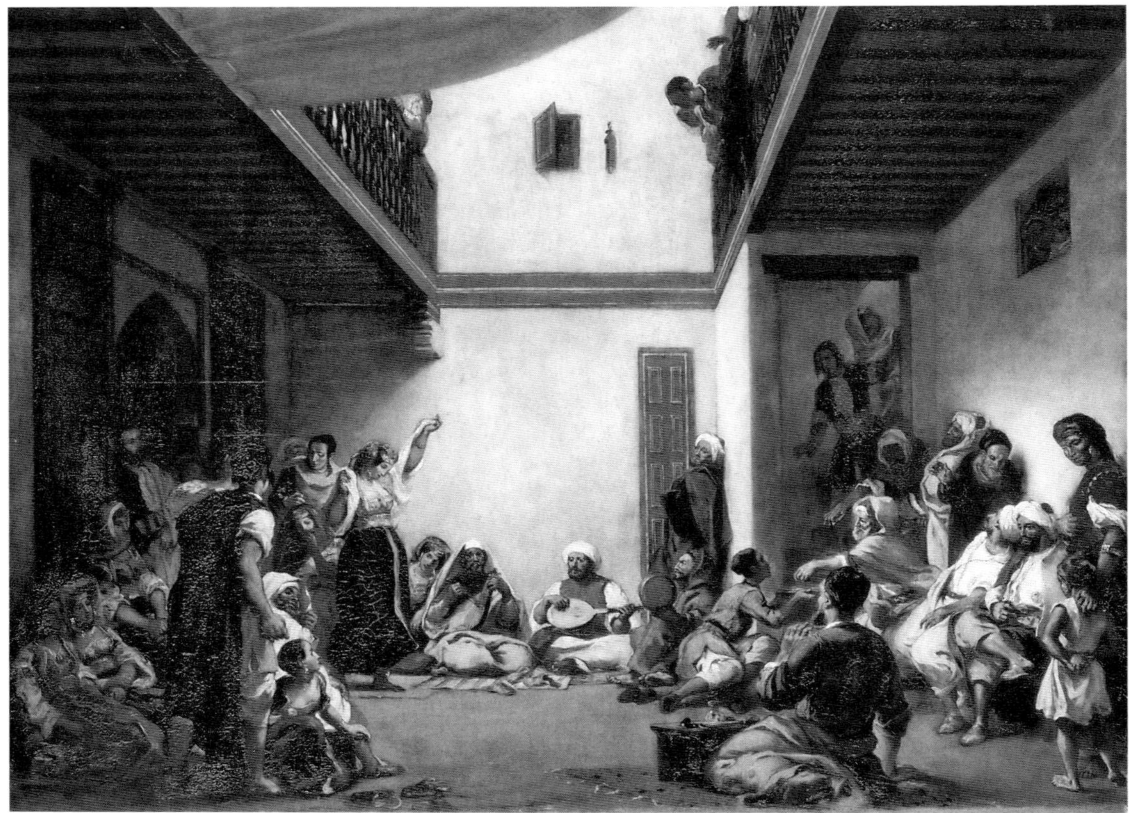

12.1. Eugène Delacroix, *A Jewish Wedding in Morocco*. Oil on canvas, 105 x 140 cm. 1837/41. Musée du Louvre, Paris. Photo: Réunion des Musées Nationaux/Art Resource, New York.

historians have argued that Delacroix contributed to the ethnographic documentation and, by that means, to the French dominance in the region.[4] In any case, there is no doubt that his paintings became an integral part of French colonial culture, which cherished the alterity of the very same North African people who were subjected politically and culturally.[5] Delacroix's famous *Women of Algiers in Their Apartment* (Figure 12.2), exhibited four years after the conquest of Algiers, could be considered as an attempt to guard the secrecy and exoticism of the Orient even after the looting and appropriation of the North African town.[6]

Nineteenth-century critics varied between ethnographic and more aesthetic responses, sometimes coalescing both, sometimes emphasizing either one. Alexandre Dumas understood *A Jewish Wedding in Morocco* as a template for his

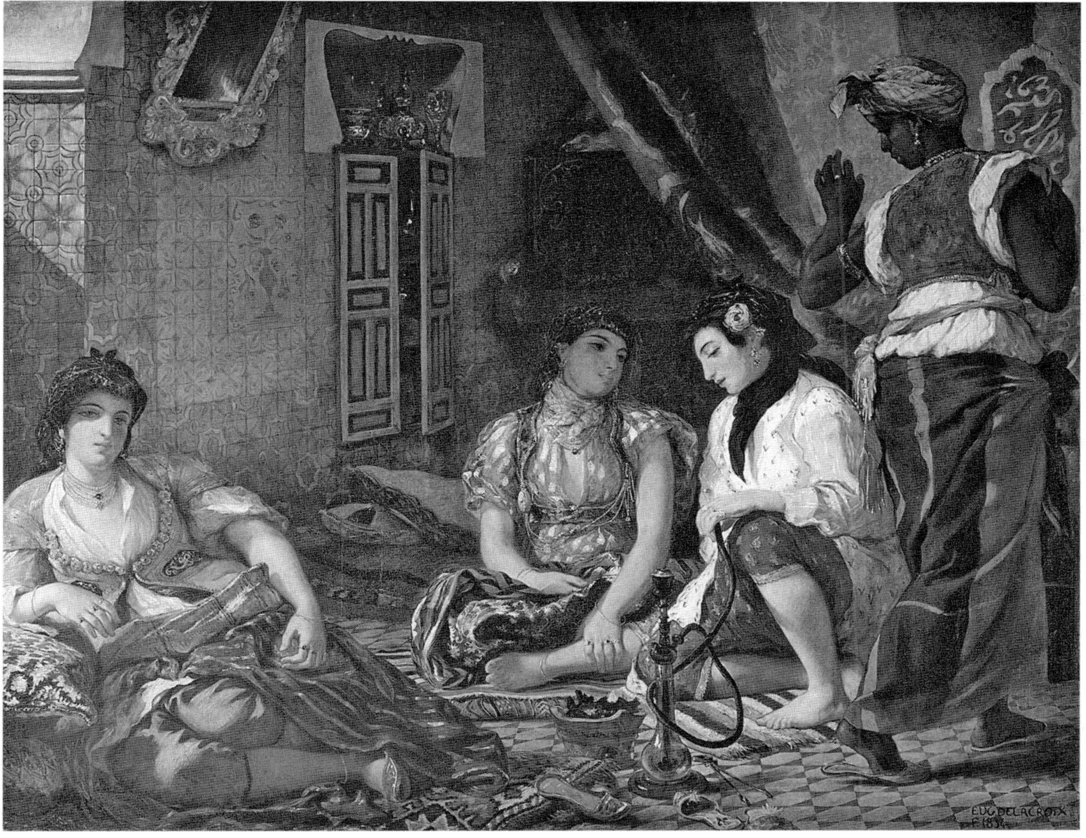

12.2. Eugène Delacroix, *Women of Algiers in Their Apartment,* 1934. Oil on canvas, 180 x 229 cm. Musée du Louvre, Paris. Photo: Scala/Art Resource, New York.

own exotist tourism in Tangiers in 1846, and Théophile Gautier stated with regard to the same painting that Delacroix had completely identified his art with the qualities of Oriental life; but as early as 1834 Gustave Planche described *The Women of Algiers* as "painting and nothing else," and shortly after Delacroix's death Charles Blanc would systematize such an immanentist approach by demonstrating the logic of the "modulation" of colors in those two paintings.[7] The conclusion I would like to draw from these responses is simple in principle but results in complicating the interpretation. There can be no doubt that Delacroix's work reflects and, in some respects, reshapes Orientalist discourse and fantasies. That said, I argue at the same time that the painting articulates a new notion of what the medium of painting is, and that the theme of a Jewish wedding is not incidental to this articulation.

It is certainly not a new claim that self-reference and the quest for alterity are interconnected, especially with regard to post-Enlightenment art and literature. I would argue, however, that the self-reflexive aspect of Delacroix's Orientalism can be related more specifically to the problem of the medium as it was raised by Lessing's *Laocoon*. In the course of Delacroix's own thorough reading of this text in the early 1820s, which has been conclusively analyzed by Michele Hannoosh, the artist rejected Lessing's restrictive notion of the medium of painting.[8] Painting, according to Lessing, subjects representation to a twofold conditioning: first, by investing it with the materiality of its means of expression and, second, by situating it in a visual space that immobilizes its objects. While the conspicuous sensuality of painting inhibits the viewer's imagination from animating the depicted scene, literature appeals directly to the imagination because it uses signs that do not display their materiality. Visual signs, instead, do not stir the imagination. They make fully visible and material whatever they represent. One might say that Lessing understood painting as a "dense" medium, in the specific sense that it possesses a resistant and immobile materiality.[9] As an art, however, painting is able to transcend these media-specific restrictions, if it takes them into account and outwits them with the help of the careful selection and shaping of its content. The most famous form of content discussed by Lessing is, of course, the "pregnant moment," which helps to animate the painting by endowing it with potentiality. But Lessing also mentioned other possibilities, such as the inclusion of a veiled figure, as in the *Sacrifice of Iphigenia* by the ancient painter Timanthes. Not least, some narratives are more suitable than others. Instead of stories that unfold a linear sequence of causally connected actions (such as Pandarus's archery), which appear frozen if singled out as themes of a painting, the artist should favor scenes of continuous back and forth, or tumultuous activity, as in, for example, the feast of the Gods.[10]

All three strategies proposed by Lessing—the choice of a festive theme, the inclusion of a veil, and, not least, the link between time and fertility implied in the term "pregnant"—should have appeared attractive to a painter preparing a wedding picture. But Delacroix disagreed in principle with Lessing's idea that in order to make a successful painting, the materiality of its medium has to be redeemed by the form of content, as if his art were dead letters awaiting to be animated by the spirit of poetry. In his early diary from 1822/24, Delacroix explores various arguments to make the case that the medium of painting in itself, due to its very materiality, is a means to involve the beholder's imagination. Or in short, as Delacroix would note in 1822, the more painting is material, the closer it is to the heart.[11] As for how to conceive of materiality's share in the imaginary involvement of the beholder, Delacroix explored two different answers. Sometimes he argued that the representation of the human body

RALPH UBL

would bring the imaginative qualities of his medium to the fore, writing that painting serves as a "magical bridge" directly connecting "the soul of the figures in the picture and the beholder". In a later diary entry elaborating on the imaginary dimension of the human body, however, he also considered the very different notion of painting as an oscillating medium, by comparing the way his art puts the imagination in motion to the aesthetics of the sea and the chant of the nightingale.[12] Both paradigms, the human body as well as oscillation, would occupy him during his entire career, but particularly after his voyage to Morocco he was strongly given to question the anthropomorphic foundation of his art.

This new alternative arose from Delacroix's use of color so as to emphasize the perceptual instability of single hues and, correspondingly, the unifying effect of a visually animated, pulsating allover. In consequence, Lessing's claim that whatever painting represents is essentially immobilized has been replaced by a notion of painting as a steadily moving, essentially dynamic medium that endows representation with a changing and vibrating mode of apparition. While Lessing identified painting's density, Delacroix transformed the medium into a more flexible state, which might be described as oscillating between different grades of intensity. Correspondingly, art critics such as Gautier, Baudelaire, and Charles Blanc and artists such as Cézanne (according to Gasquet), Signac, and Redon responded to this new notion of painting by using a vocabulary of vibration and iridescence, evoking a sensory experience of both plenitude and withdrawal.[13]

This transformation manifests itself in the themes Delacroix explored during and after his journey of 1832. We should be on guard against the supposition that Delacroix's experience was entirely determined by clichés imported from Paris, such as, for example, that since "Barbary" had never been subjected to Ottoman rule, its inhabitants had preserved ancient and biblical customs, clothing, and body language.[14] Certainly, these clichés did matter, and I show how they were used and, in some respect, reshaped by Delacroix. Of equal importance, however, is the fact that his paintings bear witness to the conditions of seeing that determined how Delacroix experienced and studied Morocco. From his letters, notes, and drawings, it can be inferred that he was interested in Morocco as a country where the visual was highly regulated, all the more for a European traveler who saw himself confronted with what he called the "jealousy" of the Muslims and whose eyes were furthermore excited, but also irritated, by the sheer force of the sun. The Muslim man and the sun are for Delacroix two instances of an overwhelming force energizing the visual field, but also dividing it into inaccessible zones. In fact, he sometimes grumbled about the concealment of Muslim women and the hostility he encountered

whenever he appeared with his sketchbook in the streets; and he also complained about the physical aching of his eyes, which he ascribed to the strong
reverberation of the sunlight from the all-white buildings. But the very wealth
of new sensations this country was offering fascinated all the more as it often
perplexed him or escaped his grasp because of these natural and social forces.[15]
As soon as he returned to his studio in Paris, he began to conceive of painting
as an art that could respond to what he had encountered in Morocco as the
unsettling intensification of the visual field; but the new works make use of the
many studies Delacroix had made while he was there of the various devices used
to mediate and shield this intensity, such as veils, folds, screens, awnings, and,
last but not least, the mazelike architecture of Moroccan buildings and cities.[16]
What he discovered in Morocco was both a shattering sublimity and means of
tempering, or (to put it in Lacanian terms) both the gaze and the screen.

Before spelling out more extensively how the transformation of the medium
was related to Orientalism, I would like to complicate this question a bit further.
Delacroix's art pertains not only to the Orientalist dualism of "European curiosity" and "Arab jealousy," but as well to the tripartite relation between Christians, Muslims, and Jews. Like other travelers to Morocco, Delacroix relied on
the help of Abraham Benchimol and his nephew David Azoncot, who served as
translators and mediators between Muslims and the French. He particularly
appreciated the invitation to their homes, where he portrayed his host's family
and, above all, was allowed to make detailed studies of the daughters.[17] He
would never experience this kind of hospitality with Muslims in Morocco, and
had to travel to occupied Algiers in order to bribe his way into the domestic
interior, which he represented as the realm of Oriental beauty in *Women of
Algiers in Their Apartment*. The highlight of Delacroix's relationship with the
Jews of Morocco undoubtedly came when he attended the wedding of one of
Abraham Benchimol's daughters. To witness a wedding was *de rigueur* for a
traveler on his quest to penetrate the secrets of the Orient and (as the deepest
of all secrets) its reproduction. He was led from the public revelry in the courtyard into the innermost chambers. Here he was allowed to study the bride; and
from here he was able to observe how the bride, in turn, was led from this
secluded interior out into the courtyard and from there across the street into
the groom's house. While he experienced the Muslims as hostile to his curiosity
and resented their unwillingness to allow him to see and study their homes,
particularly their women, he was invited to see the *arcana* of the Jewish home.
What's more, he was given the opportunity to study the regulation of visibility
of the entire feast, and how it affected Jews, Muslims, and himself as a Christian
visitor. It is my claim that this engagement with the visual order at the Jewish

wedding allowed Delacroix to redefine the visuality of his own art and of his Orientalism alike.

The painting that raises all these questions is, of course, *A Jewish Wedding in Morocco*. It was first exposed in the *Salon* of 1841, accompanied by a short explanatory text in the catalogue, which would be richly elaborated in a long ethnographic article written by Delacroix himself and published in the *Magasin pittoresque* in 1842.[18] It shows the courtyard of a Jewish home in Tangiers where Jews and Muslims have gathered and are enjoying themselves, watching a dancer and listening to music. The figures form an irregular circle that skirts the boundaries of the courtyard's space and spills into the building's interior on both the left- and right-hand sides. At first sight of the figures, with their splendid garments and their manifold interrelations, our attention is dispersed and we lose ourselves in the exuberant activities, where no figure seems to stand still or sit quietly: everything is pulsating, vibrating, circling. Despite these various foci of attention, which are reflected in the multiplicity of directions in which the figures are looking, the dancer is clearly the central visual attraction, last but not least for the beholder. In watching the dancer, we are involved in a perpetual undulation that provokes a strong agitation, or back and forth movement, all around. This kinaesthetic relationship between dance and its perception is effectively demonstrated in the depicted figures. The gesture of the Jew to our left is particularly impulsive: he stands with his right fist clenched and his left hand stretched out toward the dancer, as if to protect himself from the impact of what he sees. This gesticulation in opposing directions is all the more abrupt and powerful as the man is standing with both feet firmly on the ground. The Jewish woman sitting to his right turns suddenly toward the dancer and is moved by what she sees as if she wants to dance, too. The scribe seated in the foreground has been captured in a similar movement. He jerks his body backward and raises his left hand, while his attention is directed entirely at the dancer. A peculiar detail underscores how important these movements of arms and hands were to Delacroix. Very close to the couple looking down from the right gallery, just below the upper edge of the painting, a single right arm is reaching over the balustrade in an agitated gesture that might be read in both ways, reaching toward as well as repelling. Once again, watching the dancer and immersion into a back and forth movement are interrelated. Having said this, I also want to stress the fact that Delacroix chose a fairly small canvas—one that measures no more than forty-one by fifty-seven inches. As such, the scale of the figures does not encourage any direct bodily identification with them. What animates the scene—the bodies' back and forth motion—is transformed into perceptual motion, engaging not so much our limbs and body as our eyes, as if the visual field itself were oscillating.

So far, I have exclusively adopted the position of an absorbed beholder who imagines sitting or standing at the very place the painting has provided, between the couple and the scribe in the foreground, next to the slippers, which Delacroix often included to a painting's threshold, as if he wanted to indicate that his work might encompass those who are looking at it. But a peculiar and, for Delacroix, unusual emphasis has been placed on perspective, with a mark in the plaster of the white wall inscribing the vanishing point—situated slightly off center to the right, just beside the narrow green door against which a Muslim man is leaning, eyeing us distrustfully, as if he wants us to be excluded from the festivities. We are constrained to conceive of the scene as a perspectival representation which, by its very nature, places its beholder outside itself. The *Salon* catalogue of 1841 included an ethnographic description of the ceremony, and thus the Parisian audience was to be in no doubt that the painter had actually seen what he was showing.[19] But the relationship between seeing and showing is more complex. The painting invites the beholder to become an immersed witness, at the same time as it seats the beholder at distance, defining her or him as an onlooker at a foreign spectacle. Given the painting's format, it would be misleading to describe this shift between closeness and distance in terms of actual movement in front of the painting or two distinct physical positions we can actually inhabit. Instead, we find ourselves riven by these positions. Without changing our distance in relation to the painting, we experience an imaginary split in our role as beholder. This process of inclusion and exclusion might also be described as an extension of the oscillatory movement, from a movement animating the scene to a movement encompassing the relationship between the painting and the beholder, as if these two realms were associated in an incessant alternation between coalescence and withdrawal.

But this is to already evoke the characteristic effects resulting from Delacroix's colorism. In mobilizing the visual field, two areas of color are of especial importance. There is the pale purple floor: depending on the focus of our attention, its spatial effect changes dramatically. Obviously, the floor extends horizontally into the depth to serve as the ground on which to stand, sit, or dance. But given how critical the surface of the floor is in establishing spatial illusion, the lack of differentiation through linear or color perspective is rather unsettling. Whenever we immerse ourselves into the painting and allow our focus to be placed exclusively on the dancer, the floor contracts to a color patch and strains the stability of the illusionist depiction of space. The other area of color that needs to be mentioned is, of course, the white wall, which addresses the beholder frontally as an almost blank but all the more powerful strip of color, and thus plays its role in separating us from the scene. This distancing effect becomes evident in the aggressive gaze of the Muslim, but it is related to the wall functioning as a surface that reflects the blazing sun.[20] Looked at this way, the inclusion and exclusion of the beholder I have just described in narrative terms can be recast as an effect of the regulation of light and heat. The galleries and the brown awning are filters to create a tempered space for the wedding guests, where the beholder can imagine him- or herself to be included. The white wall transfers the force of the sun into the courtyard where it yields a twofold effect. On the one hand, it manifests itself in the pulsating motion of the dancer, the musicians, and those guests who are affected by their art. I would describe this effect as transformation of the sun in bodily movement. On the other hand, however, the sunlight expresses itself in a gaze, figured by the Muslim next to the closed green door, which makes us aware of our own physical distance from the scene.

Let's have another look at the white wall. It functions not only as a reflecting surface, but is also a screen. As such, it stirs our imagination. The staging of the glances plays its part in this. Everybody in the courtyard seems engaged in watching either the dancer or the other guests, except for the aggressively staring Muslim, on account of whose demeanor we presume that the narrow green door he is standing next to conceals something not intended for our eyes. On closer inspection, we can find another man looking out at us. He stands at the threshold of the large door in the left wall and can be identified as a Jew. Unlike the Muslim's gaze, this man's gaze is not at all aggressive and even seems to be inviting us to join him. The contrast between the Jew and the Muslim—both of them placed close to a door, the one open and in shadow, the other shut and in full sunlight—sharpens our awareness of the privilege our entrance into the interior would be, and reminds us that in order to attain this privilege, we would have to rely upon the hospitality of the Jews and challenge the jealousy of the Muslims.

But even without these narrative clues, we might be tempted to muse about the interior of the house, since a white surface in the center of a painting, being in itself a rather unusual pictorial element, points to an absence. Of special interest in this regard is the detail of the small half-open window high up in the wall. On its sill stands a vase. The fact that this is only apparent from close up entices the viewer to reflect on the hidden interior of the house. The white wall provokes us to turn our imagination to what lies concealed within and to presume that there is a particularly valuable object enclosed. Through considering the white wall with great attention, we will certainly not discover this imaginary object, but we will discover an imaginative dimension of the painting, which is presented at the precise location where the painting most strikingly presents its own materiality and density. When we begin to imagine what lies behind the screen, our imagination becomes aware of the physicality of the screen itself.

This fantasmatic object that makes our imagination wander from the courtyard to the interior, from the interior to the screen, and from the screen to the painting itself is identified in Delacroix's text for the catalogue of the Salon exhibition. In the second sentence he mentions that it is the bride who is hidden in the interior, behind the white wall.[21] In a much longer article published in the popular *Magasin pittoresque* in 1842, Delacroix gave an extensive description of the wedding, including a detailed account of what happened to the secluded bride: she was relegated to the darkest corner of a dark room, she was veiled and enveloped in woolen fabric, and before she was to be brought to the groom's house, her face was heavily painted with kohl, cinnabar, and henna. All the while, according to Delacroix's account, she had to preserve the immobility of an "Egyptian sculpture," which metaphor evokes associations of mystery and idolatry.[22]

Among the plentiful notes and drawings Delacroix brought back from Morocco, there are several dozen sheets relating to the Moroccan Jews, and many of these depict women.[23] However, with the exception of a rapid pen sketch made in the same notebook in which Delacroix recorded his observations of the wedding festivities (Figure 12.3), most of these drawings do not correspond to his description of the bride. For example, a well-known watercolor, traditionally titled *The Jewish Bride* (Figure 12.4), shows an unveiled woman without heavy makeup. Whoever she is (I do not want to rule out the traditional identification), she does not correspond to the figure that Delacroix presented in 1842 as the Jewish bride he had seen in Morocco. But there is at least a single watercolor including a henna and kohl maquillage very similar to the description in the *Magasin pittoresque*. In another, highly finished watercolor, *A Visit to the Jewish Bride*, made shortly after his return to Paris and probably acquired by (or given to) the royal family, Delacroix did not use any of the ethnographic details, such as the veil, the woolen wrap, or the makeup.[24] As with most of the other representations of Jewish women, the bride has been depicted so as to match European expectations of an Oriental beauty. Obviously, *A Jewish Wedding* does not represent the veiled or the made-up face of the bride, either. But instead of being rendered so as to seem more recognizably like an "Oriental beauty," she is conspicuously excluded. By supplementing his painting with two texts, Delacroix defined *A Jewish Wedding* as a selective representation and encouraged his audience to understand it as a screen that hides the bride and her alien traits. The *Magasin pittoresque* article contains a hint that might be read as a comment on this decision. The bride is described as the "sacrifice" of the feast. This is, of course, a topical allusion to the loss of her virginity, but it takes an unexpected turn. While Delacroix refers (ironically) to the "licentious" nature of the dance, he does not mention explicitly the

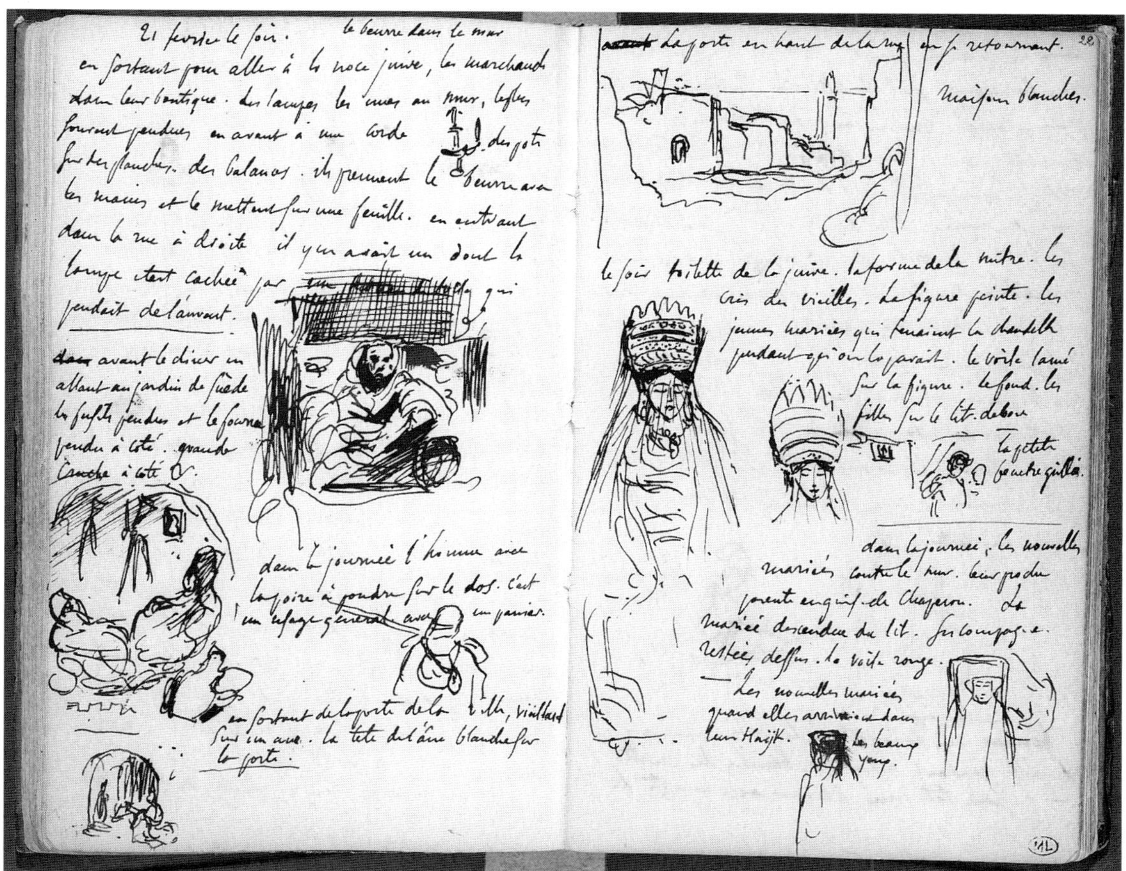

12.3. Eugène Delacroix, *Moroccan Sketchbook*, February 1832. Pen on paper, 16.5 x 9.8 cm. Musée du Louvre, Paris. Photo: Réunion des Musées Nationaux/Art Resource, New York.

sexual aspect of the bride's sacrifice. Instead, according to Delacroix, her sacrificial status consists first in her enduring all the clothing, makeup, and hourslong immobility, and second in her being shown to the crowd.[25] She is a sacrifice insofar as she is transformed into a representation. Viewed in the light of his own choice of words, the painter's decision to refrain from consummating this sacrifice in his art might indicate his wish to guard the bride's virginity.[26]

Guarding her virginity means turning the imaginary object into a symbol of potentiality. If this is the case, in what way does the bride allegorize potentiality in painting? We have already seen how, rigid as an "Egyptian sculpture," decoratively painted and put on display, the bride lends herself to figuring the visual arts. More specifically, I would argue, she refers to the allure of strong pigments and their unmediated effect, even after they have been applied to the canvas,

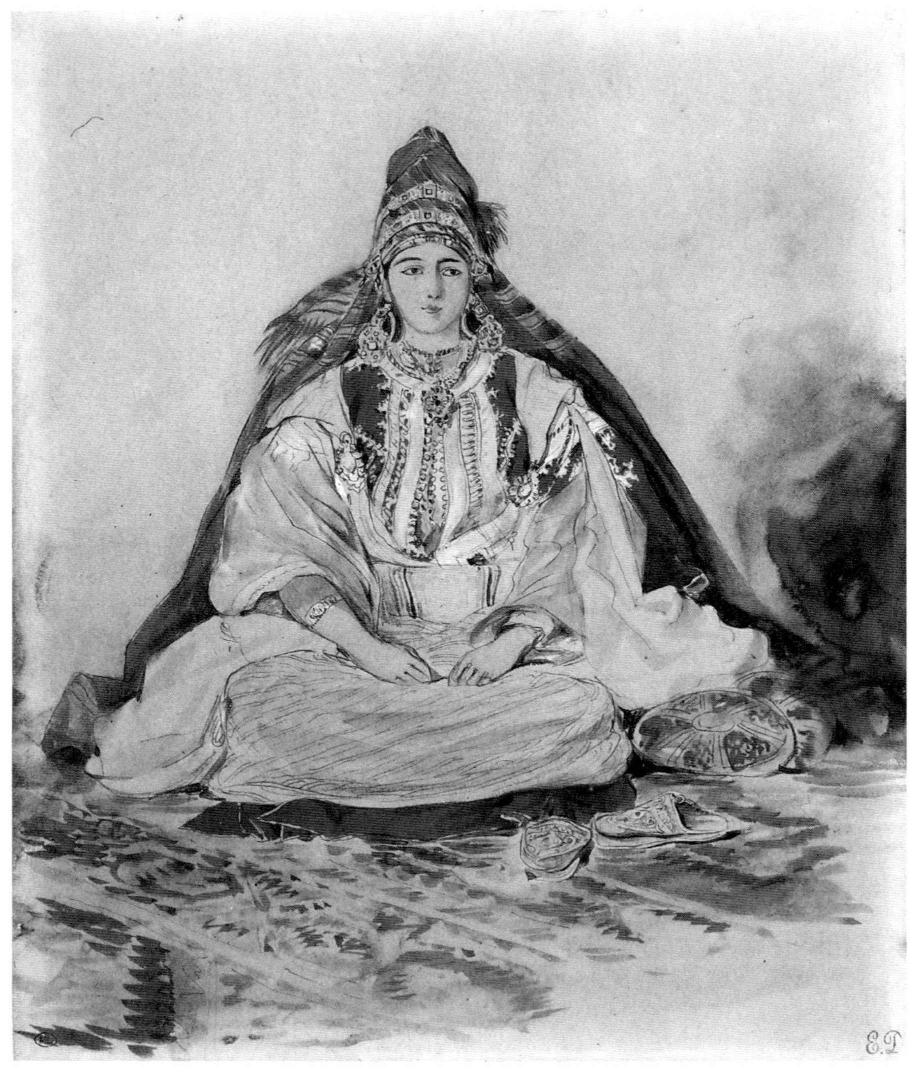

12.4. Eugène Delacroix, *The Jewish Bride*, 1832. Watercolor and pencil on beige paper, 28.8 x 23.7 cm, Musée du Louvre, Paris. Photo: Réunion des Musées Nationaux/Art Resource, New York.

dried, and, so to speak, become immobile. More generally, she figures the material aspect of the medium as a resource of painting. Being a colorist who filled his diary with careful records of his or other painters' use of pigments, Delacroix regarded his raw material certainly as the most precious resource. The interior might also be understood as the realm of the painter since, in contrast to us, he was allowed to enter the interior. It can therefore be associated with his studio insofar as both are hermetic spaces where the materials of painting are prepared

　　　　　RALPH UBL

and applied, and where only the painter is given access. As an artist who high-lighted the process of painting, by means of his open brushwork and vibrant colorism, but also by choosing an iconography which, in many cases, can be read as a metaphoric reverberation of the act of painting, Delacroix makes his viewers particularly interested in his studio. It comes as no surprise that his studio was transformed into a museum and that even his pallets have been conserved.[27] During his lifetime, however, his studio was a secluded interior, much less open to social exchange than the studios of an earlier generation, and treated as a most intimate space.[28] In defining an entire painting as a screen concealing such an inaccessible interior where an imaginary and, at the same time, alien figure is hidden—what is more, a figure of painting's material resources—Delacroix exoticizes the inner realm of his art and identifies it with certain features that disfigure the European notion of beauty, Oriental or other. This matches his approach to Orientalism as discussed in recent art historical studies, where it has been argued convincingly that Delacroix conceived his art in reference to and as partaking of a kind of alterity regarded as barbarian or impure.[29] The bride who is not sacrificed by being represented, but is enshrined as a figure of potentiality, associates this potentiality of painting with a strangely painted, rigid idol. Since Delacroix underlines in his description that the bride was not allowed to open her eyes while the henna, kohl, and cinnabar were applied,[30] we might even understand the entire painting not only as a screen, but at the same time as the displacement of the bride's face, given its conspicu-ous contrast between the closure of the white wall and the strong green, red, and orange of the galleries as well as the mingling of various colors in the courtyard.

As it is, the figure of the dancer has her share in the allegorization of the painting. For Delacroix, she marked an important difference between European and Oriental arts. Apparently, two choreographic features of Oriental dance particularly captured Delacroix's interest. For one thing, the Oriental dancer does not raise her legs but remains standing firmly on the ground. For another, all her movements originate from her hips. Both the firm stance and the circling of the hips were unknown in the Parisian theaters of the 1830s and 1840s, a time when the toe-dance held sway, with dancers such as Marie Taglioni or Fanny Elssler floating weightlessly across the stage.[31] But in the motion of Oriental dance, rotating in situ and originating from the center of the body, Delacroix recognized something that corresponded exactly to his own art: as a draughts-man he always attempted to capture the body "par les milieux," from the cen-ters and not from the external contours.[32] And as a colorist he aimed, as we have seen, at pulsating effects grounded in the materiality of the painting—like the Oriental dancer, who does not deny but instead affirms the ground. The figure of the dancer actually unites the two most prominent areas of color: the pale purple area of the floor and the white area of the wall. The stripe in the dancer's skirt picks up the purple and gives it a vertical orientation; the wide sleeves, by contrast, lead into the white of the walls; the left arm effectively functions as a distinction between the white of the sleeve and the white of the wall, while the right arm is nestled in the inner space of the folded white fabric. In this way, Delacroix took great care to entangle the dancer in the white surface of the wall or, to put it in more abstract terms, to intertwine the pulsating motion of his colorism with the material density of the painted surface. If we take into account the kinetic reverberation of the dancer's arm with arms of the wedding guests and again with the arm of the artist present at the scene, it seems plausible to read this passage from the agitated dancer to the solid wall as an allegorical passage—as an allegory for what the painter does when he transmutes the density of paint into an oscillating painting. And if we include in this allegorical reading that the visual exuberance of the courtyards reflects the force and plenitude of the sun, we might conceive of the painterly gesture as fired by this sublime source of the visual and, at the same time, as the transformation of this glare into bodily movement. The material resources of this process, however, are figured by the bride. The painter, so to speak, begins with the bride but works to capture the dancer and, through her, the oscillation of the African sun.

Going one step further, I would like to underscore that the bride and the dancer refer to a hidden and twofold origin of pictorial representation that is not rooted in the animated human body but in the materiality of the medium and the dazzling force of light. Instead of figuring the foundation of painting, the human body is now situated in a decentered representation that refers to its own origin as excluded from representation and therefore catalytic to the imagination. Given this decentering of the human figure, the comparison with Balzac's *Chef d'oeuvre inconnu* asserts itself. Balzac tells the story of how painting as an incarnated art collapsed into mere materiality. As Hubert Damisch has shown, the narrative is based on various exchanges. The thickness and the density of painting result from the interweaving of the lower and the upper layers of the paint; this exchange of 'dessus' and 'dessous' corresponds to a twofold economic transaction told in Balzac's story: thanks to his gold, Frenhofer has taken possession of the artistic secrets of his teacher Mabuse; and thanks to the beauty of his fiancée, Gilette, Poussin is allowed to see the "unknown masterpiece" hidden in Frenhofer's studio.[33] As is well known, the only recognizable element in this painting, which was supposed to present life itself, is the exquisite foot of a woman in one of the lower corners. For the rest, it exhibits nothing but "a wall of paint." Much more needs to be said about

Delacroix and this novel, but in our context it suffices to indicate two major motifs linking it with *A Jewish Wedding in Morocco*: the theme of exchange of women and the inclusion of a female figure within the materiality of paint. That said, it is even more illuminating to point out how differently Delacroix dealt with the crisis of the human figure as the origin of painting. Balzac's narration starts with the claim that the animation of painting originates in the human body and that it unfolds as a sequence of transactions that should help to attain this ideal but eventually will result in subverting it. If everything is tradable and put into circulation, the paradigmatic function of the human body is challenged. This is fatally true for Frenhofer, who is deeply involved in these transactions since he owes the secret of painting to his gold. Nevertheless, he tries to withdraw his masterwork from exchange, most obviously by withdrawing it from the gaze of other artists, but most importantly by identifying depicted and actual life (an identification he hoped to finally achieve through using Gilette as a model) . In this way, he imagines that he can overcome, once and for all, the exchange between representation and the human body that underlies the art of painting. Of course, Delacroix did not emulate this self-destructive attempt to rescue the ideal of incarnation by creating an actually incarnated work of art. He instead created a painting that refers to an origin excluded from the field of representation and split into two. This split can be described as a severing of the living human body into two different functions: the function of animation, which is assumed by the sun, and the function of physical density, which is assumed by the bride. That said, it has to be emphasized, however, that this splitting results in a profound, disfiguring transformation: the North African sun points to a sublime, that is a shattering and blinding force of life, and the physical density of the bride is equally associated with an alien world where virgins are painted and immobile like enigmatic "Egyptian sculptures."

In presenting an allegorical reading of the bride and the dancer, I have ignored the essential iconographic fact that both women are Jewish.[34] In order to understand Delacroix's figuration of "Jewishness"—the Jewish woman as bride and as dancer, in relation to Jewish and Muslim men, and all these figures together as the object of a Christian painter—I would like to start with an examination of Delacroix's earlier representations of Jews and their literary sources. From this comparison, I hope to gain a new perspective on the bride and the dancer as they relate to the highly charged topical figure of "la belle juive."[35] Shakespeare's "fair Jessica," object of exogamic desire, and her father himself, abject embodiment of Jewish literalism who withholds his daughter, have been enormously influential, not least because of the anti-Jewish theology materialized in both figures. However, in the most successful recasting of their topical configuration, Walter Scott's *Ivanhoe*, the strongest affect of the father is paternal love, not avarice. In becoming Rebecca, Jessica was thus turned into an object of a twofold fascination, not only as a figure of exogamic desire but equally because of her loyalty to her origin. For some of Scott's English readers, Rebecca even announced a kind of reconciliation between the modern state and what was regarded as Jewish particularism.[36] In Paris, Jewish artists such as the composer Jacques Fromenthal Halévy (a close friend of Delacroix) and the writer Eugénie Foa used the figure of the "belle juive" to dramatize the liberal critique of patriarchal order and of religious intolerance, as well as to make a Romantic point by contrasting the communitarian strength of Jewish life and tradition with the individualism of modern society.[37] As Diana Hallman has argued, Halévy's opera *La Juive* "touched on a contemporary social paradox: the vacillation between the embracing and rejection of Jews in the land that promised *fraternité* to all its citizens," but, in so doing, did not refrain from exploiting clichés about Jewish money and fanaticism and "concurrently reinforced ideas about the Jewish Other already present in the minds of its audiences."[38] To be sure, Hallman also points out that *La Juive* contrasted clearly with antisemitic adaptations of these stereotypes, be it in socialist or Catholic literature. To mention just one example, the character of Scott's Rebecca gave rise to Chateaubriand's infamous speculation that the beauty of Jewish women resulted from their not having been involved in the killing of Jesus.[39]

Three years before he traveled to Morocco, Delacroix made a series of lithographs illustrating *Ivanhoe*. He did not adopt Chateaubriand's theological sophism, but not unlike him he exploited Scott's contrasting of ugly Isaac and beautiful Rebecca for his own ends. In one of the lithographs (Figure 12.5), the main field shows the moment when Front-de-Boeuf pressures Isaac for money by threatening him with torture, which is to be carried out by two African slaves. On the artist's proof, the left and the right margin each include a sketch of a female nude, presumably Rebecca. This alludes to a turn in the episode, but distorts the text's implication. As soon as Isaac learns that he cannot rescue his daughter by conceding to Front-de-Boeuf's extortion, because she has already been given to another Templar, he braves his tormentor, "rendered desperate by paternal affection."[40] In representing Rebecca as a nude captive, however, Delacroix has endowed his representation of impending violence with sexual implications, as if Isaac were being threatened not for money but for his beautiful daughter. Since the margins of his lithograph are the very space that is reserved for the free play of artistic inventions, one might infer that Delacroix identified his own art with this sexualization of violence. This comes as no surprise if we think about his most notorious painting of the 1820s, *The Death of Sardanapalus*. Rebecca is one among many female trophies of an art that receives its own force from sexual violence exerted by and on exotic figures.[41]

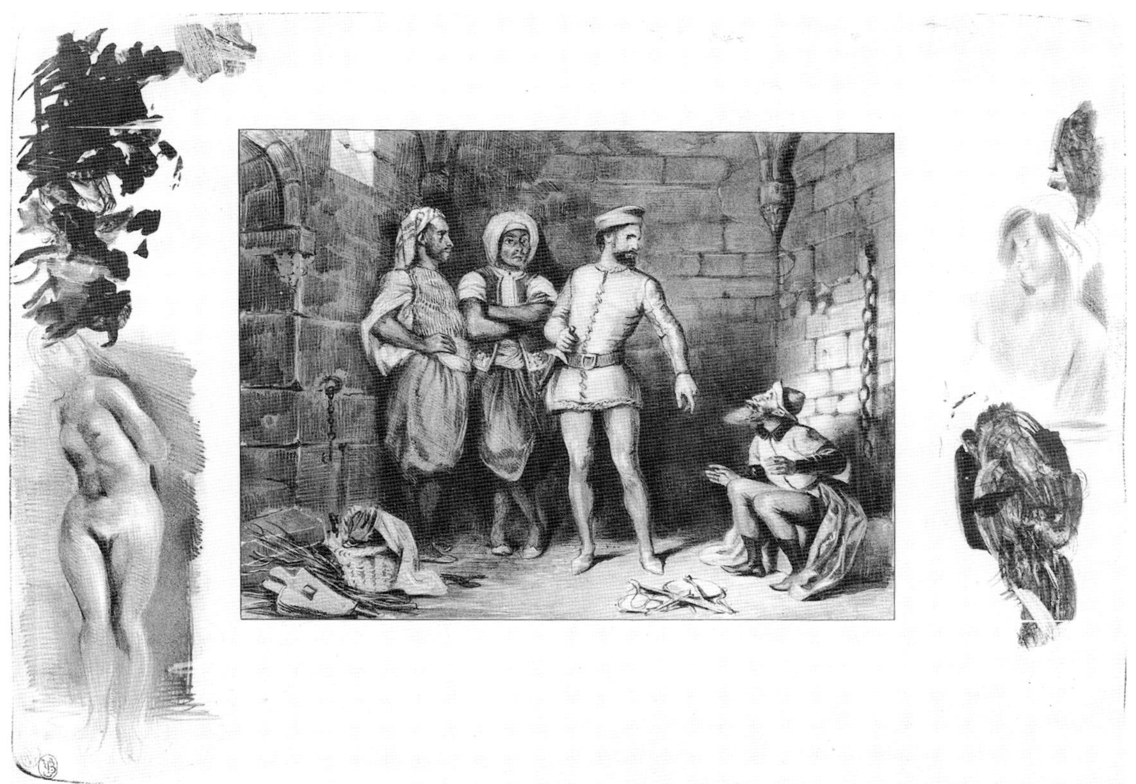

12.5. Eugène Delacroix, *Front-Boeuf and Isaac of York*. Lithography (Delteil 85), 16.7 x 21.5 cm. The William McCallin McKee Memorial Collection, The Art Institute of Chicago. Photo: Jennifer Anderson.

The voyage to Morocco brought no immediate change to Delacroix's representation of Jewish women. Shortly after his return he made the watercolor *A Visit to the Jewish Bride*.[42] As already mentioned, the bride does not show any of the alien traits, such as the strong makeup or sculptural rigidity, that Delacroix would go on to describe in his article of 1842. Instead, she is rendered as an Oriental beauty admired by Muslim notables who stand in the foreground while the Jewish men hide themselves in the second row. The black slave sitting at the bride's feet underscores that the bride pertains to the same erotic world as the Oriental harem, and is being portrayed as another object of what was known as the despotic and polygamous sexuality of the Muslims.[43] This iconographic scheme identifies the "belle juive" as an object of exogamic desire and, allusively, as an object of sexual violence, thus presenting the same though less graphic coalescence of "belle juive," violence, and sexuality as in the *Ivanhoe* illustration (Figure 12.5). As for Delacroix's written statements, his letters from

Morocco betray a purely aesthetic interest in Jewish women. From a memoir on the journey he probably wrote in the early 1840s, we learn that he holds to the anti-Jewish stereotype that the beauty of Jewish women contrasts with the ugliness of Jewish men, ascribing this ugliness to the suppression of Jews by Muslims (and implying that male beauty cannot thrive but by exercising political power; in presenting the male Jews in their black coats, Delacroix actually reminds us of their subjection to despotic laws, including clothing regulations).[44] That said, it is evident that *A Jewish Wedding* departs from Delacroix's previous interpretations of "Jewishness." Most obviously, the painting refers to an elaborate engagement with the Jewish ceremony, and therefore exhibits how much it owes to the relationship with David Azencot and Abraham Benchimol, who guided Delacroix into the inner realm of Oriental life. Jews are introduced in the painting as mediators who give access to an otherwise hostile Muslim world.[45]

But what does this redefinition of Jews as mediators—which, of course, draws on the traditional distinction between the Muslim as enemy and the Jew as "in between" and which also reflects the actual function of Jews for European merchants and diplomats—mean for the medium of painting? In his article from 1842, Delacroix placed great emphasis on the fact that at the wedding celebration only the women dance, or, to be precise, only one woman dances at a time, one after another. The single dancer seen in the painting, then, stands for various Jewish women who have already danced or who are yet to dance. According to Delacroix's description, the rhythm by which the dancers appear determines the rhythm by which money is collected from the Muslim men, who are depicted on the right side of the painting. The money goes to the musicians. But each man who gives money singles out the dancer who pleases him most by touching her shoulder with a coin.[46] Therefore, the dance and the money belong to the same order, in that they both motivate movement—the pulsing movement of the bodies and the glittering of the coins in transit. The coins reflect the sunlight; the women transform its dazzling force into bodily convulsions. Viewed from this position, the painting represents the courtyard as the realm of exogamic attraction, defined by the African sun, Muslim power, and Oriental dance. The force of the latter even affects the scribe who is conspicuously placed in the foreground, isolated from the other wedding guests. Delacroix certainly knew that, from a purely ethnographic point of view, this is a barely plausible position (and an even less plausible moment) to set down the marriage contract. But making the scribe part of the mingling of Jews and Muslims (and the Christian traveler, if we include him in the scene) underscores that in the courtyard, nobody from any of the three religious groups can resist the movement of pulsating bodies—not even the man who is professionally

committed to the endogamic exchange of women. The reaction of another figure I have not yet mentioned further underscores this point. I mean the sudden
gesture of the man who, accompanied by a Jewish woman, is descending the
staircase in the right corner of the courtyard. I would interpret this gesture as
an attempt to keep his balance, as if it is necessary for him to grope his way
from the half shadow of the staircase into the bright sunlight of the courtyard.
In passing from the interior to the courtyard, he is exposed to the African sun
and, at the same time, transgresses a social boundary beyond which Jewish men
and women are not necessarily promised to each other. To be sure, the two
figures in the left foreground who respond strongly to the dancer might form a
couple, but they are an exception since most Jewish men and women in the
courtyard do not belong exclusively to each other. The "belles juives" sitting at
the left are looking toward the Muslim guests on the right, among whom the
man with the crossed legs seems to be responding to their attention. In leaving
the house, the couple descending the stairs is also leaving the endogamic interior
and entering a realm of exogamic desire and danger. As opposed to them, the
bride does not participate in this back and forth of glances, bodies, and coins.
She embodies endogamic self-identity and therefore assumes the very function
hitherto reserved for the father of the "belle juive." Like Isaac in the *Ivanhoe*
illustration, she is placed behind a thick wall, but unlike him she is not exposed.
In concealing her, Delacroix not only kept hidden a figure that would have been
a challenge to European viewers, but he also oriented his entire painting toward
an excluded center that entices the imagination and lends itself to an allegorical
interpretation of the resources of painting.

While Jewish men are presented as mediators, Delacroix related his own
medium to the "belle juive" by imagining her both as a decorated virgin hidden
from view and as a dancer whose art is praised by touching her shoulder with a
coin. The "belle juive" figure is endogamic as well as exogamic, merely material
as well as highly animated; she guarantees self-identity and transgresses identities at the same time and can refer the painter's own secluded space as well as
to the sun as the source of the life of painting. Given this identification with
"Jewishness" as a figure of mediation, first in the colonial context and, furthermore, as an allegory of painting, I would like to come back once more to Delacroix's critique of the *Laocoon*. He took up and radicalized some of Lessing's
suggestions. He chose a festive theme, selected a moment foreshadowing the
climax of the story, and, instead of including a veiled figure in order to address
the viewer's imagination, he defined the entire painting as a screen hiding a
likewise veiled figure. Thus, a white surface turns out to be the most important
pictorial element to address our imagination. But as for how the medium of

painting is figured, Delacroix departed radically from Lessing's dualism of relegating the medium of the visual arts to the realm of the merely material, dead, and deadening letter. And he did it with a "Jewish" turn. The bride and the dancer who both belong to the very group that has been stigmatized to adhere to the mere letter are introduced as an allegory of mediation: between the material and visual aspect of his medium, its density and materiality on the one hand, and its visual pulsation between different degrees of intensity on the other hand. To sum up: pictorially, the white wall serves as common ground for either understanding of what constitutes the medium of painting. It is the element that most conspicuously foregrounds painting's material density, and, at the same time, it is the element that emits painting's oscillatory force. With regard to the structure of beholding implied in the painting, the two aspects of the medium are both linked to painting's ability to address the imagination, though each does so in a different way, the one concerning the subject and the other the object of the imagination. Looked at as a vibrating image, the painting at once includes the beholder within and excludes the beholder from its world; and looked at as a dense and material surface, the painting serves as a screen that directs the beholder's imagination to a concealed object. Last but not least, allegorically the white wall relates the dancer and the bride to each other, and, by so doing, turns a twofold figuration of "Jewishness" into a figuration of how the medium of painting works, transforming its materiality into phenomenality and, vice versa, referring the emergence of its colorism to the hidden resources of paint. Looked at that way, *A Jewish Wedding* creates an Orientalism of painting that unsettles the deeply rooted Western ontology of "Jewishness" as figure of failed mediation.[47]

In a final step, I ask how Delacroix's tripartite Orientalism relates to his ambition to create a painting equal to the works of the Old Masters. An obvious way to approach this question would be to conceive of his journey to Morocco as a primitivist experience that seeks to rejuvenate painting by relating it to an older and deeper source. In fact, this was an important rationale for Delacroix, who conceived of his own culture as very much in need of reconnecting with its origins.[48] They could be found in Morocco. He shared the belief of his fellow Romantics that the Jewish women of North Africa had conserved the beauty of the biblical Rebecca or Esther.[49] In his article on the Jewish wedding he pointed to the difference between the rote and emotionless ceremonies in modern Europe and the festivities of the Oriental Jews, which distinguish themselves in their ancient tradition, jubilance, and communitarian cohesion.[50] The old theological argument according to which the existence of Jews is legitimate because they remind Christians of an overcome stage of sacred history is transformed into an argument in favor of their function as a primitivist resource

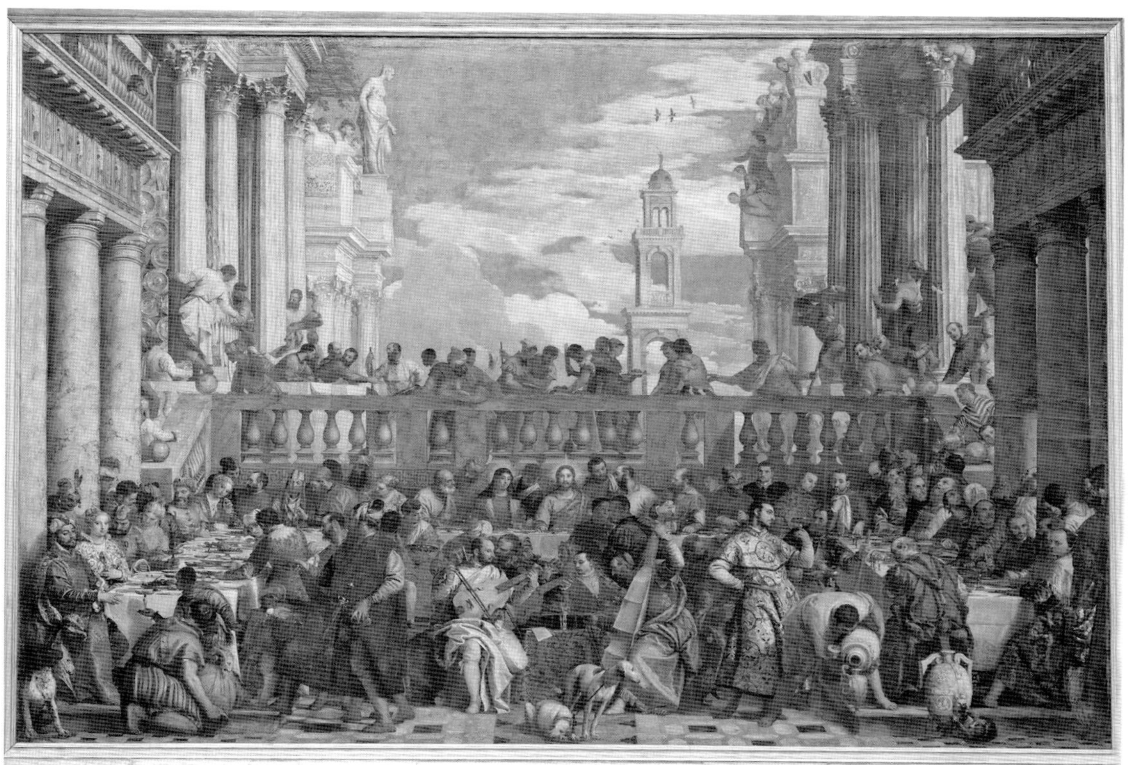

12.6. Paolo Veronese, *Wedding at Cana*, 1563. Oil on canvas, 677 x 994 cm. Musée du Louvre, Paris. Photo: Erich Lessing/Art Resource, New York.

of Western culture. From this perspective, one might suppose that Delacroix demonstrated his intimate knowledge of the Jewish wedding ceremony and tried to appropriate its visual economy of hiding and presenting in order to deepen his art's take on one of the foremost themes of Western painting: biblical feasts. At the same time, however, Delacroix's painting articulates the distance between the Jewish wedding and the modern beholders: as I have argued, the beholders are included as well as excluded and are confronted with a scene that conceals another scene inaccessible to them. What is true for the painting with regard to its subject matter also determines its relationship to the Old Masters. The primitivist reference is used to reflect upon the difference between modern painting and the masterworks of the Louvre. It is my claim that *A Jewish Wedding* revises one of the most famous representations of biblical feasts, conserved in the Louvre since 1798 and praised by Théophile Gautier as a "splendid feast for the eyes":[51] Paolo Veronese's *Wedding at Cana* (Figure 12.6). Delacroix regarded Veronese (next to Rubens) as the greatest painter of the past and searched during his voyage to Morocco for picturesque effects *à la Veronèse*.[52]

As for the specific relation of *A Jewish Wedding* to the *Wedding at Cana*, there are obvious similarities, such as the general impression of exuberance and exoticism, the stage-like setting, and the musicians in the center. On closer inspection, several more detailed points of comparison leap out, such as the giving and taking in the right corner (by the servants handling plates and vessels, respectively, by Muslims and Jews exchanging coins), the carpets hanging from the balustrade of the right galleries, and the figures placed at the same galleries. It is particularly noteworthy that in Veronese's painting a woman throws a flower down to the wedding guests with her right hand and in Delacroix's painting a single right arm performs a similar gesture at exactly the same place. What is more, both pictures lend themselves to being read as allegories of art. I have already tried to make the case for the one by Delacroix. In the one by Veronese, it is the famous group of musicians, portraying the foremost artists of Renaissance Venice—Titian, Tintoretto, Bassano, and Veronese himself—that opens such an interpretative perspective. I am most intrigued by the fact that the colors of this group of painters—Veronese's white, Titian's purple, and the green of the man close to them—matches almost the main coloristic accents of the courtyard in Tangiers, with the white wall, the purple floor, and the green stripes of the gallery.

Last but not least, not only do both paintings represent marriages, but both of them duplicate the protagonists. In Delacroix's, the bride is hidden and substituted by the dancer, who is singled out from the host of "belles juives"; in Veronese's, the groom can barely be made out in the multitude of figures, while Jesus is represented in the very moment of revealing his identity (through the conversion of water into wine). Looked at this way, it seems most striking that in the one case, the center of the picture is occupied by the central figure, while in the other, the center of the picture is a screen that hides the central figure of the festivities. Stressing this comparison further, we might ask whether Delacroix's splitting and hiding of the transcendental instance of painting indicates a challenge to the Christian foundation of the visual arts. Or to put it in slightly different words: is there a deeper connection between his Orientalism, his displacement of the paradigmatic function of the human body, and his reference to Veronese's painting?

It is safe to argue that Delacroix regarded the visual arts of North Africa as devoid of the human figure. This is at least the evidence put forward in the many drawings and notes in which he recorded the interior decoration, clothes, objects, architecture, calligraphy, and maquillage he had seen during his journey. The only exception, strikingly confirming the rule, is a drawing of vaguely anthropomorphic tombstones from the Jewish cemetery of Tangiers.[53] What is more, Delacroix understood painting as a genuinely European art. He explicitly stated that there is no place for it in Oriental culture, because of two major impediments: the Orient is ruled by jealousy, which restricts an art founded on the pleasure of seeing and being seen, and, at the same time, is immutable and therefore immune from the craze for originality.[54] While Morocco offered Delacroix countless picturesque figures and scenes and, by that means, a primitivist access to the biblical origins of European culture, and, more specifically, to the prototypes of the very beauties that had preoccupied Western painting for centuries, he also conceived of Morocco as a country alien to European painting and, therefore, as a transformative challenge to his own art. In confronting his art with the visuality of the Jewish wedding (and, generally speaking, that of the tripartite Morocco, including Muslims, Jews, and Christian travelers), he used Orientalism to question the anthropomorphic implication of his own tradition. As we have seen, Delacroix's revision of Veronese's painting results in the shielding and splitting of the constitutive instance of pictorial representation. Being the incarnation of the divine word, Jesus is the founding figure of the very possibility and legitimacy of Christian representation, and, what is more, he is in himself visibly the foundation of Christian art. This is particularly evident in Veronese's painting, since Christ occupies the central place in a scene alluding to the eucharistic mystery and therefore to incarnation. In Delacroix's painting, the center is instead occupied by the white wall, which refers to two sources of painting that are both excluded from the representation, the bride and the sun. Indeed, their exclusion is constitutive to their functioning as foundational instances: to represent the sun would have belittled its function as a sublime origin of the visual; to represent the bride would have sacrificed her virginity, exposed her as an immobile and strangely made-up idol, and thereby negated her serving as a figure of artistic potentiality. In contrast to the ideal of the living human body, the source of Delacroix's art is split into an animating force beyond any visible *Gestalt* and an immobile, sculpture-like and painted human figure deprived of any signs of animation. While Veronese supplements the visual exuberance of his work by showing the very figure who transforms this plenitude into a meaningful event, Delacroix depicts a plenitude created and, at the same time, unsettled by the absence and duplication of its origin. And it is by thus screening and duplicating the origin of his art that Delacroix marks a Romantic distance to a masterwork of Christian Europe. After all, Delacroix's art did not glorify the Incarnate Logos. As he famously stated in his last diary entry, dated June 22, 1863, the first merit of a painting lies in being a feast for the eye.[55]

NOTES

Versions of this article were first presented at the Academy of Fine Arts in Karlsruhe (May 2006), at the conference *L' objet théorique "art"* at the University of Urbino (July 2006),

Brown University (December 2006), at the University of Chicago (January 2007), and at Johns Hopkins University (April 2009). A much shorter version was published in *Tanz als Anthropologie*, ed. Gabriele Brandstetter, Christoph Wulf (Munich: Wilhelm Fink Verlag, 2007), 233–48. My thanks go to Silvia Bächli, Hubert Damisch, Gabriele Brandstetter, Catherine Zerner, and Robert Pippin for giving me the opportunity to present my arguments, to Elizabeth Tucker and (in earlier drafts) Timothy Grundy for amending my English, and to Karin Gludovatz, Stefan Neuner, and Barbara Wittmann for inspiring conversations. For their comments on the present text, I am greatly indebted to Michael Fried, Markus Klammer, David Nirenberg, and Wolfram Pichler.

1. I'm thinking of the writings of Michael Fried and Hubert Damisch: Michael Fried, "Three American Painters: Kenneth Noland, Jules Olitski, Frank Stella, (1965)," *Art and Objecthood. Essays and Reviews* (Chicago: University of Chicago Press, 1998), 213–65; *Manet's Modernism, or, The Face of Painting in the 1860s* (Chicago: University of Chicago Press, 1996); Hubert Damisch, *Fenêtre jaune cadmium. Ou les dessous de la peinture* (Paris: Seuil, 1984), 15f., 80, 275–305.

2. René Huyghe, *Delacroix* (New York: Abrams, 1963), 294: *A Jewish Wedding* "anticipates modern [pictures], for its planes, made to stand out against one another by contrasts of colour, seem a prelude to the geometrical constructions of Mondrian: the implacably white wall faces us in the picture plane, striped across the middle by two green horizontals, and divided, below, by the long vertical of a narrow door and above by a window and its shutter."

3. Linda Nochlin, "The Imaginary Orient," *Art in America* 71, no. 5 (1983): 118–31; Darcy Grimaldo Grigsby, *Extremities: Painting Empire in Post-Revolutionary France* (New Haven, Conn.: Yale University Press, 2002), 237–316.

4. Todd Porterfield, *The Allure of Empire: Art in the Service of French Imperialism 1798–1836* (Princeton, N.J.: Princeton University Press, 1998), 130–40; Albert Boime, *Art in an Age of Counterrevolution 1815–1848* (Chicago: University of Chicago Press, 2004), 352f. Boime even goes so far as to claim that Delacroix contributed directly to the military success of the French: "No doubt the visual intelligence and topographical data gathered by Delacroix and others during the diplomatic mission aided in the crushing defeat of the Moroccan troops" (390).

5. Zeynep Çelik, *Urban Forms and Colonial Confrontations: Algiers under French Rule* (Berkeley: University of California Press, 1997), 38f., 106f., 192.

6. Darcy G. Grigsby, "Orients and Colonies: Delacroix's Algerian Harem," in *The Cambridge Companion to Delacroix*, ed. Beth Wright (Cambridge: Cambridge University Press, 2001), 69–87.

7. Alexandre Dumas, *Le Véloce. De Cadix à Tunis* (Paris: Édition François Bourin, 1990), 59–71; Théophile Gautier, "Le Salon de 1841," *La Presse*, April 1, 1841, 162; Théophile Gautier, *Les Beaux-Arts en Europe 1855* (Paris: Michel Lévy, 1855), 180f.; Gustave Planche, *Études sur l'école française* (Paris, 1855), 1:248; Charles Blanc, *Les artistes de mon temps* (Paris: Libraire de Firmin-Didot, 1876), 68–82; Charles Blanc, *Grammaire des arts du dessin*, 2nd ed. (Paris: Jules Renouard, 1876), 569, 615.

8. Michele Hannoosh, *Painting and the Journal of Eugène Delacroix* (Princeton, N.J.: Princeton University Press, 1995), ad indicem "Lessing."

9. In his seminal interpretation of *Laocoon*, David Wellbery has systematically explored the usefulness of the distinction between discrete and dense signs to understand Lessing's semiotics. In the context of my argument, however, the metaphoric associations of density are more pertinent. David E. Wellbery, *Lessing's Laocoon: Semiotics and Aesthetics in the Age of Reason* (Cambridge: Cambridge University Press, 1984), 114–35.

     RALPH UBL

10. Gotthold Ephraim Lessing, *Laokoon: oder über die Grenze der Malerei und Poesie*, in *Werke und Briefe in zwölf Bänden*, ed. Winfried Barner (Frankfurt am Main: Deutscher Klassiker Verlag, 1990), vol. 5, 28 (veil), 115 (feast of the gods).

11. Eugène Delacroix, *Journal. 1822–1863*, ed. André Joubin and Régis Labourdette (Paris: Plon, 1981), 29: "L'art du peintre est d'autant plus intime au coeur de l'homme qu'il paraît plus materiel; car chez lui, comme dans la nature extérieure, la part est faite franchement à ce qui est fini et à ce qui est infini, c'est-à-dire à ce qu l'âme trouve qui la remue intérieurement dans les objets qui ne frappent que les sens."

12. Ibid., 28, 77f. I present a more detailed discussion of these entries in "Eugène Delacroix: Mit dem Meer malen," *Das Meer, der Tausch und die Grenzen der Repräsentation*, ed. Hannah Baader and Gerhard Wolf (Zürich and Berlin: Diaphanes, 2010), 75–99.

13. Charles Baudelaire, "*Salon* de 1846," *Curiosités esthétiques. L'Art romantique*, ed. Henri Lemaitre (Paris: Classiques Garnier, 1990), 105, 127; Gautier, *Les Beaux-Arts en Europe 1855*, 172; Blanc, *Les artistes de mon temps*, 28, 72f.; Blanc, *Grammaire des arts du dessin*, 613; P. Michael Doran, ed., *Conversations avec Cézanne* (Paris: Macula, 1978), 140; Odilon Redon, *A soi-même. Journal 1867–1915. Notes sur la vie, l'art et les artistes* (Paris: José Corti, 1989), 178; Paul Signac, *D'Eugène Delacroix au néo-impressionnisme* (Paris: Hermann, 1978), 75–80.

14. On Morocco and antiquity, cf. Eugène Delacroix, *Correspondance générale d'Eugène Delacroix*, ed. André Joubin (Paris: Plon, 1936), 1:317, 319, 327f., 330.

15. Ibid., 1:310, 325–27.

16. On Delacroix's interest in the North African regulation of light and heat, cf. his notes and drawings in Eugène Delacroix, *Souvenirs d'un voyage dans le Maroc*, ed. Laure Beaumont-Maillet, Barthélémy Jobert, and Sophie Join-Lambert (Paris: Flammarion, 1999), 96; Maurice Sérullaz, Arlette Sérullaz, Louis-Antoine Prat, and Claudine Ganeval, ed., *Dessins d'Eugène Delacroix* (Paris: Édition de la réunion des musées nationaux, 1984), cat. no. 1502, 1516–19v, 1524–29, 1537, 1541ff. (particularly 1547, 1559, 1586, 1606), 1755 (fols. 11–12), 1756 (fol. 23r), 1755 (fols. 14r, 16r, 18r), 1756 (fols. 10v, 18–27); more on Delacroix's poetics of heat in Ralph Ubl, "Delacroix' Wärmeräume," *Räume der Romantik*, ed. Gerhard Neumann and Inka Mülder-Bach (Würzburg: Königshausen und Neumann, 2007), 277–306. As I have already published several articles on Delacroix in German that are to result in a monographic study on the artist, I take the liberty of referring to some of my own texts.

17. On the reconsideration of Orientalism from a tripartite relationship between the three monotheistic religions, see Ivan Davidson Kalmar and Derek J. Penslar, eds., *Orientalism and the Jews* (Waltham, Mass.: Brandeis University Press, 2005). On Jews in early nineteenth-century Morocco and Tangiers, see Susan Gilston Miller, "Crisis and Community: The People of Tangier and the French Bombardment of 1844," *Middle Eastern Studies* 27, no. 4 (1991): 583–96; Daniel J. Schroeter, "The Jewish Quarter and the Moroccan City," *New Horizons in Sephardic Studies*, ed. Yedida K. Stillman and George Zucker (Albany: State University of New York Press, 1993), 67–81; Daniel J. Schroeter, *The Sultan's Jew: Morocco and the Sephardi World* (Stanford: Stanford University Press, 2002). On Delacroix's visits, there exist various accounts whose differences do not matter in the present context; cf. Miller, "Crisis and Community," 586f.; Lee Johnson, "Delacroix's Jewish Bride," *Burlington Magazine* 139 (1997): 755–59; Boime, *Art in an Age of Counterrevolution*, 355f.; Maurice Arama, *Delacroix. Un Voyage initiatique* (Paris: Non Lieu, 2006), 111–51.

18. Lee Johnson, *The Paintings of Eugène Delacroix: A Critical Catalogue, 1832–1863* (Oxford: Oxford University Press, 1986), 3:176–79.

19. "Noce juive dans le Maroc. Les Maures et les Juifs sont confondus. La Mariée est enfermée dans des appartements intérieurs, tandis qu'on se réjouit dans le reste de la maison. Des Maures de distinction donnent de l'argent pour des musiciens qui jouent de leur instruments et chantent sans discontinuer le jour et la nuit; les femmes sont les seules qui prennent

part à la danse, ce qu'elles font tour à tour et aux applaudissements de l'assemblée." Ibid., 3:176.

20. Gautier and Blanc particularly emphasized that the painting is oriented toward the sun: see Gautier, *Les Beaux-Arts en Europe 1855*, 180f.; Blanc, *Les artistes de mon temps*, 70; Blanc, *Grammaire des arts du dessin*, 615.

21. "Les Maures et les Juifs sont confondus. La Mariée est enfermée dans des appartements intérieurs, tandis qu'on se réjouit dans le reste de la maison." Johnson, *The Paintings of Eugène Delacroix*, 3:176.

22. Eugène Delacroix, "Une noce juive dans le Maroc," *Magasin pittoresque* 10 (January 1842): 8–30.

23. For Delacroix's drawings and notes, see Sérullaz, Sérullaz, Prat, and Ganeval, *Dessins d'Eugène Delacroix*, 2:365f.; Arama, *Delacroix. Un Voyage initiatique*, 135–76. For an (unpersuasive) attempt to assess the ethnographic authenticity of Delacroix's painting, cf. Cissy Grossman, "The Real Meaning of Eugène Delacroix's *Noce juive au Maroc*," *Jewish Art* 14 (1988): 64–73.

24. The watercolor of a Jewish woman with makeup is illustrated in *Eugène Delacroix* (exhibition catalogue, Staatliche Kunsthalle Karlsruhe, 2003), ed. Holger Jacob-Friesen (Heidelberg: Kehrer, 2003), 213. On the watercolor *A Visit to the Jewish Bride*, cf. Johnson, "Delacroix's Jewish Bride," 755–59, fig. 39. In an etching likewise from 1832, Delacroix isolated the figures of the bride and the black slave, emphasizing that we are invited to identify with the Muslim. Neither the watercolor nor the etching were ever shown in public during Delacroix's lifetime. Cf. Barthélémy Jobert, ed., *Delacroix. Le trait romantique* (Paris: Bibliothèque nationale de France, 1998), 129.

25. Delacroix, "Une noce juive dans le Maroc," 30.

26. A different interpretation is proposed by Maryse Violin-Savalle, "Un pan de mur blanc. Étude autour de La Noce juive dans le Maroc d'Eugène Delacroix," *Bulletin de la société des amis du Musée national Eugène Delacroix* 5 (May 2007): 33–37. Emphasizing the closed eyes of the bride, the author suggests that we understand the white wall as a symptom of Delacroix's anxiety of being blinded by the African sun.

27. René Piot, *Les palettes de Delacroix* (Paris: Librairie de France, 1931).

28. Barthélémy Jobert, *Delacroix* (Paris: Gallimard, 1998), 30; Grigsby, *Extremities*, 259, 266, 277f.; Marc Gottlieb, "Creation and Death of the Romantic Studio," *Inventions of the Studio, Renaissance to Romanticism*, ed. Michael Cole and Mary Pardo (Chapel Hill: University of North Carolina Press, 2005), 160f., 166–75.

29. Norman Bryson, *Tradition and Desire: From David to Delacroix* (Cambridge: Cambridge University Press, 1984), 176–212; Grigsby, *Extremities*, 266–89.

30. Delacroix, "Une noce juive dans le Maroc," 30.

31. After his return to Paris, Delacroix would write in a letter: "Paris m'ennuie profondément: les hommes et les choses m'apparaissent sous un jour tout particulier depuis mon voyage: très peu d'hommes me semblent avoir du bon sens: les pièces du Vaudeville ne me semblent pas amusantes ni trop morales, et l'opéra, le ballet surtout, ne me fait pas l'effet de reproduire exactement la nature. Si ce n'était les pirouettes, je préférais la danse des juives de Tanger." Delacroix, *Correspondance*, 1:337f; on the contemporary view of the aesthetics of Oriental dance, cf. Théophile Gautier, "Début de danseuses moresques" (1845), *Voyage en Algérie*, ed. Denise Brahimi (Paris: La Boîte à Documents, 1989), 124f.

32. Louis de Planet, *Souvenirs de travaux de peinture avec M. Eugène Delacroix*, ed. André Joubin (Paris: A. Colin, 1929), 33; Kurt Badt, *Eugène Delacroix. Werke und Ideale* (Köln: Dumont, 1965), 42ff.

33. Hubert Damisch, *Fenêtre jaune cadmium*, 11–46.

34. Since I have often been asked why I can be sure that the dancer is actually Jewish, I would like to underscore the fact that Delacroix believed her to be Jewish and implied this in his texts. Delacroix, *Correspondance générale*, 1:337f.; Delacroix, "Une noce juive dans le Maroc," 29. In the latter article he does not write explicitly that the dancer is Jewish, but from the description of the revelry it becomes clear that she is one of the Jewish women mingling with the Muslim men in the courtyard.

35. Luce A. Klein, *Portrait de la juive française* (Paris: Éditions Nizet, 1970); Carol Ockman, "'Two Eyebrows à l'Orientale': Ethnic Stereotyping in Ingres's *Baronne de Rothschild*," *Art History* 14 (1991): 521–39; Florian Krobb, *Die Schöne Jüdin. Jüdische Frauengestalten in der deutschsprachigen Erzählliteratur vom 17. Jahrhundert bis zum Ersten Weltkrieg* (Tübingen: Niemeyer, 1993); Sarga Moussa, "Arabes et Juives. Mythes et représentations," in *Chassériau. Un autre romantism*, ed. Stéphane Guégan (Paris: Musée du Louvre, 2002), 197–221; Nadia Valman, *The Jewess in Ninteenth-Century British Literary Culture* (Cambridge: Cambridge University Press, 2007).

36. Valman, *The Jewess in Ninteenth-Century British Literary Culture*, 33: "The figure of the beautiful, self-sacrificing Jewess makes possible a new view of Jews that accords them a place in a tolerant nation."

37. Diane R. Hallman, *Opera, Liberalism and Antisemitism in Nineteenth-Century France: The Politics of Halévy's La Juive* (Cambridge: Cambridge University Press, 2002); Lisa Moses Leff, *Sacred Bond of Solidarity: The Rise of Jewish Internationalism in Nineteenth-Century France* (Stanford: Stanford University Press, 2006), 105–17.

38. Hallman, *Opera, Liberalism, and Antisemitism in Nineteenth-Century France*, 257, 296.

39. François-René de Chateaubriand, "Walter Scott et les juives," *Oeuvres completes* (Paris, 1861), 11:764–66; Léon Poliakov, *Histoire de l'antisémitisme (2. L'âge de la science)* (Paris: Pluriel Calman-Levy, 1981), 175.

40. Walter Scott, *Ivanhoe* (1820; Oxford: Oxford University Press, 1996), 238.

41. See Grigsby, *Extremities*, 237–316.

42. Johnson, "Delacroix's Jewish Bride," 755–59, fig. 39.

43. Jewish women as objects of Muslim violence were a recurrent theme of travel accounts, as for example in Charles Didier, *Promenade au Maroc* (Paris: Jules Labitte, 1844), 156f.

44. Delacroix, *Correspondance*, 1:315; Delacroix, *Souvenirs d'un voyage dans le Maroc*, 113.

45. It may be that Delacroix was also encouraged to create an Orientalism rooted in his alliance with the Moroccan Jews as a result of his deepening personal ties with Sephardic Jews and his appreciation for their artistic achievements. Delacroix admired Halévy's *La Juive* (1835) and became a close friend of the composer: cf. Delacroix, *Journal. 1822–1863*, ad indicem "Halévy"; Delacroix, *Correspondance*, 3:19, 316; Delacroix, *Lettres intimes. Correspondance inédit*, ed. Alfred Dupont (Paris: Gallimard, 1954), 117.

46. Delacroix, "Une noce juive dans le Maroc," 29; in later literary accounts of the belly dance, this transaction is regularly described as an exchange between European travelers and dancer-prostitutes; cf. Emily Apter, "Figura Serpentinata: Visual Seduction and the Colonial Gaze," in *Spectacles of Realism: Body, Gender, Genre*, ed. Margaret Cohen and Christopher Prendergast (Minneapolis: University of Minnesota Press, 1995), 163–78.

47. As for the history of this ontology, cf. David Nirenberg's article (chapter 13) in this volume.

48. Delacroix as a critique of his own culture is studied in Norman Bryson, *Tradition and Desire: From David to Delacroix* (Cambridge: Cambridge University Press, 1984), 176–212; Hannoosh, *Painting and the Journal of Eugène Delacroix*, 173–75; Ubl, "Delacroix' Wärmeräume," 277–306.

49. Delacroix, *Correspondance*, 1:307.

50. Delacroix, "Une noce juive dans le Maroc," 28.

51. *Les Noces de Cana de Paul Véronèse* (Paris: Goupil, n.d.), 21.

52. Delacroix, *Journal. 1822–1863*, 107: "Juifs sur les terrasses se détachant sur un ciel légèrment nuageux et azure à la Véronèse."

53. Arama, *Delacroix. Un Voyage initiatique*, 142. On Delacroix's interest in the arts of Morocco, see Delacroix, *Correspondance générale*, 1:315; *Couleurs Maroc. Delacroix et les arts décoratifs marocains des XVIIIe et XIXe siècles*, exhibition catalogue, Musée des Arts décoratifs de Bordeaux (Paris: Somogy, 2002).

54. Delacroix, *Correspondance générale*, 1:310, 329f.

55. Delacroix, *Journal. 1822–1863*, 808: "La premier mérite d'un tableau est d'être une fête pour l'oeil."

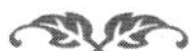

CHAPTER 13

The Judaism of Christian Art

David Nirenberg

Beauty, Aristotle tells us in his *Poetics*, consists in amplitude as well as in order. A very small creature, no matter how harmoniously arranged, cannot be beautiful, since our view loses all distinctness, and an enormously ample one cannot be beautiful either, since we lose the sense of its unity and wholeness. Could we perceive the beauty of an animal a thousand miles long? Likewise, a plot must have extension, but no more than can easily be remembered. And yet my subject—Christian anxieties about art and their expression in terms of Judaism—is indeed "an animal a thousand miles long." We may approach it on foot in order to apprehend the intricate workings of its parts. But its full magnitude, like that of Smaug the Magnificent or the Great Wall of China, can only be grasped from the air.

With an aerial view comes the risk, not only of Aristotelian ugliness, but also of disciplinary vertigo. Some of our specialized instruments begin to fail at heights high enough to encompass 2,500 years of history, and our analytical categories become blurred. The problem is only compounded by the fact that the categories that interest us most—"Christian" and "Jew"—were never as clear as we might think. The problem is not just that each category encompasses vast diversity ("Judaism," for example, includes Pharisee and Sadducee, Rabbanite and Karaite, Hasid and maskil, secular and Orthodox, to name just a few). It is also that each defined itself in terms of the other. We all know that Christianity "separated" from Judaism. But we tend to forget that in every period of Christian history, and even in those societies in which the vast majority of members were professed Christians—such as Byzantium, medieval Christendom, and modern Europe—there were strenuous arguments about what being a Christian meant, and that many of these arguments took place in terms of "Judaism."[1]

Most Christian communities, beginning with the very earliest, understood themselves as the true participants in God's covenant with Israel.[2] In their disagreements with other communities, each strove to claim the mantle of "true Israel" for itself, and to place that of false Israel—"Judaism"—upon its rivals. When Hegesippus (c. 120–c. 180) sat down to think about the origins of the many "heresies" he saw afflicting Christianity, he derived every one of them from seven "Jewish Christian" sects that arose—so he claimed—after the passing of the apostolic generation. Bishop Epiphanius of Salamis reached similar conclusions in the *Panarion*, or "Medicine Chest," an encyclopedia of schisms he compiled circa 370. He counted eighty different categories of error, many of which he explained in terms of Judaism. Insofar as a bad Christian approximated a Jew, the definition of the "Christian" was inseparable from that of the "Jew."[3]

To make matters worse, "Jew" here does not mean only a living adherent of Judaism in any of its many forms. It means also the many figures of Judaism imagined, so to speak, from the outside: by Muslims and Christians, for example, or by scholars, or even by modern antisemites. We should—and sometimes do—put scare quotes around these "Judaisms," in order to remind us that the ancient Pharisees did not subscribe to their Gospel portraits; that the Judaism described in the philosophies of a Kant or Hegel was a stranger to the synagogues of Frankfurt or Berlin; that the "Jews" who stalked Hitler's political imagination were not the same as the millions of flesh and blood whose lives he claimed. But we cannot leave these figures of "Judaism" outside our history, for they peopled Christian thought, and thereby shaped the possibilities of existence for living Jews.

Even "art" turns out to be a category whose boundaries crumble under the pressure of our pens. Can we separate the visual arts that are our subject from the verbal ones of poetry and prose? And what of "art" meaning any discrete form of knowledge, the Greek "technē"? Abetted by metaphor, our term could even expand to encompass cognition itself, often imagined in terms of the viewing of an image. Among the ancients, Aristotle was scarcely alone in claiming that "the soul never thinks without a mental image"; many a saint agreed with Augustine that our "appetite for learning" "is called in the divine language 'the lust of the eyes'"; and John Locke had plenty of modern company for his view that "the understanding of a man in reference to all objects of sight, and the ideas of them," is like a dark closet stacked with pictures obtained from the outside world of light.[4]

     DAVID NIRENBERG

At this height, where categories such as Judaism and Christianity, pictures and cognition, become indistinct, the full extension of our subject becomes visible. The broadest claim of this essay is that determining the boundary between "Judaism" and "Christianity" became a critical concern for all of Christian aesthetics, and that as a result "Judaism" became a critical term that could threaten all "Christian" art. This claim is historical: I demonstrate how basic epistemological and ontological questions came to be asked in terms of "Judaism," suggest ways in which these critiques "Judaized" specific practices in different periods and places, and point to some works of art that bear explicit traces of their engagement with these critiques. But more controversially, my claim is also about a structural potential. Insofar as the vocabulary or the underlying ontology of any aesthetics is "Christian," it threatens art with "Judaism." That potential need not be actualized historically in order to remain latent as a discursive possibility. Christian aesthetics, to paraphrase Marx, can produce the "Judaism" of art out of its own entrails.[5]

To understand why this is so, we need to take up some basic concerns about aesthetics (pre-Baumgarten)—that is, about the knowledge that humans obtain through the sensible perception and representation of objects. Those concerns long predated Christianity, and sometimes took the form of anxiety about certain types of art, as in this well-known prohibition: "Thou shalt not make to thyself a graven thing, nor the likeness of any thing that is in heaven above, or in the earth beneath, nor of those things that are in the waters under the earth. Thou shalt not adore them, nor serve them: I am the Lord thy God, mighty, jealous, visiting the iniquity of the fathers upon the children, unto the third and fourth generation of them that hate me: And shewing mercy unto thousands to them that love me, and keep my commandments" (Exod. 20:4–6). The meaning of this passage—among the most influential in the development of Jewish, Christian, and Islamic art—has been endlessly contested. Does it forbid all art, or only graven sculpture? All images, or only those of living things? Sharp differences over its interpretation mark the history of aesthetic debate between Jew and Christian, Iconoclast and Iconophile, Protestant and Catholic, even Kantian and Hegelian. But the general concern is clear: God considers certain forms of human interaction with certain kinds of things a rival form of love, and He gets jealous.

Idols are an important subcategory of these dangerous things, but they are not the only ones. Both women and wealth, for example, appear so often in Hebrew Scripture as dangerous rivals for God's love that idolatry, adultery, and greed came to be thought of in terms of each other. But the danger is in fact much broader than that. The sight or thought of any object in the world can constitute a rival to our love of God; hence we must teach our eyes and mind

how to apprehend all things properly. As "the Lord also said to Moses": "Speak
to the children of Israel, and thou shalt tell them to make to themselves fringes
in the corners of their garments, putting in them ribands of blue: That when
they shall see them, they may remember all the commandments of the Lord, and
not follow their own thoughts and eyes going astray [Hebrew, *zonim*, whoring;
Vulgate's Latin, *fornicantes*] after divers things, But rather being mindful of the
precepts of the Lord, may do them and be holy to their God" (Num. 15:37–40).[6]
This passage, so rarely cited in our histories of biblical aesthetics, suggests that
the difficulty here is not only with images and idols, but with *how we see and
think about things themselves*. The fringes of our garments serve as objects that
teach us how to look at other objects. They help us to know things chastely by
disciplining "the lust of the eyes." There is a vast ontology spun into these blue
threads, even if (perhaps because the Hebrew Bible so often expresses the problem in terms of cult rather than cognition) it does not much look like philosophy.

In ancient Greece, by comparison, questions of cognition stand front and
center in the debate about art. It is, after all, the Greek language that gave us
English speakers our own etymological complex of words derived from the root
for sight—words like "idea," "ideal," "idol," "ideology"; Greek thought that
systematized for what we call philosophy the gap between the sensible and the
real; and Greek worries about the representational techniques available to cross
that gap that produced some of the more influential statements about how art
works.

The example of Plato can here stand for many others, for he sharpened some
of the most important weapons in our philosophical arsenal. In the teachings
of some predecessors like Parmenides, Pythagoras, and of course Socrates, he
discovered and developed a fundamental distinction between the physical senses
and the reasoning intellect, between the world of sensible things (literally, aesthetics) and of "intelligibles." The latter he thought incorporeal (asômata: Plato
was among the earliest users of this Greek word), immaterial, and the truth of
things—their *ideai*, or Forms, in his specialized vocabulary—rather than of their
image or mere appearance (*eidôlon*). Theirs is the domain of "the greater mysteries": the world of metaphysics toward which Plato orients his philosophy.[7]

But although Plato sometimes imagines that the our souls once dwelt in
such a metaphysical world, "un-signed" and "un-entombed" by the body—as
he puns in the Phaedrus—he is aware that they no longer do. In this world our
soul is imprisoned by the body "like an oyster by its shell," and we must reach
truth through the senses and the sensible. The task is not easy, as Plato goes on
to explain in this same passage, because sensible things can lead away from
truth as easily as they can toward it. He uses the example of sight, "the keenest

mode of perception vouchsafed us through the body," and of beauty, of all "beloved objects" the "most manifest to sense and most lovely of them all." How does the sight of sensible beauty affect us? It can send us "after the fashion of a four-footed beast," to "beget offspring of the flesh" and "consort with wantonness" (recall the vocabulary of Numbers 15). Or conversely, it can awaken our memory of beauty in that other world, the metaphysical world "that truly is," and stimulate our soul's striving toward it.[8]

This example from the Phaedrus involves the attraction of one human being toward the beauty of another, but the ambivalence in question affects all forms of cognition that depend on sight and beauty.[9] The allegory of cognition in Book VII of the Republic makes a similar point. The prisoners in the cave know only the shadows of puppets, statues, and artifacts paraded on the wall before them. For them, "truth is nothing other than the shadow of artificial things." The prisoner who has been briefly dragged into the light—that is, the philosopher—also depends on sight for knowledge, but with this crucial difference: knowing that the sights in the cave are "idols" and "phantasms," the philosopher struggles with his soul to turn his eyes toward "that which is."

The difference does not consist in freedom from images or in keenness of sight. Both Socrates and Glaucon themselves call the entire allegory from which they are learning an "image," and they concede that in the case of a vicious soul, "the sharper it sees, the more evil it accomplishes." The difference, according to Plato, lies in the orientation of the soul, which needs to be "turned around toward the true things," and away from their mere appearance (*Republic* 514–19). It is the task of philosophy to effect this conversion of the soul's habits of perception. Philosophy seeks to make of every soul an art critic.

This is true both at a very general and in a more narrow sense. First the general: since things appears to us in our embodied state only as representations—or images—of "true things," movement toward truth requires criticism of the representations. But not all appearances and representations are the same: some are more dangerous than others. A physical shoe, for example, may be only a phantasm of the true or ideal shoe, but it is more real for Plato than "shoe" the written word or a painting of a shoe. Because their function depends upon a fiction or falsehood (the Greek root is *pseud-*), a substitution for a referent for which they can then be mistaken, things that stand for something else—things like words, pictures, money—are more worrisome than the things they stand for.

This does not mean that we must or can abandon our most basic tools of mediation and representation. But the philosopher uses these tools while at the same time cultivating an awareness of their dangers in order to avoid misleading the soul. Others, like the sophist, cultivate an awareness of these dangers in order to deliberately mislead the soul: to make the weaker argument the stronger. And still others tend to suppress the awareness all together, making their appeal directly to the world of things through the senses, rather than calling attention to the gap between appearance and reality.

Among these last, according to Book X of the Republic, are the practitioners of the mimetic arts of theater, poetry, painting, sculpture. Mimesis—a Greek word sometimes translated as representation, sometimes a bit more reductively as imitation, and sometimes left untranslated—is the key term here. Plato considers many arts to be mimetic in that they make things at some remove from the truth. The couch maker, for example, makes a couch, not the ideal form of a couch, and in this sense his product is but a shadow of the real. But some artists are more mimetic than others, among them the painter and the poet, who make representations of everything. He "produces earth and heaven and gods and everything in heaven and everything in Hades under the earth." This promiscuity insults Plato's sense of the proper specialization of each art *(technē)*. Worse, it means that what the painter and the poet produce are not real even in the couch's limited sense: "they look like they *are*; however they surely *are* not in truth" (596C–E).[10]

Poets and painters stand further from the truth than other craftsmen because they are "imitators of phantoms of virtue" rather than of virtue itself. Not only do their works appeal to "the soul's foolish parts," but this gratification does not lead toward any greater knowledge of things: "The painter will make what seems to be a shoemaker to those who understand as little about shoemaking as he understands, but who observe only colors and shapes" (600E–601A). The result of this preference for the sensible over the true is that painting, like poetry and theater, "produces a bad regime in the soul of each private man" (605C).

Reading such a sharp critique one might think that Plato is proposing a *polis* without painting (or poetry or theater), or that he believes in the possibility of community without mimesis. I suspect the opposite is true: Book X of the Republic stresses the dangers posed by these mimetic arts, not because they should (or even can) be banished from the city, but rather because their power over the soul is so great. Elsewhere Plato insists that if oriented toward the good, the power of mimesis can be put to positive work. In the Laws, for example, he does prohibit certain forms of mediated communication and representation (such as money) that he deems irremediably corrupting to the polity, but he does not banish painting. Instead, "the Athenian" praises the example of Egypt, which "long ago recognized that poses . . . must be good, if they are to be habitually practiced by the youthful generation of citizens. So they drew up the inventory of all the standard types, and consecrated specimens of them in their

DAVID NIRENBERG

temples. Painters . . . were forbidden to innovate on these models," with the result that "the work of ten thousand years ago . . . [and] that of today both exhibit an identical artistry" (656E–657A).

This passage would not have pleased many Athenian artists. Its praise of the truth claims of a severely stylized art was aimed directly at what Plato presents as the misguided aesthetic fashions of his own day, which celebrated painters for feats of naturalism and delighted in their invention of new techniques of illusion. But the more prophetic among them might have realized that Plato was issuing painting its passport into the age of transcendence. In a world of ideas in which matter was increasingly stigmatized and the appearance of things increasingly distant from their truth, painting was at risk of becoming the enemy of philosophy. Plato outlined the reasons for that enmity and its dangers, but he also set forth the terms by which it might be overcome. If art would submit to ontology, he suggested, it could labor in the service of the good.

Both Plato's criticism of the mimetic arts and his defense of them would have varied futures in the many schools of thought that the ancient Hellenistic world developed in order to bridge the gap between the material and the real. Indeed, both are already present in the earliest Christian writings—those of St. Paul. Chapter 1 of the Epistle to the Romans opens its brief history of mankind's knowledge of the divine with the extraordinary statement that "ever since the creation of the world, the invisible existence of God and his everlasting power have been clearly seen by the mind's understanding of created things. And so these people have no excuse. . . . While they claimed to be wise, in fact they were growing so stupid that they exchanged the glory of the immortal God for an imitation [homoiômati, counterfeit], for the image [eikonos] of a mortal human being, or of birds, or animals, or crawling things" (Rom. 1:20–23). This astonishing passage takes the Mosaic Law's concern with the worship of images and conflates it with the ontological preoccupations of Platonic philosophy in order to arrive at a general critique of gentile knowledge of things in the world. But Paul did not stop there. He went on to accuse the Jews—at least those who refused to accept Jesus—of worshipping the outer fleshy appearance of things rather than their inner spiritual reality: "The real Jew is the one who is inwardly a Jew, and real circumcision is in the heart, a thing not of the letter but of the spirit" (2:29). The Mosaic Law was itself the source of the Jews' ontological bind: "The commandment was meant to bring life but I found it brought death. . . . It is by means of the commandment that sin shows its unbounded sinful power." Because the mind can love God's law but cannot will the flesh to do it, the Law cannot free or save. At best it can make me aware that I "am a prisoner of that law of sin which lives inside my body." "Only the law of the Spirit which gives life in Jesus Christ" can set me free (7:7–25; 8:2).

In just this one letter of Paul, readers could find justification for two very different views of how our sensual perception of things in the world can relate us to God (that is, of Christian aesthetics). Chapter 1 condemned idolatry but held out the hope that through the sight of created things we can come to knowledge of the creator. Chapter 7 stressed the alienation from truth that came with embodiment and removed any hope that the law God gave to Moses could overcome the law of sin at work in our flesh. Chapter 1 would inspire those schools—sometimes called neo-Platonic because influenced by Plotinus and Porphyry's readings of Plato—that taught Christians how to ascend toward truth through things and the images of things. Chapter 7 would license those— like Marcion and other Gnostics of ancient Christianity, or Karl Barth and other crisis theologians of modernity—who preferred to emphasize the abyss between flesh and spirit, and for whom the only truth to be found in the things and images of this world was a heightened awareness of our imprisonment.

This diversity reminds us that Paul's epistles, like Plato's dialogues, could authorize very different ways of thinking about the gap between the sensible and the real, the material or corporeal and the spiritual. If in Romans the flesh is death (8:6), in 2 Corinthians it is a sheltering tent (5:1–4). And if on the one hand—in a passage with real implications for the future of Christian art— Christians (as opposed to those Jews who do not recognize Christ) "look not at the things which are seen, but at the things which are not seen" (2 Cor. 4:18), conversely the spiritual requires the physical. "If there is a physical body, there is also a spiritual body. . . . But it is not the spiritual which is first, but the physical, and then the spiritual" (1 Cor. 15:42–50). Later generations of Christians would discover the potential for these and many other positions in Paul's writings. But they also discovered in them a common language with which to debate the relative merits of their many different views about this gap: the language of "Judaism."

Most markedly in the Epistles to the Romans and the Galatians, Paul used the language of Judaism to teach about the dangers of attraction to law, letter, and flesh. He did so in order to address two basic questions: What is the relationship of the gentile followers of Jesus to the covenant of Abraham? And what is the relationship of the Jews to the promise of Jesus Christ? Paul sought to include every follower of Christ within the covenant God made with Abraham: "There is neither Jew nor Greek, there is neither slave nor free, there is neither male nor female; for you are all one in Christ Jesus. . . . And if you are Christ's then you are Abraham's offspring, heirs according to promise" (Gal. 3:28). But at the same time he did not want gentile converts to Christianity to adopt the ritual observances—such as circumcision—of the Jews. To do so, he suggested, would be to misread God's promise to Abraham, to confuse its letter or outer appearance with its spirit or inner meaning, a confusion that, according to Paul, could only result in the enslavement and death of the soul. When gentile converts to Christianity circumcised themselves, they placed significance in the sign of the promise rather than in what it signified, and thereby revealed themselves as "severed from Christ" and Spirit by the "desires of the flesh" (Gal. 5:2, 4, 16–18).

To put it in technical terms: the universalism Paul claimed for Jesus Christ depended upon overcoming the particularity of the sign. This dependence was not novel. Whether Jew or gentile, those familiar with Hellenistic philosophy had long tended to understand the relationship between sign, word, or image on the one hand, and meaning on the other, in terms of a hierarchy explicitly similar to that of flesh and spirit. The task of the seeker after truth was to penetrate beyond the outer or literal flesh of apparent signification, and into inner or spiritual meaning. What was unusual was Paul's apocalyptic willingness to suggest that the coming of Christ had overcome the need for the sign itself. As he put it in Romans (7:5–6): "Now we are fully freed from the law, dead to that in which we lay captive. We can thus serve in the new being of the Spirit and not the old one of the letter." "To set the mind on the flesh is death, but to set the mind on the Spirit is life and peace" (8:6). Or in the lapidary formulation of Second Corinthians (3:6): "The letter kills, but the spirit gives life."[11]

Paul recognized that, for some time after the coming of Christ, communication would still depend upon "the letter"—"Notice what large letters I have used in writing to you with my own hand" (Gal. 6:11). But he believed that this period would be short, for end-time was near. The gap between the corporeal and the spiritual, communication's dependence upon the mediation of signs, community's upon laws and conventions: these could not be completely overcome until the second coming. What did need to be overcome in the here and now, overcome immediately in the name of universalism, were those dangerously attractive signs of Judaism: the "letter" of the Hebrew Bible, the "laws" of Moses, the conventions of the earthly Jerusalem. It was into the vessel of "carnal Israel" that Paul repeatedly poured all the dangers of seeing, reading, and believing "after the flesh." It was in order to name this danger of slippage from life to flesh, from spirit to letter, from eternal truth to the mere appearance of truth, that Paul adopted the odd Greek verb "to Judaize" (Gal. 2:14), a word that promptly became a key term of Christian epistemological and ontological critique.[12]

The gospels, each in its own way, expanded this Judaizing critique into an ontology capable of accounting for the complexity of the world, of explaining why truth is not always triumphant, why it is so easy to confuse darkness with light, why God can be misrecognized and rejected, even by specialists in the divine. Matthew provides a terrifying example:

> The disciples, having crossed to the other side, had forgotten to take any food. Jesus said to them, "Keep your eyes open, and be on your guard against the yeast of the Pharisees and the Sadducees." And they said among themselves, "It is because we have not brought any bread." Jesus knew it, and he said, "You have so little faith, why are you talking among yourselves about having no bread? Do you still not understand? . . . How could you fail to understand that I was not talking about bread? What I said was: Beware the yeast of the Pharisees and Sadducees." Then they understood that he was telling them to be on their guard, not against yeast for making bread, but against the teachings of the Pharisees and Sadducees. (Matt. 16:5–12)

Here, at the very moment that Jesus warns his closest associates of the hermeneutic dangers of the world, they fall into the trap. Rather than understanding his statement metaphorically and spiritually, as he intends it, they understand it literally and materially, in the context of their own bodily hunger. In other words, the disciples, under Jesus' careful tutelage, become Pharisees at the very moment that they are being warned of the risks of infection.

When speaking of "yeast," of "bread," or of "Pharisees," did Jesus speak literally or metaphorically? The soul is at stake in distinguishing correctly between the material "thing" that a word referred to ("yeast," for example) and the spiritual truths it contained, but how can the two forms of meaning be separated from one another? As in Paul, the danger is partly produced by the nature of language itself. But again as in Paul, the general danger is given a specific form. Jesus does not say: "Be on your guard against the yeast of the signifier," or some such thing. He says (in the formulation of Luke 12:1–2): "Be on your guard against the yeast of the Pharisees—their hypocrisy. Everything now covered will be uncovered, and everything now hidden will be made clear." The Pharisees stand at the crossroads of Christian ontology, representing the danger of wrong choice in its purest form. But they are not merely passive signposts of the disjuncture between outer "seeming" and inner "being." They are active agents of error, hypocrites who deliberately cultivate the appearance of truth and suppress its essence in pursuit of their worldly desires. In Matthew's "woes of the Pharisees," Jesus provides a seven-point ontological indictment of the ways in which they confuse appearance with reality. Consider just the sixth woe, with its emphasis on a gap between outer beauty and inner truth: "Alas for you, scribes, and Pharisees, you hypocrites! You are like whitewashed tombs that look handsome on the outside, but inside are full of the bones of the dead and every kind of corruption" (23:25–32). The gospel's Pharisees quickly became figures for Judaism generally (cf. John), and it is not difficult to imagine the threat this "Judaism" posed to Christian art.

The church fathers systematized that threat from these intertwined strands of scripture and philosophy. Consider St. Augustine's description of the dangers of hermeneutics in *On Christian Doctrine*: "The ambiguities of metaphorical words . . . demand extraordinary care and diligence. What the Apostle says pertains to this problem. 'For the letter kills, but the spirit gives life.' That is, when that which is said figuratively is taken as though it were literal, it is understood carnally. Nor can anything more appropriately be called the death of the soul than that condition in which the thing that distinguishes man from beasts, which is the understanding, is subjected to the flesh in pursuit of the letter" (III.v.9). This, he explained, had been the error of the Jews. Similarly in his *Confessions*, the Jews provided a vivid illustration of the perversion of images: "That first-born people . . . worshipped the head of a quadruped in your place . . . bowing your image, that is, their soul, before the image of a calf that eats hay" (VII.9).

Like Plato in the Phaedrus, with his condemnation of those who respond to beauty "after the fashion of a four-footed beast," Augustine is here criticizing those who fail to "raise the eye of the mind above things that are corporeal." Again like Plato, Augustine understands every act of seeing and thinking to be afflicted by this "lust of the eyes." As he puts it in Book X of *The Confessions*, "The eyes delight in fair and varied forms, and bright and pleasing colors. . . . There is no rest from them given me. . . . But that corporeal light . . . seasons the life of the world for her blind lovers with a tempting and fatal sweetness." Visual absorption in the delights of creation brings about the death of the soul. This fatal attraction cannot be broken, not even (as in Numbers) by attaching blue threads to the fringes of our garments. Neither our will nor our prayerful attempts to orient our sight toward God are enough to overcome it; only God's grace can save us: "I resist the seductions of my eyes, lest my feet be entangled as I go forward in thy way; and I raise my invisible eyes to thee, that thou wouldst be pleased to 'pluck my feet out of the net.' Thou dost continually pluck them out, for they are easily ensnared. Thou ceasest not to pluck them out, but I constantly remain fast in the snares set all around me" (X.34–35).

The danger is everywhere and afflicts every human. Nevertheless, Augustine does not hesitate to give this universal error a specific name and face. Because it was this error that led the Jews to reject Jesus, the Jews serve the world as the best example of its dangers. They are "vessels of wrath," living memorials to the difference between reading the outside and the inside of things, which is also the difference between damnation and salvation. It is as "blue fringes" on the garments of the godly, as peripatetic reminders of the punishment that await every Judaizer whose eyes are not lifted by grace out of the snare cast by the sight of things in this world, that the Jews walk onto the stage of Christian art.[13]

Because of Israel's place in Christian salvation history, the Jews' roles on that stage are more varied than one might expect. On any number of questions—including the relationship between outer and inner, material and spiritual—figures of Judaism can serve simultaneously as thesis, antithesis, synthesis. They are at once the bearers of an eternal truth, exemplars of an equally enduring falsity, and typological representatives of the Christological overcoming of the opposition. Thus on the subject of images, the Jews provide Christians with examples of the most sublime rejection of the eye's attraction to the material object ("Thou shalt have no graven image"), of the most degraded submission to it (the Golden Calf), and even (typologically) of the bridging of the gap between spiritual and material in the Incarnation (e.g., in the art of the Tabernacle, which prefigured Jesus as material dwelling place of the divine). So varied are these roles, so flexible is this dialectic, that virtually any visual relationship to the object can be mapped onto the figure of the Jew.[14]

The mapping seems already complete in the debate between St. Jerome and Nepotian in 394 over the decoration of churches. Nepotian had obviously used the example of the Jews and their Temple to justify Christian decoration, because Jerome attacked precisely that point in his counterargument: "and let no one allege against me the wealth of the temple of Judea, its tables, its lamps . . . and the rest of its golden vessels." Those things of the Temple, Jerome explains, were "figures typifying things still in the future." But for Christians, who *live in that future*, "the Law is spiritual." If Christians "keep to the letter" in this, they must keep it in everything, and adopt the Jewish rituals: "Rejecting the superstition of the Jews, we must also reject the gold; or approving the gold, we must approve the Jews as well. For we must either accept them with the gold or condemn them with it." In other words, those who choose to decorate churches must become "Jews." Epiphanius—he of the "Medicine Chest"— made much the same argument at much the same time, but with a slightly different vocabulary. Criticizing church wall paintings of the saints, he reminded his readers of Paul's characterization of false priests as "whited walls" (Acts 23:3). To paint a fresco is to become a Pharisee.[15]

These were the weapons with which the Iconoclasts entered the civil war over the use of devotional images that shook the eastern Roman empire (Byzantium) in the eighth and ninth centuries. So far as we can tell from the arguments attributed to them by their victorious enemies, the Iconoclasts charged that the advocates of devotional art were either worshippers of the picture, in which case

　　　　　DAVID NIRENBERG

they were idolaters, or else they were worshippers of the image of Jesus' human body, in which case, like the Jews, they were overlooking his divinity. After all, painters could represent only the humanity of the savior, not the divine presence which had been consubstantial with that humanity. In this world (according to the Iconoclasts), the only thing that could truly represent this consubstantiality of matter and divinity is the body and blood of the man-God in the consecrated bread and wine of the Eucharist. Everything else is merely matter without presence. The worship of such matter is a confusion of God's nature, a confusion just like those of the many Judaizing heretics of the past.[16]

The Iconoclasts gave these old weapons a new edge, but the defenders of images turned that edge against them. According to a "myth of origins" propagated by Iconophiles, Iconoclasm was the invention of "a leader of the lawless Jews, a sorcerer and the agent of demonic soul destroyers called Tessarakonta-pêchys" (the name means "forty cubits tall"), who convinced the Muslim Caliph Yazid to order all Christian images in his land destroyed. When some unworthy Christians heard of this, "they imitated the lawless Jews and the unbelieving Arabs, and began to insult the churches of God." This is a polemical "tall-tale," of course, but behind it there is a refined dialectical hermeneutics at work. The Iconoclasts are "Jews" not only because they interpret the commandment against graven images literally, but also because they perceived only the outer beauty of the images themselves, without realizing that this beauty was meant to turn the inner eye toward God. The Jews were led by this error into crucifying Christ, the Iconoclasts into destroying his image. The ninth-century Khludov Psalter illuminates the point by juxtaposing an image of two Jews tormenting the crucified Jesus with long-poled sponges of vinegar and gall, with an image of two Iconoclasts using the same instruments to whitewash an image of the savior. To deface a fresco is to become a Pharisee.[17]

In Byzantium, both the defense and the critique of images were conducted in terms of Judaism. This is why a conflict *between Christians* over images produced an explosion of *anti-Jewish* polemics. That explosion conforms to what I would formulate as a rule: because of the theological centrality and dialectical utility of figures of Judaism in Christian discourses about representation, periods of heightened anxiety about representation are also marked by heightened anxiety about Judaism (and vice versa). The more Western reaches of Christendom are not an exception to this rule. They did not experience as violent a civil war over the use of images as Byzantium did, but the variety of roles available for Judaism in their debates was much the same.[18]

When Abbot Suger of Saint- Denis wanted to justify the visual program of his church (c. 1144), he did so, like Nepotian in Jerome's letter 52, by appealing to the typological precedent of the Tabernacle, with its statues of cherubim and candelabra of gold. Such decoration, he claimed, draws our "dull minds" to the sacred, "urging [the mind] upward from material things to the immaterial."[19] When St. Bernard of Clairvaux wanted to criticize the same program, he invoked the same proof text but emphasized, like St. Jerome, the other side of the typology. The Tabernacle and its religious art belonged to those ritual parts of Judaism that were meant to be overcome in its Christian fulfillment. Even more forcefully than St. Jerome, Bernard insisted on the Jewishness of those who decorate churches. The true Christian regards "all things . . . as dung" in order to win Christ (Phil. 3.8; Jerome, Letter 52.10), whereas those who fill sanctuaries with material beauty have reversed these priorities. "Does not avarice, which is the service of idols, cause all this?" Seeking earthly rather than spiritual treasure, they have become like Jewish moneylenders, hungry for both principal and interest. Small wonder, Bernard suggests elsewhere, that there are many who confuse churches with synagogues.[20]

For Bernard, like many critics of images before him, art is in close proximity to "Judaism."[21] And like many Iconophiles before them, the supporters of devotional art in turn criticize Bernard's critique as literalizing and Judaizing.[22] Already venerable in the twelfth century, this dialectical double-bind still had long life before it. Martin Luther perceived the dilemma some four centuries later and tried to protect himself from it. It is true, he wrote in 1525, that those who destroy images Judaize as much as those who adore them, because they seek to gain God's approval through *law*. "They do away with outward images while filling their hearts with idols . . . false justice and fame through works. . . . The Jews shun outward idols . . . yet in their hearts they are for God full of idols." But, Luther continues, "I who as a Christian command no power on earth" do not rely upon the law. Removing the idols first from the people's hearts through preaching, I "see to it that images are removed . . . without fanaticism and violence." Yet despite insisting on his distance from Judaism, Luther too was Judaized, and not only by Catholics in their defense of images, but also by reformers more radical than he in their opposition to them. Within a system of thought that stigmatizes as "Jewish" the material forms of communication and community on which it simultaneously depends, there is no way to escape the danger. Every utterance remains potentially too literal, every representation too material, every invocation of spiritual authority too imbricated with earthly power. As the herald of this ontological scandal, "Judaism" attends every Christian claim to truth in this world.[23]

Despite this ubiquity or, rather, because of it, the deployment of the critical language of Judaizing both reflected and effected subtle and dynamic distinctions that repeatedly transformed the history and philosophy of art. In Bernard's twelfth century, it drew attention to differences in the "Judaism" that threatens consumers of art and the "Judaism" that threatens its producers, and it suggested new ways to understand and combat both. Bernard's critique, for example, distinguished between those audiences for whom images were spiritually appropriate (the ignorant, who have few other means with which to approach knowledge of the eternal) and those for whom they were not (such as monks and other learned experts in the sacred, who possess many less crude and dangerous tools). It distinguished as well between the potential motives of patrons and artists, between those driven by a love of gold, and those driven by godliness. In other words, Bernard staged the "Jewishness" of Christian art upon the image itself, as an interplay between the spiritual state and intention of the artist or producer, and the spiritual state and intention of the viewer or consumer.

This staging was scarcely Bernard's alone. On the contrary, it was a key attribute of Gothic phenomenology. We find it not only in the writings of theologians like Bernard, but also in those (much rarer) of artists like Theophilus, whose "how to" manual stresses to other artists the importance of treating technique as an expression of God's grace in the production of a Christian work of art. Above all, it is the objects themselves that perform the fear of slippage across the line between "the Gothic image" and "the Gothic idol." Sometimes the performance was achieved through words inscribed on the image, such as the common distich "It is neither God nor man, which you discern in the present figure,/ But God and man, which the sacred image represents." More often, the image warns without words. In two gilded folios (35v–36r) the reader of the St. Louis Psalter proceeds (left to right) from Moses receiving the tablets of the law, through his casting them down before the Israelites as they adore the Golden Calf, to his praying before God (marked by a cruciform nimbus) among the sculptures and art objects of the Tabernacle. The illumination simultaneously declares the dangers that the Psalter's pictures pose, and adumbrates the typological polemic that proclaims the salvific potential of those same pictures. Similarly, on a portal of Chartres's cathedral, the image of faith is carved directly above idolatry. Faith sits full frontal to the viewer, while idolatry, in profile below her, is represented as a statue with the viewer kneeling before it. The sculpture reminds the audience that it must view the cathedral's visual program with its inner eye, rather than linger like idolaters in its materiality. And it also announces that although the patrons and producers of this program have quite literally sculpted an idol, they are nevertheless not idol makers.[24]

These objects work simultaneously to declare the intentions of their makers and to orient the intentions of their viewers. They do so in order to avoid the charge of "Judaism," the accusation that—like the Pharisees—they conceal a charnel house beneath the beauty of their surface. One way to achieve this, eagerly embraced by artists of the twelfth and thirteenth centuries, was to place Jews within the artwork, as exemplary figures whose misdirected gazes teach the Christian viewer how *not to look* at the sacred scene before them. Sara Lipton has taught us how, unlike earlier generations of Christian artists, those of the twelfth century learned to equip their Jews with special hats, distinctive clothes, and deformed faces. For the viewer, these figures provided abject lessons about the dangers of seeing after the flesh. And for the artist they served as points of projection, "vessels of wrath" into which he could pour all the dangers of "Judaism" that haunted his practice.[25]

The emergence of the blind and hyper-marked Jew as a guarantor of Christian truth within the Gothic image provides yet another example of our rule that transformations in Christian thinking about representation are linked to transformations in Christian thinking about Jews. In the later Middle Ages, perhaps the most central transformation in Christian thinking about representation involved the nature of God's presence in the bread and wine of the Eucharist. The twelfth and thirteenth centuries placed new stress on that presence, assigned it new roles in Christian devotion, and underwrote those roles with new resources of representation. Insofar as the eucharistic body of Christ had long served as the limit case in debates over the nature of God's presence in the material, these transformations not only encouraged the development of new visual programs, but also provided those programs with new grounds for the claim that art can approach the reality of its object, that representation leads toward divine presence.[26] And with these new claims came new anxieties and new types of attack—such as accusations of ritual murder and host desecration—on the Jews, who represented the original misrecognition of God's presence in the material body of Jesus. Figures of "Judaism" in Christian media affect the possibilities of existence for real Jews of flesh and blood. But that is a subject for another book.[27]

It is important to recognize these links between transformations of artistic practices, of discourses about those practices, and of figures of Judaism within those practices and discourses, with other transformations: not only theological, but also demographic, economic, political, sociological, technological. But we should not forget that the reverse is also true: developments within representational media, that is, within the practice of art itself, can transform ontological anxieties. We have seen how the fixed canon of the Egyptians, with its abstracted and ideal poses, provided Plato with an antidote to the dangers of realistic illusionism he thought rampant in his day. Byzantium also built bulwarks against the fear that the desires of artists might overcome the demands of divine truth. Among these we might count the elaboration of a canon of iconic styles, many of them imagined to derive from originals either authored by God or divinely

DAVID NIRENBERG

inspired—cloths miraculously imprinted with the visage of Christ, St. Luke the Apostle's portrait of Mary the Mother of God. Similar strategies flourished in western Christendom, albeit with more emphasis on the artist's role as intermediary. (Among the many exceptions is the striking image in Alfonso X of Castile's Cantigas de Santa Maria, which depicts God himself carving the Mother and Child of Gethsemane into a pillar of stone with his finger.)[28]

Isidore of Seville's famous complaint that, when artists strive to make things more real, they bring forth more falsehood is only one of many reminders that both artists and their works were thought of as agents of ontological change, and that the direction of the change they effected was thought to be legible in the object itself.[29] Style and ontology were inseparable in the work: the critique of one was also a critique of the other. These critiques were not monopolized by opponents of art. On the contrary, the patrons and producers of Christian art also conducted debates about style—debates about color and line, paint and material support, abstraction and naturalism, artistic self-consciousness and citation. And all parties in these debates could draw on a critical language steeped in "Judaism."

Consider the example of Jan van Eyck (c. 1385–1441). Van Eyck was not the inventor of oil painting, as Giorgio Vasari and other sixteenth-century Italians believed, but he was certainly a precocious master of oil and its glazes. The resulting pictures made new claims as objects, not only because of the enameled shimmer of their surfaces and the iridescence of their jeweled tones, but also because of the feats of detailed realism that van Eyck's techniques made possible. Through the single arch that separates mother and child in the Louvre's "Virgin of Chancellor Rolin" (c. 1435), an entire city recedes into the distance. Such feats were accompanied by new assertions of artistic subjectivity, as in Berlin's "Holy Face," so boldly inscribed "Jan Van Eyck made me" on its frame as if it were Van Eyck who had accomplished the miracle of imprinting Jesus' visage on the veil. (The painting, which exists in several contemporary copies, appears in fact to be pseudonymous.) And along with these new claims of artist and of object, came new anxieties about the *potential* Jewishness of artist, art, and audience.

"The Fountain of Grace," variously attributed to Van Eyck or his followers, provides a good example of how a painting addresses these anxieties (Figure 13.1). The upper story of the painting is an enclosed paradise, God sitting at its apex. To his right and left sit Mary and John the Evangelist, each absorbed in the reading of a book. A lamb lies at his feet, and a river flows from his throne through the garden: a pictorial representation of the verse from the Apocalypse, "procedentem de sede Dei et Agni" (22:1). The river descends until it empties into a fountain outside the walls of paradise. Those walls, with turrets left and

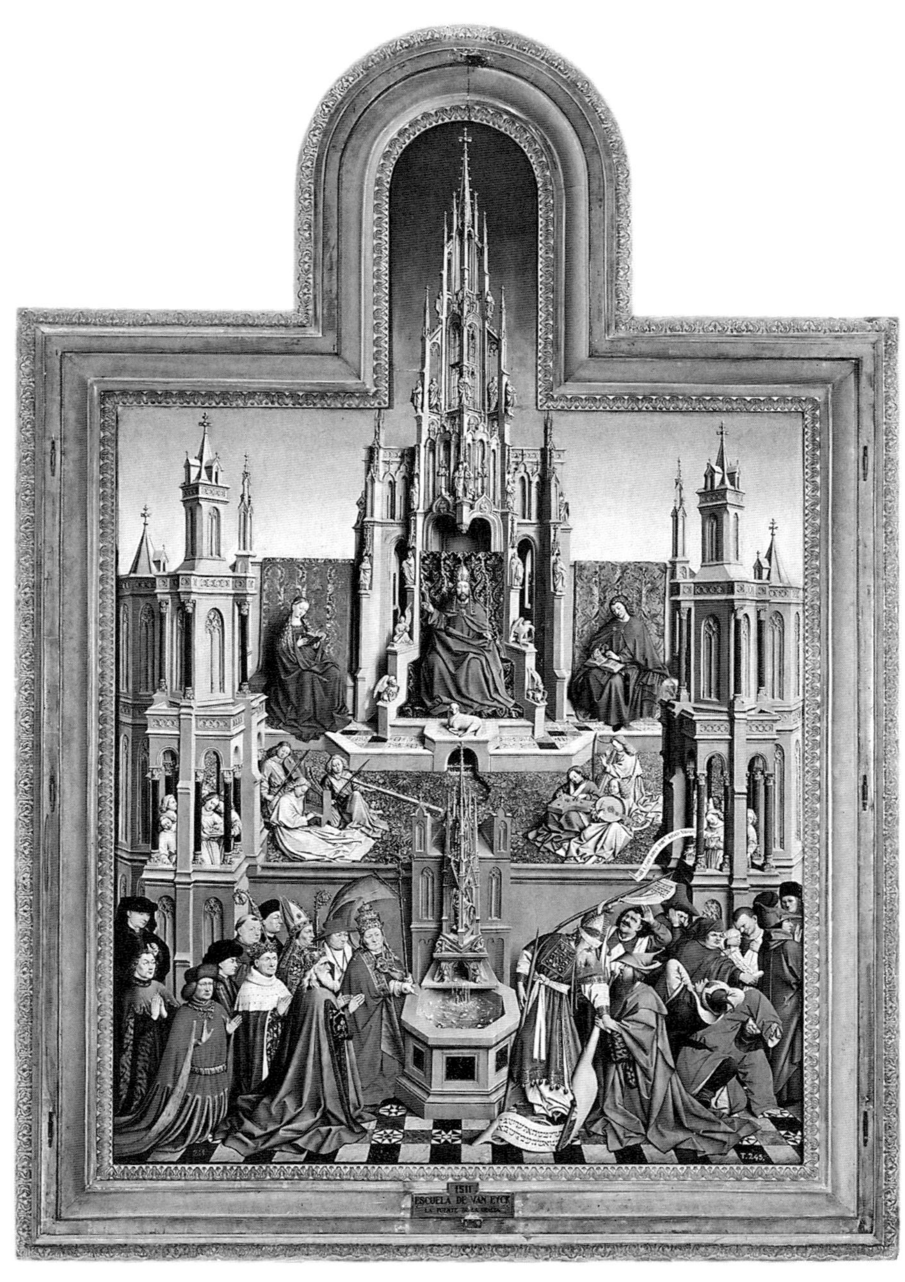

13.1. School of Jan van Eyck, *The Fountain of Grace and the Triumph of the Church over the Synagogue.* Photo: Erich Lessing/Art Resource, New York.

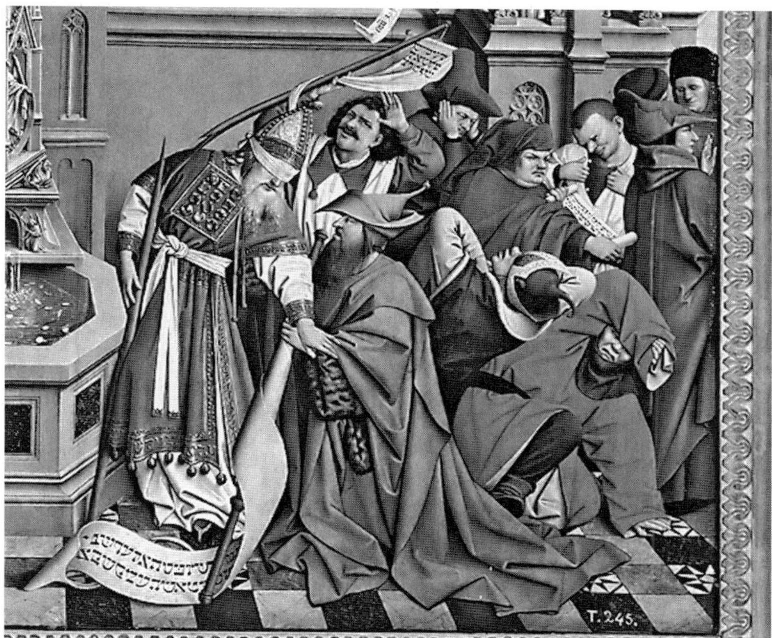

13.2. School of Jan van Eyck, *The Fountain of Grace and the Triumph of the Church over the Synagogue* (detail). Photo: Erich Lessing/Art Resource, New York.

right, separate paradise from the painting's ground floor: the terrestrial ante-chamber or forecourt of the heavenly city. The angel in the turret on the left reads from a book, while from the hands of the angel in the other tower a scroll descends bearing an inscription from the Song of Songs: "Can. Fons [h]ort-orum, puteus aquarum viventium" (4:15). Only the river and the scroll—grace mediated through scripture—break the barrier between the garden and the exterior courtyard, in which two groups are clustered on either side of the fountain. On the left a pope stands by the fountain, surrounded by Christian clerics, cardinals, and kings; on the right a group of Jews, surrounding their high priest (Figure 13.2). The Christians pray and gesture in rapt attention toward the fountain. The Jews, their high priest blindfolded, lean away from the fountain and avert their faces, vainly consulting various scrolls of Hebrew script, the largest of which lies unfurled like a fallen standard on the floor.

The painting's foregrounding of media—books and scrolls, but also music and the gestures of preaching—calls attention to our by now familiar problem. The Jews and their scrolls, painted with realistic but nonsensical Hebrew script, are a familiar embodiment of the fleshy letter and its perils. But here they embody as well the perils of a painting whose painstaking literalism is every-where evident, and perhaps nowhere more so than in the depiction of the archi-synagogus or high priest himself. In the priest's bejeweled breast plate (*ephod*), for example, the painter reveals his meticulous attention to the letter of Exodus 39. He bases his rendering of this famously obscure ritual object on a drawing provided by the biblical commentator Nicholas of Lyra, but makes slight changes in favor of an even more literal reading of the Vulgate text.[30]

Through the figure of the Jew, the painting announces its conformity to the letter. But the same figure, condemned and blind, also proclaims the Christian transcendence of that letter. The painting projects the danger of its own "Jewishness" onto the Jew within itself. In so doing, it also answers the "Christian" critic who would reproach the painter for his literalism, realism, or materialism. It places that critic—Jan Huss, for example, has been identified as the fat figure in red and blue holding an unrolled scroll—and every other viewer who fails to see the spiritual within the literal, among the Jews within the painting, standing blind before the fountain of grace. Like the St. Louis Psalter's Golden Calf or the idol of Chartres's cathedral, the Fountain of Grace hovers between the soul of its maker and the soul of its viewer, simultaneously testing and reflecting the "Judaism" of each.[31]

The Fountain of Grace may well have been painted after Van Eyck's trip to the Iberian Peninsula in 1428–29, and for Castilian patrons: that is, it may have been directly addressed to a specific context in which the recent mass conversions of Jews to Christianity had raised fears of Judaizing to new heights and had provoked new debates about the appropriateness of image worship.[32] Nevertheless, its deployment of Judaism in the defense of art is not eccentric: it is rather representative of one way in which style is beginning to legitimate itself within Christian aesthetics. This process of legitimization becomes easier to recognize as it becomes both better documented and more bitterly contested, as here, in Cardinal Paleotti's description of the function of style in 1582, at a time when the very possibility of Christian art is under Protestant attack: "The style of depiction serves a purpose. In studying this, one must distinguish the artist as such [*puro artefice*] from the Christian artist. . . . The objective of the painter as artist is to earn money by means of art . . . and to earn praise. . . . The chief purpose of the Christian artist . . . is to attain divine grace by means of his industry and skill. . . . [His work] serves the higher purpose of contemplating the eternal splendors in an act of virtue, to lead people away from vice and to the true cult of God."[33] Paleotti stresses that, unlike art *tout court*, the Christian work of art is intended as an active agent of ontological change, created with (and reflecting) the spiritual vision of its maker in order to manipulate the spiritual vision of the viewer. The work still stands poised between vice and virtue, worldly desire and divine love, material appearance and eternal truth, which is also to say between "Judaism" and Christianity.

     DAVID NIRENBERG

In Paleotti's cinquecento, Christian style still justifies itself as a flight from Judaism. By this I do not mean the narrow point that "Jew" could serve style as a critical term, though of course it could. Titian's friend Pietro Aretino, for example, liked to boast that he called the poet Brocardo a "Jew" for disagreeing with Bembo about versification, after which (in 1531) Brocardo promptly died of rage. And on the side of praise, a poem celebrating Benvenuto Cellini's statue of "Perseus with the head of the medusa" honored the artist for defeating, on the one hand, the stupidity of the Greeks, and on the other the arrogance of the Jews: "Onde 'l Greco non pur, non pur l'Ebreo/ Stupido l'vn, l'altro sdegnoso resta."[34] But these usages were relatively rare in Italy, especially in comparison to their ubiquity in sixteenth-century Spain. More important is a much broader point: the same theological claims that legitimate Christian styles of realism and naturalism also compel—with the threat of Judaism—their ceaseless change. The artist who becomes enamored of the beauty he creates, whose eyes linger on style for its own sake, becomes ensnared in "Judaism." Like Augustine in Confessions X.35, and like Goethe's Faust, he is lost as soon as he murmurs "bleib, du bist so schön."[35]

The attempts of Perugino and Savoldo to distinguish themselves from Titian, Raphael, and other painters after the "modern manner" provide a good example of what I mean by the development of style as a flight from "Judaism." According to Stephen Campbell's account of their efforts in this volume, the Brescians claimed to reject the "imitative naturalism" of the moderns in favor of a eucharistic realism. Their "mimetic mode of sacred naturalism," Campbell writes, "aspires to free itself of [the moderns'] obvious tropes of artfulness." "Christian" realism uses style to announce the incompleteness of its movement toward the real presence of the Incarnation. Judaizing imitative naturalism uses style to conceal that incompleteness. "The task of the Catholic artist/exegete is to reveal the always provisional and referential nature of the apparently literal, by inflecting his representations with the tropes of *style*."

Of course, I do not mean to suggest that Savoldo's painting was more "Christian" and Raphael's more "Jewish." My point is rather the opposite: that within this strand of discourse about Christian style, all art has the *potential* to be criticized as "Jewish," as soon as it becomes satisfied with its own artful literality. Even a framed and signed consecrated Host, if we can imagine such a hypothetical eucharistic "ready-made," could not serve as a stable end-point for Christian art. It too would be vulnerable to the criticism that it overemphasizes its own literal materiality, demanding the wrong kind of attention from its viewers.[36]

It is precisely this "transitory, fugitive element, whose metamorphoses are so rapid," that will lead Charles Baudelaire to conclude, in the mid-nineteenth

century, that "every old master has had his own modernity." But in the sixteenth century, style's flight had rather the opposite effect, of leading art back
toward the dangers of "Judaism." For now, the passage of time itself transformed works that once, in their own time and place, had the effect of orienting
souls toward the divine, into objects that misled the spiritual vision of viewers
from generations with different sensibilities. Only a century separated Michelangelo from Van Eyck, but when the Italian looked at paintings like those of
the Flemish master's, he saw "a view to external exactness," "deceiving sensual
vision," too much "stuffs and masonry, the green grass of the fields, the shadow
of trees, and rivers and bridges," too "many figures on this side and many
figures on that." Far from rescuing art from the dangers of mimesis and materiality, the evolving Christian discourses of style created new potentials for
"Judaism."[37]

These potentials extended from Christian art into the aesthetic sphere we
call the secular. The distinction itself emerged as a consequence of the increasing
Protestant insistence that only Scripture's "word allows us to see God in the
manner of a mirror" (the formulation is John Calvin's). This demotion of the
claim to presence in sign and sacrament would seem to leave a very diminished
religious role for art: that of teaching (*docendo*) through instructive scenes from
history (*res gestae*), or providing pleasing images for aesthetic enjoyment (*oblec-
tationem*). Some scholars have indeed seen in these changes an ontological
earthquake and the beginnings of the secularization of the image. But from our
point of view, two observations are more important. First, throughout these
transformations, the work of art often remains an ontological test, a diagnostic
instrument of the relation between artist, material object, and viewer. And second, the resulting diagnosis continues to be given in terms that can easily be
mapped onto theological categories of "Christianity" and "Judaism." We cannot claim, as Carl Schmitt might urge us to, that "all significant concepts of the
modern theory of [art] are secularized theological concepts not only because of
their historical development . . . but also because of their systematic structure."
But we can demonstrate that some certainly are, and these have important
implications for the ongoing "Judaism" of art.[38]

In order to demonstrate this, it is not enough to trace a given motif, such as
the Golden Calf, into modernity. No matter how much we multiply our cattle,
or extend our attention to other iconographies, the sum of examples will always
fall short of justifying my claim that the "systematic structure" of significant
concepts in modern theories of art can be usefully understood as a secularization of the theological distinction between "Christian" and "Jew." For that, we
need to show that influential ways of thinking about art charge artworks with
the task of establishing and reflecting upon the proper relation between subject

   DAVID NIRENBERG

and object; and that they evaluate the success of the artwork in terms of critical distinctions that derive from and can potentially be translated back into the theological distinction between "Christian" and "Jew."

We may start with seventeenth and eighteenth century French debates over style, taste (*goût*), and aesthetic spirit (*esprit*), for in them Pharisaism remains the governing error. Richard Neer's essay on Poussin in this volume provides an excellent example of how a particular artist could deploy a pictorial critique of pharisaic aesthetics in order to "think history painting's grounding laws of space and time and legibility . . . in order to transcend them" and thereby fit the genre into a "narrative of charity and redemption." But for a theoretical statement of the general aesthetic problem, we can turn to the most famous (albeit slightly later) representatives of the Port Royal theologians with whom Poussin was in dialogue. "We may say, in general," write Antoine Arnauld and Pierre Nicole in their *Logic, or the Art of Thought* of 1662, "that the world values most things by the exterior alone, since we find scarcely any who penetrate to the interior and to the foundations of them; everything is judged according to the fashion, and unhappy are those who are not in favor." In all forms of representation, this attention to exterior "ornamentation" leads to a falsity that is best described by analogy to sculpture or architecture: "The orator . . . disposes of [the truth] as we do the stones of a building or the metal of a statue: he cuts it, lengthens it, narrows it, disguises it, as he thinks fit, in order to adapt it to that vain work of words which he wishes to make." "All exterior things are but equivocal signs." "Accuracy of language, the use of figures, are to eloquence what color is to painting: its lowest and most material part."

The logicians of Port Royal were part of a movement (the Jansenists) eventually condemned as unorthodox. But in their concern with the dangers posed by the "letter" and the "exterior thing," they were recognizably Augustinian, even if they worked harder than some other Christian theorists of language to minimize the mediation of the sign, to make the signifier as transparent as possible to the signified. If, they argued, we are to approach things as conceived by God, without the distortion of human language and human interests, then we need to "present not only present things naked as they are, but also the very act of conceiving them." For this we need to strip down as far as possible the material supports of our cognition. "Too much attention to words and ornament . . . weakens the force of . . . thought. Similarly, painters have noticed that those who excel with color do not normally excel with drawing; the mind is not capable of mastering both, since one undermines the other." Whenever our cognitive tools of representation pay attention to the beauty of their own "surface," cognition is alienated from the object it seeks to apprehend. This misplaced attention was, for the Port Royal thinkers as for so many others, in some way essentially "Jewish": "It is pharisaic to attend to the exterior before attending to the interior."[39]

The logicians could appeal so confidently to the analogy of painting in their quest to make the letter transparent because a stylistic discourse about the dangers of color in painting was already well established. That discourse was only reinforced by the latest philosophical and theological discoveries. Descartes' argument, for example, that objectivity is extension in space and local motion, strengthened the truth-claims of drawing—*dessin*, the tracing of extension in space—and reinforced the stigmatization of color, associated with the distortions of pathos and passion. It was in these terms that the *débat sur le coloris* (debate on coloring) was carried on in the mid-seventeenth century, as when the Jansenist Philipe de Champaigne, rector of the Académie Royale, warned of the moral dangers of color, which confronts us with its *éclat*, its exterior glitter, rather than pointing to the soul of the painting, its *dessin*. We are not so far as we might think from the ontology underlying St. Bernard's critique, half a millennium before, of those Judaizers who "believe more holy, what is more colorful."[40]

A very similar ontology animated the next generation of debaters over "esprit" and the "goût moderne."[41] Bishop of Cambrai and tutor to the eldest son of Louis XIV, François de Salignac de la Mothe-Fénelon was no Jansenist, but he too advocated a self-negating style of representation, a striving after immediacy that would overcome the worldly alienation of the post-lapsarian soul and lead to a *pur amour*, a pure love of God "untainted by all self-concern." Representation that strives after truth must overcome self-love, self-interest, concupiscence. Here Fénelon's favorite painters provide a positive role-model for the writer: "One should write as the Raphaels, the Carracci, and the Poussins painted: not for the sake of seeking marvelous fancies and have one's imagination admired through virtuosity with the brush, but for the sake of painting after nature." In order for any representation to serve the "salvation" of its audience rather than the "vainglory" of its author, in order for it to make its object present in the mind of the other, it must suppress all reference to the artfulness of its own mediation. "The poet disappears: we see only what he makes us see, and we hear only those he lends a voice to. That is the power of imitation and painting."[42]

The ontology so evident in Fénelon's many critiques of theater, poetry, rhetoric, and art, is undergirded by an explicitly Christian soteriology. The salvation history disappears in the writings of some of Fénelon's Enlightenment successors, but aspects of the ontology remain in place. Diderot's writings on theater and art provide perhaps the most famous example. Here again, the art object is judged by its ability to move the soul: "Painting is the art of reaching to the

     DAVID NIRENBERG

soul through the intervention of the eyes. If the effect stops at the eyes, the painter has travelled the lesser part of the road." Like Fénelon, Diderot sees the self-assertion of the artist, the vaunting of artfulness, as an important obstacle to this goal: "The beauty of the ideal makes an impression on all men, while the beauty of making impresses only the connoisseur. If it makes him dream, it is of the artist and his art, not of the thing itself. He always remains outside the scene and never enters into it. True eloquence does not call attention to itself." And like Fénelon, Diderot draws on a venerable anti-pharisaic vocabulary to do the work of distinguishing between falsity and truth: the vocabulary of anti-theatricality. In painting as in theater, Diderot insists, "It is rare that a being who is not totally engrossed in his action is not *mannered*. Every personage who seems to tell you: 'Look how well I cry, how well I become angry, how well I implore,' is false and *mannered*."[43]

Diderot believes that the painting—like the actor, the poem, and even the word—has a dual potential. It can either reinforce the alienation of the subject from the object, of the beholder "from the objects of his beholding (and therefore . . . from himself, both in his capacity as beholder and as a potential object of beholding for others)," or overcome it. The latter is the epistemological and ontological goal of painting. Diderot seems to suggest that a radical anti-theatricality can rescue representation from its dual potentiality. Painter and actor alike must purge their self-consciousness from the tableaux—whether stage or canvas—so that it appears disinterested before the beholder. The stakes are moral as well as aesthetic. Describing a painting of "Susannah and the elders"—a subject whose theme is explicitly that of illicit beholding—he notes that the painting threatens to make the viewer complicit in the prurient crime of the elders. Executed with the proper anti-theatricality, however, the painting itself rescues both painter and viewer from danger: "When Susannah exposes her naked body to my eyes . . . , Susannah is chaste and so is the painter. Neither the one nor the other knew I was there."[44]

In *Absorption and Theatricality*, the book that has inspired these last few paragraphs, Michael Fried suggested that Diderot's reaction against the Rococo was part of a mid-eighteenth-century moment in which "the existence of the beholder, which is to say the primordial convention that paintings are made to be beheld, emerged as problematic for painting as never before" (93). The suggestion has proven revelatory, uncovering and explicating a series of powerful shifts in the "direction of the values and effects" of painting at a particular place and time. But for the purpose of this essay, it is equally important to point out the continuing power of "primordial convention." Diderot's doctrine of the relation of artifact to audience is radical, but it still leaves painting suspended between painter and viewer, as mediator in a triangular relationship. The respective responsibilities of the parties to this relationship have shifted, but the ontological outcome of the relationship remains split between two possibilities: the fantasy of overcoming the alienation of subject and object and the fear of widening it. And although the critical tools that discriminate between the two outcomes have been transformed, they have not been emancipated, either in vocabulary or in underlying ontology, from those that previously decided between the Christian and the Jew. Hence, neither absorptive nor theatrical painting is freed from the risk of Judaizing. Absorption avoids "Pharisaic" theatricality but risks the charge that—like Jews and dualists—it is too optimistic about the possibility of avoiding the alienating implicit in any mediation of the sign, and thereby destabilizes Incarnational synthesis in favor of pure spirit, divine sublimity. (In this regard it is worth remembering the ecclesiastical condemnation not only of the Jansenists, but also of Fénelon's *pur amour.*) Theatricality, on the other hand, has the advantage of calling attention to its own artifice, thereby satisfying not only Aristotle's definition of art but also heading off certain Platonic and Christian critiques. But it can be charged with overemphasizing external appearance versus internal reality, which is to say, of Pharisaism. In art as in language and cognition, the subject-object relation remains threatened by Judaism.[45]

The "new sort of beholder (or new 'subject')" of Diderot and his French colleagues was not the only conception of self that attempted to address this problem in the late eighteenth century. As Fried points out in a footnote urging comparison (p. 104), a very different idea—that of self brought before itself in the activity of representation (Vorstellung)—was emerging among the German Idealist philosophers such as Fichte. Fichte could provide a useful example for us as well, since he put his Idealism to the task of (among other things) demonstrating that the new French subject was in fact a "deadly foreign spirit," capable of believing "only in an eternal recurrence of apparent life," and that the French were, as the Prussian poet Ernst Moritz Arndt would put it a few years later, "an empty, hollow, doll-like, formless, contentless Nothing," "a Jew People." Fichte was a pioneer in the nineteenth- and twentieth-century struggle between German "Kultur" and French "Civilization," a struggle in which ideas about Judaism would play an important role. But since we have space for only one Idealist, let us focus on the one with greater impact on the future of critical thinking about art: Georg Wilhelm Friedrich Hegel (1770–1831), "The Father," as E. H. Gombrich dubbed him, "of Art History."[46]

Unlike Diderot and his colleagues, Hegel did not hesitate to cast his philosophy in a Christian vocabulary (however idiosyncratic), which means a "Jewish" one as well. This is evident already in "The Earliest System-Programme of German Idealism," probably authored by Hölderlin in collaboration with Hegel

DAVID NIRENBERG

and Schelling (1796): "The people without aesthetic sense are our philosophers of the letter. The philosophy of the spirit is an aesthetic philosophy." The Programme insisted that only beauty can move us from letter to spirit. This Platonic confidence in the power of beauty would disappear from Hegel's later writing, but the fundamentally Pauline antinomy of spirit and letter, with all its related pairs—"spirit and matter, soul and body, faith and intellect, freedom and necessity, . . . reason and sensibility, intelligence and nature, . . . absolute subjectivity and absolute objectivity"—will endure. Indeed, Hegel understood his "speculative philosophy" as the successor to Christianity in the overcoming of these antinomies, a new and higher stage in the dialectical overcoming of the opposition between "the dead concept, empty within itself, and the full concreteness of life," by the unfolding Idea as it realizes itself in "the unity of concept and objectivity."[47]

Hegel's understanding of the history of human thought was as a movement toward the "[stripping] off the forms of dualism from its extremes, rendering the opposition in the element of Universality fluid, and bringing it to reconciliation." Within this history he assigned Judaism a double role similar to the one it played in Christian salvation history. In its recognition of the sharp difference between God and the material world, it represents a crucial stage in the progress of the spirit. But once Judaism had discovered this difference, it should have proceeded dialectically to overcome it. Instead, Judaism rejected the world in favor of total subjection to a distant God. The Jews' prohibition on images, their inability to love others, their blindness to the Incarnation—these were all symptoms of this rejection, through which Judaism opposed the progress of the spirit toward synthesis. As Hegel put it in "The Spirit of Christianity and Its Fate," his early (1799) and unpublished attempt to map the history of philosophy onto the history of Christianity: "The Jewish principle of opposing thought to reality, reason to sense; this principle involves the rending of life and a lifeless connection between God and the world."[48]

"Judaism" continued to serve Hegel as a critical term that could be used to characterize the failure of previous attempts to concretize the Idea in the various domains of human activity, such as religion, philosophy, and art. In the case of religion, for example, Hegel considered the danger of "Judaism"—that is, the inability to overcome the opposition between concept and reality—inescapable, even within its most developed Christian form. In "The Spirit of Christianity" the young Hegel puts the problem baldly: "However sublime the idea of God may be made here, there yet always remains the Jewish principle of opposing thought to reality, reason to sense" (259). Hence, "in all forms of the Christian religion which have been developed in the advancing fate of the ages, there lies this fundamental characteristic of opposition." "Church and state, worship and life, piety and virtue, spiritual and worldly action, can never dissolve into one" (301). This final task, the dialectical overcoming of all oppositions, remains for philosophy.[49]

But Judaism threatens philosophy as well. There was a great deal about Kant's philosophical system, for example, that struck Hegel as "Jewish." One was Kant's famous categorical imperative. Like a Jew who can only think in terms of law, Kant misunderstands Jesus' teaching to "love God above everything and your neighbor as yourself" as a "command requiring respect for a law which commands love" (213). The resulting morality, says Hegel, is merely a "fulfillment of duty," the same as the Pharisees' "hypocrisy" (220). Similarly, Hegel objects to Kant's claim (in his *Critique of Pure Reason*) that our empirical knowledge of things is restricted to the "appearance" (*Schein*) of things, that the "thing-in-itself" (*Ding an Sich*) remains "an unknown something" (*eines unbekannten Etwas*).[50] According to Hegel, in such a philosophy, as in Judaism, the "ideal does not come to terms with reality . . . the real remains absolutely opposed." It is for these reasons that in "The Spirit of Christianity and Its Fate," Hegel associates Kant with the "spirit of Judaism," and assigns him a specific place in his historical account of the spirit's unfolding: at the Sermon on the Mount, standing not with Jesus but among the Pharisees.[51]

And what about art? Like religion and philosophy, art is for Hegel an activity striving toward the unity of concept and reality. He sees "works of fine art as the first reconciling middle term between pure thought and what is merely external, sensuous and transient, between nature and finite reality and the infinite freedom of conceptual thinking." Art can achieve this mediation in a way that "immediate appearance" cannot, precisely because it calls attention to its own deceptiveness: "It points through and beyond itself, and itself hints at something spiritual of which it is to give us an idea, whereas immediate appearance does not present itself as deceptive but rather as real and true." "Beauty" is the name Hegel gives the successful outcome of this mediation, which he sees occurring only in classical art: "When truth in this its external existence is present to consciousness immediately, and when the Concept remains immediately in unity with its external appearance, the Idea is not only true but beautiful. Therefore the beautiful is characterized as the pure appearance of the idea to sense."[52]

Hegel's classical art, in other words, is the antidote to his sublime Judaism, as Heinrich Heine (1797–1856) noted long ago: "As the prophet of the Orient [Muhammad] called them 'the people of the book,' so the prophet of the Occident [Hegel] . . . called them 'the people of the spirit.' . . . Their whole religion is nothing but a dialectic act by which matter is separated from spirit and the absolute is recognized solely as spirit. . . . In what a dreadful opposition they

    DAVID NIRENBERG

must have stood to colorful Egypt, the Temples of Joy of Astarte in Phoenicia, lovely, fragrant, Babylon, and finally to Greece, the flourishing home of art."[53] But "dreadful opposition" is not emancipation. On the contrary, precisely because of that opposition, the work of art's adequacy to the task of concretizing the Idea can be measured in terms of its distance from "Judaism": a measurement that applies not only to the individual work, but to the entire history of art itself. A logic akin to this is at work in Hegel's *Lectures on the Fine Arts*, given over the course of the 1820s, and published after his death from notes by his students. In these lectures Hegel does not map the history of art onto the history of Judaism as explicitly as he had the history of thought in his earlier "The Spirit of Christianity and Its Fate." But he does present the development of art as a progressive overcoming of oppositions that throughout his career he encoded as Jewish. As a result, his history of art can also be read as a chapter in the history of the human spirit's flight from "Judaism."

That history extends over 1,237 pages in English translation, but a brief summary may suffice to make the point:

1. The first stage of art, which Hegel called Symbolic, used natural forms to point toward the unrepresentable mystery of the divine. This art—which includes the art of the ancient Egyptians, Jews, Persians, Hindus—was abstract and "sublime." But the enormous distance between the representation and the Ideal in symbolic art (precisely the distance that led Plato to praise the art of the Egyptians!) meant that it demanded rules of interpretation. How else to determine, for example, the Ideal represented by a statue of an Ibis? Symbolic art restricts the freedom of the subject by placing her under the necessity of an external law. In this sense it was, in Hegel's own terms, too "Jewish."

2. Classical art made freedom visible in the shape of individuals—for example, in the statue of a god or hero in human form. Freedom and self-sufficiency are the Ideal expressed in the unity of form and content achieved by "classical beauty." "Classical beauty has for what is internal in it the free self-sufficient meaning, i.e., not a meaning of this and that but what means itself and therefore interprets itself." But classical art itself begins to discover that this aesthetic freedom is at odds with the finitude of the world in which it expresses itself, and soon Greek philosophy begins to point out art's inability to express what it might mean "for a finite, embodied human to be free." Classical art, Hegel concludes, possessed "spiritual individuality, but as a corporeal not inwardized, over which there stood the abstract necessity of fate" (607). In this sense, it was also too "Jewish."

3. A new stage of art emerges once the Incarnate God reveals man's vocation of freedom in the world. Romantic Art is the art that seeks to comprehend this

"infinite subjectivity" aesthetically. It is the art that has learned (from Christianity and philosophy) that the grounding assumption of art itself is false: the Ideal, the true nature of reality, has no adequate sensible form. The remaining task of art is therefore to express its own awareness of this inadequacy of art: "Romantic art is the self-transcendence of art within its own sphere in the form of art itself" (79–80). This process of self-transcendence is unceasing: "It is the effect and the progress of art itself which, by bringing before our vision as an object its own indwelling materiality, at every step along this road makes its own contribution to freeing art from the content represented" (604). Art must not pause along the road to delight in its content, settle into a style, or linger over its materiality: Hegel's Romantic Art remains in constant stylistic flight from "Judaism."

4. Yet Romantic Art cannot escape "Judaism" any more than the Christianity that birthed it can. The "Jewish" element of opposition remains within both of them (recall Hegel's claim that Christianity remained metaphysical, representing God as both transcendent and immanent simultaneously). Only in post-Kantian speculative and conceptual thought can the metaphysical divide between mind and world finally disappear, and with it the alienation that Hegel formerly called "Judaism" (104, 176). Only at this stage of Spirit's unfolding can man be said to be free. But this stage has no correlative in religion or art. Religion comes closer, because although it still "has pictorial thinking as its form of consciousness," it moves away from the "objectivity of art" to "pictorial thinking in a subjective way." But only speculative philosophy "makes its own or knows conceptually what otherwise is only the content of subjective feeling or pictorial thinking." It alone achieves true freedom, "untrammelled *thinking*" (104), escaping the shadow of necessity that Hegel cast over all "pictorial thinking," and that he, like many before him, associated with "Judaism."

Like Judaism, art has been left behind by the dialectical unfolding of the spirit that it itself set in motion. "For us art counts no longer as the highest mode in which truth fashions an existence for itself. . . . The form of art has ceased to be the supreme need of the spirit" (103). To translate the point into terms more obviously relevant to our analysis: now that the spirit, with the aid of art, has finally been freed from "Jewish" opposition and necessity, it becomes clear that art itself can never achieve that freedom. This does not mean that Hegel thought art must disappear (as he thought Judaism should have). Like other norms that no longer count as the highest mode of existence (such as law, or the Christian religion), art may still have an important pedagogical or propaedeutic role in human life.[54] But it does mean that art, like those other norms, must not forget

DAVID NIRENBERG

its belatedness. When it does so it becomes deadening rather than enlivening. Those who strive to restore lost mystery to things in order to give art a renewed claim upon the absolute—Hegel specifically mentions the efforts of neo-Catholic painters such as the Nazarenes, and French history painters like those admired by Diderot—fall into the type of necrophilia he elsewhere associated with Judaism. "Past worldviews" cannot be resurrected. "Only the present is fresh: the rest is paler and paler" (606, 608).[55]

Of course, many have disagreed: so many, in fact, that we might almost want to claim (contra Walter Benjamin) that the more the work of art seems threatened by the forces of materialism, modernity, and mechanical reproduction, the stronger grow the counterclaims of its charisma, its "presence," its mystery, its special epistemological and ontological function. One example of such a reclamation is provided by Ralph Ubl's essay in this volume, in which the romantic painter Eugène Delacroix deploys the Jewess as a trope of painting in order to redeem painting from the charge of excessive materiality. The example is fascinating, in part because it demonstrates that art's counterclaims need not be expressed as an overcoming of Judaism. But among the champions of these counterclaims there have always been many who understood the "remystification of art" as its dejudaization, some explicitly and self-consciously (such as Richard Wagner in his essay "Jewry and Music") and some less so. It is perhaps among these last that we should include Martin Heidegger's two philosophical responses to Hegel's aesthetics, "The Origins of the Work of Art" and "The Thing," essays that spurred Emmanuel Levinas to write that "the mystery of things is the source of cruelty towards men."[56]

Cruelty is not too strong a word for the crimes that intervened between the penning (1935–36) and the publication (1950) of "The Origins of the Work of Art," though we can certainly debate the extent of Heidegger's complicity in them. Among those crimes, petty as they may seem in comparison to many others, were the efforts of Nazi theorists and critics to dejudaize the fine arts. The exhibitions they sponsored—such as the "Entartete Kunst" (Degenerate Art) show of 1937, probably the best attended exhibition of "Jewish" art in history—make brutally clear the potential "Judaism" that threatens the work of art.

It may seem odd to continue insisting, in the face of a racially antisemitic art criticism, on art's "potential 'Judaism.'" The Judaism of the artwork seems here actual rather than potential, in that it seems to be the literal Judaism of the artist that corrupts the painting and threatens its viewers, rather than some "Jewish" figures of thought created by critical theories about art. But this is in fact not the case: the Nazi condemnation of artists and their works still depended on the ontological work assigned to figures of "Judaism" in the critical theories that we have been exploring, even as it claimed new foundations in the "real" Judaism (racial or religious) of the artist.

Perhaps because the Nazis' racial theories are so notorious, the familiarity of the art theories with which they collaborated is often overlooked. The development of the "Entartete Kunst" polemic itself demonstrates the process of mapping well-established art-critical discourses of "Judaism" onto newly powerful racial logics. In his *Entartung* of 1892, Max Nordau (himself a Jew) criticized a range of non-Jewish painters from the pre-Raphaelites to the Symbolists on stylistic grounds. Phillip Stauff's 1913 survey of the corrupting influence of Jews on German culture attempted to racialize the stylistic "Judaism" of non-Jewish artists like El Greco or Van Gogh by linking them to contemporary Jewish art dealers and critics who sold and celebrated their works. By the late 1920s, antisemitic critics were attempting to demonstrate that the racial corruption of the artist was legible in (and perhaps contagious from) the style of the art-object. Hans Günther's *Rasse und Stil* taught its readers how to distinguish the race-mixtures of artists by looking at their works, while Paul Schultze-Naumburg's *Kunst und Rasse* explained how the style of the work of art reveals the internal worldviews of the artist's race (he found the ugliness of modernism particularly Jewish).[57]

We might want to dismiss such writers as entrepreneurs of racist cultural politics rather than representative of mainstream art criticism. But although the power of their arguments came from antisemitism, their credibility came from their resonance with a far more respectable aesthetics. For the eminent critic Heinrich Wölfflin (1864–1945), for example—student and successor of Jacob Burckhardt, professor at Basel, Berlin, and Munich—it was more or less axiomatic that the formal analysis of art (of which he was a founding father) revealed not only the artist's "Being," but also that of the people (*Volk*) for whom the work was made. In *Italy and the German Sense of Form* (1931), he explained the differences he perceived in Italian and German realism (he found the Italian more generalized, the German more preoccupied with the particularities of its subjects) in terms of differences in the "Dasein" of the two peoples (the German spirit expects more resistance, and therefore German expression fights harder for freedom from abstraction). Within this *volkisch* theory of the art object's ontological revelations, we can already find all the mythifications necessary for "cruelty towards men."[58]

We might want to think of Nazi antisemitic aesthetics as a literalization of the onto-theological charge of Judaizing, an attempt to project onto the flesh of the "racial" Jew all the spiritual dangers that had menaced the Christian viewer ever since Paul and his successors had translated the most basic problems of

DAVID NIRENBERG

ancient critical thought into the terms of "Christian" and "Jew." But it is also important to remember that this literalization did not lessen the potential for Judaizing, but rather heightened it. This is what the Austrian politician Karl Lueger (1844–1910) recognized in his famous dictum "I determine who is a Jew," a dictum that Goebbels notoriously made his own. Of the 112 artists condemned at the "Degenerate Art" exhibit he sponsored, only 6 were Jews by "race." The rest were "Jews" only in style. As Horkheimer and Adorno put it shortly after the war: "To call someone a Jew is an excuse to work him over until he resembles the image."[59]

I say that this is worth remembering, because although the word "Jew" is no longer part of our critical vocabulary, many of the distinctions that it underwrote remain basic to thinking about art. Of some postwar artists (such as Joseph Beuys) and critics (such as Yves Bonnefoy) we might say that the recuperation of these distinctions, the remystification of art, was central to their work. Since the 1960s that centrality has expanded: Presence, Grace, and Incarnation are once again keywords in contemporary aesthetics, and literalism remains a key term of critique. I do not mean to suggest that these terms are antisemitic (whatever that might mean), or that we can do without these concepts, so basic to Western ontologies and epistemologies. But we should not forget that these concepts retain the *potential* to summon the figures of flesh and letter through which they have so often defined themselves. They continue, in other words, to threaten art with "Judaism." Perhaps this is what the Russian poet Marina Tsvetaeva had in mind when she wrote, after touring Prague's ghetto in 1924, those words later borrowed by Paul Celan: "In this most Christian of worlds,/ all poets are Yids."[60]

NOTES

The inspiration for this essay came from Michael Fried, the courage to write it from Ralph Ubl and Ricardo Nirenberg. Richard Neer sharpened its Plato, Herbert Kessler its medievals, Felipe Pereda its Van Eyck, and Robert Pippin its Hegel. To them, and to every future critic, I am grateful.

1. We now know as well, thanks to the research of scholars such as Daniel Boyarin, Seth Schwartz, and Israel Yuval, to what extent rabbinic Judaism defined itself in terms of Christianity. But it should soon become clear that I believe developments within Judaism, however dialogic, were less important than "figures of Judaism" to the development of the ontology I am exploring here, although the two certainly did have real effect on each other.

2. The Marcionites and other Gnostic Christians are the exception. They did not claim the mantle of "true Israel," rejecting both the Hebrew God and his scripture, rather than claiming any continuity with them. They did, however, attack their rivals as Judaizers and (more surprising) were themselves attacked as Judaizers by advocates of the (eventually) triumphant orthodox Christology, such as Tertullian.

3. For Hegesippus, see Eusebius, *Ecclesiastical History* 4.22. For the patristic sources on "Jewish Christians," see the useful collection by A. F. J. Klijn and G. J. Reinink, *Patristic*

Evidence for Jewish Christian Sects, Supplements to *Novum Testamentum* 36 (Leiden: E. J. Brill, 1973).

4. Aristotle, De Anima, III.7.431 (cf. Plato, Philebus 39B–40E); John Locke, *An Essay Concerning Human Understanding* (1689), book II, chap. 11, sec. 17. Francis Bacon took aim at the "idols" of the human mind in his *New Organon*, of 1620. Cf. W. J. T. Mitchell's essay on Karl Marx's analogy of the functioning of a *camera obscura* to that of ideology in *Iconology: Image, Text, Ideology* (Chicago: University of Chicago Press, 1986), 160–208.

5. Karl Marx, "Zur Judenfrage," in Karl Marx, Friedrich Engels, *Werke*, vol. 1 (Berlin: Dietz Verlag, 1981 [1957]), 347–77, quote at 374.

6. God, too, sometimes requires visual reminders of his covenant in order to know how to behave, as in Exodus 12:13, "And the blood shall be unto you for a sign in the houses where you shall be: and I shall see the blood, and shall pass over you." For a summary of the context for Israelite thought about loves that lead away from God, see my "The Politics of Love and Its Enemies," *Critical Inquiry* 33 (2007), 573–605.

7. On Plato's development of incorporeality and immateriality, compare R. Renehan, "On the Greek Origins of the Concepts Incorporeality and Immateriality," *Greek, Roman, and Byzantine Studies* 21 (1980), 105–38, with Heinrich Gomperz, "Asômatos," *Hermes* 67 (1932), 155–67. I am here following Renehan's account. On intelligibles as incorporeal, see, e.g., Sophist 246B. On the division between lesser and greater mysteries, Symposium 209E–210A (which scholars as illustrious as Cornford, Jaeger, and Guthrie have taken as marking the border between Socrates' interests [a philosophy of life in this world] and Plato's [a philosophy of another]).

8. For Plato's pun on *sema* (tomb) and *soma* (body), his metaphor of the prison and the oyster, and his discussion of sight and beauty, see Phaedrus 250A–E.

9. Which some voices in the Platonic corpus take to mean cognition *tout court*, as when Critias remarks: "All statements made by any of us are of course bound to be an affair of imagery and picturing" (107A).

10. All these points will find their echoes in the Christian tradition. Compare, for example, St. Augustine's fourth-century discussion—in dialogue form—of the falsity of tragedy, painting, and sculpture (Soliloquies II.10 [18]); or the eighth-century complaints of the Caroline books about the representational promiscuity of artists (Caroli Magni Capitulare de Imaginibus, I.2).

11. In *The Holy Family*, Marx cited this line as the most "dangerous enemy" of "real humanism."

12. Carnal Israel: Rom. 11:17–24, 1 Cor. 10:18, and cf. Augustine, *Tractatus adversus Judeos* vii.9. Judaize: the term (Latin judaizare, Gk. 'ιυδαίζειν) has received remarkably little attention, given its historical importance. See, for example, Róbert Dán, "Judaizare—the Career of a Term," in *Antitrinitarianism in the Second Half of the 16th Century*, ed. R. Dán and A. Pirnát (Budapest and Leiden: Akadémiai Kiadó and E. J. Brill, 1982), 25–34; Gilbert Dagron, "Judaïser," in *Travaux et Mémoires* 11 (1991), 359–80.

13. Vessels: *Enarrationes in Psalmos* 59:17–19, cf. Rom. 9:22.

14. Sublime: the word is Kant's, from his *Critique of the Power of Judgment*: "Perhaps there is no more sublime passage in the Jewish Book of the Law than the commandment: Thou shalt not make unto thyself any graven image" (§29, 5:274). The sculptures and objects that decorate the Tabernacle are a common focal point of both Iconoclast/Iconophile and of Jewish/Christian polemic, on which see below.

15. St. Jerome, Letter 52, chap. 10. Jerome's Judaizing strategy here is much like the one he used against St. Augustine in Letter 75, IV.13. Epiphanius of Salamis, *Testament*, ed. G. Ostrogorsky, *Studien zur Geschichte des byzant. Bilderstreites* (Breslau: M. and H. Marcus, 1929), 67, fragment 2.

   DAVID NIRENBERG

16. M. V. Anastos provides one of many versions of the arguments in "The Argument for Iconoclasm as Presented by the Iconoclastic Council of 754," *Late Classical and Medieval Studies in Honor of A. M. Friend, Jr.* (Princeton, N.J.: Princeton University Press, 1955), 177ff. For the vast bibliography, see Leslie Brubaker and John F. Haldon, *Byzantium in the Iconoclast Era (c. 680–850): The Sources, an Annotated Survey* (Burlington: Ashgate, 2001); and for a narrative of the conflict, Leslie Brubaker and John Haldon, *Byzantium in the Iconoclast Era (ca. 680–850): A History* (Cambridge: Cambridge University Press, forthcoming).

17. The "myth of origins" is from the Seventh Ecumenical Council, 787 (Mansi, XIII, 197B–200B, with partial translation in Cyril Mango, *Art of the Byzantine Empire* [Toronto: University of Toronto Press, 1986], 150–51). See especially Kathleen Corrigan, *Visual Polemics in the Ninth-Century Byzantine Psalters* (Cambridge: Cambridge University Press, 1992), 31–32. The Khludov Psalter image (fol. 67r, Ps. 68:22) is reproduced on 255. The Psalter is quoting an eighth-century anti-Iconoclast text ("Adversus Constantinum Caballinum," PG 95, 333A–336B), which made the same point without illustration: "Formerly the impious put to the lips of Jesus a mixture of vinegar and gall; in our day, mixing water and lime and fixing a sponge to a pole, they applied it to the icon. . . . They have perpetrated the work of the Jews."

18. I will skip over the Carolingian and early medieval periods here. The loudest Carolingian echo of the Byzantine controversy may be found in the *Opus Caroli regis contra Synodum*, ed. Ann Freeman and Paul Meyvaert (Hannover: Hahnsche Buchhandlung, 1998). Conrad Rudolph summarizes the Western critique of images in "La resistenza all'arte nel Occidente," in *Arti e storia nel Medioevo* (Turin: Einaudi, 2004), 3:49–84.

19. Suger of Saint-Denis, "De Administratione" 27, in *Abbot Suger on the Abbey Church of St. Denis and Its Art Treasures*, ed. and trans. Erwin Panofsky, 2nd ed., ed. Gerda Panofsky-Soergel (Princeton, N.J.: Princeton University Press, 1979), 48. Conrad Rudolph, *Artistic Change at St.-Denis: Abbot Suger's Program and the Early Twelfth-Century Controversy over Art* (Princeton, N.J.: Princeton University Press, 1990). The Temple decorations were cited by a long tradition of Western (as well as Eastern) defenders of art, on which see Herbert Kessler, *Spiritual Seeing: Picturing God's Invisibility in Medieval Art* (Philadelphia: University of Pennsylvania Press, 2000), 29–32, 192–95; Kessler, *Seeing Medieval Art* (Peterborough, Ont.: Broadview Press, 2004), 65–66; Jean-Claude Schmitt, "Les idoles chrétiennes," in *L'idolâtrie (Rencontres de l'École du Louvre)* (Paris: La Documentation Française, 1990), 107–18.

20. See Conrad Rudolph, *The 'Things of Greater Importance': Bernard of Clairvaux's Apologia and the Medieval Attitude toward Art* (Philadelphia: University of Pennsylvania Press, 1990), esp. Apologia 28, De picturis et sculpturis, auro et argento in monasteriis: "et mihi repraesentant quodammodo antiquum ritum Iudaeorum," 278; idols, dung, avarice, and usury, 280. On those who consider churches synagogues, see Bernard's Letter 241:1.

21. Indeed, Apologia 1 introduces "Pharisaic boasting" (pharisaica iactantia) as the critical theme of the entire text, not only the critique of art. The Apologia is designed to insulate his own order from the charge, while applying it to the Benedictines (or occasionally to excess within his own order, as in Apologia 12).

22. Sara Lipton discusses Cardinal Matthew of Albano's "Judaization" of the reformers in her contribution to this volume, and Herbert Kessler reads the St. Alban's Psalter as a response to Bernard in his. Yet another way to "Judaize" critics of images was to stage the debate as a Jewish-Christian polemic, much as the Iconophiles had done. Purported disputations between Christians and Jews in the twelfth century put arguments against images in the mouths of Jews so that they could be refuted as un-Christian. For one example, see Rupert of Deutz's "Anulus sive dialogus inter Christianum et Iudaeum," ed. Rhabanus Haacke, in Maria Lodovica Arduini, *Ruperto di Deutz e la controversia tra cristiani ed ebrei nel secolo XII* (Rome: Istituto storico italiano per il Medio Evo, 1979), 232–35. For the general phenomenon,

Jean-Claude Schmitt, "La question des images dans les débats entre juifs et chrétiens au XIIe siècle," in *Spannungen und Widersprüche. Gedenkenschrift für Frantisek Graus* (Sigmaringen: J. Thorbecke, 1992), 245–54; "Les dimensions multiples du voir. Les rêves et l'image dans l'autobiographie de conversion d'Hermann le Juif au XIIe siècle," in *Le visione e la sguardo nel Medio Evo*, 2, Micrologus, 6 (1998), 1–27.

23. Luther: the quotes are from "Wider die himmlischen Propheten," WA 18:62ff., here 68, 75, 78. On Luther and images, see Hans von Campenhausen, "Zwingli und Luther zur Bilderfrage," in *Das Gottesbild im Abendland*, ed. W. Schöne et al. (Witten and Berlin: Eckart, 1957); F. W. Kantzenbach, "Bild und Wort bei Luther," *Zeitschrift für systematische Theologie und Religionsphilosophie* 16 (1974).

24. On the distich, see most recently Herbert L. Kessler, *Neither God nor Man: Words, Images, and the Medieval Anxiety about Art* (Freiburg: Rombach Verlag, 2007). On the St. Louis Psalter, see Harvey Stahl, *Picturing Kingship: History and Painting in the Psalter of Saint Louis* (University Park: Penn State University Press, 2008). Faith and Idolatry: south transept porch, left inner pier on the western side, discussed by Michael Camille, *The Gothic Idol: Ideology and Image-making in Medieval Art* (Cambridge: Cambridge University Press, 1989), 11–14.

25. See Sara Lipton, *Images of Intolerance: The Representation of Jews and Judaism in the Bible moralisée* (Berkeley: University of California Press, 1999), 15–29.

26. St. Thomas Aquinas provides a good entry into later medieval attempts to provide a unified theory of the role of representation (symbolic, linguistic, artistic, and sacramental) in human cognition. His insistence on the centrality of the senses (and hence of the need for representation) in human knowledge makes room for art (*Summa Theologiae*, III, q. 25, a. 3), scriptural metaphors (I.1.9), and even poetry (albeit only literally: *Quodlibetal Questions* 7.6.16). But it does not emancipate it from "Judaism." Indeed, insofar as it treats the ritual of the mass, and even the Eucharist itself, as a "sensible figure" necessary for cognition (see ST I.II.101 for the dependence of the mass on "aliquis sensibilibus figuris"), it broadens the danger.

27. For an entry into the vast literature on the Eucharist as a model for representation in the Middle Ages, see Anne-Marie Bouché and Jeffrey Hamburger, eds., *The Mind's Eye: Art and Theology in the Middle Ages* (Princeton, N.J.: Princeton University, 2005). On the relationship between host desecration accusations and the rise of new Eucharistic practices, see Miri Rubin, *Gentile Tales: The Narrative Assault on Late Medieval Jews* (New Haven, Conn.: Yale University Press, 1999). Many scholars (such as Israel Yuval) would add another question, namely, how the actions of "real Jews" affected Christian perception of them.

28. A fundamental treatment of this theme is Hans Belting's *Likeness and Presence: A History of the Image before the Era of Art*, trans. E. Jephcott (Chicago: University of Chicago Press, 1994). On Luke as painter, see Michele Bacci, *Il pennello dell'Evangelista. Storia delle immagini sacre attribuita a San Luca* (Pisa: Gisem, 1998). On the Holy Face, see Herbert L. Kessler and Gerhard Wolf, eds., *The Holy Face and the Paradox of Representation* (Bologna: Nuova Alfa Editoriale, 1998), especially the essays by Gerhard Wolf and Jeffrey Hamburger on Veronica. The thirteenth-century Cantigas image is in Escorial ms. T.I.1, fol. 44r, illustrating Cantiga 29. On the question of what artistic originality might mean in one such context, see Lawrence Nees, "The Originality of Early Medieval Artists," in *Literacy, Politics, and Artistic Innovation in the Early Medieval West*, ed. Celia Chazelle (Lanham, Md.: University Press of America, 1992), 77–109.

29. Isidore of Seville, *Etymologiarum sive originum libri xx*, Lib. XIX.xvi, "De pictura."

30. On Hebrew inscriptions in Van Eyck's painting, see Jacques Paviot, "Les inscriptions grecques et hébraïques dans les tableaux eyckiens," *Revue belge d'archéologie et d'histoire de*

l'art 75 (2006), 53–73. The high priest's phylacteries are also a visual literalization, referring to Matthew's condemnation of the Pharisees (Matt. 23:5: dilatant phylacteria). On Nicholas of Lyra's importance as an exegete in the later Middle Ages, see most recently Deena Copeland, *The Insight of Unbelievers: Nicholas of Lyra and Christian Reading of Jewish Text in the Later Middle Ages* (Philadelphia: University of Pennsylvania Press, 2007). On Nicolas's illustrations, see Felipe Pereda, "Le origini dell'architettura cubica: Alfonso de Madrigal, Nicola da Lira e la Querelle Salomonista nella Spagna del Quattrocento," *Annali di Architettura* 17 (2005), 21–52. My observations on the artist's literalizing biblicism in his representation of the ephod are based on Pereda's discussion of the same in his forthcoming "'Ojos que no ven, oídos que no oyen.' Sentido literal y visión espiritual en la 'fuente de la vida.'" I am most grateful to Professor Pereda for making available his manuscript and discussing the image with me.

31. On Huss see Jarmila Vacková, "Early Netherlandish Painting Commenting the Contemporary Historical Reality in Bohemia," in *Ars Auro Prior. Studia Ioanni Bialostocki Sexagenario Dicata* (Warsaw, 1981), 179–226.

32. On the voyage to Portugal and Spain, see Carl Justi, *Estudios de arte español* (Madrid: La España moderna, 1908), 258–69; Jacques Paviot, "La vie de Jan Van Eyck selon les documents écrits," *Revue des Archéologues et Historiens d'Art de Louvain* 23 (1990), 83–93. On the image controversies spurred by the mass conversions, see Felipe Pereda, *Las Imágenes de la Discordia: Política y poética de la imagen sagrada en la España del 400* (Madrid: Marcial Pons, 2007).

33. Gabriele Paleotti, "Discorso Intorno alle imagini sacre e profane," in *Trattati d'arte del cinquecento*, ed. P. Barocchi, 3 vols. (Bari: G. leterza, 1961), 2:210–11. On Paleotti, see Pamela Jones, "Art Theory as Ideology: Gabriele Paleotti's Hierarchical Notion of Painting's Universality and Reception," in *Reframing the Renaissance: Visual Culture in Europe and Latin America, 1450–1650*, ed. Clare Farago (New Haven, Conn.: Yale University Press, 1995), 127–323.

34. Pietro Aretino's boast is in his *Lettere*, ed. Procaccioli, I, 199 (dated May 15, 1537). Benvenuto Cellini, *Due trattati uno intorno alli otto principali arti dell'oreficeria. L'altro in materia dell'Arte della Scultura; dove si veggono infiniti segreti nel lavorar le Figure di Marmo, & nel gettarle di Bronzo* (Florence: Valente Panizzij & Marco Peri, 1568), 4. My thanks to Ralph Ubl for this last reference, and to Glenn Most for suggesting that, by chiasmus, stupid may refer to the Jew and arrogant to the Greek (but see following note). On the widespread use of "Jew" as a critical term in fifteenth-century Iberia, see my "Figures of Thought and Figures of Flesh: 'Jews' and 'Judaism' in Late Medieval Spanish Poetry and Politics," *Speculum* 81 (2006), 398–426.

35. This flight is already hinted at in the "stupidity" of the Greeks, an allusion to Giorgio Vasari's "pittori di Grecia," whom Vasari criticized (in his life of Cimabue) for constantly repeating the same ancient style without "caring to advance themselves" ("i quali, non si curando passar piu innanzi, avevano fatte quelle opre nel modo che elle si veggono oggi"). Vasari, *Le vite de' più eccellenti pittori, scultori e architettori nelle redazioni del 1550 e 1568*, ed. Rosanna Bettarini and Paola Barocchi, vol. 2 (Florence: Sansoni, 1967), 36. On the vocabulary of Vasari's shifting distinctions between various "Greek styles" (namely, ancient and Byzantine), see Patricia Lee Rubin, *Giorgio Vasari: Art and History* (New Haven, Conn.: Yale University Press, 1995), 190–97. The important point here is that Plato's solution for the ontological problem posed by art (cultivating a fixed style, like the Egyptians) is now dismissed in favor of a requirement for constant stylistic movement.

36. In an interesting actualization of this potential, Alejandro Cifres has discovered an (as yet unpublished) early seventeenth-century inquisition in the archives of the Holy Office,

charging a painter of the suffering Jesus in the "Spanish style" with Sadduceeism, because the artist's emphasis on the suffering flesh of Jesus approximated the Jewish Sadducees' rejection of the Resurrection. Similar logic inspired Pope Paul V's attempts to ban the sale of Spanish crucifixes in Italy, a topic under research by Felipe Pereda.

37. Michelangelo's comments on Flemish art were reported by Francisco de Hollanda, who claimed they were made circa 1539. See his *Four Dialogues on Painting* (1558), trans. Aubrey F. G. Bell (1928; reprint, New York: Hyperion, 1979), 15–18, quotation at 16. Presumably Michelangelo would not have placed the Flemings among those whose eyes can rise from the mortal to the divine ("Dal mortale al divin non vanno gli occhi infermi," Michelangelo, poem 164, ll. 10–11, in C. Ryan, *Michelangelo: The Poems* [London: J. M. Dent, 1996], 152). For yet another stage in the critique of Van Eyck, see Johan Huizinga's characterization of his art as excessively detailed, allegorical, "static," and "merely mathematical," in *The Autumn of the Middle Ages*, trans. R. J. Payton and U. Mammitzsch (Chicago: University of Chicago Press, 1996 [1924]), 375–76. Such terms, in the cultural vocabulary of the 1920s, were easily associated with "Judaism" (for more on this association, see below). On the modernity of Old Masters, see Charles Baudelaire, "Modernité," in *Le peintre de la vie moderne* (1863), trans. Jonathan Mayne as *The Painter of Modern Life and Other Essays* (London: Phaidon, 1964), 13–14.

38. For the sake of provocation, I have simply replaced "state" with "art" in Carl Schmitt's well-known claim about "the modern theory of state": Carl Schmitt, *Political Theology: Four Chapters on the Concept of Sovereignty*, trans. G. Schwab (Cambridge, Mass.: MIT Press, 1985), 36. The references to Calvin are to his *Institutes of the Christian Religion*, but I have drawn them from Belting, *Likeness and Presence*, 550–51.

39. Antoine Arnauld and Pierre Nicole, *La logique ou l'art de penser* (Paris: Flammarion, 1970[1662]), part 3, chap. 20 ("On Faulty Reasonings"), 339–40. The chapter draws much, including an anti-Pharisaic flavor, from Augustine's *De doctrina* (cited, e.g., on 338). On the *Logique*, see Louis Marin, *La critique du discours* (Paris: Minuit, 1975), 67–74; Elena Russo, *Styles of Enlightenment: Taste, Politics and Authorship in Eighteenth-Century France* (Baltimore: Johns Hopkins University Press, 2007), 96. "It is Pharisaic": A. Arnauld, *De la Frequente Communion* (Paris, 1643), 169: "c'est estre pharisien que d'examiner le dehors, avant que d'avoir examiné le dedans."

40. Descartes, *Principia Philosophiae* (Amsterdam, 1644), I.68 and I.69. On the debate over color, see Bernard Teyssèdre, *Roger de Pile et les débats sur le coloris au siècle de Louis XIV* (Lausanne-Paris: Bibliotheque des Arts, 1964); Jacqueline Lichtenstein, *The Eloquence of Color: Rhetoric and Painting in the French Classical Age* (Berkeley: University of California Press, 1993). There are many non-French examples of this view, e.g., John Dryden's "Poetry and Painting" on expression in poetry, and color in painting as "the bawd" of design. See also Ricardo Nirenberg, "Metaphor: the Color of Being," in *Contemporary Poetics*, ed. Louis Armand (Evanston, Ill.: Northwestern University Press, 2007), 153–74.

41. On these debates, see Russo, *Styles of Enlightenment*.

42. "Untainted by all self-concern": "Explication des maximes des saints," in *Oeuvres*, ed, Jacques Le Brun, 2 vols. (Paris: Gallimard, 1983), 1:1011. "We must write": "Discours à l'Académie française" (1683), in *Oeuvres*, 1:535–6. The *Lettre à l'Académie* (1714), ed. Ernesta Calderini (Geneva: Droz, 1970), 78–79, praises Raphael for hiding his skill "in order to deceive the spectator and have him take his painting for Jesus Christ himself transfigured on the Thabor." Poussin is praised in "Dialogue des morts." "Salvation" vs. "vainglory": *Lettre à l'Académie*, 51. "The poet disappears": *Dialogue sur l'éloquence* (1718), in *Oeuvres*, 1:35. I have been guided here by Russo, *Styles of Enlightenment*, 85–112.

43. "Painting is the art": Denis Diderot, *Salon of 1765*, in *Salons*, II, ed. Jean Seznec and Jean Adhémar (Oxford: Clarendon Press, 1960), 174; "'The Beauty of the Ideal': *Salon of*

     DAVID NIRENBERG

1767," in *Diderot on the Arts*, trans. John Goodman (New Haven, Conn.: Yale University Press, 1995), 2:206; "it is rare": "De la Manière," in *Salons*, III, ed. Seznec and Adhémar (Oxford: Clarendon Press, 1963), 338. Like Fénelon, Diderot demands that painting be immediately intelligible, graspable "d'un coup d'oeil"; *Essais sur la peinture*, in *Oeuvres esthétiques*, ed. Paul Vernière (Paris: Garnier, 1966), 712. Like Fénelon, he admires most the work of Poussin and Raphael (e.g., *Pensées détachées sur la peinture*, in *Oeuvres esthétiques*, 825). Flemish painting, on the other hand, he criticizes as virtuosic sleight of hand, without the thematic sublimity of Poussin (*Pensées*, 793).

44. On Susannah: *Pensées*, 792. Similar ontological preoccupations are evident in Diderot's discussion of Joseph Vernet's landscapes in the *Salon* of 1767, where he suggests that these paintings pluck the viewer out of the flow of time and place him within the unalienated space of the painting: "Time no longer exists, nothing measures it, man becomes as if eternal." "Where am I at this moment? What surrounds me? I do not know, I am not aware of it. What am I lacking? Nothing. What do I desire? Nothing. If there is a God, this is how he is, he takes pleasure in himself." *Salons*, III, 134–35, 139.

45. I have revised these paragraphs with the help of a generous critique from Michael Fried, but am aware that differences still remain. On contemporary debates over the overcoming of alienation in the sphere of language, see Sophia Rosenfeld, *A Revolution in Language: The Problem of Signs in Late Eighteenth-Century France* (Stanford: Stanford University Press, 2001).

46. Johann Gottlieb Fichte, *Addresses to the German Nation*, ed. George A. Kelly (New York: Harper, 1968), 115–17. Arndt, "A Jew People," cited in Karen Hagemann, *Mannlicher Muth und Teutsche Ehre: Nation, Militär und Geschlecht zur Zeit der Antinapoleonischen Kriege Preußens* (Paderborn: Ferdinand Schöningh, 2002), 249. E. H. Gombrich, "The Father of Art History," in *Tributes: Interpreters of Our Cultural Tradition* (Ithaca: Cornell University Press, 1984), 51–69.

47. The "Earliest System-Programme" is translated in H. S. Harris, *Hegel's Development: Towards the Sunlight, 1770–1801* (Oxford: Clarendon Press, 1972). German text in *Mythologie der Vernunft*, ed. C. Jamme and H. Schneider (Frankfurt: Suhrkamp, 1984). I quote the list of basic dichotomies from Hegel's first published work, "Differenz des Fichteschen und Schellingischen Systems der Philosophie," ed. Hartmut Buchner and Otto Pöggeler, *Gesammelte Werke*, vol. 4 (Hamburg: Meiner, 1968), 13 (trans. H. S. Harris and Walter Cerf, *The Difference Between Fichte's and Schelling's Systems of Philosophy* [Albany: State University of New York Press, 1977], 90). "The dead concept": *Aesthetics, Lectures on Fine Art*, 2 vols., trans. T. M. Knox (Oxford: Clarendon, 1975), 1:53–54; *Vorlesungen über die Ästhetik*, ed. E. Moldenhauer and K. M. Michel, 3 vols. (Frankfurt: Suhrkamp, 1970), 1:80. "Unity of concept" and the Idea: *Science of Logic*, trans. A. V. Miller (Oxford: Oxford University Press, 1969), 756–57; *Wissenschaft der Logik* (Hamburg: Felix Meiner, 1971), 2:408.

48. "Stripping off" is a quote from Hegel's *Lectures on the Philosophy of Religion*, 3 vols., trans. E. B. Speirs and J. B. Sanderson (New York: Humanities Press, 1962), 1:23 (in German, Georg Lasson, ed., 2 vols. [Hamburg: Felix Meiner, 1974], 1:35), which he delivered late in his career, but he made a similar point in his early "The Difference Between Fichte's and Schelling's System," 90–91 (English), 13–14 (German), as well as in his draft "Fragments of a Philosophical System" from the same year. "Jewish principle" is from "The Spirit of Christianity and Its Fate" of 1799 (English in *Early Theological Writings*, trans. T. M. Knox [Philadelphia: University of Pennsylvania Press, 1971], 259ff.; German in *Hegels theologische Jugendschriften* [Tübingen: J.C.B. Mohr, 1907] 243ff).

49. The older Hegel of the 1822 *Lectures on the Philosophy of History* repeats this critique of Christianity's continuing "Jewish" oppositions more circumspectly, without naming them

as such. See, e.g., the work's final chapter, "The Modern Time," where he asserts that every "Ecclesiastical principle" contains within its bosom the negative principles of "slavish deference to Authority," the "adamantine bondage" of the Spirit to what is "alien to itself," "hypocrisy," etc. (413).

50. On "unbekannten Etwas" and "Dinge an sicht selbst" as noumena, see *Critique of Pure Reason,* tr. Werner S. Pluhar (Indianapolis: Hackett, 1996), 320; *Kritik der reinen Vernunft,* ed. J. Timmermann (Hamburg: Felix Meiner, 1998), 370; on "Verstand" as "der Quell der Gesetze der Natur," 173 (English), 231 (German).

51. "The Ideal does not come to terms": *Über die wissenschaftlichen Behandlungsarten des Naturrechts* (1802), in *Gesammelte Werke,* ed. Hartmut Buchner and Otto Pöggeler (Hamburg: Felix Meiner, 1968), 4:432. See also "Glauben und Wissen," *Faith and Knowledge,* trans. Walter Cerf and H. S. Harris (Albany: State University of New York Press, 1977), 72; *Gesammelte Werke,* 4:328–29. On Kant's "Judaism," see Hegel's "The Spirit of Christianity," sec. 2, "The Sermon on the Mount Contrasted with the Mosaic Law and with Kant's Ethics." Hegel's thinking about the problem of self-legislated normativity proves important in the development of his aesthetics, on which see Terry Pinkard, "Symbolic, Classical, and Romantic Art," in *Hegel and the Arts,* ed. Stephen Houlgate (Evanston: Northwestern University Press, 2007), 3–28, esp. 6–7.

52. The quotes are from *Aesthetics,* I, 8, 9, 111.

53. "Prophet of Orient": *Heines Werke* ed. Helmut Holtzhauer (Berlin and Weimar: Aufbau Verlag, 1968), 5:197–98.

54. The ongoing necessity of art for Hegel is suggested by claims like the one in the *Jena Phenomenology* that "the task nowadays consists not so much in purging the individual of an immediate, sensuous mode of apprehension, and making him into a substance that is an object of thought and that thinks, but rather in just the opposite, in freeing determinate thoughts from their fixity so as to give actuality to the universal, and impart to it spiritual life" (sec. §33, 19–20).

55. Deadening necrophilia: The centrality of Hegel's concern with the life and death of norms, and their deadening and enlivening potential, has long been recognized, though the exemplary role played by "Judaism" in that centrality is rarely noted. Hegel's colleague and contemporary Friedrich Schlegel had earlier (1803–5) concluded his own study of the Old Masters with a similar warning to contemporary artists against the two false paths by which they sought to recapture their predecessors' greatness: "Zuflucht zu manchen blos jüdischen Prachtgegenständen des alten Testaments, oder zu einzelnen Abschweifungen ins Gebiet der griechischen Fabel. . . ." See his *Gemälde alter Meister,* ed. Hans Eichner and Norma Lelless (Darmstadt: Wissenschaftliche Buchesellschaft, 1984), 118.

56. Richard Wagner's (1813–83) worries about the "Be-Jewing" of music have not been sufficiently linked to his conception of the work of art as an escape from the problem of Being. "Das Judenthum in der Musik" was published in 1850, under the pseudonym of K. Freigedank, in the *Neue Zeitschrift für Musik* 33, no. 19 (September 3) and no. 20 (September 6). A new edition appeared in 1869 (*Richard Wagner's Prose Works,* ed. and trans. W. A. Ellis [London, 1897]). But many of the relevant oppositions in his thought (such as love and law, letter and spirit) are already evident in his earliest operas, such as *Das Liebesverbot* (1834–36). "The mystery of things": Emmanuel Levinas, "Heidegger, Gagarin, and Us" (1961), in *Difficult Freedom: Essays on Judaism,* trans. Seán Hand (Baltimore: Johns Hopkins University Press, 1997).

57. Max Nordau, *Degeneration* (New York: Howard Fertig, 1968); Phillip Stauff's *Semi-Kürschner, oder Literarisches Lexicon* (Berlin: self-published, 1913), i–xi, on "The Alien Element [Das Fremdtum] in German Art: or Paul Cassirer, Max Liebermann, etc."; Hans

DAVID NIRENBERG

Günther, *Rasse und Stil*, 2nd ed. (Munich: J. F. Lehmann, 1927); Paul Schultze-Naumburg, *Kunst und Rasse* (Munich: J. H. Lehmann, 1928). Hildegard Brenner's *Die Kunstpolitik des Nationalsozialismus* (Reinbek bei Hamburg: Rowohlt, 1963) is still foundational on this topic. On the exhibition of 1937: Stephanie Barron, ed., *"Degenerate Art": The Fate of the Avant-Garde in Nazi Germany* (Los Angeles: Los Angeles County Museum of Art, 1991).

58. Heinrich Wölfflin, *Italien und das deutsche Formgefühl* (Munich: F. Bruckmann, 1931); *The Sense of Form in Art: a Comparative Psychological Study*, trans. A. Muesahm and N. Shatan (New York: Chelsea Publishing Co., 1958).

59. Max Horkheimer and Theodor W. Adorno, *Dialectics of Enlightenment* (New York: Continuum, 1972), 186.

60. Marina Tsvetaeva, "Poem of the End": "V som christianejsem iz mirov / Poety—zidy!" Paul Celan quoted the line (in Cyrillic) as the epigraph for his poem "Und mit dem Buch aus Tarussa" (1962) in the collection *Niemandsrose*. On the context of the citation, see Eric Kligerman, *Sites of the Uncanny: Paul Celan, Specularity, and the Visual Arts* (Berlin and New York: Walter de Gruyter, 2007), 11.

CONTRIBUTORS

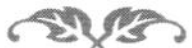

Stephen J. Campbell is Professor and Chair of History of Art at Johns Hopkins University. He is the author of *The Cabinet of Eros: Renaissance Mythological Painting and the Studiolo of Isabella d'Este* (2006) and *Cosmè Tura of Ferrara. Style, Politics and the Renaissance City 1450–1495* (1997), and, with Michael Cole, *Art in Italy 1400–1600* (2011). He is currently completing a study of Andrea Mantegna.

Jaś Elsner is Humfry Payne Senior Research Fellow at Corpus Christi College Oxford and Visiting Professor of Art History at the University of Chicago. He works on Roman and early Christian art within their complex of historiographies and receptions both in antiquity and in modernity. His major books include *Art and the Roman Viewer* (1995), *Imperial Rome and Christian Triumph* (1998), and *Roman Eyes* (2007).

Dana E. Katz is Assistant Professor of Art History and Humanities at Reed College. She is the author of *The Jew in the Art of the Italian Renaissance* (2008) and is currently working on a book that examines the Jewish ghetto in Venice as a discourse on space, surveillance, and ethnic enclosure.

Herbert L. Kessler is Professor in the Department of the History of Art, Johns Hopkins University. He is the author of many books on medieval art, most recently *Neither God nor Man: Words, Images, and the Medieval Anxiety about Art* (2007).

Marcia Kupfer is an independent scholar who writes on diverse aspects of medieval art. Her latest books include *The Art of Healing: Painting for the Sick and the Sinner in a Medieval Town* (2003) and an edited volume, *The Passion Story: From Visual Representation to Social Drama* (2008).

Sara Lipton teaches medieval history at the State University of New York at Stony Brook. She is the author of *Images of Intolerance: The Representation of*

Jews and Judaism in the Bible Moralisée and the forthcoming *Dark Mirror: Jews, Vision, and Witness in Medieval Christian Art, 1000–1500.*

Mitchell B. Merback is Associate Professor of the History of Art, Johns Hopkins University. He is the author of *The Thief, the Cross and the Wheel: Pain and the Spectacle of Punishment in Medieval and Renaissance Europe* (1999) and editor of *Beyond the Yellow Badge: Anti-Judaism and Antisemitism in Medieval and Early Modern Visual Culture* (2008).

Richard Neer is David B. and Clara E. Stern Professor of Humanities and Art History at the University of Chicago. He has published widely on Classical art, the theory of style, historiography, seventeenth-century French painting, and contemporary cinema. He is Coeditor of the journal *Critical Inquiry.*

David Nirenberg is the Deborah R. and Edgar D. Jannotta Professor of Social Thought and History at the University of Chicago. His research focuses on relations between Muslims, Christians, and Jews.

Felipe Pereda is Associate Professor at the Universidad Autónoma (Madrid). His most recent book is *Las imágenes de la discordia. Política y poética de la imagen sagrada en la España del '400* (2007).

Francisco Prado-Vilar is Ramón y Cajal Professor in the History of Art at the Complutense University in Madrid and fellow of the Real Colegio Complutense at Harvard University. His research interests include the arts of al-Andalus, medieval manuscript illumination, Romanesque sculpture, and Hispano-Flemish and Golden Age Spanish painting. His *Tears from Flanders: Memory, Philosophy, and the Consolation of Painting* will be published in 2011.

Achim Timmermann is Associate Professor in the Department of History of Art at the University of Michigan. His scholarly interests include Gothic architecture, the visual culture of the Eucharist, and the representation of Christian-Jewish relationships in medieval art.

Ralph Ubl is the Allan and Jean Frumkin Professor of Visual Art on the Committee on Social Thought and in the Department of Art History at the University of Chicago. He works primarily on art and art theory since 1800 and has written extensively on modern painting and its aftereffects in photography, collage, film, and beyond. He is currently working on a study of Eugène Delacroix.

INDEX

Italicized page numbers indicate figures and tables

Aaron, 87, 89, 93, 311

Abelard, 174

Abraham: 319; appearance of, and power of earth revealed, 164–66; circumcision of, 145, 158, 161–63, 167–69, 170, 172; penis of, as metaphor for ninth *sefirah*, 163–64; in Prudentius's *Psychomachia*, 82

Abraham Ibn Waqar, 121, 138 n12

absorption, 397, 412

Adam, sin of, 164–66

Adam Scot of Dryburgh, 90

adversos Iudaios literature, 77–78, 85, 94, 105–6

Aelred of Rielvaux, 61

Aeneas, 26, *27*, 30, 41 n56

aesthetics, 2–5, 388–90, 409–12, 417–19. *See also* Hegel, Georg Wilhelm Friedrich

Agamben, Giorgio, 132–33, 141 n30

Agobard of Lyons, 78

Aix-en-Provence, Musée Granet, Red Sea sarcophagus, *16–18*, 22, 31

Alberti, Leon Battista, 241–42

Aldonza Romeu, 134

Alexander of Hales, 215

Alexander VII (pope), 250

Alfonso IV (king), 144

Alfonso X (king), 115–21, 126, 129, 133–34, 136 n1. *See also Cantigas de Santa María*

allegory, 183, 323 n11, 369–71, 378, 380, 391

altarpieces: anti-Jewish imagery in, 225; Catalan, 99; Counter Reformation, 339–41; Cuidad Rodrigo, 218–19; Herrenberg, 208, 211, 219; *Passio imaginis,* 97–99, *98*; pre-Reformation proliferation of, 204–5; Sens, 83–86, 90–91, 102, 104; standard images for, 53; stylistic stream in Seville, 268; by Vouet, 339–40; by Zenale, 311

alterity, 253, 360, 362, 371

Ambrose of Milan, Saint, 32, 33

Amsterdam, Rijksmuseum, *Dance around the Golden Calf* (van Leyden), 217

angels: and circumcision of Abraham, 168–69; in Garofalo's *Allegory of the Old and the New Testaments,* 293; on living crosses, 188–89, 200 n16; in Moretto's *Elijah and the Angel,* 311; in Romanino's *Mass of St. Apollonius,* 325 n29; in Savoldo's *Adoration of the Shepherds,* 305; in van Eyck's *Fountain of Grace,* 405

aniconism, 1–2, 86

Anselm, Saint, 93

antisemitism: expressions of disgust, 217–20; myths, 205–6; psychology of, and hatred for the Other, 215

Antonio Paz y Melia, 151

Apollonius, Saint, 300–301, 325 n29

apostles, 53–54, 60–61, 71 n 69, 309. *See also names of individual apostles*

Arcadius, 30

architecture, 242, 247, 250–53

Aretino, Pietro, 407

Arias de Enzinas, *147,* 150–51, 153–54, 167

Aristotle, 116, 387–88

Arles: church of St. Trophime, Grignan chapel, Red Sea sarcophagus, *13, 14, 21t*; Musée de l'Arles antique, Red Sea sarcophagus, 19, *20, 21t*

Arnauld, Antoine, 409

Arndt, Ernst Moritz, 412

Ark of the Covenant, 87, 89

Arragel, Moses, *147–49*; and Alba Bible, 146, 150–58, 167, 172–73, 178 n49; and God's covenant of circumcision, 161, 163

art: as agent of ontological change, 403; beholders
    of, as problematic, 411–12; Christian anxieties
    about, 77, 80–82, 387–88; debate over, and
    excess, 57; development of, as progressive over-
    coming of oppositions, 415; Egyptian, 1; formal
    analysis of, 418; Gothic, 135–36; in image
    defenses, 87; influence of sermons on, 66 n15;
    Judaism and, 1, 406; language of Judaizing and,
    400–401; linked to the Incarnation, 80;
    meaning of, 388; as mediator of concept and
    reality, 414; mimetic, dangers posed by, 392;
    modern manner in, 295, 297–99, 308, 311–12,
    407; Nazis and, 417; necessity of, 426 n54;
    potential of, to be criticized as Jewish, 419; pre-
    Tridentine, 99, 296; questions about nature of,
    2; reform movement in, 265–68, 283–84;
    remystification of, 417, 419; Roman, 19–28,
    24–25, 30, 42 n68; secularizing tendency in, 320;
    self-transcendence of, 416; subject/object rela-
    tion, 412; as supersession, 79–86; works of, as
    ontological tests, 408–9. *See also* Christian art;
    painting and paintings; religious imagery
Atienza, Cristobal de, 273
Augustine of Hippo, Saint: and Augustinian doc-
    trine, 6, 9 n3; *Confessions,* 397; *Contra Faustum,*
    56; and *dicta non ficta,* 54–56; doctrine of wit-
    nesses, 150; and Hebrews as outsiders, 68 n42;
    on Hebrew Scriptures, 56; on Jews, 46, 144–45,
    146, 333; on the lust of the eyes, 388, 397–98;
    proof by, that Old Testament was fulfilled in
    the New Testament, 72 n86
Augustus, 33–35
Averoldi, Altobello, 297
Azencot, David, 364, 376

Bahya ben Asher, 162, 164
Balaam, 54, 61
Baldwin of Canterbury, 62
Balzac, Honoré de, *Chef d'oeuvre inconnu,* 372–73
baptism, 99, 128–31, 134, 174, 191, 270
Barbari, Jacopo de', 237, 246
Bargnani, Bartolomeo, 305
Bassano, Jacopo, 320
Baudelaire, Charles, 407–8
beauty, 387, 391, 415
Bede, 89, 92
beholders, 332, 336–38, 341, 347, 362–63, 379,
    411–12
Beirut Crucifix, legend of, 97–100, 98, 279–82
"belle juive" figure, 374–75, 377, 380
Benchimol, Abraham, 364, 376
Benedictine monks, 57, 63, 71 n66
Benevento, Arch of Trajan, 19–22, 22
Bentham, Jeremy, 252–53

Berengaudus, 91
Bergamo, 296; Sta. Maria Maggiore, *Judith
    Leaving the Philistine Camp* (after Lorenzo
    Lotto), 316, *318*
Berlin, Gemäldegalerie, *Portrait of Christ* (School
    of Jan Van Eyck), 267, *267*
Berlin, Kunstgewerbemuseum, Eilbertus Altar,
    53–61, *54–55*
Bern (Riggisberg), Abegg-Stiftung, painted cloth,
    15, 38n16
Bernard of Angers, 59
Bernard of Clairvaux, Saint, 51–52; on church
    decoration, 58, 400; comparison of secular
    clerics to unbelieving Jews, 60; on devotional
    imagery, 71 n68, 78, 401; and legitimacy of a
    pope, 174; on material ornamentation, 94–95,
    99–100, 102
Berthold of Regensburg, 189
Bible moralisée. See Toledo, cathedral
Bibles: Bury, 65 n8; First Bible of Charles the
    Bald, 46, *47*; Jean de Sy, 145–46, 168–70, *169*,
    170, 172; Jewish iconography in, 46; Leo
    Patricius, 87, *88*, 104; Lobbes, 46, *48*; Padua,
    170–72, *171*; San Paolo, 80, 90; Touronian, 109
    n31; Velislav, 170; vernacular, Jews and produc-
    tion of, 144–45
Bilderbogen, 220, 222–23
bio-theology, 126
bleeding Hosts, 206, 225–26
blood: of Abraham's circumcision, 161–63, 167;
    circumcision, 158–60, 163–64, 166; of the cove-
    nant, 161; Eucharist desecration and, 279;
    imagery of, and ecclesiastical authority,
    294–95; of Jesus and Mary, in converts, 134;
    Jewish sacrifices of, and prophecy of Christ's
    sacrifice, 90; in sacraments, 83; theology of,
    160, 163
Bonvicino, Alessandro. *See* Moretto
Bouts, Dirc, 205, *206*, 208, *211*, 226, 230 n31
brazen serpent, 82–83, 92–96, *94, 96,* 113 n87,
    222–24
Brescia, 7, 296–301, 407; Pinacoteca Tosio Merti-
    nengo, *Adoration of the Shepherds* (Savoldo),
    303, 303–5
Brescia, churches: Duomo Vecchio, *Elijah and the
    Angel* (Moretto), 316, *317*; —, *Feast of the Pas-
    chal Lamb* (Moretto), 319, *319*; —, *Sacrifice of
    Isaac* (Moretto), 318; —, *St. Luke* (Moretto),
    316; —, *St. Matthew* (Moretto), 316; San Gio-
    vanni Evangelista, *Adoration of the Eucharist*
    (Romanino), 306–9, *307,* 313; —, *Elijah and the
    Angel* (Moretto), 311, *312,* 316, *317*; —, *The Gath-
    ering of the Manna* (Moretto), 313; —, *Lamen-
    tation* (Zenale), 309; —, *Last Supper* (Moretto),

309–11, *310*; —, *Raising of Lazarus* (Romanino), 315, *315*; San Nazaro e Celso, *Resurrection* (Titian), 297, *298*; Santa Maria delle Grazie, *Adoration of the Child*, 304, *304*; Santa Maria in Calchera, *Mass of St. Apollonius* (Romanino), 300, *301*

Burgos, Cathedral, "Cristo de Burgos," 279–82, *281*

Caen, Musée des Beaux-Arts, *Marriage of the Virgin* (Perugino), 301, *302*
Caesarius of Arles, 75, 78
Caiphas, 128
canonization, 50–51, 66–67 n22
Cantigas de Santa María: anti-Jewish stories in, and authorial genealogy of, 139 n15; art of, in meaning effected interwoven vital trajectories, 123–24; genius of the illuminators of, 140 n21; *iudeus sacer* in, 133–34; patterns of misapprehension, and lack of scholarly consideration, 122–23; as performative text, 135–36; sources of, and anti-Jewish iconography, 121–22; visual language of, in context of Gothic art, 135–36.
Capriolo, Parish church, *Resurrection* (Romanino), 298, *299*
caricatures, 2, 121, 128, 133, 140 n22, 158, 211
carnal feeding, 216–17, 226–27
carnivalesque, the, 208, 245, 319
Cassiano dal Pozzo, 328
Castagno, Andrea del, 102
Castro, Américo. *See convivencia*
Cavalleria: family, 274–75; Pedro de, 282–83
Cellini, Benvenuto, 407
censorship: of Arragel's translation of Alba Bible, 145, *147*, 150–52, 156, 163, 172–73; in Seville, 268–70
Champaigne, Philippe de, 341–43, 351, 410
Chantelou, Paul Fréart de, 328
Charles V (king), 144–46
Charles VI (king), 146
Chartres, cathedral, 71 n69, 401
children motifs, 19–26, *21t, 24*–25, 29–30, 40 n41
Christ: and the brazen serpent, 92; coming of, foretold in Hebrew Scriptures, 54; continual suffering of, 215–16; on the Cross, 222; on Eilbertus portable altar, 53; in Garofalo's *Allegory of the Old and the New Testaments*, 293; gentile followers of, 3; images of, in Alba Bible, 154–56; in *Last Supper*, Passion Altar, 213; in majesty with prophets, 80–81; in Poussin's *Christ and the Woman Taken in Adultery*, 345, 351–52; in Poussin's *Penance*, 331, 339; preference for physical representations of, 78; prophecies about, in St. Albans Psalter, 79; rejection of,

3–4; revenge against Jews for death, 91–92; in Romanino's *Raising of Lazarus*, 315; in Savoldo's *Adoration of the Shepherds*, 304; Simon the Pharisee and, 328–32, 341; two natures argument, 104, 114 n104
Christian art: brazen serpent and, 92–96, *96*, 113 n87; defense of, through Hebrew Scripture, 89–90; genealogy of, 30, 91–92; Hebrew prophets in, 80; Jewish types in, 45–49; justifications of, 77–78; premise of, 104–5; style, and flight from Judaism, 407–8
Christians and Christianity: anxiety, 2–3, 34–35; authors, and Jewish questions, 3–4; in *Cantigas*, 120; conversion anxiety, 134; early, expansion into Greco-Roman world, 4; exegetical practice, 57–58; fears of impure treatment of the Eucharist, 207; in *The Fountain of Grace*, 405; idealization of ancestral Judaism, 29; identification with fleeing Israelites, 34; material instruments and, 74; preoccupations with identity, and hostility toward Jews, 297; self-understanding by communities of, 387–88; soteriology, 410; targeted assertion of identity, in Red Sea crossing, 30–31
church reform, 58, 184
Cinque Savi alla Mercanzia, 241, 247–48, 254
circumcision, 5, 160, 161, 163–67, 172, 395. *See also* Abraham; blood
Cistercian monks, 57, 61, 63
Civerchio, Vincenzo, 300
Claudius of Turin, 78, 96
clausura, architecture of, 250–52
Clement V (pope), 224
Climacus, John, 100
cognition, alienation of, from object, 409
Coincy, Gautier de, *Les Miracles de Nostre-Dame*, 121
colonialism, 143–44, 150
color: in Delacroix's work, 361, 363, 366–67, 371–72, 380; in Poussin's work, 346; stylistic discourse about, 410; in Vouet's work, 341
Comestor, Petrus, 214
communion: of Judas Iscariot, 204, 207, 214, 216; ocular, 227, 306; supersession and, 83; visual ingestion of, 279; and worthy reception, 204, 207, 214–16. *See also* Eucharist
composition: of Champaigne's *Christ at the House of Simon the Pharisee*, 341–42; of Delacroix's *Jewish Wedding in Morocco*, 365–66; of Poussin's *Christ and the Woman Taken in Adultery*, 343; of Poussin's *Penance*, 338–39; of Vouet's *Adoration of the Holy Name*, 339–41
confraternities, 204, 224–27, 297

Constantine, 14, 28–29

Contarini, Pietro, 305

convent architecture, post-Tridentine, 250–51

conventual *parlatori*, 254

conversions: bio-political strategy of, 124–26; as central theme in *Cantigas,*124; Christian anxiety about, 134; of Jews, 156–57, 174 n54; Mary as transformative mechanism for, 136; and religious identity, 141 n33; tale of, in *Cantigas,* 126–28

conversos, 126, 134, 264, 268–70, 274, 279

convivencia, 146–50

Copenhagen, Kongelige Bibliotek, MS Gl. Kgl. S. 1605 (Book of Hours), 102

Coppio, Moisé, 254

Corpus Christi confraternities, 204, 224–27, 231 n51, 297

Coryat, Thomas, 247

Councils: Fourth Lateran, 246; Quinisext, 78; Trent, 250–51

covenants, 87–89, 161–64, 420 n6

Cranach, Lucas the Elder, 294

creatura, concept of, 134–36

crucifixes: Avenging, 293, 322 n6; Beirut, legend of, 97–100, 279–82; desecration by Jews, 97–99, 274–75; physical aspect of, 77; ritual profanation of, in Zaragoza, 279

Dacians, 22–24

Daniel, 61

David (king), 54, 61, 76, 79–80, 87, 109 n31

Day of Atonement, 160–61, 167

decoration of churches, 5, 57–59, 398–400, 409

Dedeke, Wilm, 205

Delacroix, Eugène: beholders in work by, 379; as colorist, 361, 363, 366–67, 370–72, 380; engagement with modernism, 359; function of animation in work by, 373; Jewishness in work by, 378; and medium of painting, 361–62; movement in paintings by, 376–77; representation of Jewish women, 374–75, 417; representation of Jews, literary sources for, 373–74; studio of, 370–17; as witness to Jewish wedding, 364–69. Works by: *Front-Boeuf and Isaac of York,* 375, 375; *Jewish Bride,* 368, 370; *Jewish Wedding in Morocco,* 359–61, 367–68, 379–80, 381; *Visit to the Jewish Bride,* 368; *Women of Algiers in Their Apartment,* 360–61, 361, 364

Déols, Hervé de, 69 n46

depth of field, 267–68, 346, 348

devotional environments, 275

devotional images. *See* religious imagery

Diderot, Denis, 410–12

Dijon, Bibliothèque municipale, MS. 132 (Commentaries manuscript), 80–81, 81, 83

Dumas, Alexandre, 360–61

Dura Europos, synagogue, 1, 5, 31, 38 n16, 39 n33

Durandus, William, 80, 101

Ebreo, Samuel, 245

Ecclesia: in Garofalo's *Allegory,* 291; on living crosses, 183–84, 189–90, 192, 194

ecclesiastical excess, criticisms of, 51–52

Edinburgh, National Gallery of Scotland (loan from Duke of Sutherland Collection), *Penance* (Poussin), 328–30, 329, 336–39, 341–42

Egyptian army, 12–14, 28

Elizabeth of Schönau, 188

enigmas, 316

"Entartete Kunst" (Degenerate Art) exhibition, 417, 419

Epiphanius of Salamis (bishop), 398; *Panarion* or "Medicine Chest," 388

Escorial, Biblioteca del Real Monasterio, MS. T.I.1 (*Cantigas de Santa María*) 121, 129–31, 122, 124, 125, 126–28, 127, 130; MS. H.I.15 (lapidary), 116, 117–18

Espina, Alonso de, *Fortalitium Fidei,* 276–79, 283

Estella, Church of San Miguel, 59

Eucharist: Christian perceptions of Jewish threats against, 206–7; conditions attending worthy reception, 214–15; consumption of, through the gaze, 313; continuum of threats to, 205; danger of sinning Christians receiving in unworthy state, 207; desecration of, and signs of personal *virtus,* 279; equation of images and, 279; in hierarchy of naturalisms, 309; Iconoclasts and, 399; link between representation of and naturalistic elements, in genre painting, 308; in Moretto's canvasses, 316; in Moretto's *Last Supper,* 309–10; naturalism as property of, 302–3; protection required against Jews, 254; references to, in Dijon Commentaries, 83; rite of the, 204; in Romanino's *Adoration of the Eucharist,* 306–8; in Romanino's *Mass of St. Apollonius,* 300; and salvific benefits, 215; in tale of Jewish glassmaker's son, 129; theme of, in context of Incarnation, 131

evangelizing crusade, and genesis of modern Inquisition, 263

exegesis, 33–34

eyes, lust of, 388, 397–98

Ezekiel, 60

Feichtwanger, Heinrich, 191, 201 n33

Felanitx, San Salvador, *Passio imaginis* altarpiece (Guillem Sagera), 97–99, 98

Fellous, Sonia, 146, 154, 158
female figure, and materiality of paint, 373–74
Fénelon, François de la Mothe, 410
Ferdinand (king), 263
Ferrara, Pinacoteca, *Allegory of the Law and the Gospels* (Garofalo), 291, *292*
Fichte, Johann Gottlieb, 412
figura, 134–36, 291, 312–13, 316–18, 333
Florence, Biblioteca Nazionale Centrale, MS. B.R. 20 (*Cantigas de Santa María*), 118, *119*, 120, *120*, 122, *123*, 136
France: debates over style and taste, 409–12; Hebrew language in, 332–33, 336–38; Jews in, 144–46, 150, 332–33, 335; Old Testament narratives in discourse of, 334–35
Frau Venus. *See* Synagoga
Frenhofer, 373–74
fringes of garments, 390

Gallego, Fernando, 218
García, Luis ("Abraham"), 274–75
Garci Pérez, 116
Gautier, Théophile, 361
gaze: of Abraham upon his corona, and vision of the *Shekhinah*, 166; of Christian, 247; consumption of Eucharist through, 313; in Delacroix's *Jewish Wedding in Morocco*, 367; and feeding through the eyes, 326 n36; God's, upon Abraham's circumcision blood at Yom Kippur, 167; of Jews, as feared, 235, 254–55; of Jews, obstructed, 247–48; of the Pharisee and beholders, Poussin's *Penance*, 332; pornography and, 256–57 n7; reciprocity of, and social tensions, 248; sacramental, 283
genealogies, competitive, 28–36
genre painting, 308, 319–21
gentiles, 77–79
Gerald I of Arras-Cambrai, 222
German Idealist philosophers, 412
German realism, 418
Germigny-des-Prés chapel, 94
gestures, apotropaic, 216, 219, 220
ghettoization, 239–41, 243, 246–47, 252–55, 256 n4
Gilbert Crispin, 89–90, 102–4
Glossa ordinaria, 46
God: jealousy of, 389–90; representation of, in Jean de Sy Bible, 168; self-revelation to Abraham at Mamre, 167; and visual reminders of covenant, 420 n6
Godehard of Hildesheim, Saint, 50
González, André, 275–76
gospels, 204, 228 n4, 395–96
Gothic art, 135–36
Gregory of Nissa, 32–33

Gregory the Great, 77–78; the Mass of, 190
Guillaume le Clerc, 95–96
guilt, 214–16
Günther, Hans, 418
Guzmán, Luis de, 146, *147–48*, 151, 153, 156–57

Haimo of Auxerre, 101–2
Halévu, Jacques Fromenthal, 374
Hannel ben Hushiel, 162
Hanover, Niedersächsisches Landesmuseum, Landesgalerie, *Last Supper* (Master Bertram of Minden), 211, *213*
Hebrew inscriptions: in Champaigne's *Christ at the House of Simon the Pharisee*, 341–43; in *The Fountain of Grace*, 405; in Garofalo's *Allegory of the Old and the New Testaments*, 293; on Landshut Living Cross, 189, 200 n19; pictorial alternative to, in Poussin's *Penance*, 339; in Poussin's *Christ and the Woman Taken in Adultery*, 343–48, *347*, 350; in Poussin's *Penance*, 331–33, 336–38; Renaissance altar painters and, 220–22; in Vouet's *Adoration of the Holy Name*, 339–40
Hebrew language, in France, 332–33, 336–38
Hebrew prophets: in Christian art, 46, 53–54, 62, 65 nn7–8, 80–81; as witnesses, 60, 63–64
Hebrew ritual, ecclesiastical excess associated with, 51–52
Hebrew Scriptures: Castilian translation of, 146; Christ's coming foretold in, 54; in debate over art and excess, 57; defense of Christian art through reference to, 89–90; illustration of, 46; Judaizing interpretations of, 58; prophecies, 46, 54, 56, 62; Roman Christians and, 5. *See also* Old Testament
Hegel, Georg Wilhelm Friedrich, 1, 201 n33, 412–17, 426 nn54–55; *Lectures on the Fine Arts*, 415–17
Hegesippus, 388
Heidegger, Martin, "Origins of the Work of Art," 417
Heine, Heinrich, 1, 414–15
Hellenistic philosophy, 390, 395
heresy, 274, 277
Heribert of Cologne, *Vita* of, 45–46, 49–53
Herman of Scheda, 90, 102, 105
Herrenberg, Stiftskirche, altarpiece (Ratgeb), 208, 211, 219
Heschel, Susannah, 143
Hezekiah, 92, 95, 113 n87
Hildebert of Le Mans, 96
Hildesheim, Dombibliothek, HS St. Godehard, 1 (St. Albans Psalter), 65 n8, 75, *76*, 78–80
Holocaust, and Jewish scholarship, 43–44 n86

homosexuality, 270, 275

Hosea, 61

host desecrations: anxieties about, 402; Jews
accused of, 181, 183, 191, 205–6, 225, 254, 279;
Landshut Living Cross comment on, 192–94.
See also Eucharist

host miracles, 306

Huber, Joseph, *187*, 191

Hugh of St.-Victor, 46

human body: in Garofalo's *Allegory*, 291; in *Lapidary*, 116; and *yadayim*, 347–48

Hypatius of Ephesus, 86

hypocrisy, of the Pharisees, 396, 414

Iconoclasts and Iconoclasm, 97–100, 398–99

iconographic appropriations, 35

icons, 87, 89, 222, 268, 270–76, 279

idolatry, 100–103, 190, 217, 222, 389–90, 394

Idung of Prüfening, 58–59

image-worship, 276–79. *See also* idolatry

imitation, 308–9, 311–12, 320, 392

imitative naturalism, 407

imperial benefaction theme, 19–22

Incarnation, 80, 102, 126–28, 131

Ingetus Contardus, 77

Innocent II (pope), 66 n22

Inquisition, 273, 283

intarsia, 316–18

Isaac, 162, 170

Isabella (queen), 263

Isaiah, 60–61

Ishmael, 158, 162

Isidore of Seville, 101, 403

Islam, 158, 162, 389

Italian realism, 418

iudeus sacer, 126, 131, 133–34

Jacob, 60

Jacob ben Reuben, 96, 223

Jaén, Cathedral of, *Santo Rostro*, 268, *269*

Jansenists, 409

Jean de Sy. *See* Paris, Bibliothèque nationale, MS
fr. 15397

Jean le Bon (king), 144–45

Jehuda Mosca, 116

Jeremiah, 60

Jerome, Saint, 5, 58, 80–81, 398

Jerusalem, U. Nahon Museum of Italian Jewish
Art, Torah pointer, 348, *349*

Jew, meaning of, 388

Jewish Christians, 388

Jewish history, and Old Testament, 333–34

Jewish scholarship, 43–44 n86

Jews: agency of, 235, 254; baptism of, 99, 134, 174;
blindness of, 59, 66 n16, 334, 402; blood sacrifices by, 90; in Brescia, 297; in *Cantigas,* 120–21,
123, 139; as carnal viewers, 95–96, 99–100;
Christian fear of, 259 n26; conversion of, 126,
128, 136, 156–57, 174 n54; corrupting influence
on German culture, 418; Delacroix's representations of, 373–76; desecration of crucifixes by,
97–99; displacement of, 225, 233–34, 243–45; as
eye of the body, 75–77; forbidden spaces for,
246; in *The Fountain of Grace,* 405; in France,
144–46, 150, 332–33, 335; gaze of, 247–48,
254–55; hatred toward, 276–79; and host desecrations, 181, 183, 205–6, 279; as idol worshippers, 100–101; invisible, 117–24; and *jus gazaka,*
255–56 n3; of Landshut, 190–96; liberated,
19–22, *20*; as mediators, 376; obligation of, and
Alba Bible, 151; obliteration of images of, 102;
in paintings of Dura Europos synagogue, 31;
Paul on, 393; in Red Sea sarcophagi, 14, 25–26,
29, 35; restrictions on, in Venice, 259 nn24–25;
revenge against, for death of Christ, 91–92; in
salvific history, 69 n43, 69 n46; sinful carnality
of, 217; as social outgroup in Venice, 237; suspicions of violence by, 245–46; theological rationale governing status of, in Christian polities,
144–45; triumph of, appropriated as theme
Christian salvation, 30–31; as vessels of wrath,
4, 9 n3, 397–98, 402; as witnesses, 6, 45–46,
49–53, 56–57, 105, 121; women, 124, 128; worldliness and, 51

Joel, 60–61

Johan of Zamora, *147*

John Italos, 87

John of Damascus, 278

John the Evangelist, Saint, 104, 211, 301, 309,
343–45

John the Grammarian, 87

Joseph, Saint, 305

Joshua, 83, 164

Juan II (king), 144, 146

Judah ben Samuel of Regensburg, 222

Judaism: abrogation of, on Sens altarpiece, 85;
and aesthetics, 388–89; ancestral, idealization
by Christians, 29; anxiety about representation
and, 399–400; and art, 1, 406; as category,
387–88; in Christian theology, 45–46; colonizing of, by Christianity, 143–44, 150; and
errors in seeing, 3; in fifteenth-century Spain, 9
n6; figures of, in development of ontology, 419
n1; function of, in stereotypes of Christian art,
294; Hegel on, 413–14; invocations of, to justify
opposite positions, 5; as language of debate

about gap between the sensible and the real,
394; and mind-world metaphysical divide, 416;
and mystery of Incarnation, 126; Pharisees as
figures for, 396–97; questions of, in Christian
art, 2; in Red Sea sarcophagi, 34; service by
figures of, 398; style, and flight from, 407–8;
stylistic, in art, 418; theology of blood,
medieval, 160; *vasa sacra* of, 87–91, 94, 100, 112
n72

Judaizing, 5, 78, 160, 320–21, 395, 400–401, 407,
418–19, 421 n22

Judas Iscariot: and Christian fears of Jewish
aggression against the Eucharist, 214–15; communion of, as archetype of unworthy reception, 204, 207, 214, 216; in Moretto's *Last
Supper,* 309; and nose-blowing apostle, 217–19;
role of, as judaizing threat, 226; in Rotterdam
Last Supper, 211, 213–14, 216, 226; in Master
I. A. M. van Zwolle, 217, 219

jus gazaka, 255–56 n3

Kabbalah, 160, 163–64, 166, 335

kabbalism, as antithesis of carnal literalism, 335

Kalteisen, Heinrich, 191

Kant, Immanuel, 414

Klagenfurt, Kärntner Landesarchiv, Cod. 6/19
(Millstatt Genesis), 172

knowledge: of the divine, 393; recognized sources
of, 52

Lando di Piero, 104

Landshut: banishment of Jewish community,
192–94; Dreifaltigkeitsplatz, 186, 192, *193,* 198;
New Jew's Gate, 188; synagogue (*Judenschule*),
187, 187–88, 191

Landshut, churches: Dreifaltigkeitskirche, 191–92;
St. Martin's, living cross, 184–89, *185,* 191–94,
196–98, *197,* 200 nn 17, 19, 202 n44; tabernacle
altar, 196, *197,* 198

Last Supper (Lord's Supper): in Christian iconography, 203; legitimating power of, as guarantee
of Eucharist's foundation, 205; and orthodox
cult of the Eucharist, 203; sacramental interpretation of, 204; triptych by the Master of the
Legend of St. Catherine, 208; versatility of, as
touchstone of Christian aspiration, 204–5

Last Supper: as center panel of triptych, 207–9;
composition of, 209, 211; contrast between sacramental eating and carnal feeding, 216–17;
evocation of apotropaic magic in, 220–24

Leon Modena, 245

Leonardo da Vinci, 309

Leontius of Naples, 86–87, 101

Leo of Chalcedon, 100

Lessing, Gotthold Ephraim, *Laocoon* (Lessing),
362, 377–78

Leuven, Sint-Pieterskirk/Museum voor Kerlijke
Kunst (Bouts), 205, *206,* 208, 211

Levites, 87

Leviticus, 87, 104

Lisbon, Gulbenkian Collection, MS L.A. 139
(Apocalypse), 91–92, *91*

literalism, 83, 334–35, 405–6, 418–19

living crosses, 183–84, 190, 192, 194–96, 198

Locke, John, 388

London, British Library: Cotton MS D XVI (*Psy-
chomachia*), 74, 82, 105; Egerton MS 1894
(Egerton Genesis), 170, 172; MS. Roy. 6. E VI
(*Omne Bonum*), 170

Longinus, 293

Lotto, Lorenzo, 316–18, 323 n13

Ludwig IX of Bavaria-Landshut (duke), 190–91,
194

Lueger, Karl, 419

Luther, Martin, 220, 294, 400

Madonna of Mercy, 194

Madrid, Museo Nacional del Prado: *Cristo Varón
de Dolores* (Sánchez de San Román), 265–68,
266, 275, 283–84; *Fountain of Grace* (School of van
Eyck), 403–6, *404–5*

Madrid, Palacio de Liria, Alba Bible, 83, 146, *147-
49,* 153–57, *155,* 158, *159,* 160, 163–64, *165,* 167–68,
169, 170, 172, 173–74

Maestro Bartolomé, 217–18

magic, 220–24

Maimonides, 333

Malachi, 60

Mandylion and Keramion, 100

Marcantonio Raimondi, *Judgment of Paris* (after
Raphael), 311–12, 318–19

Marquard of Lindau, 188

Martin V (pope), 144

Martyrdom of Simon of Trent, 321–22

Mary: Alfonso X and, 117–18; associations devoted
to, 224; cult, 124–26, 224; miracles, 121, 129, 136,
139 n15; in Savoldo's *Adoration of the Shepherds,* 304; songs, 118 (see also *Cantigas de
Santa María*); status of, in the Qur'an, 126; in
tale of Jewish glassmaker's son, 129; as transformative mechanism for conversion of Jew
into *iudeus sacer,* 136; as vessel for materialization of God, 126; womb of, as image of the
hearth as symbol of, 131

Mary Magdalene, 315, 331

Mary/Miriam, the mother of Jesus/the Prophetess, 10–12, 14

Master Bertram of Minden, 211

Master I. A. M. van Zwolle, 217

Master of the Die, 311

Master of the Legend of St. Catherine, 208

Master of the Rotterdam-Berlin altar, 209, 211, 213, 216

material images. *See* religious imagery

materialism, condemnation of, by Christian reformers, 58–59, 63

Matthew, 2–3, 60, 104, 396

Matthew of Albano, Cardinal, 58

Meir (rabbi) of Rothenburg, 223

Melchizedek, 61, 319

Mellan, Claude, 336

Mendoza, Pedro González de, missionary campaign of, 263–64

Merlin, 128, 139 n21

Mersenne, Marin, 333

Metz, Musée de la Ville, sarcophagus, 15, 37–38 n16, 37 n13, *21t*

mezuzot, apotropaic function of, 223–24

Michelangelo, 295, 408

midrashic motifs, 170–72

Milvian Bridge, battle of, 14, 28

mimesis, 135, 309, 392–93

mimetic mode, of sacred naturalism, 308–9, 407

miracle of manna and quails, 18, *18,* 22

miracles, 49–52, 99, 118, 129, 304

modernism, Delacroix's engagement with, 359

Moretto (Alessandro Bonvicino), 296, 309–12, 316, 318–19. Works by: *Elijah and the Angel,* 311, 316; *The Gathering of the Manna,* 311; *Feast of the Paschal Lamb,* 319; *Gathering of Manna,* 311, 313; *Last Supper,* 309–11; *Sacrifice of Isaac,* 318; *St. Luke,* 316; *St. Matthew,* 316

Morocco, 363, 381

Mosaic Law, 86, 223, 393

Moscow, Historical Museum, Cod. 129 (Khludov Psalter), 399

Moses: and the brazen serpent, 92–93, 95–96, *96,* 113 n87, 222; competitive Christian interpretation of actions by, 32; and covenant of Sinai, 161; in Jewish *vasa sacra,* 89; in Leviticus frontispiece, 87; in Moretto's *Gathering of the Manna,* 311; in paintings of Dura Europos synagogue, 31; in "Pharaoh's Army Got Drownded," 10–11; in Red Sea sarcophagi, 14, 17–18, *17–18;* in Rotterdam master's Passover feast, 216–17

Mount Athos, Pantocrator Monastery, MS 61 (Psalter), 87, 102

Muslims, 126, 239–41, 363

myth of origins, 399

Nahum, 60

Nantes, Musée des Beaux-Arts, *Christ at the House of Simon the Pharisee* (Champaigne), 341, *342*

naturalisms, 308–9, 313, 317–18

naturalistic genre painting, 320–21

Naudé, Gabriel, 332

Nazis, 417–19

Neoplatonic dictum, 242

Nepotian, 5, 398

New Law, 2, 46, 270

New York, Metropolitan Museum of Art, The Cloisters, ivory cross, 93

Nicholas of Lyra, 406

Nicodemus, 92–93, 97–99, 279, 282

Nicole, Pierre, 409

Noah, 164

Nogent, Guibert de, 105

Nordau, Max, 418

nose-blowing motif, 217–20

Obadiah, 61

objectivity, 410

ocular communion, 227, 306

Old Law, 46, 65 n6, 270. *See also* Hebrew Scriptures

Old Testament: as figural, 333–34; illustration of, 46; Messiah's coming foretold in, 54; narratives of, and creative exegesis and, 32–34; narratives of, in French discourse, 334–35; Poussin's identification with figural language of, 336. *See also* Hebrew Scriptures

Olivos, Isabel de los, 273

optical seclusion, 248–51

Orientalism, Delacroix and, 359, 371, 378, 381

painters: Brescian, 7, 296–301, 407; as imitators of phantoms of virtue, 392; after the modern manner, 407; neo-Catholic, 417. *See also names of individual painters*

painting and paintings: absorption in, 412; antitheatricality in, 411; and conditions of seeing, 363; content of, 362; illusionism in, 270–72; materiality of, and the female figure, 373–74; narrative time in, 346; naturalistic genre, 320–21; as oscillating medium, 363; potential of, to reinforce or overcome alienation of subject, 411; realism, 7; Sevillian School, 264–65, 267–68, 283–84; theatricality of, 412; veiled figures in medium of, 362

Paleotti, Gabrielle, 406–7

Panopticon, compared to the ghetto, 252–53

Paris, Bibliothèque nationale de France: MS fr. 14959 (Bestiary), 95–97, *96;* MS fr. 15397 (Jean

de Sy Bible), 145–46, 168–70, *169*, 172; MS lat. 1
(First Bible of Charles the Bald), 46, *47*; MS lat.
9428 (Drogo Sacramentary), 93; MS lat. 10525
(St. Louis Psalter), 401; MS lat. 12302 (Haimo
of Auxerre), 101–2, *103*; MS Nouv. Acq. Lat.
2334 (Ashburnham
Pentateuch), 15, 38 n16

Paris, Musée du Louvre: *Christ and the Woman
Taken in Adultery* (Poussin), 343–47, *344, 347*;
Death of Saphira (Poussin), 348, *350*; *Death of
Sardanapalus* (Delacroix), 374–75; *The Jewish
Bride* (Delacroix), 368, *370*; *Jewish Wedding in
Morocco* (Delacroix), *360*, 376, *379*; *Moroccan
Sketchbook* (Delacroix), 368, *369*; *Wedding at
Cana* (Veronese), 379–81, *379*; *Women of Algiers
in Their Apartment* (Delacroix), 360–61, *361,
364*

Paris, St. Merri, *Adoration of the Holy Name*
(Vouet), 339–41, *340*

Pascal, Blaise, 333–34

Passover feast, 203. *See also* Last Supper (Lord's
Supper)

patrons and patronage, 57, 63, 115, 145, 150, 154,
156, 205, 224, 297, 305, 328, 403

Paul, Saint, 3–5, 9 n3, 82, 104, 227, 393–95

persecutory myths, 207

perspective, 317, 345–46, 351, 365–66

Perugino, 300–303, 407

Peter Alfonsi, 75–79, 86, 102

Peter of Celle, 93, 104

Petrus Christus, 220

phallus, symbolism of, 160, 163–64

Pharaoh, in Red Sea sarcophagi, 14, 17, *17*

"Pharaoh's Army Got Drownded" (Negro spiritual), 10–12, 35–36

Pharisees, 331, 346–47, 350–51, 388, 396–97

phenomenology (Gothic), 401

phylacteries, 331, 333, 423 n30

pillar of cloud/fire, 15, 37–38 n16

Pirqei de Rabbi Eliezer, 160–64

Planche, Gustave, 361

Plato, 390–93

"plomb de Lyon," 26

Poniky, St. Francis church, Living Cross, 183–84,
184

portable altars, 53. *See also* Berlin, Kunstgewerbemuseum

Port Royal theologians, 409

potentiality, 133, 362, 369, 371, 381, 411

Poussin, Nicolas, 345, 351, 409–12. Works by: *Baptism*, 328; *Biblia Sacra* frontispiece (engraved
by Mellan), 336, *337*; *Christ and the Woman
Taken in Adultery*, 343–47, *344, 347*; *Death of
Saphira*, 348, *350*; *Penance*, 328–30, *329*, 336–39,
341–42; *Penance* (Anonymous, after Poussin),
330, *330*; *Sacraments*, 328, 345–46, 348, 351

Prague, University Library, Cod. XXIII C. 124,
Velislav Bible, 170

presence, 123, 143, 215, 306, 316, 331, 333, 399, 402,
407–8, 419

Priuli, Lorenzo, 254

profane space, 321

professionalization of artists, 295–96

prophecies, 46, 54, 56, 62

prophetism, 80

Prudentius, *Psychomachia*, 74, 82, 105

Purgatory, 189

Quodvultdeus, "Sermon Against the Jews," 66
n15

Raphael, 311–12, 318–19

Ratgeb, Jörg, 208, 211, 219

realism, 7, 403, 407, 418

reality, orders of, in Bergamo intarsias, 316

Rebecca, 374–75

Red Sea crossing: 31–32, 34; adaptability of story,
10–12, 18–19; appropriation for Christian exegetic meanings, 32–34; catacomb paintings of,
15; in Jewish liturgical settings, 31; as standard
scheme in Christian sarcophagi, 12–14; Theodosian rendering of theme, 12; in various
media, 15

Red Sea sarcophagi: children and adults in, *21t*;
and Christian art, 28–30; contrast of old order
and future in, 14; genealogical anxiety present
in, 34–35; participation in appropriative and
targeted classicism, 30–31; relation to Roman
art, 25–28, *29*, 42 n68; representation of Exodus
as site of Christian investment, 32; water symbolism in, 14. *See also individual sarcophagi by
place*

reform movement, in art, 265–68, 283–84

Reims, St. Remi, 93–94, *94*

religious imagery: accusations of misuse, 274–76;
anti-Jewish, 225; Bernard of Clairvaux on, 71
n68, 78, 401; Christian anxiety about, 74–75,
104; Christian conflict over, and anti-Jewish
polemics, 399–400; Christian confusion of,
with archetypes, 102; dangers and salvific
potential of, 401–2; defense of, for devotional
utility, 270; dialectical double-bind of, 400;
Iconoclasts and, 398–99; politicization of, in
early modern Europe, 264; power to defeat evil,
82–83; prophylactic powers, 276; in public and
private spheres, 272–76, 285 n23, 287 n38; sacramentalization of, 276–77; as spurs to devotion,

religious imagery (*continued*)

59, 282; stylistic stream in Seville, 268; suggestions of ineffable Deity in, 86; and transubstantiation, 279

religious initiation, 158–60

Renaissance, 217, 220–22, 233–34, 239, 241–42

representation, 320–21, 410, 422 n26

retables, 196–98, 202 n44, 205

Richeome, Louis, 334

Rilke, Rainer Maria, 233, 247

ritual infanticide, 191–94

ritual murder, 183, 402

ritual profanation, 274, 279

Roman art, 19–26, *24–25*, 30

Romanino, Girolamo: as Brescian painter, 296, 298; and genre painting, 321; interest in art of Perugino, 325 n29; and profane space, 321; resistance to modern manner, 298–99; and sacred naturalism, 315; stylistic references by, 300–301. Works by: *Adoration of the Eucharist*, 306–9, *307*, 313; *Castragatti* or "Cat Castrator," 321–22; *Feast in the House of Levi*, 313–15, 320; *Mass of St. Apollonius*, 300, *301*; *Miracle*, 311; *Raising of Lazarus*, 315, *315*; *Resurrection*, 298, *299*

Romantic art, 415–16

Rome: Arch of Constantine, Rome, 19–22, *23*, 28; Column of Marcus Aurelius, 22–25, *25*, 30; Column of Trajan, 22–24, *24*, *25*, 30; Forum of Augustus, 26; St. Paul's Outside the Walls, Monastery of, 80, 90; temple of Mars Ultor, 26; Via Latina Catacomb, 15; Villa Doria Pamphili, fragment of Red Sea sarcophagus, 15, 39 n17. *See also* Vatican

Rome, churches: St. Paul's Outside the Walls, 15, 38 n19, 39 n33; Santa Maria Maggiore, 15, 39 n33; Santa Sabina, 15. *See also* Vatican

Rotterdam, Museum Boijmans Van Beuningen, *Rotterdam-Berlin Corpus Christi Altarpiece*, 208, 209, *210*, 211, *212*, 216–17, *218*, 220, *221*, *222–23*, 226

Rovigo, Biblioteca dell'Accademia dei Concordi, MS 212 (Padua Bible), 170–72, *171*, *172*

Rupert of Deutz: and Augustinian justification, 56; defense of Christian art through reference to Hebrew Scripture, 90; *Dialogue Between Jews and Christians*, 59; on ecclesiastical splendor, 51; on Eilbertus Altar, 61; on Jewish exegetical blindness, 66 n16; on premise of Christian art, 105; and *Vita* of Heribert, 45–46, 49–53

Ruskin, John, 242

sacramental eating, 216–17, 226–27

sacramental gaze, 283

sacraments, 62–63, 83, 99, 278, 300

sacred naturalism, 305–6; mimetic mode of, 308–9, 407; Moretto and, 316; of Perugino, 302–3; principles of, 308; Romanino and, 315

Sagera, Guillem, 97–99

saints, as figures for saved Hebrews, 17

Sánchez de Castro, Juan, 264

Sánchez de San Román, Juan, 264–68, *266*, 275, 283–84

Sandtner, Jakob, 191

Santa María, Gonzalo Garíca, 282–83

Santa María, Pablo de (Selemó Ha-Leví), 282

sarcophagi, Christian, 12. *See also individual sarcophagi by place*

Savoldo, Girolamo, 303–5, 407

Savonarola, Girolamo, 323 n13

scapegoating, 293–94

Schultze-Naumburg, Paul, 418

Scott, Walter, *Ivanhoe*, 373–74

screens, 367

scrolls, 17, 46, 50, 405–6

Scudéry, Georges de, 335

secularization, 408

sefirot, circumcision blood and operation of, 163–64

segregation, compulsory, 227, 239, 241, 248, 255

Sens, Saint Étienne (altarpiece, destroyed), 83–86, *84*, 90–91, 102, 104

senses, 52–53, 390, 392, 394

serpent, *See* brazen serpent

Setién, Isabel de, 273

Seville: Cathedral, *Virgen de la Antigua*, 270, *271*; painting in, 264–65, 267–68, 283–84; social history of, 270–76

Sextus Pompeius, 30

sexuality: fear of, in Jews, 245, 251–52, 259 nn24–25, 392; of Muslims, 375; of Synagoga, 190

sexualization of violence, 374–75

Shekhinah, 164, 166

sight: corporeal, 62, 77, 83; directional, 192, 254; Jewish, 45, 253

signs: apotropaic, 217; of Judaism, 395; mediation of, 395; tangible, 50, 53, 56, 59, 264, 278; visual, 362

Simon of Trent, martyrdom of, 321–22

Simon the Pharisee, in Poussin's *Penance*, 328–32, 336, 338

sixth seal, breaking of, 91, 111 n61

Solomon, 54

sophists, 391–92

souls, 390–91, 397

Spain, 139–40 n21, 144

spatial confinement, and the gaze, 251–52

speculative philosophy, 416
spiritual battle (*pugna spiritualis*), 74–79
spiritual enlightenment, 52–53
spirituality vs. materiality, 58
spiritual seeing, 79–80
Split, Archaeological Museum, Red Sea sarcoph-
    agus, *13*, 15–17
state of exception, 136, 141 n30
Stauff, Phillip, 418
Stephen, Saint, 83–86
Stethaimer, Hans, 186, 191
style and styles: archaisms, in Poussin's *Penance*,
    339; critiques of, and ontology, 403; debates
    about, 403; and flight from Judaism, 407–8;
    French debates over, 409–12; function of, 406;
    iconic, canon of, 402–3; reformed, 264–72;
    Roman-Venetian, parodies by Moretto, 318–19
subalterns, resistance to domination, 152–53
sublime, the, 245, 335, 372–73
Suger of Saint-Denis, 57, 82, 92, 399–400
Summerard, André du, 83–86
supernatural, signs of, in Savoldo's *Adoration*, 305
supersession, art as, 79–86
Susannah and the elders, 411
swastika, 121
Synagoga: on living crosses, 183–84, 188–90, 192,
    194, 196, 198; theme of, in conflict with Ecclesia,
    291, 293–94

Tabernacle, 90, 399–400
Talavera, Hernando de, 263–64, 268–72, 276;
    Católica Impugnación, 270, 272
taste, French debates over, 409–12
temporality, 345, 351; in typological thinking, 57
Tessarakontapêchys, 399
Theodosius, 30
Theodulf of Orleans, 78, 94–95, 111–12 n71
Thomas Aquinas, Saint, 278, 422 n26
Timanthes, *Sacrifice of Iphigenia*, 362
Titian, 297–98
Titus, 91
Toledo, cathedral, *Bible moralisée*, 121, 131, *132*, 135,
    160
tolerance, 56, 216
Torah, sacred bride of, 167
Torah pointer (*yad*), 347–48, *349*
Tournai, Bibliothèque du Séminaire, Cod. 1
    (Lobbes Bible), 46, *48*
Trajan, 19–22
transformations, linked, 402–3
transubstantiation, 62–63, 215, 279
trompe-l'oeil, 272
truth, 390–91, 395, 402–3
Tsvetaeva, Marina, 419

Turin, Museo Archeologico, Tombstone of
    Petronia Grata, 26, *27*
Tuscon, Arizona Museum of Art, Cuidad
    Rodrigo Altarpiece (Maestro Bartolomé and
    Gellego), 218–19
typological methods, and spiritual ascent, 82–83
typology, 33, 49, 56, 92, 334

Uccello, Paolo, 225, 245
universalism, 395
Urban IV (pope), 224
urban environment, and powers of social control,
    242
Urbino, Galleria nazionale delle Marche, *Com-
    munion of the Apostles* (van Ghent), 205, 225;
    Corpus Domini Altarpiece, predella cycle
    (Uccello), 205, 225

van der Heide, Henning, 205
van Eyck, Jan, 267, 403, 408
van Ghent, Joos, 205, 255
van Leyden, Lucas, 217
Vasari, Giorgio, 291, 403, 423 n35
vasa sacra, Jewish, 87–91, 94, 100, 112 n72
Vatican: Biblioteca Apostolica, Cod. gr. 746
    (Octateuch), 89; Cod. Ross. gr. 251 (*Heavenly
    Ladder* of John Climacus), 100, *101*, 102; MS
    Reg. gr. 1b (Leo Bible), 87, *88*, 104; Museo Pio
    Cristiano, Red Sea sarcophagus, 15, *16*; Old St.
    Peter's, destroyed frescoes, 15, 38 n19, 39 n33;
    Sistine Chapel, *Last Judgment* (Michelangelo),
    295
vegetation, as symbol of Israel's inheritance,
    164–66
Venice: architectonics of Jewish life in, 233; Banco
    Rosso pawnshop, 237, *239*; confinement of Jews
    in, 233–34; design and construction of, 237;
    Fondaco dei Turchi, 239–41; Ghetto Nuovo,
    233–34, *234-36*, 237, *240*, 243, *244*; Ghetto Vec-
    chio, 248, *249*; historiography, 242; mytholo-
    gizing of, 235, 237–39; Palazzo Ducale, *Journey
    of Jacob* (Bassano), 320; Piazza San Marco, 242;
    Procuratie Vecchie, 242, *243*; quays, 248, *250*;
    reciprocity of the gaze in, 235; San Marco
    (basilica of), 168, *170*; as spatial expression of
    Jewish agency, 235; travelogue about, 247;
    urban physiogonomy of, 237; as visual remon-
    stration against myth of Venice, 242–43. *See
    also* Barbari, Jacopo de'.
Veronese, Paolo, 379–81
Veronica (The), 91, 268, 278
Vespasian, 91
violence, 293, 321, 374–75
Virgin Mary. *See* Mary

vision, 3; carnal, 105, 318; corporeal, 60, 63;
domain of, 135–36; eschatological, 100; Jewish,
6, 45, 53, 59, 248; Pharisaic, 331; spiritual, 61–62,
64, 406, 408
visions, 49–50, 100, 103, 160, 166–67, 190
Vita Heriberti, 45–46, 49–53, 64 n1
von Burghausen, Hans, 186
Vouet, Simon, 339–40, 341
Voragine, Jacobus de, *The Golden Legend*, 278

Wagner, Richard, 1
Wasserburg am Inn, St. James's church, Living
Cross, 194–96, *195*
wealth, 51, 389
Weimar, Stadtkirche, *Allegory of the Law and the
Gospels* (Cranach), 294
William of Bourges, 90, 104
William of St.-Thierry, 57–58
wisdom, signs of, 54
witnesses and witnessing: Augustinian, supersession and dominance over, 80; in canonization
procedures, 50–51; Hebrew prophets, 63–64,
66; Jewish women, 128; Jews as, 6, 45–46,
49–53, 56–57, 105, 121; power of, 66 n20; shepherds, in the Nativity of Christ, 305
Wölfflin, Heinrich, 418
womb/oven metaphor, 131
women: canonization procedures and, 50;
exchange of, in *A Jewish Wedding*, 373; Jewish,
124, 128, 374–75, 417; as rival for God's love, 389;
and sensational mysticism, 306
worship: of created things, 2–3, 77, 86, 90, 92, 95,
102; of the Eucharist, 278, 399; of images, 278,
282, 393, 406

yadayim (Torah pointers), 347–48, *349*
Yazid (caliph), 399
Yehuda Mosca, 116
Yesod (Foundation), 163–64, 166
Yom Kippur, and Abraham's circumcision,
160–61, 167

Zechariah, 60
Zenale, Bernardino, 309, 311
Zephaniah, 61
Zohar, 160, 163–64, 166

ACKNOWLEDGMENTS

Many of the contributions to this volume were first presented at the third annual Lavy Colloquium in Jewish Studies at the Johns Hopkins University in 2007. When Dr. Norman and Marion Lavy endowed the colloquium some years before, they explained that they wanted their gift to support inquiry into new questions, questions that we have not yet learned quite how to ask. It is in that spirit, and in their presence, that our colloquium set out to study the figures of Judaism created by Christians in order to criticize and legitimate their art. Dr. Lavy did not live to see the completion of our work. It is therefore to his memory , and to Marion Lavy, that we dedicate this book.

We would also like to thank the Leonard and Helen R. Stulman Program in Jewish Studies at Johns Hopkins University for supporting the publication of this book, and to acknowledge participants in the Lavy Colloquium whose papers we were not able to include but whose contributions and comments vastly enriched our understanding of our subject's potential scope: Yves-Alain Bois, Madeline Caviness, Kathleen Corrigan, the late Charles Nelson, and Margaret Olin. To Jerry Singerman, who pushed us to clarify our arguments, to the anonymous readers who did the same, and to the staff of the University of Pennsylvania Press, we owe much gratitude.